Scale in miles

20

Enrile

Aguinaldo captured,
March 23, 1901

Palanan
Bay

Palanan

Tierra
Virgen

Oscaris

SIERRA MADRE RANGE

Casiguran

Casiguran Sound

Cape San Ildefonso

Baler Bay

Baler

U.S.S. Vicksburg
March 14, 1901

Manila
80 miles

----- Funston's march to Palanan

Adapted from map drawn by Philip B. King
for U.S. Geological Survey and Chief of
Engineers, U.S. Army, 1945

SITTING IN DARKNESS

SITTING IN DARKNESS

Americans in the Philippines

DAVID HAWARD BAIN

Houghton Mifflin Company
Boston   1984

Library of Congress Cataloging in Publication Data

Bain, David Haward.
Sitting in darkness.

Bibliography: p.
Includes index.
1. Philippines—History—Insurrection, 1899–1901.
2. Funston, Frederick, 1865–1917. 3. Aguinaldo, Emilio,
1869–1964. 4. Luzon (Philippines)—Description and
travel. 5. Bain, David Haward. I. Title.
DS679.B34   1984   959.9′027   84-8945
ISBN 0-395-35285-1

Printed in the United States of America

V   10   9   8   7   6   5   4   3   2   1

This book is dedicated
with love and gratitude to

MARY SMYTH DUFFY

Extending the Blessings of Civilization to our
Brother who Sits in Darkness has been a good
trade and has paid well, on the whole; and
there is money in it yet if carefully worked —
but not enough, in my judgment, to make any
considerable risk advisable. The People that
Sit in Darkness are getting to be too scarce —
too scarce and too shy . . . they have become
suspicious of the Blessings of Civilization.

— Mark Twain, 1901

CONTENTS

SITTING
IN DARKNESS

PROLOGUE

It was Mark Twain who sent me to the Philippines.

In the winter of my thirteenth year, my parents decided to divest themselves of a carton or two of old Book-of-the-Month Club selections by selling them to a used-book dealer. Instead of taking cash they asked for a credit voucher — and handed it over to me. For the entire winter and spring and summer of 1962, I would be dropped off in front of the store on Saturday mornings. I was free to spend an hour or so rummaging through that cluttered emporium, happening upon gems like *The Count of Monte Cristo, The Prisoner of Zenda,* and Nordoff and Hall's *Bounty* trilogy. But I also kept discovering and taking home more and more Twain. I tended to go on binges with writers I fancied, and Twain provided me with a banquet. Huck Finn and Tom Sawyer and the Connecticut Yankee were already mine when I began to explore the shop; soon I found his Prince and his Pauper, his Innocents, his Mississippi tales, his Celebrated Jumping Frog.

Some years later, long after it seemed that I had exhausted all of Twain's stories, I found his essays. It was like discovering an unknown facet of someone you thought you knew thoroughly. And this "new" Mark Twain — political, profane, firmly rooted in the historical events of his era — became for me more than just a cherished novelist. His commentaries, crotchety and self-righteous, took on an added significance in light of what was transpiring in the world of 1966, about which I was just becoming truly aware.

Early that year there were 215,000 American troops in Vietnam; by year's end there were nearly 400,000 and the United States itself had begun to be racked by internal strife — the demonstrations against the war, the antidiscrimination rallies of Martin Luther King, Jr., and the black power confrontations of Stokely Carmichael, the grape-pickers' strikes of Cesar Chavez's National Farm Workers.

So it was that in the year I, and many other Americans, began to understand that our country was not as perfect as had been previously thought, Mark Twain's essays were revealing to me details about our national past that had escaped general knowledge. What was more, parallels between Twain's era and mine were striking.

My ticket into this new world was a collection of once-suppressed essays, *Letters From the Earth,* each of which was at once revelatory and entertaining. The book sent me to the card catalogue looking for more. I was rewarded by Twain's own discursive *Autobiography,* his *Letters,* and the volume of sublime venom entitled *Europe and Elsewhere.* What came last was best.

Europe and Elsewhere included many of Twain's fiercest works of protest. There was, for instance, his 1900 version of "The Battle Hymn of the Republic," which began,

> Mine eyes have seen the orgy of the launching of the Sword
> He is searching out the hoardings where the strangers'
>   wealth is stored;
> He hath loosed his fateful lightnings, and with woe
>   and death has scored;
> His lust is marching on.

Was this the same Mark Twain who had so finely drawn Huck and Jim and Tom and the Boss? Knowing the characters and the mind that created them, how could one doubt it?

Religion and politics were themes he returned to again and again. In the same book I found "The War Prayer," in which an aged stranger, an emissary from God, appears to give voice to a church congregation's true prayers during wartime: "O Lord our God, help us to tear their soldiers to bloody shreds with our shells; help us to cover their smiling fields with the pale forms of their patriot dead. . . ."

Finally, I came to the essay that would eventually send me to the Philippines some sixteen years later, "To the Person Sitting in Darkness." Written in 1901, a time of renewed enthusiasm among the major world powers to plant their flags on various benighted, "backward" soils, Twain's essay excoriates the imperialistic claims of Britain (in Africa), Germany (in China), Russia (in Manchuria and Port Arthur), and the United States (in the Philippines). "Shall we go on conferring our Civilization upon the peoples that sit in darkness," asked Twain, "or shall we give these poor things a rest?" He carefully listed some twelve "Blessings of Civilization" that were currently being professed as ready for "export" to the natives of China and the Philippines as well as to the Boers in South Africa — qualities such as justice, liberty, honesty, and mercy. However, Twain went on to say, those noble attributes were actually only an outside cover, "gay and pretty and attractive, displaying the special patterns of our Civilization which we reserve for Home Consumption, while *inside* the bale is the Actual Thing that the Customer Sitting in Darkness buys with his blood and tears and land and liberty. That Actual Thing is, indeed, Civilization, but it is only for Export."

In "To the Person Sitting in Darkness," Twain wrote at great length about a war still raging across the Philippine archipelago, one that involved a great many American troops. Funny, I thought in 1966; if there had been references in our history lessons about a war in the Philippines, I could not recall them. Certainly there had been a *Spanish*-American War — Teddy Roosevelt and San Juan Hill, George Dewey and Manila Bay — something about an American battleship called the *Maine* and yellow journalists. But Americans fighting Filipinos? What was Twain talking about — and with such bitterness, as if he had been personally betrayed, along with some presumably sacred American ideals.

"We had lent them guns and ammunition," he wrote about the Filipinos, and

> advised with them; exchanged pleasant courtesies with them; placed our sick and wounded in their kindly care; entrusted our Spanish prisoners to their humane and honest hands; fought shoulder to shoulder with them against "the common enemy" (our own phrase); praised their courage, praised their gallantry, praised their mercifulness, praised their fine and honorable conduct; borrowed their trenches, borrowed strong positions which they had previously captured from the Spaniard; petted them, lied to them — officially proclaiming that our land and naval forces came to give them their freedom and displace the bad Spanish Government — fooled them, used them until we needed them no longer; then derided the sucked orange and threw it away.

It would be a number of years before I arrived at a full understanding of that war that had been relegated to the footnotes in my history books but had once stirred Twain so.

The opportunity arrived in 1979, when I handed over to a publisher the manuscript for a book on the aftermath of the Vietnam War and someone asked me what my next subject would be. Without any forethought I replied, "The Philippines," and for want of another idea, I repaired to the New York Public Library to see what I could learn about that obscure conflict at the century's turn. I saw that indeed, the United States had become embroiled in a colonial war in 1899 — the year after the five-month Spanish-American War had occurred — and it lasted officially for three years, though dragging on in sporadic "police actions" until at least 1906. During the official part of the war some 126,458 American troops took part, of whom 4,234 died and 2,818 were wounded. American military records set the Filipino military losses at more than 16,000, though some 200,000 others also died of war-related causes. This was quite a large occurrence — too large, I think, to have been given subsidiary status to the abbreviated war that President William McKinley waged against Spain in 1898. Though it was impossible to separate the two conflicts (for one could not have happened without the other), still, it was the latter — the Philippine-American War (or Philippine Insurrection, as the War Department had called it) — that was more significant in terms of the kind of nation that the United States grew to be in the twentieth century.

The deeper I delved into this project, the more I was attracted to two figures who commanded a great deal of attention at the turn of the century. Both were considered heroes of the highest sort in their respective countries; both were emblematic of their people's aspirations at the time. Twain had offered me clues that I could have seen back in 1966 had I looked for them. "To the Person Sitting in Darkness" had spoken at length about the leader of the Filipino nationalist movement, Emilio Aguinaldo; he was "their leader, their hero, their hope, their Washington." And had I gone back to the card catalogue and searched for a 1902 issue of the *North American Review*, I would have seen Mark Twain vent his spleen against the "evil notoriety" of the American general, Frederick Funston, who succeeded through a brilliant, audacious, but fundamentally dishonest scheme in capturing Aguinaldo in March 1901.

As it turned out, it was not until I had been researching the Philippine-American War for more than a year that Frederick Funston and Emilio Aguinaldo emerged as the major historical characters through whose experiences I could illuminate that period in our history. Still later, I concluded that library and archival research would not be enough, that by limiting my narrative to only the turn of the century, I would be doing an injustice. By that time I had become convinced that the destinies of the Philippine and the American people have been entwined for (at this writing) eighty-six years. I saw that what has grown between our nations is an eighty-six-year *blood compact* — engendered in our mutual conflict with Spain, born in the savage war of 1899–1902, encouraged during the forty-seven years of colonial status, maturing in the side-by-side fighting against the Japanese in the Second World War, and living on in the awkward postcolonial relationship in which we have existed since 1946.

So it was that one blustery March day in 1982 I parked my car in the long-term lot at Kennedy Airport and placed my heavy coat in the trunk before making my way to the international terminal. I was off for the tropics, to the Philippines, on an odyssey on which I would try to go beyond the history found in books to understand more about two historical figures — a rascally and heroic adventurer and a naive young firebrand of a nationalist — who have become inextricably linked in history.

I planned to literally follow in their footsteps, trying to see what they had seen, and I hoped along the way to pick up some historical reverberations among the people I would meet. In making this journey, I wanted also to come to understand the meaning of the blood compact between Americans and Filipinos, and perhaps fathom in what direction such consanguinity would be taking us in the future.

PART ONE

THE CITY

1

AN AMERICAN AND HIS COUNTRY

I

He had survived a hellish expedition into Death Valley and bitter, solitary winters in the Alaskan wastes. He had repulsed the attacks of Indian savages in the Yukon and in Cuba, weathered both Spanish artillery and the dreaded Castilian military inquisitors. He had dodged yellow fever, tuberculosis, and gangrene and ridden out malaria, typhoid, and sepsis. His horse had been shot out from under him more times than he could remember. His body had been battered and punished; his legs were crushed, his arm snapped, his hipbone seriously bruised; he had been wounded by shrapnel and Mauser bullets in the hand, lungs, arms, legs, and thigh. During this time he had risen from mercenary to brigadier general of the United States Volunteer Army.

And yes, he had been decorated and redecorated, medaled and beribboned, honored and commemorated, by a Cuban revolutionary junta and by his fellow Midwesterner William McKinley. Congress gave him the highest, the most coveted, the Medal of Honor, and at the moment that decoration was pinned to his proud, patriotic, Kansas-bred chest, he became fully a part of that heroic, historic network that stretched back through the Indian Wars, the War of the Rebellion, the Revolution, through battles and skirmishes with savages, pirates, heathens, monarchs, and tyrants, finally linking his name with those whose skill and daring had captured his imagination as a boy — Custer, Grant, Lee, John Paul Jones, Lafayette, George Washington.

He certainly had his detractors, people in high places and low —
military men jealous of his rank and politicians safe at home who en-
vied his adventurous life — but they were insignificant in the face of
all the rest. He had the respect of his men (white and colored, even
many of the dusky "little brown brothers" in this faraway Eastern land)
and had wooed and won the fairest belle of Oakland, California.
Though essentially a loner, he counted among his friends and acquaintances the vice president–designate Theodore Roosevelt, the
newspaperman William Allen White, Senator Henry Cabot Lodge,
and the Cuban *insurrecto* General Máximo Gómez.

And yet, as Brigadier General Frederick Funston sat in an office
on the dusty expanse of the great Central Plain of Luzon in the Philippines, all this was not enough.

For Funston, the five-foot four-inch, ruddy-faced, barrel-chested,
hard-as-nails thirty-five-year-old enfant terrible of the Occupying
Forces, the situation that lay outside his spare office was nearly as
dreary as the interminable collection of reports, requisitions, and
dispatches his adjutant had just placed before him. It being February 8, 1901, the second anniversary of the outbreak of war between
the Americans and the ragtag but formidable Filipino army had
passed. Any observance would be limited to a proclamation reaffirm-
ing Washington's determination to bring the war to a speedy conclusion, though perhaps certain ladylike individuals in Boston or their
few playmates in Congress, still seeing the world through rose-col-
ored illusions, might issue another manifesto extolling the virtues of
quitting before the game was won.

Not that the game was going to be won soon. Despite the presence
of seventy thousand American boys in blue, who were garrisoned at
nearly every important town and village in the Philippines, there were
nearly seven thousand islands in the archipelago that required po-
licing. And in the fifteen months since a Filipino council of war had
recognized the utter futility of organized resistance and had scattered its forces among the populace, the fitful and irregular guerrilla
war had smoldered with an intensity one could read in the sullen natives' faces. The war had become one of attrition, through which the
Americans hoped in time to grind the insurgent bands down to
nothing. But while the Americans had only suffered light losses, the
brutal climate and concomitant tropical diseases made the patrols all
the more difficult.

"We had almost worn ourselves out chasing these marauders,"
Funston would readily confess, "and it was only occasionally by affecting a surprise or through some streak of good fortune that we
were able to affect any punishment on them, and such successes were

only local and had little effect on general conditions." Those inter-mittent advances were usually made not through gallant cavalry charges or mad dashes up a hostile ridge, but from the intelligence gleaned from the network of spies, informers, and turncoats who aided the Americans. Such was the sort of war this new century had thrust upon them. Thus were insurgents captured or sent to their reward, their rifles and ammunition confiscated, their stores of rice burned or seized. At this slow rate the insurrection might continue into the next century — another hundred years of this cruel heat and con-stant air of betrayal in which the Americans stalked the Filipinos and the Filipinos ambushed the Americans.

Funston commanded the Fourth District of the army's Depart-ment of Northern Luzon, where he and his cavalrymen were faced with the inhospitable topography of Nueva Ecija province: mile after mile of ten-foot-high cogon grass, forests, and mountains, of treach-erous "amigo" villages. Funston thought of their warfare as "tiger shooting." It was dangerous work, requiring initiative and speed. But like the conditions in the rest of Luzon and elsewhere in the Philip-pines, though they were gradually filling hospitals and cemeteries, the large advances were just not being made.

Then, on that seemingly routine February morning, as the general bent over his paperwork, he was interrupted by an orderly bearing the yellow slip of a telegram. Funston scanned the dispatch and quickly dictated a reply. He was not then aware of how utterly his life would be altered.

The message was from Lieutenant James D. Taylor, Jr., the com-mander of a company from the Twenty-fourth Negro Infantry. Sta-tioned at a garrison at the village of Pantabangan, sixty miles north-east of Funston's headquarters, Taylor's troops ranged over the foothills and the western slope of the massive Sierra Madre, which separated the great Central Plain of Luzon from the Pacific coast of the island. The lieutenant's dispatch reported that his men had in-tercepted an insurgent courier. The messenger bore documents that showed indications of being from Emilio Aguinaldo himself.

Emilio Aguinaldo y Famy — the elusive incarnation of the Filipino rebellion, the Cavite province farmboy who had risen, before he turned thirty, to *presidente* and commander in chief of the scattered, invisible Filipino army. If the Filipinos were — like Kipling's Hin-dus — "half devil and half child," then certainly their leader was half devil and half saint — depending on whom one talked to, and when. Had anyone in Funston's memory been at once so praised and yet so vilified?

In that first flush of romance when the natives still welcomed the Americans as liberators from what politicians had been fond of calling "the cursed yoke of Spanish colonial oppression," when they still mobbed the hero of Manila Bay, Admiral George Dewey, and shouted *"Viva los Americanos!,"* Dewey called him Don Emilio, treated him as his protégé, and encouraged him in his fight against the Spanish. Other Americans found Aguinaldo to be clever, sincere, and ambitious; as a leader he possessed a rough eloquence and a charisma that plainly put the majority of his countrymen in his thrall. Aguinaldo was a "modern Napoleon," or, in the words of Senator George F. Hoar, he was the "Patrick Henry, Nathan Hale, and George Washington of the Philippines." The parallel to the Founding Fathers was clear to the senior Massachusetts statesman; while Aguinaldo was settling the Spaniards' hash he was, at the same time, concocting a constitutional government based on that of the United States.

But the Philippine-American romance was short-lived, gone sour upon the arrival of a multitude of American steamers bearing troops spoiling for adventure. After President McKinley's intentions toward the archipelago were revealed and Aguinaldo had shown his first resistance, the young warrior began to look more and more like a fiend incarnate to the Americans, a combination of Judas Iscariot and Benedict Arnold. Political cartoons had previously romanticized (and Westernized) his appearance; now they made him look like a precursor to the evil Dr. Fu Manchu. Dewey had changed his tune by then, telling anyone who would listen that all Aguinaldo was interested in was "revenge, plunder, and pillage." McKinley deemed "Aguinaldo and his mischievous band of troublemakers" unworthy of common diplomacy, for they were full of "sinister ambition." Secretary of War Elihu Root called him "an assassin" and "a Chinese half-breed." Vice President Roosevelt likened him to Sitting Bull, his followers no better than the treacherous Apaches. The *Hartford Courant* dismissed him as merely "a Malay adventurer," and the correspondent Frank Millet wrote in *Harper's Weekly* that "he has the keen cunning of the Chinaman, and the personal vanity and light mental caliber of the Filipino." Bitter stuff, indeed, but the pro-administration *New York Times* would not be outdone: Aguinaldo was a "vain popinjay, a wicked liar, and a perfectly incapable leader." His men were "dupes, a foolish incredulous mob."

Perhaps such vituperation was necessary to keep the home fires burning; in Luzon, Funston's own men dismissed the leader as a *ladrone*, or bandit, and no more. But Frederick Funston was inclined to agree with Governor General Arthur MacArthur: Aguinaldo was a politician skillful beyond his years, a brave and able general. More significant, the Filipino people were as one behind him. As one soldier, James Blount, wrote after he had returned to civilian life, "One traitor among all those teeming millions might have betrayed his whereabouts, but none appeared."

It had taken a combination of skill and luck for Aguinaldo to slip through their three-way pincer maneuver in November of 1899 in Pangasinan province, near the South China Sea coast. He somehow melted through the American lines and into the northern mountains with a force of only two hundred men. The rest of his army broke up into small units and, as guerrillas, commenced picking off Americans and their Filipino sympathizers. Since then, rumors about Aguinaldo's whereabouts had been sprouting like tropical weeds. MacArthur's predecessor, the hopelessly incompetent General Elwell S. Otis, assured America that Aguinaldo was dead, as did the Filipino Washington's Jefferson, Apolinario Mabini. Others claimed to have seen the chieftain's body — floating down the Rio Grande de Pampanga, lying unburied in a forest clearing in the Carabello Mountains. Some suspected "the master of disguise" had fled Luzon for Hong Kong or Singapore, where he waited and plotted a return from his Asian Elba. But intelligence from deserting insurgents suggested that Aguinaldo, traveling light, moved his headquarters back and forth across northern Luzon; using couriers and cooperative noncombatants, he was able to control virtually all the major Filipino maneuvers throughout the archipelago.

Now, fifteen months after Aguinaldo's dramatic disappearance, in whose lap had concrete news of the rebel fallen?

II

Later, when those who intimately knew Frederick Funston scrambled to get their recollections of him into print, a boyhood friend would recount an incident in the woods of southeastern Kansas some twenty-five years before Funston became a soldier-hero, when Freddy and his friends left home to hunt raccoons. Some older boys heard of their expedition and decided to have a bit of fun with them. They lay in wait deep in the woods; when the young hunters approached, they were terrified to hear ferocious noises — from bears, panthers, or whatever else they did not know — and all fled. All, that is, but Freddy Funston, who stood his ground. A few years before, he and his younger brother Burt had been frightened out of the forest by older boys making animal noises. Not fooled this time, he raised his small-bore rifle and sent several rounds into the underbrush. The

commotion ceased. Fortunately, none of the boys was hurt by his fusillade. Thus began a reputation for courage and impetuousness that
would as much advance him through life as it would hold him back.

Funston was born in New Carlisle, Ohio, on November 19, 1865,
when the assassination of Abraham Lincoln — only seven months
before — was still a raw memory. He was the son of an Irish-Amer-
ican artilleryman in the Union Army, Edward Hogue Funston, and
of Ann Eliza Mitchell Funston, a great-grandniece of Daniel Boone.
Some months after Frederick's brother James Burton was born, Edward Funston traveled by train and stagecoach to Kansas to look for
a homestead, finally acquiring a hundred and sixty acres of prairie
and a farmhouse near Iola, in Allen County, Kansas. His wife and
two small boys joined him the next spring, in 1868.

Edward Funston planted the Kansas sod with wheat and corn, and
when Freddy and Burt were old enough, he stationed them at opposite ends of the fields to help him plow a straight line. For the first
few years on that raw farm life was difficult — Ann Funston's next
two children died in infancy — but they prevailed in raising a large
family and improving the property. Ann bore four more children, a
daughter and three sons. She sent for furniture from her relatives
in Ohio and turned their prairie home into a place of middle-class
gentility: their parlor had, unlike others in Iola, a large rosewood piano
and marble-topped tables; upstairs she installed a Jenny Lind bed and
a rosewood dresser with a swinging mirror. The Funstons even bought
what seemed to be the county's first bathtub; as it was being trucked
to the farm, an elderly neighbor mistook it for a newfangled coffin
and asked who had died at the Funston farm.

Their bare surroundings began to change as Edward embarked on
an ambitious landscaping program. He had learned a smattering of
horticulture from having once traveled for a nursery firm, so he
planted cedars, cottonwoods, elms, maples, poplars, and a thousand
fruit trees; he enclosed their yard by a white picket fence, planted
roses and currant bushes, and draped a jasmine vine next to the front
door.

As his family increased and his farm became more prosperous,
Edward Funston decided to enter politics. No one was surprised when
the restless burgher was elected district representative in the state
legislature in 1872, less than five years after moving to Kansas. After
three years he stepped up to the state senate, and in 1884 he was
elected to the U.S. House of Representatives. In these political are-
nas he became known as "Foghorn Funston, the Farmer's Friend," a
relentless debater who turned on his booming voice and used his imposing frame to get his way, a power broker in the nine counties he

represented. The Funston home became a mecca for politicians, Civil War veterans, petitioners, and office seekers. When they converged upon the house — especially at election time, when a bill affecting the district was being considered, or when post offices were up for grabs — the children would be driven out of the house.

In every way, Frederick Funston grew in his father's shadow. Most remarkably, at six feet two and well over two hundred pounds, Foghorn loomed over his eldest son. Freddy grew to exactly five feet four inches — and stopped. And for most of his life, he seldom weighed more than one hundred pounds. Although he possessed his mother's size and delicate features, he became a masterpiece of overcompensation. He put himself through strenuous exercises to develop a powerful chest and strong shoulders, and he carried himself like a soldier, albeit with a slight swagger. He was seldom pugnacious, but when faced by adversity he would put his fists up in the classic boxer's stance and fight without a thought of losing. He rarely lost.

This is not to say he grew into a little thug. Young Funston also inherited his mother's love of music and literature. In the evenings one could frequently find the family grouped around their big square piano while Ann played and sang songs from her patrician father's antebellum days in Virginia or campaign songs from the Civil War. And Freddy developed an insatiable appetite for reading. He devoured his father's editions of the classics, his books on science, his histories, his volumes of poetry, and he showed a precocious interest in botany. He found he could amuse his mother by memorizing poetry and long sections of prose and amaze his father by mastering impressive amounts of statistics. What Freddy most enjoyed, though, was reading about adventure — any kind, real or imagined — from historical accounts of wars to novels about explorers and cowboys and soldiers and privateers.

To the growing boy who watched a procession of prairie schooners pass his home and head west, the world outside his eastern Kansas farm must have seemed an exciting place, for consider what took place during Frederick Funston's first fifteen years. The country constantly expanded: Alaska was purchased, the states of Nebraska and Colorado admitted to the Union, the Wyoming Territory organized. Companies threw railways across the prairies and mountains and beyond, encouraging hordes of settlers to "develop" the wild lands, opening up communication links that encircled, spanned, and began to tame the subcontinent. In those fifteen years, "the Long Drive" transferred four million cattle from Texas to Kansas cowtowns like Abilene and Dodge City. And there were the inevitable clashes be-

tween Indians and whites: when the settlers pushed a road between
Fort Laramie, Wyoming, and Bozeman, Montana, the three-year war
against the Sioux commenced, finally ending in 1868; after the massacre of a hundred Apaches at Camp Grant, Arizona, in 1871, war
began and lasted until the Apache leader Geronimo was captured in
1886; when General George A. Custer sponsored an 1875 gold rush
in the South Dakota Black Hills — including a Sioux reservation created only eight years before — and fifteen thousand prospectors
flooded the region, the resulting Sioux War eventually claimed Custer's life, and 264 others, in the Battle of the Little Big Horn. Newspapers across Kansas trumpeted the capture of Chief Sitting Bull and
Chief Crazy Horse some months later, in October 1876, when young
Freddy was just short of his eleventh birthday. The next summer
he watched as a caravan of vanquished Sioux, escorted under military guard, passed his house on the way to a new reservation in the
Oklahoma Territory.

Throughout his childhood, the family had lived in a state of mild
alert, not knowing whether strife in other territories might spread to
eastern Kansas or if Ann or the children might fall prey in an isolated incident. Once, his sister Ella recalled, a "chief" appeared at
the house when Ann was alone. He demanded to be fed, which Mrs.
Funston hastened to do, and after eating dinner and — to her horror — an entire serving dish of peach compote, he went away.
"Mother, being one of those dainty individuals who always sipped her
tea with her little finger upright," Ella remembered, "and who at all
times strictly adhered to her Ohio code of correct table manners, was
left speechless at this breach of civilized etiquette." More probably,
as a woman alone in a farmhouse, Ann Funston had been worried
about more serious "breaches of civilized etiquette." A few years later,
around 1875, a dusty wagon full of Indians stopped at their front
gate while Ann was alone with Ella and her brother Pogue. Ann hid
the children beneath her bed while the men looked around the
farmyard. Finally they left after pulling up a bed of spring onions
that Burt had planted, causing the eight-year-old farmer much grief
and tears. As minor as these incidents might seem today, the family
could know only what they heard from neighbors or read in the
newspapers. Consequently the Funston children had instructions to
hide in a hole dug beneath a hedge if strangers ever approached.
"Scratches from thorns were nothing," Freddy's sister recalled, "to
the horrors of the scalping knife."

When Frederick graduated from high school in Iola, he tried to
follow his father's example by entering the military. To his great disappointment, West Point would have nothing of him; his grades were

mediocre, he was outscored on a competitive exam, and he was too
short. Even his father's being a United States congressman made no
difference. Dispirited, he took a teaching job and spent a desultory
five months at a rural school, where the most notable event seems to
have been his thrashing a school bully who came to class with a pistol
to run off the "new little teacher." After adding teaching to the list
of things he did not want to do, Frederick enrolled in a small business college. He quickly decided that his calling was not in commerce, and, in time for the beginning of the fall 1886 semester, he
put himself into the state university at Lawrence.

Kansas State University attracted the sons and daughters of the midwestern gentry, all raised, like Funston, during a time of considerable change and seemingly unlimited opportunities, and all of them
endowed with a mission, "the tremendous desire to make a material
world out of raw material, God's great wilderness stretching up from
the Mississippi River to the Rocky Mountains," as a classmate would
later say. Into this ferment went Frederick Funston — pudgy and
apple-cheeked, sensitive about his "runty size," but determined to hide
it with a surfeit of good humor.

Frederick lodged in a boarding house and joined a fraternity. A
clerical error listing his name as "Timston" earned him an unshakable nickname. During his initiation into Phi Delta Theta, and later,
"Timmy" Funston established many close friendships, the kind of
bonds that would endure for a lifetime. His two closest friends were
William Allen White and Vernon L. Kellogg, both two years younger
and four inches taller. White came from Emporia; his father, a dry
goods store owner and an amateur doctor, had died a few years before, leaving young White's mother to follow her son after he completed a year of college in his home town and transferred to Lawrence. They lived together in a house near the campus. Kellogg, whose
father was a Kansas state senator and his mother an attorney, had
met White at Emporia, where they seemed to be the only boys on
campus interested in reading. Perhaps because of this, Kellogg prevailed upon the Whites to move with him to the larger university.
Kellogg was a smooth, natural politician, and he was immediately inducted into the fraternity, whereas White, who was thought of as being
"too damned fresh," had to wait until others had been given preference. Funston was one of them. White came in a few weeks later
after a feverish campaign to persuade the more doubtful members
by treating them to his mother's home cooking.

The three boys became inseparable, attracted to one another as
much by their high spirits as by their love of books. They made a

remarkable sight on campus: White was fat, Kellogg thin, and Funston short. There was a difference, though, between Funston and his classmates: he remained adrift and they did not; there were times when his friends withdrew from merriment to study and to plan for their futures, but such reflection was not Funston's style. His closest friends were achievers: White, though also a poor student, became a famous newspaperman, even in college balancing his studies with work as a reporter for the city newspaper and as a stringer for dailies in Kansas City and St. Louis. Kellogg, immersed in campus politics, had set himself on an academic path that would eventually make him an eminent entomologist at Stanford. And Funston's other companions showed a similar discipline that later paid off: Herbert Hadley became a governor of Missouri, W. S. Franklin a physics professor at MIT, his brother E. C. Franklin a chemistry professor at Stanford. In contrast, Timmy Funston showed little promise of making anything of himself, though he was the most energetic of the lot.

He broke up classrooms with jokes; he slyly gave professors whimsical nicknames like "Purple Whiskers" and "Zeus," names that long outlived Funston's short academic career; he was teased good-naturedly for trying to learn to dance by using chairs as waltz partners — and breaking four of them. He concocted "snipe hunts" to fool his fellow students and took part in prankish rallies that bedeviled the Lawrence constabulary. And much to the amazement and admiration of his friends, Frederick elevated the use of profanity to a high art.

There was a dark side to his character, too, for it seems to have been at college that Frederick Funston learned to drink. It is unlikely he was exposed to liquor at home, for Edward Funston was something of a temperance fanatic, known in his later years to berate strangers and neighbors angrily on Iola streets for ignoring the county prohibition laws, and doing so with sufficient zeal that he was arrested once for creating a disturbance and charged with resisting arrest. When Edward's son had put sixty miles between home and the Lawrence campus, he developed an inordinate fondness for spirits without the ability to handle them well. The Phi Delts kept a supply of homemade wine and hard cider for social occasions, and they marveled at how two drinks could transform him. Often it would take three fraternity brothers to stop him when Timmy got destructive; his friend White recalled, "We used to say that if he smelled a rotten apple he began tearing up the sidewalks," a practice he did silently, solemnly, and all alone, often when returning from taverns in Lawrence's Negro section. Most of the times the boys drank together, Funston became prey to a deep melancholy. The drinking — and the moodiness that alcohol brought — stayed with him until the end of his life.

However much his friends tried to help him after he had drunk to excess, there were many sober moments when he needed no aid. Funston had been a taciturn child in the face of a father who loved to talk, lecture, debate. Upon enrolling at Lawrence, the young man found a voice. He began airing his opinions around the campus, and when reason and debate failed to settle arguments, the "little loud-mouth" surprised those who figured that his size, physical clumsiness, and lack of interest in athletics summed up a coward or an easily defeated foe. Sometimes Funston's combat resulted from ridiculous provocations, such as the time he was the Phi Delt mess steward and he fought a fraternity brother who scoffed at his cooking. Later they became good friends. Another time, Funston was menaced by a large black man with a razor in downtown Lawrence. Funston had probably strayed into the wrong section of town, looking for some diversion from the humdrum campus life. He disarmed his assailant and marched him through the streets of Lawrence at the point of a revolver to the police station.

Even with his high-spiritedness Funston was, after all, attending college, and it would be wrong to say he learned nothing of a formal nature there. As the old truism goes, professors often remember the underachieving student — the one who fails to measure up to his or her potential — and forget those who present no problem. Funston's teachers remembered him as possessing much native intelligence but lacking in discipline. He was known as a hungry reader, spending much time in the library (often studying subjects he liked but which he refused to appreciate in the classroom). His only honors grades were in English composition, for he was a natural writer. Funston also did credible work in mathematics and economics, and he showed gifts in a field botany course. To the exasperation of those who tutored him, these courses were the exception rather than the rule.

There was another complication in Funston's college career — money. He had enrolled at Lawrence with the understanding that he would try to pay his costs himself, though his father helped in part by doubling Frederick's earnings from summer jobs. This proved not to be enough. Young Funston saved some living expenses with his fraternity cooking job, and on odd weekends he earned spending money as a university guide, taking visitors around the campus. Nonetheless, he was always short of cash — and a fancy for clothes beyond his budget made matters worse. So, after two semesters at Lawrence, the restless Funston left school to earn some money. At the end of the summer vacation, when his classmates went back to school and moved toward the adult world of careers, Frederick Funston remained, for a time, a worker of odd jobs.

These odd jobs added to his colorful reputation. During the summer months he picked up work along the roadbed of the Atchison, Topeka, and Santa Fe Railroad with an engineering crew. Then he went to Kansas City, Missouri, where he talked his way into a provisional job as a police reporter for the *Journal* — and found himself working and rooming with his school chum William Allen White, who had finished his studies and embarked upon his newspaper career. White admired Funston's high spirits; the pair became inseparable. "We roamed the city like sheep-killing dogs," White wrote a half-century later, "making friends with the cops and the dopes and the toughs, male and female, who ranged the streets at midnight."

Combing the streets of Kansas City's rough North End, hobnobbing with police and sniffing out stories in the city courts — even this "glamorous" life seemed to pale for the onetime farmboy. When the editor of a West Arkansas daily wrote to the *Kansas City Journal* with an open call for a court reporter, Funston decided to accept the job.

Taking work on the *Fort Smith Tribune* was a mistake. The newspaper, like most of the citizens in West Arkansas, was staunchly Democratic. If Funston inherited anything more than a loud voice and spunkiness from his political father, then it was certainly his Republicanism, and if the *Tribune's* editorials supporting President Grover Cleveland or denouncing high tariffs infuriated the young man, these paled before the insults he regularly overheard on the street — slanders against the martyred Lincoln, his party, his Union, and constant wistful references to "the Lost Cause" and to the Battle of Prairie Grove in 1862, in which many sons of Fort Smith had died for the Confederacy.

"I was tired of the rotten politics, and tired of the rotten town, and tired of the rotten sheet, and ready to go anyway," confessed Funston, "so I thought I might just as well wake the place up and let 'em know I was alive before I left."

He chose to tender his resignation when his editor, W. S. Murphy, went on a short business trip, leaving Funston in charge. Readers unfolded their newspapers the following day to learn that their dependable Democratic organ had become rabidly Republican. On the editorial page Funston had substituted his own prose, castigating the newspaper's readers, their state Democratic organization, and the national Democratic party. He signed off with an enthusiastic endorsement of the Republican party. An angry mob appeared in the streets outside the newspaper office. The staff and its cocky temporary chief, armed to prevent the wholesale destruction of the newspaper and, of course, themselves, withstood the town's wrath until Murphy hastily returned and printed an apology. Despite threats to tar and feather him, Funston swaggered around Fort Smith's streets for a few days, just to show he was not afraid of anyone. He did not trouble to ask Murphy for a job recommendation.

Funston was able to hold on to his next job for one year. He went back to Kansas and was hired as an assistant collector of tickets on the Atchison, Topeka, and Santa Fe Railroad, running between Kansas and Albuquerque, New Mexico.

The route between western Kansas and Albuquerque was not the most popular one to work, owing to the high proportion of rowdy passengers who made life difficult for ticket collectors. But Funston put his own stamp on the job, and people remembered his antics for many years thereafter. Once he asked a cowboy for his ticket. The passenger looked up to see, standing not much taller than eye level to him, a short, mustached conductor who had begun to grow a beard.

"Ticket?" Funston repeated.

The cowboy revealed his pistol. "I ride on this."

"That's good, that's good," answered Funston mildly, and he moved on. Some minutes later, after the cowboy had done chuckling about the matter, he heard a familiar voice, saying, "I came back to punch that ticket." He looked up — and into the business end of Funston's cocked rifle. All eyes of the passenger car stayed on him while he hastily paid his fare.

Another time, a very large, very drunken cowboy took the notion to lie down in the aisle where, staring happily up at the ceiling, he began to shoot holes through it. Funston heard the commotion, halted the train, tore into the car, kicked the pistol out of the cowboy's hand, dragged him to the rear of the train, and threw him off. Once the cowboy had recovered from his surprise, he lobbed a rock through a coach window. Funston leaped off the train and pursued him for several miles on foot, bouncing chunks of ballast off the cowboy. The train waited for his return.

In time, Frederick Funston saved enough to put himself through another two or three semesters, so he quit the Albuquerque run and rejoined his college pals in January 1889. He was a little more experienced in the ways of the world, but still showed no discernible increase in academic discipline. Consequently he did not leave much of a record behind him.

In June 1889, Funston's friend William Franklin proposed that their group spend the summer in Colorado on a camping trip. Because of Franklin's certainty that they could live for three months — including all expenses and round-trip railroad fare — for only seventy-five dollars apiece, he had no trouble enlisting nine young men, including Funston, to go along. They took one train to Denver, where they bought supplies, and another to Loveland, where they rented a burro. Then they hiked up above Estes Park to the Big Thompson River. There they found an empty cabin in which they would sleep on spruce boughs for the remainder of the summer. They were joined a few weeks later by Frank H. Snow, the young botany professor at Lawrence whose lectures and field trips had succeeded in holding Funston's attention.

"We were not a serious crowd," wrote White years later. "We lived simply [and] we had two rules, only two, as the laws of our republic: every man must clean his own fish, and no razor would be allowed in the camp. So we grew whiskers." The eleven young men spent their time hiking over several hundred miles of blazed trails and did a great deal of mountain climbing. They subsisted mostly on fish. Though game in the area was not plentiful, Funston and Kellogg went out on numerous hunting forays (with the unadventurous White tagging behind to gather wild strawberries in the canyons), and in total they were able to shoot one or two bighorn sheep, a few grouse and ptarmigan, and an occasional rabbit to vary their diet of trout. The young men had packed many books, which they traded back and forth, and took turns reading in a string hammock when they were not exploring.

One time they tramped some forty miles to a deserted mining camp called Lulu, abandoned twenty years before when the rumor of a rich gold strike down the Grand River emptied the camp overnight of its thousand inhabitants. Seeing it was like walking through a modern Pompeii. "There was the post office," White recounted, "with the letters in the boxes; the saloons with the empty bottles on the shelves; the billiard tables with their green baize, moth-eaten and rat-gnawed; the stores with their shelves like grinning skulls empty of the fleshly furnishings; in the cabins the cookstoves stood in the kitchens, and iron safes standing open, too heavy to be moved."

For years afterward, whenever business or family matters brought any of the campers together again, they fondly recalled their adventures that summer: how Henry Riggs and E. C. Franklin encountered a grizzly bear near the camp, and all three parties decided to withdraw rather than confront; how A. C. Wilmoth had left bread dough outside to let it rise in the sun, then baked it — and when he cut it open found a chipmunk inside; how Funston, who was game but clumsy, could never walk across a log bridging a nearby stream but always had to shinny across. One time the students cornered a mountain lion inside a cave, and Funston got so excited he tried to crawl inside, unarmed, to drive the beast out. His friends pulled him out of the cave by his feet and sat on him lest he try that foolhardy act again.

One day Funston and Kellogg climbed to the summit of a precipice called Table Mountain. They looked beyond, into a majestic gorge separating them from the adjacent Stone's Peak, and to a turbulent rivulet that caught their eyes. Awed by the beauty of the scene below them, they resolved to return someday to follow the glistening stream to its source.

Nine months later, in May 1890, long after the crew had gone back to jobs or college, Kellogg and Funston went to Estes Park to climb their mountain. Funston had by this time decided not to return to school; he had set in motion what he hoped would result in a permanent, or at least challenging, job. This outing was the last "boyish" venture he would make.

The previous winter had been unusually severe, and the spring sun did little to melt the heavy snows. Funston and Kellogg told their stage driver what they were planning to do, and he tried to convince them otherwise. "Boys," he warned, "wait until the sun has hammered that snow for six weeks longer; even then it won't be any picnic." They paid him no attention. The pair rented a burro, which Funston named Billy in honor of their sedentary friend White, and they bought three days' supplies.

The two hikers made camp below the treeline and near the entrance to the gorge. They passed the night "in a state of mild terror," Funston recalled, because a mountain lion prowled around just outside the light of their blazing campfire.

At six the next morning they left camp and burro behind and began their ascent into the gorge, following the watercourse that tumbled through it. They carried only a light lunch and their rifles. The gorge narrowed steadily while its side grew steeper. As they climbed, yellow pine and aspen gave way to spruce, which, as the soil grew more rocky and the terrain more exposed, gradually became dwarfed and gnarled before giving out altogether.

At eleven thousand feet they found an easier route up the side of Table Mountain, so they left the gorge to strike out over crusted snow, finally halting for lunch. While they ate, Kellogg pointed to a cloud churning over the range in a rising wind. "It was an ominous sign," recalled Funston, "and we finished our meal in nervous haste."

Moving quickly across the snowfield and making for the timberline, the two hikers were struck by the full force of a blizzard; wind-

whipped, their hair and clothing matted with ice, their hands so numb
that they kept dropping their guns, they finally came to a halt and
sat, in a quandary.

Before them stretched a field of crusted snow, "steep as the roof
of a house and smoother than the smoothest glass," which had to be
crossed though it fell unbroken for some fifteen hundred feet down
to the timberline. It seemed too dangerous to venture upon. Desperately, Kellogg leaped to his feet and cried out, "Come on, we've got
to do it. I'll take mine this way." Funston followed. They began to
cross by jamming their rifle butts into the deep snow, but suddenly
Funston slipped and began sliding. A second later, twenty feet farther down, he was able to stop himself with his gun. He looked up
to Kellogg for help, but his friend had turned his face away to avoid
seeing Funston tumble down that awful incline. A shout roused him,
but Kellogg was still powerless to help. Slowly, Funston got out his
pocketknife, opened it with his teeth, and painfully carved out hand-
holds with the blade; once he had struggled to Kellogg's side, they
resumed their escape from the mountain storm. They stumbled into
their camp fifteen hours after they had begun what seemed a care-
free hike — resolving to let the sun hammer the mountain for another six centuries before repeating the experience. Later, after the
Kansas summer had sufficiently thawed him out, Funston was able
to sell the story of his mountain adventure to Mabel Mapes Dodge's
boys' magazine, *St. Nicholas*, for seventy-five dollars.

Done with school at twenty-four, Frederick Funston asked his father
for guidance in finding a job of some sort. Foghorn was by that time
the chairman of the House Agriculture Committee. It seemed natural to hook up the restless young man's long interest in botany with
some of his father's political influence. In midsummer of 1890,
Frederick took a civil service examination to satisfy formalities, and
soon he was on the government payroll — as a special agent of the
United States Department of Agriculture, assigned to be a field botanist on an expedition gathering native grasses of the Bad Lands.
Young Funston and a team of botanical experts roamed in a caravan
for nearly four months across Montana and the Dakotas.

By December 1890, reports of Funston's good work convinced the
department to extend his service. It assigned him to another expedition, this one heading into the arid and forbidding region of Death
Valley. That blistering desert west of the Grand Canyon of the Colorado, formed by a deep, irregular trough between the Panamint and
Amargosa mountain ranges, had claimed many lives in the past half-
century. It was considered out of bounds for any sane traveler, and

not much was known about the dreadful place other than a general appraisal of its physical layout. Therefore the government dispatched a team into the valley: two botanists, a surveyor, three biologists, and a support team of nine men. On January 20, 1891, their caravan, including mounts and pack animals, followed the sulfurous Amargosa River and entered Death Valley.

For the next nine months the men ranged across the wilderness, over ovenlike deserts and through suffocating salt marshes, following canyons and climbing mountain slopes. They rationed their water severely, sometimes traveling for days without a water hole. Once, for two weeks, when provisions sent from outside failed to arrive, they subsisted "on climate," eating gophers, birds, badgers, and iguanas. In temperatures ranging from January's 88 degrees Fahrenheit in the shade to the summer's torrid high of 147, the scientists gathered voluminous data, despite the conditions, and packed away large amounts of bird, animal, and plant samples.

Funston's supervisor was Frederick Vernon Coville, a twenty-four-year-old botanist who later rose to eminence in his field, his first great work being the report of their Death Valley findings. Together they collected 2,160 plant specimens, usually on trips the pair took away from the main body of scientists. One of their earliest trips together took them nearly a hundred miles away from the camp to collect the expedition's first mail pouch, waiting for them in the half-deserted mining town of Panamint, California. Their route across the desert and over the Panamint Mountains was, of course, unmarked, and a duststorm plagued them for days. Funston and Coville were forced to leave their horses behind for one or two days while they scaled the steep Panamint slopes. They luckily found the mounts waiting for their eight-day return trip across the desert.

Later, when the team had mail to be dispatched to the outside world, Funston went out alone across the desert to the nearest post office, a hundred and twenty miles away. Foolishly, the young botanist carried only a quart of water with him, and he tried to ride his horse in the high heat of the day. He could get only twenty miles into the furnace before being forced to turn back. By then he was severely dehydrated and sunburned and probably would have perished if it had not dawned on him to wait until after midnight, when it was cooler, to return.

When the sun rose the next day, it found Funston and his bay trudging across the baking sand. Funston realized in the growing heat that he would not survive unless he kept going in the daylight. Furthermore, his horse had become so exhausted that it could not carry him any longer. So he dismounted, took the horse's reins, and walked on, going blind and delirious through midday and the afternoon. At one point he heard gun reports. Only later did he ascribe the sounds to "fever brought on by the terrible heat [which] caused the snapping of the nerves in [his] head to sound like rifle shots." He kept walking until dawn. Then he was saved — when he staggered into a fence, which led him to a ranch house and to water.

The expedition broke up in September of 1891. It had been successful in the amount of scientific information the explorers brought out of that unhappy valley. But all of the members had suffered terribly. A friend of Funston's, Charles F. Scott, who edited their home town newspaper, later claimed in the weekly *Independent* that more than half of the expedition members "were permanently disabled in mind or body by the hardships endured."

Collecting steady pay to rush into adventures: the idea seemed to satisfy Frederick Funston's nature; it spread a veneer of social acceptability over rough work, rather like being Buffalo Bill without the ballyhoo. While his government employment did not fully harness that inchoate restlessness of his, still, once the Death Valley expeditionary matters were done, he applied himself to the necessary next steps of writing a coherent report of his part, and mounting the crates of plant specimens, in a Washington, D.C., office.

He was not engaged in these sedentary tasks for long before the department approved a proposal from Frederick Vernon Coville that would take him from ruminations about Death Valley to a completely antipodal climate, one that would dominate his thoughts for the next several years: Alaska.

With his new orders in hand, Funston journeyed from Washington to Kansas, and thence to San Francisco, where he hired an assistant. Then they booked passage on a steamship for their thirty-three-day passage to the southeastern coast of Alaska. On May 19, 1892, their ship chugged through a driving rainstorm into the shelter of Yakutat Bay, about 175 miles northwest of Juneau.

Coville was intrigued by the question of what happened to the flora of an area in which a glacier, in this case the Malaspina Glacier, came to interact with the relatively warm coastal edge of land. He directed Funston to make an inventory of two separate zones: one between the sea and the limit of timber, the other extending from that point to the ice mass. For the next three months Funston and his assistant, with another helper hired in Alaska, paddled around the environs of Yakutat Bay in search of botanical specimens. He returned home only when the growing August ice floes made it impossible to travel farther by canoe.

Funston's first Alaskan trip was an unqualified success from both a personal and professional standpoint. It gave him his first chance at leadership; he came back bearing a satisfactory collection of specimens and eagerly committed his notes and observations to paper. After he had turned in his report, which detailed not only the flora he found but also had meticulous descriptions of the topography as well as useful anthropological notes on the Thlinket Indians, who inhabited an offshore island in Yakutat Bay, his pleased supervisors had another assignment waiting. "There are a great many men in the United States who know more botany than Funston does," reasoned his department chief, "but there is not one who will come closer to going where he is sent and getting what he goes after." The expedition they had in mind, however, seemed hardly to be a prize.

It seemed that the department lacked precise scientific information on the Alaskan interior. What they proposed to do was to send Funston there for eighteen months; they gave him fairly specific instructions about where they wanted him to go and offered him $185 per month, excluding traveling expenses. This was skimpy pay for such a rigorous and lonely pursuit, which they tried to offset by giving him an assistant. "I do not need anybody to take care of me," he wrote to them in refusing company, "and I do not want to take care of anybody." So Funston headed back north to "America's Icebox" alone.

As a weak sun broke behind an Alaskan coastal range buried in perpetual snow and ice on April 10, 1893, Funston disembarked from a steamer at the head of Dyea Inlet, about a hundred miles north of Juneau. Though he had vetoed an assistant, he decided it could do no harm to travel part of the way with three gold prospectors bound for the Yukon Territory. Together they hired a retinue of Thlinket Indians — seven men and women, some children, and dogs — to help them gain the summit of a steep, snow-clogged trail through the Chilkoot Pass, the only corridor across the Coast Mountains. "The Indians carried the loads," Funston wrote home, "while we dragged the empty sleds and did the swearing."

The porters held their loads with deerskin bands looped across their foreheads and burdened even their children and dogs. Every two or three hundred yards they were compelled to rest. Even so, the going was difficult. It was so hard, in fact, that along the way their chief porter, "a low-browed ex-cannibal," Funston jokingly said, threw down his load and demanded more money if he were to go any farther. "My temper had been at white heat all day," the botanist recalled,

> and without thinking what might be the consequences of such a move, like a fool, I shoved the muzzle of a cocked Winchester into the face

of the Advisory Committee of that strike, and the way that the Most
Serene Grand Master of the Amalgamated Order of Chilkoot Salmon
Biters re-shouldered his pack of beans . . . shows that it is sometimes
a good thing for every well-regulated family to have a gun in the house."

The Thlinkets did not run away at their first opportunity after this,
choosing to stay with the travelers until they reached the Chilkoot
Pass crest, three days after beginning the trek. After the Indians were
paid and discharged, Funston and his companions secured their half-
ton of supplies on the sleds, pushed them off, and climbed on board.
They descended the north slope "with the speed of an express train"
down through a wide, snow-packed gorge. At the bottom one sled
hit a bump, "and for a few brief seconds the air was filled with rolls
of blankets, sides of bacon, mining tools, and earnest, soulful profanity."

Having successfully traversed the coastal range, they saw stretching before them the beginning of the great watershed of the Yukon — a chain of six connected lakes. The men planned to manhan-
dle their sleds down the frozen lakes, hoping eventually to find timber
to construct a boat before the spring thaw deprived them of their icy
highway. Characteristically, Funston went tramping off alone in three-
foot-deep snow until he found "a spring feeding a small stream a
few inches deep, which was soon lost to sight in the snow." His explorer's soul exulted: "It was the very beginning of the mighty Yukon," the humble source of a river that would, after receiving the
waters of its many tributaries, swell to a width of three miles and a
depth of thirty feet before pouring its huge flood into the Bering
Sea, some twenty-one hundred miles distant from the trickle he could
span with his short legs.

The four travelers moved north on the frozen surface of the upper Yukon as it wound, hardly a brook, from Lake Linderman to
Lake Bennett, from Lake Bennett to Lake Nares, to Lake Tagish, to
Lake Marsh. They trudged for days between glacier-scoured granite
hills, covered with snow just beginning to melt, past small, skeletal
spruce and black pine. When a wind blew up from the south, they
rigged crude sails from blankets and coasted down the ice. To the
east, the Pelly Mountains rose in the distance.

When the lake ice began to soften, the men stopped to build a flat-
bottomed eighteen-foot skiff from scratch. They selected two straight
and fair-sized spruce trees, which they whipsawed into boards and
nailed together, filling the seams with wicking. Two weeks after they
had first addressed their trees, they launched a boat complete with
hand-hewn mast and oars. Funston loved to think up names for people, animals, and objects, usually favoring political or biblical sources,

but in this case he christened the vessel after a popular trotter in the 1892 racing season, *Nancy Hanks*. When they raised sail, the craft had been temporarily rigged as an iceboat. One day later the ice gave out at the foot of Lake Marsh, and the *Nancy Hanks* was relaunched into a melt-swollen river that was steadily growing swifter, and wider — now about three hundred feet across — all strewn with boulders, with huge blocks of ice thrown up on the shore. One mile past the place where the Tahkeena River rushed into the main, they approached what Funston knew to be "the two greatest obstructions to navigation in the whole Yukon system" — Miles Canyon and the White Horse Rapids.

There the river swept around a bend and smashed against a brown rocky ridge divided by a slit not thirty feet wide. Once the men had frantically pulled to shore, Funston observed that "the river, which has been about three hundred feet wide, suddenly contracts to about a tenth of that width, and increasing its velocity to twenty miles an hour, rushes with terrific force through a cañon with absolutely perpendicular walls a hundred feet high." On the far side of the canyon, the river plummeted through equally dangerous, rock-strewn rapids.

Funston and his friends — none of whom had been strangers to adventure — were, to say the least, extremely worried. Twelve prospectors' boats had been "swamped or crushed like eggshells" against the canyon walls, with none of the riders emerging alive from "that wild maelstrom of water." Travelers did have an alternative, and several men who had arrived at the canyon mouth before Funston were just so engaged. They had to remove their gear, windlass the boat up a hundred-foot slope, pull it over rollers for nearly a mile, roll it down a hill to water, and carry the equipment over on their backs. Faced with the choice of four days of "the most slavish work imaginable" or two minutes spent staring death in the face, they voted for the canyon. After resting for the night and watching how other daring boaters managed the next morning, and killing time discussing and debating with other quake-kneed prospectors who had beached their boats and shaken their heads in doubt, Funston and his companions pushed off into the current.

"I never felt sicker in my life," recalled Funston; but of course this was written while he was still relatively young and had not left the continent, much less fought in a war. The craft was swept like a paper boat into the turbulent notch.

> The walls seemed to fairly fly past us, and after starting we heard a cheer from the rocks above, but did not dare look up. By frantic paddling we kept in the middle and off from the cañon walls. The sen-

sation was akin to that of riding a bucking bronco. There was not a dry spot on one of us when we got through, and the boat had taken on so much water that she nearly foundered before we could bail her out.

Two days later they reached the head of Lake LeBarge. Since the lake was still frozen, though slushy, they pushed and pulled the *Nancy Hanks* on runners for three days and thirty-five miles until reaching open water. Then came the reward. "For nine beautiful, cloudless days we drifted down the river to the northwest," Funston wrote about this delightful five-hundred-mile stretch, "rowing only enough to break the monotony of lounging about in the boat."

The river threaded through rolling, hilly territory beginning to come alive with spring and picked up the Teslin and Little Salmon rivers. At this later confluence Funston bounded ashore to talk with a small camp of Tinneh Indians, but they were "guiltless of any knowledge of English," and all he could do was grin at them and admire their fur garments. Four days later — the mouth of the Pelly River, with a blackened chimney being the only remnant of Fort Selkirk, burned out by Indians forty-three years before. Farther along, the Yukon accepted the rivers White and Stewart, passed below majestic brown and red cliffs, and took the *Nancy Hanks* finally to Forty Mile Creek, "the loneliest mining camp on the face of the earth, where it is midnight all winter and daylight all summer, and where the mail comes but once a year." Funston had thus traveled seven hundred miles in forty-two days.

He bid good-bye to his friends, who went off to search for gold in the creek sandbars and gulches that had been attracting prospectors since 1884. Funston took lodging in the rude little town, which was not much more than a cluster of shacks populated by about three hundred lonely, bored, extremely dirty prospectors. There is no record of whether the sawed-off Kansan told any rough drinking companions in the Forty Mile saloon that he was there looking not for riches but for flowers and shrubs.

On August 25, 1893, Funston climbed into his skiff and put Forty Mile Creek behind him, sailing for eleven days into eastern Alaska to the confluence of the Yukon and the Porcupine. There he stayed with a missionary who introduced him to a party of Tinneh Indians. They intended to follow the Porcupine upstream to resupply a remote, abandoned Hudson's Bay Company trading post, Rampart House, hard by the Canadian border, which had been taken over by an Indian trader. After securing the *Nancy Hanks* on land for the winter, Funston piled his equipment on the Tinnehs' skiff and followed as the Indians commenced tugging it against the swift current for some two hundred miles. They waded in the freezing water for most of the way.

By the time Funston reached Rampart House, the sparsely timbered hillocks and treeless plateaus were buried by snow, and each day the sun sank lower and lower on the southern horizon. The trading post was inhabited only by an English missionary and a young English-speaking Tinneh tribesman, who had been christened David by the missionary and who had become fairly successful at trading goods for the caribou skins brought in by hunting parties. With these two men and a few Tinneh families living nearby for company, Funston settled in a log cabin and prepared himself for a long, dark winter above the Arctic Circle.

The sun disappeared at last in the middle of November. Funston amused himself for a while by studying the Indians encamped at the post. "They are well-disposed people," he noted, "although savages living entirely by the chase, and are morally and mentally much superior to the Plains Indians of the United States." The Kansan thrived on comparisons; they were forever appearing in his writing wherever in the world he strayed. The Panamint Indians he had encountered in Death Valley had also been "well-disposed," he had noted two years earlier, and far superior to the "lazy, thieving butchers," the Apaches. Mirages in the California desert were "finer than those of the Sahara," quite a pronouncement for a young man who had never been to Africa. And the Alaskan Tinneh, who had no permanent settlements, were "nomads, constantly roaming about like the Tartars of Asia, following the movements of the herds of barren ground caribou, whose flesh is their principal article of diet, and whose skins furnish them with clothing and material for their beehive-shaped lodges."

Beyond this, there was not much for the restless young man to observe. Luckily, though, soon after he had marked his twenty-eighth birthday, he was granted respite from the tedium of an Arctic winter and the likelihood of cabin fever.

Trader David wanted to barter furs at a distant post for goods he could not obtain in the Yukon. He agreed to let Funston go with him and three other Tinneh on the two-hundred-mile trip, half of it along the Porcupine, the other half striking across snowfields and the northernmost spur of the Rocky Mountains to Peel River, in the valley of the MacKenzie. On the dim morning of November 17, when the mercury was 40 degrees below zero, five fur-clad men, sixteen dogs, and four birchwood toboggans slid down a riverbank onto the hard, snow-covered surface of the Porcupine and began their hike.

One man walked ahead of the caravan to break a track in the snow;

the others kept charge of the toboggans, encouraged the animals to pull on track, and untangled them when they fought. Funston was given a sled piled high with skins for trade, with the Indians hauling the group's food, cooking utensils, and sleeping robes. There was a strategy behind this: they knew a greenhorn when they saw one and did not want to trust food or robes to his care. As it turned out, they were right. Funston was not very adept at hiking on snowshoes; after a few miles his muscles and joints began to swell, he slowed, and his companions quickly left him behind. He soon became accustomed to keeping up until after the midday meal, then losing sight of them in the bleak landscape that dimmed into darkness by two in the afternoon. He followed their broken snow and watched for flares from matches they lit and held up for him on lakes or, when they struck across land, on ridgelines.

When the caravan had covered about twenty miles, the men would halt for the night. Using a sled, they would clear away snow from a selected spot and throw down several caribou skins. The sleds were then arranged to enclose and protect them from the wind. They would gather wood and build a fire at the foot of their bed. Each night around this time Funston would wearily trudge into the light, guided by the Indians' barking dogs, and collapse in a painful heap while his companions boiled the dried strips of caribou meat they carried as their only food. While the dogs' eyes glittered in the firelight, the men would pour melted tallow on the meat and eat. Feeding the animals necessitated clubbing the more savage dogs away from their weaker fellows' share. After supper they would roll up in their fur robes — two Indians on either side of Funston — and sleep, with the dogs soon creeping on top of them for warmth. "The only drawback to this arrangement," said Funston, "was their mania for fighting among themselves. We would be sleeping comfortably when suddenly there would be a yelp as one dog bit another, and then half a dozen of them would fight all over our prostrate forms. This always made the Indians furious."

One morning they awoke and it was 50 degrees below zero. The air "stung like the cut of a whip-lash." When they left the Porcupine, the territory became mile after mile of stunted willow and frozen sloughs. They stopped to rest for a day at an abandoned trading post, Le Pierre House, which had been taken over as winter quarters for a couple of Indian families. Resuming their trek, they saw rising before them an apparently unbroken chain of spotless white mountains stretching north to south: "It was the northern extremity of the Rockies, within fifty miles of where they slope down to the Arctic Ocean." Funston's excitement grew. During their midday rest, he strayed away from the caravan to explore, taking his rifle. He went to the top of a ridge and beheld a band of caribou scattered on the opposite hillside. From a distance of five hundred yards he brought down "a big buck with tremendous antlers." The Indians heard the shot and came running up the hill. "When they saw the big buck down in the snow," Funston recalled with satisfaction, "all tried to embrace me at once."

The next morning they came to the foot of the mountains and began climbing toward a high pass. By noon they had reached the summit of the Great Divide that separated the valley of the Yukon from that of the MacKenzie. Funston was exhilarated in the cold, thin air; he felt as if he were standing on top of the world. "The view was superb," he remembered,

> and beyond description. Everywhere were mountains, all spotless white, and to the east could be seen stretching like dark bands across the wastes of snow the timber growth that marked the courses of the MacKenzie and Peel rivers. Low down in the south were the rays of the sun, peering up from below the horizon and illuminating the sky as they do with us an hour after sunset, and the light could be seen shining direct on the summits of some of the higher peaks.

The Peel River trading post, which they reached late the following day, was presided over by "a fine bluff Scotchman," John Firth, who had not been south of the Arctic Circle for twenty years. He was delighted to see the young botanist, and for four days Funston entertained him with stories from a warmer world.

Funston and the Tinneh made better time on the return trip. They merely had to follow their own tracks back to Rampart House, and Funston became more adept at snowshoe travel. Twenty-two days and four hundred miles after the walking trip had begun, on December 8, 1893, he found himself back in his little cabin on the Porcupine River.

There was little to do in the dead of winter besides keeping warm — though on at least one occasion relations with the natives deteriorated. "I had a pretty serious row with the Indians," Funston wrote to his father with some understatement, "and came very near shooting into a crowd of them who were going to knock in the door of my house because I had given a buck a crack with a dog whip." Apparently, whatever sparked the altercation was later forgotten, for Funston did go out with the Tinnehs on several caribou hunts. Otherwise the winter oppressed him; a voracious reader, he had packed only two slim books and pored over them. They were by the poet laureate of his kind, Rudyard Kipling. Funston read and reread the

seven simple dialect-choked stories in *Soldiers Three,* delighting in the
colonial adventures of Kipling's three musketeers, Privates Mulva-
ney, Ortheris, and Learoyd; and he memorized most of the verses in
Barrack Room Ballads, perhaps reading them aloud while huddled near
his stove, his flat Kansas twang twisted into a rough approximation
of Cockney, the stirring, rhythmic stanzas echoing in his tiny cabin:

> For it's Tommy this, an' Tommy that, an' "Chuck him
>   out, the brute!"
> But it's "Saviour of 'is country" when the guns
>   begin to shoot.

The words would seem, on those dreadfully long and cold Arctic
nights, to impart a martial warmth to the Rampart House quarters:

> If a man doesn't work, why, we drills 'im an'
>   teaches 'im 'ow to behave
> If a beggar can't march, why, we kills 'im an'
>   rattles 'im into 'is grave.

Finally, even literature ceased to divert him. Then a Tinneh hunting party stopped by Trader David's to get warm and exchange gossip, bringing with them a rumor from the north: a whaling fleet win-
tering in the Arctic Ocean had been crushed and destroyed by ice
floes. Funston's curiosity could not be contained. He hired an Indian
to accompany him on a 600-mile round-trip trek on snowshoes to
investigate the report. They left Rampart House with dogs and a sled
on March 10, 1894.

Seven days later the two men ran out of food, going hungry for
two days before having to slaughter one of their sled dogs. Restored
to fitness, they encountered a band of Tinneh hunters later that day.
The Indians were also heading toward the whaling fleet, seeking to
take advantage of the catastrophe by selling fresh meat to the beleaguered whalers, and the two groups naturally combined forces in that
stark landscape. They sighted the black waters of the Arctic on March
27, followed the shore to the east for two days, and found the whaling crews, happily playing baseball on the snowy shore, their seven
undamaged steamships riding at anchor nearby.

The ballplayers forgot their sport and waded through the excited,
jumping sled dogs to gather around the fur-clad Eskimos — any
strangers were welcome in the Arctic winters. They were astounded
to hear, emitted with great clouds of steam from inside one of the
Indians' furry parka hoods, words of midwestern-accented English.

The "Eskimo" then introduced himself as a government botany agent by the name of Frederick Funston, from Iola, Kansas, who had walked three hundred miles on snowshoes to pay them a courtesy call.

Back at Rampart House a few weeks later, Funston ranged around the spring-softening tundra, collecting plant specimens. By mid-June he thought he had snipped and uprooted enough of the native flora to satisfy his superiors in Washington. Leaving his winter quarters behind and taking a Tinneh along as companion, he followed the Porcupine down to its convergence with the Yukon. There the *Nancy Hanks* awaited him. On July 3, 1894, Funston set off alone in the skiff for the last leg of his assignment: a botanical survey of the fourteen hundred river miles remaining between him and the Bering Sea.

From the Porcupine, the Yukon flowed southwest between the hills, dotted with islands and occasionally treacherous, growing wider and faster with every additional tributary it accepted. Dwarfed by its magnitude, Funston paddled for two months. He made night camps, fished, and shot small game along the banks. His specimen collection grew every day.

The voyage was not entirely relaxing. Often he would be startled out of a reverie by yips and a fusillade of arrows arcing from the brush-covered riverbank out over the water toward him. A few rifle shots in the direction of the misanthropic Indians kept them at a safe distance. Otherwise, Funston saw no evidence of human beings during the entire journey. He grew morbid and slightly mad at being so withdrawn from human contact; he became convinced that he was losing the use of his vocal cords, so he talked to himself, sang, and recited Kipling as he paddled. Toward the end of his trip, in the great northwesterly bend of the Yukon, he attempted to land the *Nancy Hanks* on the nose of an island. He overturned the skiff and all his belongings spilled out into the river. With great difficulty he kept the boat from being swept away and dragged it ashore. But he lost his guns, some five hundred photographic negatives, and all the specimens he had spent two months collecting along the lower Yukon. Four days later, on August 21, 1894, Funston guided the *Nancy Hanks* through the torrent spilling into Norton Sound on the Bering Sea and went ashore in the town of Kotlik, to arrange steamship passage back home.

III

The curious transition from government botanist to professional soldier was, for Frederick Funston, a meandering path he followed without much attention to his direction, making choices at several of his life's crossroads that seemed at the time to be totally by whim. The idea of being a civil servant, even an adventurous one, lost its appeal sometime during his long isolation, and though he still was short on ideas for a career, he had begun to develop a hunger for money. "I am going to resign my job," one letter written to his father from Rampart House confided,

> and start out with an illustrated lecture and make a pile of money out of this thing. My trip is without doubt the longest on record made by a white man alone in the Arctic regions, and if properly advertised will be a big thing. Frederick Schwather, whose trip in the Yukon was child's play compared with mine, cleared $25,000 lecturing in two years, and he did not have any photographs to illustrate his talk with. I would be a rank fool to let go by such an opportunity to make money but I don't want the folks in the Department of Agriculture to get an inkling of my intentions.

After he completed the report on his second trip to Alaska, Funston tendered his resignation and returned home to begin a lecture tour around Kansas. The *Iola Gazette* had been serializing its home town boy's letters for more than a year, but local fame did not a fortune make. To his disappointment, he made nothing near what he expected to. But, his mind awash with schemes, Funston saved his modest speaking fees for a venture that he wholeheartedly believed would work; now he wanted to establish a coffee plantation in southern Mexico. Such a proposition was totally beyond his previous experience and risky at best, but he found a few backers and journeyed south to look for sites. When his money began to run out, Funston went overland to New York, arriving in March 1895. Armed with introductions to various businessmen, he enlisted the aid of a friend from Kansas, Charles S. Gleed, an attorney who had connections in the city. But as Gleed later observed, like most young men who go to New York with a scheme, eyes bright with the prospect of finding money, he found none.

All of Funston's friends wanted him to succeed at something. White, as a journalist of growing reputation (he would purchase the *Emporia Gazette* that year), was in a unique position to help. His contribution to "getting Fred settled" took the form of a laudatory thirteen-hundred-word article on Funston's adventures in Alaska, which he published in *Harper's Weekly* soon after Funston arrived in New York City. "Nothing was said of his going, and no bugles were sounded upon his return," wrote White, "yet for continued hardship, unceasing danger and uninterrupted adventure, probably this trip has not been

excelled by any other on the American continent in this century."
Funston claimed he was embarrassed by White's puffery. Nevertheless, he cooperated with his biographer and obligingly supplied a
photograph of himself in his furry Arctic parka.

In the New York literary world of a much later time, such an introduction would have produced a small flurry of cordial invitations
to lunch from editors. But in 1895, the Kansan did his own legwork
as he commenced trying to make living expenses. This was as difficult then as it would be now; he had to supplement his meager magazine sales — at least for a few months, courtesy of a Gleed contact — working for the bond department of a railroad company.

Slowly, his writing began to find a market. Taking his 1891 boys'
magazine piece, "Storm Bound Above the Clouds," to demonstrate
he was already a published writer, he was able to make a few encouraging sales. *Harper's Weekly* bought a short, somewhat colorless
article on the terrain and commercial prospects along Alaska's eastern boundary, a topic Funston continued to explore in a series for a
Wall Street trade newspaper. The next piece he sold showed more
of the Funston writing style: it was descriptive, often witty, and marked
by an air of modesty, for Funston's self-promotion was nothing if not
discreet. Entitled "Over the Chilkoot Pass to the Yukon," the article
described the first part of his Alaska and Yukon adventures with his
three prospector friends. By the time *Scribner's Magazine* published
it, in late 1896, he was far away from New York and the idea of writing — and from the security of peacetime.

By the sheerest chance, Frederick Funston happened to be strolling
about the streets of New York on a spring evening in 1896, and, near
the corner of Madison Avenue and Twenty-sixth Street, he took in
the gaudy sight of Stanford White's Madison Square Garden. Its ornate façade and Moorish tower were incandescent from electric lights,
and a lively crowd clogged the building's pilastered arcade. Out of
curiosity, he pushed through the throng and entered the great ringing, flag-bedecked hall.

Funston found a political rally in progress, part of a month-long
fair at the Garden promoting the cause of the Cuban Revolution
against Spain. The principal speaker that night was none other than
General Daniel E. Sickles, a man out of the history books. Sickles was
the hero of Gettysburg, the firebrand who had lost his leg to Rebel
shrapnel in that glorious battle; he was the "Unrepentant Cuckold"
who had, as a congressman almost forty years before, shot his wife's
lover dead on a Washington street and had gone on to win one of
the most celebrated murder cases of the era. He was the former

minister to Spain who had loudly agitated for more than half a century for the annexation of Cuba by the United States; in a few months the palsied hands of the veterans of the Grand Army of the Republic would rise as one and nominate him for the governorship of Cuba — should that island ever be taken. Leaning over his lectern, the old, white-bearded soldier whipped the crowd into a froth of patriotism and moral indignation at the barbarities perpetrated so near the American shores by a corrupt and decadent colonial power. As Funston sat amid the audience, he was transfixed by Sickles's oratory. When he returned to his room, his mind whirled with all the accumulated martial images of his lifetime. He was unable to sleep a wink, for he had decided to go to his first war.

By enlisting in a foreign cause, Frederick Funston was not operating in a vacuum. Since the beginning of the decade, America had been "drifting in the dead water of the end of the century," in Henry Adams's words, confronted by a series of crises that seemed to threaten not just the old order but the very survival of the republic. To many, a sort of apocalyptic struggle had begun, and victory over the sundry forces of darkness seemed to hinge on acquiring foreign entanglements.

Much had changed during the time Funston had lived in the frozen North. On May 5, 1893, he had been hard at work building his boat on the headwaters of the Yukon while back at home, the day was to become known as Industrial Black Friday, the beginning of the Panic of 1893 and its result, a severe and unparalleled depression. By the summer, factories, mills, and mines nearly everywhere had ceased activity. Hundreds of thousands of workers were thrown off their jobs. By the year's end, some five hundred banks and fifteen thousand businesses had failed. "Uncertainty and fear," wrote a *Washington Post* editor, "spread like a pall over a hitherto prosperous land."

The early months of 1894 ground cruelly on the unemployed. In the spring, throngs of desperate and angry hoboes under the leadership of "General" Jacob Coxey converged on Washington to demand that something be done for the poor, only to have Coxey and his lieutenants thrown in jail for walking on the grass. That pathetic defeat was not the end of the unrest, however. Within a few months, more than thirty major strikes had broken out, including the most famous one — the Chicago Pullman Strike — begun, like the others, after workers' wages were reduced. Strikers burned the trainyards and the Pullman Palace Car Company's luxury coaches standing there. Within weeks, sympathetic railway workers had also struck, paralyzing fifty thousand miles of western railroads. Over the protests of the governor of Illinois, President Cleveland ordered U.S. troops to Chicago "to protect the mails," and amid further violence and bloodshed, the strike was quelled. But there were still millions of Americans with economic grievances that had gone unheeded for years. Among the correspondence of Secretary of State Walter Gresham, a single letter summed up the frustrations of those in the social rebellion as well as the worst fears of those in power: "If this keeps on long, fire and sword will sweep the country with flames."

Any hopes that the political leaders would respond positively to agitation for social change were doomed by the disarray of the major political parties at this time.

In the two generations since the Civil War, the Democratic and Republican parties had grown fat and corrupt, the party oligarchs complacent in the knowledge that in the minds and souls of the electorate, political parties were nearly identical to religions — one was born, one lived, and one died within the fold. One's aspirations and opinions could be predicted with only the party affiliation to go on. The voters were predictable and easily managed — or so the bosses thought. But as the end of the nineteenth century loomed, their predictability began to crumble as their dissatisfaction with their leaders grew.

The 1884 presidential contest between the Republican James G. Blaine and Grover Cleveland, a Democrat, might have sounded the first alarm when progressive Republicans marched out of the national convention and into the beefy arms of Cleveland, who won. The rebels earned for themselves the derisive title of "mugwumps" ("Their mugs are on one side of the fence, their wumps on the other"). Republican stalwarts hoped this was simply an aberration, and four years later they seemed to be right, for their ranks closed behind Benjamin Harrison, who went on to the White House. Far from being a return to the status quo, a national malaise was closing in on the land, and the political bosses did not see it coming.

In the 1890 off-year elections, the Republicans watched in horror as their House majority was lost — reduced to a token eighty-eight representatives. States that had voted Republican since the first election of Abraham Lincoln cast the Grand Old Party out of power. It was the voters' penalty for Congress's cynical betrayal of them on many fronts, most notably in the increase of protective tariffs, which brought their backers great profits and ushered the nation into deeper economic trouble. Yet even such a political upset as 1890's would not turn the bosses away from the path they had chosen.

The presidential election of 1892 continued the rebuke, as Grover

Cleveland returned to the White House and his party came into full control of both congressional houses. Many perceived this as a solid Democratic victory, but they were wrong, for the vote simply reflected the widespread loss of public confidence in *any* party's ability (let alone desire) to reverse the tide of riches and power flowing into the hands of a select few. Any Democratic confidence should have been tempered months before the election, at the national nominating convention. The progressives, who hoped for an enlightened approach to easing a worsening financial crunch, had seen their interests betrayed in favor of Cleveland and the status quo. It became the turn of this progressive bloc to bolt the party, which voters did in large numbers, joining the fledgling People's, or Populist party. Launched and backed only one year earlier by southern and western farmers, the Populist platform called for such radical changes as unrestricted silver coinage, the nationalization of all transportation and communication lines, a graduated income tax, the direct election of U.S. senators, and a shorter working day. The Populist presidential candidate, James B. Weaver, received more than a million votes. It was far fewer than those for the major parties, but it still represented a substantial threat if the party continued to grow.

The message from the hinterlands in 1892 was clear. Two years later the point was driven home. By 1894, President Cleveland had demonstrated to all how fully he remained in the thrall of the industrialists and gold-hoarding bankers. The Democrats were thereupon dealt the most stunning censure of any party and its president in an off-year election — losing 113 seats in Congress. It seemed as if the Democratic party was destined to join the long-dead Whigs in ignominious extinction.

Meanwhile, the depression deepened, the rural states floated free from the system in intense unrest, and labor agitation increased; an unprecedented 1,394 industrial strikes were recorded in 1894.

As the relationship between the politicians and the voters changed precipitously in that last decade of the nineteenth century, so did the national perception of exactly where salvation lay. From the year 1890 — when the Massacre at Wounded Knee ended three centuries of warfare against America's aboriginal inhabitants as well as when the U.S. Government declared that the American frontier was closed — attention began to turn outward. "The frontier had dissolved suddenly into the past," wrote the historian Walter Millis, "and we looked up to find nothing before our eyes save salt water and the nations of the earth which lay beyond it."

The United States had shown a pattern of small foreign interventions before 1890, in Nicaragua, Japan, Uruguay, China, Angola, and

Samoa, for instance. Mostly, these incidents involved the protection of American lives and commercial interests when the natives got troublesome.

In 1890, following their party's electoral upset, members of the Republican oligarchy became convinced that they would somehow have to transform the United States into a major world power. Also, they would make foreign affairs the preeminent concern in voters' minds. The following year gave them a country — Chile — and a test case. A street mob in Valparaiso attacked a group of American sailors on shore leave. Two Americans were killed and several more stabbed. Certainly, it was not the first time that foreign sailors looking for diversion after weeks at sea fell out of grace with their hosts. But President Harrison escalated the brawl nearly to the brink of war, which was narrowly averted by Chile's conciliatory payment of $75,000. Having won this truculent episode with little more than talk, the Republicans formally committed themselves to a national policy of expansionism in their 1892 party platform: "Achievement of Manifest Destiny of the Republic in its broadest sense."

In the desultory lame duck months of early 1893, another foreign chapter began. On January 17, American commercial interests under the leadership of Sanford Dole overthrew the Hawaiian government of Queen Liliuokalani and appealed for annexation. The American minister to Hawaii, F. L. Stevens, connived to help the plot. President Harrison quickly signed an annexation treaty with the coup leaders only to have Cleveland withdraw it when he came into office a few weeks later, on March 4. The "Hawaiian Pear" so ripe for the plucking, in Minister Stevens's phrase, would have to wait for another change of administration before it would be taken.

Cleveland may have appeared to be a man of unshakable principles who would not stoop to cheap posturing in foreign affairs. But he really had only one belief in his mind: that firm reliance on a gold standard would draw the nation out of the darkness of panic and depression. Repeatedly announcing this simplistic credo, he watched his popularity dwindle and agitation for social change increase. Worse, with Democrats beginning to swell the ranks of the heretical Populists, the threat of free silver loomed. So Cleveland became a born-again expansionist — but not with Hawaii, which had been snared by the Republicans as their issue. As he approached midterm, Grover Cleveland chose to engage none other than mighty Great Britain by muscling in on an obscure South American boundary dispute.

For more than fifty years, Britain and Venezuela had squabbled over a boundary of British Guiana that ran through little more than wilderness. President Cleveland entered the quarrel in December 1894 as a "disinterested party," concerned by what he characterized as the bullying of a small, weak neighbor nation. Securing the endorsement of his outgoing Democratic Congress, Cleveland directed his new secretary of state, Richard Olney, to draft a document that would simultaneously provoke Britain and raise the temperatures of newspaper editors and the great body of voters. Olney's previous governmental incarnation had been as attorney general, in which role he had masterminded the brutal suppression of the Chicago Pullman Strike. The document he produced, on July 2, 1895, was a masterpiece of sophistry. Employing the most bellicose tone imaginable, Olney threatened war if Britain did not submit to arbitration of the entire boundary matter. He warned that by occupying disputed territory in its own colony, Britain was in danger of being considered an "invader" of Venezuela, and thus in violation of the seventy-two-year-old Monroe Doctrine — a specious argument that left the British Foreign Office in complete befuddlement. In the four months it took for the British to compose a suitably haughty reply, furious anti-British sentiment surged on all levels across the nation, as party bosses and party newspapers agitated for English blood with a manipulated public following suit, fueled partly by a dislike of all things British and partly by innocent altruism for the Venezuelans. It is likely that there would have been a war in early 1896, with the United States fighting for a corrupt South American dictatorship, but an imperial dispute on another continent intervened. Had Kaiser Wilhelm of Germany not chosen January 3, 1896, to send a telegram to President Paul Kruger of the Transvaal Republic, congratulating him on turning back the British-led Jameson raid on Johannesburg, London would not have turned its back on Washington's thrown gauntlet. Instead, Great Britain faced the more threatening menace of the German Empire and ultimately decided that its troubles in South Africa were more pressing.

Once excited, however, the Americans' new appetite for war — any war — was not going to be assuaged. "It is time that some one woke up and realized the necessity of annexing some property," declared Senator Shelby M. Cullom of the Foreign Relations Committee. "We want all this northern hemisphere, and when we begin to reach out to secure these advantages we will begin to have a nation and our lawmakers will rise above the grade of politicians and become true statesmen."

The patrician and intellectual Republican senator from Massachusetts, Henry Cabot Lodge, agreed. In a highly influential article that appeared in *Forum* magazine as the British Guiana dispute was heating up, Lodge spelled out a specific program for the nation:

From the Rio Grande to the Arctic Ocean there should be but one flag and one country. . . . For the sake of our commercial supremacy in the Pacific we should control the Hawaiian Islands and maintain our influence in Samoa. England has studded the West Indies with strong places which are a standing menace to our Atlantic seaboard. We should have among those islands at least one strong naval station, and when the Nicaragua Canal is built the island of Cuba, still sparsely settled and of almost unbounded fertility, will become to us a necessity.

Much of Lodge's program was prophetic, especially his feelings about Cuba. That Caribbean isle would become a major Republican issue in the 1896 presidential election.

Americans had advanced the idea of annexing Cuba since as early as 1823, when Thomas Jefferson proposed taking it. After all, it lay only ninety miles off the Florida coast, one of the last remaining colonies of the decaying Spanish Empire. Large communities of naturalized expatriate Cubans in Florida and New Orleans continually clamored for intervention, as did a vocal and vigorous Cuban settlement in New York City. Revolutionaries had, over the years, fomented a number of rebellions. All had been miserable failures, but none so badly conceived as the Revolt of 1850–51, led by an ambitious Spanish general, Narciso López. He landed an army of volunteers composed chiefly of American, German, and Irish mercenaries and notably devoid of Cubans. The oppressed islanders were indifferent to their saviors, and the army was cut to pieces by the Spanish. Until 1860, the slave states in America were one in calling for Cuban annexation, but of course the Civil War frustrated their hopes. In 1868, a guerrilla campaign broke out on the eastern end of the island that would come to be called the Ten Years' War. As before, most of its supporters plotted strategy and lobbied for aid from the safety of New York. Despite the war's length, it never engaged the Spaniards' full attention. Though Washington flirted briefly with the notion of entering the fracas in 1873, nothing came of it and the revolution fizzled out.

Then, on February 24, 1895, a small band of expatriate Cubans led by José Martí and Máximo Gómez landed on the island's eastern coast. Martí soon died during a Spanish ambush, and the command passed to Gómez, a passionate old Santo Domingan with superb skills as a guerrilla fighter. Gómez's single revolutionary tactic was to stop the economic life of the island by burning canefields and starving out the garrisoned towns. In so doing, he hoped to force civilian refugees into his ranks, invoke suffering among those who remained, and invite Spanish countermeasures so harsh that they would arouse the Americans to intervene.

"Without a press, we shall get nowhere," the old general pro-claimed, so in New York the Cuban junta established a press office, which churned out inflated reports of Spanish atrocities — prisoners thrown to the sharks, civilian women defiled, babies torn from their mothers' arms. Throughout 1895 the American press carried these stories, which vied for attention with those decrying Great Britain's perfidies against Venezuela. When Gómez ordered all intraisland trains to be derailed and wrecked, while the smoke from burning crops moved implacably across the island until it stained the skies around Havana, Republican newspapers in the States somehow made it seem as if this was the work of the Spanish. Senators read these "dis-patches from the front lines" into the *Congressional Record,* perhaps not fully aware that their information was coming from junta type-writers in Lower Manhattan or being whispered in Havana hotel bars by rebel agents.

President Cleveland showed no inclination to drop his anti-British posturing for a squabble with Spain, despite an alarming clamor of mass rallies held around the nation in late 1895 and early 1896. He refused to grant belligerancy status to the Cuban rebels, an act that would surely have drawn the United States into war with Spain. But as soon as Congress convened in 1896, with Cleveland's Venezuelan question conveniently solved by Kaiser Wilhelm, it focused its con-siderable attention on Cuba and preparedness — the two great is-sues of the moment. The congressional docket was clogged with bills calling for new battleships, revenue cutters, torpedo boats, coastal defenses, new rifles for the military, and for Cuban aid.

"What is the occasion for all this militant insanity we do not know," fretted the *Journal of Commerce.* "Some of it is probably due to the fact that a generation has elapsed since we have had a war, and its unspeakable horrors are largely forgotten." While this might have explained away the ferocity of the masses, what about the politicians, whose angry peroration lay at the heart of the people's anger?

Senator Lodge called for Cuban independence "by any means nec-essary" — though only a year before he had urged its annexation. His good friend Theodore Roosevelt took time off from his job as New York City police commissioner to dispatch a flurry of letters to Lodge and other Republican friends, wondering how they could in-duce the country into war; in Chicago for a speech, he warned his audience to be ready to uphold America's honor "by an appeal to the supreme arbitrament of the sword." Meanwhile, the Republican senator from Maine, William Frye, lambasted the Spanish: "Spain is the most wicked despotism there is today on this earth. I have but one desire and that is to see Cuba an independent Republic."

In this cacophony was heard the lonely voice of George F. Hoar, the longtime Republican senator from Massachusetts and as different from Lodge and Roosevelt as he could be. He speculated as to what was going on around him in the Senate chambers and across the land. "I have sometimes been inclined to think that when you saw uncommon activity in our . . . somewhat sleepy Committee on Foreign Relations," he said, "it was circumstantial evidence, not that there was any great trouble as to our foreign relations, but that a Presidential election was at hand."

Indeed there was. Over Cleveland's objections, Congress passed a nonbinding resolution favoring recognition of the Cubans' belligerency status. During the summer's heated campaign, the Democrats and Populists forgot about foreign affairs, swept up in a romance with free silver coinage and inspired by William Jennings Bryan's "Cross of Gold" speeches. The Republicans' platform called for the annexation of Hawaii, the enlargement of the U.S. Navy, and "the ultimate union of all the English-speaking parts of the continent by the free consent of its inhabitants." And the Republican plan for Cuba? Independence, by "peaceful means."

When William McKinley was washed into the White House, the tide of boundless greed and bellicosity that helped put him there abated for a time. In his inaugural speech, McKinley vouchsafed a policy of diplomatic caution and reason: "We want no wars of conquest; we must avoid the temptation of territorial aggression."

Meanwhile, Cuba waited. The Philippines waited. Frederick Funston waited.

All during the frenetic campaign weeks of the summer of 1896, the summer that he decided to enter the martial life, Funston was prepared to leave for Cuba on a moment's notice. He had obtained an introduction to the Cubans' New York junta and they accepted him as a filibuster (as gringo mercenaries were called then), telling him to visit their office once a week until all the arrangements were made. Though he was unable to interest the *New York Sun* in commissioning him as a war correspondent earlier in the year, with his leave-taking imminent, *Harper's Weekly* promised to consider any stories he could send. As it turned out, however, none of his dispatches got through.

During one visit to the junta, the Cubans said they particularly needed artillery officers. This appealed to Funston — his father had been an artillery officer in the Union Army. Even though his own experience was limited to once "having seen a salute fired to President Hayes at a county fair in Kansas," he signed on with that des-

ignation and busied himself in learning what he could of field warfare. He visited an arms dealer, learned to take apart and put together
a Hotchkiss twelve-pounder breech-loading rifle, and committed its
velocity tables to memory. The junta was so pleased by his nascent
talent that he was set to instructing Cuban volunteers in a hall above
a Third Avenue saloon.

All of this was done with the utmost discretion. Though stump
speakers and newspaper editorials called daily for American involvement in the Cuban war, filibustering was still illegal under U.S. neu-
trality laws, as was the supplying of war materiel to the Cuban rebels.
So when Funston received an unsigned telegram instructing him to
appear at the Cortlandt Street Ferry, he stepped aboard the Hudson
ferry knowing only that he was going across the river to Jersey City.
The rest was a mystery.

His underground railway was the Pennsylvania, by which he and
four other filibusters were taken to Charleston, South Carolina. There
they joined thirty volunteers, all Cubans. Charleston was full of
Pinkerton detectives working for the Spanish government and also a
number of U.S. federal agents, all eager to catch the volunteers in
proximity to a boat and its damning cargo of rebel armament. By a
circuitous route, the volunteers evaded the agents and took a train
south to the coastal town of Woodbine, in southeastern Georgia, where
they met their ship, a sturdy tugboat called the *Dauntless*. For four
days the little ship rolled and tossed on the journey to Cuba. "We lay
about day after day in our water-soaked blankets," Funston recalled,
"getting such snatches of sleep as we could, and now and then staggering to the rail to make the required contribution to Neptune. We
certainly were an unhappy and as unheroic-looking a lot of adventurers as ever trusted themselves to the sea."

On the night of August 16, the *Dauntless* unloaded her passengers
and cargo on the sparsely populated northeastern coast of Cuba.
Funston and his American friends had made a pact before they
landed: should they be captured by the Spanish — which, they assumed, meant "swift and inevitable death" — the volunteers would
follow Kipling's advice:

> Just roll to your rifle and blow out your brains,
> And go to your God like a soldier.

After waiting several tense but uneventful days, the beached volunteers were found by a rebel detachment belonging to General
Máximo Gómez. Joining these soldiers, the recruits marched thirty
miles into the island's interior, a long and hard day's march for all.

After some gruff questioning, General Gómez put Funston in charge of two field guns and told him he could consider himself a provisional officer until he proved his worth. Then he would be commissioned. Funston confessed that his skills in artillery were somewhat limited. "Well," answered Gómez, "you cannot know any less than another American who came down here and said he knew it all." Funston did not inquire what had happened to that other American.

Thus, knowing no conversational Spanish and thus able to converse only with Cuban interpreters or other *yanquis* and having little acquaintance with artillery save what he had gleaned from instruction booklets, Funston became a gunnery officer in the Cuban *insurrecto* army.

He became ecstatic at the upland scenery — the heavily forested, rolling blue hills as yet unspoiled by war — and in the first few days of campaigning he drank in all the romance of the tropics and the cavalry in which he rode. Beef cattle and vegetable gardens were plentiful in those placid hills, and the army ate well.

All was uneventful until the column of three hundred infantry and six hundred cavalry reached the garrisoned town of Cascorra, in the eastern province of Camaguey. General Gómez ordered his forces to prepare for an assault. As artillery officer, Funston circled the town on his belly with a Cuban general to reconnoiter. What he saw worried him. "It was plain, even to a layman in the art of war," recalled Funston, "that we had a big job cut out for us." Most of the noncombatants had fled the town, leaving a force of about a hundred and sixty Spanish infantry. These defenders were well fortified. Three stone or brick buildings — a tavern, a church, and a municipal hall — were strengthened by sandbags, trenches, redoubts, and a maze of barbed-wire fences.

Funston's mood darkened when his superior ordered him to place his artillery entrenchment only four hundred yards away from the defenders, behind a simple earthen parapet the Cubans built for him under the cover of night. Funston realized, after his American artillery crew joined him, that they were expected to load, aim, and fire their piece while standing in an opening in the parapet the size of an ordinary door — completely exposed to enemy fire. When they had retired to their hammocks for the night, none slept a wink.

Daybreak found them crouching anxiously behind the parapet, flanked by fifty Cuban infantry lying exposed on each side. From across the flat expanse of knee-high grass they heard enemy sentries calling to one another as their last watch ended. A dog howled in the town. Otherwise, Funston noted that Cascorra was "as quiet as death itself." As the dawn began to drive away the shadows, he pulled a lanyard: a deafening crash, a burst of flame and smoke, and bricks tumbling down.

Then: "The air was suddenly full of those peculiar popping noises that we were soon to know so well, leaves dropped from the trees, there were odd movements in the grass, a patter against the opposite side of our shelter . . . a bullet struck the tire of one of the gun wheels with a sound like the blow from a hammer." The battle was joined.

Their "fighting blood" aroused and nervousness forgotten, the yelling Americans sent shell after shell crashing into walls and sandbags while the Cuban rebels cheered them on and entrenched Spanish soldiers replied with a withering fusillade. There seemed to be as much smoke in the air as in a Kansas prairie fire. Suddenly, as he was squinting through the sight, Funston was knocked off his feet by a hard blow to his left foot. A bullet had split the sole of his shoe and knocked off the heel, leaving him with a "considerable" bruise. Other soldiers were hit more severely; they were carried away to the rebel field hospital. Meanwhile, the Hotchkiss gun was being fired so rapidly, its barrel grew too hot to touch and its breech block expanded until they had to pour water on it to keep it firing. Throughout, two men loaded while another held the lanyard; Funston did most of the sighting — hopping up behind the gun and ducking bullets for the few seconds it took to adjust the screws — until a bullet came within millimeters of striking his nose and he retired for a time, his nerves spent.

The artillery siege of Cascorra lasted for five days, until Funston's crew ran dangerously low on ammunition. Hardly anything had been accomplished other than the destruction of most of the village buildings. At that point the rebels' heavy armament consisted of only direct-fire field pieces and common shells, which were fine for straight trajectory shots at fortifications, but did nothing against the enemy soldiers protected in their trenches; without mortars or shrapnel the fight was deadlocked, for Gómez did not want to risk his untested infantry against that maze of barbed wire and that desperate force of the Spanish. With hardly any more shells, the *yanqui* artillery battery was out of the battle until the last day of the siege. During this period of rest Funston was called just once to aim his gun at the battered church — but ordered not to fire until ten o'clock in the evening, when the Spaniards had crept into the building to sleep. "I did not exactly like this task," Funston confessed, "for it savored somewhat of assassination, but [I] carried out my instructions." He learned later that when the single shell roared out in the darkness, it killed or wounded four sleeping men.

Except for this incident the siege continued in sporadic fashion, with attackers and defenders shooting occasionally across a burned and blasted field. On the tenth day, Gómez put his Hotchkiss gun back into action. His men erected a parapet less than two hundred yards from the enemy trenches, and at this proximity they poured out their last shells. Then, as heavy tropical rains began to fall, the battle slowed to a halt. Learning from scouts that a large Spanish relief force of twenty-five hundred was approaching Cascorra, the *insurrectos* withdrew, leaving behind little more than an ugly demolition job.

Gómez's infantry harassed the reinforcements as they arrived to evacuate the embattled town; when the Spaniards proceeded to steal out of Cascorra in the night, getting a two-hour start on the Cubans, Gómez pursued. By the evening, Gómez and his six hundred cavalrymen had left the infantry troops behind and succeeded in circling in front of the bivouacked enemy force. In the darkness of the early morning of October 8, they waited for the Spanish.

As the eastern horizon began to show the slightest hint of light, the Cubans emerged from a patch of woods onto a level savannah as a thick fog settled around them. Unable to see more than thirty feet, the soldiers whispered nervously to one another, their voices trembling under the stress of waiting. Funston, who had volunteered for cavalry duty, realized he would have given any amount to be elsewhere.

> We now began to hear noises in our front, sometimes the neigh of a horse or the bray of a mule, but more than anything else the sort of undefinable sound made by more than 2000 men splashing along the muddy road, with the accompanying jingle and rattle of their arms and equipment. The rumbling grew louder and nearer, and all of us were straining our eyes to pierce the fog, when suddenly it ceased, and all was as silent as ever.

The rebels felt a breeze at their backs. It began to roll back the fog. Finally they made out what at first looked like a hedge or a picket fence about four hundred yards away, then they realized they were facing the massed enemy infantry; the Spanish soldiers stood in two lines forming a right angle, with a pair of artillery pieces standing in the center. The Cubans murmured in surprise and consternation.

For thirty seconds the armies contemplated each other across the savannah.

"From where Gómez and his staff were waiting came the quick, jerky ra-ta-ta-ta-ta of the headquarters bugle sounding the charge," Funston would write.

The effect was magical and instantaneous . . . the whole line moved
forward, first at a trot, and then at a gallop. The Cubans were firing
over the heads of their horses as they advanced, with Winchester and
Remington carbines, while above the terrific din rose the yells of *Viva!
Viva Cuba! Adelante, adelante! Arriba, arriba!* We had covered scarcely
forty yards when a blaze of light broke along the whole front of the
Spanish line, followed in a few seconds by another, and then another,
while at each discharge the air about us seemed full of the spiteful
crackling of Mauser bullets. . . . Men and horses were falling on every
side, while above the crash of rifle volleys and the booming of cannon
rose the frantic cheers of the Cubans and the thunder of nearly two
thousand hoofs.

The Spaniards ceased firing orderly volleys and now wildly shot
their carbines from the hip. The rebels rode furiously up and down
their lines shooting into their faces. It occurred to Funston that the
Cuban army would be cut to pieces before too long.

"Suddenly a lively scattering of fire opened on our right," he recalled, "and the woods 500 yards distant were being flecked with the
white smoke of the Remingtons." It was Gómez's infantry, advancing
at a crouch and firing upon the heretofore unassaulted Spanish flank.
Seeing no possibility of winning, the Spanish commander ordered his
men into a slow retreat — which they did, taking along their two
hundred dead and wounded.

In the exultant flush of victory, Funston swore he would never
forget the thrill of "that wild charge across the Cuban savanna." In
a quieter moment he would write confidently, in that comparative
mood he affected when considering his adventures, that the Cuban
charge at Desmayo more than equaled one of the most famous battles of the past.

At Balaklava the Light Brigade charged against men armed with muz-
zle-loading flintlocks and batteries of old-style cannon. In the ride of *
half a league they lost thirty-seven per cent of their number in killed
and wounded, and the world will never forget the story of their valor.
At Desmayo that little force of 479 Cubans rode against magazine rifles, firing twenty shots a minute, and breech-loading artillery, and held
their position in the face of that pitiless fire until fifty-two per cent had
tumbled from their horses, killed or wounded.

"But nobody has written a poem about us," he finished, "or ever
will."

Perhaps after this assertion appeared in a magazine, someone gently
corrected Funston: in the famous one-and-a-half-mile charge of Lord
Cardigan's Light Brigade in the Crimea, fewer than 200 returned of
the 673 who began that suicidal dash against thirty Russian cannon.

Because the quarter-mile gallop under fire at Desmayo was Funston's first cavalry charge, he should be understood in his enthusiasm at trying to insert this event, indelibly impressed as it was on his memory, into the historical record. Years later, while writing his memoirs, Funston seemed to regret his youthful impulsiveness by dismissing "Desmayo — the Cuban Balaklava" in one sentence, admitting that the Cuban loss that day was only three killed and sixteen wounded. Regrettably, he omitted the otherwise crisp and vivid account of his first "wild charge" entirely.

One artillery siege and one cavalry charge closer on the long path from Kansas to the Philippines, Funston grew to be an adept warrior in the continuing months.

Soon after its small triumph at Desmayo, Gómez's force joined the army of General Calixto García in an assault upon the strongly fortified town of Guáimaro, a place of deep emotional significance since 1869. It was there that the revolutionaries had written their constitution and designed the flag under which they fought during the Ten Years' War.

In a furious siege, Funston was promoted to major, succeeding an American officer shot between the eyes by sniper fire. Under his leadership, the Cuban artillery slowly demoralized the Spanish troops. After ten days the rebels captured Guáimaro and its defenders, and the Spanish commander was mortally wounded during Funston's cannonade. In the flush of victory, when the Kansan happened to be walking by the field hospital where the prisoners were being cared for, he was pointed out to the dying Spanish officer by a Cuban soldier. "That American is the man who gave you your wound," the Cuban exclaimed in what Funston thought was "wretched taste."

"I slunk out of sight," he confessed, "my peace of mind pretty badly disturbed."

When the Spanish governor of Cuba, Don Valeriano Weyler, rode out from his palace in Havana in late 1896 to survey the countryside, he noticed that many canefields had somehow escaped being torched by guerrillas. He deduced correctly that the fields remained green only because of a blackmail "tax" that the estate owners paid to the rebel Gómez, so Weyler ordered all sugar-grinding halted. This deprived the rebels of some support and the last gainfully employed Cubans of their livelihood.

Weyler's next move continued this line of reasoning. He rounded up the entire civilian populace of the province of Pinar del Río and imprisoned them in "reconcentration" camps in the garrison towns.

Attempting to starve the insurgents by depriving them of their civilian support, Weyler visited that same lamentable condition upon the helpless peasants. Hunger and disease moved through the camps, but misery would not be confined there for long.

As Pinar del Río was swept clean, the encircling Spanish cordon in that province surprised and killed a popular rebel general, Antonio Maceo, who had tried to flee the devastated region for the relative safety of eastern Cuba, which was less populated. With Maceo's death, Weyler drew new confidence. He began pushing eastward in early 1897, destroying or seizing everything in his path that might aid the rebels. The number of reconcentration camps grew.

In the midst of a worsening famine, the army of Calixto García, to which Funston had been assigned, did little between November 1896 and March 1897 but wander aimlessly across eastern Cuba. The few civilians left in the countryside had little to share with the soldiers, who nonetheless confiscated whatever they could find. Spanish supply convoys were ambushed or isolated posts attacked whenever possible.

In desperation, García ordered a massing of forces — more than four thousand men — to participate in an assault against a nearly impregnable commercial center, the large town of Jiguaní.

The siege began on March 13, 1897. Funston fired the first salvo with a high-velocity naval landing gun that had been presented to the insurgents by the sympathetic cigar makers of Key West, Florida. For two days he and his men dueled with a Spanish artillery crew. The Spanish cannon fired projectiles at a velocity slow enough that the rebels were able to dodge the shells when they saw them coming. Once, though, on the first day, Funston was knocked off his feet by a shall fragment that struck him in the chest and left an ugly bruise.

On the evening of March 13, Funston proposed two schemes to García. They were reminiscent of his daring and foolish boyhood attempt to follow the mountain lion into its den. His first idea was to lead his American artillerymen in a nighttime sortie against the enemy's major fortress. Taking only pistols, crowbars, and twenty-five pounds of dynamite, they would creep to the base of the walls and detonate the explosives. After thus alerting the soldiers within, they would shout up to the Spaniards to surrender, claiming that fifty men with similar charges were poised to destroy the fort. García thought the idea was insane. Funston's other plan was for him to assault the fortress, alone, with a homemade bomb made of cotton camphor and gunpowder, which would signal a concentrated artillery barrage. García doubted this plan would throw the Spanish into a panic and overruled it.

The next day's fight proved to be a disaster. Funston was standing away from the protection of his parapet, calling directions to his crew, when he saw a dark object flying toward him. He threw up his hands to shield his eyes and there was an explosion — a hot piece of shrapnel struck him, breaking and mangling his left arm.

Funston finished directing the artillery that day with his arm splinted, bandaged, and tied across his chest, but even a renewed bombardment could not shake loose the enemy. García ordered an infantry charge against the town, but the force was repulsed after a hellish fight. Of the Cuban rebels, about four hundred were killed or wounded.

General García rewarded his American artillerymen with a month's furlough after the aborted siege of Jiguaní. In the wake of all the excitement, Funston's morale began to plummet. Besides the problem of his broken arm, he had contracted malaria in January and was subject to periodic fevers and chills. Food had been scarce for five or six months, so, like everyone else, he was perpetually light-headed from hunger.

The romance had disappeared from war. No longer did he write friends and family to exclaim how right Kipling had been in describing the glory of battle — such as the aesthetic thrill he received when reading in "Gunga Din" about the bullets "kicking up the dust spots on the green" and seeing that very thing only hours later. Now he wrote to his sister Ella that he had been "a pretty big fool to . . . mix up in this War," and he hoped he could return home in five or six months. In a letter to an Iola friend, Charles F. Scott, he bared all. One by one their old friends were getting married and settling down, thus in Funston's mind shutting themselves off from true comradeship forever. "I have gone past that period in my life when I can make new friendships," he confided. "I am soon to be alone in the world. . . . Yesterday I thought of this so hard that I shed some unmanly tears. . . . The best of my life is behind me."

Lonely and in a morbid mood that made him half wish that a Spanish Mauser bullet might speed him "from the full vigor of manhood into Eternity," Funston was swept back into the routine of the war, the endless foraging for food, the harassing attacks against isolated posts and army units.

Then, on June 20, in a skirmish with a detachment of Spanish soldiers, Funston got his Mauser bullet — he was shot through both lungs. Transported into the mountains by two Cubans, who carried him in a hammock suspended from a pole, he recuperated in a jungle hospital. Then, the guerrillas' medical facilities being what they were, he contracted typhoid fever. Not until ten weeks later was he able to rejoin Gómez, just in time to take part in the *insurrectos'* fall offensive. It would be his last major engagement in Cuba.

In late August there occurred another massing of rebel troops under García. This time nearly six thousand ragged, hungry, and determined Cubans lay siege to the town of Victoria de las Tunas, in northern Oriente province. García's army effectively sealed off the garrison from all possibility of outside help. Funston's crew seized an unprotected ridge that overlooked Tunas; the rebel battery was equipped with six weapons, including a type never before used in warfare — a Sims-Dudley dynamite gun that fired a canister containing a bursting charge of five pounds of nitroglycerine. Having such a terrible weapon and a clear view of all the town's defenses, the rebels were certain of success.

As the artillery barrage advanced, reducing the fortified buildings to rubble and emptying trench after trench of Spanish soldiers, the rebel infantrymen dashed in to take over the abandoned positions while Funston directed his shells over the heads of his advancing comrades. "I fairly shook with excitement," he recalled, "and kept saying to myself, 'Keep cool, keep cool.'" Dodging enemy artillery shells and bullets and dancing from behind the smoky parapet to see the action below him, he watched as an American friend, Lieutenant Colonel Napoleon Chapleau, led a small Cuban detachment against the garrison barracks. Chapleau was wounded in the neck and quickly carried to the rear. Funston hastened over to see how his friend fared.

> I saw the general and his staff, standing uncovered and with bowed heads [Funston would write], while the blood gushed in torrents from the wounded man's throat, drenching the surgeon who was attempting in vain to stop its flow. Chapleau, perfectly conscious, was muttering, "It is finished," "It is finished," "It is all over," his voice growing gradually weaker until his head sank down on his breast, and another brave man had died a soldier's death. The scene just described is such a one as we have all seen on the stage in melodramas and military plays, and have always thought overdone and unreal. But within a stone's throw was a battery in action, and as Chapleau sank into his last sleep with the silent and uncovered men about him, the last sounds he heard were the booming of the guns and the crackle of the Mausers and the whistling of their bullets while the wisps of smoke blowing back from the battery gave a setting that could not be had on any stage.

Not all of what he saw in the two-day siege struck Funston so romantically. As victory seemed assured, the rebels — who had fought their way into the town and taken the enemy positions one by one — confronted two besieged blockhouses with Funston's dynamite gun, which had been pulled into the town. The blockhouses sheltered about forty Cuban loyalists who had long fought beside the Spanish and who were known for their merciless slaughtering of wounded rebel countrymen both on the battlefield and in field hospitals they had overrun. These traitors knew well that they could expect no quarter from the *insurrectos,* Funston saw. They threw down their carbines and marched out into the street, where they stood while the rebels waded among them with machetes, killing them all. "It was a shocking spectacle, but it was retributive justice if there is such a thing," Funston rationalized, "for these men had never known what mercy was." It was the sort of excuse the Kansan would hear again, and be heard to utter again.

Promoted to lieutenant colonel after the victory at Tunas, Funston nonetheless increasingly yearned to leave the island. But General García pleaded with him to remain a while longer.

Another accident intervened during a cavalry rush in October, when Funston's horse was shot out from under him. He hit the ground a few seconds before the mount rolled on top of him, crushing his legs and deeply impaling his thigh upon a dry stick. Thrown back on the mercy of the rebels' surgeons, Funston languished in a remote hospital with a badly bruised hipbone and a wound that developed a nasty abscess. By late November he believed it possible that he might die of the infection or, if he survived the tropics, that he might be a cripple for life. While talking this over with an American friend, James Pennie, who was severely ill with malaria, Funston suggested they leave together for the mainland.

Their petition for a medical furlough was immediately approved by General García, with the understanding that they would return to fight after proper treatment in the United States. To Funston's disappointment, the general's permission was overruled by the revolutionary civil government, which saw no reason why the *yanquis* should be permitted to sail away from the collective misery if the tens of thousands of Cuban *insurrectos* could not.

There seemed to be no other choice for the weakened men but to leave anyway. Taking García's worthless transit passes, they rode north. They hoped that once they reached the coast, the documents would be taken for real and get them aboard a filibustering ship returning to the mainland.

On December 12, the two were intercepted by a Spanish patrol. Pennie evaded them; Funston found himself at last a prisoner. Staring into the muzzles of his captors' rifles, knowing he could be shot at any moment, Funston told his story as quickly as he could dream it up:

Yes, he was an *insurrecto* but *(wringing his hands)* now he was a deserter — he had been looking for Spaniards *(straining to get the Spanish words right)* to whom he could surrender. He was tired of war *(taking his grimy handkerchief out, and with it, the pass from García that would condemn him)* and he hated the revolutionaries *(swabbing his sweaty face with the handkerchief);* he had information to exchange for his life *(slipping the crumpled pass into his mouth),* valuable information *(swallowing it).*

The Spaniards bound him hand and foot and took him before the local commander at Puerto Príncipe, to whom Funston told his story. He was then taken before a board of court-martial, where he repeated his tale, and the convened Spanish officers believed him. Escaping execution, he kept his bargain by concocting an elaborate fabrication of information they already knew and plausible lies. The Spaniards made him swear he would never again aid the *insurrectos.* It was an oath he was able to keep, for before the year's end they had conveyed him to Havana and the enfolding protection of Consul General Fitzhugh Lee. Soon he was put aboard the first available ship for New York. The year 1898 — a turning point for the fortunes of Cuba, Spain, the United States, and the Philippines — had commenced.

When his spirits had been lowest, when Funston had despaired of ever returning home, he had written several bitter letters wondering why the government of William McKinley was "playing a damnable dirty part" by ignoring "one of the most merciless and cruel wars in the history of mankind." Funston had no idea how much attention had been paid to the Cuban situation by certain parties in Washington all during 1897 — and no way of knowing, as his ship steamed athwart of Key West, Florida, on his return home, that the U.S.S. *Maine* lay at anchor there, awaiting the coded telegram from Consul General Fitzhugh Lee that would summon the warship to Havana Harbor.

President McKinley — the genial, ambiguous, long-winded former congressman from Ohio — struck most of his contemporaries as an enigmatic figure of limited ambition, known to hold no values dearer or more complex than protectionism and patriotism; most saw him as essentially a weak politician. Actually, as Henry Adams astutely observed, McKinley was the "first genius of manipulation." He was a mandarin who let others do his maneuvering for him, seeming only reluctantly to acquiesce to forces outside himself. McKinley was actually seldom surprised by the rush of events because he was only very rarely not in control of them. Seeing clearly the threat to party stability that widespread voter discontent almost guaranteed, Mc-

Kinley's every action was calculated to keep his party in control and minimize trouble from Democrats, Populists, and any splinter groups within the Grand Old Party. His "antiboss" presidential campaign, which successfully kept Republican mugwumps in the fold, had actually been supported and financed by the state political machines he seemed to be against. To the voters he appeared to favor restricting the business trusts, though after his election he did nothing to hinder the growing concentration of wealth and power in the hands of a few. And though he privately told friends like Carl Schurz that "there will be no jingoistic nonsense in this administration," he resolutely set about instituting a policy of expansionism. The president's inaugural speech ("We want no wars of conquest; we must avoid the temptation of territorial aggression") was the last public utterance he would make about pacifism.

McKinley's subsequent actions puzzled many. As a seemingly peace-loving Republican president who had once been a major in the Union Army, he retained Cleveland's Cuban consul, Fitzhugh Lee, despite the fact that Lee, a former Confederate cavalry officer and a nephew of Robert E. Lee, was a Democrat with a well-publicized eagerness to involve the United States in a Spanish war. The president shifted the senile (but nonetheless bellicose) John Sherman from a seat in the Senate to his Cabinet, as secretary of state. This move had the added utility of bringing McKinley's campaign manager, Mark Hanna, to Sherman's vacant place in the Senate. Of the two changes, the appointment of Sherman, who fulminated against Spain until the outbreak of war, would be more significant to American foreign policy.

One of McKinley's most interesting new lieutenants was none other than Theodore Roosevelt, who was given the post of assistant naval secretary. His superior, John D. Long, was a notoriously weak administrator. Two months after taking his new job, Roosevelt made a bellicose speech at the Naval War College: "No triumph of peace is so great as the supreme triumph of war," he said, earning a mild rebuke from Secretary Long and a private, discreet assurance from McKinley that he "heartily endorsed" Roosevelt's sentiments.

With no more than hints from the president that he was following the right course, Roosevelt quickly became the administration's most prominent spokesman for expansionism. Nearly every day he met for lunch at the capital's Metropolitan Club with other influential politicians, military officers, editors, and intellectuals — men such as the senators Henry Cabot Lodge, W. P. Frye, and W. E. Chandler; the naval intelligence chief, Charles H. Davis, Captain Alfred Thayer Mahan, and Commodore George Dewey; Judge William Howard Taft; Brooks Adams, the philosopher; Dr. Leonard Wood, a veteran of the

Indian Wars and now the president's assistant attending surgeon; and others, all of whom pined for one version or another of Manifest Destiny and who waited impatiently for the president to do something forceful about Cuba.

While shrewdly seeming to resist this clubby cabal's pressure, McKinley proceeded to follow its preferred national course faithfully, though at his own slow pace. Fourteen weeks after his inauguration, McKinley signed a new treaty annexing Hawaii. It was submitted to the Senate and tabled until the following spring, when the expansionists were confident they would have enough votes at last to acquire that foothold in the Pacific.

All through his first ten months in office the president pushed and pushed against the Spanish government, seeking to force them to enact measures that rather than alleviate Cuban suffering, would ultimately ensure American intervention. On May 17, 1897, he called for a $50,000 appropriation in answer to Fitzhugh Lee's wild claims that "a large number of American citizens [in Cuba] are in a state of destitution." The required legislation was swiftly passed. On June 26, he dictated a note to the Spanish ambassador, Depuy de Lome: if Spain did not revoke its reconcentration orders and enact reforms in Cuba, the American government would intervene "in the name of common humanity." Three weeks later he ordered his new ambassador to Spain, Stewart Woodford, to inform Madrid that the United States would wait only "a reasonable time" before stepping in. Then the president sent Woodford to the capitals of Europe to see if any would come to Spain's aid after such an American intervention. Woodford's poll suggested that the way was clear, for most nations wondered why McKinley was making it harder for Spain to do what he demanded; of intervention Europe said nothing.

By this time, a stumbling block had reared up in McKinley's path. On August 8, the Spanish premier was assassinated by an anarchist in Madrid, which precipitated an abrupt change in government: the Spanish Liberal party took over under the leadership of Práxedes Sagasta, who had long been the champion of relaxed rule over Cuba. The new premier immediately pledged that Cuba would be granted Canadian-style autonomy. He recalled the notorious General Weyler and ordered an end of reconcentration in October; by November 14, Sagasta's new governor general had revived farming outside the miserable reconcentration camps and started to care for the neglected peasants.

To these reforms McKinley had nothing to say — at least not until his annual message to Congress on December 6. Using rhetoric so reasonable and pacific in tone that warmongers in the opposition

Democratic party condemned him for his lack of backbone, the president discounted Madrid's reforms as well meaning but insignificant, the autonomy proposal as unacceptable. In addition, despite Spain's attempts to avert war, McKinley deliberately moved up his deadline for a peaceful settlement. Previously he had specified a "reasonable time"; now he warned that Spain should, for all intents and purposes, yield its sovereignty "in the very near future." Otherwise, he threatened, "it will be a duty imposed by our obligations to ourselves, to civilization and humanity, to intervene with force." Thus the president sent a message to the Cuban rebels: if they continued to fight for a few more months, they would soon have American troops on the island to fight their battles for them.

A little more than one week after McKinley's congressional speech, on December 15, the United States battleship *Maine* arrived at Key West, dispatched by the president at the request of Consul General Lee. "An extensive and dangerous" anti-American conspiracy had reared up in Matanzas province, Lee claimed, and he required naval support close at hand. McKinley placed his battleship at Lee's disposal; all that was required was one telegram from Havana.

The opportunity came on January 12, 1898, when for one brief hour, Spanish army officers stoned several Havana newspaper offices and wrecked their presses, complaining of biased reportage. Lee telegraphed home a series of alarming reports: "mobs" roamed Havana at will, he said; he had heard "rumors" that they might march on the consulate. As the days passed, Washington waited tensely for more news, but the choleric old diplomat seemed to have lost his nerve when it came down actually to precipitating a war. McKinley took matters into his own hands on January 24, ordering the *Maine* to Havana. He reassured the public that he was only doing so as a friendly act of courtesy, but what could be made of this maneuver? As the historian Walter Karp has succinctly said, "After warning the Spanish ambassador that an anti-American outburst in Cuba would compel him to send in troops, the President ordered the warship to Havana to provoke an anti-American outburst."

For two weeks the *Maine* rode the swells at her mooring in Havana Harbor while Spanish dignitaries nervously showed her officers every courtesy. They even sent aboard a case of sherry for the Americans' comfort. Privately, of course, the Spaniards prayed that the ship would leave before trouble appeared.

It seemed that everyone in America favoring war with Spain — by now not just editors of the sensationalist party press, the Democrats, and Roosevelt's expansionist friends, but also a considerable segment of the citizenry — was pleased at this turn of events, though if the warmongers could have had their way, the *Maine* would have gone in with guns blazing, backed up by the rest of the North Atlantic coastal squadron. By then, that fleet had been sent at Roosevelt's importuning to Key West. The assistant naval secretary, never one to mince words with his friends, chafed at McKinley's caution and complained that the president had "no more backbone than a chocolate éclair."

In the face of such gathering tension, what, one might ask, could Henry Cabot Lodge have meant by the curious statement he made on January 31: "There may be an explosion any day in Cuba which would settle a great many things," he wrote to a friend in London, the diplomat Henry White. "We have got a battleship in the harbor of Havana, and our fleet, which overmatches anything the Spaniards have, is masked at the Dry Tortugas."

Exactly how candid were Senator Lodge's words? It will never be clear. On the night of February 15, the U.S.S. *Maine* blew up in Havana Harbor, with 262 killed of its 350-man crew.

A collective shudder ran though the American public, but most people refrained from making instant judgments until a hastily convened Naval Board of Inquiry released its findings. Not patient enough to wait for its report, Roosevelt assumed the disaster "was an act of dirty treachery on the part of the Spaniards." That opinion was echoed on the yellow editorial pages of the sensationalist press, but regardless of what the publisher William Randolph Hearst and others would say, it was generally recognized that the group standing to gain the most from the disaster was not the Spanish, for they would lose everything, but the Cuban rebels. Though subsequent theories, offered away from the heat of war, have pointed to an accidental cause within the ship (such as a boiler explosion or a seaman smoking too close to the forward powder magazine), the Inquiry Board released a report on March 28, suggesting on very flimsy evidence that the explosion was due to an external force: a mine. That absolved the U.S. Navy of any blame.

The report stopped short of assigning guilt to anyone, but it arrived too late, for regardless of what had sent the *Maine* to the bottom of Havana Harbor, the urge toward war had developed its own momentum. In the wake of the explosion, a dead calm had fully descended upon Washington. McKinley maintained his guise as a victim of circumstance. He appeared to have been profoundly shaken by the weight of events. His actions, however, spoke louder than anything he might have said. Presidential emissaries sent to sound out the economic titans in New York and Boston reported a growing eagerness to bring matters to a head — for the improvement of the economy a war would generate. A more confident McKinley persuaded a crony, Joe Cannon, chairman of the House Appropriations Committee, to put forth a $50 million bill for national defense but shrewdly made sure his name would not be attached to it. Cannon introduced the bill, which swiftly passed in both chambers without a single dissenting vote. To the world it looked as if a militant Congress was prodding its reluctant president into action.

The Spaniards were stunned by the popular support for the "$50 million Bill," but more shocks were to come. On March 17, Senator Redfield Proctor of Vermont rose to address his colleagues. He was a former secretary of war, under Harrison, a stern Yankee politician. He claimed, as he began speaking, that he had been an antiexpansionist. This in itself was curious, since the few who knew him well were aware that he was solidly in agreement with Roosevelt's expansionist cabal. Having made that claim, which was widely circulated, Proctor related his findings during a cursory inspection of Havana, from which he had just returned. He had found untold miseries, he reported, and had heard many reports of Spanish atrocities. He had become convinced that there was no path for the country but "humane intervention."

Proctor's speech was a propagandist's dream. In one stroke it dealt a mortal blow to the crumbling congressional peace faction, all but silenced the protestations of Wall Street, and renewed the public hunger for revenge.

On March 29, the Spanish government received an ultimatum from Washington. Madrid was to lay down its arms while the United States negotiated between the rebels and the Spanish government "through the friendly offices of the President of the United States." In addition, reconcentration was to be revoked immediately. The ultimatum demanded an answer within two days.

The Spaniards agreed to lift reconcentration within the deadline. However, they balked at disarming, for that was simply too humiliating. Only when the pope interceded, out of pity for their plight, did they agree to put down their weapons.

Unmoved, McKinley rejected the Spanish offer, now claiming the matter was out of his hands: "I cannot assume to influence the action of the American Congress," he said. Despite this intransigence, Spain formally announced an armistice on April 9. It was too late for even this gesture to avert war.

McKinley's response to this latest Spanish move — the culmination of extraordinary concessions of one sovereign nation to another in peacetime over what could be considered internal affairs — was to begin drafting his war message to Congress. He delivered it before a joint session on April 11:

> Gentlemen, in the name of humanity, in the name of civilization, in behalf of endangered American interests which give us the right and the duty to speak and to act, the war in Cuba must stop. . . . I have felt constrained on repeated occasions to enter the firm and earnest protest of this government. Of the untried measures there remain only neutral intervention to end the war by imposing a rational compromise between the contestants; and intervention as the active ally of one party or another.
>
> I speak not of forcible annexation, for that cannot be thought of. That, by our code of morality, would be criminal aggression.
>
> I have exhausted every effort to relieve the intolerable condition of affairs which is at our doors. I now ask the Congress to empower the President to take measures to secure a full and final termination of hostilities in Cuba, to secure in the island the establishment of a stable government, and to use the military and naval forces of the United States as may be necessary for these purposes. . . .

That Spain had already surrendered he neatly ignored, but for an oblique reference buried far down in his long text, where he claimed that Madrid had made only the vaguest movements toward ending the strife.

Handed this politically popular issue, Congress debated for just one week before passing, on April 19, a favorable joint resolution calling for the "forcible intervention of the United States as a neutral to stop the war, according to the large dictates of humanity." However, expansionists desiring to add the island of Cuba to American territory were thwarted by a clever amendment inserted by a Colorado senator, Henry M. Teller, which expressly forbade the United States from exercising "sovereignty, jurisdiction, or control" over the island. In the jubilation of the debate, the Teller Amendment passed unnoticed.

By the time the Spanish government learned that the resolution for intervention had passed, with McKinley's signature affixed to it, there was nothing left for them to do but declare war. The next day, April 25, McKinley sought and received the preordained reply, his joint congressional declaration of war against Spain. It was backdated — to April 23, 1898.

IV

Across the State of Kansas there was an unprecedented rush to buy flags and patriotic bunting, for the citizens' excitement had been rising steadily for months. With each new episode unfolding in this international drama, throngs of jayhawkers gathered around the bulletin boards of the newspaper offices to learn the latest news: THE MAINE BLOWN UP! FIFTY MILLION DOLLARS FOR DEFENSE! SENATE FOREIGN RELATIONS COMMITTEE RE-INTRODUCES HAWAII ANNEXATION BILL! KEY WEST FLEET STRIPPED FOR ACTION! The bulletins were welcome in rural towns and farms grown dim in the long economic recession.

In early March, handbills and posters appeared up and down the streets of Topeka:

On the Inside of the
CUBAN REVOLUTION
by
FREDERICK FUNSTON
Lieutenant-Colonel and Chief of Artillery
of the Cuban Insurgent Army
The Real Facts about the Struggle for
Independence told by one who
Marched and Fought in the
Armies of Gómez and García

On the day advertised for his lecture, Frederick Funston stepped off the noon train into a large and effusive crowd; his hand was pumped enthusiastically by the mayor and all the leading citizens of the capital, his back pummeled by college acquaintances and family friends, his coattails touched by children half crushed in the crowd. He was whisked into a ceremonial carriage draped with the Cuban revolutionary flag and taken to the best hotel in town, where he held court over wellwishers and squads of reporters. Like a true showman, Funston saved his most dramatic yarns for the evening performance, though he spoke freely about recent events. He believed the *Maine* had been accidentally blown up; the Spanish could not be so foolhardy as to cause that tragedy. As for the looming war, he had his doubts it would come to pass — there had been, after all, so many false alarms in the past ten years. But if war came, he declared, he was ready to do his part.

Funston had arrived in New York City on January 10, 1898, in the midst of a snowstorm. He had only what the charitable Fitzhugh Lee had given him: a white tropical-weight suit and six dollars. Weak and feverish, Funston weighed about ninety pounds. He coughed up blood into his handkerchief from time to time and limped badly from the unhealed abscess in his hip. He checked into a hospital, his bills paid by the New York Cuban junta, and after a surgeon cleaned out his infected hip, he recuperated for three weeks.

From the day of his return to the United States through his train trip back to Kansas, reporters had dogged his heels; his firsthand reports guaranteed headlines, especially because he was one of the small American fraternity of mercenaries for the Cuban cause.

Once, during a reunion with William Allen White, the young war hero pondered whether he should consider following his father's example and enter politics. White persuaded him with apparent relief that he should seek some other way of making a living. While Funston considered his various options, there was the more immediate problem of raising cash. He decided to take advantage of his celebrity by once again going on the lecture circuit. Securing the services of a manager, Funston spent the next ten weeks spellbinding audiences under Chautauqua tents and in Elks' lodges in Missouri and Kansas with his personal account of the Cuban revolution, receiving up to fifty dollars per night. The pinnacle of his tour was in Topeka: he stood in front of a huge map of Cuba tacked to the wall and held his audience completely in thrall for two hours while he outlined in stirring rhetoric the causes for Cuban discontent and, modestly, it was noted, related his part in the conflict.

A member of the crowd jamming the Topeka Elks' Hall during this speech summoned Funston back to the state capital after war was declared. As the telegram was signed by Governor John W. Leedy, Funston hastened to comply.

The president had called for 125,000 volunteers to augment the existing regular army strength of 28,000 officers and men. Kansas had been directed to furnish three infantry regiments of about a thousand men each. Governor Leedy, a Populist, distrusted the regular army and even his own national guard — of which he was, of course, commander in chief — and he had decided to build his volunteer regiments from the ground up. While national guardsmen were free to enlist as individuals, Leedy wanted his own men in command. After witnessing Funston's performance as a speaker, the governor wanted him to help fight for Kansas. When Funston walked out of the governor's office, he did so with an appointment as colonel of one of the three Kansas regiments, the Twentieth Kansas Volunteer Infantry.

There was no shortage of volunteers. On May 13, a motley crowd of three thousand jayhawkers assembled on the State Fair grounds in Topeka to be mustered into service. Funston had not yet been outfitted with a uniform, like many volunteers, and he ran into a problem. "I was staying at a Topeka hotel," he recalled,

> and on going out to the camp to participate in the ceremony, was halted at its boundary by a sentry in the national-guard uniform, who informed me that visitors were not allowed within the limits of the camp. I replied somewhat icily that I was the colonel of the regiment. The sentry was a very tall man, and altitude has never been one of my charms; so the man bent his head until his mouth was within a couple of inches of one of my ears, and, as a most engaging grin overspread his features, whispered, "Try the next sentry. He's easy." And he was so stubborn and immovable that the officer of the guard had to be called before I could join my command.

A few days later, Funston was summoned to Tampa, Florida, to be debriefed of all the information he could remember about Cuba to staff officers under Generals William R. Shafter and Nelson A. Miles, who were preparing for the massive infantry assault upon Cuba. His information would not prove to be very valuable, since the only campaign would take place in a district where he had never been, near Santiago. Nonetheless, many of the gathering soldiers plied him full of questions. William Allen White later claimed that

> when the regular-army men at Tampa began to question him about his range with the artillery Funston told them, with a boyish innocence too sweet to poison with military science, that he pulled his guns up within four or five hundred yards of his mark before firing. Whereat the army men laughed quietly, winked at one another, and listened dubiously thereafter. Later, when some Spanish officers were taken prisoner at Santiago they told in horror of "a little damn fool American," fighting under García the year before, who poked the nose of his gun so close to the Spanish fortifications that his powder burned their eyebrows. Then the American regular-army men remembered Funston, and laughed again.

While in Florida, Funston learned that his regiment was to be sent to San Francisco — obviously not a staging ground for an assault upon Cuba. He hated the prospect of sitting out the war on the American mainland while others with no experience in fighting the Spanish were sent in his place. He implored General Miles to give him detached service with the Cuba-bound Fifth Army Corps, but Miles told him his place was with his own regiment.

"I supposed that to be its finish," Funston recalled, "so far as any participation in the war was concerned."

Five months later he would find himself in the Philippines, and soon thereafter in a war — not against the Spanish, but in a war anticipated by only a select few in Washington at the very moment Colonel Funston stood in the warm Tampa sun, kicking the dust in frustration at the untimely demise of a promising, glory-filled, soldierly career.

Theodore Roosevelt, the most industrious of McKinley's unofficial spokesmen, was also the government's most ardent lobbyist for lassoing the Philippines into the American corral.

The young assistant naval secretary had long been a Social Darwinist, championing the destiny for world domination of what he and many others called the Anglo-Saxon race; in his ceaseless call for war as a method to improve masculine character and ensure American strength, he repeatedly followed the theme he expressed in his multivolume work, *The Winning of the West*. "The most ultimately righteous of all wars," he wrote in 1893, "is a war with savages," for it established "the foundations for the future greatness of a mighty people . . . it is of incalculable importance that America, Australia, and Siberia should pass out of the hands of their red, black, and yellow aboriginal owners, and become the heritage of the dominant world races." Much as he had celebrated "the rude, fierce settler" as instrumental in sweeping the "savages" from their own lands, Roosevelt now espoused the necessity of a strong and aggressive navy for extending American majesty abroad.

While still a student at Harvard, Roosevelt had begun work on a book, *The Naval War of 1812*, that would affect his own career and the destiny of his country. The product of detailed historical and technical research, the book became extraordinarily popular within the navy after its publication in 1882. A copy was ordered for every ship's library, and the Naval War College made it required reading, thus influencing an entire generation of naval officers with its implicit call for a strong naval force to ensure America's greatness. Roosevelt's subsequent books and articles continued to pound the theme home.

One reader who was profoundly influenced by the young Roosevelt's views was a middle-aged career officer, Alfred Thayer Mahan. He and Roosevelt shared many sentiments and were more or less in constant communication from the time the book was issued. In 1890, Mahan collected his own lectures delivered at the Naval War College into a book, *The Influence of Sea Power upon History*, which eclipsed Roosevelt's earlier work in reputation while extending its message and influence. Mahan's book urged that the United States Navy should be used to ensure foreign markets for a revitalized American industrial economy.

After spending much of the 1890s in pursuit of this goal of mercantile imperialism, Mahan found himself a respected naval strategist at the Naval War College when, in June 1897, his ideological twin, Roosevelt, addressed the college. The martial phrases that rolled off Roosevelt's tongue ("Peace is a goddess only when she comes girt with a sword on thigh," and "the diplomat is the servant, not the master of the soldier") may have struck his boss, Secretary Long, as foolish and intemperate peroration. The words signaled quite something else to Mahan — and to the eager young theorists who worked with him.

One such officer, Lieutenant W. W. Kimball, had produced a blueprint for naval strategy in June 1896 as one of the regular Naval War College war games scenarios. His report had postulated a war with Spain over Cuba. It envisioned a blockade in the Caribbean and even proposed a contingency plan for sending the North Atlantic fleet to bombard the Mediterranean shores of Spain. Significantly, it also suggested that the navy's Pacific fleet attack the Spanish colony in the Philippines — for the express purpose of seizing the archipelago: "We could probably have a controlling voice, as to what should become of the islands when a fixed settlement [with the Filipinos] was made."

Kimball's report had been duly submitted to the Democratic administration; Secretary Long's predecessor had treated it with as scant attention as he had blueprints for a war with Japan, Russia, and Germany. It was filed away and forgotten until the change of administration brought the department a jingoistic new assistant naval secretary, who displayed great zeal in rescuing the document and returning it to his strategists for updating.

Roosevelt soon began to have ready access to the president's ear. McKinley, a master of innuendo, had by then informed him that their views were in accordance. In September 1897 they met once for dinner at the White House and twice went riding through the streets of the capital in the presidential carriage, during which times the personal warmth between them grew. Roosevelt announced that he intended to enlist in the army should war break out, since he felt it was the baldest hypocrisy to advocate war without a willingness to take part. Having introduced the subject in such a personal way, he avidly launched into a discussion of a war memo he had sent over to the White House that suggested a strategy for a Cuban offensive. It also specifically recommended that the Asiatic squadron should "blockade, and if possible, take Manila." America would retain the Philippines. This was just the sort of strategy McKinley wanted to hear, for Roosevelt presented tantalizing possibilities as by-products of the inevitable war with Spain.

Discontented groups in the Philippines had been troubling the Spaniards off and on for the past twenty-five years. Revolution had

finally flared up in August 1896, which resulted in the Spanish authorities' imposing harsh penalties on the Filipino civilians. The situation was similar to that in Cuba: an unstable colonial power was
bogged down in a guerrilla war with nationalists who would never
rest until they had driven their oppressors from their country. As in
Cuba, the Philippine revolution was in a stalemate, with the only solution seeming to be intervention from a foreign power — such as
the United States.

By ending three centuries of Spanish rule over the islands, Mc-
Kinley stood to gain more than simply a coaling station. The future
of Asia seemed to be in doubt in that autumn of 1897, and with its
teeming millions in ignorance of American mercantile products, it
could not be ignored in the growing call for new markets. As a brash
but popular new senator, Albert Beveridge, had said, "American factories are making more than the American people can use; American soil is producing more than they can consume. Fate has written
our policy for us; the trade of the world must and shall be ours." In
the clarity of that sort of reasoning, Asia could not be ignored — especially since the imperial powers were lately showing such interest.
There were, for instance, indications of Japanese ambitions in the
Pacific, for in their temerity, even the Hawaiian islands had not escaped Japanese notice. The partition of China seemed at hand, a
suspicion that was fueled in November when Kaiser Wilhelm seized
Kiaochow and the Russians sent their fleet to Port Arthur. France
was in Indochina, Great Britain in Hong Kong, the Dutch in the East
Indies, Spain in the Philippines, Germany and who knows who else
in China; it was obviously time to strike *somewhere* before America
was left out of the game entirely. In urging the president to consider
the Philippines Roosevelt was not alone; there was Lodge, backed by
the rest of their Metropolitan Club cabal, and other influential men
such as the powerful New York State boss Senator Orville Platt, who
advised McKinley in November that Manila was the key to the whole
Asian "crisis."

Having done everything but tack his Asian naval strategy to
McKinley's forehead, Theodore Roosevelt continued throughout the
autumn of 1897 to work both in the spotlight and behind the scenes
to see it implemented.

The post of commander of the Asiatic squadron became vacant.
Roosevelt had his candidate. Commodore George Dewey had served
with the illustrious Stephen Decatur — no small recommendation to
the hero-worshiping historian in Roosevelt. Dewey was only three years
shy of retirement, but he looked to be far more than just a museum
piece to the assistant naval secretary. Roosevelt recognized an ideol-

ogy and ambition similar to his own, qualities needed for the player of the key role he envisioned.

Learning that another officer's name had been advanced for the job, Roosevelt slyly kept the recommending letter off Naval Secretary Long's desk. He called in Dewey and asked him if he knew any senators. Certainly, said the commodore; he knew the senator from his own state, Redfield Proctor of Vermont — the man who became so instrumental in delivering a Spanish war the following year. Proctor visited the White House that very afternoon, and it was not long before McKinley sent over a letter requesting that Secretary Long appoint the commodore to the Asiatic post. Only then, after his choice was assured, did Roosevelt "remember" to show his superior the other nomination.

Informed by Roosevelt and Senator Lodge of their strategic plans, Dewey plunged into a study of "all the charts and descriptions of the Philippines that I could procure, and put aside many books about the Far East to read in the course of my journey across the continent and the Pacific." He sailed from San Francisco for Hong Kong, where the fleet awaited, on December 8. That was, of course, four days after the president had ordered the *Maine* to the Florida Keys and two days after McKinley had made conflict inevitable with his annual message to Congress.

With all the players in this drama acting at once independently and in concert, the elements of a grand and complex scenario were in place — except for some minor details, which Roosevelt saw to in the days following the *Maine* explosion.

On Friday, February 25, Secretary Long decided to take the afternoon off, complaining of tiredness and several vague ailments that were no doubt partly a result of the strained atmosphere in the capital. He left Roosevelt in charge, fully empowered as acting secretary of the navy.

Shortly after Long left, Senator Lodge was telephoned, and he hastened over to lend the acting secretary a hand as cablegrams began pouring out of the Navy Department as if it were the central transmitting station for Western Union. In three or four hours Roosevelt sent a message to Congress requesting authority to add fifteen hundred additional seamen to the navy's ranks; he ordered three hundred thousand tons of coal sent to Key West to be used in a possible invasion of Cuba; he dispatched carloads of projectiles to Fort Monroe and Fort Hamilton; he put the South Atlantic and European stations on a war alert; he requisitioned guns and ammunition and ordered squadron commanders worldwide to "keep full of coal," especially his key officer across the Pacific:

DEWEY, HONG KONG: Order the squadron, except the *Monocacy,* to Hong
Kong. Keep full of coal. In the event of declaration war Spain, your
duty will be to see that the Spanish squadron does not leave the Asiatic
coast, and then offensive operations in Philippine islands. Keep *Olympia* until further orders.

ROOSEVELT

Secretary Long felt well rested when he returned to his office on
February 26, but no amount of sleep could have prepared him for
the fait accompli presented to him by an unrepentant Roosevelt. So
bewildered was the mild-mannered "old dear" (his assistant's sobri-
quet for Long) that he let all of Roosevelt's orders stand and could
only remark in his diary entry for the day that "during my short absence I find that Roosevelt, in his precipitate way, has come very near
causing more of an explosion than happened to the *Maine* . . . the
very devil seemed to possess him yesterday afternoon."

On April 24, five days after the Cuban intervention bill passed Congress with its Teller Amendment forbidding the retention of Cuba,
McKinley summoned Secretary Long to the White House to set in
motion the process for acquiring a different piece of colonial real estate. The president would not go before Congress to ask for a formal war declaration until twenty-four hours later. Yet there he was,
knowing full well that he had forced a fifth-rate power into war the
way a bully would push someone off the sidewalk, issuing his directive before hostilities had begun. Small wonder McKinley would request Congress to backdate the declaration to the day *before* April 24,
when the historic cablegram went winging its way toward the waiting
Asiatic squadron:

DEWEY, HONG KONG: War has commenced between the United States
and Spain. Proceed at once to Philippine islands. Commence operations at once, particularly against the Spanish fleet. You must capture
vessels or destroy. Use utmost endeavors.

LONG

The warships sailed out from Hong Kong into the China Sea at
two in the afternoon of April 27. Dewey's departure for the Philippines prompted bulletins that would be the first public announcement in America that the war to liberate Cuba would begin ten thousand miles away in an Asian archipelago.

The battle began in Manila Bay with Dewey's famous words to a
subordinate, "You may fire when you are ready, Gridley," just before six in the morning of May 1; it would be one of the most lop-
sided battles in naval history. Awaiting Dewey's formidable squadron

was the pathetic Spanish fleet: seven unarmored ships, three of them with wooden hulls, including one wreck that had to be towed. The Spanish naval commander, Admiral Patricio Montojo, knew well ahead of time that his force would never prevail against anything larger than an outrigger canoe. He ordered his ships to anchor close enough to shore so that when they were sunk, his crews could cling to the rigging and escape drowning.

As Dewey's armored cruisers stayed out of the Spanish guns' feeble range, the destruction was fairly uncomplicated. Salvos during the morning set most of the Spanish ships afire; the American fleet withdrew for a time to take an inventory of its ammunition and to let the smoke clear before resuming the bombardment. By noon, all the Spanish ships had been sunk. Three hundred and eighty-one sailors were killed or wounded. On the American side, Dewey's ships were barely scratched — twenty or thirty times in all — and besides one engineer who died of the considerable heat belowdecks, only eight men were slightly wounded.

During the battle, shore batteries in Manila had been booming out at the Americans rather ineffectively; the commodore sent word to the Spanish governor that if the guns did not stop he would bombard the city. All became quiet. Dewey demanded use of the submarine cable to send notice of his victory, but the Spanish governor refused. In retaliation, the commodore ordered one of his ships to drag the harbor until the only means of telegraphic communication with the outside world was severed.

In the United States on the day of the battle each shred of news sent circuitously through Madrid was picked over and dissected by prodigious crowds. The newspapers on the morning of May 2 reported the total destruction of the Spanish fleet, and though no information was known about Dewey's squadron for nearly a week, the nation immediately erupted in a frenzy of celebration. Brass bands marched in the streets, joyous crowds broke into spontaneous bursts of patriotic songs, and that night the American skies were crimson from bonfires and skyrockets.

By then, President McKinley's council of war had met and resolved to send up to fifty thousand troops to Cuba. As Secretary of War Russell A. Alger recalled, the decision "to send an army of occupation to the Philippines was reached before Dewey's victory occurred." We know for certain that during the afternoon meeting on May 2, McKinley issued verbal instructions to Alger to dispatch "an army of occupation" to the Philippines — the first American soldiers to leave the Western Hemisphere.

On May 19, in a letter to General Wesley A. Merritt, who had been appointed commander of the Philippine expeditionary force, the president codified his verbal instructions: the Spanish were to be driven out of the Philippines. Again McKinley used that curious term "army of occupation," curious when the term "army of conquest" would have been more accurate. Only Manila Bay was in the possession of Dewey (who had since been promoted to rear admiral). This left the fortress-like capital, countless Spanish garrisons scattered across an archipelago that would be found to possess some seven thousand islands, and a vast, oppressed native people. The president's concept of occupation thus reflected not the present state of affairs, but his plan for the future.

McKinley was inscrutable to the last; nearly everyone around him continued to believe he had been conquered by his government's own war faction, whose leaders, Roosevelt and Lodge, celebrated their victory after what Lodge called their "constant work and anxiety." From San Antonio, newly appointed Lieutenant Colonel Theodore Roosevelt paused from his task of assembling a Cuba-bound regiment of cowboys and college men into what would become the Rough Riders. "Give my best love to Nannie," he wrote to Lodge in Washington, "and do not make peace until we get Porto Rico while Cuba is made independent and the Philippines at any rate taken from the Spaniards." Lodge replied: "They mean to send not less than twenty thousand men to the Philippines. As to Cuba I am in no sort of hurry. Our troops are fresh and new. . . . Porto Rico is not forgotten and we mean to have it. Unless I am utterly and profoundly mistaken the administration is now fully committed to the large policy that we both desire."

Lodge was mistaken only in thinking that his president had ever needed converting. Until the day he died, William McKinley would consistently maintain that "the truth is I didn't want the Philippines and when they came to us as a gift from the Gods, I did not know what to do with them." But found among his private papers many years later was his handwritten memorandum, written just after Dewey's squadron demolished the Spanish fleet: "While we are conducting war and until its conclusion we must keep all we get; when the war is over we must keep what we want."

V

The first contingent of troops bound for the Philippines sailed out of San Francisco Bay toward a sun setting over Asia on May 23, 1898. Colonel Frederick Funston and his regiment, the Twentieth Kansas, remained behind at Camp Merritt, in the western suburbs of the city, and were told they would stay until the unit could master elementary training. This proved to be a difficult task. Fewer than half of the men had any military experience. Funston, being a self-taught soldier, had to rely on subordinates to instruct the men in close-order drilling and the manual of arms. Moreover, as civilians were not restricted from entering the camp and as the fleshpots of San Francisco were but a short trolley ride away, too many of Funston's farmboys had to be constantly reminded that they were preparing for war and not being indulged in a colossal lark. One exasperated general complained directly to the War Department about the poor quality of the Kansas fodder provided him.

The entire army division turned out for a parade through the city streets on the Fourth of July. Because the quartermaster had not yet issued horses to the officers, Funston hired one from a livery stable. Much to his chagrin, it proved to be skittish. With his regiment formed and prepared to step out, the colonel hopped onto the ugly-eyed brute just as the army band struck up a march. "That horse quivered in every limb for an instant and then bolted," Funston would recall ruefully. "I might as well have tried to hold a cyclone. In front of the tent that was my home was a large fly, and under this the animal went, and I was ignominiously scraped off in the presence of some thirteen hundred grinning and delighted patriots."

Fortunately he was not impaled on his saber, a gift from the proud citizens of Iola. Later in the day, after he had struggled to guide the madly dancing steed up Market Street, Funston's already shortened temper broke when he saw the spectacle of civilian paradegoers — "hoodlum men and big boys" — tossing firecrackers at the hooves of the officers' horses while the policemen stood by like "so many cigarstore Indians." Funston decided to try to dispense some military justice.

One big ruffian . . . lit another large cracker and under the very nose of a policeman ran out into the street and tried to throw it under my horse [he would write with unabated rage a dozen years later]. Right then and there murder came into my heart, and I made a hard and conscientious effort to kill him. Of course, I was carrying my sabre, and . . . cut at him with all my strength. Only a quick jump backward saved him from death or a severe injury, as the point of the blade passed within six inches of his throat. I deeply regretted my failure, and would have been willing to take my chances with any American jury as to the outcome. I have seen too many good men go down to death to have had any more compunctions about killing a hoodlum of that type than over despatching a savage dog.

As little as Funston enjoyed his Fourth of July, the rest of the country found much to celebrate. It would be called the greatest Independence Day since the one thirty-five years before, when the bulletins from Gettysburg and Vicksburg had arrived simultaneously upon the national birthday.

For a country newly embarked upon an aggressive foreign policy, the United States had done quite well. All congressional opposition to the president's Hawaii bill had crumbled when McKinley threatened to annex the islands as a war measure, and the little archipelago was formally taken into possession on June 15. In another part of the Pacific, the Philippine-bound expeditionary force stopped on the president's orders at the tiny isle of Guam in the Spanish Marianas, seized it, and took aboard the small Spanish garrison as prisoners. On the southeastern shore of Cuba, American troops landed unopposed at Daiquirí; they routed a Spanish contingent at Las Guásimas the following day, June 23. Then, on the first day of July, came the hallowed battle of San Juan, the brilliant capture of a ridge overlooking the city of Santiago. It was a day Lieutenant Colonel Theodore Roosevelt would call "the great day of my life. I rose over those regular army officers like a balloon," a feat not unnoticed by the newspaper correspondents he kept close by his side. The ink had hardly dried on American headlines when word arrived that Admiral Cervera's imprisoned fleet had attempted to run a blockade of Santiago Harbor only to be burned, ship by ship, to the water. So it is not without irony that on the day memorializing American independence from a foreign power, the citizens went wild at the prospect of their new American empire.

What the Spaniards could not do to the Americans, however, would be accomplished by microorganisms, for by the time the Spanish troops surrendered unconditionally on July 17, malaria and yellow fever had begun to decimate the expeditionary force in Cuba. It was weeks before the men could be extricated from the island, but by that time the shocking toll of deaths from disease was temporarily buried by an avalanche of other news: Spain sued for peace on July 18, and President McKinley replied by ordering the invasion of Puerto Rico, instructing his troops to hoist the Stars and Stripes over the island. Meanwhile, by the end of July, some twelve thousand American soldiers had landed on Luzon in the Philippines. The president cabled Dewey in Manila Bay, requesting more information on the Philippines, particularly about industry, farming, minerals, and other natural resources; the secretary of state appointed a representative to "investigate and report on financial and industrial conditions in the Philippine islands."

The summer was not even over yet. In those heady two months, Theodore Roosevelt had been catapulted to a place of extreme popularity. "I hear talk all the time about you being run for Governor and Congressman," Lodge had written to him in early July, "and at this moment you could have pretty much anything you wanted." The Massachusetts senator thought it not impossible that his heroic friend might eventually join him in the august Senate chamber. Who could know the limit?

As the summer weeks wore on, Camp Merritt in San Francisco seemed to be at the antipodes, so far as action was concerned. Word trickled back from Manila that the Americans had blockaded the enemy in the city's high-walled medieval fortress; it was only a matter of time before the starving Spaniards surrendered. But despite that foregone conclusion, expedition after expedition continued to sail through the Golden Gate, off to Asia. Far from all possibility of glory, Funston's Kansas boys squirmed under army discipline and grew increasingly restless. Fights and brawls broke out; the troops were plagued by an epidemic of bronchitis and pneumonia, and thanks to swarms of prostitutes, a growing number of cases of venereal disease were reported. In an effort to rescue the farmboys, a veritable deluge of letters and telegrams poured out of their home state and onto the already overburdened desk of Secretary of War Russell Alger in the capital; he had become forced to conduct the war "during the greater part of the night and Sundays" as he felt obliged to attend to correspondence and visitors bearing petitions during office hours. TWENTIETH KANSAS DISAPPOINTED AT NOT BEING SENT TO MANILA, read one such telegram. SAY CALIFORNIA AND IOWA ASSIGNED AHEAD OF THEM. THEY ARE AS WELL DRILLED AND EFFICIENT AS OTHER REGIMENTS. The Twentieth Kansas stayed where it was.

Meanwhile, the president had waited until the possession of Puerto Rico had been confirmed before responding to Madrid's suit for peace. His conditions: Cuban independence, title to Puerto Rico, and in the Philippines, the city, bay, and harbor of Manila. Spain balked at the "overly harsh" terms, but had no choice but to agree. The truce between the countries was proclaimed on August 12, the same day that the governor of Manila threw open the city gates to the Americans after a mock battle arranged to allow the proud Spaniards the opportunity of surrendering under fire. Somehow, during all of the negotiations, one group was totally ignored: the Filipinos.

The ranks of soldiers in San Francisco grew so depleted that troop positions were consolidated; Funston's regiment was moved to a campsite on the Presidio reservation. The patriotic women of the city, having blessed the recruits with ample contributions of cakes, pies, and garlands of flowers, encouraged a number of liaisons. It was only a matter of time before the little colonel, who according to William Allen White had fallen "desperately in love every six months with a new girl" in college, fell desperately in love again. In early October he met the petite Eda Blankart, of the nearby city of Oakland. She was a music teacher, "a woman of marked beauty, great strength of character, and a high degree of culture as a musician," in the words of the suitor's home town friend Charles S. Gleed. Much as Edward Funston had courted Ann Mitchell in the anxious weeks before he left to fight the Confederacy, his son met, wooed, and proposed to Eda within the space of two weeks. It was, Funston swore, "by all odds the smartest thing I ever did in my life." They were married on October 25, 1898.

Two days later, Colonel Funston left his bride, to sail with the second and third battalions of the Twentieth Kansas on the transport *Indiana,* bound for Manila.

"Nobody supposed that we should ever see any fighting," Funston would recall, "as it was thought that our duties would consist in helping to sit on and hold down the 'little brown brother' for a few months." With the war over and the president's peace commission in Paris working out terms with Spain, several officers took advantage of the tropical cruise by taking their wives along on the transport ship; Eda Funston would follow on another troop carrier several weeks later.

The Spanish war might have been over, but it was quite evident once Funston arrived that more trouble was brewing. From as early as the middle of May, General Merritt had warned McKinley that "it seems more than probable that we will have the so-called insurgents to fight as well as the Spaniards" and that "the majority [of Filipinos] will regard us with the intense hatred both born of race and religion." And by the time the *Indiana* had arrived with its cargo of Kansas volunteers on November 30, friction between the coexisting armies had increased to the point where it seemed only a matter of time before war would break out.

"Almost without exception," an American major reported to Washington, "soldiers and also many officers refer to the natives in their presence as 'niggers' and natives are beginning to understand what the word 'nigger' means." Tempers flared at racial epithets, but there was more. Houses were searched without warrant by Americans brandishing guns; at checkpoints it became common to knock

Filipinos down at the first hint of "disrespect," though some Americans showed anything but respect when searching Filipino women. Shopkeepers saw their wares "confiscated" or bought with Confederate money; sentries regularly shot at Filipinos if they did not like their looks: "We have to kill one or two every night," wrote an army private to his father in January. For their part, many Filipinos began to respond in kind, hissing threats in their own tongue, drawing their fingers across their necks in unmistakable hostility, pushing back when they were pushed. Filipinos were reported to be shoving American generals off sidewalks, though this seems an exaggeration. Knifings were a nightly occurrence. Fights on street corners and at the mutual army checkpoints by day were inevitable. After one such altercation between a South Dakotan sentry and a Filipino soldier, the American emerged with his face badly cut by a bolo knife while the Filipino's head had been blown off by a Springfield rifle at close range. Colonel Funston, serving as officer of the day, took at face value the wounded sentry's statement that he had been assaulted without provocation. Funston dryly observed after viewing the Filipino's body that "if a bullet from [those old Springfields] hit a man he never mistook it for a mosquito bite."

On November 29, 1898, Spain agreed to all of McKinley's demands, including the cession of sovereignty over the entire Philippine archipelago to the United States for twenty million dollars. Of course McKinley had signed the treaty and submitted it to Congress for ratification. Then he had issued his famous Benevolent Assimilation proclamation, which left no room for doubt that "the future control, disposition, and government of the Philippine Islands are ceded to the United States."

North of Manila, in the market town of Malolos — where the patriots had set up their constitutional convention, elected the charismatic young firebrand Emilio Aguinaldo president, and ratified their declaration of independence — the Filipinos heard about the "benevolent assimilation" of their new nation only through the most roundabout means. Though certain elements in the government favored declaring war immediately, others prevailed, arguing that they should hold to their last hope: that the American Congress would heed their endless flowery appeals by rejecting the treaty.

About thirty-six hours before the fateful vote was scheduled, on the night of February 4, 1899, Colonel and Mrs. Funston were disturbed just after they had retired by a vigorous pounding on their door.

"Come out here, Colonel," shouted Major Wilder Metcalf, a fellow Kansan, "the ball has begun."

"I scarcely realized at first what he meant, but hastily slipped on a few clothes and came out into the hallway," Funston remembered. "Metcalf conducted me to a window, and asked, 'Did you ever hear that racket before?' And sure enough, from a little north of east, floating over the housetops of the great city, came the distant rattle of the Mausers. There was no mistaking it, and we realized that a war had begun."

"They have commenced," the colonel told his wife; "that is firing at the outposts." After Funston left, "not knowing whether for hours or forever," as Eda confided to an interviewer, there came another tap at her door. "A major entered," she recalled,

> telling me to get ready at once to go to the barracks, for it was safer there. I calmly packed my tooth-brush, towels, and other necessities; the other ladies marveled that I should think of such things at such a time, but I had learned a lesson from my husband. I shall never forget that walk to the barracks. Every step seemed to add a century to my life, the guns on the *Monadnock* boomed in our ears, and the signals from the fleet lighted the way. My husband's cousin and a soldier who escorted us did their best to lessen our fears. At the barracks all was quiet save the clicking of the telegraph-machines, and now and then the sound of firing . . . I sat day and night at the operator's elbow, dreading, yet insisting on learning every bit of news.

In Washington on the following Monday morning, February 6, 1899, the senators took their places in the Capitol in an air of barely suppressed excitement. The newspapers brought in by some carried sketchy dispatches of skirmishes in Manila. On the day scheduled for a vote on the McKinley peace treaty, after weeks of wearisome debate on the matter of the "benevolent assimilation" of ten million souls at two dollars per, the hubbub among the senators ceased as William McKinley appeared in the hall. He stood ready to address them.

"The first blow was struck by the inhabitants," the president said. "They assailed our sovereignty and there will be no useless parley, no pause, until the insurrection is suppressed and American authority acknowledged and established."

McKinley retired to the White House to await the Senate's decision. His speech was followed by a few more hours of debate, during which time Senator Lodge could be seen vigorously lobbying for passage, twisting arms, applying pressure. Then there was a motion to end the discussion.

In Albany, New York, Theodore Roosevelt waited for a bulletin from Lodge. Upon the strength of his enormous popularity after San Juan Hill, Roosevelt had been elected governor of the State of New York the previous fall. As he waited, perhaps a stanza from a popular new poem by Rudyard Kipling passed through his mind. It had just been published in *McClure's* and he had recommended it to Lodge as "mediocre poetry but uncommonly good sense":

> Take up the white man's burden —
> Send forth the best ye breed —
> Go bind your sons to exile
> To serve your captives' need;
> To wait in heavy harness,
> On fluttering folk and wild —
> Your new-caught sullen peoples
> Half devil and half child.

Finally, late in the afternoon, Roosevelt received the news: the McKinley treaty had passed — by one vote.

With no useless parley and no pause, the American expeditionary force slashed through an unprepared, ill-equipped enemy. In the short time between the outbreak of fighting and the passage of McKinley's treaty, perhaps as many as 3,000 Filipino soldiers had been killed; the American losses were 59 dead and 278 wounded. Projecting those figures indicated the war would be over by the advent of the rainy season, some four months later.

While Eda Funston remained in the city at the elbow of an army telegraph operator, she listened especially for word of the U.S. Second Division, which was composed of seven regiments including the Twentieth Kansas. Aided by long-range artillery support from Dewey's flotilla, it pushed northward up the coast of Manila Bay and then inland. The division was commanded by Major General Arthur MacArthur (whose son Douglas was even then preparing to study war at West Point). For the most part, his men were all volunteers, but months of drilling in the States had given the soldiers a nominal amount of discipline. There were, of course, exceptions — the most visible being the Twentieth Kansas. On Sunday, February 5, the Kansans had to be called back a thousand yards to keep the firing line from bulging; when shells from the U.S.S. *Concord* began falling around his troops, Funston saw the wisdom of pulling his men back to rejoin the other regiments. After the little town of La Loma was overrun, the division fought its way trench by trench toward the fortified town of Caloocan. The Kansans were always at the head of each massive charge. "There goes Kansas," exclaimed MacArthur as the regiment swarmed, yelling and shooting, toward Caloocan, "and all Hell can't stop her." Funston's men routed the Filipino defenders, in their excitement ignoring orders to halt inside the town and chasing the retreating enemy far into the outskirts. CALOOCAN TAKEN, wired MacArthur to headquarters. KANSAS A MILE IN ADVANCE OF THE LINE. WILL STOP THEM IF I CAN. Funston's immediate superior, Brigadier General Harrison Gray Otis, sent a message forward inquiring how long he could hold his position. The colonel's reply passed into legend: "Until I am mustered out!"

This sort of attitude was the stuff of headlines — indeed, war correspondents quickly discerned Funston to be good copy — but the little colonel's recklessness did not sit well with Otis, who was, ironically, himself a newspaperman, being the editor and proprietor of the *Los Angeles Times* in civilian life. Otis (who was not related to the corps commander, General Elwell S. Otis) had served during the Civil War in the same regiment as Major William McKinley. As brigade commander, Otis kept warning Funston that he was interfering with the overall war plans; Otis was forever reining in the Twentieth Kansas. He complained that Funston could not control his men, which sometimes was true, especially early on in the campaign. One night the entire regiment panicked in their bedrolls and began firing into the darkness at no discernible targets. Blowing bugles to signal a halt did no good; Funston and his officers could only get the volunteers to cease after repeatedly kicking them. But if rambunctious and undisciplined, the Twentieth also mirrored its colonel in courage, however reckless. "When I tell them to charge," Funston wrote a home town friend proudly, "the trouble is not to get them to come on, but to keep from being run over by them."

Continual squabbles with General Otis did Funston no harm, for he had come under the protection of the first of his two great mentors. Major General Arthur MacArthur had, like most of the corps' senior command, served in the Civil War. At seventeen, he had volunteered for duty with the Twenty-fourth Wisconsin Infantry, served as a lieutenant under Sheridan in the battle of Perryville and as captain at Stone's River. At the battle of Missionary Ridge he had led a charge up that terrible incline, later receiving the Medal of Honor for gallantry. MacArthur had commanded a regiment at twenty, and after the war he continued in regular army service, coming to be known in his youth as "the boy colonel of the West." To the hero-worshiper in Funston, MacArthur was an ideal commander: the elder soldier, still made of iron, had lived since the beginning of his military career with a maxim: "Sometimes one has to decide for oneself the relevancy of orders." This, of course, reflected the colonel's sentiments exactly, and between the two a sort of father-son rapport sprang up. Bypassing his immediate superior, Funston repeatedly

approached MacArthur with proposals that he be sent with small detachments on what were obviously foolhardy missions; on the night
hostilities first broke out, he implored the general to be allowed to
take a platoon out across the Filipino lines in a blind search for Emilio Aguinaldo. "If anyone can do it you can," MacArthur told him,
"but I cannot spare the men."

Up the trackbed of the Manila-Dagupan Railroad lay Malolos, the
seat of the Filipino republic. By then Aguinaldo had withdrawn with
his government some 30 miles north to San Isidro, in Nueva Ecija
province. The revolutionary leader's home province of Cavite, on the
shore below Manila, was already under the control of General Henry
W. Lawton, and forces under General Loyd Wheaton had pushed
eastward through the farm country of Laguna before being recalled.
Reinforcements from the American mainland had already begun arriving as early as the end of February. Against all this opposition,
Aguinaldo's losses continued to be heavy, with only a few minor victories to console him; a column under General Antonio Luna had
been displaced from Caloocan by the Kansans, and it darted south
to burn some suburbs of Manila. But Luna was repulsed. The Filipino forces could only withdraw slowly into Luzon's central plains,
fighting all the way as the Second Division followed relentlessly. At
the outskirts of Malolos, MacArthur gave Funston a singular honor,
that of taking a few men and "feeling his way" into the town. As it
turned out, the defenders of Malolos had already retreated, but
Funston became known as the first man into Caloocan and the first
man into Malolos. The bantam colonel's stature was increasing daily.

The hot season descends upon Luzon without mercy in late March,
with the tropical sun baking the central plains until midday temperatures in the high nineties, the low one hundreds, are commonplace.
The heat came hard that year, especially to troops who had never
experienced a Philippine summer — which is to say, the entire
American expeditionary force. The soldiers had been issued uniforms of heavy khaki; shoes began to fall apart and supplies were
slow in coming. Moreover, they had been given unpalatable rations — especially cans of nauseating salmon, nicknamed "goldfish,"
which was so oily that it ignited like a torch when dry. Whenever a
unit passed into a new village, there was a wholesale riot to steal
whatever chickens or livestock could be cooked. As if this were not
enough, nearly everyone suffered from dysentery; and malaria,
cholera, and dengue fever were steadily depleting the ranks. Hospitalization for infected wounds was common.

Except for disease, over which they had no control, most of the soldiers' problems were caused by gross mismanagement. Despite the energetic efforts of Lodge, Roosevelt, Alger, and the rest of the expansionists in Washington, the army had entered this war unprepared. Compounding the problem to an incredible degree was the man overseeing all military operations in the Philippines, Major General Elwell S. Otis.

Tall, taciturn, his bare pate offset by white muttonchop whiskers that seemed to hang from his mustache and sideburns and flap in the wind, Otis had graduated from Harvard Law School in 1861. He had been a hero in the Union Army and had transferred into the regulars after the war; a veteran of the Little Big Horn, Otis had written a book called *The Indian Question* — its point of view can be inferred.

During the Civil War, Otis had been shot in the head and in the many years since had suffered from insomnia. He found his relaxation in work, the more tedious the better. Arriving in the Philippines some weeks before the Spanish surrender, the commander buried himself in paperwork and was so unable to delegate authority that his staff was paralyzed. After the hostilities commenced, Otis never visited the battlefields, busying himself rather with approving supply requisitions and other details. More than one military historian has characterized him as a prototype of today's desk general rather than the dashing cavalryman typified by the likes of Arthur MacArthur and Frederick Funston.

His contemporaries held more scathing opinions of the general. MacArthur said Otis reminded him of a locomotive bottom side up, its wheels revolving at full speed. Admiral Dewey quipped that the major general was a "pincushion of an old woman." The papal delegate to the Philippines, Archbishop P. L. Chapelle, maintained that Otis was "of about the right mental caliber to command a one-company post in Arizona."

His heavy-handed soldier's diplomacy had done much to alienate Aguinaldo and his cabinet in the six months leading up to war. Once the shooting started, he deployed units with maddening inconsistency, often sending brigades to take territory at a great loss only to be withdrawn, allowing the Filipinos to reoccupy their lost ground. When the war began, Otis was shown to be hungry for publicity for his expeditionary force, but only of the right sort: pro-Republican, pro-McKinley, pro-army. His press releases made ridiculous claims of victories and used inflated battle statistics; nearly every sheet spoke of another "disastrous blow to the enemy" that would presage the imminent collapse of the "rebellion."

In his desire to allow only "good" news out of the islands, Otis had been censoring news dispatches heavily since his arrival. Every press report was blue-penciled, and since he controlled the only cable terminal, his power was nearly complete. Critical reporters were not allowed at press briefings; the most troublesome were deported. Newspapers in Manila were shut down and their publishers and other personnel jailed after unfavorable articles appeared.

One of the general's subordinates, Brigadier General Henry W. Lawton, was infuriated by the Otis style. At his suggestion, eleven journalists prepared a statement of protest that they all signed, realizing as Lawton had that there might be strength in organizing. The document complained that official press releases presented an overly optimistic view of the situation, an optimism that the officers in the field did not share, for hardly anyone thought the situation was well in hand. The journalists contended that the Filipinos' will to resist remained firm, that the American volunteers' morale was dangerously low, and that even a great increase in troops would not remedy the situation. Finally, the correspondents stated that all previous newspaper dispatches had been censored and made to come into line with the administration's view.

When the correspondents presented this document to Otis and asked that he transmit it, he refused. "Gentlemen," he told them, "you have served an extraordinary paper upon me; you accuse me of falsehood. This constitutes a conspiracy against the government. I will have you tried by court-martial and let you choose the judges."

However, Lawton's theory about safety in numbers proved correct. The document was sent by mail to Hong Kong and cabled to the United States, where it was widely reprinted in many newspapers. The editorial reactions depended on the party affiliation of each particular journal, but it would soon be seen that the floodgates had begun to open. General Otis escalated his censorship, though the eleven offending journalists escaped serious harm. Recalcitrant to the end, Otis continued to spin out his fantasies until a new secretary of war, the Wall Street lawyer Elihu Root, replaced him in May 1900 with Arthur MacArthur.

Try as he might, Otis could not totally control the journalists, who began to show great ingenuity in smuggling reports out. Even less under the general's thumb were his own soldiers. Within six weeks of the war's outbreak, American newspapers began to reprint letters sent from the battlefield. The writers were a diverse lot of soldiers: some were horrified at what they witnessed or even participated in; others reveled in the "fun" that this foreign war provided.

"We make everyone get into his house by seven P.M., and we only tell a man once," wrote Corporal Sam Gillis of the First California.

"If he refuses we shoot him. We killed over 300 natives the first night. They tried to set the town on fire. If they fire a shot from a house we burn the house down and every house near it, and shoot the natives, so they are pretty quiet in town now." A private in the Utah Battery wrote home of a "Goo Goo" hunt: "With an enemy like this to fight, it is not surprising that the boys should soon adopt 'no quarter' as a motto, and fill the blacks full of lead before finding out whether they are friends or enemies." Another soldier reported that "our fighting blood was up, and we all wanted to kill 'niggers.' . . . This shooting human beings beats rabbit hunting all to pieces."

Shock waves rippled slowly back in the States as these letters appeared, for the practices they revealed seemed unbelievable to a citizenry that less than a generation before had turned deaf ears to the barbarities at Wounded Knee. The world was growing vastly more complicated, along with the people in it, and only so much could be assimilated at one time. What, for instance, could a civilized being think about the "water cure," a practice used to extract information from Filipino prisoners (whether soldiers or civilians): a soldier would hold a person on the ground while several gallons of water were sluiced down the throat. The prisoner's midsection would be horribly distended; the water would be removed by kicking or punching the stomach until all the water was expelled. The procedure was excruciating and was very effective in making the Filipinos talk.

It has passed into general understanding that the first major instance of reprisals against civilians in the Philippines occurred at the order of General Loyd Wheaton after two of his companies fell into a trap and disintegrated. Wheaton ordered his men to burn every town in a twelve-mile radius to the ground. In another incident, a soldier from Kingston, New York, reported that "last night one of our boys was found shot and his stomach cut open. Immediately orders were received from General Wheaton to burn the town and kill every native in sight; which was done to a finish. About 1,000 men, women and children were reported killed. I am probably growing hard-hearted, for I am in my glory when I can sight my gun on some dark skin and pull the trigger."

Soon after the war started, a representative of the International Red Cross was summoned by Emilio Aguinaldo to document the conduct of the war. Evading a phalanx of public relations men sent by Otis to keep him in Manila, the official visited the American lines, where he found villages burned to the ground and "horribly mutilated Filipino bodies, with stomachs slit open and occasionally decapitated."

Of course, war being what it is, the Filipinos began to reply in kind, despite their reputation for having treated Spanish prisoners with civility. At each instance General Otis added the new account to his propaganda campaign: Americans tortured, buried alive; Filipinos who did not respect "the laws of civilized warfare"; Filipinos whose innate jungle savagery had forced Americans "in only the most isolated of instances" to imitate them.

Like so many important facts about the war, most details did not see the light of day until it was too late to change policy or establish guilt high up in the chain of command. It was only much later, in 1902, that congressional hearings looked into American conduct in the war — and only then after committee members such as Albert Beveridge had exerted prodigious energy in keeping them from happening at all. Even with such official attention, the conviction rate was very low, with only token sentences passed out. One Richard T. O'Brien described to the Committee on the Philippines what happened in the town of La Nog, on Panay Island:

> How the order started and who gave it I don't know, but the town was fired on. I saw an old fellow come to the door, and he looked out; he got a shot in the abdomen and fell to his knees and turned around and died. . . . After that two old men came out, hand in hand. . . . They had a white flag. They were shot down. At the other end of the town we heard screams, and there was a woman there; she was burned up, and in her arms was a baby, and on the floor was another child. The baby was at her breast, the one in her arms, and this child on the floor was, I should judge, about 3 years of age. They were burned. Whether she was demoralized or driven insane I don't know. She stayed in the house.

There seems to be some evidence that a fair proportion of the crimes committed during the war could be laid at the feet of the volunteer soldiers who came to their adulthood on the American frontier — the "Western States, where the school-house has made literacy universal and intelligence high," as William Allen White often described the territory. Even volunteers from White's home state admitted participating in activities that chilled patrician anti-imperialists in Boston; a few letters from the Twentieth Kansas were published in 1899, including one from a private who admitted, "With my own hands [I] set fire to over fifty houses of Filipinos after the victory of Caloocan. Women and children were wounded by our fire." Another soldier reported his company took four prisoners at Caloocan. Men asked an officer what to do with them, and later reported, "He said, 'You know the orders,' and four natives fell dead."

The Twentieth's own colonel loudly disputed these and other accounts. "The stories of brutality on the part of volunteers were sent out by correspondents whom no one knew either in Manila or on the firing line," Funston claimed. "As for the soldiers who tell such tales, they are simply liars."

But the ugly stories could not be dismissed so easily — especially when the colonel himself had his name linked to the atrocities. Some junior officers and soldiers in the Twentieth charged that he "maintained and supported an advertising bureau to build up himself and tear down other men; that he commanded, condoned, and rewarded rapine and murder simply because they sprung from his own partisans and associates." One embittered lieutenant, John F. Hall, went before a crowd of anti-imperialists in Boston after his mustering out and charged that a number of officers, including Funston, had given secret orders on February 2, 1899, to precipitate a conflict with the Filipino army. Another Kansas soldier, Private Charles Brenner, wrote home to complain that during the fierce battles around Calumpit in February, Colonel Funston had ordered that all prisoners be shot, an order enforced by Major Wilder Metcalf and Captain William H. Bishop. When an American news clipping carrying this charge reached the desk of General Elwell S. Otis, he sent it on to Funston with a suggestion that the private might be persuaded to retract his charge, a policy that Otis had found frequently worked. In this case Brenner refused to take back the charge; indeed, he produced a corroborating witness, Private Putnam, who told a military investigator that either Bishop or Metcalf had ordered them to shoot two Filipino prisoners. Otis ordered Brenner court-martialed "for writing and conniving at the publication of an article which contains willful falsehoods concerning himself and a false charge against Captain Bishop."

Rumors about the Twentieth's colonel continued to surface, some of them from a source as close to Funston as Funston himself. After a small American detachment was lured into an ambush by civilians claiming to know of an insurgent weapons cache, Funston bragged to reporters that to avenge the American deaths he had ordered twenty-four prisoners summarily executed. But when he heard rumors that he might be subject to court-martial, he insisted that the prisoners had "attempted to escape" and were killed in the chase.

There was one common final defense that the American military commanders gave. The stories of atrocities were not true, they would say; even if they were, they only represented payment in kind. "The natives have no idea of honor," Funston told a reporter for *Harper's Weekly*. "In our fighting with them they violated all the rules of civilized warfare, and they knew perfectly well what they were violating. They would bring forward flags of truce, and when our men went forward under similar flags the insurgents would fire upon them. . . .

Yet in return our men were wonderfully kind and considerate to the wounded and the prisoners." Or, as he told a *New York Times* correspondent,

> I am afraid that some people at home will lie awake nights worrying about the ethics of this war, thinking that our enemy is fighting for the right of self-government. The word independent, which these people roll over their tongues so glibly, is to them a word, and not much more. It means with them simply a license to raise hell, and if they get control they would raise a fine crop of it. They are, as a rule, an illiterate, semi-savage people, who are waging war, not against tyranny, but against Anglo-Saxon order and decency.

Burning houses? Shooting prisoners? Torturing civilians? What, people might have asked, had happened to American youth?

What had changed little Freddy Funston, who had played cowboys and Indians through the orchards of his father's Kansas farm? What transformation had been worked in the young man who had enlisted in the Cuban revolution and emerged without a shred of evidence that he had violated any articles of war? Perhaps one can only point to the nature of the Asian war, the collision of cultures and race, and to the rampant messianism abroad in the United States that made all American actions good and all others' bad.

More questions must surface at this turning point in Funston's life, these about a change in personality. Lifelong friends would claim no matter what was published that Funston was the soul of modesty. "Not only is Funston modest in appearance," wrote Charles S. Gleed, "but also in conversation. . . . There is little use of the pronoun 'I,' an entire absence of anything like arrogance or boastfulness." Charles F. Scott would write that "he is not a notoriety seeker. He is not an adventurer, a mere soldier of fortune. . . . The real man, as his intimate friends know him, is the very opposite of all these. In social life . . . Funston is modest to a most unusual degree. His friends cannot imagine him doing anything deliberately spectacular." Yet despite what Gleed or Scott or White might claim about his personality, at the very least Funston employed, as a *Harper's Weekly* columnist noted, a "graphic use of language" that "leads to his sentiments being quoted more, probably, than he would approve."

Whether it was due to that era of demagoguery at the century's turn, to an impressionable young Freddy Funston tagging along during all his father's political stumping, to the soldier's fast rise to command men taller, stronger, and smarter than he, or to a combination of all of the above, the public Frederick Funston at thirty-three had a penchant for uttering statements that delighted some and angered many, thus at once making him more famous and infamous, a precise balance that he seemed to relish — much like a contemporary, Theodore Roosevelt. The two men had begun a regular correspondence, for each represented to the other a certain ideal: Roosevelt had, after all, conquered his youthful illness and frailty to the point where he seemed capable of almost any achievement, and Funston saw himself as having risen above his mediocre education and his height to the place where he commanded large groups of soldiers and repeatedly came into the public eye. A comment that Joseph Bucklin Bishop, an editor of the *New York Evening Post,* made about Roosevelt applies equally to the Kansas colonel. "He has to talk," said Bishop. "The peculiarity about him is that he has what is essentially a boy's mind. What he thinks he says at once, says aloud. It is his distinguishing characteristic, and I don't know as he will ever outgrow it."

From a modern vantage point, it seems as though there was some sort of preposterous liars' contest going on, with Funston and Roosevelt standing at opposite sides of the globe and outdoing each other by turn, taking the value-skewed Social Darwinism that was then commonplace in the Western world and making one outrageous statement after another.

To Roosevelt, the Filipinos were "Tagal bandits," "Malay bandits," "Chinese halfbreeds," or "savages, barbarians, a wild and ignorant people, Apaches, Sioux, Chinese boxers." His view on warfare, it will be remembered, was that "the most ultimately righteous of all wars is a war with savages," which establishes "the foundations for the future greatness of a mighty people."

Meanwhile Frederick Funston stood surrounded by reporters who gleefully took down his every word. Did the colonel think the American army should remain in the Philippines? Of course, Funston would reply, "and rawhide these bullet-headed Asians until they yell for mercy." But once begun, how hard it was to stop talking. "After the war," he would say, "I want the job of Professor of American History in Luzon University, when they build it, and I'll warrant that the new generation of natives will know better than to get in the way of the band-wagon of Anglo-Saxon progress and decency." And did the colonel have any words about his Kansas boys? "The boys go for the enemy as if they were chasing jack rabbits. . . . I, for one, hope that Uncle Sam will apply the chastening rod, good, hard, and plenty . . . until they come into the reservation and promise to be good 'Injuns.'" And what, they asked, did the colonel think about the Filipino citizens? "A Filipino is chronically tired," he would reply; "he is born tired; he stays tired and he dies tired. If you hire him he will labor a few days, and then he goes out of the work business for about a week, while he attends a fiesta or two. It doesn't matter how much you pay him; a Filipino will work as hard for 50¢ a week as he will for 50¢ a day." With pencils scratching madly to catch every intemperate word, the questioning would continue. Colonel, your views on Aguinaldo and his army? "A cold-blooded murderer and a would-be dictator" presiding over "a drunken uncontrollable mob" with "the minds of children."

Funston did not always spout nonsense; sometimes buried among his colorful opinions were some that made sense. Once he told reporters that he had decided he was an anti-expansionist, "though not a bitter one," and could see no benefit to be derived from the Philippines save for those going to a few "big syndicates and capitalists." And though he had a blind spot concerning his own country's involvement in a colonial war, his powers of observation about other roots of the Filipinos' discontent encompassed their long-standing hatred for the Spanish clergy, who owned enormous tracts of land and took cruel advantage of the peasants. "I am a Protestant," Funston said,

> but I have no feeling against the Catholic Church, and my sentiments in regard to the Dominican friars are shared by many army officers in Manila who are devout Catholics. The Dominicans control all the Church property in the island of Luzon, and they have used their influence against us from the outset. They are so bitterly hated by the insurgents, as well as by the great body of the people, that I am convinced if our government would confiscate the property of the Dominicans and expel them from the islands the insurrection would fall to pieces. These friars have been active in fomenting trouble and they are very powerful because of their enormous landed interests. They own square miles of the richest land in all the districts, which they rent to tenants. They are experts in rack-renting, for if a tenant makes improvements they promptly raise the rent. The Jesuits have done good work, but even among Catholics in the Philippines I found no one to speak a good word for the Dominican friars, because the evil influence of these men was plain on every hand.

Regarding his foes on the battlefield, Funston was certainly capable of dismissing them as a "mob," but occasionally he would admit that "the real test of the morale of troops is the ability to bring them time and time again to face the music, to suffer almost inevitable defeat, and to have their ranks decimated by appalling losses. Judged by this standard, the Filipino does not by any means stand at the foot of the list."

These calmer opinions did not get as many headlines as the words he spoke as "Funston the Loudmouthed Colonel," and whether it was due to the selectivity of newspaper editors or Funston's own desire for attention, he was more often found to speak words that belittled, intimidated, and infuriated others. If some of his speeches resembled those of Theodore Roosevelt, the telling difference was that Roosevelt knew when to shut up. It would come as quite a blow a few years later when Funston would be muzzled by Roosevelt, by then his commander in chief.

William Allen White, whose *Emporia Gazette* had become an important Republican newspaper, regularly advised Roosevelt, who asked him to intercede. Recalling the instance later, White offered another interesting explanation for Funston's sea change:

> Funston, who was rising in the army, was talking too much. Kellogg and I guessed why: Funston, who to us was still "Timmy," still could not carry his liquor. Roosevelt sent me to Timmy to tell him that he must quit talking, or the President would have to rebuke him publicly. When I told my message, Timmy looked at me and grinned: "Oh, Billy, look not upon the gin rickey when it is red, and giveth color in the cup, for it playeth hell and repeat with poor Timmy."

MacArthur's Second Division continued to press northward from Malolos, across a plain bisected by creeks, streams, and rivers, toward its next objective, the town of Calumpit. On the way, Funston was joined by the "well-known correspondent" James Creelman, who stayed close enough to come under fire repeatedly as Funston strode among his troops, shouting orders and occasionally blazing away with his revolver at the enemy.

Another newspaperman had stepped out of Funston's life, to his relief. Harrison Gray Otis resigned his appointment after Malolos to return to civilian life. He was under the impression that the war would be over soon, and he was anxious to be at the helm of the *Los Angeles Times* when that happy event occurred.

Succeeding the publisher as brigadier general was an old soldier who became Funston's second great mentor and protector, Loyd Wheaton, whom Funston worshiped as "a dashing and aggressive soldier" and "without a doubt the most striking individual and the most interesting character among those who served in our army in the Philippines." Wheaton was of slender build and sported a long, bristling beard that hid his mouth and lower features as effectively as if he wore a bandit's bandanna. With a jaunty cavalryman's hat and his habit of wearing a cloak around his shoulders (in the style of Ulysses S. Grant), Wheaton was for Funston the quintessential soldier. During the Civil War, he had been a lieutenant colonel in an

Illinois regiment and was wounded at Shiloh. During the storming of Fort Blakely, he was the first soldier to enter the Confederate works, "leaping sword in hand through a gun embrasure," as Funston admiringly recounted. Wheaton had received a Medal of Honor for that trick, but in the years after the war he failed to distinguish himself. For twenty-five years he remained a captain in the regular army, only seeming to awaken like a military Rip Van Winkle at the beginning of the Spanish war. Wheaton's detractors estimated his military mentality at somewhere near the level of his former rank, but everyone agreed he was a colorful soldier. His most-quoted remark came in a mess hall, when a war correspondent tried to get him to admit that Filipinos were brave soldiers. Wheaton slammed a fist on the table. "Brave! Brave!" he shouted. "Damn 'em, they won't stand up to be shot!"

"He seemed to enjoy fighting for its own sake," Funston recalled fondly, "and had a positive contempt for danger." More significant to the young Kansan's career, Wheaton was generous in giving recognition to the men under his command. He felt no pangs of jealousy when a junior officer like Frederick Funston was acclaimed for his exploits — which after Malolos came with increasing frequency.

The division was temporarily halted in its progress at the bank of the Rio Chico by a partially collapsed steel bridge and by heavy gunfire directed at the Americans from the opposite bank. Funston led about ten men in a mad rush to be the first to cross the river; dodging bullets, they ran to the bridge and edged out for fifty yards by clinging to the girders on one side. At the collapsed part they dropped into the stream to swim the rest of the way. "Although I had got into the water first," Funston admitted ruefully, a lieutenant "beat me to the bank, being a faster swimmer." As they were unarmed and barefoot, it was fortunate that the insurgents had by then withdrawn.

The next day, the combined brigades were forced to halt again at the bank of the broad Rio Grande de la Pampanga. Four hundred feet away, on the opposite bank, waited the strongest resistance they had yet encountered — a formidable entrenchment of four thousand Filipinos backed by artillery and the dread Maxim machine gun. After a day and a night of reconnaissance, the only way of establishing a beachhead on the enemy bank seemed to be by a combined artillery assault to cover the activities of a small unit in the river.

Therefore, on April 27, 1899, one hundred sharpshooters began raking the tops of the Filipino trenches, joined by several machine guns, a Hotchkiss revolving cannon, and the division artillery. Two Kansas privates named Trembley and White stripped naked, dashed out of a clump of bamboo to the river carrying the end of a long coil

of rope, and plunged into the swiftly moving water. Finally reaching
the opposite bank, only inches below the enemy trenches, they fumbled until the rope was securely tied. Two other soldiers started across
in a leaky dugout canoe, pulling themselves along the rope, but they
capsized, losing their arms and the clothing and weapons of the waiting White and Trembley.

Meanwhile, Funston was on the riverbank near a partially burned
raft his men had discovered. "I realized perfectly well that according
to the rules of the game a colonel should not leave the bulk of his
regiment on one side of a stream and accompany a detachment smaller
than a company in size," Funston recalled, but of course he had been
doing precisely that for nearly three months. Generals MacArthur
and Wheaton, who stood some yards distant, directing the barrage,
had their eyes on Funston. "I had initiated this enterprise," he rationalized, "and felt that I must see it through. I could not but consider the outcome as doubtful, and knew mighty well that if I should
send a small force across and sacrifice it I would be damned in my
home State all the rest of my life, and held up to scorn by all the
corner-grocery tacticians in the country."

He took seven men across on the raft and, ordering the rest of his
troops across in stages, he dashed with a half-dozen men into the
trenches — to find only dead and wounded. Returning to the bank,
they followed it until their progress was halted by a sixty-foot-wide
stream that emptied into the Rio Grande at that point. Though they
came under heavy artillery fire from MacArthur's guns, the Filipinos
on the far side of the stream sent a withering fire across toward Funston's men, who were pinned down. Just then the insurgents' machine gun opened up. An American yelled out, "It's the Maxim —
we're goners," only to receive a kick from Funston, who told him to
keep his views to himself. The colonel stood up and saw that the
Maxim nest was three hundred yards away, beneath a railroad culvert, and commanded his prone men to rise. "Under that culvert,
rapid fire," he yelled, and the gun was thereupon silenced.

The insurgents, having seen that their position was tenuous, began vacating their trenches. Funston and a dozen men piled into
canoes, crossed the stream, and ran toward the works of a half-de-
stroyed bridge. They reached it just as two companies led by General
Wheaton succeeded in crawling across the girders to join Funston and
his comrades.

"There were some vigorous hand-shakings and mutual congratulations," the colonel recalled. The real honors, however, would come
later.

On the following day the Americans were attacked by a large contingent led by Aguinaldo's most gifted officer, General Antonio Luna. Two Kansas soldiers standing next to Funston were shot in the head, and a few minutes later, when Funston was giving orders, he himself was hit.

"I felt a most terrific blow on my left-hand," he wrote, "in which I was holding a pair of field-glasses. At first I did not realize that I had been shot, but Lieutenant B. J. Mitchell, who for some years afterward served me as aide, picked up the glasses . . . took me by the arm, and called a man of the Hospital Corps. Blood was splattering all over me, and I had no desire to look at the offending hand, and so held it out to the man, looking the other way in the meantime."

"Is there anything left of it?" Funston asked.

"Clean shot," replied the corpsman.

A few minutes later, he was running after his men to participate in another skirmish. Afterward, the divisional commander came by to see him. "Well, Funston, you got it at last," said MacArthur, "I am glad it is no worse."

He was sent back to Manila to recuperate from the minor wound. On his way he was handed a telegram, congratulating him upon being promoted to the rank of brigadier general of the volunteers. "I was highly gratified" at this recognition from MacArthur and Wheaton, Funston wrote later, "and nearly forgot the throbbing in my hand."

Some time later, Funston was presented with a Medal of Honor for his part in the crossing of the Rio Grande de la Pampanga. The two privates, White and Trembley, also received the award.

Funston succeeded his mentor, General Wheaton, to command the First Brigade of the Second Division; his Kansas regiment continued under him. At the end of June, he was directed back to Manila with the Twentieth and told to prepare to accompany them on a steamer back to the United States. "In a year and a half of service it had but two desertions, both of these occurring shortly after its muster-in," he wrote. "It lost thirty-five men from disease, fourteen of whom were victims of a small-pox epidemic that broke out in the barracks of the First Battalion shortly after our arrival in Manila. Its battle losses were three officers and thirty enlisted men killed, and ten officers and one hundred and twenty-nine enlisted men wounded."

After a hero's welcome in San Francisco and Kansas, Funston left his wife with her parents and returned to Manila. He was given command of a brigade in the central Luzon plains, with headquarters in the dusty town of San Isidro, Nueva Ecija province. San Isidro had for a time been the capital of the Filipino republic, until its president had been forced to retreat into the north. Emilio Aguinaldo had instructed his armies to disband, adopt civilian clothing, and continue the war as guerrillas. He himself had disappeared into the northern mountains and from some remote hiding place continued to direct his forces. Only the vaguest of rumors had surfaced about his whereabouts — until February 4, 1901, when an orderly handed Brigadier General Frederick Funston a telegram.

VI

In the fifteen months following Aguinaldo's dramatic disappearance, some seventy thousand American troops had not been able to halt the insurrection or catch its human inspiration. Having now received such promising news that Captain Taylor in the Pantabangan garrison had apprehended a courier from Aguinaldo himself, Funston lost no time in directing Taylor to have the messenger escorted to San Isidro "with all possible speed."

Two days later, his sentries hustled a bedraggled courier into his office. Dressed in rags and obviously hungry, exhausted, and demoralized, the Filipino clutched his wide-brimmed straw hat in his hands as the general began a preliminary interrogation.

His name?

Cecilio Segismundo.

His village of origin?

Dupax, Nueva Vizcaya province.

His "tribe"?

Ilocano.

His occupation?

Policeman in the native constabulary of Manila under the Spanish, later an insurgent corporal under Major Nazario Alhambra and official courier to *el presidente,* Emilio Aguinaldo.

And his story?

Segismundo's tale explained his general dishevelment. A small party of insurgents consisting of Segismundo, one sergeant, and four privates had made a punishing trek, traveling in a generally southwest direction for nearly one month through unforgiving mountains and jungles without adequate supplies or civilian support. They had attempted to slip around the American patrols at the garrisoned Pacific coastal village of Baler, but, characteristic of the bad luck that had plagued them throughout the journey, they had strayed into an ambush by an American scouting party on the Plain of Tuntunin, near Baler. Two of them were killed. The survivors ran out of food, became desperate, and clambered through a high mountain pass through the Sierra until they finally came down onto the Central

Plain. They hid in the outlying fields of the barrio of San Juan, near Pantabangan. Segismundo sent a messenger to contact the mayor. That official had, unbeknownst to Segismundo, sworn a loyalty oath to the Americans, so his reply took the form of an earnest appeal that they hitch themselves to the cart of Anglo-Saxon progress and decency. Footsore, exhausted, and hungry, unable to muster any resistance even if they had chosen to, Segismundo and his fellows were persuaded to present themselves to the Americans. At this last reverse, the tired messenger decided he had seen as much of the revolution as he could stand.

"I am glad to wash my hands of this business," Segismundo told Lieutenant Taylor in Pantabangan, and he had handed over a dispatch pouch.

Having been awakened at midnight by his captors in Pantabangan and hustled the seventy miles south to San Isidro in great secrecy, Segismundo wondered nervously how much more he should tell the bearded little general to whom he had been conducted. He watched as Funston flipped through the contents of the travel-worn pouch.

Most of the documents were ordinary missives scrawled from homesick insurgents to their loved ones. Then, as Funston continued his examination, there leaped before his eyes the names of all the major insurgent military figures in Luzon: There was General José Alejandrino, once sent by the Spanish into exile in Hong Kong with Aguinaldo for rebellion; he had always been a highly placed figure in the insurgency. There was General Teodoro Sandico, the former director of diplomacy in the Aguinaldo-Mabini revolutionary cabinet. There was General Urbano Lacuna — the canny guerrilla general whom Funston had chased all over Nueva Ecija for the better part of a year and who, only a few months before, narrowly missed shooting Funston during a frantic dash to escape the Kansan's cavalry patrol. There were the brash young brothers Pablo and Simon Tecson, swift tacticians who had been rewarded with field promotions by their commander in chief. Finally there was Baldomero Aguinaldo, Don Emilio's second cousin and commander of the revolutionary forces in Cavite province.

These official dispatches were written in Tagalog; they were encoded and largely indecipherable without further study. But Funston soon spotted one significant detail: the correspondence was signed Colon de Magdalo or Pastor. These were, Funston realized with mounting excitement, noms de plume used by Emilio Aguinaldo.

Were the letters genuine or bogus? Funston wanted to know more. He directed a squad of burly soldiers to hustle the hapless courier away and persuade him to round out his story.

There are several accounts of what happened next. One of Funston's aides related what seems to be the most doubtful version; he claimed to have escorted Segismundo to an empty house, where over the course of a peaceful and agreeable afternoon the courier told most of what he knew. In contrast to this pacific version, Aguinaldo would later assert that Segismundo had been tortured twice by being given the "water cure." Finally, the last version came from Funston himself, who noted only that they used "forceful" means. He declined to go into detail.

The story extracted in whatever way from Segismundo ran as follows. Emilio Aguinaldo fled from the Americans with a small escort; narrowly avoiding capture twice and hampered by malaria and insufficient food, the insurgents finally went through the Cagayan Valley and climbed into the Sierra Madre. Descending the eastern slope toward the sparsely inhabited Pacific coast, they reached a tiny, unimportant, and isolated village in northeastern Luzon called Palanan, which was surrounded by mountains. Hardly anyone ever cared to go there, especially American soldiers. On one occasion, however, not long after Aguinaldo and his company arrived, lookouts posted in the hills ringing the village warned of an approaching American column. *El presidente* hurriedly gathered his staff and military escort, his treasury records and archives, together with all the Palanan townsfolk and their cattle and foodstuffs, and climbed into the neighboring mountains. When the Americans arrived they found the village deserted, and, not even suspecting that Palanan had recently sheltered their preeminent foe, they went away. Aguinaldo returned to Palanan, said Segismundo, and there, in perhaps the most inaccessible spot in Luzon, was where he remained to that day.

Before Segismundo would be fed and allowed to sleep, Funston wanted the answers to four more questions, and he got them. No, said Segismundo, he had no idea what his dispatch pouch had contained, nor what the secret of Aguinaldo's cipher might be; yes, he was willing to renounce Aguinaldo's cause and take the American oath of allegiance; yes, he wished very much to avoid imprisonment, return to his home in Nueva Vizcaya, and live a peaceful life; yes, to secure his release he would cooperate with Funston and do him some "service."

Segismundo was locked up for the night.

Funston thereupon turned his attention to the next order of business, the wearisome task of deciphering the small stack of captured documents. His great hope was to discover if Segismundo had spoken the truth about Aguinaldo's stronghold in Palanan.

Funston summoned two aides to his headquarters. Captain E. V. Smith, his adjutant general, had fearlessly ridden through the Luzon forests with him and had more than demonstrated his intelligence during their association. The other aide would become, after the general himself, the most important figure in the weeks that followed.

Lazaro Segovia y Gutierrez, an intelligence officer who had served under Funston for less than a year, was only twenty-two years old, a dashing "secret service" operative who relished his important position in Funston's command. Clean-shaven and handsome, with a prankish sense of humor but gifted in administrative duties, Segovia had been born in Madrid to a genteel but less than well-to-do Spanish family. He was precocious in education, earning his Bachelor of Arts degree at fifteen. Wanting to continue his schooling but lacking the means to do so, he enlisted as a volunteer in the Spanish army to reap the educational benefits it offered. He enrolled in a private college, but his studies were cut short by the Cuban revolution. His educational privileges were retired; he was recalled to his army company and made a corporal, but as luck would have it, he escaped being drafted for Cuba. He had heard about a military academy in the Philippines and petitioned the secretary of war for a transfer to the islands, which he received in 1895. Once in Manila, he was attached to a regiment composed of mostly Filipino troops, and again he enrolled in classes. One year later, the first Filipino insurrection broke out and Segovia joined his regiment. During the next eighteen months he fought in Laguna, Batangas, Cavite, Bulacan, and Nueva Ecija provinces as well as in Manila, and he later told his biographer he had been decorated seven times for gallantry — an assertion that in light of his activities during the next two months should not be doubted.

When the war between Spain and the United States began he was at Manila, bottled up in the walled city along with the rest of his garrison until the Spaniards' final capitulation in August 1898. Though the defeated Castilians were ultimately shipped back to disgrace in Spain, Segovia remained in Manila, having been unsuccessful in securing permission for his Filipino wife to emigrate with him. "Impelled by his love of adventures," as his biographer wrote, Segovia cast his lot with the Filipino army in October 1898. He became a lieutenant and the aide to General Mariano Llanera, coincidentally coming under fire at one time from the Twentieth Kansas as it swept toward Caloocan.

The Spaniard saw which way the military winds were blowing by the spring of 1900 and surrendered directly to General Funston in

May of that year. Always able to recognize a kindred spirit, Funston made Segovia a trusted aide, translator, guerrilla strategist, and spy. Later, the general would owe his life to his subordinate.

Funston, Smith, and Segovia took off their coats and shirts and sat down in the general's office to examine the insurgent documents closely. The three amateur cryptanalysts were fueled by an occasional drop of whiskey and copious amounts of strong coffee supplied by the general's personal cook. They toiled through the night. Funston, who was well acquainted with the Spanish language, sat at Smith's right side and dictated his translation while the subordinate officer pecked away at his typewriter; at the same time, Segovia labored to find a clue to the cipher using his knowledge of Spanish and Tagalog. Three mind-numbing hours later, Segovia isolated a key word, "ammunition," in a letter to General Sandico by finding a sentence that read: "Here we can manufacture - 14 14 , 13 : 6 (13," and listing all the possible "bad things" that the *insurrectos* could manufacture, finally realizing it could only be "ammunition." Following that breakthrough he worked out the rest of the code, a rather simple one that substituted numbers for the alphabet in reverse order, with a few exceptions to confuse any unauthorized readers. Funston treated his two aides to a celebratory glass of whiskey and they then jubilantly translated the bulk of the dispatches, finishing shortly after dawn.

Funston was disappointed but not surprised to see that any mention of the town of Palanan had been scrupulously avoided in the letters. He still had only Segismundo's word as to the actual whereabouts of Aguinaldo. But among the many messages that detailed the various mundane aspects of running a scattered guerrilla army — troops moved, supplies allocated, funds transferred — one letter positively shone. It was addressed to Don Emilio's cousin Baldomero and signed with *el presidente*'s old Masonic name, Colon de Magdalo. It mentioned the remote valley that Segismundo claimed Aguinaldo had used to gain access to the Pacific coast — and Palanan. The letter proved, in Funston's words, to be "the one that was the final undoing of its writer."

> After many and risky adventures we were able to reach Cagayan Valley, where we are at present. I have not sufficient people of my confidence to garrison this province. I want in the first place, that you take charge of the command of Central Luzon, residing wherever you deem it best. Send me about 400 men at the first opportunity with a good commander; if you can not send them all at once, send them in parties. The bearer can serve as a guide to them until their arrival here; he is a person to be trusted. We are preparing a large arsenal in this

camp, which can furnish Central and even Southern Luzon with ammunition. Some of the commercial houses of Cagayan and Isabela have
promised us machinery and tools. . . .

Colon de Magdalo

Clearly Aguinaldo had remained in charge since his disappearance and was prepared to continue the struggle indefinitely. But the
early morning hours were not an ideal time to ponder this, for the
bleary-eyed men had reached the point where they could no longer
function without rest. Despite all the coffee, Funston said, "we were
nearly done for — we had been without sleep or food for twenty
hours." He dismissed Segovia and Smith.

Returning to his quarters, Funston retired, but his mind refused
to let him sleep. He restlessly conjured a series of questions that had
no certain answers. What did it all mean? Were these documents,
which by the hand of providence had been dropped square in his
lap, as significant as he hoped? Could they be as important to him
personally as they might be to his country? Was there some way to
"tidy up" the package before passing it on to army headquarters in
Manila?

Even as he lay staring at the ceiling of his bedroom, the pieces of
a large, complex, and very important jigsaw puzzle began to fall into
place.

Again and again Aguinaldo's words came back to him: *"I have not
sufficient people . . . send me about 400 men . . . [Segismundo] can serve
as a guide. . . ."*

At four in the afternoon he finally got up. He went over to the house
in which the courier had been locked up and disappeared inside.

It was not until the next morning, February 12, that Funston's
thoughts were sufficiently organized for him to bring his staff fully
into his confidence. He summoned Lazaro Segovia to his office for a
private conference. A short time later Captain Smith and another aide,
Lieutenant Burton J. Mitchell, were called.

He had devised, the general told them enthusiastically, "no slouch"
of a plan. Having been presented with information pinpointing
Aguinaldo's whereabouts, naturally he could see no alternative but
to dispatch a party of men forthwith into Isabela province, to Palanan, and to capture Emilio Aguinaldo alive. Thus with one bold
stroke he would remove the heart, soul, and inspiration of the Filipino rebellion.

Certainly it would not be easily accomplished. According to Segismundo, all trails leading to Palanan were carefully watched by no-
madic Negrito and Ilongote tribesmen who eked out an existence by

hunting and gathering food. Should an American war party approach, no matter how large or small, these primitive savages would
swiftly alert the insurgents. Landing a party on the Pacific coast and
dashing the seven miles overland to Palanan was no solution, either.
With the appearance of smoke from an American steamship funnel
on the horizon, an alarm would sound and the insurgents would
scatter into the mountains before the landing party had so much as
lowered its boats.

The key to success lay in Aguinaldo's own words: "Send me men."
What if the relief troops were not his own?

There was only one way to ensnare Aguinaldo, said Funston, "to
get him under false colors."

Galvanized by the boldness of this venture, the four men pored
over the military maps of Isabela province. The maps were sketchy;
they had been drawn using antiquated Spanish charts nearly old
enough to have illustrations of sea serpents in the water off the eastern coast of the island. Despite their lack of concrete knowledge of
the terrain, the men concocted an elaborate and hazardous plan,
adding details here and there, and as they worked it began to take
on a shape and a life of its own.

Aguinaldo had asked his cousin for reinforcements. Funston would
deliver them. The troops would be Macabebes, ruthlessly effective
Filipino scouts from the village of Macabebe in Pampanga province.
Some people thought the Macabebes were descendants of the Mexican Indians brought to the Philippines as slaves by the conquistadors; whether or not this was true, their origins might as well have
been on another continent, for they had never fit in with the other
Filipinos. For generations they had fought in native battalions under
the Spanish flag — even against their own countrymen when the
Revolution of 1896 had begun. When the Americans had appeared,
the villagers asked the Spanish government to relocate them en masse
to the Caroline Islands if Aguinaldo's revolution succeeded. An
American captain urged that his superiors continue the policy of divide and conquer by enlisting native scouts — just as they had with
American Indians twenty years before — but after the fall of Manila
the redoubtable General Elwell S. Otis had resisted the idea. He was
afraid they would remain "true to race" and turn traitor; but he should
not have worried, for there was a blood hatred between the Macabebes and Tagalogs like Aguinaldo and his crew. The Macabebes had
been forced upon Otis by a forward-thinking War Department. As
far as Funston's scheme was concerned, the Macabebe scouts would
not be distinguishable from loyal insurgents. With proper prepara-

tions they could fool Aguinaldo, even at close range, until the noose had tightened around him.

Don Emilio's "relief column" would bring some guests he would not expect — five American officers who would, the conspirators decided, play the part of prisoners of war.

It was a brilliant and audacious plan. To bring it off required a complicated scenario that would be believed by the insurgent chief. Aguinaldo expected his detachment to travel from Baldomero's headquarters, somewhere in the Central Plain of Luzon, across the eastern cordillera to the coast and then north to Palanan. Any American column could certainly duplicate that itinerary, but the men plotting in Funston's office decided that the journey would be too long, too risky. Instead, they would eliminate two hundred miles of hard marching by planning on sea transport to a place where the relief troops would have come down onto the beach after scaling the mountains. That place was near the village of Casiguran, twenty-seven miles north of the last American garrison at Baler. The area was totally out of the American sphere of control and known to be sympathetic to the guerrillas. Between Casiguran and Aguinaldo's stronghold at Palanan lay more than a hundred miles of uncharted, unexplored, and unpacified terrain. Funston's group — and there was never any question in the general's mind but that he would go along — would be leaving the safety of occupied Luzon. They would be utterly cut off from any possible outside aid, constantly at risk of betrayal, ambush, starvation, sickness, injury, and the cruelty of the elements.

It was, to be sure, an extremely daunting prospect. Nevertheless, none of the men in that room wanted to be left out.

2

MANILA, 1982

I

The No Smoking light blinked on and the barnlike interior of the jet was filled with annoying jaunty music. The pilot dropped us below the clouds in a long approach toward the Philippines. My seat, in the center of the aircraft, had no view but that of flight-stunned seatmates, so I bolted out of place, ignoring admonitions from the attendants, and darted up and down the aisles. A pilot's chart flapped in my hand. Trying to manage port and starboard glimpses of the many islands that had appeared below out of the green ocean (my first tropical sea), I leaned over strangers' laps to peer outside. My map rustled in their faces. I hardly appeared like someone who had spent thirty-six months in the library learning about the country he was approaching. More likely, I presented the image of an overexcited standee on a Hollywood tour bus.

Finally I returned to my seat just as we flashed over the brightness of Manila Bay and landed. During the claustrophobic milling toward the exits, I took comfort for the last time from the Filipino stewardesses' dazzling smiles. After years of studying their country and events that had eventually shaped not only their lives but mine, I was at last about to set my feet upon Philippine soil and into the footsteps of two turn-of-the-century antagonists, to attempt to see simultaneously through the dead eyes of Frederick Funston and Emilio Aguinaldo as well as through my own. What had changed? The Manila of the past still lived for me; what about the Manila of today? Nervous, anticipating, I felt rather like a mail order bride about to meet a suitor. As I stepped from the plane onto the roll-away stairs, I was greeted by three things: the wave of heat of an early Philippine summer; the sight of a multitude of brightly dressed people pressing themselves against chain-link fences and roaring out a welcome to my fellow passengers; and, below me on the tarmac, a man in a dazzling white shirt with epaulets, cradling a submachine gun in his brown arms.

V. S. Naipaul once remarked about India that "to see its poverty is to make an observation of no value; a thousand newcomers to the country before you have seen and said as you." In Manila, the government seems willing to do everything it can to prevent visitors from seeing (and mentioning) the poverty, for if it is out of immediate sight, painted over or walled in, then perhaps it will go away. But paint blisters and walls warp more rapidly in tropical Third World countries, and though Manila tourist maps neglect to show a district such as Tondo, or the shantytown that sat directly across from the airport, they are still there, and so far as the Philippines is concerned, observing its poverty is becoming more of a political act as its existence is denied by those in power.

Speeding down the bayside corridor linking the International Terminal and downtown Manila, we passed squads of municipal street-sweepers, men and women in red trousers, straw hats, and school-bus-yellow T-shirts announcing they were METRO MANILA AIDES. Even at the godly hour of seven on a Sunday morning they were zealously clipping foliage and sweeping dirt out of our way and wake, possibly grateful to have jobs even if it meant attending church on Saturday night so they could keep the avenue clean for Sunday tourists. The palm-fringed thoroughfare used to be called Dewey Boulevard, but, of course, after independence the roster of heroes changed as did some of the street names. Rechristened Roxas Boulevard, it commemorates the first Filipino president to serve in the post–World War II days of independence, Manuel Roxas. Our driver shouted over the din of a tape of an Elvis imitator singing his medley of Presley songs to a disco beat; finally the driver made himself understood: we were approaching the tourist belt of the Malate and Ermita districts. Sure enough, as the traffic and atmosphere thickened, we began passing a strange international mélange of tourist joints: here the Ginza Supper Club, the Aloha Hawaiian Hotel, the Playboy Club; there the Bachelors Three Sauna and Massage, Kentucky Fried Chicken, the Starlight Disco, and even Uncle Mark's Chicken-in-a-Bikini Restaurant.

Filipino friends in the United States, whether exiles or expatriates, had advised staying with their relatives or former classmates (or, in a few cases, former cellmates) as the best way of seeing the capital. While this was reasonable advice, I was unwilling to impose too much on the famous Filipino hospitality. Besides, I cherished my independence in a new city; I could always see more clearly that way. It was fortunate that I was traveling with my brother, Christopher Bain, a photographer whose commercial and magazine work had enabled him to engineer a swap of his services for our lodging.

Our hotel revealed itself to be the showcase of the capital, the Manila Hotel. My friends predicted its opulence would eventually embarrass or dismay me, and they were correct; but of all city hotels, it has an air of history about it and so seemed to be the best place for a historically minded person. Built to overlook Manila Harbor in 1912, the hotel still exudes a colonial ambiance despite its recent renovation and the addition of a modern tower. Perhaps its being owned by the government explains the absence of hustlers and hawkers from its perimeter, as is not the case elsewhere. We passed through its courtyards unmolested, only to be halted by a phalanx of polite but firm security men who searched our bags and patted our persons. They were looking for bombs or weapons, the entry of which used to make staying at the hotel hazardous.

Douglas MacArthur, the illustrious son of Arthur MacArthur, lived at the Manila Hotel between 1935 and 1941, a fact that does not escape one for very long in the hotel. According to a brochure in my room, MacArthur accepted the position of military adviser to the Philippines after naming several conditions, the most interesting of which was that he be given a residence equivalent in comfort and elegance to the Presidential Palace of Malacañang. His suite at the Manila Hotel is maintained approximately as it was when he and his family lived there and is available for wealthy transients at a price one would expect. During part of the time I was in Manila, the current U.S. defense secretary, Caspar Weinberger, was staying there. The hotel's general manager, a courtly and avuncular Dutchman (born in Java) by the name of Frans Schutzman, told me later that Weinberger's aides had relayed the secretary's strong desire to sleep in MacArthur's rooms. However, the aides feared they could not justify the expense since their administration had, so recently, slashed Health and Human Services budgets, and if someone like the gadfly Senator William Proxmire learned of the extravagance, their chief would be greatly embarrassed.

Weinberger got to sleep with MacArthur's restless ghost and his office was billed at the lowest single-room rate, for Schutzman knew publicity value when he saw it. More than twenty years before, as manager of the Raffles Hotel in Singapore, he had obtained Somerset Maugham's permission to use a line from one of his short stories in the hotel's advertisements: "Raffles Hotel in Singapore stands for all the fables of the exotic East." In return, the author was promised a free stay whenever he was in town. Maugham eventually took him up on it, but when the hotel owners refused to honor the agreement, saying Maugham was wealthy enough to pay his own bill, a furious Schutzman settled it himself and immediately resigned. In the subsequent years he was general manager of the Nile Hotel in Cairo, the Cavilieri in Rome, the Hyatt Regency in Toronto, United Nations Plaza in New York, and since 1976, the Manila Hotel — not unfitting residences for a former spy, as Schutzman might admit, for he had served with British Intelligence during the Second World War.

Whether or not he keeps his hand in his old trade, Schutzman is a skilled hotelier, and his Manila Hotel has attracted "heads of state, nobility, literary giants, and cinematic legends," as he immodestly told me. Indeed, I found a piece of paper in my room entitled "the Hall of Fame." Among the names were those of Lyndon Baines Johnson, Richard Nixon, John Lennon, Ernest Hemingway, and Dame Margot Fonteyn. About halfway down, someone had cleverly filled in a blank space with my own name in matching type. I appeared between James Michener and Tyrone Power.

On the days I ventured into unknown Manila neighborhoods with a willingness to become lost, I naturally employed caution, especially upon learning that 80 percent of the urban road fatalities involve pedestrians. Presumably most of the accidents are caused by the traffic-dominating, rambunctious jeepneys. Legacies of the Second World War, jeepneys were originally surplus military jeeps, which were converted by the blowtorch and hacksaw into public transport vehicles of the most gaudy and frightful sort.

Jeepneys remind me of pinball machines on wheels: they are buttressed, on the average, with no less than a dozen each of chrome rearview mirrors and colored lights. Streamers, ribbons, and pennants dangle from their many antennas, and a herd of nickel stallions stampede across the hood while credible paintings of "typical" Philippine scenery — waterfalls, volcanoes, and lagoons are the most popular, though religious themes also dominate — adorn port, starboard, and aft panels. With ten or twelve passengers jammed into the back compartment, the jeepney lurches in and out of traffic almost as though it were in a chariot race. The passengers, left to shift for themselves, hang on to overhead rails for dear life, sweating companionably, hips wedged against their neighbors' and knees commingled with those of the riders on the bench opposite. Without having completely deciphered the placards that designated each jeepney's route through the city, I began climbing aboard anyway. Surviving a few narrow scrapes, I wished I had found a place beside the driver so I could abandon ship when disaster seemed imminent. This front seat usually being taken and well defended, I sat in back in a kind of stoop (since headroom is not built for Westerners) or twisted my torso so I could lean out into the open air. The jeepney driver honks his horn every few seconds, but the effect struck me not as Western aggression, when motorists lean on their barrel-chested horns as they cut someone off (and roundly curse the drivers who do unto them a block later). In Manila, as the jeepney driver turns to cut off others, he seems to accept with equanimity that sooner or later he must slam on his brakes when a competitor swerves across two or three lanes and stops dead ahead to discharge a passenger. When the jeepney driver honks his horn, he is not saying "Get the hell out of my way" but "I see you!"

Perhaps some of those frequent pedestrian deaths fall among the ubiquitous, skinny cigarette boys. Somehow I doubt it. They are too nimble at what they do, which is to stalk boldly between traffic lanes as autos go roaring by. No younger than eight or nine, they persist in making an annoying kissing sound as they dart toward oncoming motorists, their hard-eyed stares daring them *not* to buy their cigarettes, which are kept in wooden trays and sold singly or by the pack. Most of the time they sell a couple of cigarettes at a time; a jeepney driver will purchase two, tucking one behind his ear for later and accepting a light from the cigarette boy's proffered disposable lighter. The boy then scampers away through the cars, kissing the noisome air to make as many sales as he can before the traffic light changes. As the chariot race begins anew, he is enveloped in the noxious clouds of black exhaust smoke that pour from every vehicle in Manila, which knows nothing of the muffler and less of the catalytic converter.

It is impossible for anyone aware of history to travel through Manila without being constantly reminded of the past. The effect can be strange. In the drab but clamorous shopping district of Cubao, as I forged my way through the noontime crowds, I suddenly passed into a gigantic shadow and looked up to see the Araneta Coliseum, a stage for visiting rock and pop stars and, some years ago, the site of the third boxing match between Muhammad Ali and Joe Frazier. Then, as if a hand had been planted on my shoulder, I became aware that I was standing on General Emilio Aguinaldo Avenue. Another time, searching for a bookstore in Ermita, I felt myself settling into the sidewalk rhythms enough to know confidently when I could sidestep into the street to bypass a knot of people and not get flattened by a truck — but then I came upon something so incongruous to modern Manila as an avenue named for William Howard Taft. My street savvy wouid crumble before the dissonant images of present and past.

The effect stayed with me throughout my stay and it was not unpleasant, only constant, since there does not seem to be one road in the capital that does not commemorate someone from the past. I have always "collected" street names anyway. For instance, in a development in Lanham, Maryland, there is not only an Elvis Road but also a Presley Avenue. In the Magnolia Gardens district of Jacksonville, Florida, hard by the Ribault River, one may find Calloway Circle, Ellington Road, and drives named Poitier, King Cole, Mahalia, and Campanella. In a Brooklyn, New York, neighborhood surveyed and laid out, I believe, in the 1880s, there are two parallel streets, President and Garfield, that honor the chief of state assassinated in a Washington railroad station in 1881.

This twin fascination with history and urban planning allowed an unparalleled history lesson in Manila. The most modern district, Makati, boasts several top-flight hotels and a commercial center that might be useful if the city telephone system worked. Radiating from this gleaming hub are several expensive developments, complete with watchtowers and armed guards, within which the Manila jet set lives and relaxes. Yet these areas of upper-class comfort, these paragons of modernity, have taken their names from the earliest colonial times. One, Magallanes Village, commemorates the Portuguese explorer we know as Ferdinand Magellan, who shifted his allegiance to Charles I of Spain and set out on September 20, 1519, from San Lucar, Spain, with a fleet and 237 men. After encountering the South American continent, he sailed around it through what became the Strait of Magellan and struck out across the Pacific. Four months later, on March 17, 1521, the crewman sighted an island called Samar, part of an archipelago they called St. Lazarus. Visiting other islands, they were welcomed by the Indios (as the Spaniards viewed the natives), who seemed to have no objection to being converted to Catholicism, for it brought them beads and other goods. The Spaniards found an exception on April 27, when Magellan intervened in a tribal dispute at a place called Mactan. There, Magellan and sixty men, together with twenty or thirty reconstructed Indios, tried to land their longboats. Rocks and coral reefs forced them to anchor as far as two hundred yards from shore. They waded toward the beach in thigh-deep water only to be confronted by some fifteen hundred natives. The defenders of the beach at Mactan forced them back, pelting them with spears all the way, seemingly unafraid of the Spaniards' muskets. What happened is related by an Italian crew member, Antonio Pigafetta:

> The natives continued to pursue us, and picking up the same spear four or six times, hurled it at us again and again. Recognizing the captain [Magellan], so many turned upon him that they knocked his helmet off his head twice, but he always stood firmly like a good knight, together with some others. Thus did we fight for more than one hour, refusing to retire farther. An Indian hurled a bamboo spear into the captain's face, but the latter immediately killed him with his lance, which he left in the Indian's body. Then, trying to lay hand on sword, he could draw it out but halfway, because he had been wounded in the arm by a bamboo spear. When the natives saw that, they all hurled themselves upon him. One of them wounded him on the left leg with a large cutlass, which resembles a scimitar, only being larger. That caused the captain to fall face downward, when immediately they rushed upon him with iron and bamboo spears and with their cutlasses, until they killed our mirror, our light, our comfort, and our true guide.

The tribal leader who defied Magellan was named Lapu-Lapu, and he has since become a symbol of Filipino resistance to Western domination. It is a fitting irony that within the Makati development of Magallanes Village, there is not only Magallanes Avenue but Lapu-Lapu Avenue, where the two warriors are wed forever inside that playground of the rich.

Elsewhere in Makati, one finds other walled compounds where lawn sprinklers work all day and where one often hears the unmistakable sound of children splashing in backyard swimming pools. Three of these compounds are named Urdaneta, Legaspi, and Salcedo villages, and together they symbolize the tying of the knot, as it were, of Spanish colonialization. Urdaneta Village is named for an Augustinian explorer, Andres de Urdaneta, whose writings enlivened King Charles's interest in the Philippines, as the Archipelago of San Lazarus had come to be called. The new name for the islands honored Felipe, crown prince of Spain, who became King Philip II in 1556 and set into motion the fourth and most successful Philippine expedition. Urdaneta was to be the pilot, and an official of the Mexico City government, Miguel López de Legaspi, commanded the fleet, which arrived at Samar in 1565. Legaspi founded a thriving Spanish colony on the islands of Cebu and Panay. Together with his teenaged grandson, Juan de Salcedo, Legaspi explored other places to settle.

In 1570 and 1571, Salcedo encountered a settlement of Muslims on the island of Luzon. (Muslims had begun to migrate north from the Malay peninsula, Java, Sumatra, and Borneo, among other places, throughout the previous century and established communities on many Philippine islands.) This location in Luzon, with its large sheltered harbor, seemed very desirable to Legaspi when he heard about it. It was called May-nilad, after *nilad,* a common native shrub, and was defended by a formidable fort on the headland between the sea and the Pasig River. The sultans of Manila were of two minds about striking any agreements with Salcedo, who was something of a firebrand, so their early dealings alternated between skirmishes and unsatisfactory parleys. Legaspi, however, was known for his diplomacy. In April and May of 1571, the older explorer appeared in Manila Bay, and by strenuously employing his talents he was able to strike bargains with the Muslims. However, all did not go smoothly. At least one other tribe was not so easily swayed; the inhabitants of an inland village called Macabebe insisted upon a token battle before they would be convinced to come under the governance of King Philip of Spain. With that impediment gone, the settlement at the mouth of the Pasig River eventually became the center of Spanish power in the Pacific.

The people and the culture of the Philippines were already a rich and varied stew when the Spaniards arrived. The archipelago had been inhabited by humans for at least twenty-one thousand years, a figure established with the discovery in 1962 of a fossilized skullcap in the southwestern part of Palawan island; tectites and tools from the Paleolithic era have also been found in many places around the islands, and depth-age estimates place these at fifty thousand years. The most popular theory suggests that during the Pleistocene epoch, the level of the ocean was lower by some 156 feet, which exposed a broad lowland where the South China Sea now exists. Across this land bridge wandered the first inhabitants of the Philippines as well as those of Malaysia and Indonesia. Later, after the earth's ice cap retreated and brought the exposed land masses to their present configuration, other settlers and traders arrived by boat from Malaysia, Indonesia, China, Borneo, even India; each contributed to the precolonial civilization, which was primarily agricultural, though trade flourished among all the western Pacific islands and with the Asian mainland.

Under Spanish rule, the settlement at Manila became a way station relaying the riches of Asia by way of one or two galleons each year to Acapulco, and thence to Mexico City and Spain. A Jesuit historian, Father Francisco Colin, lovingly catalogued the goods leaving Manila during the Spaniards' Golden Age:

> The pearls and precious stones of India, the diamonds of Narsinga and Goa, the rubies, sapphires and topazes and the cinnamon of Ceylon, the pepper of Sumatra and Java, the cloves, nutmeg and other spices of the Moluccas and Banda, the silks of Persia, the wool and

carpets of Ormuz and Malabar, the rich hangings and bed coverings
of Bengal, fine camphor from Borneo, balsam and ivory of Abada and
Cambodia, civet of the Lequios, and silks of all kinds from China —
raw and woven in velvets and figured damasks, taffetas and other cloths
of every texture and design and color. . . .

Such shipments were a strong temptation to privateers, especially
those of the British, whose relations with Spain were not very good.
In 1587, the pirate Thomas Cavendish captured a galleon off the coast
of America that was worth as much as two million Mexican pesos,
and during the famous round-the-world privateering expedition of
Captain George Anson (1740–44), a Spanish ship was waylaid off
the coast of Samar, yielding up to $1.5 million worth of pure silver
and pieces of eight. This hardly endeared Britain to Spain (nor did
the two-year English occupation of Manila, which began in 1762,
during the Seven Years' War in Europe).

By then the city had expanded outward from the original settlement at the mouth of the Pasig River, and it had survived much worse
than the temporary embarrassment of British rule. Only four years
after Legaspi's founding of the city, a fleet of three thousand Chinese
pirates landed a war party ashore; although the corsairs were repulsed, Manila was laid to waste in the process. Rebuilt, it burned to
the ground in 1583, when funerary candles ignited the San Agustin
Church during services for a Spanish governor general. The succeeding administration ordered that all city buildings be rebuilt of
stone or adobe, but even this solid construction was vulnerable, for
earthquakes repeatedly devastated Manila, particularly those in 1645,
1863, and 1880.

Despite the threat of fire and cataclysm, Manila acquired a nearly
permanent physical appearance during the administration (1590–93)
of Gómez Pérez Dasmariñas (whose name, by the way, graces yet another compound in the modern district of Makati). Dasmariñas constructed a medieval fortress on the spit of land at the river mouth
and raised formidable stone walls to enclose the city entirely. It is
interesting to note that the governor paid for Fort Santiago and the
walls of Intramuros, as the district came to be called, by taxing Chinese
imports and all merchandise shipped to Acapulco, and he assigned
to the project all the proceeds from the government's monopoly on
playing cards.

By the nineteenth century, the center of gravity had shifted beyond the medieval walls of Manila; suburban villages had taken on
their own importance, each satellite with its own particular identity.
Even at the coming of the Americans, Ermita was known for its embroidered piña (pineapple) cloth; Malate, for its elegantly decorated

slippers; Tondo, for its milk, butter, and cheese; Binondo, for cigars and its concentration of commercial streets; and Paco, for its circular cemetery. Today, they have all been swallowed up by the greater body of Metro Manila, with the greatest loss being each district's individuality. Admittedly, a few have maintained distinctiveness: Binondo has its crowded Chinatown; Quiapo, its ozonous thoroughfares; Tondo, its depressing slums; Ermita and Malate, their bars and bordellos.

Defining heroes is a subjective business, and the collection of martyrs, saints, and long-gone governors that suited the Spaniards seemed inappropriate to Manila's new proprietors at the beginning of the twentieth century. The Americans remade the capital in their own image, throwing up war memorials everywhere to commemorate some of the forty-five hundred soldiers killed by the Filipinos between 1899 and 1902, turning old Fort Santiago into the headquarters of the modern U.S. Army, and transforming the medieval moat around the Walled City into an eighteen-hole golf course. The memories of two major paternal figures — Admiral George E. Dewey, who had pronounced Emilio Aguinaldo and his government "like a pack of boys," and Judge William Howard Taft, who had coined the expression "little brown brothers" — were enshrined in the two major boulevards girding the bayside districts. One plaza commemorated William McKinley. Another was named after General Henry W. Lawton, killed in 1899, a fate also visited upon Colonel John M. Stotsenberg, whose name was memorialized in the massive military base north of Manila now known as Clark Field; both men were considered at the time to be as close to certifiable martyrs as one could expect of Americans. Elsewhere in the city, the Filipinos in Malate puzzled over new signs designating Calle Nebraska, Calle Dakota, Calle Kansas, and Calle Georgia; across from the old Spanish promenade, the Luneta, they studied the antics of the baseball players in Wallace Field.

All the American war memorials established at the turn of the century were pulled down after independence in 1946. Justifiably, many of the geographical names were changed to accommodate the Filipinos' own crowded pantheon of heroes. If one excludes a modern neighborhood in Quezon City, where for some reason the streets are named after American presidents, I found that of all the American soldiers, of all the administrators whose deeds shaped the Filipinos' lives (for better or worse), only genial old Willie Taft and two fellow governors remain. A major exception has been made in the case of a second lieutenant in the army who served in "police actions" in Samar and Panay in 1903 and 1904. Forty years later, after his career and deeds had been firmly linked to the fate of the Philippines, Douglas MacArthur became, for the Filipinos, the only genuine American hero.

On the eastern edge of Rizal Park (formerly Burnham Green, formerly La Luneta), in a crowded concrete building, resides the national memory in the consolidated form of the National Library, the National Historical Institute, and the National Archives. During my work there I met the director, a rumpled, gray, sly-humored historian, Dr. Serafin Quiason.

"I have just returned from installing a plaque in Kawit, the birthplace of Emilio Aguinaldo," he told me, "for yesterday was his one hundred and thirteenth birthday." Aside from his administrative tasks and his research, Quiason often presides over such ceremonies. In the coming weeks, I would stumble across many plaques.

"Manila is such a place of history for me," I told him. "I was somewhat surprised that most of the people I've met so far seem to have only a partial understanding of their own past."

"You should not be surprised," replied Quiason, and of course he was correct, for almost everybody everywhere shows the same lack. "We're trying to correct it in the schools," he said, "but it is a long process, and we have many obstacles. Some of that blame, it is sad but true, rests with you Americans."

"Besides the fact that we kept the Philippines as a colony for nearly half a century," I said, "what do you mean?"

"Well," he said, sinking lower into his seat, "there is much to be said about how a colonized people are educated, but I was referring to a couple of important facts. First, after the Philippine-American War, all of the thousands of original records of the Philippines, all the so-called insurgent documents, were crated and shipped to Washington, D.C. Any Filipino researching the period had to bear the expense of going all that way to your National Archives. It was not until 1957 — *just twenty-five years ago!* — that your Congress voted to return them to us. And who knows what might have been lost in all of that time?"

He smiled and shrugged. "Have you been downstairs to our National Library?"

I admitted that I had found less than I had expected in the rare books section, where leprous patches on the ceiling indicated a leakage of water and where the bindings of old volumes had been gnawed by mice. A young student researcher told me that sometimes she could hear them running and squeaking behind the stacks. "Actually," I told Quiason, "I think I have found more books on the Philippine-

American War in New York, in the New York Public Library's research building."

"That is probably true," Quiason said, shaking his head sadly. "I have been there." He named a few other institutions, including the Library of Congress, with superior collections of Filipiniana. "Again, sorry to say, we have to thank the Americans," he said. "Remember that story from the Vietnam War era, about 'destroying a village to save it'?" He pointed to the wall over his head, where an oil painting had been hung that showed a Greco-Roman edifice, the former home of the Philippine National Library. The building looked as if it were a rather elaborate sand castle that had been partly destroyed by a large foot lowered from the sky. Half of the building had collapsed into rubble.

"The liberation of Manila," he explained. "At least, in this painting, a mixed blessing. Douglas MacArthur and the Americans found it necessary to blast the Japanese out of the city. Our books got in the way." He was genuinely grieving. "As I said, a mixed blessing. We lost so much, so many irreplaceable volumes. Perhaps someday our holdings will be replaced, but probably not."

As I was leaving, Dr. Quiason called me back.

"If you should happen to come across any Filipiniana in your research, any books in the out-of-print stores in America, let me know. If they are the right price, maybe we can buy them." But he did not sound convinced.

Old men — Americans — appeared in the hotel lobby one day, some of them infirm, all looking pale in comparison to the Asians and to the raw, sunburned Australians who can be found swaggering through hotel lobbies all over the East. Gradually, the number of these American tourists, and their blue-haired wives, grew to the point where they could no longer be ignored. Many of the men took to wearing the Filipino national costume, the *barong tagalog,* a loose-fitting shirt of nearly transparent cloth that is worn with its tails outside the trousers. The shirts recall the age when the Spanish overlords decreed that all male Indios wear them as a badge of their nativity; the transparent fabric served also as a political tool, for it was impossible to hide weapons beneath such a shirt. *Barong tagalogs* look extremely informal to eyes conditioned to seeing social acceptance in a jacket and tie; tourists wearing them never seemed to be totally at ease in the fancy restaurants of the Manila Hotel — and I had to stifle an urge to whisper "Tuck in your shirt!" when they looked most vulnerable.

Their numbers grew. On my way to breakfast in the morning, I would find cardboard signs opposite the concierge station that announced group tours to Fort Santiago or the Pangsanjin Falls; heading back upstairs in an unusually crowded elevator, I would overhear snatches of war stories being recounted for perhaps the thousandth time. The fortieth anniversary of the Fall of Corregidor and the Bataan Death March was approaching, and soldiers from three nations were beginning to converge upon Manila for the observances. Knots of Filipinos from the provinces, groups of loud Japanese men and their docile wives, appeared; the Japanese, recognizing the faces of old comrades in restaurants and lounges, hailed them loudly, embraced them, and laughed while their wives looked on shyly.

I have never understood how former mortal enemies are able to gaze at one another without antipathy, but I saw no hostility among the old American and Japanese soldiers in the weeks preceding the commemoration; indeed, while there seemed to be no instances of intermingling, the groups looked curiously at one another, stealing glances while struggling over the huge hotel menus or peering at their neighbors' foreign necks while standing in line to change their money. I overheard, at least among the Americans, repeated references of the "some of my best stereo components are Japanese" variety and begrudging confessions that these soldiers-turned-businessmen wished they could "open up" Japan to their products or services. As for the former allies, it was a pleasure to witness a few Filipinos and Americans renewing acquaintances of forty years earlier. Their shared hardship had obviously imprinted itself upon these wan or falsely hearty men, more than one of whom I came upon in the corridor of my high tower floor, where a floor-to-ceiling window near the elevators overlooks the vast expanse of Manila Bay. The Mariveles Mountains on Bataan would be barely visible across the haze, but these men would stand and look out over the water, losing themselves in thought as the elevators came and went nearby, their discreet chimes failing to rouse the men from their reveries.

Four hours after the sneak attack on Pearl Harbor, on December 7, 1941, the Japanese began their offensive in the Philippines. The American naval commander, Thomas C. Hart, had been notified of the destruction in Hawaii through official channels, but Douglas MacArthur learned of it only when a news bulletin from a California radio station alerted his staff. There would be no time for preparations.

When the Philippines had moved into a commonwealth status in 1934 as a prelude to independence, President Manuel Quezon requested that his old friend General MacArthur be appointed military adviser. President Roosevelt acquiesced, and MacArthur, who had earlier assured Quezon that "I am prepared to devote the remainder of my life if necessary to securing a proper defense for the Philippine Nation," arrived in Manila in late 1935. He faced a Herculean task. The Philippines was preparing for its eventual freedom by laboring to readjust the economy before favorable trade agreements were ended. Thus, the commonwealth government allowed for only a limited military budget, and Quezon's support for his American adviser proved to be spotty once he began to understand that MacArthur, being outside Roosevelt's sphere, could not deliver miracles.

With almost no money for an effective naval or air force, MacArthur's program concentrated on creating an army. This plan soon bogged down, hampered by language problems, the lack of skills and education of the Filipino recruits, and most of all by limited funds — not only were the soldiers paid next to nothing, but their training was woefully inadequate. MacArthur, however, was blind to these issues, and being a great believer in the efficacy of public relations, he asserted that the army was making great progress. Through official channels he agitated for more support from Washington, not realizing until too late that Roosevelt and his advisers were formulating contingency plans in which there was no effective place for the Philippines.

By July 1941, the Japanese had moved into southern Indochina. The United States responded with economic and diplomatic sanctions, and Roosevelt placed the Philippines under American control, with MacArthur as commanding general of the combined Filipino and American units, the United States Army Forces in the Far East (USAFFE). Within three months Washington articulated its priorities: European defense was of the first importance, to be followed by attention toward Asia. A perimeter stretching from Alaska to Hawaii to Panama would be defended, with token forces in the Philippines guarding only Manila and Subig bays.

Thus it was that on December 7, 1941 (December 8 in the Philippines because of the International Date Line), the entire American air force at Clark Field and other installations was destroyed in a lightning Japanese air raid. Within two weeks the port area of Manila was bombed; to spare the capital further damage, MacArthur withdrew from Manila and declared it an open city, but the Japanese ignored the designation and dispatched their bombers for more raids.

MacArthur moved his command to the fortress island of Corregidor, at the mouth of Manila Bay, and his armies to the parched terrain of the Bataan peninsula, which enfolds the western shore of the bay. Meanwhile, Japanese forces had landed at numerous points in the archipelago to little opposition. Manila was occupied on January 2, 1942. For the next three and a half months, the combined Filipino-American troops repulsed attempts to overrun them while medicine and food supplies ran short and disease took its toll. When Roosevelt decided to shift MacArthur to the defense of Australia and the southwestern Pacific, the general was evacuated from Corregidor by submarine on February 18. It fell to General Edward P. King to surrender his Bataan defenders, some seventy-eight thousand troops, on April 9; less than a month later, on May 6, MacArthur's successor, General Jonathan Wainwright, ended the resistance of the forces on Corregidor. By then the Bataan troops had been forced to walk the grueling "Death March," which resulted in the deaths of at least six thousand men. The survivors of both sieges were imprisoned in the Philippines until the commonwealth was recovered and in Japan and Manchuria until the close of the war.

When I was in Washington at the National Archives, I came across a collection of photographs of Manila after its liberation in early 1945. Then it was clear why Dwight Eisenhower had said that of all the world's capitals, Manila was surpassed in devastation only by Warsaw. In the terrible, month-long battle, which was fought not only block by block but building by building, entire neighborhoods were reduced to ashes.

From the day he stepped into the knee-deep surf of Red Beach, Leyte, on October 20, 1944, MacArthur strove toward the symbolic recapture of the capital. The Americans landed northwest of Manila at Lingayen Gulf on January 9, 1945, and it took nearly a month before the first units were able to fight their way to the city limits. What awaited them were some four thousand Japanese army troops and seventeen thousand naval troops, who had decided to make their last stand behind Manila's concrete fortifications and inside the numerous government buildings of the southern Manila bayside districts. All the bridges spanning the Pasig but one were blown up to hamper the American advances. As the historian Teodoro A. Agoncillo, then a young man living in the capital, recalled,

> Japanese troops, aided by the Makapalis [collaborators], poured kerosene on many houses and set them on fire. The resulting conflagration turned the houses and buildings in the Ermita and Malate districts into ashes, debris, and twisted iron. From the north, the fearful inhabitants could feel the tongues of flames licking at the houses that dated from the Spanish period. Men, women, and children caught between angry flames rushed to the nearest plaza or open space to save themselves. Others found their way to the Pasig and swam to the north bank for

Ann Mitchell Funston
(Kansas State Historical Society)

Edward H. ("Foghorn") Funston, "the
farmer's friend"
(Kansas State Historical Society)

The Funston homestead, Iola, Kansas, now a historical landmark
(Kansas State Historical Society)

Frederick Funston, age twenty-four,
wearing his fraternity pin
(Kansas State Historical Society)

Below: Funston at Kansas State University
(standing, far right); William Allen
White, wearing a hat, reclines below.
(Kansas State Historical Society)

Though this picture was probably taken in a Kansas City studio, it shows Funston in his "Esquimaux" garb. *(Kansas State Historical Society)*

Below: Summit of Deer Mountain, Estes Park, Colorado: Funston (third from left) and his friends entertain some sisterly visitors. *(Kansas State Historical Society)*

Opposite: "Bird's-Eye View from Summit of Chilkoot Pass" shows the Alaskan route as Funston would have seen it. *(By Winter and Pond; Library of Congress)*

Right: "By all means the smartest thing I have ever done in my life," Funston said of marrying Eda Blankart. Taken in Manila, 1898 *(Kansas State Historical Society)*

Below: Eda Funston with her sons Frederick Jr. and Arthur MacArthur Funston, 1904 *(Kansas State Historical Society)*

On the Inside of the . . . Cuban Revolution,

— BY —

FREDERICK FUNSTON,

Lieutenant-Colonel and Chief of Artillery of the Cuban Insurgent Army.

A Short Account of the Cause of the Revolution with Character Sketches of a few of the Leaders. . . .

The Composition, Organization and Equipment of the Patriot Forces, and how they March and Live and Fight. . . . .

THE Real Facts about the Struggle for Independence told by one who Marched and Fought in the Armies of Gomez and Garcia. . . . .

Broadside used to advertise Funston's lecture tour after his return from the Cuban revolution, 1898 *(Kansas State Historical Society)*

Below left: President William McKinley, "easily first in genius for manipulation," in Henry Adams's words, 1901 *(By C. M. Bell; Library of Congress)*

Below right: Admiral George Dewey, "the Hero of Manila Bay" and sponsor, for a time, of Emilio Aguinaldo *(By George Prince; Library of Congress)*

Colonel Roosevelt in his Rough Riders uniform—tailored by Brooks Brothers, New York *(By Rockwood; Library of Congress)*

While others went off to war, Funston and his Kansas regiment cooled their heels at the Presidio in San Francisco. *(Kansas State Historical Society)*

At the Presidio, Colonel Funston (seated second from left) waits for Philippine transport orders with the Twentieth Kansas regiment's field officers and staff. *(Kansas State Historical Society)*

WHAT WILL HE DO WITH IT?

"What Will He Do with It?" Uncle Sam shackles the Philippines in this *New York Herald* cartoon, 1898. *(Library of Congress)*

The headquarters of Emilio Aguinaldo's Magdalo revolutionaries, Cavite province, 1898 *(National Archives)*

Adoption of the Philippine Constitution, Malolos, September 15, 1898, during Aguinaldo's address *(National Archives)*

Emilio Aguinaldo y Famy, president and spiritual leader of the Filipino nationalist movement, in late 1898, shortly before the Americans made war on their former allies *(National Archives)*

José Rizal, who influenced the revolutionaries of Bonifacio's Katipunan but refused to join it. The Spanish executed him anyway. *(National Archives)*

A Filipino outpost before the nationalists learned that they had been benevolently assimilated. *(Library of Congress)*

A Filipino infantry squad. Though all are shown with carbines, the great majority of combatants had only bolos. Those with rifles often removed the sights as a hindrance, giving rise to the American joke that they could hit a target only if they used the gun as a club. *(National Archives)*

General José Luna, Aguinaldo's chief military strategist. He was assassinated, probably under the orders of the Manila elite, who wanted to swerve the revolution away from social change.
(National Archives)

General Gregorio del Pilar, "the boy hero of Bulacan"—a dandified military genius who died gloriously, protecting Aguinaldo in the Battle of Tirad Pass, 1899 *(National Archives)*

"Dining on the battlefield": Colonel Funston pauses in his meal of beans and Philippine chicken to appear resolute for the photographer, 1899. *(Library of Congress)*

"Street barricade held by Kansas boys, Feb. 4, 1899": taken before the outbreak *(Library of Congress)*

General staff officers, Manila, 1899: Funston (left) stands with General Arthur Mac-Arthur and General Elwell Otis (center left and center right, respectively) *(Library of Congress)*

'Taking it easy during a lull, Oct. 2, 1899": Funston's Kansas volunteers *(Library of Congress)*

The occupation of Malolos, March 31, 1899. Soldiers of the Kansas regiment march into Aguinaldo's first capital as smoke billows from the church in which he was installed as president. *(National Archives)*

The Twentieth Kansas Infantry bringing in the dead on carts, March 15, 1899, village of Pasig *(National Archives)*

safety. Those caught between the raging flames and the maddened Japanese were massacred.

In the frenzy of killing, rapine, and destruction, more than a hundred thousand Filipino civilians were killed by the Japanese, who then retreated behind the centuries-old walls of Intramuros for their final battle. Under a furious American artillery bombardment, the last conflict for the first district of Manila raged. As Agoncillo recalled,

> The American troops inched their way painfully and dangerously from one building to another, using machine guns and flame throwers to flush out the enemy lurking in the crevices and dark corners of houses and buildings. Intramuros, sanctified by age, the priceless product of centuries of fear, preparedness, glory, and romance — Intramuros, where thousands were trapped, withered from the deadly bombing and bombardment of the Americans who could not persuade the Japanese to surrender in the name of humanity and history. And so, what more than three centuries of history built up to house Spain in the tropics was destroyed in a few days. Nothing was left standing except the old San Agustin Church and convent: Intramuros was a debris, a tattered memory.

Much more was debris and tattered memory than the once-picturesque medieval district. The Philippines was faced with a staggering rehabilitation problem; its very civilization had been torn to shreds by the war, the Japanese occupation, and by the liberation.

With 80 percent of the capital destroyed and many other cities and rural areas laid to waste, the rebuilding of homes, schools, hospitals, bridges, and roads became paramount. Food distribution, broken down during the Japanese period, when plantations were converted to growing cotton for Tokyo and the reduced rice production diverted to feed the imperial troops, had to begin again from scratch; it would be years before rice exports would exceed imports. Losses of livestock would never be replaced. Industry had been ravaged; in once-bustling Manila, the only large-scale commercial activity in 1946 (besides a thriving black market) centered around a brewery, two soft drink bottling plants, some cigarette factories, and a few sawmills and soap factories.

Rehabilitation was slow. Emergency food distribution and other social services were initially handled by a civil affairs unit of the American army until financial aid from Washington began arriving in mid-1945, together with loan guarantees and the gift of the American army surplus.

However, rehabilitation did not come without a price tag — nor did

Philippine independence, which would be proclaimed on July 4, 1946. In return for war damages totaling $620 million (signed into law by President Truman on April 30, 1946), the Philippines was forced to accept an onerous economic agreement, the Bell Trade Relations Act. This provided for an eight-year period of free trade relations followed by a twenty-year period of gradually rising tariffs. "Free trade" in the act, however, levied quotas on Philippine sugar, lumber, tobacco, and coconut oil, with other products subject to American protectionism; currency exchange would be set solely by Washington.

Moreover, Americans were granted equal rights to exploit and develop Philippine industries, which in effect crippled any development and kept the new nation an economic colony. As Teodoro Agoncillo and Milagros Guerrero put it, "The United States . . . played the role of a man who, having been aided by a friend who lost everything in defense of the former, now brashly demanded that he be given the right to live with his friend's wife in exchange for his financial help."

Despite the flood of American carpetbaggers into the Philippines and the problems caused by an inflation rate of nearly 200 percent, some Filipinos flourished in the early postwar years, particularly those profiteers who had thrived during the Japanese occupation. Graft and corruption are no strangers to any country in the world, especially during and after national emergencies, and the Philippines was (and is) no exception. People who had been encouraged by wartime stringencies, and who took advantage of the situation when hunger and need were commonplace, saw no reason to alter their course; together with more honest but no less skillful entrepreneurs, they emerged as the new wealthy in the postwar era to replace the agricultural land barons as the country's upper class.

This elite, created and conditioned by the Second World War, has now come to dominate Philippine politics as well as the economy. To be sure, there have been changes in the cast of characters in nearly thirty years of independence. Six presidents have served, each change of administration giving another group of ministers a chance for profits while other plutocrats have controlled the Congress; the nation has, in Robert Shaplen's words, "swung from periods of profligacy and corruption, during when little or nothing was done to cope with its many deep-seated economic and social problems, to moods of great zeal for reform, when the nation seemed suddenly to rediscover its capacities for growth and to realize the potential of its human and material resources."

At the bottom of society remain the very great numbers of economically dislocated, for whom life has not changed a great deal; they have looked — in vain — for nearly twenty years to one man for a remedy to society's inequities.

II

If anyone has been shaped by the war years and then adopted the postwar ethos, it is Ferdinand Edralin Marcos, president since his election in 1965 and dictator since his seizure of the constitution in 1972.

Born in 1917 to wealthy, educated parents in Sarrat, in the province of Ilocos Norte in northern Luzon, Marcos inherited the unrelenting ambition that is culturally typical of Filipinos of Ilocano extraction. Unlike other groups, such as Tagalogs or Pampangans, Ilocanos have historically been willing to migrate from ancestral lands, to sever their ties to families and neighbors; they are known for their opportunism and frugality. Added to this cultural bequest was the particular indoctrination employed by Marcos's father, a politician, and grandfather, who both worked to toughen the boy. Before he was ten he could ride, wrestle, box, and shoot with proficiency. An equally rigorous education made him fluent in Ilocano, English, and Spanish. Marcos did well in high school and college, deciding then to follow his father into law if not politics; during law school he was at the top of his class, finding time also to be an ROTC cadet and a national rifle-shooting champion, which later got him into trouble.

In 1935, after a bitter election resulted in Marcos's father being beaten in a congressional race, the young man was plucked out of his final year at law school and arrested — charged with the assassination of his father's rival. Someone had stood outside the man's house and shot him as he brushed his teeth. Police instantly suspected young Marcos, who had won his sharpshooter medals using the same type of rifle and who happened to be in the province at the time. The case attracted national attention. Marcos was found guilty after a long and complicated trial. However, he successfully appealed his case before the Philippine Supreme Court, convincing it that the government's chief witness had been bribed to name him as the murderer. He emerged from jail a national celebrity.

The Second World War made him a hero. An army intelligence officer during the battles on the Central Plain, Marcos distinguished himself after the retreat to Bataan. He survived the Death March and the long Japanese interrogations in Fort Santiago, later escaping into the mountains and joining the resistance as a guerrilla. By the close of the war, he claimed to be the most decorated Filipino soldier. (Researchers in 1984 contend, however, that many of his American medals seem not to have been awarded to him at all.) The young officer, after beginning to practice law, attracted the attention of officials of the Liberal party, who saw him as a potent vote getter. The party arranged for his candidacy in the 1949 congressional elections, which nationally became the most corrupt of all Philippine races. Marcos, running in his father's old district, counted heavily on the veterans' vote. Of surpassing importance was his regional appeal; linguistic groups tended to vote for their own candidates, and Ilocanos traditionally did so most heartily. Marcos promised to give them an Ilocano president within twenty years.

In 1965, after sixteen years as a congressman, senator, and as president of the Senate, Marcos bolted his Liberal party to run for president on the Nacionalista ticket. The campaign was particularly vicious as rhetoric and accusations flew between one-term President Diosdado Macapagal and his former political colleague. Marcos's old murder charge was resurrected along with rumors that he had enriched himself at public expense, evaded taxes, padded his payroll, defrauded businessmen, and, worst, that he had stolen land from helpless farmers by employing his encyclopedic command of the law. Despite these accusations, Marcos soundly defeated Macapagal after spending a fortune in political advertising that more than matched the incumbent's.

Not an inconsiderable force in his election was the presence of his wife, Imelda Romualdez Marcos, who had enraptured the people as Jacqueline Kennedy had done in America several years before. From a less than wealthy branch of a rich and powerful family in Leyte, Imelda Romualdez found herself, a young college graduate and beauty queen, being strenuously courted by a thirty-seven-year-old congressman who would not take no for an answer. Their marriage was one of glamour wedded to power, attributes they both possessed in great amounts. The Romualdez clan controlled more than half a million votes in the Visayan islands and had amassed a financial empire; Marcos had grown rich in legal fees, family land holdings, and the perquisites of public office: he controlled more than one million votes in northern Luzon, and his mastery of the country's laws had given him further power. The couple became a constant presence in the society columns. Imelda accompanied her husband on his political junkets, singing folk songs in the appropriate dialect before his speeches. With her beauty, her expensive wardrobe, her charm, and with his gruff handsomeness and eloquence, it seemed to the rural people of the Philippines that a vote for them was a vote for Hollywood and the wish-fulfillment it (and glamorous politicians) presumed to offer.

To his credit, Marcos in his first term presided over the construction of hundreds of schools and thousands of miles of roads, including a national highway network, and great leaps were made in research on rice production. However, he claimed these projects as his own, though they had been financed by the American government and private foundations; also, untold portions of the money were waylaid by intermediaries. Nothing was done about land reform. Poverty and inequity still ruled the lives of the majority. Corruption in government remained entrenched, with Marcos's army of supporters — from ministers down to barrio lieutenants — enriching themselves. Meanwhile, the First Couple, as the Marcoses had come to be called, lived extravagantly, regally, far, far beyond their modest salary and expense allowance, setting unequaled standards of greed and self-aggrandizement for those below them.

In 1969, Marcos became the first president in Philippine history to win reelection, a feat he ensured by spending a fortune — he acknowledged more than $100 million — in buying advertising, votes, and muscle. Some two hundred people were killed during the campaign. Despite the president's campaign assurances, life in the Philippines failed to improve after his reelection. Corruption all but paralyzed business and government. Despite a national rice surplus, large segments of the debt-ridden rural population continued to suffer malnutrition, if not hunger. The crime rate rose as the standard of living plummeted, with robberies and ransom kidnappings becoming especially commonplace in cities swollen by those migrating from the depressed countryside. As citizens saw they could no longer rely on the police for public safety, they began arming themselves; in the upper strata of society, oligarchs and politicians maintained private armies. It seemed to the average Filipino that society had broken down to a level lower than even the chaotic, penurious years immediately after the liberation.

Unrest in the country was without precedent. The newspapers reported the flagrant derelictions of public servants as if they were covering daily gossip. The nation's clergy called for justice in land reform and were joined by university students and teachers, who stepped up their protests against the government — criticizing not only its domestic policies but also its participation in the Vietnam War. By this time, two political groups had begun their violent opposition to the Marcos government. One, the outlawed Communist Party of the Philippines (CPP), had been in existence since 1930. After the fall of Bataan, some twenty thousand left-leaning tenant farmers of central

Luzon organized themselves into a guerrilla force called the Huk-balahap (roughly, the People's Anti-Japanese Army). During twelve hundred engagements with the Japanese and their "puppet" forces, the Huks (as the guerrillas came to be called) were credited with inflicting some twenty-five thousand casualties. In the postwar era, the CPP passed into the hands of the Huks, who drew their political inspiration from Russia. Seeing that there was no place for them in the newly independent nation, they mounted an insurrection against the government that began in 1948 and lasted some six years before it was finally quelled. By the 1970s, most of the surviving Huks had degenerated into racketeering, explaining away their scams with empty rhetoric. But a new generation was on the ascendant. Other, much younger Philippine communists, many college-educated, who leaned toward Mao Zedong's model of cultural revolution, appeared and took up the banner. The term "Huk" was dropped as tainted. The CPP acted in concert with its military wing, called the New People's Army (NPA), to inaugurate a new campaign against the government. They found some sympathy among the peasants in the mountains and forests of northern Luzon; NPA guerrilla units began to harass the Philippine military. Elsewhere, on the nation's southernmost island of Mindanao, militant Muslim separatists had begun to revolt against the provincial government and Christian landowners and against outposts of the national army.

The government's first response to the revolutionaries and lawful dissidents alike was to suspend the writ of habeus corpus for all for a period of four months. This followed a grenade attack upon a rally of the opposition Liberal party. Marcos restored civil liberties in January 1972, but if anything, both nonviolent protests and terrorist actions increased in the ensuing months. Homemade bombs exploded in numerous government and private business buildings. By then the great mass of Filipinos had become so cynical that each incident prompted many to doubt whether the communists or Muslims were in every instance responsible. While some bombings were claimed by the outlawed groups and a few resulted in injuries, such as the explosion at Quezon City Hall in September, many occurred at night or on weekends, when there were few people around. Others resulted in rather more flash or noise than damage. Speculations arose that the government itself might be setting at least some of the bombs as an excuse for further crackdowns, since Marcos had continued to claim that the communist menace, though serious, was under control.

The citizens had become so fatalistic, their government's credibility had become so eroded, that each headline came under public scrutiny, becoming merely the stuff of gossip. The climate of doubt and political trivialization worsened as the president seemed to be trapped by his own dishonesty. Marcos had repeatedly denied that either he (or his wife) had ambitions for another presidential term, noting that the constitution limited him to two terms. Under his direction, however, in July a constitutional convention approved a change from a presidential form of government to a parliamentary one, which opened the way for Marcos to skirt the law and rule as prime minister.

Other political events underscored the blurring lines of truth. The same month as the convention's decision, a ship with North Korean registration was reported to have landed weapons in northern Luzon, provoking a furious government assault on that remote countryside. With no information to go on, some people in the capital immediately assumed "the boat was Imelda's." Within two months, the motorcade of Secretary of Defense Juan Ponce Enrile was sprayed with automatic rifle fire, riddling the secretary's limousine. But Enrile happened to have changed a long-standing habit that day and took a rear car in the procession. Some saw this as another setup.

On September 21, 1972, President Marcos imposed martial law in the Philippines, citing the growing threat of "lawless elements," which he defined as communists, Muslims, rightists, and professional criminals. He disbanded Congress, and military commanders moved in to take over all local and provincial government functions. Marcos assumed all overriding government powers, including the sole right to issue edicts and decrees that had the force of law, which in the next decade would approach a thousand in number. He imposed a midnight to 4:00 A.M. curfew, curtailed the rights of assembly, free association, travel, and expression, and put all newspapers and radio and television stations out of business, replacing them weeks or months later by government-controlled institutions with approved staffs. The schools closed for nearly a month. Utilities and critical industries such as steel mills were nationalized. With firearms and other weapons prohibited, during the next ten months the government claimed the confiscation of more than half a million unauthorized weapons.

In the early weeks, opposition leaders were conspicuous by their silence, a curiosity that was later explained by their all being in jail. Arrests began even days before the martial law decree was publicly announced on September 23. A number of senators, representatives, and two provincial governors joined the priests, nuns, students, teachers, artists, and journalists in prison. The government estimated that some thirty thousand people were arrested and detained in the weeks immediately after the proclamation. (The number rose to fifty thousand within three years.) Almost all were detained without charges or benefit of trial.

As an adjunct to his imposition of such rigid control over all areas of Philippine life, President Marcos announced the inauguration of a reform program called the New Society. Corruption was to be extirpated, warlords and oligarchs eradicated, downtrodden tenant farmers elevated — this by granting each farmer twelve acres of land and putting limits on the size of landowners' holdings. In his crackdown on government corruption and inefficiency, Marcos ordered hundreds purged from their jobs.

Initially, the government announcements promised that martial law was only a temporary measure to make it safe to walk the streets again "and preserve the public order." The attitude of average, nonimprisoned Filipinos toward the strictures was therefore tolerant. From their point of view, the crime rate plunged dramatically. Perhaps the firm hand of Marcos seemed preferable to moral anarchy and political unrest, confirming as it did the nearly universal fatalism toward personal control of their lives. Since gossip had been declared a crime, doubtful Filipinos chose their audiences carefully before speculating whether Marcos might have issued his proclamation not to clean up society but to extend his hold beyond his constitutional term. Then, on October 20, an announcement was made — so quietly that most citizens were unaware of it and its implications. The constitution had at last been revised, making Marcos both president *and* prime minister indefinitely. The president was thus in control of a constitution of his own making, which lent authority to dictatorial rule by decree. Several months later, a sham national referendum underscored the shift of government.

The week following the announcement, in an address before the Philippine Historical Association, Marcos confided that he had made the decision to impose martial law after consulting with God. The president had, he asserted, received "several signs" from God to act. The members of his audience, all historians, could have reminded Marcos of an interesting precedent. Seventy-four years earlier, William McKinley had told a visiting delegation of Protestant ministers that he had decided to acquire the Philippines after a similar conference with the deity. In all probability, none of the historians sitting demurely before Ferdinand Marcos in 1972 elected to point this out to him.

III

I arrived in Manila fourteen months after martial law had been lifted, a "normalization" enacted in January 1981, after President Marcos claimed that the government had "significantly defused the dangers of subversion, sedition and rebellion." Despite the fanfare, most saw the lifting as merely cosmetic and probably due in part to the anticipated ceremonial visit of Pope John Paul II. Actually, recent tinkerings with the constitution had granted Marcos an unlimited number of six-year presidential terms. Moreover, he had announced that all of the orders and decrees he had issued during the nine years of martial law were still in effect, and the revised constitution authorized him to rule by decree whenever he found it necessary. Backing Marcos was an army that had been swollen since 1972 from 60,000 to 155,000. An enlarged corps of officers created by the president ensured its loyalty. Having made good on his promise to depose some of the most flagrantly corrupt oligarchs, Marcos had installed his cronies in their places, drawing political and economic power from them as they grew wealthier from his "favors."

In the detention centers, approximately a thousand political prisoners languished. Cautious opposition groups circumspectly urged for a restoration of true democracy, but because they were not unified, people did not hold much hope for their success. Meanwhile, NPA guerrillas had enlarged their presence from isolated regions in northern and southeastern Luzon to where they were active in forty-one of the Philippines' seventy-two provinces, though their numerical strength was still estimated at less than five thousand. In the far south, nearly thirty thousand guerrillas of the Moro National Liberation Front (MNLF), who advocated creating a separate Muslim state in Mindanao, had tied down the greater part of the Philippine military.

So not much had changed since military rule ended when I arrived in Manila. All the newspapers had been spawned in the months immediately after September 1972, and in a decade their staffs had plainly grown used to printing what passes for news: government bulletins, crime stories (mostly sordid), and gossip. The country had been deprived of its greatest columnists ten years before; the ones who still had a forum were cautious, cautious, cautious. A few timid tabloids provided a modicum of opposition. One felt isolated from real events occurring within and without the Philippines; even a developing wire service story — such as the Argentine seizure of the Falkland/Malvinas Islands, which happened while I was in Manila — lost all its drama and significance. For local news, one had to read between the lines of the boring newspapers and otherwise subsist on gossip.

Even gossip, tending as it does toward the personal, proved unsatisfying and trivial. Manila was still vibrant with speculation about the disappearance earlier in the year of a thirty-two-year-old professional basketball coach named Tommy Manotoc. While in the United States in December 1981, Manotoc had secretly married the twenty-six-year-old daughter of Ferdinand and Imelda Marcos, Imelda Junior, or Imee. The problem was that Manotoc had been married once before, to a beauty contest winner. He obtained a divorce in the Dominican Republic days before his second marriage, but divorce is not recognized in the Philippines.

Imee's parents, apparently crushed at the news, had hoped to marry their daughter to someone with more social standing and in a ceremony that properly reflected their dynastic leanings. In 1983, their other daughter, Irene, would be married to the scion of the nation's highly prominent Araneta family. The ceremony, held in the bride's father's home town of Sarrat, Ilocos Norte, cost $1.3 million in private and government funds to stage. The town was restored to its seventeenth-century Spanish style by hundreds of workers. The government airline flew in five hundred guests and accommodated them in an ocean liner moored off the coastal town or in specially constructed "People's Halls" in Sarrat. One hundred thousand Ilocanos flocked to free fiestas nearby. Welcome banners, tens of thousands of potted plants, and thousands of flowering shrubs made Sarrat look like a massive movie set. When some of the bushes proved to lack blossoms, workers tied white crepe-paper flowers to their branches. The government provided Irene Marcos with three wedding dresses, designed by Givenchy, Balestra, and Valentino.

Apparently Imee Marcos could have received such a wedding if she had chosen the right man. When Tommy Manotoc disappeared from his white sports car on December 29, 1981, shortly after dining with his young wife, his family immediately blamed the bride's family. Marcos denied this, saying that the sportsman was probably "in the hands of kidnappers who are either subversives or criminal elements who have sent a ransom note to the family." Later, his spokesman added that the Manotoc disappearance might be a plot to embarrass the Marcos government, since the sportsman was distantly related to exiled opposition figures.

A little more than one month after he vanished, Tommy Manotoc reappeared, claiming that the abductors from whom he was rescued were insurgents who had demanded $2.5 million in ransom. But NPA spokesmen, including the incarcerated party chairman, José Maria Sison, denied any part in the kidnapping; an officer of the Philippine Constabulary admitted later that he could not recall the NPA ever holding anyone for ransom. Defense Minister Enrile arranged a press conference for Manotoc; the young man read a statement exonerating the president — a statement that seemed to many to have the mark of a government speechwriter.

By the time I arrived in Manila, one month after Manotoc's reappearance, he could be seen on evening television coaching a basketball team. He still looked ill at ease. In social gatherings around the capital, people I met took pleasure in assuring me that whatever had happened to Manotoc, nobody had ever thought he was actually in danger. "Imee looked like a cheerleader the whole time he was missing," said one woman. "She was happy and bubbly. I think she and Tommy arranged it all themselves to force Marcos and Imelda over to their side." Other acquaintances pointed out the suspicious fact that the presidential spokesman had predicted Manotoc's reappearance more than one week before it occurred. "I think Marcos kidnapped him as a warning," said one man. "He wants Tommy *out*."

While most of this reasoning seemed plausible, given the personalities and politics involved, still, after listening to Manotoc-Marcos gossip for three nights running, I asked the people I was dining with whether these theatrics were the only "political" opinions I was going to hear from them. There was a short, embarrassed silence, which was broken by a man who happened to hold a minor bureaucratic job in one of the ministries.

"I have a *political joke* for you," he said. The others clamored for him to tell it.

"This is about Carlos Romulo," he said, referring, of course, to the eighty-three-year-old foreign minister, who during the last war was an aide to Douglas MacArthur and later a brigadier general; he had also been an ambassador and for three terms president of the United Nations Security Council. While Romulo was doubtlessly a member of the present government and had never shown a desire to put any light between himself and the president's policies, still, I could think of at least a half-dozen more deserving butts of jokes.

"Once upon a time," said the man, and people snickered in anticipation, "Carlos Romulo was in Madrid on diplomatic business and he decided to go to the opera. He got himself a nice private box and had just settled in when the audience below him turned around, looked up, and began booing and catcalling at someone in the adjacent box. Romulo leaned out to see who was receiving the crowd's anger and was surprised to see Evita Perón. She was livid herself.

When she recognized Romulo she said, 'Ambassador Romulo, listen to what they are shouting. After all I have done for my country, how can they have the nerve to malign me — to call me a *whore?*'

" 'Please don't let it bother you, madam,' replied Romulo. 'Back home, people still call me *General.*' "

To be fair to my acquaintances, perhaps they limited their political opinions to jokes and trivia for a reason; maybe they felt they could only speak their minds when they knew whom they were talking to. After all, my introductions had come from very different sources and some Filipinos were confused by them, thinking they were receiving mixed messages. One endorsement I brought had originated on the Delaware River in southern New York State; during a canoe trip with Herb Gordon, an adventurer, writer, and veteran newsman, we had gotten talking about my Philippine trip. Gordon offered to introduce me to an old friend and must have detected my lukewarm reception to the idea of having to contact, I thought, his old war buddy or business partner. "Perhaps you've heard of him," he said. "Are you familiar with the name Carlos P. Romulo?" Of course I was, I said. Gordon went on to explain that he had been a diplomatic correspondent at the same time that Romulo had been the ambassador in Washington; the families had grown close in those years. After that canoe trip I had written to Romulo, mentioning Gordon's name, and gave a sketchy outline of my historical research; the foreign minister politely endorsed the idea of my trip to retrace Funston's and Aguinaldo's footsteps, and in turn arranged for me to meet Teodoro Agoncillo and other pertinent people once I arrived.

The mention of two other endorsers, equally generous, often elicited the catchall phrase I heard whenever someone wanted to change the subject to basketball or the weather: "Oh, that is *very* controversial." The two people were a married couple: Heherson ("Sonny") Alvarez and Cecile Guidote-Alvarez, both political exiles in the United States. Sonny had been the private secretary of President Macapagal, and as a liberal democrat he had been elected to the 1970 Philippine Constitutional Convention. His frequent criticism of President Marcos made him an enemy; to avoid arrest after martial law, he went underground. The government agents looking for Alvarez interrogated his father so harshly that he suffered two heart attacks, dying after the second. They also arrested Sonny's apolitical younger brother Marsman and tortured him to death. By then, Sonny had escaped by stowing aboard a ship bound for Hong Kong. Cecile Guidote, a recipient of the Ramón Magsaysay Award and a bright light in Philippine drama, was prevented from joining her husband in the United

States until she sneaked aboard a commercial jet with forged documents. They are both active in several American anti-Marcos groups, but in Manila, it is their reputation and former social standing that have endeared them to a small but wide spectrum of Filipinos, from government apologists to aboveground activists.

"To get anywhere in Manila you have to have names," friends in the States had told me, so I came with enough names to fill a small hall, sufficient to endorse me into, I hoped, almost anyone's presence. As I began meeting people in the capital, nearly everyone had another introduction he or she wanted to make. After a while my wallet bulged with business cards with phone numbers scrawled on the back, and I began to feel desperate each time someone said, "And you *must* talk to. . . ."

I was sitting in a restaurant on the roof of a hotel on Roxas Boulevard, watching, of all things, a fashion show. Many fashion shows are held in hotels in Manila, and I had successfully avoided all of them until I was dragged to this one by some tourism officials who wanted to discuss a magazine piece over lunch. Not far from our table, a dozen American models — each one half of a set of blond and lanky twins — displayed the fashions of a Danish designer to an audience of Filipinos and Japanese, accompanied by disco-pop renditions of Glenn Miller. This happened to be the prelude to a heavily choreographed display of Japanese kimonos. It had all been arranged by a gushy Philippine tourism representative stationed in Tokyo. He could be seen beaming and clapping his hands while seated at a table with some of the wealthiest women of Manila. These fashion-conscious wives of cabinet ministers and industrialists glittered with jewelry and rivaled the young models for artfully applied makeup; in these postwar years, cultural and economic relations between Japan and the Philippines have grown strong, and the ministers' wives showed appropriately polite interest in the show. Normally, Madame Marcos would have been there, outglittering them all, but she had flown to Saudi Arabia with her husband and his retinue for a few days. The Philippines sends more than half a million workers abroad every year — since jobs are unavailable at home — and these workers are said to send back more than a billion dollars yearly. Some 220,000 Filipinos work on construction projects in the Middle East. What with the trouble in Mindanao with Muslim secessionists, the Philippine government was eager not to antagonize King Khaled or anyone else in the Islamic world who was in a position to interrupt that flow of foreign exchange.

"I could never work for the government," said Carmen, throwing a glance toward the ministers' wives as she exhaled her Marlboro smoke. I looked at her in surprise. She did, after all, work for the Tourism Ministry as a promotional writer. For her, apparently, being paid as a free-lancer rather than as a staff member did not constitute official "work." Carmen belongs to a sophisticated group of intellectuals, all with family or social connections, who make their living in government but do not consider themselves a part of it. She remains in the Philippines, she said, "because it's my *home*," though for reasons of her own she chose to have her child born abroad. I had met Carmen before I had wearied of the Manila Name Game, and on this occasion I mentioned that I wanted to meet a historian, Alejandro Roces, whose revisionist work interested me.

"He was just let out of jail," she said. "He refused to vote last year — in protest — so they arrested him." She sent a cloud of smoke toward the ceiling and emitted a dry chuckle. "That is the Filipino style of democracy for you," she said. "If you don't vote you're locked up!"

Beside her, her companion laughed nervously. He also worked for the government, but he was never heard to utter a dissenting word.

"Isn't she a card," he said.

One morning I went with my brother to have a look at what was going on within Intramuros, where the sounds of construction could be heard seven days a week. The fifty-hectare space inside the walls had been reduced to rubble during the 1946 liberation, with the sole exception of the San Agustin Church. In subsequent years, the area had been desultorily rebuilt but neglected, with squatters settling in, but those destitute tenants had been forced out in 1979, when work was begun to restore the Walled City as a tourist attraction. Imelda Marcos supervised the planning, as she did for most government cultural projects.

We saw a group of boisterous American children swarming over the Fortin de San Pedro, an independent structure that was originally linked to Intramuros by a wooden bridge spanning a moat. The building was intended to shelter bombardiers, who could protect the moat from being breached by attackers. It has now been filled with religious artifacts and resembles a chapel. As we neared the children, who were trying to balance themselves on the Fortin parapets, we met a pretty American woman named Jennifer. Her bright-eyed manner betrayed her position as an elementary school teacher — an art instructor, it turned out — for the children at Clark Air Base. She had been in the Philippines for fourteen years and was married to a

Filipino. She introduced us to a young architect standing a few yards away. Bernardo worked for the Intramuros Restoration Administration and had been pulled away from his blueprints to escort Jennifer's class. We tagged along.

Within the walls and two blocks away a few minutes later, the children scattered to buy ice cream and fruit from vendors who appeared before our school bus had come to a halt. Bernardo told me he had been trained in modern architecture but had just begun working for the consulting firm in charge of reconstruction. "It was such a shock," he said, "to be trained in the use of concrete, steel, glass . . . and now find myself concerned with these old buildings dating from the sixteenth century."

I indicated a group of laborers who bent over huge stone blocks, slowly fashioning them with rudimentary tools. "I suppose that sort of technology was a letdown after college," I said. He pointed to a courtyard in front of the San Agustin Church. "Those pavement stones were shipped from Europe and the Asian mainland as ballast for galleons," he told me. "They're very much like granite. Even our own modern cutting equipment cannot get through them." He led me across General Luna Street to show me a building being reconstructed. "We've incorporated elements from old buildings we buy all over the country. We ship them back here," he said. "But underneath the outer skin, where no one can see, we use prestressed concrete and other modern materials. We've got electrical cables, even sprinkling systems. But no one would be able to tell."

We entered the church. Those two Spanish conquistadors, Legaspi and Salcedo, are interred in a side chapel, and a large repository of Spanish culture is exhibited in the adjoining monastery. Most of the church is a museum — a showpiece, it is intended, for the entire district — which should be completed within a decade. In one room, filled with religious statues and tools of the trade, was a grotesque, carved wooden statue of a reclining, contorted Jesus. His scourge marks dripped profuse rivulets of wooden blood. His eyes turned up toward the ceiling. A rope had been carved out of wood and was knotted loosely around his neck.

"Isn't it funny," I said to Bernardo, "how the Spanish, who perfected the art of the garrotte on Filipino nationalists and other troublemakers, would create and venerate a similar symbol for worship?" I heard no reply. Turning, I saw that Bernardo had been upset by my irreverence. He sorrowfully moved away, blushing, to rejoin the American schoolteacher and her hyperactive charges. My brother and I finished the tour by ourselves.

Later, after nightfall, I went back to the Walled City and entered Fort
Santiago, which is now picturesquely in ruins. Manicured lawns dotted with trees filled most of the enclosed space. Benches and a foun-
tain heightened the placidity of the once-martial grounds, which were
well populated on that pleasant, breezy night. Couples strolled along
the walks, sat on benches, looked at the incongruous collection of colonial limousines set inside velvet ropes, or ascended ramps leading
to relative privacy on the battlements. Surrounded by such couple-
dom I felt especially alone, having gotten out of the habit of attending the theater or of wandering about in contented solitude. That
night I was doing both — so I suppose I was feeling twice as lonely —
but at least I had the challenge of understanding a Tagalog drama,
which would take all my attention.

The Philippine Educational Theater Association (PETA) was the
brainchild of Cecile Guidote-Alvarez before she found herself in political hot water. She had prevailed upon park administrators to give
her space in the fortress for indigenous theater; thanks to her energy, PETA is housed in a roofless barracks between the Bateria de
Santa and the Bastion de San Francisco. I filed in with the rest of
the audience as the entire cast warmed up in an antechamber by ser-
enading us with Tagalog folk songs.

The play was entirely in Tagalog, or rather "Taglish," the corruption of both languages. By listening for the occasional English word,
like "gymnasium" or "working for the people" or "parasite," and by
interpreting body language, I could easily decipher it. A young man
is torn between filial loyalty and his sense of duty to the people. After
much soul-searching, he quits his establishment job and opts for
working for the masses, who forgive him and convey their welcome.
The play was slightly on the tame side compared to what actually goes
on in the Philippines. However, it had a rousing nationalist, pro-union
spirit, and I was certain that everyone in the audience inferred the
intended messages from it. In six months, when the government
cracked down on labor unions, the play was very likely banned.
Something about the spirit of the performance suggested other theater I might have seen in a Greenwich Village coffee house in the late
1960s.

Interest in drama is quite strong in Manila — and elsewhere in the
country. A fierce play about the nineteenth-century revolutionary
Andres Bonifacio had recently ended its run to great acclaim. In a
nation where freedom of expression is still rigidly curtailed, playwrights have deftly moved to historical allegory or to modern nationalism to explore their themes, which unsurprisingly seem to center around the chafe of a sequestered people.

I went to see Ernesto, a friend who lived in the outlying districts of Metro Manila. Six months before, I met him at a lecture in New York. It had been snowing then, and he, my wife, and I sought shelter in a coffee shop for a few hours after the talk. The last I had seen of him was when he waved good-bye as we dropped him off on a street corner; by then the snow was coming down so furiously, he vanished before we could return his wave. Now, as I turned off a shabby boulevard onto his street and saw him waiting in front of his house, it was hard to believe all that time had gone by.

Ernesto was a social worker with a private agency, and I asked him to tell me about his experiences in 1972.

"When I was younger, working in the slums, we thought there was no limit to the things we could do," he said. "We could strike, we could boycott, we could demonstrate in front of Malacañang Palace with impunity — rights you Americans take for granted. We even thought we could peacefully displace the regime by our moral force alone! How naive we were!

"Then 1972 came. Thousands were rounded up and thrown into jail. I myself was picked off the street by plainclothesmen, driven around, beaten, and tossed into a cell with twenty other guys. Some of them were moved within a few days to other prisons. Some others none of us ever saw again. It was three years before I went up against a military court on charges of violating the public order — attending demonstrations — and possessing subversive literature — books and pamphlets. It was another two years before they let me go, but those charges hang over my head to this day. They had pictures of me holding a Down with Corrupt Marcos sign, and had taken things from my house. And I was a small fry!

"We were all sure that the president had been planning martial law for a long time — maybe from the first term — because it was done so professionally, as if the details, the surveillance, were all ironed out way before. And the way they humiliated us, ground us into the dirt, could not have been the case of individual soldiers without discipline, but rather a concerted program to terrorize us out of our opposition, and to take others down with us by betraying them. I was beaten, burned, choked, but I consider myself lucky that I am still alive, that my scars do not prevent me from going on.

"Funny . . . before 1972 I was scared to death of communists. I honestly thought they would have horns! In prison I met my first communists — they ate the same food, drank the same water. Though I never would have known it before going to jail, I saw that moderates, and progressives like me, have many similar aspirations to those people with horns and tails. We lost many friends in those years. But those of us who came back are in many ways stronger, more united, than we ever would have been otherwise. So maybe the laugh is on the president after all."

Since his release, Ernesto still works at providing services for squatters and slumdwellers, though he is careful "not to go too far," as he says, by involving himself in mass activities or by being seen in public places with old cellmates, even socially. The threat of being invited back to Fort Bonifacio or Camp Crame for questioning lives with him every day, as does the possibility that one day he might vanish, with no government agency admitting to his arrest. "That they might kill me for the little I do I can accept," he said, "but that I might lie anonymously in unconsecrated ground — for some reason, that terrifies me even more."

Ernesto is not alone in his concerns, as a delegation from Amnesty International showed during a visit in late 1981, just four months before my visit. Their 127-page report noted:

> The Philippines Government has constantly affirmed its commitment to the rule of law and has introduced extensive measures intended to uphold principles for the protection of the rights of people in the custody of its agents. In practice, the mission found there is overwhelming evidence that the principles enunciated by the government on the treatment of people suspected of crimes of a political nature are systematically disregarded.

During an earlier visit to the Philippines, in late 1975, representatives from Amnesty International were told that 6,000 political detainees remained from the high of 50,000 arrested under emergency regulations since 1972. In depositions taken during that two-week visit, 71 of the 107 detainees interviewed claimed to have been tortured by government agents — most often while they were being interrogated and held incommunicado, often in secret holding centers known as safehouses. The news of violations received after 1975 gave rise to the concern that though the number of detainees fell to about 1,000, there had been an alarming increase in reports of disappearances and extrajudicial executions. Moreover, the few official investigations of human rights abuses were grossly partial and tended to dwindle into nonaction.

The 1981 mission was able to examine 49 new cases in its seventeen-day stay. It found 26 cases of arbitrary killing where it could be proven that the victims had been taken into government custody of some form; 6 cases in which the disappearance of the victims precluded confirmation that they had been in fact killed by government agents, though such a circumstance seemed likely; and 32 cases of alleged torture. The 49 represented "only a small proportion of the total number of reported cases," the mission noted.

During my stay in Manila, I talked to at least fifteen people who had been detained, tortured, and intimidated after their release. All had been initially arrested within months of September 1972. To protect them from further harassment and to place the emphasis where it should be — on the situation since martial law was lifted and "normalization" reinstituted — I decided to follow Ernesto's suggestion that I substitute cases publicized by Amnesty International's 1981 report for those of the people I came to know and respect. Here, then, are eight cases chosen at random:

Reynaldo Borromeo: 33-year-old agricultural worker, resident of Banga Caves, Ragay, Camarines Sur. Shot dead in early morning of 15 September 1981 on coconut estate where he worked by members of Integrated Civilian Home Defense Force (ICHDF) and police, of whom S.G., O.R. and G.P. were identified by name. Believed to have been killed as a New People's Army (NPA) suspect.

Loreto Castillo: 23-year-old former student employed by Ecumenical Research Center. Arrested without warrant in Barrio Garrahin, Pitogo, Quezon, on 18 July 1981 by members of Philippine Constabulary (PC). Taken to Camp Assena Natividad, Gurnaca, Quezon. Detained until 16 September 1981. During this period tortured, threatened with death, forced to sign "confession" and denied access to legal counsel and friends.

Rudy del Carmen: 31-year-old farmer, married with one child. Arrested without warrant on 16 August 1981 in home in Barrio Bacuyangan, Hinoba-an, Negros Occidental, by combined unit of Task Force Canlaon and local PC detachment. Tortured in Ilco PC detachment barracks. Fled area after being permitted to go home on 19 August. Shot dead on 30 August 1981 by PC soldiers, allegedly while trying to escape, in Sitio Labao to where he had fled with wife and family.

Milagros Lumabi-Echanis: Arrested with child in Sampaloc, Manila, on 14 August 1980 by PC unit. Held incommunicado in Maximum Security Unit, Fort Bonifacio, until located in March 1981. Granted temporary release February 1982.

Manuel Marbid: Aged 33, farmer. Wife executed affidavit stating that she had witnessed the killing of her husband by six named members of the ICHDF on 15 September 1981 in Sitio Saogan, Barrio Tabgac, Ragay, Camarines Sur. Affidavit also alleged that wife had seen one of the ICHDF members taking 2,000 pesos received in payment for carabao from her husband's body. It was announced on the radio that Manuel Marbid had been shot as an NPA suspect. Authorities undertook no investigation of case.

Sampatu Maulana: One of approximately 40 Muslims arrested in Manila in June 1981 in connection with an alleged conspiracy to assassinate President Marcos. Arrested on 21 June 1981 by men in plain clothes identifying themselves as members of the Metropolitan Manila Philippine Constabulary Command. Missing until located in the Maximum Security Unit, Fort Bonifacio, on 24 September 1981. Reportedly held immediately after arrest in "safehouse" for three or four days where tortured with repeated punches and electric shocks.

Jaime Nierra: Aged 19, a market vendor, from Bansalan, Davao del Sur. Arrested without warrant by policemen in Davao City on 8 June 1981. Taken to "safehouse" in Bansalan where tortured under interrogation. Tortured again on 9 June in ABC Gym, Bansalan. Died as a result of torture.

Silvestre Vijer: Aged 32, resident in Barrio Naddungan, Gattaran, Cagayan. Killed by members of 17th Mechanized Infantry Battalion commanded by Lieutenant M. accompanied by ICHDF member M.B. The 17th MIB were on an operation in the area. Shortly before a soldier of the 17th MIB had been killed in an encounter with the NPA. Silvestre Vijer was ordered out of his house and interrogated about presence of NPA in the area. While being interrogated he was repeatedly beaten with rifle butts. He was ordered to run and was shot dead. The soldiers subsequently claimed that they had shot an NPA commander.

On my way to visit Ernesto I had seen a few of the squatters' settlements with which he is concerned. The crowded, gimcrack houses — of wood scraps, bamboo, odd pieces of metal, and with no electricity or running water — line the banks of the Pasig River and those of other streams and drainage canals. They can appear overnight on any vacant lot in the city, the occupants having been forced to move from wherever they lived the day before. Entire abandoned warehouses have also been taken over.

The problem of squatters has steadily risen since after World War II, when migrants from rural areas flocked to the cities, seeking jobs and other benefits of urban living. Today Manila, with a population of more than two million, is plagued with the health, welfare, and crime problems of a third of its residents, all of whom are squatters.

The government sees distinctions within these blighted "communities." Some residents are supposedly "illegal" squatters; that is, people who have erected their shacks without building permits or who might demand payment upon being told to evacuate private or public land. Enforcement of the rule regarding "legal" and "illegal" squatting is always arbitrary, with punishments of up to one year's imprisonment and fines that might be five times a family's annual income of, perhaps, $120 a year. Occasionally, with fanfare, the government will transfer title to some kind of undesirable land to its illegal tenants, but more often crews of municipal workers backed by police will arrive to demolish the shacks and send the people back to the streets, looking for a new home.

Attempts at correcting the housing problem have been spotty at best. In fact, nearly all the new housing projects across the country are too expensive for the people who most need them, and many developments are strategically chosen to drive up land values for the benefit of well-connected private parties or members of the government. The most flagrant example is in the waterfront area of the district of Tondo, only ten years ago known as Southeast Asia's largest slum; there, a multimillion-dollar redevelopment project was inaugurated. However, the cost of new housing has put it out of reach of nearly all the area's former residents, who have been squeezed into greater squalor in the margins of the district.

This is also the case in a housing scheme with the acronym of BLISS, a pet project of the minister for human settlements, Imelda Marcos. Model communities are built to provide "the eleven basic needs of man" in a rhapsody of cooperation between citizen and government. These needs are: shelter, livelihood, power, water, food, medical attention, mobility, ecological balance, education, clothing, and recreation. One BLISS project I found off Ramón Magsaysay Boulevard was built on the right-of-way of the main railroad line. The concrete buildings looked airy and solidly constructed, and certainly represented a unique use of urban space, but one must note that of the eleven basic needs of man, "quiet" is not included, thus allowing these units to exist perhaps ten feet from where the trains thunder by. I visited another BLISS development, the San Vicente Complex in Quezon City, which is in a less hectic setting. Its benefits to the poor and displaced are limited. Out of 175 units, more than half (95) were set aside for "high-income" residents, with those classified as "poor" receiving only one fifth (35) of the apartments. These units are bare, with a toilet, bath, and plain cement flooring — certainly better than a shack on the banks of the Pasig, but low-income BLISS residents have rarely been subjected to that sort of life. "Low income" as designated by BLISS is five hundred to fifteen hundred pesos of gross monthly income; for 40 percent of Manila's population, the *annual* income is less than twelve hundred pesos, or $140. Around Manila, BLISS and other housing projects are regarded as pork barrel programs, social developments with political strings attached.

I recall a most startling image that showed me the substance of the efforts to help "the truly needy" in Manila. Shortly after I left the city, a BBC crew was shooting footage for a documentary on the Philippines in its *Third Eye* series on developing nations, and they filmed the ceremonial opening of a new urban housing project.

Madame Marcos was on hand to make a speech, and a chorus of little girls wearing light blue uniforms for the occasion sang her a specially composed song. It went something like: "Thank you, First Lady, for giving us this wonderful home." (The Marcoses attempt, whenever possible, to give the illusion that government projects are their personal gifts.) As the First Lady's eyes began to brim with tears at the moving choral performance, the BBC camera began to pull away, showing, in turn: the muddy street, the new apartments' picturesque façade, and, moving farther still, that the sides and rears of the houses were patched-together planks, tin sheets, and cardboard.

So much of the government of the Philippines is only façade — maintained not only to hide its serious financial woes but also to portray the nation as something it is not.

Part of its economic predicament has been due to depressed worldwide prices for commodity exports (such as sugar, minerals, and coconuts). Still more blame must be directed to its dependence on foreign oil, though this has lately been reduced; in any case, the president claims that the impact is worse than it actually is. But as the Philippines has fallen into the rut of importing more than it exports, it has paid for this imbalance with borrowed foreign money, meeting interest payments with still more borrowed money and choosing to inaugurate all sorts of costly schemes to enhance its credit rating. When Ferdinand Marcos took office in early 1966, the national debt was only $600 million. But by 1982 it had soared to $18 *billion*, giving the country one of the highest per capita debts in Asia.

As he has become more beholden to international financiers like the World Bank and the International Monetary Fund, so also have they begun to balk at Marcos's way of doing bu ness. They have begun to insist on concessions for more loans — such as sharp reductions in tariffs, which hurt some local industries — and they have levied pressure on the president to expand employment somehow and to accelerate the growth of industry and nontraditional exports. Though he has taken small steps toward increasing the national export industry, Marcos plainly sees his salvation in foreign investments. Critics see this emphasis as ultimately self-defeating, since money will continue to flow out of the country in greater proportion than the amount remaining at home. Marcos will hear nothing of this criticism. It is as if he were an inexperienced head of a household who, having gotten into deep water with his mortgage, loans, and credit cards, hopes for a winning lottery ticket to set his life in order again. Meanwhile, his creditors are on the telephone; they besiege his front and back doors and are hauling away his automobile even as he is offering his own children as collateral for a loan he will use to buy a new wardrobe to keep up his façade of prosperity.

From their palace, the First Couple has presided over a bizarre campaign to transform the small part of the country that foreigners see into a place that will make foreign investors feel at home, a place that reflects the Marcoses' good taste and breeding, a place that will ensure their social standing — not their historical standing — for all time. In the process, they have constructed what has become the Disneyland of Asia, a nationwide theme park of progress that is about as durable as a papier-mâché house in a monsoon.

One could envision a progression, a sort of imaginary tour. Visitors landing at the costly new Manila International Airport are encouraged to stop at a nearby attraction that will acclimatize them to the Philippines. It is the Nayong Pilipino, or Philippine Village, a landscaped miniature of many of the country's regions. There it is possible to buy the arts and crafts of minority groups without having to endure uncomfortable travel to remote places that are colorful but lack essential human services and excel in discontent. After checking in at one of Manila's thirteen new four-star hotels and presumably conducting some business, visitors may be treated to entertainment "just like home" — if home happens to be the Lincoln or Kennedy Center or Boston's Symphony Hall. The First Lady has presided over a panoply of expensive cultural projects. On landfill in Manila Bay stands the Cultural Center Complex, which a friend once described as "Mussolini-style architecture updated to the present, and pure self-aggrandizement for Madame Marcos." Originally intended to support an aquarium and playing field, the reclaimed land was quickly seen as too valuable for so plebeian a use.

Instead, one may now visit a Folk Arts Theater (built for the 1974 Miss Universe Beauty Pageant), art galleries, the Design Center for the Philippines, the Philippine Center for Industrial and Trade Exhibits, the Philippine International Convention Center, and the Philippine Plaza Hotel. Several months before I arrived, an army of eight thousand workers toiled feverishly to complete the Philippine Film Center, a $21 million palace styled after the Parthenon, in time for the January 1982 opening of the First Manila International Film Festival. Madame Marcos has always been rather open about desiring to paste a cosmopolitan veneer over her country, hoping, in effect, to be able to attract her jet-set friends to Manila so that she will not have to travel so often to Beverly Hills, Manhattan, Washington, Paris, and London. For the film festival, she flew in more than three hundred guests — including George Hamilton, Jeremy Irons, Peter Ustinov, Priscilla Presley, Jack Valenti, Lord Lew Grade, Michael York, and Pia Zadora. She held lavish parties at Malacañang Palace and at Fort Santiago; the latter included a glittering and bejeweled medieval religious pageant, fireworks, and dinner for two thousand. In order to duplicate the atmosphere of the Cannes Film Festival, an ersatz beach resort was placed on the landfill near the Film Center. Complete with imported white sand and a manmade pond that quickly took on the form of a carabao wallow, the area failed to attract starlets and photographers.

The avowed purpose of the film festival was to find outlets for Philippine films — which are heavily censored — and to develop Asia as an audience for Western films. But since Philippine films (so far) are of limited interest, being mostly romances and kung fu epics and featuring scripts in Tagalog, and since Hollywood already dominates the Asian market, many critics saw the festival as the First Lady's attempt to promote herself to the society she most admires while consolidating her own wealth and power.

Some months after that extravaganza, Imelda Marcos's Cultural Center entered into a five-year agreement with the Boston Opera Company and its artistic director, Sarah Caldwell, to establish an Opera Company of the Philippines in Manila. In return for $100,000 annually, the Boston Opera would train young Filipinos in their home country and offer some of them internships in Boston. As with the film palace, critics such as the exiled Cecile Guidote-Alvarez charged that it was the "penchant of Madame Marcos for ostentation and her obsessive desire to be received by international high society that is behind the government's efforts to build cultural palaces all over Manila and to recruit a never-ending parade of celebrities and artists to give the dictatorship an aura of glamour." This "frivolity and wealth is scandalous," the critics said, in light of the poverty of most Filipinos. As it happened, the hue and cry raised by activists in Boston proved too embarrassing for the troupe. The arrangement was allowed to lapse in the fall of 1983, though an opera spokesman denied the move had any political implications.

We were sitting in my hotel room, my brother and I, when a knock on the door announced the steward from Room Service. He was a very polite young man, an Ilocano from Bulacan province, just outside Manila. He had once told us how glad he was to have left Bulacan — where the job prospects were limited to peonage on a sugar plantation or dreary and unhealthy work in a tannery — and how lucky he had been to find a place in that elegant hotel. On this afternoon, as our steward set down the bottles of San Miguel beer, he lingered and asked us how we were finding his country. We told him that we liked it very much.

"The Filipino women, they are very pretty," he said shyly.

It was not exactly an original statement. The Filipino women *are* very pretty; I had been assured of their great beauty from the first day I walked into the tourism office in New York. An office manager handed over a stack of promotional literature, each brochure showing a winsome young woman in the tiniest of bikinis. "The Filipino women are very pretty, you know," the office manager had said, and the phrase doggedly began popping up everywhere once I arrived in the country. Government officials, flight attendants, hotel clerks, service station owners, museum guides, elevator operators, librarians, maître d's, historians, sociologists, anthropologists, playwrights, lefties, righties, males, females — all found it necessary to season their small talk with this verifiable statement, to elicit from me my confirmation, my playful grin. Cabdrivers found it an especially important remark — only they followed it with questions as to my marital status, my relative freedom at the time, my possible loneliness, and my desire to meet a girl. Of course, except for cabbies, pandering was not always the intent. Filipinos enjoy getting affirmative answers to questions much more than negative, and they often construct their conversations in order to receive an imbalance of yeas. Before I had been in Manila very long, I began to suspect that the rote lessons started in elementary school:

"Repeat after me, class: Filipino women are very pretty."

"FILIPINO WOMEN ARE VERY PRETTY."

"Very good."

To our steward I nodded my agreement but politely confessed that I was growing weary of hearing it everywhere, that it contributed to a cheapening of womanhood and encouraged a state of mind in which all Filipino women would be considered available.

He thought for a moment before he spoke, hesitating with his English stretched beyond the platitudes spoken to tourists, stammering slightly with the strain of speaking a truth to a foreigner. "Your country — many countries — are much richer than our country," he said. "It makes many of our women turn to prostitution." He paused and looked at the floor. "It is too bad, you know?" he murmured. "It should not be."

The marketing of sex as a tourism incentive is extraordinary in the Philippines; it is generally agreed that the phenomenon is as marked as one might find in Bangkok, for instance, or, compared to Seoul or Taipei, perhaps more so. Searching for statistics, I found that back in 1976 the Manila Health Department listed some 528 cocktail lounges, clubs, bars, and massage clinics in Metro Manila that were registered for prostitution. As tourism has recently passed the one-million-visitors-per-year mark, so the number of establishments has grown. In Manila's tourist belt alone — the districts of Ermita and Malate — there are about 120 flesh shops, with 21 accredited by the Ministry of Tourism and licensed by City Hall. Each of these shops has between 100 and 200 hospitality girls, who work for accredited tour agencies. The city government has issued prostitution licenses to about 100,000 massage attendants, hostesses, waitresses, and go-go dancers, but certainly many others prefer to work outside the health regulations and taxation by avoiding registration altogether. "The pre-occupation for tourist dollars has turned Manila into a flesh-pot," wrote the editor of *Ibon*, a fortnightly journal of statistics and facts about Philippine life. She continued by noting that even the country's last resource — the youth — was being corrupted: in one month, she noted, some 115 children between nine and thirteen years old, male and female, were rounded up in the Ermita-Malate districts for suspected prostitution.

After a while it became a cliché to see a foreign man walking by the bars and souvenir shops in Ermita with a young Filipina on his arm, whether he was a sunburned, toupéed Australian in walking shorts, an overweight businessman, or a shy and gangly close-shorn American serviceman. Most noticeable, however, were the Japanese — who must hold the All-Asia Prize for Boorish Tourists. With their penchant for efficiency, the Japanese have streamlined the entire exchange. Japanese package tours are said to have an unusually high ratio of male tourists, mostly middle-aged businessmen. These tours generally arrive in the early afternoon and are transferred from the airport to a hotel by limousine. Almost immediately, the group is picked up by a bus sent by a club. Once at the club, women are displayed — sometimes behind glass panels — and after making their choices, the Japanese treat their dates to dinner and perhaps a floor show before retiring with them. Kickbacks from drinks, food, and entertainment revert to the Japanese tour agency, as does the major portion of what the prostitute has earned. The Japanese Women's Christian Temperance Union has reported that of the sex tours' $50 prostitution charge, $14 goes to the local travel agent, $16 to the hotel, and $10 to a Japanese tour guide, leaving $10 for the prostitute.

The Ministry of Tourism's emphasis on sex for hire — and also the sexiness of the average Filipino — has thus corroded social situations between locals and visitors. One night I went to meet Trinidad, a former girlfriend of a Filipino friend of mine in the States who had asked me to say hello for him. She worked for a film company in Manila, and even over the telephone I could tell she was brassy and assertive in a way more common in New York than Manila. This proved to be less than totally true, as I found out after we had chatted about our mutual friend for a while and I asked if she would meet me for dinner later in Ermita. She hemmed and hawed, briefly considered asking another woman along, balked at first when I suggested that my brother join us, and finally agreed to meet us both at a restaurant on Maria Orosa Street.

Trinidad arrived fifteen minutes late, striding quickly to our table and somewhat rudely beckoning to our waiter before she sat down. She ignited the first of a constant chain of cigarettes, ordered a drink, and dismissed the waiter brusquely. After we had small-talked our way out of her nervousness, Trinidad explained her earlier hesitation.

"When one sees a Filipina with an American man," she said, "there can be only one conclusion drawn."

We had an exceedingly pleasant dinner that was drawn out by many cups of coffee. When it was time to go, Trinidad rushed off into the tumult of Ermita's strolling night life to find a cab for herself. "It's okay, don't bother," she said when we offered to help her find one, and after waving to us over her shoulder, she disappeared into the sidewalk crowds.

Mutya was doing research at a private university in the Manila suburbs, and she had been helping me decipher the occasional Spanish texts I ran across. She so patiently took time from her own work that I offered lunch as the only way to thank her adequately.

Again came that hesitation. Then: "Perhaps I could," she said, "if I brought along my friend," and she pointed to a woman several tables away who happened to be looking our way.

I was in a teasing mood and asked why a mature woman needed a chaperone.

"Maybe you are right," she said doubtfully. "Why should a forty-two-year-old mother of six children have to take along a chaperone? If people talk, let them!"

In a Chinese restaurant not far away, she told me her story. The eldest of eight children, she had married at fourteen — interrupting school, of course. She and her husband had had six children. One day he announced that without consulting her, he had applied for an American visa and planned to find a better job in California. The money he could send home would make his absence easier, he reasoned. After he had gone and found work in the States, the money eventually stopped coming. He divorced Mutya and took two other wives in America. Prevented from marrying again since divorce is not recognized, Mutya raised her children by herself. She returned to school at night, working for the university during the day to support herself, her mother, and her three youngest children. After getting her high school and college diplomas, she was now well on her way to finishing a master's degree. Her employer had offered her a better job when that time came, which pleased her. As it was, she was paid a little less than half of what men received in comparable jobs. This would also be the case after her promotion, but she could only shrug at that.

Mutya did not remember whether she had actually loved her husband. "That was too long ago, several lifetimes," she said. But several years ago she met a foreign man with whom she had dinner a few times — always chaperoned. "He was such a gentleman," she told me. "Before he even knew me he came in on a Monday and said, 'How was your weekend?' and I could only tell him that it was tiring. When he asked me what I had done, I said, 'Cook, clean, scrub the floors, mend my daughter's dress.' 'That would keep you out of trouble,' he said, and I answered, 'What trouble? I don't have *time* for trouble,' and he laughed."

She became less animated. "He went back to Argentina," she said, "and we wrote back and forth for a while. Then the letters stopped. After a few months I gathered all my courage and telephoned. A woman answered. She said, 'Oh, he moved from here a long time ago.'" Mutya smiled and shrugged. I saw that it was a habit of hers, that shrugging.

"And that is my story," she said.

Later we stood at the bus stop. It was a Friday, and the afternoon rush hour had begun early. "I really wanted to do this but I was afraid," she said. "Everyone talks, talks, talks. They make fun of women who fall in love with foreigners and want to move away." She glanced at the people in a jeepney that pulled up at the curb to take on passengers. The driver beeped his horn, wondering if Mutya wanted to squeeze on. She abruptly turned her back to the street.

"They are all looking at me," she said.

Dolores worked for a government ministry; she had been present at a number of informal get-togethers, including the ones where people told Tommy Manotoc jokes and grew reticent when I tried to draw from them any firm opinions they might hold. When I announced that I planned to spend the next few days at the University of the Philippines in Quezon City, Dolores offered to give me a guided tour of the institution. I agreed to meet her there the next morning, though something in her manner suggested she had been asked to keep an eye on me.

The next day I took a taxi out to the campus. My driver was talkative, telling me he read many American novels and saw American movies whenever he could. He had especially liked the films *Apocalypse Now* and *The Deer Hunter*. I had by that time noticed a white washcloth draped over the taxi meter; every time the driver spied my eyes straying toward that obscured device, his conversation took on renewed energy. I decided to go along with his game to see how much he would charge me. He was forty-seven, he said, with one daughter studying chemistry at the university. He confided that he had "given up women five years ago — it was too hard on my constitution."

"You're probably living wrong," I returned. "Give up smoking, eat right, get some exercise."

He only sighed. Since he had introduced the subject of sex, I waited for him to ask me if I wanted a girl, but after inquiring about my wife and whether she was with me, he apparently decided I was not fair game. He only overcharged me slightly when we reached the campus.

The University of the Philippines had moved after the war to Quezon City, the district created to house many of the institutions destroyed during the liberation. Now, instead of being confined within a downtown compound, the university sprawled across beautiful lawns in a mile-long oval pattern with the freshly painted Quezon Hall at its head.

Dolores was waiting at the faculty center with her sister Ophelia, an anthropology student. Together they walked me through the History Department. It was semester break and all the offices were closed, which was regrettable because I had read the publications of most of the faculty and would have enjoyed comparing notes with them. In the Anthropology Department, a listless young instructor gave me some information on tribal minorities on the northeastern coast, but he seemed either too unimaginative or too torpid from the heat to understand the expedition I planned to make. The young women next took me through a dusty little anthropology "museum," a few cluttered rooms, where the exhibits were falling apart from neglect.

This tour was turning out to be profitless, and I began to wish I had gone directly to the library. Dolores spied an older man on the far side of a crowd of students who were enduring registration. She

pulled me over to meet him, telling me that he was a prominent
playwright by the name of Behn Cervantes.

"David is writing a book about Agoncillo," she said, after getting
his attention and introducing us. He looked at her sharply, then glared
at me as if I were a moron.

She blushed, realizing she had misspoken. "Oh, no, I meant
Aguinaldo," she amended.

Cervantes snorted. "Same thing — Aguinaldo, Agoncillo." He refused to look at either of us. Such rudeness and arrogance in a country where hospitality is universal can ruin one's entire day. I would
not let that happen, so I turned my back on Cervantes and went outside, not caring to know why he treated an elderly historian and a
deceased warhorse with the same disdain. Later, I mentioned the exchange to a friend of mine who had spent five years in prison after
martial law was imposed. "Don't take Behn's attitude seriously," he
said. "He was arrested with the rest of us, but he didn't handle prison
very well — spent five years there, I think, came out very bitter, unable to adjust to outside life again. Behn can't reconcile his earlier
activist life with the kind of quiet social change we're working for
now. He writes ultranationalist plays. He hates the Americans, he
hates the government, he hates the past — but his heart is in the right
place." A few days later, my friend told me that he had passed the
word to Cervantes that my heart was in the right place, too, and the
playwright sent his apologies. But I had no appetite to look him up
again.

Across the street from the university building, Dolores and I sat
down on some steps near a soft drink stand. We were surrounded
by undergraduates.

"I feel like an old lady," she said, laughing. She was twenty-five. I
told her that I had gone to college at the same time as her older
brother, during the protest years of the Vietnam War. The students
in the Philippines and in the United States had shared many preoc-
cupations then, I said, and I wondered how her generation of students had appeared to cope with the events after 1972.

"I'm a child of martial law," she answered. "I was fourteen when
it was declared. I really don't remember what it was like before."

I asked her what made her different from her brother and older
cousins.

"More conservative, less outspoken," she said. "And apolitical. We're
more willing to take government jobs. But you know, we're not so
different from a lot of the people who demonstrated outside Malacañang Palace in the sixties. Now some of them are as conservative
as I." She seemed to find satisfaction in that belief, although it was

only partially true; I had met some who continued to work — albeit quietly — for changes in the status of women, for the improvement of slum life, for the establishment of rural cooperatives or home industry, each taking small but important steps.

"Tell me your life story," I said.

"What do you want," Dolores replied, "the tragedy or the funny parts?" But she would say no more. She stared at the students lounging in the shade of a big tree, particularly at a knot of chattering, effeminate young men.

"There are too many gays in Manila," Dolores said, still looking at the students. "Even in school. There are many, many more gay men than gay women. It cuts out most of the available men — half are gay, a quarter married, a quarter going steady." She sighed. "You know what? I think a lot of men in Manila, especially students, have become gay because it is the only safe way left they can protest." She had not had a boyfriend in "years," she said.

The last thing we talked about before she left was her hope for the future. Dolores wanted an overseas post with the government, and she had applied for assignment to the Philippine mission in Toronto. I had no doubt that her plans for that job also entailed meeting someone, anyone, who would rescue her from her solitude.

During my stay in Manila, I saw in the back pages of the newspapers many personal advertisements from men all over the world looking for a Philippine bride as well as ads from agencies that specialized in arranging such long-distance partnerships. Dolores, and others like her, are too sophisticated for such appeals, but more than seven thousand Filipinas became export brides in 1981. West Germany and Australia lead the world in such arrangements, though they are by no means the only countries; the United States has, not surprisingly, emerged as the most desired destination of all. It is unfortunate that some of the agencies recruiting wives are actually fronts for prostitution, which has resulted in some rather cruel shocks for women who leave the Philippines expecting to find a new home for themselves.

One Sunday we arranged to go with Renato Perdon, a curator of monuments with the National Historical Institute, to Cavite province, just south of Manila, to visit the Emilio Aguinaldo birthplace and museum. After he met us at the hotel, we took a cab down Roxas Boulevard to the district of Paranaque, still within Metro Manila, from which we would take a bus.

Renato led us through a maze of refuse-filled streets (the Metro Manila Aides are concentrated along the tourist routes). Announcing a shortcut, he turned into an alleyway that gave onto a hidden, crowded marketplace. As we squeezed between stalls selling T-shirts, straw mats, cheap shoes, and clothing, I felt as though we were underwater, perhaps beneath lily pads. The glare and noise of the outside world were muted. Sunlight diffused through the multicolored awnings and made the cheap dyes glow. Proprietors and customers alike smiled as we moved by them, a few uttering the universal greeting "Hey, Joe," which has been handed down since the war. Abruptly we were on another street — radios blasting and horns tooting, now deafening after the murmur of the alley. Renato pointed to a minibus. He told us to watch our wallets on this sidewalk with pushcarts and staring passersby.

The bus ride was uncomfortable — far too many passengers, far too many vehicles on the Cavite Boulevard ("beach traffic" was Renato's explanation). The seats had not been designed for Westerners. We were jammed in with eight other people in the rearmost row, all of us beginning to adhere to one another in the damp heat.

Renato told me how the study of history was changing. "Partly it's from new scholarship, which is from the Philippine rather than the American sentiment. After so many years of colonial mentality, finally we are breaking away. Also, with changes in Filipino culture, this independent way of thinking sees new interpretations of old facts."

I related to him the experiences of three Filipino friends who now lived in the United States: John Silva, the product of a durable marriage between an American navy officer and a Cebuano woman, now a dealer in rare books and photographs; Bernardo Lopez, Jesuit-trained, who was a writer and photojournalist in New York; and Richard Fernandez, who was studying international management at Harvard. All three had not known anything about, for instance, the Philippine-American War and the deeds of figures such as Aguinaldo, Bonifacio, and Mabini until they moved to the United States. "I remember memorizing the fifty states and their capitals," Silva said to me once, "and also the presidents — Adams, Jefferson, Millard Fillmore. *Nothing* about the Revolution of 1896. *Nothing* about the San Juan incident that started the war in 1899. *Nothing*." Lopez had said the same thing, adding that his literature classes emphasized American and English writers. Fernandez said he was shocked at what had been left out of his textbooks back home — especially since he, as well as my other friends, was born after independence. "Talk about a colonial mentality!" Silva had said. "What an outrage!"

Renato Perdon said he agreed with my friends. He also said he hoped that high school and college students were following a more original curriculum now, though he was not sure how much was sinking in. The present generation of published historians was aging, too, he said; mostly they were in their fifties, sixties, and seventies, which made him worry about the future. Renato, who is in his thirties, easily named his contemporaries, who were not many. "And there are no new young scholars coming up," he said, "which is unfortunate. The trend has been toward business, science, and so on."

We finally got off the bus in the town of Kawit and entered the grounds of the Aguinaldo Shrine, as it is called. Whitewashed, red-roofed, three stories high with a tower emerging from its center roof, the building is at once picturesquely homey and impressive, its lines an amalgam of Spanish, Victorian-gothic, and tropic-colonial architecture. Inside, the luster of the hardwood floors and dark walls reflected the sunlight streaming in through the windowpanes. Walking through the shrine with a great-grandniece of the old general ("He was very reserved, very soldierly" was all the remembrance she imparted), I was amazed at how many portraits of American dignitaries hung on the walls. There was Franklin Roosevelt and Truman and assorted generals, but few Filipinos represented in the living quarters. Did this reflect Aguinaldo's taste or that of some sort of fawning decorator let loose there after the general died? I never found out. Only on the first floor, which had originally been used for storage but now is a small museum, did I find a photograph of Aguinaldo's fellow revolutionaries, his Galeria ng Makasalanan (Gallery of Sinners). Not far away was a formal portrait of five American officers; Frederick Funston was seated in the center. All around me were rusty old sabers, moth-eaten uniforms, torn and bloody battle flags, and straw hats returning to dust. In a generation, all of it will have crumbled, and by then perhaps no one in the country will know anything of the past — and that stately old house will have become a nightclub, perhaps another Chicken-in-a-Bikini restaurant.

I saw a small coin box in the center of the museum. It was next to a guestbook that was filled with the appealing scrawls of young visitors. The box had a sign: PUT DONATIONS HERE. My hand automatically went into my pocket and withdrew some coins, but it was halted in midair by Renato.

"Don't waste your money," he said. "It goes directly into the Treasury. None of it is used to keep this place maintained. Our budget stays the same regardless."

Another petty sham, the taking of the money of schoolchildren and pensioners, of tourists and pilgrims. I said I wanted to go.

IV

I *was* ready to go. The time I had allotted for Manila was nearly gone. My research in various archives had reached the point where I was saturated with history; the sources were beginning to repeat themselves — the signal for any writer that it is high time to stop taking notes and to begin the actual writing. I had paced out all of the historical sites I could find in the capital; went on a three-day drive into the Central Cordillera for the incongruous double duty of retracing Aguinaldo's wanderings through the rice terraces of Mountain province as well as searching out the site of General Yamashita's 1945 surrender to the Filipino and American forces. In these last few days, more and more of my time was concerned with helping my brother complete plans for our own expedition — our hike which would parallel that taken by Frederick Funston in 1901 — a hundred-and-ten-mile walk, or thereabouts, which would take us about as far spiritually from the raucousness of Manila as one could get.

I had not met one person in Manila who was not gloomy about our intended trek. Dr. Quiason at the National Historical Institute said that he would not consider going to *any* remote place in the Philippines "without notifying the armed forces for an escort." Philippine Tourism officials, seeing no profitable way that foreigners could be induced to travel to the inhospitable northeastern Luzon coast, unanimously suggested we stay in Manila or take in a provincial religious festival. Members of the nightly dinner merry-go-round, librarians, teachers, priests, and cabdrivers — all of them mentioned Aurora-Quezon and Isabela provinces with reverence and in the same breath as their talk of guerrillas, guerrillas, guerrillas.

Even though President Marcos had gone on television recently to claim that "subversives no longer pose a danger or threat to the nation's internal security," apparently no one had thought to inform members of the New People's Army. As in the case of many other remote provinces, the NPA has a significant presence in Quezon and Isabela, both of which are lightly populated and mountainous, with shorelines completely cut off from the rest of the island. Marcos discounted their strength. "They are carrying rifles but they are not soldiers — meaning, they are not ready to pit their strength against the armed forces," he said. "Most of them are hit-and-run guerrillas. They will not be able to hold territory."

Despite the president's statement, his provincial military leaders had been announcing alerts for weeks — in Leyte, Bohol, Ilocos Sur, Da-

vao del Norte, North Cotobato, Quezon, Surigao del Sur, and Kalinga-Apayo provinces. Of those eight areas, the box scores reported
in the newspapers were: for the government, 18 killed, 5 wounded,
and 29 disarmed; for the dissidents (presumably including innocent
bystanders), 17 killed, 1 wounded, 17 captured, and 75 surrendered.
In addition, headlines screamed out a warning that a rebel plot had
been "bared" that had been aimed at subverting national barangay
(barrio) elections for district council members and barangay captains, which were intended for some time the following month.

In view of all this unrest, my mind was certainly not eased by news
bulletins that an unidentified submarine had been sighted off the
eastern coast of Aurora-Quezon province. The military authorities
were certain that it carried military hardware for the rebels, though
the fishermen who actually witnessed the unloading of crates admitted that they could not say for certain whether the crates contained
weapons or contraband Scotch. Later, radios and other electronic
equipment washed ashore on the island of Polillo, off Quezon province, though it seemed unlikely that they had anything to do with
the submarine sighting.

As if this were not enough, the newspapers announced that a series of unseasonal typhoons had begun to strike the islands south of
Luzon, killing at least fifty-nine people. The first storm, which was
called Bising, generated winds as high as 185 kilometers per hour,
prompting the president to declare a state of calamity in the stricken
provinces. Bising moved so fast that I began to wonder whether it or
another storm might hit the unprotected northeastern coast of Luzon during the weeks we would be pinned to the seashore by the
coastal mountains, with only tents for shelter. I knew already that
casualty rates from storms were high in the area we were going to,
and I had made sure that the typhoon season would be safely over.
Now we had these out-of-season storms to think about.

While nothing could be done about the weather, I was given the
chance to do something about our presence in a contentious military
zone. Having gotten to know a fellow with contacts in the underground, I confessed to him that I was slightly worried about running
into NPA guerrillas who might mistake us for someone else and shoot
or abduct us before asking questions.

"I would worry less about guerrillas," my friend told me, "and more
about government soldiers or police. They're not used to outsiders
poking around in their territory; they operate pretty much as they
please. We've heard of at least one Western journalist — an American — being wiped out by PC soldiers in Mindanao. That was in '74.

So if any one official asks you what you're doing there, say you're a tourist. They don't like journalists. Drop as many 'approved' names as you can. Maybe they'll believe you."

My friend asked whether I wanted to meet any members of the NPA while I was up north. "If I was alone," I replied, "then I'd say yes. But I'm going to be going with five others, including my brother" (I almost said "little brother," protectively). "I feel responsible for them. I don't want to drag them into a political scene they don't understand, or meet people they might jeopardize unknowingly later, or put them in danger themselves."

My friend said he understood, and he promised to try to spread the word to his contacts in the north that we were to be left alone. If it seemed possible for me to leave my companions for a few days and rendezvous with anyone hiding in the mountains, he said, someone would contact me.

It had become apparent that whenever my energy level was low — especially directly before a meal, but also if I found myself rushing about too much in the hot sun — I became prey to despondency and paranoia. I began to think about microphones in my hotel room and have odd, frightening daydreams of the worst possible things happening to me, or to my brother, or to my four friends from the States who were to accompany us, or even to my wife back home. So much of the country seemed, at times, to be disconcertingly barbarous, what with the daily reports of kidnappings, terrorism, banditry, political repression, nighttime arrests, casual threats — the seemingly complete and arbitrary power of the government. My mind would sometimes be filled with images of the work bolos and machine-gun bullets could do on a human body, and I would drift off from a book or a half-eaten sandwich for minutes at a time.

A few days before our friends arrived, I had a rather bad reaction to the malaria prophylaxis I had been taking regularly. Foolishly downing the pills on an empty stomach, I soon became violently ill with all the symptoms of food poisoning. When it was all over, I was five pounds lighter and pretty weak on my feet — which was hardly good preparation for a strenuous hike.

But then there were the four familiar faces of my jet-lagged friends, who appeared in my room with my brother as I was drinking what seemed like my twentieth milkshake, to rebuild my strength and my weight. Around my bed were piled cartons and trunks that disgorged tents, backpacks, freeze-dried food, climbing rope, cooking utensils, lightweight hiking boots, medical supplies, and several quarts of a fruit-flavored powder called something like URK (or more likely

ERG; which they assured me contained electrolytes, potassium, and glucose, meant to replace a stressed person's lost salts during a hike).

"Mix me up some of that stuff," I said, rising to the occasion, "and let's get this expedition on the road." I wondered if, wherever they were, Frederick Funston and Emilio Aguinaldo were laughing at me for presuming to plant my footsteps in theirs or for even daring to think that I could understand what manner of men they actually were.

If any more knowledge was to be gleaned, it would be far off the beaten track, away from books, libraries, and historians, along a coast where it might be possible to scrutinize Funston's and Aguinaldo's end of the twentieth century from ours. And there was always the chance I might at the same time obtain some reflected light on our own noisy and complex age.

3

A FILIPINO AND HIS COUNTRY

I

Emilio Aguinaldo y Famy was born on Holy Monday, March 22, 1869, in the town of Cavite el Viejo (which later came to be known as Kawit) in Cavite province, on the eastern shore of Manila Bay. He was the sixth of eight children born to Carlos Jamir Aguinaldo, an employee of the Administration of Public Lands, and Trinidad Valerio Famy, once directress of a government tobacco factory.

His mother suffered unbearable labor pains for three days prior to his birth, and a midwife and her attendants could do nothing for her. "They were just ready to give up when my father thought of a most extraordinary plan to save my mother," wrote Aguinaldo in his memoirs. "Surreptitiously, he went downstairs to light a *berso* (giant firecracker). The sudden loud explosion startled my mother and, without much ado, I saw the light of day."

In choosing a name with which to baptize the infant, Carlos Aguinaldo consulted his calendar to find that the saints for the day were Deogracias and Bienvenido, which the father thought ostentatious. He settled instead for Emilio, a martyr's name. Being born during the saddest week of the year and saddled with a martyr's name made an indelible impression on the boy — and the man. "This probably explains," he would say, "why from childhood, my life has always been fraught with hardships and sadness."

He was a meek boy, considered small for his age, and his parents were forever indulgent. "Among my brothers and sister, I was said to be the most loved by my father," he recalled, "maybe because I was the youngest among the boys and the ugliest among them." Doted on by his family, it came as a blow when, during a smallpox epidemic, the nearly three-year-old Emilio contracted the disease. "I was seriously ill and given up for dead," he wrote, "so my mother, brothers, and sister started crying over my hapless condition. When my father arrived and saw I had a high fever, he gave me a cold bath. In no time I stirred and gave a low moan. . . . How happy everybody was at my miraculous cure, surely a grace from the Lord Almighty." The disease scarred his face for life.

In the three centuries since the Spanish conquistadors had landed in the Philippines, brandishing a cross in one hand and a sword in the other, a dark night had settled upon the lives of generations of Filipinos — the Indios, as the Spaniards called them. Instituting a feudal system that guaranteed power, land, and wealth to the colonists, the Spaniards levied taxes and tributes upon their vassals, conscripted them into forced labor, and established government monopolies of tobacco, wine, and other products. Vast estates were carved out and mercilessly ruled by not only the Filipinos' secular conquerors, but by the friars as well. These ecclesiastics became the most hated authorities on the islands. Their power was unchecked, their influence on daily life pervasive. They instituted taxes, cheated peasants out of their land, and imposed harsh penalties for the most minor offenses, all the while preaching Christian charity, meekness, and forgiveness. The friars became the center of each Filipino settlement and town, and it became their responsibility to educate the poor Indios. Their curriculum, such as it was, relied heavily on Christian doctrine and a fear of the Lord's appointed servants on earth. Many of these so-called educators resisted the idea of teaching the Filipinos the Spanish language (there was no national Philippine tongue until the twentieth century); instead, the Filipinos conversed in one or more of scores of tribal dialects, such as Tagalog, Ilocano, or Visayan. Giving the people a common language might unite them or "pave the way for the coming in of Protestant ideas."

The government authorities made life worse. The islands drew the dishonest like a magnet, and it became impossible to pass through life as a peasant without making heavy contributions to the pockets of corrupt officials as well as to the bottomless coffers of the colonial government.

Despite the agreeableness and hospitality that has always been deeply rooted in the Filipino character, no people could endure these miseries for long without revolting. Peasant uprisings occurred in the latter half of the eighteenth century in Batangas, Cavite, Bulacan, and Ilocos provinces, all of which were quashed and which resulted in little betterment of general conditions.

With the onset of the nineteenth century, dim rays of light began to fall upon the archipelago. In 1814, the Spanish governor in Manila opened the port to foreign trade. A lively commercial business was established, trading in sugar, coconut, hemp, coffee, and tobacco, which resulted in the evolution of a Filipino middle class. Slowly, education began to improve — at least for those who could afford it. Then, in 1869, the opening of the Suez Canal shortened the sea voyage between Spain and the Philippines. This encouraged more contact between Europe and the islands; thousands of Spanish immigrants arrived, some bringing word of the beginnings of a wave of Western liberalism to the Philippines. Books became more available. In response to a very brief liberalization of the Madrid government, the burdensome laws were relaxed slightly. However, in 1872, a new regime took power and the light began to dim again — the beginning of another slide into feudalism.

The incident that would signal the beginning of the end occurred in Cavite province. The Spanish governor, General Rafel de Ezquierdo, ended the old policy of exempting Filipino military and civilian employees of the Cavite port and arsenal from paying certain taxes or from being drafted into public works projects. Mutiny broke out among the Filipino soldiers. Though it was quickly suppressed, Governor Ezquierdo instituted draconian reprisals. He arrested a number of mild reformists who had become too outspoken for his taste. Three nationalist Filipino priests were executed by garrote, and many others were exiled to Guam. Persecution was stepped up. Scores of people were jailed and tortured. Units of the Spanish army fanned out across the countryside to frighten the Indios into submission. As Agoncillo has written, those students and intellectuals who were "unable to steer through the thick darkness in their native land, sought light in Europe."

On the evening of January 15, 1872, the townspeople of Kawit were thrown into confusion by the sounds of fighting directly to their north, around the Cavite arsenal. The next morning, news spread that musketeers from Manila were sweeping down on the town. The dread *juez de cuchillo,* or "judgment by the knife," had been instituted, which called for anyone standing in the path of the soldiers to be shot or beheaded. Everyone fled in panic.

Emilio was not yet three years old and only a few days cured of the smallpox that had nearly killed him. "During the scamper for safety, I was separated from my mother who entrusted me to the care of Eugenio Valerio, my cousin," he recalled. "We were to cross a river, but being afraid that we might be overtaken by the enemy, Eugenio left me in the thickets and crossed the river by himself. When the infantry had passed by, he felt it safe to go back for me. So he crossed back . . . and found me hoarse from crying because I was being devoured by giant ants." The boy was painfully swollen from the bites and suffered a relapse of his smallpox. "To my young mind," he recalled, "these . . . were added proof to my being a martyr."

Less than a week later, Carlos Aguinaldo was arrested in the massive Spanish dragnet to eradicate anyone who might have had anything to do with the Cavite Mutiny. The elder Aguinaldo, because he was educated and moderately well-to-do, had drawn the Spaniards' suspicions. He was soon released from custody, but simply his having been picked up enlarged his reputation as being anti-Spanish. By then, Carlos Aguinaldo had grown in local prominence. He was known as a capable barrister and a politician, having once been the temporary mayor of San Isidro, Nueva Ecija, and he was elected mayor of Kawit many times. When he took young Emilio on his official rounds, the people of Kawit would smile and point and call the shy boy "Little Captain." When Carlos died after a stroke in 1878, he was forty-eight and Emilio was nine. His burial, recalled Emilio, "was the best ever witnessed in our town."

Although the future revolutionary leader learned the alphabet early, it was the last precocious thing he would do about education; when he began school he showed no enthusiasm about learning. "Instead of attending to my studies," he said, "I spent my time playing the common games of the times [and] playing with toy guns." From a kindergarten managed by his grandmother, he went to public school where, he recalled, "although I was not very good in arithmetic and I could not understand the two Spanish textbooks, my teacher loved me and I do not remember having been punished." Later, he attended four different private high schools in Manila, but he was too homesick to study. In 1882, when a cholera epidemic closed the schools, he went home — this time for good. Aguinaldo was thirteen.

Returning to his widowed mother's house — a genteel, two-story affair of limestone and hardwood set between the Camino Real and the Marulas River — Emilio helped with various family interests: small real estate plots, a farm, and a little sugar factory in the town of San Francisco de Malabon.

After several years, Emilio and his brothers bought a ten-ton outrigger sailboat, which they christened the *San Bartolomé*. With it they began what became a prosperous trading business that carried them between Luzon and Mindoro island, and several others in the Visayan islands, taking loads of Kawit salt and bolo knives, returning with rattan, tallow, and even cattle — which Emilio used to start a small but successful ranch in Cavite.

While helping to erase the debts left after his father's death, Emilio had also begun to follow in his father's path. When he was seventeen, the young man was notified that he was to be conscripted into the Spanish army. This could have been avoided with a simple payoff, but instead his mother chose to use her family ties and political clout to get Emilio appointed barrio captain. The position deferred him from military service, but it had its own drawbacks. One of his functions was as local tax collector — and he was expected to pay the difference out of his own pocket whenever he was unable to collect. However, he escaped the odium of the job through his easygoing, diplomatic personality. After eight years of service (during which time he continued to operate his lucrative trading business), he was elected mayor of Kawit.

Emilio Aguinaldo swore not one but two oaths on the day he became mayor, for he marked his elevation in society by being inducted as a Freemason. In some ways, it was a standard move for a young businessman and politician; belonging to such an organization was a way for the bourgeoisie to show some slight independence from the confines of Catholicism. There was, however, another reason the lodges were becoming increasingly popular: they were following the examples of those established in Barcelona and Madrid by Filipino expatriates, who saw the secret society as a means of disseminating nationalist propaganda.

The young mayor of Kawit began to recruit assiduously. His first Masonic convert was his cousin Baldomero Aguinaldo, a justice of the peace; not long thereafter, he approached a childhood friend, Santiago Alvarez, for the same purpose. But Alvarez, the son of the mayor of Novaleta, Cavite, was on a mission of his own, for he asked Aguinaldo to join another secret society, the Katipunan, which was even more anti-Spanish. "Alvarez found no difficulty in convincing me," he wrote later, "because this was the kind of society I was looking for. I was merely waiting for the opportunity to join it."

Several days later, on a Sunday in March 1895, Aguinaldo and his sponsor journeyed from Kawit to Manila by *banca* and steamship ferry, and under the cover of night they were conducted on a long *calesa* ride. Aguinaldo was made to wear a blindfold. When their buggy finally reached the place of initiation, the mayor of Kawit went through a series of rigid tests not unlike those given him at the Masonic Lodge.

He was baptized with a new code name, Magdalo, after the wanton Mary Magdalene, the patroness of Kawit. Removing his blindfold after the ceremony, he found himself in a house in the Binondo district of Manila owned by the *supremo* of the Katipunan. "That was the beginning," recalled Aguinaldo, "of my acquaintance and friendship with Andres Bonifacio."

Bonifacio's life offered a strong contrast to that of Aguinaldo. He was born in 1863 in Manila's squalid working-class district of Tondo, where "the streets were as crooked as the administration," according to one historian, "and as dirty as the conscience of Spanish officialdom." One of three children, Andres had reached only the fourth grade. He showed, however, a talent for penmanship and an innate desire for self-betterment. As a boy and an adolescent, he manufactured paper fans and canes, which he sold on the streets of the capital; later he joined a commercial firm, first as a messenger and then as a broker of rattan and tar. It was said that Bonifacio habitually read late into the night; his small library included law books, a history of the French Revolution, a volume of the lives of American presidents, and novels by Dumas, Hugo, and the eminent Filipino writer José Rizal.

The former slumboy became as attracted to nationalism as he had been to the middle class, linking these impulses before he was thirty by joining a Masonic Lodge and helping his idol, Dr. Rizal, to found a reformist organization called the Liga Filipina. When Rizal was arrested by the Spanish authorities and exiled to an island in the southern Philippines, Bonifacio attempted to keep their *liga* intact. It failed to generate any excitement among those he knew, so he turned to organize the more radical and plebeian Katipunan. With his blunt single-mindedness, the young man from Tondo was able to build the secret society from nothing to three hundred members. He found particular success after assuming the leadership himself, becoming the society's third *supremo*. The Katipunan's objective was the separation of the Philippines from Spain, but only as a last resort, if the friars were not expelled and political rights not granted to the Filipinos by the Spanish government. The Masonic trappings of procedures and codes were taken extremely seriously by the members, who risked harsh punishment if their connection to the society was discovered. Even the sacrament of marriage took on political overtones. After Bonifacio lost his first wife to leprosy, he married again in 1893. He and his bride were wed in two ceremonies: one in a church, one before their fellow Katipuneros.

The addition of the young mayor of Kawit to the society's roll pleased Bonifacio, for Aguinaldo became an avid, though discreet, recruiter. Once, during a Katipunan meeting in the Kawit mayoral headquarters, Spanish officials interrupted to ask Aguinaldo why so many people were gathered. He replied that they had all been arrested for playing cards. He brought in so many prominent citizens from Kawit that Bonifacio set up a local branch of the Katipunan, known as the Magdalo faction.

The year 1896, which would be so significant in the life of Emilio Aguinaldo, began on January 1 with his marriage to the eighteen-year-old Hilaria del Rosario, from Tinabunan, Cavite. Aguinaldo had previously been unlucky in love while trading among the islands. He had abandoned one infatuation with a maiden on the island of Mindoro after the girl's parents objected. On Tablas Island he was attracted by a group of young women "displaying their beautiful legs as they frolicked with the waves" and vowed to marry one of them, but his mother made him promise never to return to the island. Though at the time he wondered "if I was really destined for martyrdom, even in love," presumably he conquered any parental objections to a union with Hilaria del Rosario. Their first child, Miguel, was born in October 1896. The baby was welcomed with fireworks into a province newly freed and to a world also witnessing the birth of a rebellion.

By mid-1896, Katipunan councils had been formed in many provinces. In Manila, Bonifacio wished to receive the blessing of Dr. Rizal — whose name he had already appropriated (without permission) as a sponsor — and he sent an emissary to Dapitan in the far south. Several weeks later, the Katipunan leaders had their answer, but it was not one they expected; Rizal sent word that he wished to have nothing to do with their revolution, which he felt to be ill advised and, at the very least, premature. Crushed by this rebuff, the *supremo* and his councilors attempted to enlist other prominent Filipinos, whose money might be used to finance the rebellion and whose influence would attract more members. This attempt also failed. Bonifacio might have excused Rizal for his indifference, but he became vindictive against the other members of the *illustrado* class. He ordered his right-hand man, Emilio Jacinto, to prepare forged letters linking the *illustrados* to the Katipunan. At a crucial time Bonifacio would release the documents, each of which alleged that a rich Filipino had contributed to the Katipunan war chest — each in effect a death warrant when it fell into Spanish hands.

As the rebels had failed to attract support from the community's intellectuals and wealthy, they were still faced with the problem of obtaining arms. Overtures to a visiting Japanese dignitary raised the hope of acquiring guns from that country, but their appeal was never officially answered. Some Katipuneros were able to steal odd revolvers and rifles but hardly enough to go around, for the membership had risen into the thousands. So it was that when the Revolution of 1896 began, it would do so principally as a rebellion of bolos, knives, pikes, spears, sticks, and stones against the formidable weaponry of the Spanish.

Throughout July and August, rumors began to drift into the governor general's palace in Manila regarding a mysterious subversive society. Nothing much was done about this information until a weak-willed Katipunero disclosed everything he knew about the society to a clever priest on August 19, 1896. Father Mariano Gil of Tondo then did some investigating of his own and turned up incriminating documents hidden in a Manila printing shop. He hurried to the police with the news.

The authorities began rounding up suspects for torture and interrogation, and with each new revelation sending the guards out after more rebels, the reign of terror began. Hundreds were arrested and imprisoned — not only Katipuneros but innocent Filipinos, including those of the middle class who had scorned the revolution and thus earned Bonifacio's enmity. Many were quickly exiled to the Carolines or to penal colonies. In Manila's Walled City, some six hundred prisoners were incarcerated in dungeons that became awash at high tide; though the hapless prisoners were able to keep their heads above water during these long stretches, a Spanish soldier tossed a rug over the dungeon's only ventilating shaft. Within a few days most of the prisoners had suffocated.

Other deaths came more quickly. Massacres of peasants were reported in the outlying provinces, with many being tortured before death. An American observer told of the arrival of a new load of prisoners, bound for the cells of Fort Santiago:

> In Vigan, where nothing had occurred, many of the heads of the best families and moneyed men were arrested and brought to Manila in a steamer. They were bound hand and foot, and carried like packages of merchandise in the hold. I happened to be on the quay when the steamer discharged her living freight with chains and hooks to haul up and swing out the bodies like bales of hemp.

By this time the rebellion had fully erupted. Despite the paucity of modern weapons, a Katipunan war council had declared August 29 as the day of reckoning. The first blow was to be struck by Bonifacio's faction in Manila. Therefore, on the designated night, Aguinaldo gathered with his men, waiting on a bridge in Kawit that af-

forded an unobstructed view of the capital's waterfront. Their signal —
the dimming of lights on the Luneta promenade — would summon
them to join the attack.

"Our hearts beat fast," recalled Aguinaldo. "I was restless and
worried." Hour followed hour as they strained to see a signal in the
darkness, but none appeared, so they left the bridge at dawn to get
some rest.

It turned out that Bonifacio's plans had been thwarted by a series
of Spanish raids and arrests, but if bad timing and ill luck were responsible for his first disaster, that would not always be the case. The
following day, Bonifacio led several hundred rebels in an attack on
a Spanish powder magazine in the suburbs. When his men failed to
subdue the handful of defenders, the supremo was revealed to be a
poor tactician, and when Spanish reinforcements arrived in due time
to relieve the magazine, Bonifacio's men were routed, with some eighty
killed and more than two hundred taken prisoner. It was not until
several days later that his Katipuneros were able to regroup, but when
they engaged the enemy again they were repeatedly defeated.

While Bonifacio's cachet as a military leader was disappearing, the
reputation of Emilio Aguinaldo was beginning to soar as a separate
rebellion in Cavite province took place. There, local Katipuneros
agreed upon August 31 as the day for their uprising. That morning,
Aguinaldo presented himself before the Spanish governor of the
province in the town of Cavite. Acting in his capacity as the mayor
of Kawit, he requested a detachment of infantry marines as reinforcements against the "bandit" rebels. He learned then that all the
soldiers excepting cne company had been dispatched to defend Manila — along with all the arsenal's available guns. With this important strategic information, Aguinaldo hastened to his comrades in
Kawit.

Meanwhile, in the towns of San Francisco de Malabon and Novelita, the rebels had begun to disarm the town police and civil guards
and capture the municipal buildings. Emboldened by this news,
Aguinaldo led a contingent against the civil guards of Kawit, overpowering all three without firing a shot. By that afternoon, all three
towns were under revolutionary control. In Kawit, about a thousand
civilians gathered in the town plaza, and at Aguinaldo's suggestion,
they dissolved the local Spanish rule by electing a new revolutionary
government. Candido Tirona became mayor, with Emilio Aguinaldo
as flag lieutenant. In the flush of these first victories, the Katipuneros of Kawit issued a revolutionary manifesto, urging all provincial
towns to "break the chains of slavery that have bound us . . . to rebel
against this tyrannical race."

Even as couriers fanned out across the province with this call to arms, preparations were being made to attack the town of Imus. A force under Aguinaldo's cousin Baldomero left for the town, but they were turned back by the enemy about midnight. This reverse ended after daybreak on September 1, when Aguinaldo left Kawit to aid his cousin, making a combined force of some two thousand bolomen. The Spanish defenders of Imus were forced to retreat — to the fortress-like *casa-hacienda* of the friars, where they refused to be dislodged. Even the priests fired volleys out upon the rebels, and though the place was surrounded, it seemed to be a stalemate. Finally, after Flag Lieutenant Aguinaldo ordered an adjoining grain warehouse set afire, inundating the enemy with smoke, the Spanish surrendered.

On September 2, Katipuneros from the town of Bacoor appealed for aid in turning back a column of Spanish troops. Aguinaldo had the bugle sounded and the Kawit church bell rung. Five hundred rebels responded almost instantly. "When I arranged them by fours," the young leader recalled, "it was fascinating to see many brave men ready to fight for our Motherland! We had nine guns only. Our men carried wooden stakes and nipa sheaves which looked like guns at a distance. Others had bolos and daggers."

This ragtag army marched for an hour until they reached Bacoor. Aguinaldo ordered entrenchments dug, which an engineer fortified with mortar and banana trunks; he stationed his soldiers beneath houses and along the banks of the Zapote River. Soon they were confronted with their first serious threat — a massed contingent of Spanish infantry, cavalry, and artillery. When a disciplined volley tore into the rebel ranks, they disintegrated.

"I shouted to my men, 'Fire, Lie Flat! Crawl! Fire! Fire!'" Aguinaldo remembered. "I shouted again. I could not order them to advance as the enemy was still far. When I looked behind me, I found that only the dead were left, for the rest had retreated. I thought of running, too, but I noticed that the cavalry had surrounded us. . . . I pretended to have been shot and fell near the body of Lieutenant Mariano Maigue, one of my policemen. I covered my face with his blood and made believe I was dead." When the enemy had passed, he escaped through swamps and fish ponds to rejoin the survivors of his troops, now in Imus. They thought he had been killed.

All that night, the rebels prepared to meet the Spanish column when it appeared in Imus, and it was because of these precautions that Aguinaldo scored his first major victory. He ordered the construction of pillboxes and entrenchments. A bridge leading into the town was cut in such a manner that the enemy would not discover it until too late; a captured cannon was placed with a clear view of the bridge and camouflaged with leaves. At daybreak on September 3, he stationed his ill-armed soldiers so that they were hidden in trenches or lying flat on the ground behind cover.

The Spaniards appeared — some five hundred strong — and, seeing no rebels around the town, marched toward the bridge. At the moment the soldiers in the lead saw they were trapped on a bridge with no way to cross the damaged section, Aguinaldo's troops fired their few weapons, provoking a furious volley in reply. Pressing his advantage, the flag lieutenant sent a group to wade across the shoulder-deep river in pursuit, but the rebels floundered, and many were carried away. So Aguinaldo took a group across himself, this time ordering his men to grasp their comrades' arms. The rebels reached the far side, attacked the Spanish flank, and panicked the enemy, who fled across the newly planted rice fields toward the cover of a distant estate house. They became mired in the thick mud, and Aguinaldo's soldiers waded among them with daggers, spears, and bolos. The Spanish commander, Brigadier General Ernesto de Aguirre, mounted his horse to flee, dropping his sword in his haste.

"When everything was clear, we surveyed our booty," said Aquinaldo. "We had two cartloads of tattered dead bodies, 70 Remington guns and other equipment. When I examined General Aguirre's sword, I found these words inscribed: *Made in Toledo, Spain, 1869*. This was the year when I was born. The coincidence made me happy. From that time on I brought this sword in all my battles."

Within a week, nearly all the towns in the province had been liberated. Emilio Aguinaldo, now acclaimed as a general, had become a hero overnight.

II

For six months and more the province of Cavite continued under rebel control, with many towns in six other provinces also troubling the Spanish government. Dissatisfied with Governor General Ramon Blanco's lack of success, Madrid replaced him with a real barbarian, General Camilio de Polavieja, who began his reign by ordering mass executions of the captured rebels and the shooting of a number of prominent moderates — including José Rizal, who was killed on December 30. Outside the capital, Polavieja's forces began to nip away at the liberated zones but were bitterly contested in every operation.

By February, the Spanish had weakened the Katipunero armies in central Luzon to the point that Polavieja could direct his cavalry and infantry to concentrate on the most troublesome province, Cavite. By then, the Katipuneros there had become seriously divided into factions. With the whole province on the alert, it was hardly the time to be arguing political nuances or getting bogged down in personality cults. Nonetheless, the Katipunan had arrived at an important turning point.

Before the revolution, so many Cavitenos had flocked to the Katipunan that two factions evolved. In northern Cavite, there was the Magdalo council — named after Emilio Aguinaldo's nom de guerre and headed by Baldomero Aguinaldo. In southern Cavite a separate council was later organized at Novelita. It was called the Magdiwang faction and was led by the mayor of Novelita, Mariano Alvarez, who happened to be the uncle-in-law of Andres Bonifacio. Normal competition began to grow unhealthy after the rebellion began, for both factions scored decisive victories against the Spanish; each became convinced that if Spain were to be defeated for good, one faction would have to gain control over the other Their mutual suspicion intensified to the detriment of the war effort. On March 22, 1897, an assembly of the Cavite Katipuneros convened in a former friars' estate house at Tejeros to consolidate the two fractious councils. Emilio Aguinaldo was absent — not because it was his birthday, but because he was leading his Magdalo forces against the enemy in a barrio near Imus called Salitran.

The atmosphere in the Tejeros estate house was nearly as combative as that on the battlefield. Because most of the Magdalos were busy fighting the Spaniards and others had not been invited, those present were greatly outnumbered by the Magdiwangs. So far as the Magdalo chieftains were concerned, the bitterness had hardly been improved by the choice of mediator, Andres Bonifacio, who had been summoned from a mountaintop roost. He had arrived in late December with a small entourage consisting of his wife and two brothers, Ciriaco and Procopio. At that time, the Magdalo leaders observed that Bonifacio strutted about and "acted as if he were a king." He also attempted to have one of their number arrested for a military blunder committed four months earlier. As *supremo* of the Katipunan, Bonifacio believed honors and prerogatives were due him as natural leader of the rebels, but it was not meant to be. His order to arrest the errant soldier had been ignored by the Magdalo rebels, and he was treated as a rather poor relation who had appeared on the doorstep uninvited. Perhaps desiring to leave the chilly climate in northern Cavite, Bonifacio had journeyed to the Magdiwang bastion of Novelita, where he was welcomed as a king and placed at the head of a parade as townspeople shouted, "Long live the ruler of the

Philippines!" Bonifacio took up residence in his supporters' territory; from that point on, the supposedly impartial leader showed a marked bias toward the Magdiwang faction.

At the Tejeros convention, the mood among the delegates was so tense that a recess was declared to keep the members from solving disputes with their revolvers. After tempers cooled, with Bonifacio presiding, the delegates voted to abolish the old Katipunan organization in favor of a new republican government. The estate house rang with the cheers of all who were present at this birth of the Republic of the Philippines.

Voting for officers took place. Elected president in absentia was Emilio Aguinaldo, whose victory over Bonifacio and Mariano Trias was loudly celebrated. Though a Magdiwang supporter suggested then that Bonifacio, as runner-up, be declared vice president, the will of the delegates was plainly with a popular vote. Bonifacio again lost, this time to Trias. In due time the positions of captain general and the directors of war, state, finance, justice, and the interior were filled, the last by Andres Bonifacio.

Then, at the instigation of a single Caviteno — a Magdalo follower grown haughty with victory, whose name was Daniel Tirona — a mortal rift was opened. Despite the popular election of Bonifacio, which should have been accepted with grace, Tirona stood and shouted, "The position of director of the interior is an exalted one and it is not right that a person without a lawyer's diploma should occupy it." Thus snubbing the former Manila slumboy, whose pride was great, Tirona called for a new vote for a Caviteno attorney, José del Rosario.

Only one person in the assembly paid any attention to Tirona: Andres Bonifacio. Everyone else ignored the breach. During a shouted exchange amid the milling crowd, Bonifacio demanded satisfaction; Tirona turned his back and began to melt away in the crowd. Enraged, Bonifacio produced a pistol and tried to shoot his detractor, but his hand was stilled by an onlooker. The delegates had begun to leave the hall. A frustrated Bonifacio stood, no longer a king but an insulted, impotent cabinet minister; determined somehow to have the last word, he screamed out over the tumult: "I, as chairman of this assembly, and as President of the Supreme Council of the Katipunan, as all of you do not deny, declare this assembly dissolved, and I annul all that has been approved and resolved."

With his men, he shouldered his way out of the hall.

The delegates at Tejeros, deciding to ignore the vanished Bonifacio and to pass over his protestations as merely pique, summoned Emilio Aguinaldo to come before them to take the oath of office. The general declined to leave the battlefield at Pasong Santal, for the Spanish were firing furiously at his men from a distance of two hundred yards. Only when his older brother Crispulo offered to relieve him did Don Emilio agree to leave his troops.

Upon his arrival at the estate house, Aguinaldo was mystified at being denied entrance by a guard; Bonifacio and his followers were now barring the delegates from their meeting place. The convention had removed to a church nearby, so it was by candlelight and before a crucifix that Aguinaldo and his ministers took their oaths on the evening of March 23.

One unpleasantness marred the event. General Artemio Ricarte, a stocky schoolteacher from Ilocos Sur province who had settled some years before in Cavite, had been elected captain general, but when it came time for him to be sworn in, he could not be found. After the ceremonies, someone spied Ricarte in the rear of the hall as he tried to slink out. With great acclaim, he was propelled through the crowd to stand before the newly installed *presidente*. When asked to take his oath, Ricarte demurred. He protested that it was too early to take oaths after what had transpired with Bonifacio.

After some arguing, another voice was heard, that of Daniel Tirona. He jeered that it was no use to discuss anything with Ricarte: "It is clear that he has compromised himself to someone else."

"I have made a promise to fight for the redemption of the Philippines," countered Ricarte, "but unlike you and others here, I have not made any promise to serve a person or persons belonging to only one province of the islands!" Amid angry mutterings, Ricarte knelt and swore his oath of office. Then, pleading dizziness, he left without saying good-bye.

"I was amazed at such behavior from a general of our army!" Aguinaldo confided later. He did not know at the time — and did not learn until two days later — that on the morning prior to the induction ceremony, Ricarte and forty-two other supporters of Bonifacio had met with the *supremo* and issued a resolution declaring the Tejeros election null and void. When he found out, Aguinaldo chose to ignore the action in the hope that tempers would cool with time. "I patiently accepted this difficult situation," he would say later, "so that petty jealousies and recriminations of brother against brother [could] be stopped."

Not long after he learned of this new wrinkle in his political troubles, Aguinaldo dispatched a large body of reinforcements to join the forces of his brother Crispulo. Only later did the news reach him that Bonifacio and Ricarte had intercepted these troops and ordered them

to protect Malabon, the town the *supremo* was in; as a consequence
of denying reinforcements to the beleaguered rebels at Pasong Santol, the Spaniards had overrun the village. Among those killed was
Crispulo Aguinaldo.

Bonifacio's countermanding of his orders and the subsequent death
of his brother were to Aguinaldo black spots in the history of their
struggle for independence, incidents he would never forget. The
grieving general traveled to Pasong Santol in a fruitless quest to recover his brother's body (which had been dumped into a mass grave
by the Spaniards); afterward, he rejoined his troops in Bayang Luma.
There, in battle, the charging Spaniards "fell like cards" before the
Filipinos' sturdy defense lines, though after several hours the rebels
were outmaneuvered and forced to retreat.

"Had the enemy pursued us, we could have been overtaken," wrote
Aguinaldo, "and surely I would have been placed in the iron cage
intended for me and left on the Luneta for the public to ridicule.
The enemy could have easily captured me because I could hardly
crawl on the rice paddies as my malaria fever which I acquired in
Bayang Luma was again sapping my vitality."

Through a feverish haze and occasional delirium that consigned
Aguinaldo to bed for several weeks, more and more bad news reached
him. It was enough to make him despair of ever reaching an agreement with the prideful *supremo*.

Contrary to promises he made, Bonifacio had pulled troops out of
Malabon and retreated south into Magdiwang territory, thereby
making it possible for the Spanish to roll down the Cavite coast and
gobble up the territory liberated by Aguinaldo and his comrades eight
months earlier. Bacoor and Aguinaldo's home town of Kawit were
burned to the ground; the Spaniards also occupied Novelita, Rosario, and San Francisco de Malabon. Then, Aguinaldo's delegation
under Colonel Agapito Bonzon returned from a conciliatory mission
to Bonifacio. They carried the *supremo*'s reply: Bonifacio said he had
been treated intolerably and planned to move to another province
where people would be glad to have him.

Then, on April 19, the recuperating Aguinaldo heard startling news
that got him out of bed and strapping on his revolver. A loyal major,
Lazaro Macapagal, rushed in to report that his unit had been detained at the headquarters of Bonifacio as it passed nearby. Macapagal had escaped, but not before learning that other companies in
Aguinaldo's command had also been assembled there, all without the
president's knowledge.

Taking Baldomero and Tomas Moscardo, both generals, and a

regiment of troops for safety, Aguinaldo approached the *supremo*'s *hacienda* that evening. His men surrounded the building. Though initially denied entrance by the guards, Aguinaldo wheedled his way past them and tiptoed to a place just outside the room where the *supremo* and his supporters were meeting. "How shocked I was upon seeing my favorite and best-loved generals — Pio del Pilar and Mariano Noriel — in the meeting," recalled Aguinaldo, but moments after he recognized them, he was discovered by Procopio Bonifacio, who had come up behind him in the dark hallway.

Procopio loudly announced that Aguinaldo was eavesdropping, bringing the meeting to a halt. The startled *supremo* feigned hospitality, asking him to join them. Aguinaldo declined: "If you really needed me in this meeting, you should have invited me." He excused himself and went downstairs. Unlocking a few doors at random, he found his sequestered soldiers and released them.

Ciriaco Bonifacio appeared with another invitation to the meeting in progress. Aguinaldo again went upstairs to say that he did not want to intrude on a private meeting. A few minutes after he left the building, Aguinaldo and his soldiers heard the sound of running feet. The Bonifacios and their men ran outside and in the darkness eluded the surrounding cordon of troops.

Rumors of betrayal, sedition, and lawlessness were left in the Bonifacios' wake as they fled to the barrio of Limbon, in the town of Indang. Some reports were true: they planned to go to the neighboring province of Batangas and set up their own revolutionary government, with Andres Bonifacio as president, and their own revolutionary army, with soldiers and weapons gathered "by persuasion or force." Aguinaldo's own errant generals, del Pilar and Noriel, who elected to stay behind, confessed they had been blinded by Bonifacio's promises and testified to his plans. Then news reached Aguinaldo that a handful of rebels from Bantangas had formally recognized Bonifacio as their leader. Though Bonifacio's repudiation of the revolutionary government could not be disputed, other stories floated about that were just gossip: that he had looted friendly towns and that he was secretly in the friars' employ.

Faced with a problem that had to be resolved, Aguinaldo ordered the Bonifacios arrested. On April 28, half a battalion of soldiers surrounded the dissidents' compound at Limbon. Colonel Agapito Bonzon had been explicitly instructed by Aguinaldo not to harm the soldiers; nonetheless, he fired upon the brothers, sparking a brief skirmish that left Ciriaco Bonifacio and two of Bonzon's men dead. The *supremo*'s arm was wounded, at which point Bonzon rushed up and cravenly stabbed him in the throat with his dagger. Despite this grave wound, Bonifacio lived. He was placed in a hammock, his brother Procopio was hog-tied, and his wife escaped assault at the hands of the brigand Bonzon only at the intercession of the colonel's own men.

The prisoners were conveyed to a military tribunal, where they were examined and confronted with the testimony of other witnesses; their subsequent trial has puzzled and bedeviled historians to this day. The prosecutors had, in addition to a wealth of circumstantial evidence, documents prepared by the *supremo* and his followers that utterly repudiated the legality of Aguinaldo's revolutionary government during wartime; further, Bonifacio had been anything but discreet in his denunciations to many people. This in itself would seem to have been enough to convict a defendant of sedition. To this could be added, certainly, many of Bonifacio's military decisions, which might have been seen as dereliction of duty.

Why, then, Filipino historians have repeatedly asked, was it necessary to pile up spurious charges on an already tight case? Why, then, did the Bonifacios receive a trial that, even under wartime conditions, would be considered a kangaroo court? Only the most partisan observer could deny the trial was legalistic overkill. The prosecutor's chief witness was drawn from Bonifacio's own camp; Lieutenant Colonel Pedro Giron seemed to have perjured himself in a number of ways, including his contention that the *supremo* offered him money to kill Aguinaldo. When Bonifacio demanded that Giron be produced to accuse him in person he was told the officer was dead — which was a lie. When Colonel Bonzon took the stand as arresting officer, he claimed the Bonifacios had fired first, which though not true was accepted as fact. Throughout the trial, the brothers received no adequate defense from their counselors, who plainly condemned them as much as their judges. The Bonifacios' main defense against the sedition charge was lukewarm and legalistic: they were "ignorant" of the government's legitimacy, they said, because they had repudiated it. They claimed they could not be guilty of conspiracy against an entity they felt did not exist.

Everyone could see that their denials held no force in the face of the guilt the court had decided was preordained. Andres and Procopio Bonifacio were condemned to die. Although Aguinaldo initially commuted their sentence to banishment, he was persuaded to rescind his order after strenuous lobbying by the two generals who had almost succumbed to the *supremo*'s temptations. Therefore, after the guilty and righteous generals del Pilar and Noriel had been joined in their denunciation by several of Bonifacio's deputies, who had scurried to cleave to the prevailing side, the commutation was withdrawn.

On May 10, 1897, the prisoners were escorted to a woody area near Mount Tala by a contingent of soldiers under Major Lazaro Macapagal. Andres Bonifacio still suffered from his wounds and was carried in a hammock, but when his brother was taken out of sight and shots rang out, the *supremo* tottered away into the trees. Macapagal and a few men followed, there were shots, and Andres Bonifacio fell dead. With the founder of the Katipunan martyred in the face of regionalism and personality politics that seemed to endanger the revolution, a part of the revolution he had helped spawn died also. It is tragic and beguiling to think what course the struggle might have taken had the rift between him and his Cavite protégé not opened.

By the time of Bonifacio's death, a change had been made in the colonial administration; Governor General Polavieja had retired from the field, pleading illness, to be replaced by Fernando Primo de Rivera, who had arrived in Manila on April 23. His declaration of a short amnesty was ignored by most Filipinos, so he unleashed his troops across Cavite. Aguinaldo and his soldiers were forced to retreat to the adjacent province of Batangas, and when subsequently pursued, the revolutionary leader slipped through the Spanish cordon by heading north with only five hundred troops. With much of his home province in ruins and under Spanish control, Aguinaldo took his family with him, for he had decided to flee to central Luzon, where his ally, General Mamerto Natividad, waited with his army.

The advent of the rainy season all but halted the hostilities. During the interim, the rebels established a republican government at a mountainous place in Bulacan province called Biaknabato, with Emilio Aguinaldo as president and Mariano Trias as vice president. Their secretary of the interior, Isabelo Artacho, drew up a provisional constitution based on one prepared by the Cubans at Jimagayu in 1895; it included a bill of rights guaranteeing freedom of religion, education, and the press. Shortly thereafter, Aguinaldo issued two manifestoes, written for him by General Natividad. The first echoed most of Bonifacio's earliest demands of the Katipunan: expulsion of the friars, press and speech freedoms, the restitution of land, parliamentary representation — with continued guerrilla war threatened if the demands were ignored. The second manifesto showed off Natividad's skills at their fieriest:

> On the inauguration of the second epoch of our struggle, from these mountains, ever faithful to our liberty and independence, we raise our

voices to all those in whose breasts beat noble hearts; to all those who have courage and honor, dignity and patriotism.

We make no racial discrimination; we call upon all who possess honor and the sense of personal dignity; the Filipino, the Asiatic, the American and the European all alike suffer; and we invite all those who suffer to aid in lifting up a fallen and tortured people, a country destroyed and sunken in the mire of debasement. . . .

To arms, noble hearts, to arms! Enough of suffering! . . . We fling back into their teeth the name which our enemies give us. We are the faithful sons, we who, scorning life and money, and comfort, we who, scorning all kinds of hardships, give our blood for the good of our country, for the welfare of our fellow-citizens and the redemption of our children.

Viva the free Philippines!

These were brave words, but a reconciliation of sorts was already in the making. In Manila, a Hispanicized Filipino attorney named Pedro A. Paterno approached the governor general with an offer to mediate. The *illustrado*'s offer was not altruistic; he had his eye on a Spanish dukedom and a reward and he also wanted a title for his brother, Maximo. He appeared at Aguinaldo's mountain retreat, regally borne on a hammock carried by servants, on August 9. During the next several months, Paterno traveled thus between Manila and Biaknabato as an agreement was hammered out. The negotiations were rife with tension, both between the arrogant Paterno and Aguinaldo and among members of the rebel camp. Aguinaldo's provincial host, General Natividad, bitterly opposed any resolution short of complete independence, but his voice was lost in November, when he was killed in a battle with the Spanish. The so-called Pact of Biaknabato was born.

An agreement in which neither party showed good faith could hardly be expected to last, but for the signatories it came at a crucial time. Rebel contingents across Luzon maintained their resistance against the Spanish troops, but their soldiers were becoming demoralized; some were even lured back into the colonial fold with promises of amnesty and future tax concessions. Those who remained committed to the revolution had to contend with declining stores of weapons. So far as Governor General Primo de Rivera was concerned, if the pact endured long enough for him to retire back to Madrid, victorious in halting a rebellion, its primary purpose would be served.

Under the terms of the agreement, Aguinaldo and nineteen associates agreed to be exiled to Hong Kong in return for the sum of eight hundred thousand pesos, to be paid in three installments — half upon leaving Biaknabato, one quarter upon the surrender of a certain number of weapons, and the remainder after the "Te Deum" was sung in the Manila cathedral and a general amnesty proclaimed. Spain additionally pledged to distribute nine hundred thousand pesos among the civilian victims of the war. Strangely, after so many revolutionary manifestoes crying for freedom, there was no mention of any Spanish reforms in the final agreement. Aguinaldo would soon claim that Primo de Rivera had reneged on his verbal assurances of freedom of the press and speech, the expulsion of the friars, the release of all political prisoners, and an end to banishment. But since the rebel leader was unable to secure a written promise from the governor general, some historians have suggested it is doubtful that Aguinaldo saw the agreement as anything other than the borrowing of time and the obtaining of funds to buy more guns and ammunition when the pact unraveled.

On December 27, 1897, Emilio Aguinaldo and his deputies ascended the gangplank of the British steamer *Uranus* in the Lingayen Gulf, and soon the ship was on its way toward the western horizon and the British Crown Colony of Hong Kong.

III

In early 1898 — at the same time that President William McKinley stepped up his pressure on the Spanish government, as the battleship *Maine* steamed toward Havana on its "friendly mission" and a battered young filibuster in Cuba named Funston recovered from his tropical illnesses — the signatories of the ill-fated Biaknabato Pact watched their agreement wither even before the echoes of the peace celebrations had completely died out.

Exiled to Hong Kong, Aguinaldo deposited the government's four hundred thousand pesos in a bank, sternly informing his deputies that the principal would remain untouched while the rebels bided their time, living on the interest, to see what would happen at home. Resistance by the rebels remaining in the islands continued in a decentralized fashion, and many of the weapons surrendered to the colonial government were, contrary to the terms of the agreement, ancient, rusty, and inoperable. No relaxation of Spanish rule was apparent; indeed, arrests of Filipinos began to increase.

In Hong Kong, the exiles were reunited with others in the city's Filipino community who had been called the Hong Kong junta by the Biaknabato government. Even while Aguinaldo and Paterno were negotiating the pact, the junta had been attempting to forge a foreign alliance that would enable the revolution to continue. Felipe Agoncillo, an associate of Aguinaldo and the junta's leader, had approached the American consul, Rounseville Wildman, in October and November with the offer of an "offensive and defensive alliance" in the event of a war between Spain and the United States. Agoncillo had asked for twenty thousand stands of arms and a like number of ammunition rounds. He proposed putting up two provinces and the Manila Custom House as security, but after conferring with Washington, Wildman turned down the strange proposal. Other members of the junta next suggested approaching Japan for protection, an idea turned down by the majority, including Aguinaldo, all of whom believed that they could recover their country if the U.S. Navy would only prevent Madrid from sending reinforcements to the Philippines. Throughout February 1898, rumors and news bulletins gave the rebels hope that a Spanish-American war was imminent. The following month they heard the first concrete word that an alliance with the Americans might come to pass.

The Filipinos were elated at the sudden arrival of the U.S.S. *Petrel*, whose skipper, Captain Wood, had been sent to find Emilio Aguinaldo. During the course of several conferences in March and April, Wood urged Aguinaldo to return to the Philippines and reassemble his army; with American arms and advice he could help liberate the country. Naturally cautious, Aguinaldo inquired what intentions the Americans had toward the Philippines. "The United States, my general, is a great and rich nation," replied Wood, "and neither needs nor desires colonies." This sounded fine to Aguinaldo, but he wondered if such a promise might be made in writing. Wood, suddenly demure, responded that only Commodore Dewey could speak for the government.

A pesky matter of legalities intervened, bringing the discussions to an abrupt halt. Some months before, the members of the Biaknabato cabinet who had not been exiled to Hong Kong demanded a share of the Spanish payoff. Primo de Rivera complied by giving them the second payment of two hundred thousand pesos. One rebel minister had not been present to receive "his" part of that money: Isabelo Artacho, the interior minister. In a maneuver that might have been encouraged by the Spanish governor general, Artacho traveled to Hong Kong, where he brazenly and selfishly demanded two hundred thousand pesos from Aguinaldo for "services rendered" to the revolution. *El presidente* was so infuriated to learn that his ministers at home had conspired to keep the money intended to finance the renewed revolution that he deposed them. Artacho, however, was close at hand and proved to be unshakable; he filed suit for the money in the Hong Kong Superior Court. Aguinaldo was forced to flee the port under an assumed name to escape subpoena.

Along with an aide, Colonel Gregorio del Pilar, and his secretary, Lieutenant José Leyba, Aguinaldo slipped out of Hong Kong on April 7, traveling by ship to Saigon and Singapore, where he arrived on April 23. *El presidente* lodged at the house of a fellow countryman, Dr. Isidoro de Santos, but his disguise was penetrated in only four hours. A wealthy English planter named Howard Bray appeared at the doctor's door, asking for Don Emilio. He was turned away. The following day he reappeared, this time assuring the servants that he was no process server but a man who had lived for many years in the Philippines and who sympathized with the revolutionaries' goals. Bray added that he had been sent by the American consul general in Singapore to set up a meeting with Aguinaldo. This news admitted Bray to Aguinaldo's presence.

The meeting with the American diplomat, E. Spencer Pratt, was held in a Singapore public house; Aguinaldo recalled that they met in a "cloak and dagger atmosphere."

With Howard Bray interpreting, Consul General Pratt suggested an alliance. "As of the other day, April 19th, Spain and America have been at war," he told Aguinaldo, who was completely taken aback. "Now is the time for you to strike. Ally yourselves with America and you will surely defeat the Spaniards!"

Still overwhelmed at the mention of war, Aguinaldo remained silent.

"America will help you," said Pratt, "if you will help America."

"What can we expect to gain from helping America?"

"America will give you much greater liberty and much more material benefits than the Spaniards ever promised you."

Aguinaldo wondered aloud if such an alliance could be honored with a written document stating the terms and promises. The consul general hedged; only Dewey could sign such an instrument, he said. But, he went on, "you need not have any worry about America. The American Congress and President have just made a solemn declaration disclaiming any desire to possess Cuba and promising to leave the country to the Cubans after having driven away the Spaniards and pacified the country. As in Cuba, so in the Philippines. Even more so, if possible. Cuba is at our door while the Philippines is ten thousand miles away!"

Aguinaldo was elated. He replied that if Dewey would honor him with an official invitation, confirming Pratt's assurances, he would return to the Philippines "and fight side by side with the Americans."

At noon the following day, Consul General Pratt sent the Englishman to fetch Aguinaldo to his residence at the stately Raffles Hotel. When he arrived, Aguinaldo saw that Pratt held in his hand a telegram from Dewey. It said, simply, SEND AGUINALDO AT ONCE, but Pratt enthusiastically extemporized on that minimal theme. He told *el presidente* that Dewey said the United States "would at least recognize the independence of the Philippines under the protection of the U.S. Navy." There would be no need for a formal agreement, he assured the young Filipino, for the word of a commodore and an American consul was equivalent to the most solemn pledge.

"If I can secure arms," said Aguinaldo, "I promise you that my people will rise as one man against the Spaniards." Pratt volunteered to help the rebels secure guns; he asked that in return they appoint him as their representative in the United States, a favor the grateful Aguinaldo promised to take up with his government.

The three Filipinos sailed from Singapore on the night of April 25, reaching Hong Kong early in the morning of May 1. They were chagrined when no one from Dewey's squadron was there to meet them; Dewey had already sailed for Manila Bay to sink the Spanish fleet. This Aguinaldo learned from Consul Wildman, who thought that the commodore would surely send a cutter back for his illustrious new ally.

While he waited for news from Manila, Aguinaldo wasted no time. He paid Wildman fifty thousand pesos for two thousand rifles, two hundred thousand rounds of ammunition, and a launch for traveling between islands in the archipelago. They would be delivered in due time.

On May 7, the revenue cutter *McCulloch* arrived in Hong Kong, breaking the gathering tension with news of Dewey's gallant victory; Aguinaldo and his staff prepared to sail. *El presidente* handed over another sixty-seven thousand pesos to Wildman for more arms — items that never arrived and that were never accounted for by Wildman. But, blissfully unaware of this and everything else except the warm glow of a revolution that they seemed sure to win, Aguinaldo and seventeen associates boarded the *McCulloch* on the night of May 16, escorted by Wildman and the U.S. minister to Siam, John Barrett. The two diplomats waved encouragingly as the little boat puttered off toward the Philippines.

"It was past noon on May 19 when the *McCulloch* dropped anchor in Manila Bay," remembered Aguinaldo.

Almost immediately, the Admiral's launch carrying his adjutant and private secretary came alongside to convey me to Dewey who was waiting on his flagship. Accompanied by Colonel Del Pilar and Lieutenant Leyba, I boarded the launch and in no time I was being piped over the *Olympia* and being greeted cordially by the Admiral himself. I was given the honors due a general officer. . . . Ushering us to his private quarters, he was effusive with hospitality and cordiality. He might well be, with his Manila Bay victory and immediate promotion to Rear Admiral — and the prospect of getting the Filipinos as allies.

What took place during that and subsequent meetings is rife with controversy. According to Aguinaldo's notes, Dewey told him that "the United States had come to the Philippines to free the Filipinos from the yoke of Spain," that it needed no colonies, and that "the Filipinos and Americans should act toward one another as friends and allies." The admiral offered sixty-two captured Mauser rifles, all the guns seized from the destroyed Spanish warships, and thousands of rounds of ammunition to seal their bargain; he also promised to send a steamer to pick up the first shipment of arms bought through Consul Wildman.

Again Aguinaldo asked if such an alliance could be sealed in writing. The benevolent, patriarchal seaman smiled gently in answer. He pointed out that Aguinaldo's own pact with the Spanish had been documented in such a fashion, though it held no force; "the word of honor of Americans," Aguinaldo recalled being told, "was more positive, more irrevocable, than a written agreement."

As the impressionable — or gullible — young revolutionary learned after it was too late, Dewey, Pratt, and Wildman categorically denied that any promises regarding independence, or independence under a protectorate, were ever made. However, it is significant that none voiced any corrective words as Aguinaldo reorganized his army, drove the Spaniards into tenuous sactuary in Manila's Intramuros, and issued numerous proclamations extolling independence and the great alliance with the United States. Only later — with legions of American soldiers landing in the country — did America's real intentions emerge, and with them the resolute but nonetheless hollow denials from the admiral and the two diplomats. Somehow their promises had been misconstrued as genuine, they said. The naive young Filipino firebrand, the "Malay adventurer," could hardly be believed when disputing the word of an American gentleman.

"Go ashore and start your army," the admiral had told Aguinaldo, and to the leader's delight there was no lack of volunteers. The Hong Kong junta, learning of Dewey's plans to sail for Manila, had had the foresight to send along two of its number with a proclamation. The text had galvanized all who read it:

> COMPATRIOTS: Divine Providence is about to place independence within our reach, and in a way the most free and independent nation could hardly wish for. The Americans, not from mercenary motives, but for the sake of humanity and the lamentations of so many persecuted people, have considered it opportune to extend their protecting mantle to our beloved country, now that they have often obligated to sever relations with Spain, owing to the tyranny this nation is exercising in Cuba, causing enormous injury to the Americans, who have such large commercial and other interests there.
>
> At the present moment an American squadron is preparing to sail for the Philippines. . . . The Americans will attack by sea and prevent any reinforcements coming from Spain. . . . There, where you see the American flag flying, assemble in numbers; they are our redeemers.

In the few heady weeks after Aguinaldo's triumphant return to his homeland, proclamation after proclamation blossomed forth. "The great North American nation, the cradle of genuine liberty," enthused Aguinaldo, "has come to us manifesting a protection as decisive as it is undoubtedly disinterested toward our inhabitants, considering us sufficiently civilized and capable of governing for ourselves our unfortunate country." He made it plain that all foreigners — including the Chinese and Spanish — were to be protected, that his men should harm no prisoners or property, with any infractions such as murder, rape, or robbery punishable by death.

Soon Aguinaldo's fresh and eager troops had cleared Cavite province, all but surrounding Manila. By June 30, nearly every province in Luzon was under revolutionary control; some nine thousand Spanish prisoners of war would soon be held under strictly humanitarian conditions. But by then things had begun to crumble, much like an old building will begin with a piece of cornice falling or a crack appearing in the masonry. Nearly delirious with joy, the Filipinos proclaimed their independence on June 12, complete with a Declaration of Independence written by one Ambrosio Bautista, who based it on the American document. Strangely enough, Admiral Dewey, the ally and protector of Aguinaldo, did not deign to attend; it was "mail day," he said, and he would be too busy. No other invited American dignitaries appeared either, though *el presidente* did find an American colonel who agreed to sign the declaration alongside the ninety-seven Filipino signatures.

Several weeks later, the first contingent of American troop ships steamed past Aguinaldo's headquarters at Cavite and came to anchor. What was the young leader supposed to infer from this? He met General Thomas M. Anderson, the first of three senior commanders whose dignity and status and age awed Aguinaldo to the point of his being blind to their patronizing. On July 4, a day of no little historical significance, Anderson assured him that the United States had "entire sympathy and most friendly sentiments for the native people" and wanted "most amiable relations" with the revolutionaries. Nonetheless, *el presidente* could hardly avoid being suspicious, seeing transports teeming with American might, and pointedly asked if the United States intended to hold his country as a dependency. Anderson's reply fell upon ears that wanted to hear soothing words. There had never been a colonial dependency in all of America's history, Anderson intoned, and Aguinaldo, relieved, confided that in his careful study of the U.S. Constitution, he could find no authority for seizing colonies.

Before the end of July, General Wesley Merritt arrived to take charge of the growing number of American troops. He began with a series of curt orders for the revolutionaries to give way. Aguinaldo's pathetic counterdemands were glibly answered by Merritt, who told him to trust "the good will and the sense of justice of the American people." But, *el presidente* wondered, when was the justice going to begin? He had interposed fourteen thousand troops between the hostile Spanish and the Americans, saving untold American lives at the cost of many of his own men, and his thanks had been rude commands to step aside to allow the Americans to make the final assault on Manila. The revolutionaries, thus denied their rightful share of the victory, began to grumble; their bitterness rose to the point where it began to deafen all reason. With the arrival of Merritt's successor, General Elwell S. Otis, arrogant orders were issued to displace the Filipino columns. Once, after Otis issued one of his "requests," Aguinaldo complied by ordering General Mariano Noriel to move his headquarters from a forward position in Pasay to Makati in the rear. Noriel was crushed but reluctantly obeyed. When he saw the Americans replacing the Filipino flags over the trenches with their own, he turned to Aguinaldo almost in tears. "Look, general," he said, "look what they are doing! If we don't look out, they will be replacing our flags with their own all over the country!"

"You are being tragic," replied Aguinaldo. "They're our allies, always remember that!" But there was no force in his words. With each embarrassing concession, Aguinaldo attempted to save face, but there was no way to avoid the sinking feeling that he had lost control, that perhaps martyrdom of one sort or another was truly his fate, and more poignant, perhaps that was also the destiny of his new nation.

Hoping in his fatalistic way that if he demonstrated the Filipinos' capacity for self-government, their cause would attract sympathy and they would be left alone, Aguinaldo busied himself with preparations for a constitutional convention, to start in Malolos on September 15. He leaned heavily on a new councilor, Apolinario Mabini, who from outward appearances seemed to be anything but a revolutionary theorist.

Mabini was thirty-four and sickly — paralyzed from the waist down and confined to an invalid chair. When Aguinaldo had first met him on the eve of their day of independence, Mabini had been carried in a hammock to the chief's presence. He looked too frail to live through the next few months, but his firmness of voice convinced Aguinaldo to make him his most trusted adviser, for his reputation for brilliance had preceded him. Mabini had been born into an impoverished Batangas family, but his scholarly talents raised him out of his desperate circumstances. He had studied at San Juan de Tomas in 1894, intending thereafter to use his education to defend the poor. Drawn easily into the nationalist movement, he had worked in Rizal's prototype reform organization, the Liga Filipina, and had been briefly jailed by the Spanish. Then, with the revolution in its first phase, Mabini had been stricken with what seems to have been infantile paralysis, but the resulting infirmity had, if anything, sharpened his zeal.

On their first meeting, the paralytic was appalled to learn that Aguinaldo had secured no written agreement from any of the Americans. Despite the gnawing worry that they were operating fruitlessly and without protection, Mabini's advice was that "the first duty of the government [was] to interpret faithfully the popular will." It was perhaps comforting for them to busy themselves with cleaning and straightening their house — something over which they had power — even in the dawning realization that it was being stolen from under their noses, and in more ways than one.

The Malolos Congress convened with Aguinaldo's call for "the Philippines for the Filipinos." The populist philosophy hammered out so carefully by Mabini (with a great deal of inspiration from the eighteenth-century French philosophes and the American federalists) was adopted by his chief. But their plans were sabotaged at the start by Aguinaldo's naiveté. He had worked for months to court the wealthy, Hispanicized Filipinos, the *illustrados*. *El presidente* was, despite his charisma and military skills, still a provincial farmboy and merchant at heart, and he thought the *illustrados* would add a veneer of culture and learning to his government, thereby making it like the "best" elements of Western governments. Nearly all the *illustrados* had

sneered at the revolutionaries in 1896 and were outright collaborators; these wealthy Filipinos, headed by Pedro Paterno, worked to
capture the revolution before their security was threatened by the
"rabble" elements represented by Apolinario Mabini.

During the course of the Malolos Congress, any hope for an egal-
itarian government was ended during the writing of the Constitution. Crafted by an *illustrado,* Felipe Calderon, it did guarantee basic
freedoms, but it also ensured a weakened presidency and limited
suffrage, which was extended to only the landed gentry. Aguinaldo
would be proclaimed president, with Mabini as premier, but the posts
had been stripped of their power. At the end of the convention,
though Aguinaldo could say proudly that "the Republic we established was the first crystallization of democracy in all the east," the
revolution was doomed.

The nightmare continued — seeming to predict a gloomy future,
not only for the Filipinos' government, but for the existence of independence itself. For a few months after Independence Day, Philippine vessels flying the flag of the republic plied the waters of Manila Bay. They were accorded the rights and responsibilities of any
national fleet and received salutes from American men-of-war. Then
Admiral Dewey grew impatient with the mosquito fleet's presump-
tuousness. He ordered two Filipino gunboats seized for flying "unauthorized" colors and confiscated their guns and flags; he threatened to "blow them to pieces" if they crossed his path again. When
a delegation of Filipino captains went to protest this treatment, Dewey
told them their flag was "a piece of bunting" of about the same worth
as "a yacht pennant." The admiral saw one Filipino officer muttering
under his breath; he insisted upon hearing a translation. "He said he
will get even with you," said the interpreter. Dewey had the officer
tossed from the *Olympia*'s main deck into the harbor.

Meanwhile, American troop ships kept arriving and tensions rose
between the two armies; only great restraint on the part of the
Americans and Filipinos alike averted bloodshed. Hoping to hold his
troops back through will alone and to cement the different factions
of his government by the sheer force of personality, Emilio Aguinaldo continued to pray, passively, that some outward force, or fate,
would intervene on his behalf. Aware that Washington and Madrid
were holding peace talks in France, he directed Felipe Agoncillo to
go to Paris to give the Filipinos' side of the story. Agoncillo had no
better luck in Paris than he had had in Washington; the talks concluded as if the Filipinos did not exist.

There was one chance remaining: whether the American Congress would ratify the treaty or repudiate it, a decision the Filipinos hoped would be affected by a burgeoning anti-imperialist movement within the United States.

Upon Dewey's victory in Manila Bay, only a few dissenting American voices had been heard in the resulting ferocious gush of nationalism. The first to brave the tide were two men: Moorfield Storey, a Boston attorney and reformer, and the German refugee-reformer Senator Carl Schurz. Then, at a mass meeting in Boston's Faneuil Hall on June 15, 1898, the New England Anti-Imperialist League was born; under the direction of Storey and others like the businessman Edward Atkinson, it struck responsive chords outside the northeastern states, causing it to take a less regional name. As the Anti-Imperialist League, with chapters in most major American cities, the group attracted some twenty-five thousand members by late 1898. It would ultimately swell to three times that number. Though the membership of old abolitionists, reformers, Republican Mugwumps, Democrats, Populists, and labor organizers hardly had the strength to sway many elections, still, they had a disproportionate influence across the country. As the historian Stuart Creighton Miller said, the roster of anti-imperialists read "like a combination of the *Social Register* and *Who's Who in America*." There were politicians, such as former President Grover Cleveland, House Speaker Thomas B. Reed, former Treasury Secretary George S. Boutwell, Senators George F. Hoar, Benjamin Tillman, R. F. Pettigrew, and J. B. Weaver, and Democratic presidential hopeful William Jennings Bryan (who would soon begin to wander away from the fold). There were educators, such as Yale's William Graham Sumner, Harvard's Charles W. Eliot, John Fiske, Charles Eliot Norton, and William James, and Columbia's Felix Adler, Frederick W. Starr, and John Burgess. And there were writers, such as Edgar Lee Masters, Mark Twain, Edwin Arlington Robinson, William Dean Howells, Ambrose Bierce, Lincoln Steffens, Finley Peter Dunne, and William Vaughn Moody. Even such diverse figures as the reformer Jane Addams, labor leader Samuel Gompers, and the industrialist Andrew Carnegie were united, at least, in their denunciation of the government's developing foreign policy.

Despite the eminence of the anti-imperialists, their influence could go only so far, for the McKinley administration claimed it could match them writer for writer and educator for educator; in Washington, where policies were made, dissenting voices could be quieted by political pressure or name-calling. Indeed, words such as "traitor" and "sedition" began to be bandied about, increasing in direct proportion to the number of weeks before the Senate vote on McKinley's Treaty of Paris. "Whatever may be thought of the judgement and

motives of the Boston school of national slanderers," the editors of
the *Boston Times-Herald* would write in a typical broadside somewhat
later in the fray, "there can be no doubt as to the treasonable nature
of their acts." About the same time, the *Philadelphia Press* wondered:
"What would have happened during the Civil War if a public meeting had been held . . . to cheer Jeff Davis and denounce Lincoln as
a murderer?" Of course, no reasonable thinker would try to compare the War Between the States with the War to Extend Anglo-Saxon
Progress and Decency (as Funston and Roosevelt were wont to call
it), but to the minority of Americans attending protest meetings,
writing broadsides, and lobbying their elected officials against taking
that distant archipelago, there seemed to be a scarcity of reasonable
thinkers across the land — especially in the Senate. In that august
chamber, the debate over McKinley's Paris Treaty began in January
1899. Felipe Agoncillo scurried from office to office in Washington,
submitting memorials and documents in a vain effort to influence the
vote. Meanwhile, in the Philippines, Manila seemed like a powder keg
about to blow.

Emilio Aguinaldo was coming to the end of his patience. In Manila,
handbills and posters had appeared overnight trumpeting Mc-
Kinley's strange, almost laughable words about "benevolent assimilation," which apparently were too direct for Governor General Otis;
he rewrote and toned down the American president's language so
the Filipinos would be deceived into thinking they still had a chance
to prevail. This doctored proclamation had been torn down and
trampled by patriotic Filipinos, whose rage was then doubled a few
days later when McKinley's original document was inadvertently
smuggled out of Iloilo to the capital. Aguinaldo's response was to denounce the Americans as the "true oppressors of nations and the
tormentors of mankind." He stated categorically that he had never
recognized the sovereignty of the United States. "My government is
disposed to open hostilities if the American troops attempt to take
forcible possession," he said, ending with the dark words: "upon their
heads be all the blood which may be shed." It was the Americans'
turn to deface and tear down a proclamation on the streets of Manila.

The war of words did not last much longer. On January 16, Admiral Dewey shifted the anchorages of his warships so that they
flanked the Filipino positions on the periphery of Manila. Some observers on land might have noticed that the ships' crews were no longer
attired in their dress whites but in their combat khakis. Apparently
the significance of this was missed by the Filipinos.

Five days later, General Otis moved a unit of the Nebraska volunteer regiment to an area called Santa Mesa, a high protuberance of land bordered on three sides by the meandering confluence of the San Juan and Pasig rivers. It also gave the volunteers a clear sight into the Filipino trenches, squeezing the unfortunate revolutionaries between the Nebraskans and a Washington regiment. Aguinaldo protested this move "one and a thousand times," and he was certainly not mollified by Otis's bland assurance that he needed the area "for sanitary reasons only," for soon the Nebraskans were joined by an artillery battery that happened to be aimed directly into the Filipino trenches.

By the end of January, a steady stream of refugees was pouring out of Manila, choking the roads leading north in barefoot chaos. Of the Filipinos who remained, a few were secretly organized into a "fifth column" of sorts, with instructions from their chief to fight fiercely with their bolos and staves should war break out. (Most of these fighters were shot or imprisoned a few days later.) Outside the city limits, Aguinaldo's ill-armed, untrained troops stuck to their positions ringing the capital.

On February 2, General Otis fired all the Filipino workers from their jobs behind the American lines. He ordered his troops to maintain a "full alert" and warned Admiral Dewey that the time was nearly upon them. Then Otis sent a message to Aguinaldo. It called for vigilance in keeping the peace.

Perhaps the general's words lulled the Filipino into a false sense of security. Aguinaldo and all his officers made plans to travel the 25 miles north to Malolos on February 4, leaving their posts in charge of subordinates. They planned to celebrate the formal adoption of the Philippine republic's constitution with an unparalleled patriotic convocation. A lavish ball would follow. Tailors and seamstresses worked overtime to prepare properly elaborate costumes for the officers and politicians and their wives and sweethearts.

The night before the Malolos ball was to occur, the Americans in Manila placed a sentry detail at a post near the Santa Mesa position recently vacated by the Filipinos. The post was in a disputed area called the pipeline, where earlier attempts to irritate or nudge the Filipinos had provoked shouting matches between the two camps. On this occasion, however, the American sentry detail was ordered to shoot any intruders.

At half-past eight on the night of February 4, while the Philippine commanders were forgetting their troubles in Malolos, Private William Grayson of Company B, First Nebraska Volunteers, strolled through the darkness near the Santa Mesa pipeline. Nearby was his friend Private Miller. Suddenly, four figures loomed out of the night. "Halt!" Grayson ordered. The strangers were Filipinos, for one of them mimicked the private's words: "Halto!" They may have been drunk.

"I challenged with another 'Halt,' " Grayson testified later.

> Then he immediately shouted "Halto" to me. Well, I thought the best thing to do was shoot him. He dropped. Then two Filipinos sprang out of the gateway about fifteen feet from us. I called "Halt" and Miller fired and dropped one. I saw that another was left. Well, I think I got my second Filipino that time. We retreated to where six other fellows were and I said, "Line up fellows; the niggers are in here all through these yards."

Almost immediately, a line of rifle fire erupted along the entire American line, soon to be joined by the army and navy heavy artillery. The war had begun.

"Armageddon was loose," Aguinaldo recalled, "against our desires and in spite of our earnest and sincere efforts to befriend America." Thunderstruck when their party was interrupted with news of the fighting, the officers hurried back to Manila at first light on Sunday, February 5, but by then the American artillery had scattered the panicky Filipino troops. Then the overeager volunteers began to chase and slaughter them. The toll of dead that day was some three thousand Filipinos — and sixty Americans.

Under a flag of truce, a Filipino staff officer appeared at General Otis's command post with a message from Aguinaldo. The shooting had commenced despite the president's orders, he said. Don Emilio wished to end hostilities and create a neutral zone between the two armies "wide enough so that accidental contact would be impossible." Otis haughtily replied that "the fighting having begun must go on to the grim end."

When he heard the American's reply, Aguinaldo knew they were at bay. "We had no honorable course but to resist," he would write, "and sell our lives dearly."

IV

"On the night of February 4th, two days before the U.S. Senate approved the treaty," claimed Secretary of War Elihu Root in the only version of the story the world would know for some eighteen months, "an army of Tagalogs, a tribe inhabiting the central part of Luzon, under the leadership of Aguinaldo, a Chinese half-breed, attacked, in vastly superior numbers, our little army in the possession of Manila, and after a desperate and bloody fight was repulsed in every direction."

Leaving aside the truth of who had attacked whom, it was true that with some sixteen thousand armed soldiers in battle, the American army was outnumbered by the Filipino strength of eighty thousand, but the revolutionaries were scattered across the islands, with only half of them armed with rifles. The Filipinos had no artillery save a few untrustworthy Spanish cannon, which fired solid shot. Most of the soldiers did not know how to use their rifle sights, consequently firing so inaccurately that it became a joke among the Americans that their enemy could hit nothing unless they used their rifles as clubs. Against the Americans' well-coordinated and rehearsed attack plan, the Filipinos had only the most general ideas about strategy — ideas that had done wonders with the Spaniards but countered the new enemy only sporadically.

As the Americans' three-pronged maneuver cut Aguinaldo's forces in half, pushing them north and south of Manila, it seemed to Aguinaldo that "the original beachhead begged from us was expanding like an explosion." Soon reinforcements arrived from the United States "in torrents," bringing American troop strength to more than one hundred thousand. "As we yielded ground, we moved our government farther north behind our crumbling lines," Aguinaldo remembered.

The outcome of the war seemed to rest on one gifted — but supremely flawed — general, Antonio Luna. Of Ilocano forebears, he had been born into a cultured family and studied at two Manila universities before becoming a pharmacist. In this genteel social niche, Luna identified with the complacent upper class to such an extent that he denounced the Katipunan in 1896, becoming an informer; it was later said that on his testimony, José Rizal and other prominent moderates were executed. The colonial governor rewarded him with "banishment" to Spain — hardly terrible in comparison to the draconian punishments meted out to other Filipinos in 1896.

In Spain, Luna studied military tactics; after the outbreak of the Spanish-American War, he began his long journey home. Stopping in Hong Kong, he procured a recommendation from Felipe Agoncillo; on the strength of this and his newfound military knowledge, Aguinaldo made Luna a brigadier general and director of war in September 1898. He was ultimately promoted to commander in chief of central Luzon, a position that helped bind Aguinaldo's southern Luzon men to Ilocanos like Luna, who, though a product of Manila, still had regional ties in the north.

Luna was "a fiery and fanatical commander," in Aguinaldo's words, but his effectiveness as a leader was crippled by a ferocious temper. He had labored long and hard to instill discipline in his army of peasants, but the outbreak of war intervened before he could mold them sufficiently. After the town of Caloocan had fallen to the Kansas volunteers, Luna led a column back to try to retake Manila. During the fighting, he ordered a Kawit battalion to replace a unit that had grown too exhausted to fight. Regionalism — which was forever rearing its ugly head among the Filipinos at the worst possible moments — intervened. The Kawit officer, Captain Pedro Janolino, refused to commit his men, claiming he had been instructed to obey only Aguinaldo. Infuriated, Luna disarmed the Kawit soldiers and sent them to Malolos for punishment. Days later, he learned that Aguinaldo had reinstated the soldiers. Luna angrily submitted his resignation.

Aguinaldo maintained his support of his Kawit men. Then Premier Mabini interceded, worried about their unsteady best general; though the paralytic agreed that some discipline was necessary lest the morale of the entire army suffer, he argued that Luna was "a despot" who had committed abuses against his men, against civilians — and even against the government — by issuing extrajurisdictional orders that threatened overall stability. Mabini saw Luna's resignation as an opportunity to get someone else they could depend on. *El presidente,* in awe of his temperamental general, ignored Mabini's counsel. He was able to convince Luna to remain at his post, not fully aware that for Antonio Luna, any insult rankled beneath his skin and was never fully forgotten.

Subject to frustrated rages at his soldiers' lack of professionalism, the self-taught general rode them too hard and easily lost sight of the larger picture. During the defense of Malolos, Luna withdrew two battalions from the firing line at Bagbag to discipline a subordinate, General Tomas Mascardo. Luna's officers warned him this was a mistake, for the maneuver left a large breach in the line, but Luna did not heed them. While he was gone, MacArthur's troops poured through the opening, causing a general Filipino retreat. This led directly to the fall of Malolos on March 1.

With its army in tatters, the Philippine republic's government was becoming bitterly divided, but for political — not military — reasons.

One month after the shooting started, an American peace commission landed at Manila armed with McKinley's instructions to seek "the humane, pacific and effective extension of authority" and to "secure with the least possible delay the benefits of a wise and generous protection of life and property." Two members of the peace commission were already familiar names in Luzon: Admiral George Dewey and General Elwell S. Otis. Presumably the other members were expected to supply the wisdom and reason. Jacob Gould Schurman, the president of Cornell University and head of the commission, was the single voice of anti-imperialism. Dean Conant Worcester, an anthropologist from the University of Michigan, had spent several years studying the non-Christian tribes in the Philippines, and he viewed all Filipinos with a combination of disdain and scientific detachment; he favored annexation. Charles Denby, a former minister to China, was also an enthusiastic imperialist. Despite their general agreement with Otis, as commander of the military, he said he would brook little interference from the Schurman Commission.

Word of their desire for the islands' future, however, filtered across the blasted battlegrounds to San Isidro, where Aguinaldo and his Malolos cabinet had established themselves. The Americans proposed something they called autonomy, which included some few freedoms but no independence. Aguinaldo and Mabini immediately denounced the Schurman Commission's proposal as insulting, but a time bomb built into the Philippine Constitution was ticking away, waiting to blast their hopes and expectations.

The Malolos Congress reconvened. It was fully controlled by *illustrados* such as Pedro Paterno and Felipe Buencamino and began with a shocking lack of a quorum: only twenty out of a hundred members were present. The congress voted for the cessation of war and the acceptance of peace under autonomy — which of course held the promise of the resumption of profitable lives for the attorneys and merchants of the *illustrado* class. President and premier were thus made fully aware of how little power they held. In the end, one resigned and one gave in.

Mabini argued that "since war is the last resource that is left to us for the salvation of our country and our own national honor, let us fight while a grain of strength is left us." The packed congress answered by calling for his resignation; he was replaced by Pedro Paterno, the sleek attorney who as premier took control of a cabinet that was then reorganized and packed with *illustrados* like Buencamino, who became interior minister.

Emilio Aguinaldo had agreed with Mabini, but his weakness before those more sophisticated and educated won out again. He acceded to the prevailing *illustrados*, retaining an optimism not warranted by the events.

Their political troubles were not over, for who should appear at Aguinaldo's side but the mercurial Antonio Luna, whose energetic call to resist the Paterno clique went unheeded by the conciliatory *presidente.* At the end of a long debate about accepting the Americans' offer, General Luna lost his temper and the debate descended into a personal argument. He told Buencamino that he was no better than his son, whom Luna said had shown cowardice in battle. The suave Buencamino replied by reminding Luna that his withdrawal of the troops at Bagbag had caused an even greater defeat. Stung, Luna slapped Buencamino hard, knocking him down, and would have thrown himself upon the others if Aguinaldo had not restrained him.

Several days later, Luna slyly ordered his soldiers to arrest most of the cabinet on the charge of treason without informing his commander in chief. Aguinaldo soon learned that Paterno and the others were behind bars, and though he promised Luna that he would "investigate" the general's complaint, sending him back to his men at the front, Aguinaldo released the prisoners. He would learn that they, too, knew how to harbor grudges.

On June 4, while General Luna was at his headquarters at Bayambang, Pangasinan, he received a telegram summoning him to Cabanatuan for a conference. The message bore Aguinaldo's name. Luna departed immediately with an aide and some soldiers, arriving at the newly established seat of government the following day.

The general entered the convent that Aguinaldo had made his home and office. He startled the sentry, who was attached to the very Kawit battalion that Luna had disarmed and tried to punish some four months earlier. The nonplussed sentry apparently failed either to salute or present arms, for Luna slapped him across the face, shouting, "Don't you know what you are doing?" Grumbling, the general proceeded upstairs to his chief's office.

Instead of Aguinaldo, the general beheld Felipe Buencamino, which filled him with hatred and rage. They began arguing when Luna was informed that *el presidente* had left that morning for troop inspection in San Isidro and Tarlac. "Why call for me when he could not keep his appointment?" Luna shouted, and, characteristically, he began to berate Buencamino and insult, perhaps threaten, *el presidente.*

Suddenly, the two heard a rifle shot outside. Luna turned his back on the minister and rushed down to investigate. At the bottom of the stairs he encountered Captain Pedro Janolino, the insubordinate Kawit officer, and the ugly and frustrating memory of Janolino's escape from punishment made Luna almost froth with anger. "You fools," he screamed in the enclosed space in which they stood, "don't you know how to handle a rifle?"

Fearing that the general would harm him, Janolino pulled out his bolo and slashed him across the head. Other soldiers from the Kawit battalion appeared and, seeing Luna reeling from the blow, crowded in to stab and fire at him. Luna staggered outside, hissing "Cowards! Assassins!" and fell in a heap in the convent yard. His aide ran toward him but was shot down. Still muttering his defiance, Luna died, having received some forty wounds.

Felipe Buencamino came outside. Looking over at the gory bodies of his enemies, he spoke: "At last they are dead. Go see the body and get all the papers from his pockets, especially the telegram." He saw something in the faces of the soldiers as they realized what they had done. "Don't be afraid," said Buencamino. "We will take care of you."

Immediately upon learning of Luna's death, Aguinaldo ordered an official investigation. He had grimaced through the general's many tantrums and stood by him when another leader would have court-martialed him for desertion (at Bagbag), dereliction of duty (on numerous occasions Luna had defied Aguinaldo's edicts on the humane conduct of war), or disloyalty (rumors had recently abounded that Luna was eyeing Aguinaldo's job and planned to depose the executive cabinet with one of his own). Despite the counsel of advisers such as Mabini, *el presidente* had set a high value on his choleric general. "The loss of Luna," Aguinaldo would say, "was, of course, a very heavy blow to our armed efforts." But when the investigation was finished, the report blamed Luna for instigating the attack and absolved the Kawit soldiers of any guilt. In accepting the verdict without comment, Aguinaldo betrayed his regional bias and his naiveté — but no culpability in a plot. There is no evidence that Aguinaldo had anything to do with the assassination. This does not seem to be true of Felipe Buencamino, who had become Luna's blood enemy. The *illustrado,* and any of his colleagues who might have helped in a plot, escaped any blame. By confiscating the dead man's papers — including the mysterious telegram that had summoned the general without the knowledge of the purported signer, Aguinaldo — Buencamino had removed a damning piece of evidence that could have linked him to the assassination.

After the death of Luna, dissension grew, endangering the already splintering Filipino ranks. Discipline, always poor, crumbled, with many soldiers beginning to lose faith in the cause and surrendering to the Americans. During a short period of amnesty, Pedro Paterno and other *illustrados* retreated to Manila; it was the rainy season, and with whatever scraps of nationalist zeal they harbored in their hearts having melted away, they were welcomed into the American embrace.

The remaining members of the revolutionary government shifted west across the Central Plain to Tarlac. By then Aguinaldo had resumed the combined tasks of president and military commander, harassed on one front by the steadily advancing Americans and worried on another by the constant problem of holding his men together. He was particularly bothered about whether the soldiers of Ilocano extraction might bolt or rebel in reaction to Luna's death. More and more he relied on a dashing young general to keep dissidents in line and to replace or transfer those whose loyalty was in doubt.

Gregorio del Pilar, who had served as Aguinaldo's trusted aide ever since the days at Biaknabato, had been born in Bulacan province in 1875. He was the nephew of Marcelo H. del Pilar, one of the earliest propagandists of Philippine nationalism, who had fled to Spain to escape arrest in 1888, thereafter publishing a nationalist newspaper that helped fuel the revolution. As a teenaged student, Gregorio had helped the movement by distributing anti-Spanish literature. Once, at the parish church of Malolos, he and some friends appropriated religious tracts from the sacristy, replacing them with political pamphlets that they cleverly bound into the covers of the tracts. The following Sunday, the priest followed his usual practice of taking the pamphlets from the sacristy and distributing them among the worshipers. "Read these booklets, my brothers and sisters, and pass them on to others who can read them," the unwitting Spanish priest instructed. "You shall gain indulgences by reading them, and you shall be good in the eyes of God."

Gregorio del Pilar received his Bachelor of Arts degree from Ateneo de Manila University in 1896, the year of the outbreak of the revolution. He joined the Katipunan the following December, soon finding himself in battle, for Bulacan was among the first provinces to rise against the Spanish. During the Spanish attack upon Kakaron, del Pilar acquitted himself well despite a wound in the forehead where a Mauser bullet grazed him. He was promoted to lieutenant, subsequently capturing many weapons during raids and ambushes.

In August 1897, he appeared at Aguinaldo's stronghold at Biaknabato to request authorization for a raid upon the Spanish headquarters at Paombong. Some days later, Aguinaldo's troops confronted and nearly shot a small group of men in Spanish uniforms — who revealed themselves as del Pilar and his Katipuneros. They had attacked the Spaniards at Paombong while they were relaxing, unarmed, near the town church, driving them off without their weapons. Del Pilar proudly brought fourteen of the scarce Mausers back to Biaknabato. It was not long before Aguinaldo promoted the fearless young officer to lieutenant colonel. Later, during their Hong Kong exile, del Pilar had accompanied *el presidente* to Singapore, where he witnessed the secret negotiations between Aguinaldo and the American diplomat. When Aguinaldo returned home to reorganize his army, del Pilar was made military head of Bulacan and Nueva Ecija provinces, which he quickly cleared of Spanish troops. For this service he became a brigadier general.

Young, educated, and handsome, Gregorio del Pilar possessed a charisma that made him an idol among the troops and civilians alike. He cherished the best horses and the most expensive clothes and riding boots, and, not surprising for such an eligible bachelor, he had sweethearts wherever he went. "His traveling bags and his wallets were always replete with mysterious and perfumed letters, capricious and artistic memoirs of women," said del Pilar's biographer, Teodoro M. Kalaw. The boy general, as he was universally called, enjoyed the affections of so many women that they were continually vying for his undivided attention, something that he, at the pinnacle of his youth and strength, was unable to give.

As Aguinaldo's eyes and ears, del Pilar ensured loyalty toward the beleaguered revolutionary government among the men he commanded. In the ensuing weeks, this counted for a great deal as the government became sorely tested. On October 12, the Americans began a massive three-pronged offensive to pin Aguinaldo down on the Central Plain in Pampanga. *El presidente* retreated once again, moving his government north on November 12 from Tarlac to Bayambang, in Pangasinan. The American cavalry rushed in pursuit, for they recognized that he was making for the mountains of northern Luzon, where there awaited a large force of insurgents under the command of General Manuel Tinio. If the two armies united in such territory, conquest would be slow in coming.

By that time, Aguinaldo and his generals had realized the futility of organized resistance. They still possessed active military units in the far-flung provinces of Luzon, in areas like the islands of Panay and Mindanao, and around Iloilo, but their center was lost; communications were destroyed. During a war council on November 13, Aguinaldo decided to break up his armies into small, irregular guerrilla forces that would discard uniforms for the clothes of peasants and harass the Americans with sabotage, raids, and ambushes. Accompanied by his family, three cabinet ministers, and a column of twelve hundred men that included del Pilar's brigade, *el presidente* headed north toward the mountains, which were now in sight. He was absorbed not just by the thoughts of a commander in retreat but by those of one who has sustained a personal loss; his infant daughter, Flora, had died of fever en route between the towns of Villasis and Bayambang. The grieving father had been forced to attend to the baby's burial at the Bayambang church with only the briefest of formalities, keeping her death from his wife until he could tell her privately. Then, for expediency, *el presidente* ordered his troops to be divided into two columns. Under del Pilar, the advance guard numbered only two hundred and fifty; it escorted Aguinaldo, his wife and sister, and various commanders and their families. The rear guard fell behind, as the way was hard and rain fell constantly. Between the towns of Manaoag and San Manuel, the Americans overtook the rear guard and captured everyone, including Doña Trinidad, his mother, and Miguel, his son.

The advance column of soldiers had, by then, left the Central Plain to continue north up the hilly corridor, which was flanked on one side by the Lingayen Gulf and on the other by mountains that began a steady eastward rise into the formidable Central Cordillera. Clinging to the coastal foothills, the soldiers passed through the villages and towns of Pangasinan and La Union provinces at a forced pace, only rarely stopping to rest or eat and losing their strength in consequence. They fought through monsoon forests and climbed laboriously over the mountains in their path, receiving word almost daily that the Americans were relentlessly closing the gap between the two groups.

"It rained continuously, and it was very muddy," noted Colonel Simeon Villa, an ophthalmologist who had served under General Luna and was close to Aguinaldo during the flight into the mountains. "A strong wind and the cold air made our teeth chatter as we climbed [and] when we reached an altitude of more than 500 meters, we thought we were high up near heaven. . . . We were all wet but we could not change, for our clothes [were] with the soldiers of the rear guard."

In the town of Naguilian, the soldiers were greeted by an immense crowd, including the municipal band. There they stayed for two days to gather strength, until word of foreign troops sent them on again at midnight on the nineteenth.

They struck the seacoast north of Balaoang and joined the national road, on which they made good time to the town of Candon in Ilocos Sur province, arriving on November 21. There, with abrupt mountains narrowing their chances of escape to the north, Aguinaldo's column turned east, across a small, soggy coastal plain, and then, finally, up into the towering Central Cordillera. They forded streams and passed among the famous tiered rice terraces, heading toward a high mountain cut through which they would enter the heart of the cordillera. The passageway was called Tirad Pass.

Above the hill villages of Concepcion and Lingay — the latter on a little plateau about two thousand feet above sea level — the narrow trail zigzagged dizzily up the mountainside, finally crossing the summit of the pass at forty-five hundred feet. As Aguinaldo's column crossed, forced into single file by the narrowness of the passage between massive boulders, General del Pilar paused to alight from his white horse to survey the strategic possibilities of the perilous trail. "The Americans could never take this place," he said, "and if they ever take it, it would only be over my dead body." He ordered a detail to construct trenches at several places along the length of the pass and assigned troops to guard them. Then he followed Aguinaldo to camps in the settlements of Angake and Cervantes, on the opposite shoulder of the mountain.

They were still hidden in the mountain fastness and unmolested a week later. Del Pilar, knowing that the Americans would soon be knocking at the door of Tirad Pass, left Cervantes to return to his soldiers. Aguinaldo tried to persuade him not to go, saying that the trail could be held without him, but del Pilar said his duty was to prevent the foreigners from capturing his chief whatever the personal cost.

"We arrived in Angake after midday," recalled del Pilar's aide, Vicente Enriquez, who had known the general since the earliest days of the Katipunan. "Towards dusk, we noticed that the guard stationed at the highest point of Tirad, whom we could see from where we stood, was nervously waving a red flag, a signal that the enemy had been sighted. We hiked towards that place and spent the night in a makeshift hut at the summit." At dawn on December 2, they heard rifle shots below, from the direction of Concepcion.

Major Peyton C. March and his battalion had recently been attached to the flying cavalry brigade of General Samuel Young in the long chase to capture the rebel chief. Aguinaldo's trail had disappeared for a time, leaving his pursuers to wallow through the mud along the coast, offering bribes to anyone who would give *el presidente* away. Apparently someone found the price to be right, for on November 30, Young learned that Aguinaldo had gone through the precipitous Tirad Pass some five days earlier. He ordered March to strike inland from the coast and try to cut off their elusive quarry.

Leaving immediately with three hundred soldiers and an Ilocano guide named Januario Galut, March reached Concepcion in less than one day. There the "half savage, nearly naked tribe" of mountain dwellers told him that, as the war correspondent John T. Mc-Cutcheon reported in the *New York Herald*, "the insurgents were holding the pass, that it was heavily intrenched and barricaded at various points. There was a massive stone barricade at the summit, and in places the trail was exceedingly narrow and so steep one could hardly climb it. It was suspected that in many places the trail was destroyed. Major March began to see that a proposition of a desperate character had to be considered."

The next morning, December 2, Major March led his soldiers to the mesa town of Lingay, where they first drew fire. "A sharp clatter of Mausers was heard," observed McCutcheon, "and bullets began singing overhead." The advance company, having made it another fifteen hundred yards to the first slope of the pass, was pinned down by del Pilar's invisible soldiers, somewhere far above; a support company was sent through rice fields to attempt a different route toward the top. "It was at this time that those watching from Lingay first caught sight of the insurgents," McCutcheon wrote. It was plain to those in the town that the soldiers ahead could not see their enemy, so March took two more companies to join them. Under a furious hail of fire the Americans slowly climbed the zigzagging trail, sustaining heavy losses at every turn. Finally, though, they saw they could go no farther, for the trail led to a wide opening where there was no cover and no possibility of a charge. March was forced to send one of his companies back down the awesome route with instructions to flank the trail — and the rebels — by scaling the heights. "Far down the trail," reported McCutcheon, "the company of men, numbering between forty-five and fifty, swung up the ravine and disappeared from the view of those who were waiting in the protection of the ledges beneath the Filipino barricade." Except for occasional shots from sharpshooters on opposing crags, it became quiet, "an interminable wait which was as trying as active fighting." The sun beat down on the quick and the dead.

General del Pilar's aide-de-camp had taken off his insignia of rank when he arrived at the trenches; he had been sent forward to find out what was happening. Captains in the trenches told Enriquez that their soldiers had "heroically and successfully resisted heavy shelling of the American cavalry. . . . Our soldiers, lacking ammunition, limited ourselves to shooting at very close range during the assault." At another position near the summit, he found twelve men. "From the peak, I could see some Americans resting below, their rifles piled in stacks," recalled the aide. "Our men reassured me of our impenetrable position, pointing out to me our enemies below. They said that we could cause damage to the enemy just by rolling big stones from the mountain. . . . We all agreed about our excellent position and that we had the upper hand."

Gregorio del Pilar shortly joined his aide at the trenches and took over direct command of the fighting. Some time later, during the stalemate that pinned down Major March, the lazy pattern of firing picked up momentarily, then abated somewhat. The general ordered a cease-fire and his men signaled that Americans were directly ahead; del Pilar stepped onto a promontory to survey the enemy position.

From his vantage point in the relatively safe position in the village of Lingay, Richard Henry Little, a war correspondent, could see what was transpiring as if it were on some vast canvas on which the tiny figures could move, duck, and die. His description of the battle is one of the classic examples of reporting, and deserves to be cited at length:

> We had seen him cheering his men in the fight. One of our companies crouched up close under the side of the cliff where he had built his first intrenchment, heard his voice continually during the fight, scolding them, praising them, cursing, appealing one moment to their love of their native land and the next instant threatening to kill them if they did not stand firm. Driven from the first intrenchment he fell slowly back to the second in full sight of our sharpshooters and under a heavy fire. Not until every man around him in the second intrenchment was down did he turn his white horse and ride slowly up the winding trail. Then we who were below saw an American squirm his way out to the top of a high flat rock, and take deliberate aim at the figure on the white horse. We held our breath, not knowing whether to pray that the sharpshooter would shoot straight or miss. Then came the spiteful crack of the Krag rifle and the man on horseback rolled to the ground, and when the troops charging up the mountain side reached him, the boy general of the Filipinos was dead.
>
> We went up the mountain side. After H company had driven the insurgents out of their second position and killed Pilar, the other companies had rushed straight up the trail. . . . Just past this a few hundred yards we saw a solitary figure lying on the road. The boy was almost stripped of clothing, and there were no marks of rank on the blood-soaked coat. . . . A soldier came running down the trail.
>
> "That's old Pilar," he said, "we got the old rascal. I guess he's sorry he ever went up against the Thirty-Third." "There ain't no doubt its being Pilar," rattled on the young soldier. "We got his diary and letters and all his papers, and Sullivan of our company's got his pants, and

Snider's got his shoes, but he can't wear them because they're too small, and a sergeant in G. Company got one of his silver spurs, and a lieutenant got the other, and somebody swiped his cuff buttons before I got here or I would have swiped them, and all I got was a stud button and his collar with blood on it."

So this was the end of Gregorio Del Pilar. . . . A private sitting by the fire was exhibiting a handkerchief. "It's old Pilar's. It's got 'Dolores Hoses' on the corner. I guess that was his girl. Well, it's all over with Gregorio."

"Anyhow," said Private Sullivan, "I got his pants. He won't need them anymore."

The man who had the general's shoes strode proudly past. . . . A private sitting on a rock was examining a golden locket containing a curl of woman's hair. "Got the locket off his neck," said the soldier. . . .

As the main column started on its march for the summit of the mountain a turn in the trail brought us again in sight of the insurgent general far down below us. There had been no time to bury him. Not even a blanket or a poncho had been thrown over him.

A crow sat on the dead man's feet. Another perched on his head. The fog settled down upon us. We could see the body no longer.

And when Private Sullivan went by in his trousers, and Snider with his shoes, and the other man who had the cuff buttons, and the sergeant who had the spur, and the lieutenant who had the other spur, and the man who had the handkerchief, and another that had his shoulder straps, it suddenly occurred to me that his glory was about all we had left him.

Vicente Enriquez had tried to take his general's corpse with him when he retreated, but he was forced to leave it when the first Americans approached. He removed a diamond ring from del Pilar's finger, which he kept for some time before giving it to another commander. He hid in a forest to escape the enemy, coming upon the cadaver the following day. "We placed him in a canal and covered him with stones and dry leaves," Enriquez said, adding that a proper burial was impossible because the Americans were so near. The task of laying del Pilar's remains to rest would be performed several days later by an American lieutenant, who provided a headstone inscribed with the general's name and the legend: "An Officer and a Gentleman."

At about five o'clock in the afternoon of December 2, the survivors of the Tirad Pass battle reported the death of their leader to Aguinaldo. There was much mourning in the camp, but there was no time to be lost, for the Americans were said to be approaching quickly.

El presidente and his remaining force set out from Cervantes to cross
a succession of higher mountains, moving deeper into the Central
Cordillera throughout the night, struggling blindly in a numbing lunar chill to outdistance their pursuers, ascending higher and higher
into the clouds before disappearing, finally and utterly, into the dark,
rocky core of Luzon.

4

MANILA, 1901

I

Somber and resplendent, evolving and decaying, buffeted by two successive, overpowering colonial tides and the clash of many disparate cultures, the city of Manila sat in the year 1901 as it had for two centuries on the eastern bank of Manila Bay, a paragon of endurance. Beneath a swaying forest of masts in the deepwater harbor, tiny Filipino *bancas* and *cascos* competed for room with majestic merchant ships and freighters, with hemp barges and tugs. But there were no disputes for right-of-way with the flotilla of the U.S. Asiatic Fleet, whose cutters, launches, gunboats, and destroyers cruised and moored wheresoever they desired, imperiously bearing witness to who maintained control of the harbor and of Manila itself.

The imposing but singularly squat medieval walls of the fortress they called Fort Santiago and the district called Intramuros loomed over the harbor and the mouth of the Pasig. The river was fairly wide and navigable, simultaneously separating the ancient Spanish garrison from the rest of Manila and serving as the principal commercial thoroughfare. Guarding the river, the gray stone fortress walls rose some thirty feet, capped with parapets and bastions, and varied from ten to twenty feet in thickness. Entrance could only be gained through one of eight gates, their drawbridges spanning a dry moat. One historian maintained that the ancient trough had for decades gradually filled up with "mud and filth of the consistency of cold molasses, sustaining a rank growth of noxious vegetation and breeding abominable stenches." Fearful of releasing untold horrors, the Spanish had delicately left the moat undisturbed, but the new Yankee inhabitants of the Walled City were enthusiastically sanitary and drained it as soon as they took control. Aside from other hygienic efforts and the tentative restoration of an overgrown botanical garden to an approximation of its former splendor, the Americans' presence had so far only slightly changed Manila — that is, in a physical sense. But on its wide boulevards of Intramuros there had been a noticeable increase in the hustle and bustle of those who had business in the numerous square, two-story stone government offices, at the custom house, and at the central post office. Early in the morning on a typical day, bright-eyed and fervent civil servants imported from the American heartland dodged around their laconic Filipino and Spanish counterparts. Blue-uniformed soldiers, a multitude of them, moved with purpose between the ministries on courier duty, passing yet others on guard duty at the old arsenal and other military buildings.

Church and state operated side by side in the Walled City. In front of the Manila Cathedral, which was built on the ruins of a predecessor destroyed by an earthquake, acolytes would adjust the surplice of a Catholic priest, ignite the incense, and another somber religious procession in honor of one of many saints would begin to make its way past the eleven other churches in the district (most of which resembled factories more than places of worship), past the convents, rectories, monasteries, cloisters, and colleges. The forces of God and government never ceased to dominate life inside those picturesque, venerable, useless medieval walls; it did not matter that most of the Spanish bureaucrats had been sent packing back to Madrid. With the Americans' arrival, the silent, somber, and austere atmosphere had deepened. The streets echoed with the firm tread of Yankee boots while the air rang with a constant melody of pealing church bells. No number of shops, stores, or parks — and there were many — could diminish a visitor's impression that burning onto the red tile and corrugated metal rooftops of the city were the unrelenting, patriarchal twin gazes of William McKinley and God Almighty, creating that constant, inescapable gloom.

Life was not so gloomy in the districts of Manila where commerce had a firmer hold and where wartime and the new presence of American merchantmen had quickened an already frenetic pace. The capital was scored with a busy network of canals, streams, ponds, and lakes. Indeed, Manila might have qualified for the name some journalistic boosters had given it — "Venice of the Pacific" — had its water not been so vile and odoriferous with waste and garbage. But that aesthetic judgment certainly did not affect business, for on every day save the Lord's each navigable watercourse was choked with vessels of every description loaded to the gunwales with strong tobacco, bales of hemp, mountains of raw sugar, ripening fruit and vegetables, and cheap textiles. The streets of the main business district, Binondo, were equally congested with freight vans and carts pulled by whipped and underfed ponies or stolid, ungainly carabaos, or even dragged along by gangs of grunting, nearly naked Chinese coolies. One traveler noted the diverse nature of business in the district, marveling that

> not only do the grant shops, millionaire merchants, all the banks but one, the money-lenders, the money and produce brokers, mass themselves in Binondo, but hither one must come to find civil and mining engineers, insurance agents, marble dealers, implement dealers, artificial ice plants, brick-making plants, silversmiths, lithographers, printers, newspaper offices, shipping offices, railway and tramway headquarters, ship chandlers. . . .

The list could go on.

The luxurious commercial showplace of Binondo was the thoroughfare called the Escolta, along which six thousand or more vehicles rolled by every twenty-four hours over cobblestones imported from Hong Kong. The stores defied earthquakes by using plate glass windows instead of the small panes of nearly transparent oyster shells used elsewhere. European proprietors sold almost everything available on Fifth Avenue and the Champs-Elysées: French millinery and perfume, Swiss watches, fancy jewelry of Spanish or Moorish design, dependable American shoes and dry goods. For sustaining weary shoppers, the Escolta offered cafés and restaurants comparable to those in Europe; bakeries were fragrant with croissants and sweet Italian pastries, and confectioners served candies and ice cream sodas made with fresh native chocolate.

There were also hundreds of stores presided over by their Chinese entrepreneurs, and they were similar to any in Canton and Hong Kong. On Rosario Street, which angled off the Escolta and which was considered the great mart of the common people, hawkers urged passersby to examine their handmade basketwork, beaded shawls, tin religious items, and gaudy, illuminated portraits of the Virgin Mary and Admiral George Dewey.

When in Manila, visiting journalists, dignitaries, politicians, and brigadier generals habitually sought lodgings at the Hotel de Oriente, in one guest's mind the only establishment in the city worthy of the name "hotel." Small by American standards, the Oriente contained eighty-three rooms for public service and accommodations for twenty-five horses. While eating in the dining room under broad, ornate fans swung by Chinese punka boys, it was difficult to forget that Manila was one of the great crossroads of the world, especially while sampling the cuisine, which ranged from Spanish and French to Mexican and Indian dishes. "Its most popular curry," remembered one hearty eater, "is one made of camerones or large prawns, and the side dishes served with it included the Bombay duck, the Macassar red fish, fried breadfruit, fried onions, granulated roast peanuts, Spanish anchovies, grated young cocoanut, green and red chile ribbons, mango chutney, green chutney, English pickled walnuts, English mustard pickles, and palm farina."

After such a meal, one of the finest pleasures available to, for instance, a visiting brigadier general was hiring a carriage for himself and his lady and joining the nightly throng down on the Luneta, the lovely public promenade that overlooked the harbor. All Manila society turned out each dusk in stylish landaus and victorias, in four-wheeled *calesas* and small two-horse barouches. Even Filipinos in less elegant circumstances were present, having hired the two-wheeled, top-heavy *caromatas* (which always seemed on the point of turning bottom up), whose drivers, eager to squeeze another customer aboard, would direct their horses from a passenger's lap. No one seemed to mind.

In the years before the Americans arrived, folk assembled on the Luneta to watch the Spanish execute insurgents, who stood on the sea wall with their hands bound, looking out onto the water as they awaited the firing squad volley. From a bandstand, a small military band would play jaunty marches for the amusement of the onlookers during the bloodletting. Marches were still part of the evening's entertainment in 1901, though those gathering on the Luneta had come to admire only the sunset and to find some respite from the heat in the sea breezes. As a myriad of electric lamps blinked to life along the graceful curve of the strand and as gentlemen reflectively touched matches to cigars, the sun would sink gloriously behind the Mariveles Mountains, transforming the sky and the great, muddy yellow gulf with hues of gold and vermilion. Confronted with such a magnificent spectacle, it was easy to forget there was a war going on.

II

When William Jennings Bryan (who personified the "ray of hope" for peace to Aguinaldo) was soundly defeated by the incumbent William McKinley in November 1900, it signified approval of the "forward" policy in the Philippines while signaling the Americans in Manila that their efforts should be stepped up. Arthur MacArthur announced in December that henceforth Filipinos who failed to aid the American troops actively would be considered on the wrong side of the conflict and punished accordingly; their property was subject to confiscation, and the long-standing unofficial practice of torching suspect villages was given the highest official sanction. Aguinaldo's old adviser, the paralytic Apolinario Mabini, and thirty-eight others were deported to exile and the worry of deprivation and disease on faraway Guam in January; and in the three-month period ending on the first of February, some six hundred Filipinos were arrested in Manila — many said to be members of the insurgent army.

If there were any peaceable method to defuse this long insurrection, the Philippine civil commissioner William Howard Taft — the portly, handlebar-mustached, genial former circuit judge from Ohio — believed he had the solution. In February 1901, he proudly sponsored the creation of the Federal party much as a latter-day businessman would coach a Junior Achievement chapter. It was an approved political organization that all Filipinos were encouraged to join. The party platform, which called for the immediate surrender of Aguinaldo's forces, representation in the United States Congress, and eventual statehood, received a lukewarm reception. Only Filipino businessmen and propertied conservatives could be induced to join, and cynics promptly dubbed them Americanistas. It was not certain whether or not the American military held out much hope for the fledgling political party. However, it was common knowledge that the civilian Taft and the military man MacArthur constantly feuded, so presumably the army was confident that any military solution would come long before Taft's wealthy little Americanistas could convert their poorer countrymen.

An item appeared in the February 22 edition of the *Manila New American* that sent a chill of urgency through the palatial headquarters overlooking the Pasig River — particularly through the bones of Brigadier General Frederick Funston, newly arrived in the capital to finish preparations for his secret expedition. On that day a local correspondent disclosed that during a recent American raid on a pharmaceutical shop, a packet of letters from the insurgents was confiscated along with a cipher key. The reporter breathlessly revealed that the dispatches put Emilio Aguinaldo's presence somewhere in Isabela province — precisely (though the scribe did not know it) in the neighborhood of Funston's ultimate destination. In truth, an American patrol had discovered these documents in Manila around the time that Funston was quizzing his captive and evolving his plan. The men in Manila, expecting reward or recognition, were instead instructed to forget about the matter. Funston and his superiors, Generals Wheaton and MacArthur, hoped the readers of the *New American* would also forget it. Reports were frequently printed placing Aguinaldo just about everywhere but inside Malacañang Palace, MacArthur's own headquarters. Nonetheless, to all of Funston's worries was added the possibility that if *el presidente*'s couriers brought him word of that new report, their leader might deem it prudent to move his headquarters yet again — making pointless Funston's elaborate scheme.

Malacañang Palace sat on the north bank of the Pasig, one and a quarter miles east of the Walled City. The former residence of the Spanish governor general was easily the most splendid mansion in Manila, summoning a sense of the immense grace and wealth of its colonial past. A stroll in its magnificent gardens was always on the itinerary of visiting dignitaries: who could resist walking along paths paved with seashells, below rustling fruit trees heavy with coconuts, bananas, lemons, and mangoes, or be immune to the sensual assault of the splashes of floral color, the perfume of a thousand exotic blooms?

Amateur botanist though Funston was — he could still rattle off accurate descriptions of the flora of Death Valley and Alaska — there was no room in his busy Manila days for lingering anywhere, especially in MacArthur's back yard. But if he had allowed himself a little swagger a few weeks earlier, when he first visited the palace, certainly no one would have blamed him for it — or for savoring the pleasure of being ushered past sentries and appointment secretaries through the opulent halls, being given preference over petitioners of every stature to spin out his proposal to his immediate superior, General Loyd Wheaton, and then to be whisked past yet others and be asked to tell it all over again to Governor General Arthur MacArthur.

In the weeks following their bemused but nonetheless warm blessing, Funston passed again and again under the imposing Malacañang porte-cochère as the many details of his expedition were settled.

While in San Isidro, the general had decided on at least two other American officers who, like himself, would play the role of prisoners of war of the column of counterfeit Filipino insurgents. These two Funston knew personally.

Lieutenant Burton J. Mitchell was not only the general's personal aide, he was in addition a first cousin. Mitchell shared Funston's birthplace of New Carlisle, Ohio, where he was born in 1871, and also called Iola, Kansas, his home. His parents had moved there when Mitchell was seven and Funston thirteen (the two families lived on adjoining farms). Burton's father had served with distinction during the Civil War in an army unit known as the Mitchell Battalion, so called because of the number of Mitchells in its ranks. At the outbreak of the Spanish-American War, young Mitchell had been working for the federal government in Washington; he went home to enlist as a private in the Twentieth Kansas. In Manila he was detailed as a clerk in the adjutant's office, later being promoted to quartermaster's sergeant; he had escaped his desk when the shooting started and was promoted to second lieutenant while the Twentieth fought at Caloocan. Soon thereafter Mitchell became his cousin's aide-de-camp. Short, slight of build, and apple-cheeked, Burton Mitchell looked to be the consummate farmboy, and he was content to live in Funston's shadow.

Captain Harry W. Newton had been chosen because he had once been posted to the garrison at Baler, on the northeastern coast of Luzon, and therefore knew a smattering about the area. Newton had been born in 1867 in Superior, Wisconsin; his parents were among the city's first settlers. His education and job experiences were coincidentally similar to Funston's: he had attended Racine College for three years and worked as a baggageman, ticket clerk, and cashier for the Northern Pacific Railroad, subsequently being appointed deputy city clerk and comptroller in Superior. In the last couple of years before the war, Newton had found time to work nights as manager of the Celebrated Superior Minstrels and weekends as captain of a state militia unit. In May 1898, Newton's company had followed the call of President McKinley; it was absorbed into the Third Wisconsin Volunteers, which saw service during the Puerto Rico expedition. At the close of the Spanish war, Newton decided to continue in the military. He secured an appointment as first lieutenant in the Thirty-fourth Infantry and arrived in the Philippines in September 1899. Four months later found him fighting in the trenches around Panay; later he became a brigade adjutant, first under General Lawton during the failed pincer operation to capture Aguinaldo in 1899, later under Funston in central Luzon. Newton was superintendent of the Manila security police when he received an order to join Funston in his secret operation — "A great scheme," the captain would write home, giving only the barest of details though he knew it would take a month for his letter to reach Wisconsin, "and if successful it will be the greatest piece of work done in the islands."

Another of Funston's staff was the Spaniard Lazaro Segovia. He had been chosen to play the part of an insurgent officer of the relief

column by dint of his inventiveness and capacity for leadership —
for after everyone had assumed his role, Segovia would command a
trio of turncoat Tagalog soldiers, men who were necessary to lend
veracity to the scheme. "The selection of these men was a very delicate matter," Funston said, "as they would have it in their power to
ruin us by disclosing our real character."

At least one of these soldiers was known by Aguinaldo. He was a
corpulent and rather weak-willed former rebel by the name of Hilario Talplacido, who had served under General Antonio Luna as a
major in 1899. During the battle of Caloocan, Talplacido had been
part of a nighttime operation that had attempted to sneak up on the
slumbering Twentieth Kansas. The Filipinos had been overheard by
an outpost, provoking the long and hysterical fusillade by the entire
regiment that Funston's staff had been able to halt only by kicking
the volunteers back to sanity. By then the Filipinos had changed their
minds about attacking and withdrew with their wounded, including
Talplacido, who had been shot through the lungs. After he recovered, he had served under General Pantaleon García, finally being
arrested with his chief in the town of Jaen, Nueva Ecija province, by
Funston's adjutant, Captain Smith, in May 1900. After several months
in jail, Talplacido had been converted to the American way of looking at politics; he took the loyalty oath and was released in his wife's
custody. He became an informer, seldom venturing out of San Isidro for fear of assassination. Now, Hilario Talplacido was told only
that his presence would be required by Funston for a month or two;
as yet he did not know any details nor that he would be posing as
the leader of the reinforcements.

Equally in the dark were two young soldiers — Dionisio Bâto, who
had been captured, and Gregorio Cadhit, who had tired of the rebellion and surrendered three months earlier. Both had sworn the
required American oath, as had the recent Ilocano convert Cecilio
Segismundo. Funston pressed the failed messenger into service to
guide the relief column to Aguinaldo — just as *el presidente* had ordered. Segovia told Segismundo to keep his mouth shut.

On the day these men were to leave, young Dionisio Bâto had arranged to be married in the San Isidro church. The wedding party
emerged from the ceremony to see a U.S. Army ambulance wagon
parked in the churchyard. Without a chance even to kiss his bride,
Bâto was put into the vehicle, joining Lazaro Segovia, Segismundo,
Talplacido, and Cadhit. The Spaniard would only hint that they might
be going to Manila to arrest a revolutionary officer. This, said Talplacido, could hardly be expected to take two months. Segovia would
say nothing more.

Of course Bâto — the fresh, young bridegroom — was not alone among the Tagalogs in worrying about his fate.

They had no way of knowing that, as the horse-drawn ambulance wagon rattled south toward Manila, someone had penetrated to the heart of General Funston's plot. Despite the pronounced secrecy in San Isidro, the information had leaked out to the compound containing the brigade's prisoners of war. One Crisanto de la Fuente was a major in the revolutionary army who had recently been captured near Pangasinan. Unlike Funston's turncoats, he had refused to swear the oath. When the awful news of his president's betrayal was whispered to him, the major wrote two messages on cigarette paper:

My dear Presidente:
I have definite information that Colonel Hilario Talplacido and that officer Lazaro Segovia have met with the American army, and there is a rumor, which is true, that these officers will go to your place, accompanied by soldiers.

CRISANTO DE LA FUENTE

He smuggled the warnings to a confederate, hoping that they would reach his leader's headquarters before it was too late. Aguinaldo never received them.

Funston had arranged for Segovia, the three "reformed" rebels, and the failed courier to lodge together in a hotel in the Walled City. Segovia soon found that his charges had attracted their innkeeper's concern when the owner of the establishment anxiously drew him aside. The Spaniard was obviously a gentleman and a man of some learning, said the innkeeper, but what of the four bumpkins who shared his room? The hotel had never lodged such ill-bred, rough-looking Filipinos before; was there not going to be some trouble? Talking fast but politely, Segovia placated his questioner by assuring him of the high moral character of his companions.

The Spaniard had been instructed to supervise his roommates closely and never to let Segismundo be alone with the others or venture outside by himself. Burton Mitchell visited daily and kept them well supplied with money, which they were encouraged to spend freely. Despite the comfortable room and their generous allowance, the Filipinos continually bombarded Segovia with questions: who was this strange little Ilocano, Segismundo, and what, for the love of the Virgin, would they be called upon to do? Segovia's only answer was silence.

For Talplacido, this confirmed his worst suspicion — he and Bâto and Cadhit were doomed to join the others deemed a threat to American sovereignty, exiled to the godforsaken island of Guam. Ever since Talplacido had been conducted into the ambulance wagon in San Isidro, the possibility had gnawed at him. He had lugged all his worldly possessions along, and for a few panicky moments during a rest stop in San Fernando he had almost tried to run away. Now, pent up in a hotel room in the capital and closely scrutinized whenever he ventured outside, his anxiety grew — and was transmitted to Bâto and Cadhit like a lurking fever. The three glumly resigned themselves to deportation. When it was finally time for the men to leave, Segovia had great difficulty convincing Talplacido to leave his baggage behind.

At Malacañang Palace, where greater cares and concerns confronted Frederick Funston and his sponsors, other crucial elements were being added to their scheme.

MacArthur prevailed upon Admiral George C. Remey, the successor to Dewey as commander of the Asiatic squadron, to lend him a light-draft gunboat and a close-mouthed crew. Remey complied with the trim little *Vicksburg*, a relatively new steel vessel of two thousand tons skippered by Commander Edward B. Barry.

Meanwhile, General Wheaton notified Funston that he had assembled a detachment culled from Company D of the First Battalion of Macabebe Scouts. The unit had been organized for less than two months, but the rawness of the scouts would be mitigated by the presence of a grizzled old first sergeant named Pedro Bustos. He had fought his brother Filipinos in the southern islands with such ferocity that his former employers had sent him to Spain for an awards ceremony.

The Macabebe detachment had been organized by two American officers from Claquato, Washington. Brothers with an appropriate name for adventurers — Hazzard — they were the sons of an Indiana family who had migrated west to establish a farm a few miles south of Tacoma. The elder brother, Captain Russell Train Hazzard, had been a mechanical engineer for the Southern Pacific, later establishing himself in the hops business. Lieutenant Oliver P. M. Hazzard had been a schoolteacher and had also attended the state university. At the outbreak of the Spanish war, they joined a National Guard company as corporals, but the unit had to be disbanded after a rambunctious disagreement among the men over the qualifications of their captain. After the unit was reorganized into Company M of the First Washington Volunteers — with a new leader —

Russell was made a second lieutenant and his younger brother a corporal.

Sent to the Philippines, Russell became part of General Wheaton's staff, where he won distinction in several engagements. The tropics caught up with him before long and he became ill, but after a medical furlough in the States, he took part in the American expedition to put down the Boxer Rebellion. He returned to the Philippines at the close of the celebrated march on Peking.

By then, both brothers had been promoted to their present ranks. They soon transferred from the Washington Volunteers to the Eleventh Cavalry after their original unit was mustered out. Oliver Hazzard, whose nickname was "Happy" and who had gained attention as a sharpshooter, commanded the company while Russell was absent. In time, the Eleventh was also retired, so, again choosing to remain in the war, Russell and Oliver had volunteered to organize the new battalion of Macabebe scouts. Tall, raw-boned, and fearless (and both devastatingly handsome), they struck General Wheaton as being well suited for the expedition. Funston agreed, and thus the Hazzards rounded out the ranks of his small band of bogus prisoners of war.

Incredibly, with all the elaborate preparations — which involved both branches of the military and the cooperation of hundreds in the ranks — only five American officers knew of the mission besides Funston and his retinue.

On March 4, while, on the other side of the world, William McKinley and Theodore Roosevelt stood before a glistening, flag-draped Capitol and took their oaths of office in a prolonged Washington drizzle, the planners of the Funston expedition were nearing their own inauguration. Supplies and uniforms were stowed in anonymous crates and sent to the steamer rather than risking the comic but perilous alternative of having the Macabebes don their costumes on the morning of the day they would leave. "All Manila would have gone wild with gossip," Segovia soberly noted, "at seeing the scouts marching in such a guise through the streets." The mystified Macabebes watched as their shiny new American-issued Krag-Jorgenson rifles were taken away from them, only to be replaced once they were at sea by captured Mausers and Remingtons that were much used and battered — and, with a few exceptions, serviceable.

Readying himself for the journey, Frederick Funston eased his wife's curiosity — and increased her alarm — by taking her into his confidence; shortly thereafter, he parked Eda with friends in the capital and bid her a fond good-bye, knowing, as he later admitted, that all through his long absence "the poor woman had to keep her council." Then he left to pay his final respects at Malacañang Palace.

"Funston, this is a desperate undertaking," General MacArthur told him somberly. "I fear I shall never see you again." With these cheery words to give him courage in the dangerous weeks ahead when he would step off the edge of the civilized world, Frederick Funston took leave of his commandant to join his comrades at their point of embarkation.

At three in the afternoon of March 6, 1901, the conspirators began to arrive at their assembly point at the Anda Street wharf on the Pasig River. First, Lazaro Segovia arrived with his four charges, as mystified as ever about their destination. In no more than a half-hour Funston and his cousin Mitchell appeared, carrying their bundles of old uniforms to serve them as make-believe prisoners. A few minutes later, Harry Newton walked up. In a short time several horse-drawn wagons halted at the wharf, bearing boxes of clothing and uniforms for the scouts and crates of rifles. Finally, at four, the Hazzard brothers brought up their company of scouts, all marching unarmed.

Thus assembled, the men piled into their riverine transport, a launch for the American and Filipino officers, which towed in its wake a barge full of scouts. The late afternoon light was failing as the little convoy left the turgid waters of the Pasig for Manila Bay.

Ahead, riding the yellow swells, lay Commander Barry's *Vicksburg*.

III

The anchor of the *Vicksburg* was raised at half-past seven on the evening of March 6, 1901. There was a light breeze, and the moon had begun to rise behind scattered clouds, which sailed from over the darkening Bataan peninsula.

Even as the crew hoisted the steam launch and gig and secured all boats for sea, Lazaro Segovia left the company of his general and made his way through the bustle of sailors; he was intent on gaining a perspective on the first chapter of their long voyage. He climbed one of the tall iron masts to smoke a cigar and enjoy the view. Below him, the Macabebe company was sprawled in various stages of repose on the throbbing deck. Funston disappeared into the ship's interior with its staff to tell them of his scheme.

Funston had come aboard with his men in the late afternoon, with the few who knew their destination pretending that what they were doing was only routine. This boarding was considerably less eventful than one earlier in the day, when he had come out to the ship for the last of a series of preparatory conferences with Commander Barry. Funston had received a bad shock then. As he had walked up the gangplank, he was utterly startled when naval guns boomed across the bay. It had been a salute, but not to him; an Austrian man-of-war coming to anchor began a thunderous exchange of twenty-one-gun salutes with Admiral Remey's flagship, the *Brooklyn,* followed by a personal salute of thirteen guns. In the afternoon, the exuberant Austrians fired off another salute in honor of their Manila consul; and if they had known what was transpiring on the *Vicksburg* that evening, they would have doubtlessly created a noise for Funston, too.

Leaving its mooring, the thousand-ton *Vicksburg* cruised past Cavite peninsula and its hulking fortifications, past the spongy littoral marshes below, then nosed to pass rocky Corregidor Island through the south channel. Finally, the ship came out of the shelter of Manila Bay. The men standing on the deck could see, behind them, the light atop Corregidor, revolving in its regular arc as if bidding farewell.

A gnawing disquiet in Lazaro Segovia's innards proved to be the early rumblings of *mal-de-mer,* a condition exacerbated, no doubt, by his Manila cigar, and he shakily descended from his perch. The green-visaged Spaniard took a marine's advice and settled amidships until the nausea dissipated. Lieutenant Mitchell found him during the night and asked why he did not take advantage of the cabin assigned to him. "I can't do it," Segovia told Mitchell. "The atmosphere is too strong for me. I am very delicate." Most of the scouts were snoring away on the deck, but several who were not approached Segovia for information. As different curious Macs sidled over, the Spaniard waggishly varied his answers; he told some they were bound for Hong Kong, others Guam or even San Francisco. The resulting confusion of gossip, which occupied the scouts throughout the night, was not really the stuff of great comedy but nonetheless helped Segovia forget his sickness and pass the time.

When the men awakened the next morning, they were steaming through the busy Verde Island Passage, which separated Luzon from the smaller island of Mindoro. Over the stern loomed the mountainous coast of Batangas province. The Sibuyan Sea lay only a few hours ahead.

Funston and his men amused themselves while the ship's crew was put through the daily exercise drills on the main deck. Then Commander Barry, who was a strict disciplinarian, dispensed punishment to some members of his crew: five days in double irons to a seaman for leaving clothes on a hatch, five days of bread and water rations and solitary confinement to another for impudence to an officer, reduction of rank to two sailors who had returned from the Manila fleshpots forty hours after their leave had expired.

Another bit of shipboard discipline occurred next, when the general decided it was time to disclose the overall plan to the Filipinos. He summoned Segovia from his place on the sunny deck and asked him to help. They began with the three officers. When told of Funston's intention to capture Emilio Aguinaldo alive, Talplacido, Cadhit, and Bâto were thunderstruck. *Capture Emilio Aguinaldo alive? This was the supreme betrayal, compared to which their earlier perfidies shriveled to nothingness,* they protested. *How could they survive in Luzon — or anywhere else in the Philippines — after doing such a deed?*

Funston allowed their sputterings to subside. Then he sternly reminded them of their American loyalty oath. So, if they preferred not to help by accompanying him on his mission, they should begin to say their prayers and otherwise prepare to meet their Maker. Hilario Talplacido halfheartedly offered another obstacle to his going along: *el presidente* was no doubt aware that Talplacido had taken the oath and would look upon him with no end of suspicion. Funston told him not to worry; he had anticipated every possibility and was prepared to deal with even Talplacido's reputation. The sagging, dismayed Filipino next voiced doubts that he could adequately portray the colonel and leader of an insurgent reinforcement column.

"Don't worry," Segovia reassured him. All Talplacido had to do was behave as did all insurgent chiefs. "Clear your throat after every few words," the Spaniard advised, "and if we meet people ask them about the behavior of their headmen and how everything is getting on in their hamlet." As their leader, Talplacido must give "sweet words" to the municipal authorities, inquiring in detail about their conduct; Segovia would take care of the rest.

Funston and the Spaniard left the three to their thoughts. They went outside, where, on the *Vicksburg*'s deck, the Hazzard brothers had assembled their company of scouts into snappy formation. Soon the Macabebes' mood had been transformed into what an observer might have called uneasy; it seemed very doubtful to them that they would ever return from such a dangerous journey. Also, the scouts distrusted Talplacido and the other Tagalogs, for surely they would betray them all to Aguinaldo at the earliest opportunity. Before the nay-sayers reached their chorus, old Pedro Bustos stepped forward to exhort the valor back into his fellow scouts. He had spent his whole life fighting against his own countrymen, first for the Spanish, then

Rice terraces in the mountain provinces of northern Luzon have changed little since Aguinaldo toiled through them during 1899 and 1900.

The intrepid adventurers at Palanan: Sulimon, Christopher Bain, Bersosa, Benchan, Udeng, Dario Gonzalez, Paul Kirtland, David Bain, Erich Vogt, Bill Allen. The man on the ground, the Agta headman at Palanan, insisted upon being included.

NATIONAL PARKS DEV'T. COMMITTEE

Above: This homage to foreign investment graces a park in Metro Manila. Filipino workers are the lowest paid in Asia.

Right: Boys in Manila sell ammunition they claim was dug from the battleground at Corregidor.

OPPOSITE

Top: The ubiquitous jeepney, Metro Manila

Bottom left: Homeless children sleeping in Rizal Park, downtown Manila, a stone's throw from the city's most elegant hotel

Bottom right: The final resting place of Aguinaldo, Kawit, Cavite

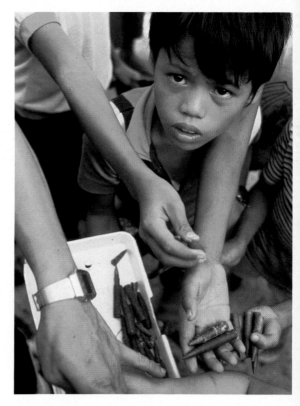

This panorama of Casiguran also shows the Sierra Madre shrouded in rain. *(David Bain)*

Above: Udeng and Sulimon

Left: Bersosa, "seventy years old and spindly, all white whiskers and gristle, and full of betel juice that kept him going fast in a loping gait over sharp rocks"

Outside Casiguran: Bersosa, Erich, Bill, and David

This elderly Ifugao in Banaue may be the son of one of the warriors who hectored Aguinaldo in 1899.

An Agta woman peeks from her hut with two children, near Calabgan.

Above: Trekking up the beach

Right: "An abrupt escarpment of volcanic rock some forty feet tall stood perpendicularly across our path like a large black ship thrown up onto land": Erich climbs to join Bill and Bersosa.

OPPOSITE
Top: At Danny Mangalapus's rattan-picking camp. "Our caravan was like a traveling carnival."

Bottom: Palanan street scene on market day

The National Historical Commission's monument to Aguinaldo in Palanan has been defaced. It will topple into the river within five years. *(David Bain)*

Palanan is one of the most isolated villages in Luzon. Opportunities for these children will steadily narrow due to the lack of educational and medical facilities.

All photographs, unless otherwise indicated, are by Christopher Bain.

for the Americans. There was not an atom of fear in his whole system, in Funston's view.

"My general," he piped, "I care not for these others, but as for me, I am an *American soldier* and am ready to do your bidding." The Macabebes were apparently rallied by this brief speech, but Funston was taking no chances. He privately instructed Segovia to keep his eyes and ears open: it would fall to the Spaniard to maintain discipline during the trek.

Before Funston dismissed the scouts, he delivered one final lecture. Any slight betrayal or disobedience, he said, would be rewarded with summary execution.

Second thoughts evaporated.

Under Commander Barry's direction, the *Vicksburg* chugged across the warm and tranquil Sibuyan Sea, no sooner passing one forested island than sighting another. Little fishing villages sent out their flotillas as the gunboat passed, but no *bancas* came near. The barometer began falling as the vessel pulled toward the quickening currents rushing through the San Bernardino Strait. Meanwhile, Funston retired with Lazaro Segovia to the privacy of Commander Barry's cabin to enact a neat piece of forgery: a letter of introduction, so to speak, that would help in duping and eventually trapping Emilio Aguinaldo.

The previous November, an American party including Funston, Burton Mitchell, and Segovia had come upon a temporary insurgent headquarters in an abandoned farmhouse. They routed the occupants, but after a brief exchange of gunfire the rebels escaped. Only after Funston had made an inventory of the Filipinos' abandoned possessions did he realize he had come face to face with his archrival in Nueva Ecija province, General Urbano Lacuna. From the small treasure trove of captured documents Funston turned in, he retained two pieces of official stationery, which were crudely marked with a rubber stamp to read Brigada Lacuna. He had no sooner received permission for his expedition to go after Aguinaldo than he gave one of his Filipino interpreters the task of counterfeiting Lacuna's signature on the blank stationery, using genuine documents as a model. As the *Vicksburg* neared the entry to the Pacific, Funston and Segovia bent over a desk to concoct two letters that they hoped would seem to be responses from General Lacuna to his commander in chief's bidding. For authenticity, they used information from the documents captured with the messenger Cecilio Segismundo.

The first letter, dated February 24, 1901, indicated that it had been

written by Lacuna at his mountain hideout at Buloc, in eastern Nueva
Ecija, a place they suspected Lacuna actually used from time to time.
The letter acknowledged receipt of Aguinaldo's correspondence of
January 13 and 14 and thanked *el presidente* for confirmation of Lacuna's appointment as brigadier general, which had been made some
time previously by Aguinaldo's subordinate General Alejandrino.
Letting his imagination flow while inhabiting the persona of Lacuna,
Funston continued dictating to Segovia some "airy persiflage," as he
later called it, about the great progress Lacuna's men had accomplished and some rather immodest mention of how he, Lacuna, was
doing his part to expel the hated invader.

So much for the first letter, which was aimed only to set the scene,
and provide the authenticity, for the second letter, which contained
the real payoff. It was dated February 28 and claimed the receipt of
orders from Aguinaldo's cousin Baldomero. Of course, Baldomero
would have assumed command of the "Centre of Luzon" had he received the message borne on poor Segismundo's back. Since his mail
had been interrupted, Funston anticipated what his response would
have been as new commander of the rebels of central Luzon: he would
have ordered his subordinate Lacuna to send reinforcements to
Aguinaldo. So Lacuna, in writing this letter to Aguinaldo, would announce that he was sending one of his best companies to join *el presidente* at Palanan. This group had been swiftly assembled, the letter
claimed, and the assigned reinforcements were leaving under the
command of the gallant Hilario Talplacido, who, in case the leader
was not aware, had for a time sworn the American loyalty oath after
his capture, but he had now returned to fight under the nationalist
banner. Accompanying Talplacido's column would be the "loyal insurgent" Spaniard Lazaro Segovia. Funston dictated "some mere
rubbish, just to fill in space down to the bogus signature," and their
work was done. Only with the passage of time would Funston know
whether this elaborate web of lies would help them — or trap them.

As the *Vicksburg* entered the San Bernardino Strait, it passed and
exchanged colors with a French streamer also bound east, then continued through the passage between the southernmost tip of Luzon
and the cultivated northern shore of Samar Island. They were seldom out of sight of the mile-high cone of Bulusan volcano. Then
they came out into the open Pacific and heavier seas. The ship turned
into the wind and proceeded to skirt up the eastern flank of Luzon;
Funston and his band of conspirators became incapacitated with
seasickness.

Days passed and preparations continued. The Macabebes received
their uniforms — such as they were — for the trek. Since the guer-

rillas had long before discarded their regular issue to blend in with their surroundings, only a few scouts donned the blue insurgent uniforms. The rest put on the raggedy, soiled clothing that had been collected around the seamier sections of Manila. The few articles that looked too new were effectively aged and weathered by being used along with the harshest navy soaps to scrub the *Vicksburg*'s hold.

The scouts assembled on deck for classes, snickering at first to behold their sorry getup. Their teacher, Lazaro Segovia, lectured in Tagalog, which became their mandatory dialect on the ship, and they were given the yarn they were to parrot during any contact with the inhabitants of the eastern coast. Segovia drilled and drilled, questioned them, and drilled again while the diminutive general from Kansas looked on with stern approval:

They were one of General Urbano Lacuna's companies.

They had operated in Nueva Ecija province against the Americans.

They were ordered to join el presidente *and had begun their northward journey in February.*

Crossing the mountains between Pantabangan and Baler, they surprised a party of ten American soldiers, who were making maps. They killed two and wounded three of the Yankees; the wounded were left to die. The remaining five, who surrendered, were taken prisoner.

Though the reinforcements had not been so instructed, they brought along their prisoners because the company could not spare any of their number to take the captives back to General Lacuna.

Segovia knew well that the Macabebes usually treated civilians with contempt if not cruelty. As an American officer, Gregory Batson, said after working with them, "They are terrors. Word reaches a place that the Macabebes are coming and every Tagalog hunts his hole." So, over and over, the Spaniard repeated the refrain: "Treat all men as your brothers and hurt nobody."

Segovia feared there would be a lack of discipline on the trek. The whole venture depended on a series of "ifs" to succeed. *If* the Macabebes were disciplined and *if* they remembered always to speak in Tagalog (even when seemingly alone). *If* they never for one minute slipped a nod or a knowing wink to a comrade or overplayed their roles, then perhaps they had a chance. *If* Talplacido had the physical and mental strength to play colonel, then perhaps they might stay alive a little longer. *If* the Americans could survive a hundred miles without their tins of bully beef and beans, without the copious amounts of food they were accustomed to putting down each day, then perhaps their mission would not fail on some deserted beach. *If* all the Filipinos they encountered on their way to Palanan chose to believe their fantastic story, then perhaps General Funston would emerge from this with his exalted prisoner and everyone could go home and risk their lives no more. These misgivings Segovia never voiced. If their venture depended on all those "ifs," then the less the percentages were worked out, the better for all.

Frederick Funston had his own worries. One was how to avoid being seen by someone on the shore near their planned landing point below the town of Casiguran. He asked Commander Barry to follow the eastern coast to Tabayas province and the sleepy village of Atimonan. The town had an American garrison and was considered pacified, which would make the procurement of sailboats for the mission easier and more discreet. These native craft could be towed along and eventually used to transfer the members of the expedition to the beach. This would be done far enough out to sea to eliminate the possibility of the *Vicksburg*'s being spotted. Even a telltale smudge of smoke on the horizon would send the rebels scampering for a new hiding place.

On the night of Saturday, March 9, the ship worked in for an anchorage in Atimonan Harbor. Lookouts spied the lights of the village through a mist and soft rain at half-past eleven. Barry took the helm and followed the shore at a distance of a mile. He used caution for good reason. His charts were useless, set at a scale of ten miles to the inch, and there was only one depth sounding indicated, which proved to be off by forty feet. His sailing manual's tide chart for Atimonan was wrong by twelve hours.

Sailors at the fore were rapidly lowering their chains for soundings when they called back that the bottom was coming up fast. Barry ordered his engines reversed, but it was too late. The ship settled sideways against a soft mud shoal and stopped dead.

There was no discernible shock to wake the slumbering soldiers. But when the commander ordered the engines into forced draft and began to back them hard, how could anyone sleep? The engines roared and whined at their limit, making the whole ship shake; the screws churned the water into an angry froth; navvies went out in their rowboats to drop mud anchors in the hope of enabling the *Vicksburg* to winch itself free, to no avail. All around the ship, sailors called out their depth soundings while, on the bridge, Commander Barry raged and Funston fretted: would this signal the early demise of his plans?

For Frederick Funston, watching helplessly and muttering a curse or two at their predicament, perhaps banging his fist against the ship's rail, such a reversal must have rubbed his nerves raw. Much more than the success of his mission, the capture of Aguinaldo, the ending of the insurrection, was at stake. Back in MacArthur's palace, when the governor general had confessed he was afraid he would never set eyes on the Kansan again, Funston had been given some disturbing news. The War Department had notified MacArthur that they wanted Funston mustered out of the army, an order to which, as a volunteer officer, he was subject at any time. This constant uncertainty had always rankled him; back in September of 1899, after the department had shipped him home with his regiment for mustering out, he and Eda Funston were in San Francisco, at her parents' home, trying to decide what sort of new career was suitable for a relatively young retired brigadier general. Funston still had not lost sight of his dream to make a fortune somehow, continually going to Eda with a new scheme for cornering one market or another in the Philippines. To each plan she had the same answer: an officer's job was more dependable, so he should concentrate on rising in the ranks of the regular army. When Washington sent Funston a telegram saying they were retaining him for further Philippine duty, he had gone back without a murmur and handled his brigade post well. In time, he put civilian life completely out of his mind. He relished his post and entertained ideas of further glory and promotion. Then, on the verge of this bold maneuver that had the feeling of history about it, he had been told by an unappreciative War Department that his services were no longer required. MacArthur had, of course, received permission to retain the Kansan for a short time for unspecified "special duty" without a hint of the reason. Unless this crazy venture worked and gave Funston an argument for his permanent retention, his army career was soon going to end. Funston would be free to take his medals and search — at thirty-five years of age — for a new career. No wonder he had left Malacañang Palace with bitterness crowding out the excitement of the chase. Now, how the plight of the grounded *Vicksburg* must have excoriated his soul!

Some four clamorous hours after the *Vicksburg* went aground, the ship's executive officer, Lieutenant J. R. Glennon, had a brilliant suggestion. The crew prepared the *Vicksburg*'s heavy steam launch for lowering. When it had been rigged out over the side, the big gunboat heeled over slightly. Barry backed his engines at full speed. The vessel pulled clear — undamaged. Barry found an anchorage in a respectable sixty-eight feet of water and waited for daylight.

Burton Mitchell took Segovia and a few scouts ashore the next morning and conferred with the head of the American detachment, who helped them search for native boats. Alas, the villagers had no *bancas* to spare. Loath to return empty-handed, Segovia brought back to the ship a load of fresh vegetables and a quantity of bolo knives. Since the bolos were carried by nearly every insurgent, serving both as weapons and as tools in hacking brush and firewood, they would enhance the counterfeit rebels' costumes.

Commander Barry continued the search. He steered away from the coast to the island of Polillo, which the authorities considered too unimportant for an American garrison, since it had but one village. As the ship nosed into the harbor, guided by a church tower rising above the palm trees, Barry — now shy of uncharted waters and unpacified shores — took many precautions. He ordered his men to prepare for resisting attack. Proceeded by a cutter that took soundings and guided the *Vicksburg* around shoals and sandbanks, the ship anchored opposite the town, bristling with its formidable howitzer and four-inch quick-fire guns. Two cutters went to shore, both with armed crews. With this show of force, Segovia and the Americans, including Funston and Barry, walked into town. Many of the citizenry fled into the woods upon seeing a huge gray warship approaching. The few who stayed behind to guard their meager possessions displayed white flags in front of their homes. The other townspeople soon returned, for they saw a chance to make a slight profit that day selling chickens and coconuts to the landing party. Mitchell, charged with finding the needed *bancas*, returned to the ship in triumph with three large, two-masted sailboats. He had paid 160 pesos for the lot.

Before they weighed anchor on the showery Tuesday morning of March 12, Barry held court again and gave a sailor ten days in double irons for striking the boatswain. With its enlarged brig population, the *Vicksburg* sailed out of the lee of Polillo Island and struck a northward course. The three fragile-looking vessels trailed in its wake, connected to their mother ship by hawsers, each *banca* holding two Macabebe scouts who steered, kept the lines clear, and bailed. In two hours, the ocean's moderate swells had swamped one of the *bancas*, and the gunboat was forced to halt while it was bailed out. Barry ordered the ship to resume progress but at a slower speed. Funston realized that in addition to the days spent searching for the boats, they would now lose another in trying to hold on to them.

The sea grew rougher. Around five in the afternoon the swells became too much for the frail Filipino sailboats, and one sank. The two scouts in it barely escaped drowning by hauling themselves through the waves on their towlines to another *banca*. It was apparent that the others would not remain afloat for much longer, so a vessel was lowered to rescue the miserable crews. The operation, hampered by the high seas, consumed two hours, during which time the steel lifeboat was tossed repeatedly into the wooden *bancas*, nearly splintering and capsizing them. After the six shivering scouts and their rescuers were at last helped on board the *Vicksburg*, the little sailboats fought the seas for a few hours more — the first disappearing beneath the waves after sunrise on Wednesday, the more hardy craft finally going off its hawser at dinnertime. When a sailor entered the captain's stateroom to announce this loss to the assembled officers, what could the general have done but bang the table in front of him in frustration? How could the expedition be safely landed on the coast without *bancas*? By this time, the *Vicksburg* had drawn too near its destination on the mainland to chance foraging for more native boats, so the original plan was reluctantly scrapped. Funston's men would have to risk being put ashore in the steamship's regular landing boats under the cover of night, and they would have to trust to fate that they would be seen by no one — and that the unmistakable form of the warship could be hustled far away from land by daylight.

At one in the morning of Thursday, March 14, beset by a thick squall, the *Vicksburg* approached the melancholy coast under a low head of steam, its lights carefully screened. It passed the high, dark prominence of the San Ildefonse peninsula and halted just inside the entrance to Casiguran Sound. Unassisted by moonlight, starlight, or any other illumination, ninety men quietly and hastily slipped into cutters. Immediately there was a cry, and they had their first casualty: while making the leap from the *Vicksburg* into a launch, a Macabebe accidentally dropped a bolo on his foot and cut himself seriously. He was sent back to the ship's infirmary. Later Funston discovered that another scout, too frightened to leave the ship, had hidden himself in the hammock nettings belowdecks, thereby avoiding the venture altogether.

The launches were lowered into the rough sea. Huddled in the boats, Funston and the other American "prisoners of war" were dressed as enlisted men, in blue shirts with no insignia, khaki breeches and leggings, and campaign hats pulled low over their heads to keep the wind from taking them. Each officer carried a day's ration of rice and a rolled half-blanket, inside of which was stowed a towel, comb, and an extra pair of socks. The "insurgents" were dressed in ragged clothing; their colonel, Hilario Talplacido, brought along a wedding outfit, securely wrapped in oilcloth, to be used for any ceremonial occasions that might occur.

The landing boats pulled through the clouds of fog and rain toward land; the men could see no evidence of life ahead. Drawing nearer to the dark beach, they negotiated through a barrier of coral reefs, and soon the boat hulls were scraping up onto sand. The eighty-nine men disembarked and gingerly passed their supplies and rifles up above the high-water mark to the place they would spend the night.

With a muffled "Good luck, lads," the sailors shoved the longboats back into the dark froth and disappeared into the night.

The men on the beach were left utterly alone — or so they hoped. Ten thousand miles from home and shivering wet, they could make no fire for fear of being detected. They put their backs to the sea. Sheltered insufficiently from the steady rain by palm fronds drawn over their heads, the men remained awake, anxiously peering into the gloomy jungle before them.

PART TWO

THE WILDERNESS

5

DINALUNGAN, AURORA PROVINCE, 1982

I

Today there is only one road from the great Central Plain to the town of Baler on the northeastern coast of Luzon. It winds through the Sierra Madre cordillera and is subject to washouts and landslides with every tropical rainstorm. During the dry season, it has a tendency to crumble away into nightmarish gorges. Usually only logging trucks or dilapidated public buses grind through the mountains, splashing through streams that tumble across the road from the heights and then drop into chasms, passing beneath enormous ferns, towering dipterocarp trees, and feathery pandanus pines that crowd the margins of the road. On one particular day in 1982 at the beginning of the hot months, two rented jeepneys threaded through the foothills on the cordillera's western slope, their American passengers inhaling great quantities of dust as they prepared to retrace history.

Ten hours earlier I had risen from starchy hotel sheets and breakfasted on eggs Benedict, croissants, a sliced mango, and Batangas coffee. I planned to sleep that night on the barren beach of a coastal area seldom visited by any outsiders save missionaries and the occasional anthropologist. The next morning, with my five companions, I would begin a hundred-mile trek up the mountainous eastern edge of Luzon.

It is a place populated only here and there by people whose remoteness from the very mainstream of Philippine life, whose daily acquaintance with hardship, have enforced a stoic self-reliance that still can encompass a remarkable courtesy extended to their very few visitors. Physically, the coast has not altered much in a millennium, nor have the lives of its inhabitants been affected in any clear way by the ripples of changing civilization. But though life repeats its patterns from year to year and generation to generation — affected chiefly by the cycles of planting and harvesting, dry heat and wet heat — the northeastern coast has not been without drama nor has history passed it by.

Near where the miserable Bagabag-Baler road plunges into the Sierra, the twisted wreck of a steel bridge lies uselessly in the riverbed, torn away by a typhoon-flood of unimaginable proportions, and the road dips into a rivulet drying up in the early summer heat. Roaring through a tiny hillside village, our jeepneys raised choking clouds of dust that rolled toward lines of newly washed clothes flapping like banners and enveloped a little girl in a pink dress standing at the roadside next to a pile of ripe melons. A sharp turn, a steep climb, another turn, and as we entered the jungle that covers the cordillera, the sky shrank to a thin blue ribbon directly overhead. We drove carefully around two large earth-moving machines rumbling down the road toward us. For some undiscernible purpose, they were pushing large boulders from the road shoulder to its center. Everywhere was the sound of tropical cicadas — a thousand buzzsaws nearly drowning our engines' roar. At every switchback the narrow, carved-out road crumbled away a little beneath our tires, sending earth and gravel showering over the snarled vegetation climbing the ravines below.

Several hours after entering the mountains, a slight opening in the jungle flashed a glimpse of the sea — its brilliant blue momentarily exciting eyes grown weary of dun-colored dust and the green, green forest. Descending now, following a stream that flowed beneath red clay cliffs, we passed a roadhouse called Villa Imelda nestled among ferns and pines. Then we came out on a long, sloping alluvial fan planted in ricefields and coconut palms.

The drivers became emboldened by a paved road, a sign announcing Baler, five kilometers away, and by the prospect of getting paid and starting back home. They sped down toward the ocean at an incautious clip, past nipa palm huts, tin-roofed shacks, a mud-colored church with a green-tiled roof (from which emerged a procession carrying a statue of the Virgin Mary), past carabaos that ignored us and children who cried, "Hey Joe," scattering roosters and chickens before gliding to a halt before a two-story government building with a sign that read: PROVINCE OF AURORA, BALER MUNICIPALITY, HON. LUIS

ECUBAÑEZ, GOVERNOR. Walking by a group of idle, gawking men, we six dusty Americans clumped upstairs in our hiking boots and passed a dozen startled secretaries, to be met finally by the smiling governor in pressed pants and Banlon shirt who ushered us into his office.

As we talked, my eyes were repeatedly drawn to the gaudy, larger-than-life portraits of Ferdinand and Imelda Marcos that hung over his head; they looked like the sort of art available in shopping malls back home. For his part, the governor noticed and commented on the portrait I had printed on my T-shirt: a bearded American army officer, turn-of-the-century vintage — the man whose exploits had beckoned me to the northeastern coast of Luzon.

"Ahhh, Frederick Funston," the governor said thoughtfully. "Probably in your textbooks an American hero who single-handedly brought about the end of the Philippine-American War by capturing the man who in *our* textbooks was the Filipino George Washington — Emilio Aguinaldo, a brilliant general, diplomat, first president of the Filipino republic." He smiled genially and ordered another round of warm Pepsis. "Frederick Funston must be an important figure to you Americans."

I was not about to disturb the exalted image of that long-dead and forgotten war hero in the governor's mind. That would make the loss of the first Asian republic seem even more tragic.

But the governor would not dwell on history, though he alluded to the stories of Chinese pirates settling centuries ago in the mountains north of Baler and, more recent, to the experiences of American and Filipino guerrillas receiving supplies from submarines off Baler during the Japanese occupation in the Second World War. Governor Ecubañez had, instead, much to say about a famous American film director whose company had filmed a Vietnam War epic near Baler for ten months. "It was very good for our economy," the governor said. For me this produced images of trucks laden with beer, pâté, and cocaine threading through the Sierra Madre toward Baler while humming portable generators powered air-conditioned trailers and tape decks. Ecubañez told me that the film director had been very meticulous about authenticity; learning somewhere that Vietnam villages contained no dogs, he had all of Baler's dogs removed — to what fate I did not learn. Pressed beneath glass on the governor's desk was a photograph of Ecubañez with the film producer's second unit of technicians. The governor still recalled with pleasure the names of most of them.

Later, below a bridge spanning a sluggish river, we boarded the last outrigger *banca* to leave Baler before the Easter weekend halted

all commercial traffic. The captain of this thirty-five-foot diesel passenger boat was anxious to get started and rushed over to help us
get our baggage aboard. But when he lifted one of our backpacks,
he grunted under its weight and set it back down, laughing at us for
expecting to carry it for very long. We put out and followed the river
as it meandered through a tangled jungle, spilled through a gap in
a sandy beach, and emptied into the Philippine Sea. The pilot steered
straight out through the waves breaking several dozen yards off the
beach. Behind us, the governor stood on a sandy point and waved
from a place that seemed to resemble that used by a film crew several years before during the Sturm und Drang orchestration of a
helicopter attack upon a fake Vietnamese village — of which there
now seemed to be no trace.

Before we had gone very far, the outrigger turned toward a stone
jetty, where a group of travelers stood next to their belongings, waiting for us. While these people climbed aboard, an overweight and
loutish young man sitting near me sent a boy down the Baler jetty
with a 20-peso note for some gin. Seeing me watching him, he insisted I look inside his plastic wallet, where he displayed an identity
card attesting to his membership in the national police. He flashed it
to everyone on board, and I saw people exchanging uneasy looks:
watch out for this bozo. When the boy reappeared with a bottle, the
policeman drank from it as though it were water.

"Here," the sergeant said to me, pushing the bottle in my face.

I declined. He looked at me with a familiar accusatory light in his
eye — I had seen it in bullies everywhere. "You don't want to drink
with me?" he said, and again I refused, as did my brother and our
friend Dario Gonzalez, both of whom had sized him up. Our three
other comrades, however, obliged him by drinking his cheap gin but
saw that their politeness was wasted. He showed a felon's interest in
our various possessions, but after four or five pulls on his bottle, the
gin worked on him before he could make any grabs. He asked us
our destination, and when we told him Casiguran and then Isabela
province he squinted at me. "Isabela is full of communists," he slurred.
"Are you a communist?" I shook my head and he drank some more.
"Hey you," he said to my friend Erich Vogt. "Are you a communist?"

"No, man."

The sergeant's glare swept briefly across the Filipinos in our boat.
They shifted uncomfortably. "We know what to do with communists," he said.

Soon his drinking made him incoherent. He lapsed into Tagalog,
which none of us understood. When he shouted something, two

boatmen led him aft, stumbling and groaning. For a moment I thought they were going to ditch him in the darkening Baler Bay — and for a crazy split second I half approved — but they only held him upright while he urinated into the sea. I emptied his gin into the ocean while his back was turned. Soon he was back among us, collapsed on the deck in a sodden heap to sleep it off, a threat no longer to any of us.

While the cop snored, a young man made his way over to sit beside me on the gangway. "I hope you won't assume," he said, "that all Filipinos are like that fellow."

"Of course not," I replied. "There are drunks everywhere, especially in the United States. It's just too bad that he's in a position of authority somewhere. I feel sorry for the people he's supposed to be watching over."

"He's usually pretty harmless," said the young man, who introduced himself as Gerry Imperial. He was college-educated and worked for the Food Management Authority, a government agency in Baler; though only twenty-six, he supervised a staff of ten. With a candor unusual in the Philippines, he asked me a question: "Did you see how I walked down the jetty to our boat?"

As a matter of fact I had. Gerry had a pronounced limp.

"I had polio," he confided, "but I try to master my infirmity through my contact with other people — by fighting my shyness and shame, by making new friends." He questioned me closely about American culture and the details of my life there. During our long trip to Dinalungan he managed to sit down next to each of us six Americans, sailing effortlessly into friendly and frank conversations that, more than any others we had experienced, bridged the wide dissimilarities of our two cultures.

The sun went down behind the hulking cordillera in characteristic tropical splendor, turning our faces and those of our twenty fellow passengers the same rosy hue as we chugged north across an unruffled sea. A full moon began to climb across a sky of brightening stars. Accompanied by the steady pinpoints of Jupiter and Saturn, the moon illuminated Baler Bay but not the dark mountainous coast, where from time to time a light would flash onshore as if people were coming out of their isolated houses to look at the sky. At the stern of our *banca,* the other passengers leaned companionably against each other and talked quietly over children sprawled asleep across their laps. Several people reclined on the narrow bamboo gangways and blew cigarette smoke into the breeze.

I picked my way over the dark pile of baggage and came out from under the canvas awning to stand on the prow. Leaning out, I could see phosphorescence streaming away in our wake. Ahead and to my right, a black shape rose in the darkness. It was the tip of a long, narrow, finger-shaped landform called Cape San Ildefonse, which pointed southerly — toward me, toward Baler, toward the road home. I didn't take it for a sign but for a portal — into a place where the present would recede enough to let the past intrude.

In my mind's eye was a vivid sight of three dark longboats pulling through rain and fog off that coast no darker eighty-one years ago than it was now, passing as we were the craggy peninsula that stood in the night skirted by a faintly white, crashing froth of breakers. I could almost make out the faces of the men in those tossing boats — faces grown familiar from faded photographs, but looking anything but confident or triumphant as they peered through the mists at land they knew to be more dangerous than any they had trod upon — having embarked on a mission perhaps less the stuff of adventure than that of nightmares. I shivered, though the night was balmy. The vision faded under the moonlight as we turned to starboard and headed in toward land.

After we had put ashore, at the end of a Wednesday that had begun with my struggling to answer a 4:00 A.M. wakeup call, I lay awake in my sleeping bag on the beach. A few hundred yards away, a small village lay below the still silhouettes of palm trees. There was a strange glow from the sand. As I stared up through the transparent, summer-weight fabric of my tent at the stars, I listened to the eerie voodoo chorus of roosters and dogs befuddled or enchanted by the declining full moon. Before I finally fell asleep, my thoughts naturally flew back to one of the men on those silent rowboats so long ago: the midwestern soldier of fortune, Frederick Funston.

II

The tide was high and the sun already climbing in a cloudless sky when we poked our heads outside the tents. It was six in the morning. Twenty-five yards away a Filipino family stood in the dunes, looking at our three bright space-age tents in astonishment, for we had set them up long after these people had gone to bed. A gaunt man with uncombed hair slowly approached us with a worried expression. Trying to smile, he politely asked me where we were going. I indicated north, up the beach.

"You are missionaries?" he asked.

"No, historians," I replied.

He looked puzzled but introduced himself. He was Florentino E.

Araza, Sr., a minor official of the village nearby called Dinalungan. Araza's wife, sisters, and children approached us curiously and he introduced me.

"I am writing a book," I explained to him, "on the Philippine-American War."

"Ah," Araza said, "the Philippine-American War."

"Yes. Eighty-one years ago an American general landed here, when it was only jungle. He went by foot north to Palanan after Emilio Aguinaldo."

"Ah, Emilio Aguinaldo," he said, smiling. "The Americans came with some scouts. They stayed in Casiguran along the way!"

I nodded, pleased he knew this. "Yes. In fact, they landed right here on this beach, near Dinalungan."

"We have a place in history!"

By this time ten more villagers had walked up, then a half-dozen children. A dog sniffed my feet but growled when I stooped to scratch behind his ear.

"We plan to duplicate the Americans' hike to Palanan," I said.

Araza winced. "That is a long way," he said doubtfully, and he looked gloomy for a few seconds. Then he brightened. "But this is an *important mission* you are on, to re-create that event! History is *very important!*"

These words were the nicest welcome I could have hoped for. Araza told me he would return later, and he hustled his family back to his house, a one-story wooden structure with a corrugated metal roof that sat behind neat hedges about sixty yards away. A few others wandered off, leaving the rest to withdraw to a respectful distance, from which they squatted and watched us.

We set about getting our day started. To be truthful, when I had said we were historians it was only for convenience, for of all of us, only I could claim the title after my years studying Philippine and American history. My brother, Christopher, the photographer, who is fair-haired and bearded and often mistaken for my twin though he is six years younger, had expressed an interest in reading something about our predecessors on that coast. But in the months prior to the trip there was little time for history, much less for a briefing on the current Philippine political scene. His time had been occupied by planning the nitty-gritty details of the expedition — what backpacks, tents, or stoves to carry and what to eat, such as the foil packs of freeze-dried cheese omelettes we began preparing for breakfast.

Christopher's evident pride in the utility of our aluminum cooking gear, in the incongruity of our futuristic tents and all our other gadgets on that primitive beach, was tempered somewhat that morning owing to the loss of a hunting knife during our nighttime unloading of the outrigger. He had borrowed it from our father for the trip; in addition to feeling its sentimental value, he was chagrined at the prospect of his beginning this expedition without the camper's most useful tool, so he moodily scuffed around the dunes for a while in a fruitless search before giving up. Stirring the watery mess in the frying pan, he listened glumly as our friend Bill Allen said he might have a spare to lend. My brother and Bill have been friends for many years, and Chris knew well that of any traveling companion he might have, Bill was the most likely to possess an extra hunting knife. A gangly, red-bearded, and freckled cabinetmaker by trade, Bill had more wilderness camping and hiking experience than all the rest of us put together; when he was little, his parents thought nothing of setting off with children in tow into remote bear country in Canada or of teaching them the finer points of mountain climbing. Now a father himself, Bill was conscientiously seeing to his own son's education in the wilds, and he plainly regretted being separated from his family by half a world. He seemed to be most at ease when depending on his wits and upon the well-used equipment in his travel-stained backpack. To Bill's credit, he looked upon Christopher and me — with our factory-fresh gear and hiking lore gleaned mainly from guidebooks — without amusement. Bill had set foot in the Philippines only a few days earlier and knew nothing of the country beyond what he had seen at the hotel and during our dusty ride to Baler. Still, he inspired confidence in me with my minimal acquaintance with the outdoors, and in Christopher, who despite a strenuous life was, like me, on his first wilderness expedition.

We were scraping the last morsels of cheese-flavored library paste from our aluminum plates when a terrible rumbling made us turn in time to see a huge olive green vehicle bounce through the scrub growth at the top of the beach and churn its way through the sand, halting near our camp. It was an ammunition carrier, one of the thousands of old jeeps and trucks abandoned by troops during and after the last war. Araza sat in the passenger seat next to another middle-aged man. "This is the mayor's truck," Araza said. "The mayor is in Manila on business, but we would like you to come and meet Mr. Bote. He is temporarily in command." I left my friends and hopped into the back of the truck, squeezing onto a bench next to several women and children who smiled shyly but said nothing.

The village was built on perpendicular gravel lanes. The houses were small and unkempt and looked poor. People looked out from their glassless windows at us; a few waved. Araza's friend pulled up next to an unadorned house built of concrete and they ushered me into a fenced-in yard. I shook hands with Pablito Bote — twenty-six, married with two children, whose title was municipal development coordinator. We sat on a bench in his yard. A distrustful dog kept his eye on me while a pig and some chickens wandered around our feet.

"Our village is very poor," Bote told me, "but of course you and your friends will stay with us as our guests until after Easter."

"I'm afraid we can't," I said, thanking him for his kindness. By Easter, three days away, we hoped to be many miles distant, in the village of Dinapiqui.

"What? It is impossible to travel on Holy Weekend — there is no transportation."

"But we plan to walk."

"Walk to Casiguran?" Why would anyone *walk* to Casiguran? Especially in the summer?

"Yes, and from there to Dinapiqui and Palanan."

Bote looked embarrassed. He was too polite to tell me I was a fool. He stared at the ground for a long while. "But you should rest," he said, "and participate with us in our observances. We have many interesting . . ."

He went on, but I began thinking of another conversation that had taken place in Manila ten days earlier, in the grand old colonial building in Rizal Park that housed the Ministry of Tourism. There, in offices so bare that two secretaries' chairs were appropriated for our interview with their boss, my brother and I met a tourism promotion official by the name of Ting de los Reyes. He had a laconic manner until he addressed his staff, when he adopted an exceedingly brusque tone. He knew vaguely of our mission but soon grew numbed by the immense detail of plans, requests, time demands, and suggestions. He flatly warned us about the coastal provinces of Aurora and Isabela: "It's very dangerous there. A real hotbed. I myself would not go there for fear of bandits, guerrillas." He looked at the floor. "No, what I think you should do is spend Holy Week with me in Pampangas province. We have many interesting sights there. After that, a visit to Baguio, and perhaps later a trip to go rafting at Pansangjin Falls."

"Yes, that would be very nice," I said. "Perhaps later if we had time — but back to our expedition." De Los Reyes looked down at the floor again, seeming to stare at something. He smiled, sighed, and paid attention to us for a few minutes. Then he brought up the beaches at Cebu, the volcanoes in southern Luzon, and — certainly — Holy Week observances in Pampangas. Hearing this, *we*

looked down. De Los Reyes looked down. There was an embarrassed silence while we all stared at the office carpet.

"Well," I said finally, "back to our expedition."

Now, sitting on a wooden bench and examining the packed earth
of Pablito Bote's small compound after the third go-around of politely expressing regrets at not being able to stay the weekend, I felt
the same welling of claustrophobia: trapped by Filipino hospitality
and your own good manners!

"Look, it just won't work," I said, impatience welling up in me as
I labored to keep an even tone. "We left a schedule behind with friends
in Manila. If we don't reach Palanan by April twentieth, they're going
to get alarmed. And when they get alarmed they're going to send
out search parties to look for us in the mountains!"

This did the trick — and caused no insult.

Not long after, the man who had driven me into the village took
me back to the beach. His name was George Robert, certainly an unusual name for the Philippines, where most names derived from the
Spanish. "I think," Pablito Bote had wryly opined, "that George Robert is indirectly a by-product of the Philippine-American War." The
women standing nearby laughed lewdly. George Robert grinned a
gap-toothed smile. He had another reason to smile. He was going to
make a month's wages for two days' work. After a spirited negotia-
tion, he had agreed to haul some of our camping supplies to a food
drop in Dinapiqui, about sixty-five miles north over a very rough
mountain road.

Our two orange rectangular tents and blue dome were being rolled
up when I returned to my friends. A little boy stood nearby, on his
leg a fresh gauze bandage that had attracted the curiosity of his playmates. Dario Gonzalez, our curly-bearded and husky companion,
sternly told the children not to touch the boy's wound. Dario was
dressed in a light green scrub shirt because it was light and comfortable in the growing heat and because that was what he wore in his
home town of New York City, where he was the chief physician in
the emergency room of a hospital. He would have readily admitted
that, before I invited him to join us, the last thing he could have
imagined doing for a vacation was living out of a backpack on a foreign coast. If tramping through jungles and mountains was a totally
new experience, he was at least open to the prospect of seeing if he
was up to it. Along our way he would be well equipped for the many
kinds of medical emergencies that might befall us, from mild infections to traumatic amputations. The suppurating wound on the little
boy's leg had naturally drawn his attention; he had quickly cleaned

and covered it and had given a packet of antibiotics to the boy's mother for further treatment.

All of the villagers had left the beach for whatever shade they could find when we finally shouldered our backpacks. To make up for lost time, we foolishly decided not to heed the rising sun and so struck off along the soft baking sand.

The marching order divided naturally, almost by age. Up in front was Erich Vogt, looking something like Errol Flynn with his olive Australian bush hat and pirate's mustache as he strode forcefully up the center of the beach. Some years before, Erich had renounced the suburbs from which he had sprung in favor of a more natural existence in and around Glenwood Springs, Colorado, where he did his best to make a living as a carpenter in a severely depressed housing market. Business being what it was, it afforded him perhaps more opportunities for camping and technical rock climbing than he would have preferred, but at least he excelled in these pastimes, and on the few occasions he had returned East, he was full of tales of adventures in avalanche country and pioneer-style revelry in the raucous taverns of Colorado. The life appeared to agree with him. I had not seen him in years when I sent word that I was putting together a hiking party destined for the Philippines, but Bill Allen and Christopher swore that Erich's skill in the outdoors would be valuable, and I would see later that they were right.

Following Erich was Paul Kirtland, who, like all of our party but Dario, had been raised in Port Washington, New York. An engineer for a Long Island aerospace firm, Paul had spent more free time on the water racing sailboats than he did on land, and perhaps because of this he did nearly everything with a languorous economy except drive cars, which he did as if he were the featured attraction at a stock car race. The fact that our trip up Luzon's northeastern coast would be made on foot lessened the chances of head-on collisions and such, and consequently Paul, with his half-Chilean good looks and wry smile, inspired us all with confidence. Together, Erich and Paul had the strength of four or five men, and it was as much for this as for their companionability that I had asked them along. Within minutes of our striking camp, they were forging ahead in the sand as Erich began the delivery of another Glenwood Springs anecdote for which Paul was an avid listener.

Bill — all practicality — walked down where the sand was still wet and hard from the tide, making his path easier. Being the fairest-skinned, he had the most to fear from the tropical sun, so he had taken precautions and glistened from sweat and lotion. He wore a shapeless straw hat, a hobo's headgear. Behind him trudged Christopher, whose camera bag hung on his chest like an orange marsupial pouch and stood ready to disgorge his Nikons at the least provocation. He walked without a hat despite my admonitions. Next was myself, still a fresh and eager sightseer of this bright terrain, one part of my mind focusing on our predecessors. I carried a handsome hardwood staff acquired two mountain ranges away, in Ifugao province. Sweat had begun to transfer the black stain from the staff to my hand. A brass idol — Busao, the rice god — had been fixed to the top end and caught the sun nicely. Dario followed a few paces behind, content to bring up our rear; from under his hat, he looked at the waves slapping onto the sand. Across a calm sound, the peninsula presented itself as a regular series of mountain humps of exposed brown rock and a patchy carpeting of scrub growth and trees. It stretched from southwest to northeast for eighteen or twenty miles, a spiny tail of the cordillera we would live with for an unknown number of days.

From Cape Engano at the northeastern tip of Luzon to Dingalen Bay south of Baler, the land emerges abruptly out of the Philippine Sea to form a massive uplifted and tilted block some two hundred miles long: a veneer of twenty-million-year-old Tertiary sedimentary rock over an igneous foundation. The cordillera is heavily timbered, fringed by cliffs, inaccessible, mysterious. It is drained by rivers and hundreds of swift streams that have sculpted the heights but have neglected to deposit their alluvium at the mountains' feet; that is, with the exception of the sheltered coastal bay plains at Baler and Palanan and the vaguely spoon-shaped one we were following now toward Casiguran. About eight miles over my left shoulder the mountains rose, bulwark over rampart, to more than six thousand feet, with untrammeled jungle creeping down the flanks toward this beach, giving way on level ground to occasional groves of coconut palms and untended irregular garden plots.

By the time an hour rolled by, I was beginning to fret. The group was becoming separated by lengthening distances. Those at the front — now some two hundred yards ahead — were least acquainted with the Philippines (and Third World countries in general), having arrived only five days earlier. I worried briefly that because they were so far in front they might meet someone when I was not nearby; because of their ignorance of this complex culture and its murky political climate, they might get us in some sort of difficulty.

We left the beach and entered a shady coconut grove for a break at half-past twelve, setting our packs down near a tumbling hovel. It may or may not have been owned by the ancient man who crouched in the bushes a dozen yards away and refused to come near. I reminded my friends that we had agreed to be ruled by the buddy system. Paul and Erich reluctantly agreed to a slower pace and to initiating a break every hour. Then they wandered off to forage for fallen coconuts, which were plentiful and still sloshing with milk.

We tossed the last drained coconut into some bushes and hoisted our loads, feeling refreshed, but fifteen minutes later I was back down on the beach, soaked with sweat and dehydrated. Panting, with half my water supply gone, I couldn't resist gulping down more. My feet baked and chafed. My backpack bit into my shoulders and hips. I could hear Dario gasping behind me and stopped to let him catch up. The distance between us and our friends was lengthening.

"Why are they walking so fast?" Dario asked. For a minute I could not reply. Having watched them grow up, six years behind me, I considered now all their wrestling tournaments, track meets, gymnastic matches, karate matches, competitive sailing; their softballs, footballs, and Frisbees tossed at every looming quiet moment in their lives. They were active people. They even relaxed aggressively.

"They like to compete" was all I could reply.

"Funny time to prove yourself," he grumbled.

We walked on. The tropical sun could shorten one's temper, as we were discovering, for the farther our comrades drew ahead, the angrier Dario and I grew. After an hour of plodding under the sun and railing furiously at their backs, we halted when Dario put his hand on my elbow.

"Show me your watch," he said.

I complied and he took his own pulse rate.

"Damn them!" he raged. His heart was going at 120 beats per minute and he felt nauseated — the first signs of heat stroke. "Where are those guys?" he asked, and we squinted across an empty expanse of hot white sand. Christopher was a dot on the beach; the rest were not visible. I pointed to a shady patch of sand beneath a palm tree and we staggered over to it. Between us, we finished a liter of water.

Twenty-five minutes later Christopher returned. He was wearing a hat finally, and he had left his load up ahead. We flung bitter words his way and he turned around, penitent, to rejoin the others. We followed and later found them sitting in some shade near a pitted concrete loading dock, abandoned on the beach like a useless boat. My brother knew well the fulminations to which I am sometimes prone and tried to intercede, assuring me he had passed on our complaints to his chums. But I would have nothing of it. I was still angry and insisted on having my say: on this first day of hiking they were running us into the ground, and to what purpose? They sprawled on the sand, as blasted by the heat as we.

Munching on peanut butter and crackers, we drained our canteens and regained our good humor. When Erich got up to look for more coconuts, Paul and I volunteered to find water.

We followed a sluggish creek for several hundred yards through the trees, hoping to find clean water. But the creek meandered into reeds, then a swamp. We turned away at the suggestion of a glowering carabao that lumbered out from a thicket and confronted us. Aside from the vegetation fringing this unpromising creek, the ground was a wasteland of dust with no topsoil to support trees, just sand and brown weeds.

From there the mountains looked green and inviting, so we struck off across that blasted field toward a furrow in the mountainside. A half-mile later we could see it was an old, dry streambed. Paul said we had already walked so far, we might as well go all the way. Then a young man appeared amid dying, scraggly brush. He knew no English and was frightened of us, but when we held up our string of twelve empty canteens, he motioned for us to follow. At the edge of the tree line we passed through his vegetable patch and stepped over a stick fence into his yard. A rooster and chickens pecked at the ground and pigs snuffled nearby. On the front porch of his thatch-roofed cottage the young man's pregnant wife sat husking rice. She was lovely, but when she smiled in welcome, I saw she had no front teeth. Down in a hollow shaded by bushes and perfumed by wildflowers, the farmer showed us his secret, a bamboo sluice that ran up the mountainside to a high hidden spring of sweet water.

I learned later that the desolate place we had walked through had been created by outsiders who had come to the coast looking for minerals. Their workers had aggressively strip-mined acres of land, much of which had been reclaimed from jungle only a few years before they arrived. The crews had invaded the farmers' homes, sunk deep pits in their yards, and claimed that their commercial rights prevailed over the impoverished farmers' property rights. Those rapists of the land had been surprised, though; the farmers had banded together and sent a petition to their provincial governor, and the miners were evicted. But this dusty, infertile land could never be reclaimed.

Although an unpaved lane runs all the way from Dinalungan to Casiguran, we had elected to avoid it whenever possible in order to retrace Funston's path literally. This hot afternoon made beach-walking wearisome, so we turned inland to follow the road for several miles through a wild, wooded area. A few people passed us and looked askance at our bandits' bandannas tied around our foreheads to catch sweat, and they winced at the sight of our ridiculous loads. But everyone exchanged greetings with us. We came to a creek and gingerly crossed it on rotten logs to keep our boots dry. At the same time, a couple walking in the opposite direction simply removed their rubber sandals and splashed across. I saw a snake swim away from them in our direction and was glad to be looking silly and fastidious on that soggy and unsteady bridge.

We followed the lane into a cleared area. Four or five modest houses on stilts with nipa palm roofs stood well off from us; faces appeared at every window as soon as we walked into the open. They began calling out to us and waving.

"Hello!"

"Where are you going?"

"Hey, Joe!"

"Where are you going?"

"Casiguran," we shouted back. A few people left their suppers to follow us. It was an hour before sunset, time for us to make camp. The road curved past the houses and a tiny gristmill, finally depositing us back on the beach. Everywhere the sand was littered with monument-sized red luan logs, each about twenty or thirty feet long, six feet across, and split neatly in half. They would have fetched a good price at a lumber mill for whoever had troubled to drag them down the mountainside and across the narrow plain to this beach. But the government had belatedly realized that years of lax regulation and bold corruption had permitted unrestrained logging. A few families had gotten rich, but erosion had resulted all over the country, most seriously in the Cagayan Valley and Ilocos and Batangas regions of Luzon and on the large islands of Mindoro, Cebu, Bohol, Leyte, and Masbate. Though it may be too late for many regions, the eastern watershed of the Sierra Madre seems to be safe — for the time being. Commercial logging was recently forbidden along many areas of the littoral, causing some enterprises to withdraw, such as the one responsible for these gigantic luan Lincoln Logs. The people who followed us pressed the logs into service as bleachers; the crowd swelled to forty or fifty men, women, and children as we put down our loads for the last time that day.

"Hello, my friend, what is your name?"

I turned to see who spoke; it was a man in his mid-twenties — shirtless, wearing khaki shorts, with a long bolo knife hanging from his waist. His hair was long, longer than fashionable among young men, and a mustache drooped from his upper lip. His name was Jessi. He was a farmer and sometime fisherman with a wife and children.

He told me he had, unlike most of the people here, been to Manila several times. While we talked, he stood with his shoulders held back confidently; he was an able conversationalist, and I felt that he might be just as at ease in the smoggy bustle of the capital as he was on this quiet beach.

Jessi noticed that Bill and Erich were trying to get some dense kindling lit and told them he had an easier way. He led us into the underbrush and gathered an armful of dead palm branches. Dumping them near our unsuccessful campfire, he demonstrated a trick that we used for the rest of our expedition. With two quick slashes of his bolo he stripped the frond of its dried leaves, then broke it partway through and ground the fibrous ends together. He produced a disposable lighter and the branch caught fire immediately. He added dry leaves until he had a flame. The process had taken less than two minutes. "*Now* you can burn that wood," he said, smiling. Bill, who was usually slow to let his emotions show, looked delighted to learn a new trick.

Looking over his shoulder and over the heads of the crowd, I saw a familiar figure approaching — it was Gerry Imperial. Seeing him wave at us as he skirted a log, approaching slowly, was like being greeted by an old friend.

"I see you have met my cousin," he said, indicating Jessi. "Some people told me there were Americans camping here and I assumed it could only be you." His parents lived nearby, "in a simple nipa house." He had not seen them or his home in a year and was making a surprise trip in time for the Easter weekend. "You do not look as if your hike was easy," he observed, and he was right. My calves, face, and forearms had been burned bright crimson during the afternoon's search for water; Bill, Erich, and Chris had developed bad blisters on the bottoms of their feet and now hobbled around the campsite. We were all fully wrung out, a sorry group of adventurers on their first day's march.

"Everyone here would be so happy if you would just say a few words to each, personally," Gerry told me. I thereupon wandered the length of our spectators' gallery, meeting the entire hamlet. Most of the people were relatives of our friend, and all were extremely curious about the supplies coming out of our seemingly bottomless backpacks. By then the orange two-person tents were up and Christopher was carefully threading a folding flexible pole into slots in the blue dome. He stood up with his fingers full of limp fabric, gave his hands a sharp upward twist, and the cloth flew up in the air and popped open, settling down onto the sand — a tent, a Bucky Fuller marvel. Our crowd moaned in appreciation. Atop a mahogany log, a tiny Svea stove was quickly bringing water to a boil. Bill, our chef of the evening, produced a bright yellow foil packet of dehydrated beef Stroganoff and the people leaned forward to see what he would do next.

I began to feel uncomfortable and then realized why. Though here the sea yielded an abundance of food and the alluvial soil was fertile, the people in this settlement lived for the most part as their ancestors had, impoverished in cash, material goods, and security beyond the present day. With each of the flashy gadgets we produced, I felt more and more embarrassed at the superfluities of richness. Certainly we all lived very modestly in the States, but in the Filipinos' eyes we had come to this beach with the equipment and toys of kings. And though I knew that as Bill poured dessicated chunks of meat and noodles into a pot, Jessi and his friends watched with an interest borne not out of hunger but novelty, I sensed that, nonetheless, to watch this marvel in action was to want to sample it. After some anguished minutes of indecision I took Gerry aside to explain my problem: we had calibrated our food needs down to the last meal. I knew his fourscore relatives wanted at least to sample our magic food, but I was worried about the week ahead, when we would enter a wilderness with no settlements at all, with no chance to replenish our supplies.

"Say no more," he said. "I understand." But I could tell from his crestfallen face that he was disappointed. "I will tell them what you have told me." The people withdrew at his suggestion and he disappeared.

I did not enjoy the meal at all, wishing I had handled the matter better.

Later, in my tent, I was awakened by someone calling my name. I unzipped the tent flap and looked out to see that Gerry had returned with his nephew, holding a beautiful fish. It was at least 14 inches long and gleamed in the moonlight.

"I thought you could add this to your dinner," he said. But everyone was asleep, our pots were put away, our bellies full, and we had nothing to stow the fish in until morning. He stood awkwardly holding the fish while I made my apologies. Then he asked if I was sure. I was. We talked for a short time more, both of us embarrassed at this slight collision of cultures. Finally he said goodnight and limped back down the beach.

The first Westerner to set eyes on the craggy eastern coast of Luzon was a Spaniard now called "the last conquistador," Juan de Salcedo. He was the grandson of Miguel de Legaspi, the man who planted the Spanish flag on Philippine soil in February 1565. Salcedo had been dispatched from Mexico to Cebu island in 1567 as the commander of an expeditionary group. He was all of eighteen, but already very good at war and plunder. He quickly subdued the large Muslim towns on the islands of Mindoro and Lubang and in 1572 shifted his attention to Luzon, becoming the first Spaniard to sail into Manila Bay. Later, when Grandfather Legaspi had conquered the Tagalog forces and established Manila as the center of Spanish vassalage of the archipelago, the old man dispatched Salcedo to help consolidate his control.

While Salcedo was exerting muscle in Taytay and Mayhayhay he heard rumors of gold, and he importuned his grandfather to commission an expedition to northern Luzon. Legaspi had no men or ships to spare, so the determined Salcedo obtained eight or nine *bancas* and Filipino helmsmen. With forty-five Spaniards, he sailed out of Manila Bay, around the Bataan and Pangasinan peninsulas, and straight up the little-known western coast to Vigan, where he left most of his men in a fort. Salcedo then took fifteen companions in two open boats of shallow draft and sailed around the northern coast, then through perilous seas down the entire mountainous eastern coast. He returned to Manila in the late summer of 1572 with a promising cargo of fifteen pounds of gold. Thereafter, the race to pacify the Philippines' major isle picked up speed.

Sixteen years after Salcedo's triumphal voyage, two Dicalced Franciscan fathers, Fray Estevan Ortiz and Fray Juan de Pórras, founded missions in the sleepy coastal villages of Baler and Casiguran, an area of heathens ripe for conversion. The eastern coast was known in those days as the Contracosta, the opposite coast. Ortiz and Pórras were succeeded by "the venerable martyr," Fray Francisco de Santa Maria, who consolidated his missions "with a sufficient number of the faithful who were withdrawn from the darknesses of paganism by the influences of a zeal so seraphic," according to contemporary chroniclers. By 1662, the Franciscans had come to see that this lonely and mountainous coast was more of a burden than they had originally thought. They asked another order, the Dicalced Augustinians (or Recollects), to take over the responsibility for the souls in the two villages. "These missions were not very desirable," the Augustinian friars groused, "both because of the wretchedness of the earth, and because of the small number of tributes that they contained." Religious orders elsewhere in Luzon had annexed large tracts of farmland for plantations, amassed valuable real estate in Manila, and exacted tribute from gold mines in the Central Cordillera. But the Recollects in Baler and Casiguran had been charged with occupying "the least

profitable posts so far as earth is concerned, but the most merito-
rious in the heavens," so they had to content themselves with poor
farmers and religious backsliders, typhoons and marauding pirates.

Because of the continuing raids of Moro privateers, the soldiers in
the small, neglected garrisons on the Contracosta erected forts as well
as watchtowers to give early warning so that the civilians could escape into the mountains above their villages. I heard that a crumbling old Spanish fortress lay somewhere on Cape San Ildefonse, but
there seemed to be no way to visit the cape. When Gerry Imperial
and his cousin Jessi told me on a rubescent Friday morning that they
knew where an old watchtower sat, guarding the passage between the
sound and Casiguran's inner bay, the chance of seeing it gave me
another reason to buy us passage on a *banca* that would leave our
beach that morning for Casiguran. I doubted that some of my blistered friends were in shape to do much walking, and I was glad to
have an opportunity to see how a small Philippine town would observe Good Friday, the people's most solemn religious day.

We climbed aboard the motor-powered outrigger *banca* at seven in
the morning with about twenty other people. Gerry pulled himself
aboard unaided and cheerfully introduced me to the pilot, his uncle.
Erich sat near several children and noticed that one boy was wearing
a T-shirt with a cartoon drawing of two characters from a popular
American children's television show.

"Hey, *Sesame Street*," my friend said, grinning down at the little boy.
He pointed at the two characters on the boy's shirt. "Bert . . . Ernie
. . . *Bert* . . . *Ernie!* Right?" The boy did not understand the signif-
icance of his shirt. But he smiled back, wanting to be polite.

"These kids don't know about *Sesame Street*, Erich," I said. "They
don't have television sets. They don't even have electricity."

On the coral-fringed peninsula, one knobby peak fell before another; on the mainland opposite, coconut palms grew down in some
profusion to the beach. Behind a space of reeds and mud, the braided
rivers Didinagyan, Calabgan, and Caengrean emptied congruently into
the sound. As we puttered evenly across the calm water, flying fish,
called *bolador* here, leaped in long, glimmering arcs into the sun. A
dark *pating*, or shark, trailed us for a time before turning away. As
we approached the narrow entrance to Casiguran's inner bay, where
the sandy Motiong Point reached like a hook to within four hundred
yards of the cape, Gerry shouted something to his uncle at the wheel.
We turned aside toward the peninsula.

"There is your Spanish tower, David," Gerry cried, pointing to a
shamble of mud-colored stone that had fallen in on itself. Then we
were past it and into the clear, shallow water of the bay, gliding above

a forest of swaying undersea plants and an occasional crab scuttling over pale, submerged rocks. On the far side of the bay, several boats were anchored offshore from a cluster of white buildings and large fuel tanks. Our pilot told me that this was the headquarters of the local Philippine Constabulary unit; I sighed in relief. Although I had letters of introduction from scholars and a few officials, no one had issued us a permit to travel on this coast because in Manila no one knew whether permits were required. Therefore the chance of being turned back or, just as bad, escorted along our route by armed government soldiers was always on my mind. Contrary to my expressed wishes, the Tourism Ministry had cabled ahead of us, requesting the PC to escort us; Governor Ecubañez had shown me a copy of the order in Baler. Since then, I had been trying to figure out how to dodge police checkpoints, so sailing past the PC on this placid bay pleased me greatly.

At the head of the bay, a number of brightly painted *bancas* were tied up at the muddy confluence of the Casiguran and Casalogan rivers. Soon, after some good-natured shouting, some men onshore came over to grab our lines and haul us into a place between two other boats. We all disembarked.

Just then a skiff pulled in, and among its passengers were two young white women. Paul and Erich quickly got over their surprise, adjusted their bedraggled clothing, combed their hair with their fingers, and rushed over to help them ashore. The women could not believe their eyes when they saw two tall handsome Americans, with four others waving from their place next to a pile of camping gear.

"What are *you* doing here?" they exclaimed in unison. Upon hearing who we were and a brief explanation, they introduced themselves as Iris Harrison, from Michigan, and Anne Kueffer, from California. Both in their late twenties, Anne and Iris had attended divinity school in the United States and language school in Manila to prepare them as missionaries for the New Tribes Mission, a group with headquarters in Florida that desires to spread Christianity among tribal or minority groups in distant places. These two young women had lived by themselves on the San Ildefonse peninsula for two years.

"We had a really bad typhoon awhile back," explained Anne, "and after it was over, some people who worked with us decided they weren't cut out for this life — it can be pretty harsh sometimes — and they left. We moved from our hut into their house." Their roof was still of nipa leaves, she said. Anne and Iris lived near a place where members of a migratory tribe frequently camped. These hunter-foragers called themselves Agta or Aeta. The Tagalog word for them, however, is Dumagat, "those by the sea," which is the term the missionaries used. The women held literacy classes, provided rudimentary medical help, proselytized, and studied Agta culture.

We squirmed into our backpack straps and began walking under a cruel sun toward the central barangay of Casiguran, two miles distant. Anne and Iris stayed with us, chatting animatedly with Paul and Erich. We told them we needed to hire guides and they promised to help.

Our group was hobbling so slowly that even Gerry outdistanced us. He waved as he limped on ahead. I was leaning heavily on my walking staff, since my badly burned calves chafed at every step. Christopher and Bill grimaced as they walked on their blistered, barely usable feet; Dario, as our doctor, had had to painstakingly remove sand that had been ground into a popped blister on my brother's foot, and Christopher was now obviously in great discomfort. It grew hotter as we walked by a succession of green fields; weighed down as we were by seventy-pound backpacks and perspiring heavily, we grew ever more dehydrated. It was not yet ten in the morning.

We began passing a number of shacks built of weather-beaten planks and tottering on stilts. Heat-stunned chickens and dogs and pigs huddled in the shaded spaces underneath the houses. Faces appeared at windows, and at gates people leaned out to touch us. Some laughed scornfully; some crossed themselves as I passed — a Moses or a pariah leaning on my ornamented Ifugao walking staff with its strange brass headpiece that drew their attention like a magnet. Two, three, then four men on rickety bicycles fell in behind us. Staggering and panting under our loads, we were unaware that a rumor was already flashing ahead of us: we were pilgrims on a penitential crusade to Casiguran for Good Friday, mortifiers of the flesh on this most holy of holy days.

6

CASIGURAN SOUND, 1901

At dawn, the rains ceased falling upon Frederick Funston and his men, left on that strange beach by the departed steamship in the midst of a squall on March 14, 1901. As the morning brightened slightly into an overcast and gloomy day, the sodden adventurers rose stiffly from the sand and took in the view. Across the bay were the mountains of Cape San Ildefonse. An empty beach stretched north for what seemed to be five miles, ending finally at the mouth of a narrow entrance to an inner bay. Three or four thatch houses could be discerned with the unaided eye, though even when using an old pair of field glasses, Segovia could see no signs of a living being anywhere ahead of them.

"Now we were full-fledged insurgents," the Spaniard recalled thinking. With daylight, Funston had undergone a metamorphosis, losing his bearing of command and assuming the guise of a captured and dejected army private. He and his American comrades would have to remain in character day and night until the march was ended.

No one slept that first wet night. The Hazzards had, by sheer exercise of will, kept their scouts from panicking at every stray nighttime sound, and Segovia moved from sentry to sentry, cautioning each to maintain his guard while refraining from firing should any stranger approach. "I was so scared," the Spaniard confessed later, "that I thought they had already forgotten my lessons and advice given on the steamer." One slip of discipline, such as an unwarranted shooting, would have instantly lost them their credibility, possibly their lives.

Their confidence in their roles grew when they started the march, at half-past five. "Everything was now in our favor," wrote Funston, "as we felt positive that our landing had not been discovered." With Segovia at the head of the men, with Funston and the other "prisoners" marching under guard in the center of the column, they maintained a steady, easy pace, though it soon became evident how sinuous was the shore; as their path unwound before them, they assumed what had seemed to be an easy five-mile trek would actually be ten or twelve miles. They followed the empty beach for three miles, crossing two creeks and halting at a third to boil fresh water for breakfast. The Americans looked sourly at their fare — a handful of rice per man. Rice was considered exotic native food in those days, and most American soldiers scorned it as unpalatable. Burton Mitchell claimed it upset his stomach, and though General Funston and Captain Newton did not have such delicate constitutions, they showed little enthusiasm when eating the "native dish." The Hazzard brothers, meanwhile, lustily devoured the grains and came up for more. The failure of the expedition's first breakfast was changed to triumph when Oliver Hazzard produced a tin of bacon he had abstracted from the officers' table on board the *Vicksburg*. Its contents quickly disappeared. Segovia prudently buried the empty tin in the sand, "to awaken absolutely no suspicion in the future," before they took up their march again.

Presumably many of the inhabitants of Casiguran were fishermen, but there was not a single *banca* on the surface of the sound. This raised the men's suspicions; where were the people? Several miles later, the men found their first trace of human habitation on the coast — a rude shelter made of nipa palm leaves thrown over sticks propped against a low tree branch. This small structure was apparently an outlook, as it commanded a view of the ocean and beach. Its recent occupant must have seen their column from afar, assumed it to be the enemy, and taken flight; his footprints in the moist sand pointed toward distant Casiguran, the plantations and coconut groves of which they could now see down the beach. This explained the dearth of human souls in the neighborhood. They slowed their pace cautiously, hoping by an unaggressive demeanor to induce one of the "savage Balugas," or Negrito hunters, to approach them in curiosity or friendship.

At least one other member of the expedition besides Cecilio Segismundo was familiar with this stretch of coastline south of Casiguran. Harry Newton had been a member of the first American garrison established in Baler by Funston the previous year, and he had roamed the area immediately around Baler for some five months. It had been a quiet period: the insurgents had withdrawn to Casiguran, and for the most part the two contingents ignored one another, separated as they were by about forty miles of jungle-fringed coast. Newton had spent his time shooting fish in the streams above Baler, exercising his horse on the beach, and writing letters. Once, he wrote home, he had encountered a party of mountain folk — Ilongotes — while taking a rowboat along the cliff-fringed beaches south of Baler. "They thought their last days had come," he noted. "We were probably the first white men they had ever seen, and as they live, it is kill and get killed. As we had the best of it — guns against bows and arrows — they began to cry and pray and when I pulled my kodak on them they were prepared to die. Their dress consisted principally of cocoanut oil and bushy hair."

In June 1900, the Americans at Baler learned that the villagers in Casiguran had thrown their Spanish priest, Father Mariano Gil, into jail some two years before, during the second uprising against the Spanish. Father Gil was the last imprisoned priest in the islands. Newton set out with five soldiers and a Filipino guide in an open eighteen-foot skiff to row up the coast and rescue the padre. The captain and two others went into the town at night and captured the mayor. After assuring him that Casiguran was completely surrounded by American troops and forcing from him the information they needed, Newton waded across one and a half miles of mud and water until he found and liberated the priest. On the return trip, Newton followed the rowboat of his companions; alone in a dugout canoe, he carried with him Father Gil's library. The weather turned squally. He fell behind and finally retreated to dry land when the party ahead disappeared. Newton lay on a rock projecting into the sea for three days until a search party returned to rescue him.

As Frederick Funston's expedition continued its first day's walk toward Casiguran, the tide rolled up the beach. In some places, mangrove jungles grew down into the water, their overcrowded boles and tangle of upthrust prop roots too dense and overgrown to pass through, so the column took to wading through the surf for long distances, perhaps five miles altogether. When they regained dry land, there were numerous streams to ford. The sandy beach came to an end with an expanse of some two miles of sharp stones, which slowed the barefooted Macabebes. At one small rivulet of sweet water, they halted to fill their single earthen pot with rice while fatigued, groaning scouts sat on the ground, nursing their bruised and cut feet.

One of the men discovered a *banca* concealed in the heavy bushes that hung low over the stream. After a furtive consultation with Funston, the Spaniard ordered his men to make ready to send an advance message to Casiguran. The town had seen Americans only when they were interested in liberating friars, as Captain Newton had done, or wanted to relieve the townspeople of food and valuables, as had happened on other occasions. Cecilio Segismundo had once been garrisoned in the town under the command of Major Nazario Alhambra until his troop had been ordered, in December 1900, to join Aguinaldo. Funston decided that the little messenger appearing again in Casiguran would ease any doubts about their group being insurgents. So Segismundo was ordered into the canoe, followed by Cadhit and three scouts. The Macabebes had been told to kill the courier and Cadhit should they betray the mission, a threat the former rebels had no doubt they would enjoy carrying out; so they, as Funston put it, "entered into the spirit of the thing." Segismundo carried a message with him:

> Local Presidente of the village of Casiguran:
> I send you the bearer, Cecilio Segismundo, who is our guide, accompanied, by a sergeant and three soldiers of my detachment to seek quarters for the troops who will arrive this evening. I also pray of you to have food prepared for our arrival. We are, 1 commanding officer, 1 captain, 4 lieutenants, 77 soldiers and 5 American prisoners. I beg of you to have sufficient food ready as my soldiers are greatly fatigued, having marched for the last fifteen days over mountains. May God guard you many years.
>
> At the beach of the bay, March 14, 1901
> The Commander — Hilario Talplacido

Once offshore, the *banca* was turned to cut across the head of the bay. Segovia estimated it would reach Casiguran in perhaps two hours, time enough for the column to eat and rest.

They resumed marching at half-past two. About ninety minutes later Segovia, leading the column, saw a lone figure some distance down the beach heading in their direction. The Spaniard wheeled and hastily ordered his soldiers into the undergrowth before the approaching man could spy them and run away. The eighty-three soldiers crouched for some minutes in a tangle of shrubs and screwpines. When the man drew close and Segovia jovially hailed him, the Spaniard was told the man had been sent to guide them into the village.

As they walked, Segovia questioned their escort closely. Much as he had expected, his column had been seen by a Negrito lookout, who ran to the village reporting an approaching American detachment. Most of Casiguran had run into the forest to hide but were now returning at the assurance of Segismundo and Cadhit, who had arrived at the village without incident. The Spaniard asked the guide if their insurgent column would be welcome in Casiguran.

"Yes, very much so," the villager replied. "If we have troops we will not be afraid of the Americans. They came once, but we could not fight them because we had only three guns which the [mayor] has for the protection of the town. But now since you are here, we will not run away but stand to our posts; we will take prisoners like those you have, and you will see how brave the people of Casiguran are, what fighters!"

No doubt the guide's bold self-assurance chilled Segovia, for he changed to the subject of their quarry, Aguinaldo, and inquired whether the village was seeing to Don Emilio's needs.

"President Aguinaldo is well content with us," the villager told Segovia, for Casiguran patriotically dispatched rice, sweet potatoes, and chickens to Palanan twice monthly. "He has written a letter to our president telling him that when we are independent he was going to confer honor upon Casiguran for the help we had rendered him and his soldiers."

"Well, you must keep on," replied the Spaniard, "and then the honor is certain."

They had by now reached the head of the bay and were in sight of Casiguran. Soon they encountered four villagers who were preparing to go fishing. The play-acting was now earnestly pursued. Hilario Talplacido called to the fishermen, saying he was too fatigued to walk farther; as soon as they learned they were being addressed by the commander of the insurgent unit, they abandoned all thoughts of fishing and hoisted the portly officer "like a bale of merchandise," as an amused Segovia noted. They carried him up a narrow, muddy trail through the woods and into town. As they passed the first thatched dwellings, villagers curiously approached them, asking where the Americans had been taken prisoner and then why they had not been killed to be rid of all bother. Ignoring the latter question, the scouts made a great show of guarding the five captives and took delight in impressing "the yokels" with tales of their ferocious engagements with the Yankee invaders. Indeed, a couple of the Macabebes exchanged knowing smiles with each other. Their expressions were wiped clean by a murderous glare from Funston, which may have reminded them of the general's lecture aboard the *Vicksburg*: *Any slight betrayal or disobedience will be rewarded with summary execution.*

"We entered the town in great style," noted Funston, for among the receiving crowd appeared the Casiguran municipal bamboo orchestra. Segismundo had apparently kept busy after delivering his message to the townsfolk, for he now greeted his fellows, one arm smugly wrapped around the shoulders of a village girl he had be-friended during his earlier stay in the area. His sweetheart had given him a welcome gift of two chickens, which he had with him. He told Segovia that the mayor had gone to Palanan with a delegation of vil-lagers to deliver provisions to Aguinaldo and join in celebrating Don Emilio's birthday. *El presidente* would turn thirty-two on March 22.

Casiguran was a moderately large settlement of perhaps a hundred board and thatch structures, bounded on three sides by farm plots and groves. In the center of town, an old Spanish stone church and an attached rectory stood next to the town square. Here Gregorio Cadhit and the two Macabebe guards rejoined the group. Frederick Funston, who was heavily guarded halfway back in the column and was carrying his own blanket roll, returned the villagers' gazes. "They crowded around us, and there were some black looks and some re-marks not of a complimentary nature," Funston noted, "but in gen-eral there was nothing in their conduct to criticize." Within minutes, he and the other prisoners were locked up in the house of the absent mayor.

"We had now stepped into a hornet's nest," Segovia mused. Great care had to be taken during every waking moment to ward off the doom that hovered over their heads. He saw to it that his soldiers were billeted in houses, with orders not to stir.

Attended by the fulsome vice mayor, Segovia learned that while Casiguran was a poor town, the villagers would give the soldiers all the provisions they could. The only problem was time, said the vice mayor. Their recent shipment to Palanan had depleted their stores. Segovia speculated that Don Emilio must have had quite a force with him to deplete Casiguran of its rice.

"Has he many soldiers with him?" Segovia made the question sound casual.

"Yes sir," replied the official, "very close to a hundred. There is no danger because the Americans cannot approach on any side with-out being discovered, and the soldiery are determined to resist should the enemy come. Now with your arrival all danger will be past, and no matter how many Americans may be sent against you, you can kill them all."

The odds were not great — Aguinaldo's hundred against Fun-ston's eighty-eight — but surprise would be the deciding element.

The vice mayor was still talking.

"When will we be independent?" he asked Segovia.

"Very soon," the Spaniard answered. "Before the month is over something important will happen."

"Our *presidente* tells us the same thing," exclaimed the delighted official, "that before long we will be independent. He tells us to have a little more patience and keep working."

The vice mayor took his leave, instructing four villagers to prepare some sixty pounds of rice for the soldiers. Segovia tried to wake his men, but many preferred sleep to food.

The flickering lights of Casiguran began to be extinguished, one by one, as the Spaniard slipped past his guards to confer with his American "captives." Their room was unfurnished but for two wooden chairs; consequently, the five were reclining on the bare plank floor. Segovia had sent over two cooked chickens he had purchased and a small quantity of rice. All had eaten well but Lieutenant Mitchell, whose queasy stomach would accept only a small piece of chicken.

The Spaniard crouched over Funston and in low tones told him what had transpired with the village headman, especially of the vice mayor's plea of poverty in provisioning the column for its week-long march to Palanan. This presented a problem; the soldiers had bought a good supply of rice during a stop on the sea voyage but had carelessly stored it in cloth bags in the three *bancas* they obtained for landing. When the *bancas* were lost to the high seas, so was the rice.

"Very well, Segovia," whispered Funston, "but it is necessary that you hurry matters up." This was spoken with some urgency. The general reminded his subordinate of their agreement with Commander Barry and the *Vicksburg*. Directly following the unloading of its stealthy cargo of counterfeit insurgents, the warship was to steam south to anchor off the coast near Baler. Three of its passengers were to disembark to carry on business with the American garrison — which ostensibly had been the official reason for deploying the *Vicksburg* out of Manila. After laying at rest for four days, Commander Barry planned to sail directly to Casiguran and land a party of marines, who would claim to be searching for the Americans taken prisoner in the mountains above Baler. Should something have gone wrong in the village, Funston's group could be rescued. If not, the fiction would have been enforced, and the marines would search and bluster for a time before withdrawing to the ship.

"The *Vicksburg* will be here in four days," Funston whispered to Segovia, "looking for insurgents, and it would be rather strange if the marines found us here, instead of being en route to Palanan."

"Do not worry, General," Segovia reassured him. "I shall arrange our journey before that time."

Lazaro Segovia had slept his last full night's sleep aboard the ship, and it would be another day before he would have more than a catnap. He spent the greatest part of their first night in Casiguran making rounds to prevent his scouts from breaking quarantine. "I know the Philippine soldier too well," he wrote later, "and it is no secret to me that the first thing he does on his arrival at a village is either to seek a friend or a girl, and this done, they prefer to sleep with them; for a native soldier to seek and find a friend, male or female, in [an] entirely unknown village, is a question of half an hour."

Early the following morning, Segovia set about collecting enough provisions for the long march to Palanan. He had decided to keep in reserve one third of the food they were given to eat in Casiguran, for the village poverty was self-evident, and he knew the civilians would furnish them with only so much. He sent Segismundo out to buy all the chickens and eggs he could; still, he doubted very much that there would be sufficient provisions for eighty-nine men on such a long and difficult hike. By previous agreement with Funston, Segovia started over to wake Talplacido so they could compose a letter to go out over the Filipino's signature. This would be added to the Lacuna correspondence concocted aboard the *Vicksburg* and taken by a Negrito runner, who was conscripted by the vice mayor to make the journey to Palanan in advance of the column. Outside the mayor's dwelling, several village dignitaries approached the Spaniard and begged him to show them his American prisoners. He obliged by escorting them upstairs.

The five Americans were lying on the floor when the door opened and the assembly trooped in. Without rising, the general grinned laconically up at the men.

"Hello, *hombres*," he said, but the villagers paid the Kansan less attention than they did his cousin, who was the focus of their curious stares. A villager explained to Segovia that Lieutenant Mitchell resembled the Spanish friar who had once been in charge of their parish. No one recognized Captain Newton, despite his earlier visit to the village to rescue the padre. After a quarter of an hour, the townsfolk left. Before Segovia could settle down to his letter, he was again interrupted by the sentry, who announced another visitor. It was an old man, with vigor belying his age, who completely surprised Segovia by addressing him in Castilian, a tongue he had not expected to hear in that rural setting.

"When I heard yesterday that the Americans were coming," the old man said, "I took my family out in the woods. Upon my return this morning I heard the captain was a Spaniard, and as I have always had a great regard for Castilians, I come to call on you and the commanding officer." Such charm had to be reciprocated, so Segovia lost no time in bringing his visitor before Talplacido, who by that time had arisen. The villager told them he was a native of Manila but had resided in Casiguran for thirty years; by dint of the wisdom his age and travels had given him, he was highly respected by his fellow townsfolk.

"I would like to see the prisoners if you will allow me," remarked the old man. "I have never seen an American in all my life; when they came here once before, I ran away. What tongue do they speak?"

"English," Segovia replied.

When brought before the reclining captives, the old man instantly began to speak. "One, two, three, four," he pronounced carefully, "five, six, seven, eight, nine, ten."

"Hello," said General Funston from the floor.

"You speak *mucho ingles*," Segovia said as a compliment to the visitor.

"Yes, I was an employee of an English firm in Manila, half a century ago," returned the old man, but this he said in Spanish, his English not extending beyond counting to ten. They chatted away for half an hour; the old man was certain that Don Emilio would be pleased to see the American prisoners, and he congratulated Segovia for his unit's valor in capturing them.

The time for socializing was over. Segovia and Talplacido closeted themselves to begin work on a new set of letters, which were written in Spanish by Segovia. One, over General Lacuna's forged signature, served as Talplacido's directive from his superior. In addition to carrying a copy on his person, Talplacido included these official orders in another letter, which, like the first, was written in Spanish by Segovia and signed by Talplacido. This second missive, addressed to Aguinaldo, read as follows:

General Urbano Lacuna, under date of February 26, communicated to me the following:

MAJOR HILARIO TALPLACIDO: In virtue of the superior order received from the commanding General of Central Luzon, you will tomorrow start out on a march with the company of Captain Segovia in the direction of Northern Luzon and the Province of Isabela towards Baler, which is the safest route. Mr. Cecilio Segismundo will accompany you as guide and take you to the place where our Honorable President E. Aguinaldo resides, under whose orders you will be in the future. May God guard you many years. The Military Commander of the Province of Nueva Ecija, U. Lacuna, Bulac, February 26, 1901.

Having set out on the 27th, last, in compliance with above instructions, we arrived yesterday, after a march of 16 days at this village of Casiguran, where I intend to remain until the soldiers are rested and I am able to procure the necessary provisions for the journey. The command is composed of one captain, four lieutenants, four sergeants, eight corporals and sixty-five privates, making a total of 1 captain, four officers and seventy-seven soldiers.

We have furthermore, five American prisoners of war, of whose capture I shall render a separate report. I also forward the correspondence which was handed to me by General Lacuna with orders to deliver it to Your Honor so as not to delay it as we will not leave here before three or four days, because this village is poor and it is very difficult to procure what we need in a day or two. May God guard you many years. Casiguran, March 16, 1901.

The Officer in command of the expedition, Hilario Talplacido

It was necessary to write a separate report of their purported skirmish with the Americans, so this they proceeded to do. Again, it was addressed to Aguinaldo:

On March 3rd, when marching through the mountains of Pantabangan in the direction of this village, we surprised a group of 10 Americans, who judging by their actions were taking photographs of the country and seemed to be engineers. We opened fire and after a skirmish which lasted for twenty minutes, killed two, wounded three and the remaining five surrendered to us. Having collected their guns, ten in number, we left the wounded in care of some hunters with instructions to hand them over to the American detachment in Pantabangan and had the two dead buried. Owing to the difficulty of returning with the prisoners to General Lacuna's camp, I decided to bring them with us and this is the reason why they are now in our company.

I also inform Your Honor that by the same hunters I forwarded a report on this matter to General Lacuna, which report by this time must have reached him.

A short time later, after he had tied the letters into two bundles for their bearers, Segovia appeared at the vice mayor's door. The official told him that runners would leave late that afternoon and were expected to reach Palanan in only three and a half days, being very fleet of foot. He then showed Segovia what food had been procured for the soldiers: a few hundred pounds of rice and Indian corn and a quantity of sweet potatoes. The vice mayor said he expected to collect more, but not much. Segovia inquired whether he could purchase any of the carabaos he had seen about the village. The official doubted this was possible, saying that all he could do was accompany the Spaniard while he asked people if they could spare any of their water buffaloes. As they made their rounds, all the villagers claimed that they needed their animals for work in the rice fields. Finally they met an old woman who agreed to sell Segovia two yearlings at the bargain prewar price of eight pesos a head. While the beasts were being led away by two scouts to be slaughtered and salted, Segovia took leave of the vice mayor, urging him to do his best in adding to the food supply. If this was not done by nightfall, Segovia warned, he would have the houses searched and take what was found, though he would pay for it.

"I have no intention," the Spaniard explained heatedly, "of allowing my soldiers to die of hunger on the road simply to save the people of Casiguran a little rice."

Two runners left Casiguran in late afternoon as predicted bearing the packets of letters, each wrapped securely with plantain leaves. Segovia promised to reward each Negrito with one peso when next they met. Then the Spaniard instructed several Macabebes to begin to search for food hoards among the villagers; he gave the scouts money for purchasing what they found and cautioned them not to abuse anybody.

At about five o'clock in the evening, a village constable was seen patroling the streets of Casiguran, though whether he was protecting the townsfolk from outside enemies or from the counterfeit insurgents was not certain. He carried a Remington rifle, much to the annoyance of the Macabebes. One drew Segovia aside to complain.

"Captain, take the gun away from him," the scout urged. "It is a pity that such a fellow should be carrying so good a rifle."

"NO," exclaimed an exasperated Segovia, "you must not even *think* of such a thing! We are not here for this purpose, and do not trouble the man even if he carries a dozen rifles!"

Sometime after that exchange, an alarming rumor swept through town: the insurgent General Manuel Tinio had moved four hundred of his men from Ilocos in the far northwest to join Aguinaldo in Palanan. This nearly completely unmanned the Macabebes, and they lost whatever confidence they had gained by play-acting. It was only through vigorous argument that the Spaniard and his timid Filipino assistants convinced the scouts that surprise would win over any force they would face.

The Americans, being locked up, were prone to chew over rumors until they were thoroughly digested, and they became agitated when the news about such a formidable number of enemies was whispered to them. "This yarn caused us much uneasiness," confessed Funston, "until it was finally set to rest."

Later that night, Segovia visited the prisoners and brought Funston up to date on what had transpired outside his bare cell. They agreed the column would leave Casiguran in thirty-six hours, in the early morning of March 17.

Their central problem remained — food for the officers, soldiers, and local guides, a total of a hundred and one stomachs to fill. Segovia's men succeeded that evening in locating about twenty pounds of rice, forty of cracked corn, and a quantity of sweet potatoes. For his part, Cecilio Segismundo had somehow wheedled sixteen chickens and five pounds of dried fish from the impoverished townsfolk. This meant that, all told, the column would carry with it only enough food for five and a half days at best, though if the Americans insisted on restricting their diets to buffalo and chicken meat, without supplementing it with the hated rice, they would run out of meat in three days.

"All right," said Funston, "we have six tins of beef extract," disclosing that the officers had been holding out on Segovia, "and this I think will carry us through." As if there was a choice. The men were faced with the prospect of abandoning the mission and with it their quarry. They had learned that only one Westerner — a Spanish priest, a generation before — had ever walked the distance to Palanan. He had, however, been well supplied with food, which they were not. Their prospects seemed dubious at best.

The Americans held a brief conference and voted unanimously to take their chances with short rationing and a forced march that, with luck, might get them to Palanan in less than seven days.

"Though I must confess," remarked Funston in retrospect, "it was with considerable misgivings so far as I was concerned. As will be seen, the result came near being disaster."

7

FROM CASIGURAN TO CASAPSAPAN BAY, 1982

Today, Casiguran is a drab collection of perhaps a hundred unpainted, two-story buildings roofed with metal. It is surrounded by fields that give way to mountains. In the center of the town is an open square, which is flanked on one side by a concrete church with a red corrugated roof that is next to a good-sized parochial school. On another side is the two-story church rectory. Here we sought sanctuary from a priest I had fortuitously met a few weeks earlier in Manila, Father Florentino Santiago, of the Dicalced Carmelite order. He furnished us with two rooms on the second floor of the building, which belonged to priests who were "out on their rounds along the coast." Replenished by a much-needed cold bail shower and several chilled sodas from the rectory icebox, I went downstairs to keep an appointment with Anne and Iris, who had agreed to help arrange some guides for the trek to Palanan. Dario, Erich, and Bill tagged along.

Walking across the square, Anne told me she thought we should hire six Agtas — specifically, two older men who knew everyone on the coast, three young men to help carry supplies, and another to serve as interpreter. This sounded reasonable. I had been told by Father Santiago and a colleague in Manila that we could not expect to hire any Agtas at all unless they were accompanied by "diplomats" who could smooth our way through strange or unfriendly territories.

Not far from the church, we ducked our heads and entered a poorly lit, earthen-floored cantina. Awaiting us were twenty dark-skinned

Agta men, dressed for the most part in mission pants or loincloths. They looked at us with interest as Anne carefully made introductions. As I shook their hands, I detected gin fumes on their breath; though they were not Christian, they had evidently been celebrating the Christians' holiday exuberantly and for some time. They had trouble focusing but were nonetheless in high spirits.

The American adventurers sat on one bench, the Agtas on another. They were: an old man with white grizzled hair, a young mustachioed man, a dignified middle-aged man with many beaded bracelets and armlets, an ancient skinny fellow in shorts who draped one of his legs companionably over those of his neighbor, and another white-haired patriarch. The rest stood behind in the shadows and watched. Anne and Iris took stools between the two groups and the negotiations commenced.

"They say they can make thirty pesos a day picking rattan," Anne told me, "and I'm going to reply that work doesn't come every single day." This she did, and they agreed with her. But why walk all that way? Everything they needed was here. She turned back to me: "They like Iris and me a lot, and I'm asking them as a *personal favor* to make the walk with you." The men seemed to scoff for a while, but they grinned, obviously under the spell of those two effervescent missionaries.

"Tell them I'll throw in ten kilos of rice at the end," I said, and she did. Their resistance seemed to be crumbling, and when I added boat passage back to Casiguran, the bargain was struck. While Anne left to find the three young men she had in mind, one of the patriarchs got up to sing us a song. His high, nasal, atonal singing reminded me of a muezzin. Though the only word we understood was "Americano," Bill sang an improvised translation into my ear, a reflection, perhaps, of his nervousness: *"We will string them up by their thumbs, those Americanos."*

Later, Anne returned with two boys in shorts and T-shirts and one slightly older boy who wore only a bright loincloth. "They'll do the hunting for themselves and the old guys," Anne assured me. This was good, since our freeze-dried food supply had not been figured for such a retinue. "And," she said, "they'll share whatever they get — crabs, fish, roots, berries, deer, wild pigs."

Our Agta interpreter, a man in his twenties named Lito, took me outside for a private conference. "Don't trust these other people," he slurred in a conspiratorial tone. *"They are not honest."* He looked up at me earnestly and I got a whiff of *bino*, the locally produced fermented coconut juice. I thanked him for his candor. "And don't give them any money in advance," he said. Then he proceeded to ask me

for his pay so he could give it to his mother. Iris said she thought
this was all right. Lito made me promise not to tell the others of this
transaction, and I handed the money over without a doubt about this
young man. Thanking me, he added that as his friends were very
lazy, I should stress their arriving on time the next morning.

When the Spaniards came to the Philippines, they classified the natives into three separate racial stocks: the Indios, the majority of the
population, descended mostly from Malaysians and Indonesians; the
Moros, basically of the same background but clinging to the Muslim
religion and culture; and Negrillos or Negritos, a dark-skinned, kinky-
haired pygmy group that was very likely the first to inhabit the islands. The Negritos' name for themselves was Agta (or a variation,
such as Aeta), and they lived a migratory life of hunting and foraging. Never very numerous, the Agtas began declining with their first
encounters with Westerners, for their mobile, active lives and ani-
mistic beliefs did not square with the values the Spanish imposed on
the Philippine population.

All the friars' attempts to convert the tribes to Christianity failed,
as did their efforts to make the Agtas stay in one place and take up
farming. With the advent of the American era, those governing Luzon's eastern coast were as disturbed by those tribal free spirits as the
Spaniards had been. In 1912, the authorities forced a hundred and
fifty Agta families to move onto a reservation at Calabgan, near Casiguran. To encourage the tribesmen to farm, the Agtas were sent
out each morning in chain gangs to clear the forest for planting. Even
this did not work. The reservation was closed in 1923 "due to the
expense involved and the small number of Negritos that could be
kept in this reservation."

One would think that previous failures to put the Agtas on reser-
vations and make them shift to farming and a year-to-year existence
instead of a day-to-day one would have discouraged the Philippine
government from trying again. However, in 1975, a government
foundation called the Presidential Assistance on National Minorities,
or PANAMIN, asked the Philippine army to move some fifty tribal
families onto cleared land — actually, the identical reservation doomed
in 1923. Within a few years, this enterprise was also all but defunct.
Nowadays, PANAMIN aid is confined to relief after typhoons and
infrequent medical help.

Although the Agtas have shown little interest in changing their lives
and abandoning tradition to the degree that various institutions have
desired, they still have evolved a firm and complex relationship with
the Filipino townspeople based on the bartering of food. Originally,

the tribal hunters exchanged meat from their wild pig and deer kills for rice. But because of the growing scarcity of wild game and fish during the last several generations, the position of the Agtas has changed. More often today they are day laborers, swapping their work for rice, clothing, and money.

Though the Agtas have always resisted the paternalistic attempts to reduce them to reservation life, unfortunately the clash of civilizations is taking its toll among them. The primary activity of the Agta men used to be hunting, but as one American anthropologist who lived among the tribes in Casiguran for more than fifteen years discovered, the practice has declined severely. He found in 1962 that all able-bodied men owned bows. Fourteen years later, less than half of the men owned bows, with one in five confessing they had not shot any game in more than a year. (We would later learn from a personal perspective about this decline in the practice and skill of Agta hunters.)

I asked that anthropologist, Dr. Thomas Headland of the Summer Institute of Linguistics, what he saw as the future for the Agtas.

"Pretty bleak," he answered. "The number one problem for them is the Philippine population explosion. The Agta to non-Agta ratio in Casiguran has gone from two to one at the turn of the century to forty-three to one today. [The population of the Casiguran Agtas in 1977 was 954 versus some 30,000 "lowland" Filipino peasants.] Game, fish, and forest (the primary Agta resources) have been drastically reduced during my twenty years in Casiguran," Headland said. "Many Agta have given up hunting completely as an occupation. Agta birth rates are high, but death rates are, unfortunately, higher. Our preliminary analysis (based on a comparison between the census of 1977 and Morice Vanoverbergh's census of the Casiguran Agta in 1936) shows a population decline of twenty-two percent in that forty-year period."

The main killer, at least among the Casiguran Agta, is tuberculosis, a disease introduced by Westerners; Headland told me that 19 percent of the adults die of it. Sickness and malnutrition have put the death rate of children before puberty at a staggering 48 percent. Other reasons for the high mortality are pneumonia, alcoholism, and among females complications from childbirth. Also, I was surprised when Headland told me the homicide rate among adult males. "Our 1977–1978 data show fourteen percent of the adult males die of homicide," he said. "And homicide has been very high over the last six years, with roughly about twenty-five to thirty percent of the adult male deaths in that period from murder."

In short, the story of the Agtas in Casiguran is similar to those of other Agtas on the remote fringes of Philippine civilization. Whether they are in Luzon's northeastern coast and mountains, in the western Luzon provinces of Bataan and Zambales, or in the upland jungles of Samar, Negros, and Leyte islands, these aboriginal Filipinos seem doomed to extinction.

Two hours after I hired our guides, I walked back to the rectory under a steady mist with a pair of rubber sandals I had bought in the marketplace. I rounded a corner of the churchyard just as the congregants poured out of the church. The crowd followed a phalanx of elders bearing effigies of the Black Nazarene and the Virgin Mary — their bases fluttered with peso notes — and a coffin-shaped reliquary. Just after two men playing a dirge on dented old trumpets passed, I saw Gerry Imperial again and took this opportunity to fall in line beside him as the procession wound through town.

"You do us honor to join us today," Gerry said. With his uneven gait, he could not avoid bumping against me in the crowd. I saw that he was also regularly colliding with a pretty, wide-eyed young woman on his left. Gerry introduced us; her name was Evelyn and her family lived in Casiguran. She was another cousin of his and they had attended school together. Nearby, her mother or aunt smiled a toothless chaperone's smile, and I wondered if Gerry and Evelyn thought of each other as more than cousins. I hoped so.

The line of worshipers moved at a funereal pace along muddy, potholed lanes flanked by open drainage ditches and silvered old walls of houses. After bisecting, then encircling Casiguran, our crowd headed to the base of a tall knoll that rose incongruously from the plain. A chapel with a grand view of the countryside stood on its summit, but those in front did not mount the steps leading to it. Instead, the people ahead broke from a solid mass to small clumps, heads now looking down and shoulders moving tentatively sideways, as if their footing were uncertain. I surmised that our cratered road had come to a place of great sogginess, but I was wrong.

When we drew near, I found no mud puddle but instead four young men lying face down on the wet ground. I could not see their faces, but their hair was long and extremely matted, like that of the war-damaged panhandlers one encounters in American cities. These Filipinos were wounded: their bare backs were bruised blue, with a mass of cuts as if someone had flogged them. They were clad only in skirts and head coverings made of banana leaves, and they wore bracelets fashioned from fish hooks. Everywhere was blood.

"You're supposed to step on them," said Gerry, and I realized with horror that the entire crowd was passing over the backs of these men. "It's part of their penance."

"I could never step on another human being," I replied, now uncomfortably close to tripping over their bodies as the crowd pressed me forward.

"Ah, but you might hurt their feelings if you do not," Gerry said. The very words to spur me to action. At my feet, the first flagellant turned his head and looked up at me with one glazed eye. His nose was pressed into the mud. Shrugging, I gently nudged the man's arm with my shoe and stepped across. "That's good," said Gerry approvingly, and his cousin smiled at me. She wore a pretty embroidered and frilly blouse of white cotton. I went on to nudge and step over the other recumbent penitents, knowing that the countless bare feet or flopping sandals of the townsfolk were hardly doing the open cuts on their backs any good. Later I learned why these men did this: in times of famine, economic reversals, or sickness within the family, some men vowed to become penitents for a certain number of holy weekends if their prayers were answered.

When the conquistadors and friars arrived at this archipelago four hundred years ago, they were confronted with multitudes of *infideles;* with the exception of the people of the southern islands, who were Muslim, all the others were animists. In the rural areas of the islands, Christianity is still tinged with animism, and to a certain extent seminary-trained clerics do not work hard at discouraging this. But what is most striking is the number of arcane practices left over from those early Hispanic times and the vast numbers of Filipinos who are affected by them — not only in rural places but in the cities, not only among the peasants but among sophisticated city dwellers.

I remember having lunch with a young woman named Margie David, the public relations director for the government-owned Manila Hotel. I had only been in the country for two days and was just beginning to recover from jet flights that totaled some twenty-three hours. Margie was very much the overworked career woman. Sitting with her in the Champagne Room of the hotel, picking at some sparse and indifferent examples of nouvelle cuisine, I found her hungry for literary discussion. She had arranged to have *The New Yorker* flown in weekly from the Manhattan office of Philippine Airlines. "Otherwise I would starve," she said, "from a literary point of view." She had met the magazine's editor, William Shawn, several times, and its peripatetic Asian correspondent, Robert Shaplen, "stays with us whenever he is in town," she said.

Somehow — probably due to the wine, which I never would have ordered because of its absurdly high price in the Philippines, but at this meal it was on the house — our conversation segued from the arts into matters of the spirit. Many people's minds were turning that way with Easter Sunday only a few weeks away. Conversations were peppered with references to "going home for the festival"; evidently everyone in the city had rural roots or else claimed them during that time. In nearby Rizal Park, an evangelical caravan had attracted large crowds all week. Their music and testimonials boomed across the park and floated throughout the hotel. On the television, commercials with religious themes fought for space with those for Australian watches, Manila gin, and gadget-packed gas ranges. My favorite announcement with a religious theme had been: "Holy Week Programming Featuring the Six-Hour Re-creation of the Book of Genesis, Filmed in Locations Closely Approximating the Originals. . . . And next [the announcer continued, switching gears to secular programming without so much as a discreet pause], "The Murderer Who Would Not Die."

"We have a tradition of spiritualism in this country," Margie explained to me, her face very intent. "It is a part of our Catholicism but yet apart from it." In the north of Luzon, she said, were faith healers who used only their fingers to open the skin of their patients before operating with their bare hands. They were so famous that Pentecostal Europeans flocked to Luzon regularly on faith-healing package tours. I wondered whether miracle cures were guaranteed. Margie then told me about Nostradamus, whose sixteenth-century prophetic verses were enjoying particular popularity in the Philippines of the 1980s. To amuse her, I quoted one of his apocalyptic quatrains that I had memorized many years before:

> In the year 1999, seventh month
> Terror will rain from the skies
> To resuscitate the great king of Anglemois
> Around this time Mars will reign for the good cause.

"We have spiritualism in our country also," I added. "For instance, we have a radio preacher named Reverend Ike, who used to sell pieces of terrycloth he called 'prayer shawls' and vials of 'holy incense oil,' with which one could pray one's way to the hereafter — or at least to financial solvency."

"Oh yes," Margie cried delightedly and clapped her hands. "Here we have someone named Johnny Midnight. He broadcasts a weekly prayer show. He tells his listeners to place a tumbler of water next to the radio. After a half-hour of music and sermons, they're supposed to drink the water and receive a holy blessing that way."

It was appealing that this sophisticated woman — with her knowledge of Europe, fashion, the literary world, and even fresh gossip from New York and Los Angeles — was also so obviously a part of Filipino culture that to her, life could also encompass such mysterious and arcane religious rituals as faith healing, passion plays, pageants, miracle working, and flagellation. She told me about tiny villages that became boom towns during the holy weekend, when thousands of Filipino tourists descended upon them to witness Lenten processions, such as the one on Bantayan island near Cebu, or restaged crucifixions, such as what occurred in the town of Mandaluyong, in Pangasinan province on Luzon. In the latter barangay, tradition had a man donning a wig and false beard to enact the crucifixion of Jesus by arranging to be nailed to a wooden cross. This was done to atone for the victim's sins. Then, in 1980, a thirty-three-year-old mestizo peasant named Donald Rexford, Jr., grew his hair and beard to the required length and had himself crucified not for his sins but in the name of being reunited with his American father, an army truck driver who had disappeared after a hurried acquaintance with the Filipino's mother. Rexford, a manual laborer with a mien of inchoate fervency, twice repeated the painful imitation of Christ's three hours on the cross, but he has yet to be reunited with his father.

Margie David told me that Rexford, and other self-mortifiers such as the flagellants I encountered in Casiguran, heal themselves quickly with holy water and oils. There are, she said, no scars.

Whether or not this is true, I saw no evidence of miraculous healing in Casiguran — only backs and legs bruised purple and torn bloody by long strings of heavy wooden beads that went *clack, clack* as the penitents ran in circles through the crowd in front of the church. One ran up and stopped not 5 feet from me. Breathing heavily, he looked through me with glazed eyes. He was covered with welts, and his rosary (if that is what it was) dripped blood into the sand. *Clack* his beads rattled as he raised them high and brought them down on his thigh. He turned and ran, scattering the squealing children who tried to dodge the drops of blood that flew everywhere.

Gerry came over and apologized for leaving me; he had wanted to spend more time with Evelyn and I did not blame him. I wondered how he will fare in this world — a sensitive intellectual, crippled in a society that depends on strength. I wish him well.

Upstairs at the rectory, Father Santiago produced bottles of cold beer, which we drank sitting around a long table while two young acolytes

prepared dinner. Santiago had grown up in Baler. His round face
and gentle demeanor had a distinctly Castilian air, and I could easily
imagine him in a friar's hooded cassock in place of his casual secular
clothes. He told me that the Carmelites planned to withdraw their
priests from the Aurora province coast, and priests from another order would inherit Casiguran. It seemed that, four hundred years after
the Spanish had begun reduction of the Contracosta, this remote place
was still a burden to those administering it from afar.

"If they must send me elsewhere, I hope it will be to the mountains," Santiago said. "I feel more at home in the boondocks than in
the city, and I think I can do more good there — it would be more
of a challenge. In the time left I want to expand my work with the
Dumagat tribes here. They are scattered and have no real government and they are often taken advantage of — they are the, what was
the term, the *niggers* of Filipino culture. And then there are my rounds
to take care of." He smiled. "We keep pretty busy here."

Indeed, the three priests in Casiguran only occasionally see each
other. They each have a motorcycle and cover the needs of the tiny
villages between Baler and Dinapiqui. In addition to their regular
duties, they have attempted to set up a program of educational classes
for teenagers and adults, but they have run into problems with the
military authorities. In one instance, a colleague of Father Santiago's
began an encounter group for married couples, "to explore and then
surmount the difficulties in the home," I was told, "starting with simple budgeting and management. Then, moving into problems between husband and wife — even drinking and beating up the man's
wife and children. We got some open discussions going." But the local Philippine Constabulary commander ordered the program dis-
continued because it encouraged communist thought and rebellion
against authority.

The parish at Casiguran is isolated, and for that reason the priests
are constantly under the watchful eye of the government. It is the
same in every city and remote settlement in the islands; where once,
in the Spanish era, church and state were indistinguishable, now they
have diametric goals. The tension became most pronounced in the
1960s, that time of nearly worldwide ferment.

In the wake of Vatican II's call for a renewed church commitment
to social action and social justice, the hierarchy of the Philippine
Catholic Church, which represents 80 percent of the country's population and therefore is its most powerful religious institution, embarked upon a series of initiatives. The first grew out of a week-long
Rural Development Congress (RDC) in February 1967, with the full

participation of the government. It envisioned the organization of the poor, social amelioration, and fundamental changes in government attitudes. But by 1969 it was plain that the RDC programs had not touched the real problem of land distribution or of widespread government corruption, and so they were only marginally effective. Some two thousand church-sponsored projects (such as credit unions, cottage industries, and agricultural improvements) were only partially successful because not enough funds or personnel were made available. The church hierarchy was open to criticism because of its conservatism — borne of its vast land holdings, its ties to landlords, and its immense wealth. It effectively lost its cachet with the failure of its reformist initiatives.

Priests and nuns and layworkers turned their hopes to a number of Jesuit-influenced moderate secular movements, such as the Christian Social Movement and the Federation of Free Farmers, whose inspiration was said to be found in Martin Luther King's Southern Christian Leadership Conference and Cesar Chavez's United Farm Workers. Scattered demonstrations, picket lines, and nonviolent actions protested not only feudalism and government actions but also Philippine compliance in the Vietnam War. They were countered by arrests — but no change resulted.

In 1969, shortly after Ferdinand Marcos was inaugurated for his second term, he looked to a visit of Pope Paul VI to Manila as an opportunity for papal endorsement. The First Lady's well-publicized social welfare projects seemed outwardly to be in line with the pope's call for attention to the poor, and it was clear that Marcos desired the Philippine Catholic Church's imprimatur for these projects before the papal visit. Instead, seven bishops wrote a "Message to the President," which pleaded with him to cease tolerating "graft and corruption, self-enrichment, vote-buying, goon-hiring which make a mockery of democracy, almost unlimited over-spending in campaigns. . . ." The prelates asked Marcos to become a "deeply moral person whose honesty and integrity are beyond reproach."

The government responded furiously in an official broadsheet: the church was "the single biggest obstacle to progress . . . having grown immensely rich through the centuries mainly at the expense of the citizenry." The church and not the government, it said, was responsible for "the sharp social cleavage between the rich and the poor."

When the pope arrived in the Philippines, his speech criticized the uneven distribution of wealth and asserted that Catholic tradition was not simply doctrinal but stood for "the defense of the poor and the weak against every form of injustice."

The church hierarchy was unable, as the new decade began, to summon up more than words in defense of the poor and weak. The clergy in moderate secular organizations were similarly powerless; the groups began splintering, losing support, as there was a gradual trend toward radicalization among socially concerned reformers, students, and clergy. One progressive group, called the Philippine Priests Incorporated (PPI), which had been formed in 1968 and was quickly branded by the government as being full of rebel priests, held three widely publicized congresses that helped to clarify the role of the religious in a developing nation like the Philippines. An offshoot group, Christians for National Liberation, was formed in February 1972. It declared that a radical renewal of Christianity cannot be separated from efforts to free oppressed citizens from feudalism, imperialism, and bureaucratic capitalism.

Seven months later, when martial law was declared, elements within the church became more polarized as members of Christians for National Liberation were hunted for sedition and the group went underground. In contrast, a council of Philippine bishops endorsed the Marcos move. More confusion resulted during a December conference of representatives from the nation's religious orders, where members voiced "critical approval" of martial law stringencies.

Events took on a seesaw quality. At the top of society, a liaison committee was established by the church hierarchy and the military to air complaints and foster communication; it failed early after its first test in a 1974 inquiry into the torture of an imprisoned priest from Jolo, when the military deflected all discussion to other matters. Some months later, the government cracked down and arrested a number of Philippine Protestant ministers and others for consorting with an anti–martial law personality; in a separate move, a hundred and fifty paratroopers raided a Jesuit novitiate and arrested twenty-one persons (including a priest) for similar reasons. In an act that surprised many, the newly installed archbishop of Manila, Jaime Sin, sent a letter of protest to Defense Secretary Juan Ponce Enrile and later called a press conference in which he told foreign reporters about instances of detainees being tortured. Then the bishops' council reversed itself and called for an end to martial law.

After a prominent progressive theorist, Father Edicio de la Torre, was arrested in downtown Manila, he called from prison for an investigation into allegations of detainees being subjected to electric shock, beatings, cigarette burning, and sexual abuse. When the hierarchy joined this priest's call, a military investigating panel dismissed twelve soldiers. Observers claimed this was only the tip of the iceberg.

In late 1976, the rank-and-file clergy who had moved into the area now known as the Christian Left were working openly for the resumption of a banned labor movement, the restoration of civil law, the rights of poor farmers, and the boycotting of national referendums to expand presidential powers and endorse martial law. The government answered with a program of intimidation of church activists. After mass arrests and the deportation of foreign missionaries, the government closed the religious radio stations and newsletters. After 1976, the Christian Left accustomed itself to a life lived in the catacombs.

The end of martial law in 1981 changed the situation only a little. All released detainees, religious or secular, lived under the threat of being picked up again. In trouble spots such as Mindanao, Samar, Bataan, Kalinga-Apayo, and Isabela, authorities kept a close watch on the nature of religious programs. And a new cycle of arrests began in April 1982, including that of Father de la Torre, who had been at liberty just over a year.

While some priests attempt to build up their parishioners' self-reliance and awareness of their human rights, a few others have opted for armed struggle. Four clergy in northern Luzon have joined units of the New People's Army, and others have taken up arms elsewhere in the Philippines.

All of this keeps the church in a quandary. A Jesuit, Father Benigno Mayo, recently recalled the 1981 visit of Pope John Paul II to the Philippines, when the pontiff "admonished us . . . to involve ourselves with the problems of the people but not to undertake political causes. This is almost an impossibility in the Philippines."

I awoke at five on Saturday morning after an uneasy sleep. Throughout the night, churlish dogs roamed the streets of Casiguran, howling and barking and fighting incessantly. I wanted to go out with my heavy staff and dispatch them all, but I knew they would tear me to pieces for trying.

Lito, our Agta interpreter, and Bersosa, our elderly diplomat, had promised to appear with their crew at the stroke of six, but as six, then seven, eight, and nine o'clock passed, we saw how ridiculous it had been to make appointments with people who did not own watches. My colleagues passed the early morning juggling odd objects in the rectory to entertain Father Santiago and his acolytes, then they played a spirited Frisbee game in the churchyard. They drew a crowd of several hundred people who had never seen a Frisbee before. I cooled my heels.

When the missionaries arrived at ten trailed by hungover Agtas, the women were full of apologies. "It's so hard getting them up on time," Iris told me, "and then we had to wait for the tide to come in to get our boat across the river." I counted heads and came up short; Lito seemed to be missing. "We looked all over for him," said Anne. "He just plain disappeared."

"Well," I said, exasperated at this revelation of human frailty, "he's already been fully paid for the trip." Comprehension flooded into Iris's face as she remembered that she had provided Lito with a character reference. Anne insisted on repaying me, saying, "I'll shake it out of him when I see him next!" I believed her. It seemed that we could afford to lose our interpreter anyway, since Bersosa had an adequate supply of about a hundred English words. The rest of the communicating could be by sign.

Anne told me that the Agtas insisted on being paid in full before walking one step. I balked. "Maybe half," I said, "but no more."

"Hey, absolutely not!" It was Christopher, who had been standing nearby. He drew me aside and heatedly argued against any further trust; if Lito had absconded, so would they. I was inclined to give them the benefit of the doubt. "Nope," my brother said, "not a single penny until Palanan." Paul and Bill, who were listening to our conversation, agreed. "They obviously can't be trusted," said Paul, worried. But it seemed we would get nowhere without some sort of exchange, and — since it was my money we were talking about — I overruled them. Bersosa got two thirds of his pay by dint of his advanced age and status. A princely looking middle-aged man, Seanbuyan, and the three young men, Sulimon, Udeng, and Benchan, each got half. Still, of course, it was a pittance.

The guides promptly disappeared into the town. Anne assured me they were only getting supplies for the trip. Sure enough, they soon came back and stood ready beside the cloth rice sacks we had filled with equipment for them to carry. The boys wore bright new mauve loincloths they had bought from a lowland merchant.

Father Santiago gave us a silent blessing and we hauled up our gear. Anne and Iris waved prettily, extracting promises from us to write to them. As we moved through the crowd jamming the churchyard, a man grabbed my wrist and would not let go.

"My friend, where are you going?" he asked.

"To Palanan," I answered.

"Oh, very bad," he said, "too long way. It will take you a week!"

Some children ran along with us as we passed a number of little stores, each of which displayed little but a few bars of laundry soap, and odd package of candy, a small sack of cornmeal. People had gathered in front of each one to trade and gossip, and they turned to stare as we approached. A boy darted ahead and ran from one cluster of people to another. *"They are walking to Palanan!"* he shouted. The men shook their heads in disbelief or smiled and saluted us; the women averted their faces or looked at us with disarming interest. Soon Casiguran and its citizens were behind us and all was still.

The muddy lane we followed gave out in a rice field. We crossed that wide, marshy patchwork on a network of low earthen dikes, the three young men leading us with their rice sacks balanced on their shoulders. We paused while they went at saplings with their knives; stripping bark, they tied it to their sacks to form shoulder straps. Then we rejoined the waist-deep Casalogan River, which had, down-stream, welcomed us to Casiguran. We forded its sluggish meander six times — which, of course, required our exchanging our hiking boots for the sneakers we had brought for such a purpose. (One of the cardinal rules for treks is to keep boots dry — or feet will dete-riorate quickly.) Our guides, being barefoot, simply crossed the water and waited, watching the spectacle of Bill crossing piggyback on Paul, his poor feet encased in white bandages that Dario forbade getting wet. At one crossing, a family traveling with a carabao the size of a Volkswagen negotiated the river with much drama, and we let them go ahead of us. A little boy climbed on top of their animal and started yelling and swatting the beast's hindquarters. With a lot of mooing and splashing, the bull entered the stream at a fair gallop and was across in a thrice.

Those desiring to walk north from Casiguran must follow a nar-row and unmarked trail that often seems to disappear into the brush or becomes lost in a maze of deer trails and tribal hunting paths. Stepping away from the last bend of the Casalogan and leaving the sun for the bright green, tiered canopy of the jungle, I spied Bersosa and Seanbuyan, who had sat down for a rest on a fallen log. The rest of our column had passed them and were now disappearing into the undergrowth.

"You go 'head," rasped the old man, who sat with his spindly legs underneath his chin. His friend, whose loose shirt had been loomed into bright stripes of yellow, white, and red and resembled an Afri-can dashiki, nodded, smirked, and signified that they would be along in time. I left them in a spotlight of sun.

Soon our column was following a muddy path that descended some five to seven feet to the floor of a narrow trench that snaked through the undergrowth at the level of the tree roots for more than a mile. Hopping across old mounds of carabao dung the size of three-layer cakes, I saw long scuffs in the reddish mud, traces of the sledges that had worn this trail far beneath the surface of the soft earth over generations. I decided to go barefoot for a while, relishing the mud oozing between my toes.

No one talked. In those quiet woods I heard the soft padding of feet behind me and turned to see that Bersosa and Seanbuyan had finally caught up with us. The old man, his shirt hanging way past his loincloth nearly to his knees, slithered up in the ankle-deep mud and put his arm across my shoulders.

"You my friend," he said reassuringly. "I did not know it back there but I know now. You my friend." I knew a companionable drunk when I saw one and realized what supplies he had purchased back in town; he gave off gin fumes that pushed me back against a tree. But despite five days' worth of white whiskers bristling from his face and rheumy eyes that betrayed his long holiday celebration, I felt affection for this seventy-year-old coot. I clapped him on the back — chicken bones and gristle — as he neatly slid past me and walked unsteadily up the muddy trough. He and Seanbuyan linked arms and began singing a tribal drinking song. I shrugged and followed.

My brother heard the noise and turned to see what was going on. "Terrific," he said. "I told you we shouldn't have given them any money. We're going to make real progress with these two bozos plastered all the way." He was standing on the crown of a slippery embankment. When Bersosa showed signs of not being able to make it, I pulled and pushed him up.

"Great guides," said Christopher.

"Thank you, my friend," Bersosa said to me. He looked at my scowling brother and patted his arm. "You my friend too."

"Terrific."

Sometime later, Seanbuyan indicated he wanted another rest stop. My brother suggested that we search the Agtas' bags for booze and confiscate it, a motion seconded by our friends, but at this I drew the line. I reasoned that this dense jungle with its multiplicity of pygmy trails was no place to start treating our guides like children. "Let them drink," I said. "It will all be gone before long. They're keeping up with us, at least." Which they continued to do, despite the dire predictions of my friends.

The ground began to fall away in a gentle decline as we joined a creek, and we followed its course for several miles toward the sea. When fallen trees intersected our path, there was little to do but crawl beneath them in the mud since, in that ancient forest, they were often too big to climb over with our cumbersome gear. Erich brushed against a shrub, bruising a stalk that gave off a stinging juice. Some minutes later he had what appeared to be an acid burn on his arm that would mark him for days. Meanwhile, Bill despaired of keeping his feet dry. He announced this by splashing across the creek, drawing a protest from our staff physician.

Five and a half hours after leaving Casiguran, I saw an opening in the jungle. The creek we followed ran out of the woods and emptied into the estuary of a small river that in turn spilled across a grand, crescent-shaped beach of fine white sand. Palm trees tilted out picturesquely from the jungle, their leaves swaying in a breeze coming off the warm and green Philippine Sea. We stopped here, hot and sore, and rummaged for our bags of dried fruit and trail mix. Our guides built a fire as soon as they came out into the sun. Sulimon, in his early twenties, who bore himself with grace and dignity, suspended our cooking pot from a tripod they built out of sticks and sapling bark.

To my surprise, a sobered-up Bersosa asked us for rice. We reminded him that our bargain called for them to provide for themselves. He then grudgingly pulled out a bag of rice from his own possessions but accepted dried fruit from Erich with a curt nod.

All in all, I was pleased with the way things were going. We had hiked a good day's distance, had weathered the drinking issue without bad feelings, and had reaffirmed the terms of our agreement at this late afternoon meal. Chewing on a dried apricot, I lay back on the sand and relaxed, wishing I had not left behind in Manila a book that would have read well under a palm tree on this deserted beach.

The book, *A Question of Heroes,* is a collection of historical essays written by a prominent novelist, poet, and playwright, Nick Joaquin, whom I had met in a bookstore, La Solidaridad, in that cacophony of dives and tourist hangouts that is the Ermita district in Manila. Nick is a vigorous man in his sixties, a former newspaper columnist who is enough of an iconoclast to make the government worry about what he might do next while they call him one of the country's great literary treasures. Nick likes La Solidaridad because it is the last bookstore in Manila that caters to progressives and intellectuals and carries an eclectic range of titles (including all of his). It publishes a journal of opinion that boasts a worldwide subscription list and often holds a variety of cultural events such as readings and lectures. It is Nick Joaquin's second home.

We went with a mutual friend — Virgilio Reyes, who was working then as Carlos Romulo's special assistant — to a smoky bar next door called the San Miguel. Nick ordered beers all around and launched into a rowdy and far-ranging monologue. Before our glasses were empty, he had touched on the relative merits of New York and Europe, the state of Filipino arts, choice political gossip, and a quick but detailed character analysis of Emilio Aguinaldo.

"Aguinaldo was our second greatest antihero," Nick told me. (He said the other was José Rizal, martyred at the hands of the Spanish authorities in the early months of the 1896 revolution, in which he had declined to take part.) "Aguinaldo was of the middle class — the gentry. Because of his youthful timidity and a habit of self-pity, he became deficient, lacking. He never allowed himself to reach the gentry standards of that era. If he had stayed in Kawit and remained mayor of his home town, those deficiencies wouldn't have mattered."

"What deficiencies?" I asked.

"Education, mostly. Imagine — the first president of the Philippines, a dropout! At thirteen! As an old man, he said it was because his classmates tormented him. But forever after, he was crippled in dealing with his intellectual betters. He deferred, yes. But with resentment. And a lack of trust. Really, I think he *hated* intellectuals."

He was momentarily distracted by the maître d', who came over to empty Nick and Virgilio's ashtray. The young man received a good-natured poke in the ribs from the restaurant's reigning literary star. "How are you doing tonight, my friend? Will you join us for a drink?" Nick asked. "No? Suit yourself." He ordered another round.

A pretty young woman vocalist joined the band as they vamped an introduction for her. She waved to Nick, her eyes and teeth flashing in the spotlight. I asked him to return to his Aguinaldo theory — what else had the president lacked?

"Boldness," Nick replied. "A bourgeois trait. Oh, yes, he was courageous! A good general! But his prudence kept him from being *truly great!*"

The band began playing a song about New York, and Nick wheeled around in his chair with a pleased cry. "Start spreading the news," he sang and waved to the band. "My current favorite song," he told me. "They play it just for me."

With that we lost track of history, certainly of time. But in *A Question of Heroes*, Nick Joaquin continued the thought by recalling that Aguinaldo's memoirs cite the story of the moth and the flame without understanding that for him, the flame signified not the lure of the bright and the glorious, but only *danger*. "The crucial point of his career — and of our history — must be read as *his* reading of the moth-and-flame story," Joaquin asserted, writing about an Aguinaldo flushed with victory over the Spanish in his home province. "Down the Camino Real he rushed, during the summer of '98, until he reached the very gates of Manila and victory was his for the taking. But the city blazed before him like a flame — not the bright, beautiful, splendid flame of glory, but only the flame of danger that a good bourgeois doesn't dare like a moth. So he retreated from the blaze of the flame. And bourgeois prudence lost us the Revolution."

A growing tide rushed up the estuary at an alarming clip. We scurried to haul our gear across this Philippine Bay of Fundy. Tepid seawater was already up to our abdomens and rising. On the far side, we realized that sly Seanbuyan had made no move to follow. As a wave dashed across twenty-five feet of dry sand to separate us by a great distance, Seanbuyan laughed, waved, and began trudging south. His bows and arrows bobbed in the late afternoon light as he walked away and disappeared.

"He will go hunt," Bersosa told us. "He will come back in morning."

"He'd better," muttered Christopher. "That's my little daypack he's got on his back."

Two miles up a wide sandy beach, the land was covered with scrub brush and palms falling from the approaching cordillera down to a small plain. To our left, coconut palms, an entire grove, appeared. Below them two nipa houses stood among tall bushes — the homes of the pioneers who had escaped the confines of the Casiguran Bay plain for this fertile and unpeopled frontier. The houses were separated from each other by a stream that flowed out of the darkening trees and meandered through sand dunes toward the ocean. A dog barked in the yard of one hut, which had apparently been emptied of its occupants by the Easter festivities taking place one day's walk south. In the second house, the family had remained home because of illness, as we learned when we met two shirtless men who welcomed us to their beach and invited us in. They were Bert and his cousin Esteban, and they had malaria. So did Bert's wife, Rosada, and their children, four-year-old Emelita, her year-younger brother Robinson, and a wailing infant boy, Rodriguo.

Bert invited us to sleep in his house that night. As there were ten of us and such a tiny house, he agreed to shelter our guides while we set up tents in his neatly swept yard. The family grew their own tobacco, and Bert offered a cigarette rolled in notepaper to Bill. Dario went into the house to examine the family and emerged shaking his head.

"These people are in bad shape," he said. "I've got to do something. I can't just stand by and listen to that baby cry." He commandeered from each of us our plastic vials of fansidar and chloropinoquine — our malaria prophylaxis for the entire trip. "I'll give you guys back one — no, two — pills each," he promised, "and you can buy more back in Manila."

"Will we get back in time?" Paul wondered.

"How the hell do I know," Dario replied edgily. "Don't worry about it now. That baby might die tonight." He cursed himself for not thinking to bring pills for situations like this, for in the capital malaria pills are reasonably inexpensive. But we would have had to bring many: there is no satisfactory distribution system for malaria prophylaxis in the isolated settlements of eastern Luzon, still less chance for fighting the parasite or its mosquito hosts on the banks of this unnamed stream far from civilization. We could save this family tonight and next week, but what about next month, next year?

Later, we all gathered inside the house to watch Dario. He had retired for a quarter-hour inside the dome tent with a flashlight to calculate dosages and a timetable for administering the medicine. The wooden house had large windows, and the roof was made of closely packed nipa leaves over wooden beams. Inside it was intimate, comforting, dry, and warm. A large iron kettle bubbled on a stone hearth. The only illumination came from the orange coals and from a small candle placed on a low table. We all sat on the floor, since there was no furniture to speak of. The malarial children were restive and feverish. Beads of sweat stood out on the forehead of Rosada, who cradled tiny Rodriguo. The baby's face glimmered damply. As Dario knelt and used a gentle, soothing professional manner I had not had the occasion to see before, he gave the pills to the adults and, splitting the tablets in half with a penknife, to the weeping children. He gave explicit directions for subsequent treatments. The dim orange light reflected in these patients' faces an unqualified gratitude and reverence and filled me with exultation.

Still later, we Westerners emerged from the house into swarms of fireflies. On the beach we passed around a bottle of dark Manila rum. Waves thundered against the beach. Above, a bat swooped from the trees to dive in curious arcs between our upturned, dizzy heads and the myriad pinpoints of stars.

8

THE ODYSSEY TO PALANAN, 1899–1901

I

High in the Central Cordillera of northern Luzon, on the summit of one small, bristly mountain dwarfed on two sides by its taller fellows, perched a village of sturdy thatch houses. Their rightful owners had abandoned them in favor of a ragged detachment of soldiers. These guerrillas had struggled up the heavily forested ramparts the previous day, and now, on the late morning of May 20, 1900, those not assigned to guard duty or the lookout posts industriously pounded unhusked rice grains while others tended smoky cooking fires or looked after their tethered packhorses. In the largest house, its entrance flanked by sentries, two men had recently concluded their rather silent breakfast. Orderlies removed the dishes. The younger of the pair sat preoccupied and thoughtful beside a small window, his mood uninterrupted by his deferential companion. After a while the younger man said, "Look!" A black butterfly with small dots on the border of its wings was resting on his left hand, which was on the windowsill. He gently brought his right hand over, as if to touch the undulating wings, and the butterfly flew away. It came back and flew away again, never to return. The silence continued. After a long while President General Emilio Aguinaldo y Famy looked over to his friend and adviser, Dr. Santiago Barcelona.

"I'm getting more nervous each day," he said.

The five months and eighteen days of incessant travel since their escape through Tirad Pass had not been kind to the revolutionaries and less so to their leader. Aguinaldo despaired at being out of contact with the world outside the mountains and at having only sporadic direction over his guerrilla forces, which were spread wide through the provinces. To this was added his personal losses, each of which had struck him with shattering intensity. First the gallant death of del Pilar, to whom he had felt bonded as brother to brother. His mother and son were captured; then, days before Christmas, he made the painful decision to send back his wife, his sisters, and all the other women in the fleeing column to give themselves up. His wife had lately been subject to fainting spells due to the climate and fatiguing pace, and though she would be better off in the lowlands, their parting was difficult. Word reached him later that his only son, Miguel, had perished of smallpox. It would be many months before he learned this was false, but until then he bore the guilt of this death with that of his infant daughter, whom he had buried himself as the Americans closed in. At each succeeding blow Aguinaldo reminded himself that these were sacrifices "for the revolution" and he would say a silent prayer. But the cause was exacting a high price.

For the better part of five months they had not been in a Christian town — five months of zigzagging from village to village through the highest reaches of the Central Cordillera, where their unenthusiastic hosts worshiped trees, snakes, spirits, clouds. Lowlanders called these warlike pagan tribes by the collective name of Igorots, mountain dwellers. Actually, the Igorots represented three separate cultural groups, the Bontocs, Ifugaos, and Kalingas, though some in individual communities, or *rancherias*, answered to other names. Though each was distinct, the different tribes had much in common. They were renowned for cultivating food in a land with no level surfaces, a problem they had mastered perhaps a thousand years earlier by creating complex terrace systems that crept up the mountain faces, on which they grew rice and sweet potatoes. If they wore clothes at all, they chose tiny loincloths, but they decorated their bodies with earrings and necklaces from which dangled boar's teeth and pottery shards. Tattooing was popular among both men and women. The Igorots wore their straight hair to the shoulders and kept it glossy with animal fat. They hunted with murderous-looking lances and poison-tipped arrows. And they vigorously defended their *rancheria* borders from their neighbors' encroachment.

Outsiders from the lowlands who ventured into the mountains were constantly in danger of treachery. During the earlier colonial era, the Spanish army established outposts on the fringes of the highlands. From these small fortresses they sent expeditions to search for gold and made occasional punitive incursions to even the score after Igorot raids on the lowlands. After some years, they even established a few posts and the obligatory missions in the fastness of the cordillera itself. Despite these measures, the Spanish were never able to control the area, much less convert its inhabitants to Catholicism. Now that the Spanish were gone and the Americans in their place, Emilio Aguinaldo's unprecedented call in 1898 for Filipinos to unite despite language and cultural differences had largely fallen on deaf ears in this place where the stars seemed close enough to touch. The political realities of war and revolution had not penetrated these heathen altitudes, making the presence of Aguinaldo's soldiers of liberation questionable if not completely untenable. The Igorots just were not very interested in the cares of outsiders. But the nationalists were not in the cordillera to convert apolitical heathens. They needed, rather, to attempt a regrouping against the foreigners. During the first weeks of their flight from Tirad Pass, Aguinaldo and his troops looked warily about them as they marched, avoided straggling too far behind the main group, and slept — despite the reassurance of sentries — with one eye open and one ear cocked. This was because all the mountain tribes had in common one disagreeable custom.

They collected heads.

When the nationalists reached and took shelter for a time in the *rancheria* of Banaue, soon after they entered the mountains, they witnessed a ritual called the *kānao* that chilled them. Their memory of it stayed with them during the long months of travel ahead.

The *kānao* took place whenever a warrior succeeded in beheading an enemy, whether a Christian or an Igorot of another settlement. The visiting soldiers watched, fascinated and repelled, while some 50 Igorot warriors — each wearing a feathered headdress and brandishing a spear and a short baton — danced in a line to the rhythm of beaten sticks. Leading the swaying procession was a man carrying a pole, at the end of which sat the severed head of an enemy warrior. The celebrants and their grisly trophy finally came before a particular house, where the warriors danced for a long time in a circle, crouching, bending, each hopping on one foot with a leg extended, rhythmically waving their arms. Some brushed the dirt with the severed hands and feet of the victim as if they were using brooms. An Igorot informed a nervous aide, Simeon Villa, who was standing protectively near *el presidente*, that the rite would last for six days, and there would be plenty of food and drink to keep them going. Not until the end of that time would the head be buried. Then, after decomposition was complete, the skull would be disinterred and used to decorate a warrior's house.

The soldiers never heard their hosts say so outright, but it was understood that despite an uneasy truce negotiated upon the troops' arrival, the Igorots would be glad to hold the *kānao* in their honor and add some revolutionary heads to the existing trophy collection. As Colonel Villa confided to his diary, "Those in Banaue are just waiting for an opportune moment to behead us." The men were careful never to be caught alone in the outskirts of Banaue. When Aguinaldo commissioned a captain to take a small detachment to investigate the route that lay ahead, warriors from a neighboring *rancheria,* not knowing or caring about any pacts between the soldiers and the occupants of Banaue, ambushed the patrol and wounded four people before they were driven off, clutching three captured rifles.

When Aguinaldo moved his troops from Banaue, deeper into the mountains, the harassment continued as they scrambled up and down the steep slopes. Early on the rainy morning of December 28, *el presidente* rose from his stony bed to answer nature's call and beheld through the gloom a tribesman who had crept past the sentries and was poised with his spear to slay them. Aguinaldo cried out in alarm. The soldiers grabbed weapons, instantly awake. The Igorot abandoned stealth and escaped by stumbling and rolling down the mountainside. The exhausted and jittery troops got safely under way after daybreak but were attacked three times in the next two days. Once, on a narrow path that snaked through a jungle, a barrage of lances flew out at them from behind impenetrable walls of foliage. Later came another attack with the Igorots now bold and visible, screaming aggressively as they launched their missiles. They seemed undaunted by the soldiers' guns, possibly realizing that the nationalists had no quarrel with them and were thus unwilling to release the full power of their weaponry against naked warriors armed only with spears and bolos. Still later, while descending a mountain by following the rocky banks of a rapidly flowing river, a hail of stones pelted down upon them from the cliffs overhead, and Aguinaldo's men were forced to take cover beneath rock outcroppings until the savages went away. Somehow the soldiers escaped serious injury in the attacks. They were not unmindful of the irony of these encounters: one group of guerrillas, in rough and unfamiliar terrain, being harassed and driven away by another guerrilla force.

These hundred soldiers of the Philippine nation had left on their meandering and hard-paced journey with the simple purpose of putting as much distance, and no small number of mountains, between them and the concentrated American forces that had pursued them to Tirad Pass. While they were still in Banaue, spies told them that the Americans — some three hundred in number — had picked up their trail. This spurred the soldiers to resume their trek as much as did the threat of pagan beheadings. Once he was satisfied that the larger force of Americans was far enough behind, Emilio Aguinaldo called together his officers for a conference; together they decided to continue in a generally easterly direction until they contacted another American column. Then they would fight, and there, they decided, in a final, glorious fray they would die.

But they were hardly feeling suicidal; in fact, their overriding desire was to survive the terrain. Climbing barren, rocky mountains in the punishing heat, they would reach one summit and behold another, higher peak in their path. Overcome by fatigue, hunger, and thirst, many men fainted on the steep inclines; others could only crawl, crying, fearful lest they be left behind.

One month after the sortie at Tirad Pass, the soldiers emerged from a forest to see that they had reached the cordillera's eastern flank. After having crossed three provinces and the highest mountain chain in Luzon, they saw below them the lush and vast Cagayan Valley, with its promise of food, rest, and regrouping. Thus, as the soldiers came down off the mountains, they marched nearly in columns and even sang to the rhythm of their steps. "We did not mind the hunger, thirst, or heat," recalled Villa. "We were filled with enthusiasm."

The Magat River flowed down to the valley floor from the cordillera and its foothills, passing the village of Oscaris before intersecting in the north with the mighty Cagayan River. Food was plentiful in that small barrio on the rich alluvial soil of the valley's southwestern edge. Also in good supply, the nationalist soldiers discovered, was patriotism. They were welcomed as heroes. Aguinaldo, Villa, Barcelona, and their officers lodged in a rectory while their troops were billeted in the church. On the morning after their arrival in Oscaris, crowds gathered from the neighboring towns to present *el presidente* with the valley's bounty of rice, corn, sweet potatoes, pork, and fish.

They spent ten idyllic days thus, basking in the outpouring of nationalist sentiment, nursing those in their number who were enfeebled by malnutrition and malaria. On January 18, reality intruded with word from Ilagan, a town 40 miles away, where the Cagayan River received its Magat River tributary. Four hundred American soldiers had learned of the visitors in Oscaris and were preparing to sweep up the river toward them. Aguinaldo put his troops on full alert. The next day a messenger ran in to the barrio to report that a small American convoy was leaving the town of Echaque, about fifteen miles southeast of Oscaris, and it intended to travel out of the valley toward the Nueva Vizcaya provincial capital of Bayombong. The temptation to waylay an enemy convoy was overwhelming. While he waited for confirmation that the larger force was advancing on them from the northeast, Aguinaldo dispatched a patrol — a captain and forty soldiers — to meet the convoy. By late the next evening his patrol returned — with five captured carabaos and twenty horses. They had killed two Americans in the ambush and had retrieved their rifles. In addition, they brought a prisoner, a Chinese man working for the foreigners. After being examined by a military tribunal the following day, the Chinese was executed for collaboration.

When they heard a rumor that a large Filipino force was operating only a day or two's march away in Nueva Vizcaya province, the officers in Oscaris decided to wait as long as they could. Perhaps, after contacting and joining their compatriots, Aguinaldo's men would be a better match for the Americans. So they waited, perhaps longer than was prudent. On the afternoon of January 30, Aguinaldo rode up into the mountains until he arrived at a place where he could stand on an outcropping and see the great green expanse of Isabela, with all its barrios and planting fields slashed out of the woods bordering the glistening rivers. He detected no enemy maneuvers, though spies had informed him earlier in the day that the Americans had reduced both Echaque and Carig to embers. Below him, though, he suddenly made out the shapes of his own men and all the horses hastily approaching. Why had they decamped so frantically? An aide ran up the embankment and breathlessly told him the Americans were near. With an exclamation, Aguinaldo grabbed his field glasses and beheld the line of blue uniforms. He had not spotted them earlier because the American troops had spread out in guerrilla fashion. Darting forward in short, cautious bursts, taking advantage of the natural cover, they were at that moment entering Oscaris. It was like a quail hunt, and the Filipinos were the quarry.

Hopelessly outnumbered, the prudent nationalists disappeared into the dark forest and marched into the thickest part until they were satisfied that they had shaken their pursuers. In their woodland camp, they learned from a spy two nights and one day later that the Americans had divided their forces into two columns after combing through Oscaris. Then they had fanned out to look for them. Luckily, the villager reported, the foreigners' search was taking them in the opposite direction from where the men were hiding. So el presidente bade his troops return to Oscaris in the hope that their rumored reinforcements from Nueva Vizcaya would reach the barrio soon. They were not threatened for another ten days, nor did they hear any more word of reinforcements.

In the meantime, on February 5, a lieutenant reached their camp with scandalous news. General Daniel Tirona, whose battalion had operated in the valley, had wearied of war and given himself up to the Americans in the town of Cagayan. Tirona, of course, was the Caviteno who, as a member of the Tejeros Convention in the heady days of the Katipunan in 1897, had insulted and provoked the *supremo*, Andres Bonifacio, into an irreconcilable split. Tirona went on to prove himself "infamous, cowardly, and shameless," as Colonel Villa noted, for the general had mercilessly taken advantage of the peasants in the valley by robbing some and monopolizing necessities such as rice and salt. But his true colors were flown when he surrendered, for Tirona seemed to turn into a vassal after joining the Americans. The lieutenant told Villa and Aguinaldo that his former general was now employed in an American captain's household, where he washed dishes, cleaned shoes, and bore the insults of his former soldiers and civilians with the most unmanly lack of pride.

Hope for more troops finally evaporated. Protected by their outposts and a network of sympathizers across the upper valley, they enjoyed the last truly leisurely days they would have for many months to come.

The soldiers amused themselves by inaugurating a series of horse races, pitting two steeds against each other and enthusiastically cheering for both winner and loser. Aguinaldo attended each boisterous match, knowing how well they improved his soldiers' morale. Their spirits would have to be as high as possible, he knew, for after a private meeting with Barcelona and Villa, *el presidente* had decided they could not tarry in Oscaris without a larger army. His network of guerrilla mail had finally caught up with him, bringing old Manila newspapers and letters from agents in other provinces, in the capital, and in Hong Kong. At least now, with a sketchy appraisal of the events transpiring outside the Cagayan Valley and Isabela province, he was able to form a plan. When his spies reported on February 10 that three columns of Americans were about to coordinate an encirclement of Oscaris and a full-scale attack, Aguinaldo knew the time had come.

Rather than fight, they would leave the valley. The men would return to the harsh mountains and head for Abra province, thus facing another march of some eighty miles. But in Abra province, General Manuel Tinio commanded a strong guerrilla army. Perhaps the general could spare a contingent of five hundred men, who would join Aguinaldo's in an operation that would sweep Isabela province clean of the foreign invaders. Then, linking up with Tinio, the nationalists could roll down from the northern mountains across the great plains, recapture Manila, and send the Americans back to where they belonged, on the far side of the Pacific Ocean.

The troops walked north through forests and over foothills for two days. A hot rain fell steadily for most of the journey; their horses slipped and slithered in deep mud all the way. When they arrived at the settlement of Seli, peopled by the friendly Igorot tribe known as Kalingas, the soldiers sent messengers to two Christian towns, Gamu and Reina Mercedes, requesting rice, which began arriving in satisfactory quantities within a day. Early on the morning of February 15, they regretfully turned their backs on the level plenitude of the Cagayan Valley and began their slow ascent into the unfriendly Central Cordillera, which waited to greet them with its worst.

Insufferable heat alternating with sudden downpours that swelled the streams they forded and filled the ravines with a steamy mist . . . slippery rocks and muddy paths causing many to fall . . . in the failing light, the grunts and thuds of bodies losing their balance and crashing to the ground . . . the terrified screams of packhorses tumbling off cliffs or being swept away in torrential rivers, their owners helpless to rescue them or the provisions they carried . . . the swollen, bleeding feet of shoeless soldiers . . . entreaties from the commander to march an extra hour before their meals, to rise an hour earlier to continue the march . . . stinging flies and mosquitoes . . . malaria and other fearsome diseases striking the ranks of men already weakened by thirst, hunger, exhaustion . . . leeches creeping into their clothing, onto sleeping faces, robbing them of the blood that sustained them . . . their path made dangerous by stakes of bamboo planted by tribes who left their settlements cleaned of provisions before melting into the rocks and forests . . . the continuous threat of the barbarities of the *kānao* . . . through the mossy canyons of the rivers Malig, Tanudan, and Chico, along slippery cliffside paths, over precipices, promontories, creeks, streams, rivers, boulders, cliffs, through jungles . . . from village to village: Seli to Butigui to Balinsugan to Babalao to Banafa to Parasili to Guinabuan to Latang to Maralag to Caragdag to Malalig to Boac to Bilo to Manducayon to Dancalan to Gaang to Lubu . . . the small part of the sky visible between the high mountains seemed to be just a hundred meters away, the sun and moon only apparent for a handful of hours before disappearing over the walls that at once imprisoned the soldiers and beckoned them onward.

Aguinaldo paid and discharged two friendly Igorot guides who had led them for many days along a nightmarish mountain route between Manducayon and Gaang. The two warriors began their return journey but only got as far as the settlement of Gurong before they were waylaid by enemy tribesmen. When word of this reached the nationalists, they were resting after their lunch in the village of Lubu; *el presidente*, Villa, and Barcelona were at that moment discussing Aguinaldo's fear that they might not be able to prevent civil war in the far-flung islands of the archipelago once independence was won. But the news of the murder of their guides swiftly turned Aguinaldo's mind from politics. His patience at these irrational mountain barbarities came to an end. He immediately sent half of his troops to the offending settlement, where they discovered their faithful guides' flyblown bodies. Pierced by dozens of spears, they had already been butchered for the *kānao;* the soldiers said they looked like chopped meat. They retaliated by burning all the houses and shooting whomever they encountered.

Leaving Lubu for Mangali and then Talutoc, the column followed a river that plunged between its abrupt mountain walls in such a way that they were forced to cross the torrent some seventeen times. They had to link arms to keep from being swept away by the icy water. On March 4, at Talutoc, the tribesmen told them that they had heard all about Emilio Aguinaldo: he was "a supernatural man who flies and is usually accompanied by thunder." *El presidente* did not entertain them with displays of flight, nor did he disclose his true identity. He learned, having reached the provincial border, that despite General Tinio's large force, all of Abra was firmly in the Americans' grasp.

Four days later they had crossed uncountable mountains and finally climbed to the summit of one peak, reaching the settlement of Lubuagan. There the Gaddangs, another tribe of the Igorots, were not very pleased to see the troops, who were outnumbered by the savages by ten to one. They did not even pause from their daily tasks to welcome them, but they made room, billeting the soldiers in groups of three or four in one section of the village. The disgruntled tribe, after several days of hospitality enforced as much by their good manners as by the presence of so many guns, attempted to dislodge their guests by spreading the rumor that 300 Americans had followed their trail and had now reached the Lubu settlement. Aguinaldo did not believe them. He doubted that any Americans would endure the hardships they had suffered to get to that inaccessible place.

However, not fully discounting the rumor, he thought about reinforcements. They were at last in Abra province, so it was time to contact General Tinio. *El presidente* dispatched a squad commanded by a captain named Villareal to search for Tinio in the mountains where he reputedly operated.

While they waited, malaria began to take a firmer hold; almost a third of the men were down with it. When rain fell, keeping them indoors, Aguinaldo, Barcelona, and Villa passed the time by studying English. When the sun came out, *el presidente* ordered his sergeants and corporals to study heliography. At night, they concocted fantasies of an easy life after the revolt was won — a European state tour and then, as a reward for their toil, *haciendas* in the bounteous San José Valley in Nueva Ecija, where they would grow coffee, cacao, sugar, and palay and raise cattle.

On the afternoon of March 22, Emilio Aguinaldo, the "invincible liberator of the Philippines," celebrated his thirty-first birthday. In his honor, his men constructed a huge rectangular dining table beneath the sheltering trees. Twenty-five soldier-musicians tooted a merry greeting on their bamboo pipes as he arrived before them in his ceremonial uniform. "The greetings were solemn and splendid, because the President after receiving them affectionately, offered them sweets, cigarettes, and wine," recalled Villa. They sat down to the best meal they had eaten for months — the cooks having scoured the countryside for days to produce the feast. There was *paella,* chicken stuffed with sweet potatoes and covered with strawberry sauce, roasted pig, stews, rice wine, and sweets. They dined and listened to speeches; they toasted *el presidente* and each other, vowing to die in the mountains rather than submit to foreign domination. And all wept in memory of their departed comrades, especially when Aguinaldo's physician, Santiago Barcelona, rose to toast the memory of the gallant general Gregorio del Pilar. Despite a temporarily somber air created by the mention of the boy hero of Bulacan, the party was altogether a splendid affair, full of patriotism and merriment — a necessary catharsis for the long-suffering troops.

El presidente received a delegation of warriors from nearby Naneng on March 31, including the leader of that *rancheria,* Chief Binuañgan. He presented Aguinaldo with a gift of a small amount of rice as a token of good fellowship. While they were chatting amiably inside the house used by Aguinaldo as his headquarters, a dozen soldiers marched into the village. They were, they told the lookouts, the advance guard of a nationalist company commanded by Captain Gregorio Panel, and they had been operating in the Ilocos provinces near the China Sea coast; earlier in the month they had met Captain Villareal during his search for General Tinio, and he had told them where *el presidente* was now based. Panel, they reported, had sent them ahead and was following with sixty more soldiers to join Aguinaldo's personal guard. Moreover, these new soldiers had captured a secret document from a courier that merited their leader's immediate attention.

With news such as this, Aguinaldo's meeting with the Igorot chieftain had to be interrupted. While his guest waited, Aguinaldo curiously opened the package handed him and found a letter addressed to a major of the American army. Dated two weeks earlier, it reported that a large force of Katipuneros had arrived in Lubuagan. Sitting amid his troops in that very village, Aguinaldo read the informant's long litany of complaints of how all the settlements in the area were being victimized by the nationalists. Please expel them, the informant pleaded.

Across the room, Chief Binuañgan blanched when he saw what Aguinaldo was reading. He stood and silently edged out of the house.

Meanwhile, *el presidente* finished reading this request for American aid, with appended statements by two Christian Filipinos who apparently lived nearby. Then he realized with a shock that the letter was signed by his erstwhile guest, who seemed to have abruptly disappeared without taking his leave.

Soldiers captured the chieftain after a mile-long chase. In the nationalists' improvised jail, he joined two Christian prisoners who had been arrested as possible spies by a scouting party two weeks earlier. Spies they were, for they had helped the Igorot produce his letter of betrayal.

They stayed in Lubuagan all through April. Nearby settlements contributed food regularly, and with their successful hunting and foraging expeditions into the forests, they no longer lacked sustenance. They dined on carabao meat aplenty, rice, and even chocolate from the *rancherias*. On April 7, Captain Panel appeared with his sixty-one soldiers, swelling Aguinaldo's ranks to 168. It was a slightly more formidable number, but still not capable of inflicting much damage on the foreigners, much less expel them. Finally, on April 12, their long wait for Tinio was rewarded. The general arrived with an escort of 25 men, and Aguinaldo's entire staff went down the trail to meet them. Villareal, tired but triumphant after searching for the general in the mountains and valleys of Abra province for more than a month, was commended for his successful mission.

Though he was a welcome guest, Tinio gave no more soldiers to Aguinaldo than the seventy-three under Captain Panel. Perhaps a larger detachment could be spared later, but for the present all thoughts of *el presidente* returning to Isabela province were shelved. Tinio departed for the military zone under his command on April 16, and Aguinaldo seemed content to remain in Lubuagan. He began receiving reports of nationalist activities in Abra province and discussed various plans for attacking American outposts within striking distance. He also started composing a manifesto, "To the Filipino People," which would be distributed throughout the islands. He made several reconnaissance tours of the paths leading to nearby Guinaang and Balimbing, inspected his outposts, and supervised the building of trenches. Meanwhile, malaria continued to move through his men, finally claiming the life of a soldier of the Bulacan Battalion on April 25. Around that time, sturdy Simeon Villa came down with the chills, but he emerged at the other end of the fever by the first of May. Others continued to suffer.

"Every wail of the wind seems to bring us news of the impending arrival of the Americans," Villa observed on May 16. Two weeks earlier they heard that a hundred enemies were on their way to attack, but the Americans returned to their post at Bagued, it was said, when they learned they were outnumbered. This may have been wishful thinking on the part of the spies, for in a few days the Igorots and Aguinaldo's own soldiers stationed along various trails began sending in a flurry of messages. At least three detachments of Americans, each numbering a hundred, seemed to be maneuvering toward Lubuagan. One column had been temporarily repulsed by a guerrilla unit from General Tinio's far-flung force. As the days passed, there was great activity in Aguinaldo's trenches, all of it spurred on by reports of Americans swarming through the *rancherias* of Bucay, Labaan, Bontoc, Banao, and Naneng, threading their way through passes and over mountains toward this new center of resistance before much resistance could be organized. Like so many ants scenting the presence of food, the enemy unerringly closed in.

An Igorot from Lubuagan was waiting for Aguinaldo when he emerged from his headquarters at six o'clock on the morning of May 17. Americans were only an hour away, in Sumader, said the warrior to Aguinaldo and Barcelona. *El presidente* dispatched a courier to verify this alarming report. Sure enough, the courier returned to say that he had crept up within sight of the soldiers, who were busy with their breakfast. Aguinaldo did not have many options. Half his forces were sick, so he ordered the *rancheria* abandoned in favor of the village of Guinaang, where the bulk of his men had been billeted. Making their way slowly because of their sick comrades, they heard more bad news. One of the American units had blindly bypassed the revolutionaries' fortified trenches on the summit of a nearby mountain and was continuing its advance unchecked. The squad of nationalists holding that outpost, now flanked and useless, hooked up with Aguinaldo. They reached Guinaang an hour past noon, took a hasty lunch, and faced a heart-wrenching problem.

Fourteen of their patients, reduced by malarial fever and stomach problems, were obviously too weak to continue farther, so Aguinaldo was forced to leave the sick behind. He summoned the chieftain of Guinaang and gave him money, extracting a solemn promise that he would take care of the soldiers. He and all his people would answer with their lives for the weakened men, warned Aguinaldo. The sick lay on pallets on the ground with desperation on their faces, terrified that they would become victims of the *kānao*. Sadly, their *presidente* doled out three pesos per man and led his troops into the thick forest that surrounded the town. He believed that, if nothing else, divine providence would guard his men.

Ascending and descending mountains, they passed through Pugong and Mguilang, Aguinaldo moving ahead of the main group along with his two chiefs of staff and some soldiers. Night fell, but they did not stop, nor did they carry lights, for the Americans were still too close. They edged their way along slippery mountain trails, blundering again and again into trees with sharp spines. Deep ravines opened up at their feet, "seeming to wait for a human life to be swallowed by the abyss," thought Villa. Several horses stumbled sideways and disappeared into the darkness below. Descending finally that awful mountain, they picked their way down an almost vertical trail through a thick forest. The moon appeared, its weak light filtering through the canopy of foliage above their heads. Still, many soldiers fell and rolled down the path until they slammed against the trees in their way. At midnight, Aguinaldo and his exhausted comrades halted to eat supper. Afterward they fell into a deep sleep. The other men continued to arrive at their camp throughout the early morning.

At seven o'clock, an Igorot appeared. He had followed them all the way from Lubuagan to report that after Aguinaldo's men left the town, all the Igorots decided to flee also. When the Americans entered Lubuagan they found it deserted, and in anger some began shooting randomly into the blank wall of trees surrounding the *ranchería* while others torched the houses. Now, the warrior told them, the enemies were less than an hour away. There were as many as a thousand.

El presidente immediately ordered their departure and they left the place almost in flight. The only available route lay along a snakelike

river that boiled and tumbled against its abrupt walls. Following it
meant repeated dunkings — as many as twenty fordings in three
hours. After passing the settlements of Dupas and Naneng, both of
which were at the tumult's edge, one of his majors came up to
Aguinaldo, saluted, and reported that a soldier named Salazar had
drowned in the river. For a while the troops took to dry land but
soon came to the brink of another watercourse. They stopped short.
The memory of Salazar was heavy, for this new river was wider,
deeper, and swifter than any they had encountered. It was obviously
sure death to enter. So they changed their route, backtracking a short
distance, and turned onto the rocky trail toward Asibanlan. They
stopped early that evening inside a forest, having marched only ten
or eleven hours.

Aguinaldo and his vanguard got under way shortly after six o'clock
on the morning of May 19, and they followed a trail that continued
through the forests. After a few miles they stopped, realizing that
their rear guard was missing. *El presidente* ordered a corporal to blow
his bugle, but they received no answer. He assumed the troops had
taken the wrong trail, so he dispatched a patrol to find them. Two
hours later they were reunited, and they continued the upward march
until the trail disappeared into a thicket. Then it became necessary
to create a path through the tangle with bolos. After midday they
crossed the summit, and as they began to pick their way carefully
down the opposite side, a stinging cold rain began to fall. It soaked
and chilled the soldiers and slickened their path. Reaching the bottom, they followed a river that tumbled over big boulders and then
began climbing another peak through trees that hid them from the
sun. Finally they emerged into a level clearing where many abandoned Igorot houses awaited them. This was the *rancheria* known as
Sanga. The vanguard column used this place as their camp for the
night while the other soldiers bedded down in strategic spots and
outposts.

On the next morning, May 20, Aguinaldo and Barcelona arose at
six o'clock and walked over to visit Major Panel's installation. While
the three stood talking they heard the sound of slapping, and Barcelona went to investigate. He found an infantry officer, Major Jeciel, and a soldier of Panel's column. Jeciel, for some reason blinded
with anger, slapped and kicked the soldier, who did not resist his superior. Barcelona did not intervene but reported the incident to
Aguinaldo.

"That is not good," said *el presidente*, looking worried, and he went
over to rebuke Jeciel, who was still so enraged that he kicked and
slapped the bruised soldier again for good measure. This won him a

sharp order to desist from Aguinaldo, whom he finally obeyed.

Returning to breakfast with *el presidente*, Barcelona noticed that his mood had shifted. He was somber, preoccupied — perhaps by the memory of his young son, whose death had been relayed to him only a few days earlier; perhaps it was because of their haphazard flight from the enemy through the cordillera or because of that morning's breakdown of troop discipline — which could spread in these stressful days like a cancer throughout his forces.

At breakfast there was silence. Aguinaldo's preoccupation was unshakable. Then came the portent of bad luck: a black butterfly hovering in the air near *el presidente,* signifying death or tragedy or loss to the person it touched. Barcelona watched mutely as his leader reached out to touch this symbol of disaster, but the butterfly fluttered out of reach, flew back toward Aguinaldo's hand, then disappeared out the window.

"I'm getting more nervous each day," confessed the thirty-one-year-old incarnation of the revolution.

Several hours later, he learned that Americans had entered the village of Guinaang, found the fourteen malarial soldiers, and shot them dead as they lay on their pallets.

II

Fate, it would seem, would not allow them time to mourn those fourteen, for not long after, they were thrown into utter chaos.

In the afternoon, Aguinaldo and Barcelona ascended the mountain to inspect the places where various detachments had encamped. *El presidente,* upon passing by a watchtower built by the departed villagers, ordered that it be occupied by one of his officers. This was fortunate, for at that moment American soldiers were entering the distant lower reaches of the deserted *rancheria,* an area held only until late that morning by Major Panel's troops, now stationed near the summit. The tower lookout did not sight the enemy, who were dispersed and creeping upward guerrilla-fashion, until some time later. Just as the lookout saw them, Aguinaldo and Barcelona happened to be passing nearby, and from the top of the watchtower the soldier screamed a warning to them. Simeon Villa appeared, leading troops from below, shouting that the enemy approached. *El presidente* ordered everyone to climb. Bullets began to whistle past their heads. They began ascending, firing at will, with two of the Bulacan companies lagging behind as a rear guard. Two of their lieutenants and at least four of their soldiers were seen to die. Above, Major Panel and his men had disappeared behind cover and could not be discerned in the underbrush. The sun began to set behind the mountains, the rifle fire grew more intense, and the nationalists continued to retreat toward the nearby *rancheria* of Guday. They came to a place where their horses could not pass. As Aguinaldo and his officers squinted into the growing gloom for a path, someone shouted, "Americans behind!" and they were forced to abandon horses and saddles. They took only their rifles, satchels, raincoats, and woolen blankets.

The fleeing nationalists passed rapidly through a darkened Guday, locating a trail away from the *rancheria* with some difficulty. Because of the darkness, they became scattered in groups of five and ten. They entered another black forest, its trees slashing and resisting them at every step with spiny branches. Ravines and drop-offs yawned at their feet, claiming some men. Half a kilometer behind in Guday they saw the torches of their pursuers.

Aguinaldo, in the forest depths with fifteen men, looked desperately for a way out. Hearing a sound to the rear, he took off his distinctive white pith helmet and brandished a rifle. Barcelona protectively replaced his chief's hat with his own dark brown one. Villa was nearby. *El presidente* turned in the dark to whisper something to those behind him. But they had run away, leaving the three alone with their guide.

The four continued to walk through the night, pausing only briefly near midnight. Unsure of the correct route, they blundered into a settlement and ate a small amount of rice. Six o'clock on the morning of May 21 found them descending a deep ravine, but soon, after encountering a small creek, they retraced their steps out of the declivity, fearing entrapment. Their guide was still confused but indicated they should scale the mountain ahead of them. Halfway up, they saw a group of men at the summit. Aguinaldo obstinately refused to flee, wanting to see for himself whether the figures were friends or foes. As they drew closer he recognized the peripatetic Captain Villareal, another officer, and nine soldiers, who had been searching for their leader since the previous day's rout. All rejoiced.

From their vantage point at the mountain crest, the nationalists watched as the tiny figures of the pursuing American column entered the village in which Aguinaldo's small group had paused at dawn. Down the mountain's opposite flank the Filipinos fled. They passed two settlements, forded a river, and entered the *rancheria* of Tuctuguinoc. The Igorots there did not flee but instead cooked rice and slaughtered a pig for the fifteen visitors. Just as they had fully relaxed and their hosts had placed the food before them, their sentinel raised an alarm: seeming to have wings on their feet, the enemy had reached the nearby river.

They all jumped up and fled. Barcelona had taken off his shirt, so he hurriedly put on his black coat over an undershirt. He grabbed his cartridge belt and gun, but his hat was not in its accustomed place when he reached for it. Aguinaldo and Villa were already quite far away. He ran without his hat to overtake them.

Climbing yet another mountain toward the blazing noonday sun, Barcelona stopped, feeling giddy, then fainted from the heat. He awoke a half-hour later to find his head cradled in the lap of Aguinaldo, who fanned him with a hat and gave him water and some rice. When he was fully recovered, they continued the climb. Villa was telling Barcelona that they still had a long way to climb when suddenly *el presidente* ordered them off the path. As they crouched in the undergrowth, firing erupted and bullets began to pour in from three directions. The Americans had split into three columns, climbing nearby peaks, and now were trying to cut them into little pieces. The nationalists ran down, away from the fire, followed a dry stream, retraced their steps, ascended, descended, crossed a river filled with crocodiles, and left the enemy behind.

After having passed the night sleeping fitfully on damp and mossy stones, the fifteen continued their eastward trek through the mountains. They descended to a plain at noon, crossed a river, and rested. The *rancheria* of Tabog lay ahead in the distance. Just then they saw a column of men coming down off the mountain behind them. As Aguinaldo ordered his men to disperse, Barcelona peered through field glasses and saw a man dressed in black with a colored felt hat, armed with a rifle.

"They are Americans," the doctor said. He and his leader cautiously crept back along a riverbed to reconnoiter. They ducked when men in the column's vanguard spotted them, but instead of rifle fire, they heard a familiar voice calling to them. It was Lieutenant Teodoro Dayo, leading a group of forty-five men out of the cordillera to rejoin *el presidente*. Dayo said he had heard that at least two hundred Americans were waiting for them in Tabog, ahead.

Now sixty-one in number, they still could not account for more than a hundred missing since the rout in Sanga. Hiking on this high plain, there was not enough food for their group, and no one had eaten much in those two brutal days. "Everybody looked like corpses," observed Barcelona, "pale, weak, and with deep-set eyes!" A puppy followed the column as it passed a deserted *rancheria;* it was killed and eaten by some soldiers. Finally, in late afternoon, they were able to buy sufficient rice from the Igorots in the settlement of Magaogao, and they took a long rest inside a forest. Then the men crossed two rivers, but a third engulfed them up to their chests, its vicious current tugging at their feet. Holding tightly to one another they crossed, with Aguinaldo taking the lead and shouting, "Determination, brothers!" in encouragement. Ten men lost their rifles.

Then, while it was still dark, the nationalist column silently passed the *rancheria* of Tabog, occupied by Americans. Around dawn they saw they had reached the lower foothills of the eastern reaches of the Central Cordillera. Once again, they looked down upon the Cagayan Valley and Isabela province. As before, the sight filled them with joy and relief.

Having reached that valley of relative plenitude, the revolutionaries again enjoyed the patriotic hospitality of civilians in many towns. In Enrile, on the banks of the Cagayan River, the townspeople received Aguinaldo on the feast day of his patron saint, the martyr Saint Emilio, with a grand and festive party and a ball attended, it was noted, by "more than sixty young girls of the aristocracy of Tugegarao and Enrile." During the ball, which lasted for some eleven hours, partygoers told the soldiers that the Americans had been spreading rumors about them. The foreigners, still combing the mountains for Aguinaldo, told the villagers "they had him completely surrounded" and expected his capture very soon. On the following day, May 30, as the nationalist column began a slow march south along the great river, Aguinaldo decided to deal a small blow to the enemy. He sent Colonel Villa and a company of soldiers to attack the posts in Cabagan Nuevo, Maluno, and Tumauini, where the Filipinos inflicted twelve deaths and fourteen wounds while only three guerrillas were hurt.

By the next week, the soldiers had found a new base of operations in a forest near the town of Naguilian. There, in a campsite they christened Tierra Virgen, the guerrillas remained for two months and twenty-one days.

Small raiding parties from the camp nipped at various American installations; Aguinaldo sent messengers to his scattered generals in the mountains and in the lowlands of southern Luzon, and he began to get letters and newspapers from Manila and Hong Kong. Starting to feel as if he was regaining control of the situation, he learned on July 29 "with deep pain in his soul" the latest news about Pedro Paterno, the *illustrado* attorney who had collected double commissions for his work on the Biaknabato Pact with the Spaniards and who had later maneuvered himself into control of the Aguinaldo-Mabini government. Apparently Paterno was up to his old tricks: a Manila newspaper revealed that Paterno was, as Colonel Villa noted, "usurping the power of the Chief of the Revolution by revealing and feigning to possess ample powers" belonging to Emilio Aguinaldo. The shyster had established his own party of autonomists in Manila.

Though he was weakened by malaria and bronchitis and stomach problems, Aguinaldo finished a manifesto exhorting his people not to lay down their arms; he wrote more instructions for his generals; and he dispatched an official document to his former premier, Apolinario Mabini, giving the imprisoned paralytic the power to negotiate a peace based only on the independence of the Philippines.

On August 26, Aguinaldo learned that the Americans had taken one of his wounded soldiers as prisoner and presumably had tortured him, for he agreed to lead them to Tierra Virgen. This galvanized *el presidente* into taking actions that would safeguard his office while continuing the warfare in the valley. He had decided to leave most of his troops under the command of two captains, who would lead the men in guerrilla actions in the province. Aguinaldo would leave the valley, crossing the Sierra Madre to the eastern coast of Luzon, where there awaited an isolated sanctuary he could use as a new base — the town of Palanan.

Taking only sixteen riflemen and Villa, Barcelona, and two other officers, *el presidente* set out on August 27, narrowly evading two American war parties. "We slept with nothing as a roof but the sky over us," recalled Villa. "The earth was our floor, and for caresses we had the sting of the mosquitoes known as *nicnec*, which were present in great numbers and kept us awake the whole night."

Climbing up and down mountains, swimming streams and skirting crocodiles, bedeviled by mosquitoes and leeches and soaked continually by rain, suffering from constant hunger and succumbing to malarial chills, the revolutionaries clambered over the Sierra toward the east and the sea.

By September 6, they had come down onto a level coastal plain that was bisected by a broad, winding river. Tracts of jungle had been cleared near the settlement of Palanan, but the town itself was in great disrepair, with most of the nipa huts falling down. The villagers welcoming the nationalists told them that out of fear of their town being captured by the foreigners, they had fled to the mountains and rebuilt their huts there. "Everybody," noted Villa approvingly, "armed with spears and darts, was ready at all times to face an invasion by the Americans. They would show them that they preferred to live in the mountains than to submit to foreign domination." If the soldiers wanted to stay and protect them, the people said, they would resume life in the village with a willingness to fight for their homes as they had been prepared, in hiding, to fight for their freedom.

Palanan seemed to be an ideal place from which to reinvigorate the war without having to be on the alert constantly. Within days of the soldiers' arrival, the villagers began to repair their houses and cheerfully donated fish and chickens for their guests' comfort. To ensure that their tenure would be uninterrupted, Aguinaldo stationed lookouts near the few trails leading to Palanan through the Sierra and from the nearest village, Casiguran, ninety miles to the south. Feeling safe for the first time in many months, *el presidente* planned, not only for a long stay in the town, but for renewing communications with his various generals who, while carrying on the fight, waited for his directions.

Two weeks after industry and purpose had returned to the impregnable little town of Palanan, Emilio Aguinaldo took his doctor, Barcelona, his aide, Villa, and a small presidential escort and hiked for three hours to the shore of the Pacific Ocean. A ship had arrived with ammunition, and the party found it beached and guarded by one of *el presidente*'s lieutenants and five soldiers.

Theirs had been a pleasant and leisurely hike — for once — and after they had rested for a while, Aguinaldo, Villa, and Barcelona walked out over the hot sand to enter the Pacific surf. They paddled about, their minds clear, thinking only of the brightness of the sky, the warmth of the day, the invigoration of the ocean.

9

FROM DINAPIQUI TO NORTH OF
DINATADMO POINT, 1982

I

The frontier settlement of Dinapiqui did not exist when Emilio Aguinaldo found his way to Luzon's northeastern coast. Had Funston's band of conspirators paused north of Casiguran to strike inland from the cliffy protuberance called Dinapiqui by the aborigines, they would have found a heavily forested bay-plain overlooked by mountains. Today the area is the last place for expansion from the settlements leapfrogging from Baler through Casiguran along the narrow coastal corridor. Only recently have people elected to settle there, and the town of Dinapiqui seems to suffer from its own tentativeness. Settlers from Casiguran — Tagalogs, mostly — and Ilocanos from the western watershed of the Sierra had met here to fight the jungle with bolo and torch and carve out a place for rice fields and coconut trees. For a time a mining company came in, attempting to extract minerals from the nearby mountains, but that overly ambitious enterprise had failed. The speculators left, and with them some villagers. Only the most determined pioneers stayed behind to keep the jungle from reclaiming their hard-won land, but they had accomplished little else. The tin-roofed houses were in disrepair; each shack was made of boards silvered by the sun and frequent storms and surrounded by untended overgrowth. For the most part the inhabitants seemed too tired or dispirited to summon any curiosity about our presence.

We had come to Dinapiqui in an empty cargo boat called the M.S. *Marivie*. A forty-five-foot diesel outrigger that sailed the waters off the Contracosta, it hauled mostly rattan for its skipper, an entrepreneur named Danny Mangalapus. He was originally from Casiguran, but he had traded and bargained his way up from that quiet village to the rare stage in Philippine rural life where he could boast of a pied-à-terre in Metro Manila. Doubtless that bachelor pad, as he called it, was cramped and in a seedy neighborhood of the capital, and probably he could afford to visit it only a few times a year. On that poor coast, however, Danny made sure everyone he met knew of his money and his deals.

We encountered him on the beach a short distance north of the malarial homestead of Bert and Rosada (who, by the way, seemed to be in improved health when we said good-bye). The skipper was out recruiting Agtas for a rattan-picking job he had up north, and he saw a chance to make money on what would otherwise be a dead run by offering us transportation to Dinapiqui. I took Danny up on his offer. Bill Allen's feet, alas, were still in sorry shape; despite his being the saltiest member of our expedition, his feet had given out first, and he burned with embarrassment. Plainly a day of reduced exertion was what the doctor ordered; in fact, Dario heartily agreed. So I bought passage for eleven hikers — eleven because Seanbuyan, our errant guide, had been waiting for us when we awoke, as old Bersosa had promised.

The *Marivie* chugged under an unblemished sky out of Casapsapan Bay and the lee of another peninsula, this one pointing north, called Taregteg Point. The ocean here was rough and the Agtas, who live by the sea but do not often venture into or upon it, became seasick. We left the protection of the peninsula's steep brown bluffs, and in open sea, our boat's outriggers turned into wings as we plunged from mountainous crests into deep troughs, the fragile-looking bamboo poles slamming into the sea with tremendous crashes that made the boat shudder. Christopher and Bill perched on the *Marivie*'s soaring prow for most of this roller-coaster ride; when they returned amidships, they were drenched with spray and exhilarated.

Even as the ship was turning unexpectedly toward shore, Danny Mangalapus was clambering along the slippery gangway to tell me why. Wanting to keep within the bounds of the law, he was detouring me to the coastal checkpoint of the Philippine Constabulary at Dikabasan, where he said I could present my papers and seek permission to cross the border between the provinces of Aurora and Isabela. I tried to convince him to bypass the authorities, for having evaded the PC this long, I had no desire to take the chance of having our trip interrupted — or worse, curtailed. But Danny was adamant.

My interview with a PC sergeant in a bamboo watchtower overlooking the beach was an anticlimax. His station was so remote that no cables from Manila had arrived to command him to escort us through "dangerous rebel territory." Though we would soon be far away from civilization — even outposts like this one — I still felt having soldiers along was only begging for trouble in any encounter with rebels. The sergeant at first was reluctant to let us go without consulting his superiors. With some fast talking fueled by the momentum of a journey that had begun half the world away, I escaped with only his warning that the PC could not be held responsible for anything that happened to us in the wilderness ahead.

A downpour began soon after we resumed the voyage, with rising waves making the passage uncomfortable for everyone but Dario; he took an antihistamine and crawled into a rope locker to sleep alongside a sailor down with malaria who was avoided by all the crew with a nearly superstitious fear.

The *Marivie* finally turned in toward land in midafternoon, coming to rest where a heavy surf broke upon a black, sandy beach. We formed a line to pass our gear over the froth to dry land while from the prow our guides shot their arrows in high arcs through the rain toward the empty beach, tossing their bows after them. These important possessions transferred, they gingerly lowered themselves into the breaking waves with evident unease. Seanbuyan, however, remained on board. He had learned the skipper was treating his crew to a night's worth of gin. "If there's a party within a hundred miles," I commented dryly, "Seanbuyan will sniff it out." He promised to meet us in the morning, but it would be several days before we would again lay eyes on him.

Rain hammered down on us as we slid up a long trail to the village, arriving close to darkness and evoking no great excitement from the citizens of Dinapiqui. It was Easter night, we remembered; I found the mayor busily celebrating the feast day at his house with a few other dignitaries. They were unable to rise from their bench due to the quantities of gin they had consumed, but the mayor saw to amenities by having his little boy bring out some glasses of hot coffee for me and Bersosa. "This Dumagat I know well," the mayor said, patting the old man on the head. "We go back many years." My companions had congregated in an empty Episcopal chapel on the far side of town to wait out the storm, so there was no great hurry to break off our chat, which continued amiably as the mayor tipsily wandered from topic to topic, little of it clear to me. Christopher then appeared and brushed aside the courtesies offered by the inebriated mayor. Instead, he hoisted up one of the two trunks we had sent to the mayor's care at the beginning of our trip and left without a word.

"Your brother seems to be a man of action," the mayor observed.

"He hasn't acclimated himself to the Philippine pace yet."

The next morning I pushed open the heavy doors of the little Episcopal chapel. The heavy rains had ceased, leaving great pools of water in wagon ruts and carabao tracks, and much of the hamlet was obscured by fog. A half-dozen children were waiting outside to bid me good morning. They had risen with the roosters and walked through the dripping weeds to see the best diversion that had come to their village in ages: six sodden and grizzled Americans who tripped over mounds of equipment, stumbled into their clotheslines which were strung willy-nilly about the chapel, and groped, half asleep, for camp stoves and instant coffee. The sight was entertaining — at least to children.

Our aboriginal guides, too, were awake. They lounged in their loincloths on the church pews that, pushed together, had been their beds. They viewed with no readable expressions the two tents we had erected inside the little chapel. These took up most of the available floor space and made necessary our going through a complex series of contortions to get from one place to another. Our guides probably assumed this was another crazy affectation of ours rather than a precaution against tropical mosquitoes. Actually, despite our worries — which had been fed by the formidable insects in Casiguran several days before — the night had been free of bugs. To this we presumed we owed thanks to a family of noisy geckos, whose batlike chirpings from their upside-down places on the ceiling had disturbed our sleep until the relentless territorial crowings of roosters had begun at dawn.

After a freeze-dried cheese omelette breakfast, I strolled over to the mayor's house to return a borrowed kerosene lamp. No one answered my knock, so I left it on his doorstep. Skirting the house to avoid a furiously yapping dog, I nearly tripped over the mayor himself. He was sitting on a tree root, looking old and miserable and hung over. I nodded and left him alone in his misery.

A dozen young women were washing clothes in plastic basins at a community pump. They smiled brightly when I appeared. After I had passed, one coquettishly called out, "I love you," and they all laughed merrily when I turned to see who spoke. Finally the adult population seemed to be taking notice of us.

This was confirmed at the municipal hall, a concrete bunker with jalousie windows and apparently the only structure in town that would withstand a typhoon. Here I met Vice Mayor Razo, whose take-charge manner suggested he was the real power in Dinapiqui.

"Ah, here you are," the vice mayor said, all business. "Your friends should be arriving shortly. I sent a boy over with a note asking them to come.

"I have been reading the letters and documents you left with the mayor," Razo told me. "He has driven south for a municipal officers' conference and left me in charge." I decided to be discreet about seeing Razo's boss in desperate need of an Alka-Seltzer only a few hundred yards away.

"I am curious to know just how you assembled your party," he went on, holding one of my documents. "David Bain, a writer, and Christopher Bain, a photographer. This I can understand since you will write about your experiences and show your brother's photographs. But the others: Paul Kirtland, an engineer; William Allen, a cabinetmaker; Erich Vogt, a carpenter; Dario Gonzalez, M.D., a hospital doctor. Are you planning to build a city out of the jungle?" He laughed at his jest.

I began to explain that I had brought these others along because they were old and trusted friends when they appeared. Razo repeated his little joke about building a city. Outside the window, small boys peered in through the open louvers and made faces at us.

"Doc," the vice mayor said to Dario, "you have a Filipino name. Gonzalez is a Filipino name." A subordinate standing nearby nodded to confirm this. Dario explained that it was also a Puerto Rican name — not so much of a coincidence, he said, since the Spanish had colonized both lands.

"Well, Doc, you should stay here with us. We are very poor and many sick people are here. All we have is one nurse" — he indicated a man who had shouldered past the village men who, curious, had begun spilling into the room. Dario replied that the hospital for which he worked in New York expected him to return. "Anyway, Doc," Razo said, "you look very healthy." The vice mayor turned to me, chuckling. "We are not used to such healthy people here." Evidently he was referring to Dario's husky build. I briefly considered pointing out that Razo should see some of his well-fed countrymen working for the government in Manila who made our physician look positively slim.

"You will have to excuse us," Razo said as he handed our proffered passports to a police sergeant, who began copying down our names, dates and places of birth, and passport and visa numbers. The officer wore a very large revolver, and I wondered why he would carry such a formidable weapon in this tiny, peaceful village.

"We have to take precautions," Razo explained, referring either to the copying of our passports or to his subordinate's packing a rod nearly as big as a cannon. "Last year we had other visitors — a Swiss, a German, an American — who told us they were on vacation. They stayed in the chapel, as you did. They hired men to take them fishing off Dinapiqui Point. Finally they went into the mountains to the north, as you will. We heard nothing further from them. But then the national government sent soldiers to our village to look for these men. They told us the foreigners were spies. The mountains are full of communist guerrillas, you see."

I asked him for whom did he think these spies had worked. "I don't know, they never told us," he said. "Maybe CIA. Maybe communists." He shrugged.

The fog had lifted far above and was dispersing under the heat of the rising sun as we readied ourselves back at the chapel for our hike. The sky was clear enough to see for many miles — to the rounded, tree-covered peaks of the mountains that rose from the Dinapiqui fields on three sides of the town. After glancing at our topographical map, I saw that we were in for some climbing before we regained the seacoast. I did not need a map to know that this little burg was the last bit of civilization we would see until we reached our destination, Palanan, sixty-five miles away.

I was distracted from admiring the mountains by a commotion out in front of the chapel, where the children had taken up watch over us. I came around the corner in time to see one stocky nine-year-old plant his fist in the eye of a younger and smaller boy. Crying, the younger boy began hurling large stones at his tormentor, who ran a short distance and stood dodging them with the petulant, mean-spirited expression of the bully on his face. Once again America stepped in to police the world; I halted the barrage and sternly ordered them away in opposite directions — the bully out into a field where some carabao were grazing, the crier toward the center of town.

A short time later, when we had shouldered our gear and put the chapel behind us, the two boys reappeared together with their friends. They had somehow patched up their differences and now fell in behind us for a while. We passed a road crew of young men halfheartedly digging a drainage ditch beside our path with picks and shovels. They wore T-shirts that prominently advertised various products — Sanyo tape recorders, Caterpillar tractors, Hershey's chocolate — that were undoubtedly not available in Dinapiqui or anywhere nearby, probably Hong Kong production overruns that somehow had made their way to this frontier. The boys stopped working and stared at us.

"Where are you going?" several asked. We told them Palanan and they stared some more and grinned. "You are *crazy*," one said.

We crisscrossed soggy green checkerboards of rice paddies for about three quarters of a mile by walking single file on narrow earthen dikes. Of our guides, two of the young men — Sulimon and Udeng — looked pleased to be sporting the backpacks we had sent up to Dinapiqui with a cache of food the week before; the youngest, Benchan, who still carried his rice sack with rattan shoulder straps, looked disappointed not to have a bright nylon pack with many zippers like his friends. Old Bersosa had rigged up baggage of his own. Before we left the chapel, he eyed a five-gallon cracker tin we had filled with trash and intended to burn. He announced he wanted to appropriate the tin and carry it all the way to Palanan and back to his home in Casiguran. What about the trash inside? we had asked him. Did he want that also? He had assured us he would take care of that. The old man went out into the bushes and, to our ecological dismay, scattered foil packets and cheese wrappers until the can was empty. Some villagers who had been watching us laughed and offered to burn the trash themselves later. Bersosa had taken the shiny tin and fashioned it with sapling-bark straps. It bounced against his back with every step.

So now we walked: six Westerners in T-shirts and khaki walking pants, striding heavily under towering backpacks (from which swung various articles of wet clothing tied to dry in the air), our hiking boots leaving large, waffled prints in the dust beside the footprints of our diminutive guides, who were clad only in brightly patterned loincloths and who carried loads on their backs, bows and arrows in their hands.

We came to a deltaic river and forded its waist-deep water six times before reaching the far side. A jungle grew down the mountainside and spilled into the river. Passing into the trees, a very muddy path led up into the jungle. The breeze and sunshine quickly disappeared, and the air became thick and sour as we plodded now in zigzags up the incline, stumbling over vines, crawling on our bellies beneath the fallen trees too large to struggle over. When we fetched up at the base of a cliff sundered by a ravine that exposed the crumbling undercrust of the mountain, Bersosa indicated that our path was straight up into the scar.

There is something starkly inappropriate about most accounts of mountain climbing. The activity is invariably described as an assault, but as far as I can tell, the mountain always emerges unscathed, save for some dislodged rocks here and there, while the climber returns with bruised shins, torn knees, and lacerated fingers.

Climbing is such a solitary endeavor — the leap across open space, the thud as your horizontal flight is halted by solid rock and your fall is arrested by a lucky grab, the blind lateral movement from one toehold to the next, the straining upward for a dangling tree root. It demands so much of your conscious attention that your comrades' presence recedes; you are only aware of a disembodied hand reaching down to pull you up over an impossible stretch or latching on to you before you pitch sideways from a shifting pack load and topple over a cliff. As I ascended, the vegetation swayed in my blurry periphery. My attention focused on a succession of images — a mossy rock, a handful of leaves and tall grass, a scummy pool of water, the brown shadow of a snake. I heard only the muffled and disjointed sounds of pebbles cascading beneath me, the insect roar of the jungle, the diminishing murmur of my companions' voices. I halted on a ledge, unable to advance farther; my veins seemed ready to burst. Through a mist of sweaty self-pity I became aware that Paul was standing nearby, waiting for me.

"How are you doing?" he inquired. I grunted something about managing better on level ground. He then kindly relieved me of a fuel bottle, a coiled length of rope, and my spare canteen. When we resumed climbing it was easier — me with my load reduced to something like fifty pounds, and he with his, which must have now weighed seventy. It did not seem to slow him down; I said I'd reclaim the load when we reached sea level again.

We looked up just in time to see the rest of the party scramble over a ledge and disappear some seventy-five feet over our heads. We shouted at them to wait, not to leave us so far behind, but there was no answer. Cursing, we followed, periodically calling the high-pitched "hoo" the aborigines used to keep track of one another in the forest. Some minutes later, we made it to the top of the ravine. We saw the rest waiting for us among the trees about twenty-five yards up a steep, narrow path. I was in a scolding mood when we crossed that distance but something in their faces — anxiety, alarm, suppressed fear — made me keep silent.

"Bersosa says we shouldn't make any noise on this mountain," Erich told me in little more than a whisper. His face was ashen. "He says the people who live here are renegade Agta. If they find us on their land, he says they'll shoot us with bows and arrows."

So this was it: after months of nightmares and macabre daydreams with images of slashing knives and spears, I had arrived in this primeval jungle on a Philippine mountainside with my sense of impending doom intact, waiting for someone to tell me that somewhere out in the dense foliage, savage pygmies lusted for my interloper's blood. I thought of Michael Rockefeller, who disappeared in similar territory in New Guinea. I thought of a character in a short story by Paul Bowles: his fool of a well-meaning linguist is captured and cruelly tormented by North African nomads.

We had no firearms. It was at once an ethical and a tactical decision that we had all made during a planning meeting back in — of all places — my parents' suburban dining room. No guns. Theoretically they would only attract trouble in the provinces where bands of New People's Army guerrillas operated freely; people who needed guns desperately might not wait to hear of my anti-Marcos views and affiliations since it is much easier to appropriate weapons after ambushing those who carry them. A few of us were nervous about venturing into this land unarmed, though, and carried sportsmen's slingshots and pellets in fairly accessible backpack pockets. Then, in Casiguran, Erich had traded three packs of Camels at the marketplace for a murderous-looking bolo and Bill paid about twenty pesos for a similar one. Of course, all these lent was an empty, false sense of security. We were no match — nor did we want to be — against guerrillas with automatic weapons, with whom we at least stood a dialectic chance. But with renegade Agtas on this high, overgrown mount, the odds were slimmer that we could talk our way out of a scrape. As I stood, still out of breath from climbing, noticing that our guides were also peering warily into the bush, a brief snatch from Frederick Funston's favorite poet — Kipling, of course — floated through my mind: "And the epitaph drear: 'A Fool lies here who tried to hustle the East.' "

Weeks earlier, when I was still making the rounds in Manila, I had gone to the cathedral of the Dicalced Carmelite order on Doña Rodriguez Street in Quezon City. It was in a pleasant neighborhood of villas hiding behind high walls along a well-shaded avenue. That immense church was easily four or five stories high from pews to domed ceiling, with tall, arched doorways admitting light, air, and many birds; large banks of votive lights twinkled like cities on facing mountaintops. I was there looking for travel advice from two priests with years of experience on Luzon's northeastern coast.

Father Herman Esselman was a pale, white-haired, humorous man from Milwaukee who had spent most of his life in the Philippines. Indeed, he had been stationed in missions up and down the coast since 1942 and was now the order's national vocational director. His friend, Father Florentino Santiago, was of course later to be our host in Casiguran.

They gave me much information during our afternoon's conversation: etiquette among the villagers and among the aboriginal tribes, how to deal with the barangay police and tribal headmen, and even woods lore. Regarding the guides we planned to hire upon reaching Casiguran, Father Esselman became very specific.

"Hire three or four guides," he said, "but no more. Half the barrio would go along with you if they thought they'd get a free meal. Bring food for them. Buy rucksacks, because they'll never carry anything in their hands — their arms are too weak, but their backs can carry a hundred pounds. And always listen to what they say. If they tell you the area ahead is too dangerous, then go back, or get a boat and go around. Take their advice — especially if they say there is danger."

I asked Father Esselman what he meant by "dangerous."

"Well," he replied, "some people up there still have a headhunting ritual."

"What?" I hoped I sounded casual. "I thought there was no more of that on Luzon. I thought that the practice died out fifty or sixty years ago. That's what the guidebooks said."

"Guidebooks are for tourists," Father Esselman answered. "You're not going where the tourists go. But don't worry about headhunters. It's practiced among only a few scattered tribes now — Dumagats and Ilongotes — mostly up in the mountains between Dinapiqui and Palanan. In any case, it's done only for very special occasions." He smiled reassuringly.

"Like what?"

"Oh, marriage rites, funerals," he answered.

Marriages and funerals sounded pretty commonplace to me.

"The chief requires it," explained Father Santiago. "The head is a token of the seriousness of their rites. They catch single people unawares or surprise someone in their sleep."

"But don't worry," repeated Father Esselman. "It's usually confined to each other."

"But there *have* been cases," said Father Santiago.

"Cases?"

"Well, a few Tagalogs, a few whites . . . but only a few, not many."

I realized that while the two priests had been telling me this, their demeanor had been perfectly serious. But in their eyes was a distinctive Irish twinkle that they must teach in Carmelite seminaries. I hoped they were pulling my leg and not simply enjoying my discomfort. But after I had arrived on the coast with my companions to begin our long trek, I was told about renegade Agtas, or Ebukid, a derogatory name that meant "hillbillies." Supposedly residing in the very mountains we planned to cross, these tribal people were distrustful of outsiders who ventured into their territory. In the lowlands, mayors and policemen warned me about communists and everyone else talked about renegade Agtas. We heard a number of stories about raiding parties taking their victims away, never to be heard from again. We heard a story about a small plane that crash-landed high up on a remote mountain overlooking the ocean. The occupants — American or Belgian, depending on who told us the story, since it was repeated several times — had survived the crash, but by the time rescuers got to them, all that was left were butchered, headless corpses.

"It really depends on when you go, too," Father Esselman had told me back in Quezon City.

"When?" I said, but I knew what the answer would be.

"Oh, June . . . May . . . April," said Father Santiago.

The date on my calendar watch read April 12, a Monday, as our little party resumed climbing the path on that mountain north of Dinapiqui. I did not relish being last in line, for Father Esselman had told me that they liked to pick off stragglers. But that is where I happened to be, so I kept anxiously looking behind me.

After what seemed like hours in that oppressive forest I heard the faint dull roar of breakers ahead and to my right. A slightly salty breeze blew through the lianas and giant ferns. Abruptly, like brushing aside a curtain, we stepped through a final wall of foliage into the open sun. The menace melted away.

We found ourselves on a high, grassy plateau about three quarters of the way from the peak of the mountain we had just climbed, which despite its difficulty seemed to be the smallest in the rugged chain that stretched north and south along the coast. Below, at the foot of a five-hundred-foot bluff, was the Pacific — rather, the Philippine Sea — breakers flashing against a blueness of immense tropic intensity. Coral reefs ran parallel to the beach. Offshore rocks poked above the surface like monuments. It was an extraordinarily clear day; only a few light, cirrostratus clouds sculled lazily through the sky. Looking south, I could see all the way to the crags of Dijohan Point, at the northernmost part of San Ildefonse Peninsula near Casiguran, more than twenty miles away.

A set director could not have envisioned a better place for a break. By unanimous but unspoken consent, we shed our loads and collapsed on the grass. Sulimon and Udeng procured cigarettes from

Erich's bottomless supply. Bersosa extracted his mixture of betel nut and powdered lime from a battered little tin. He soon looked disarmingly euphoric. Unable to resist the spectacular view, Christopher pulled out one of his cameras and, on a whim, beckoned Sulimon over. With one view through a telephoto lens, the young man called excitedly to his friends. They were soon laughing and pointing and exclaiming — comparing far-off Taregteg Point with its magnified image, finding great hilarity in isolating through the lens an enlarged slice of nose, a smidgen of ear, a bit of magic.

Our descent to the beach was slow and cautious, following a dry, gravelly ravine. Sliding the final distance onto the shore, I saw that the beach was a chaos of strewn rocks and boulders — just as Frederick Funston's account had predicted. The sight of this massive field of geological debris left me awestruck.

The strand was narrow, ten or fifteen yards wide, under looming cliffs supporting only thin patches of scrub growth. At the mountains' foot, wispy and dwarfed screw pine and large-leafed rhododendron struggled to remain upright among the boulders, which tumbled thickly over a bed of fine gravel and varied in hue from grayish green to brownish orange. Our path lay straight up the beach, but there were no straight lines and no level ground. Rather than walking, we hopped from rock to boulder and boulder to rock, often having to clamber over obstacles bigger than pianos. Concentration was crucial; take your attention away from the spot intended for your next step to look at companions, mountains, or the glimmering ocean, and you found yourself on the ground and out of wind. My attention was focused so exclusively on the broken surface that the ocean's roaring movement in my periphery made the boulders seem to ebb and flow. At one point I heard a grunt behind me and stopped to see Dario lose his balance and fall — opening up a four-inch gash in his shin that immediately drew flies. We were too tired to talk, and after Dario had dressed his wound with antiseptic cream we hurried to catch up with the others. I thought about the words of the Spanish aide on that expedition exactly eighty-one years before.

"This would have been a beautiful and picturesque journey for a party of pleasure-seekers, well-provided for with all the delicacies and luxuries," Segovia had recalled of this coastline, "but for us, tramping barefoot and starved, it was certainly not a pleasure trip." Well, here were six American adventurers who had taken care to outfit themselves with all the necessities: freeze-dried food and leakproof plastic water jugs, lightweight aluminum cooking kits, camping stoves, fuel, fancy lanterns, nylon tents, fiberfill sleeping bags, closed-cell sleeping mats, Manila rum, ponchos, extra clothing, extra shoes, Swiss

Army knives, ropes, climbing wedges and carabiners, jungle-formula bug repellent, and enough medical equipment to keep a rural clinic going for a month — all zippered into brand-new expedition backpacks that had been scientifically designed to place most of the weight on your hips, where it could be borne easier, but in this cruel terrain they bounced and swung and cut into our shoulders. Constantly off balance, we simply careened from one hard, sloping surface to another like heated molecules. We may have been much better equipped than that column of ragged conspirators in March 1901 and in better physical condition, but after two hours we were reduced to a similarly uncomfortable state, with blistered heels, pinched toes, cramped backs, and glazed eyes.

Our guides were another matter. Bersosa, though barefoot like all the Agtas, kept way in front; he was old and spindly, all white whiskers and gristle, and full of betel juice that kept him going fast in a narcotized, loping gait over sharp rocks that were already wearing down our own Vibram soles. He gave us nary a glance (except to complain during a break that "you are too slow!"), but the young Agtas kept up with him and threw back an occasional nod of encouragement at us.

Then we halted. Benchan turned and signaled for us to squat low among the rocks while Bersosa began walking ahead, carrying the prized cracker tin but exhibiting his bow and arrows in plain sight across his shoulders. As the old man crossed a widening beach that was strewn with rocks as large as watermelons, Sulimon crabwalked over to us and silently pointed up the beach. There were men up there, he seemed to be signifying.

"Agta?" asked Erich. "Tagalog?"

Sulimon shrugged. He pointed at Christopher's orange camera bag, then to his own eyes, then down the beach.

"Let him look through your telephoto," urged Erich.

Camera in hand, he crouched as if he were Richard Avedon and studied the tiny figures that had just come into view far away. "Tagalog," pronounced Sulimon, adding something else that was unintelligible to us but made Benchan and Udeng relax. So we relaxed. Bersosa finally drew close to the strangers; he turned and waved us to follow. When I finally reached him he hissed out an order: "Do not stop!" We trudged by two Tagalogs wearing tattered clothes and straw hats and carrying bolos. They did not return our smiles, nor did we say anything. I felt far from civilization, far from home.

About an hour before sundown, we saw moving toward us from the northeast heavy clouds boiling above a wall of rain. The sky and the ocean were darkening as Bersosa told us that this place had the last source of water "for very long time," so we made preparations to camp near a trickle of water that fell down from the cliffs.

"Where are we going to pitch the damned tents?" Christopher asked no one in particular. Because there was no level ground — just big rocks — we would have to forgo shelter that night. Removing our bedrolls and ponchos, we covered our backpacks with tarpaulins and weighted them down with rocks. Soon a fire was blazing high. Sulimon walked out among the tidal pools (with Erich trailing behind) and returned with an octopus writhing on his spear. He threw it directly onto the fire, and when the octopus started to crawl out, he held it down. It thrashed and twisted and survived the flames longer than I thought possible. But, then, I'd never seen anything burn to death before. Benchan and Udeng returned from foraging with a potful of snails. To these they added seawater that they had brought to a boil. Earlier, as we were clambering among the rocks, I had spied a place where hundreds of empty snail shells lay in a rock cleft; confident that sooner or later its meaning would be revealed, I filed the observation away in my mind until I found myself sitting next to the fire with my nine companions, tapping boiled snail shells on the rocks until their contents were dislodged, then picking off the entrails before eating the muscular "foot." I added my empty shell to the growing pile.

"What do Agta call these?" I asked the old man, holding up a snail.

"Escargots," he answered. I could only stare at him, baffled at how he had picked up the term.

After it had gotten dark and a mist began to fall, we realized why Bersosa had not moved from his place beneath an overhanging rock; having claimed his shelter he stayed put — and dry. The young guides crawled inside with him. The mist became a drizzle, the drizzle became a steady rain, and there was nothing to do but sleep. Dario clambered up onto a flat boulder, covered himself with his poncho, and went to sleep, his legs dangling over the edge of the rock. Bill and Erich grumbled for some minutes, then disappeared beneath a plastic tarpaulin. I got into my poncho and wedged myself among the rocks. Christopher lay nearby, softly cursing. Rain seeped through our water-resistant (not waterproof) ponchos until we were only slightly drier than the rocks on which we slept. Water dribbled into my ear or down my cheek; I shifted periodically but found no comfortable position. I would drift asleep, hear a noise, wake up, look outside: gray sky, gray water and surf, recumbent figures looking in their ponchos like half-filled trash bags discarded among the rocks.

II

Bersosa had been the first to fall asleep in his dry rock cleft and, predictably, he was the first to awake. He let out a yell, summoning us from beneath our wet ponchos. The day had broken in a sky that was overcast but free of rain. The old man was in a foul mood; he curtly took a few handfuls of the granola and dried fruit we passed around, then got up without a word, picked up his cracker tin and weapons, and left without looking to see if we followed. The boys trailed dutifully behind him. Getting the rest going proved difficult. Dario and Bill aimlessly and groggily walked around the camp, and by the time Christopher and I got the group pointed in the right direction, a great distance separated us from our guides. They were no more than specks hopping and bobbing on the surface of this sea of rocks, and we struggled to shorten the gap, always mindful of the threat of renegade Agtas, suspicious rebels, or even bandits. Meanwhile, our hired "diplomat," our seventy-year-old insurance policy against mishap, outwalked us.

The repetition of boulders quickly grew wearying. I noted with alarm that Dario, who had been too tired to eat dinner and uninterested in our breakfast of squirrel food, was less sure of his balance that morning than he had been the afternoon before. He picked his way from rock to rock with what seemed to be exaggerated care, stopping often to rest. I stayed close to keep him company. This seemed to irritate him, so each time he stopped to sit down on a rock, I stood a distance removed and leaned on my staff, staring out over the ocean. At our snail's pace, the distance between us and our comrades lengthened to nearly a mile.

The sea had cast up a profusion of objects that collected between the boulders on the gravelly sand. Hopping along, I occasionally saw strewn about various battered artifacts of our faraway civilization: a sandal without a strap, a washbasket without a bottom, a deflated rubber ball, a shapeless and unrecognizable mass of plastic. Happily, these were greatly outnumbered by small, brightly colored seashells that gleamed among the pebbles, begging to be collected. From then on, for each moment of weakness or despair, I would pause, sink heavily to one knee under the weight of my pack, and pick out the most attractive shell I could find to present to my wife back home.

At midmorning Dario and I rejoined our friends, who had finally stopped to rest. No one talked very much; our uncomfortable night had shortened our patience with the terrain and with each other.

During this break, Benchan came back to us from where Bersosa had stopped, about five hundred yards ahead. The young man looked concerned, and his urgent sign language told us it was not a good time to be so separated from our guides. We followed him ahead.

We found the old man dwarfed by house-sized rocks and talking to three young Tagalogs who said they were walking with their dog and some supplies to Dinapiqui. Bersosa told us he wanted to cook rice here. I nodded and wordlessly walked a few feet to sit down and wait. But it seemed that not everyone was so acquiescent.

"We haven't walked far enough," my brother said, and Bill chimed in to agree. "If we stop to cook rice we'll lose the whole day. We'll get caught in the afternoon rainstorm."

"I cannot go farther without rice," whined Bersosa. "I am very hungry. I must have rice!"

Christopher answered by taking off his pack and extracting a bag of granola, which he placed on the rock next to the old man. Bersosa looked at it with disgust. He pushed it away toward the Tagalogs, who readily began eating the contents.

"Look at that!" Bill said. "He gave away our food!"

"Let him cook his rice," I said.

"The boys like granola," my brother answered. "If he's so particular, let him wait another couple of hours."

"Bersosa," said Erich, crouching next to the guide, "you should have eaten more breakfast." He reclaimed the bag. "This is good food!"

"Not good. I must have rice."

Erich stood, shrugged, and shifted his gaze from me to Christopher. "Maybe he should cook his rice."

Feeling increasingly detached from what seemed to be a pointless and stupid argument, I moved farther away until I was out of earshot. "Let me know how it turns out," I called, and I turned my attention to the sea.

A few minutes later my friends were standing beside me. Somehow they had compromised; the guides would stay behind and cook their meal while we would forge ahead. We would wait for them at a prominent spur of beach several miles north.

"You know," I said to Christopher and Bill after we had begun walking, "we're never going to get anywhere if we insist that the guides keep to our schedule, our convenience. This is *their* territory. And it's a mistake to expect them to eat our food."

"What's wrong with our food?"

"Nothing's wrong with it — for us. But Bersosa's been eating rice his whole life. You can't expect him to switch overnight to peanut butter and crackers, or granola. Rice is what he likes best."

"Rice takes too much time," Christopher replied stonily. "I don't like losing so much time in the middle of the day. We've got to stick to a schedule, and they should too."

"After all," said Bill, "we're paying them."

"*I'm* paying them," I answered, "and what are you going to use, then, diplomacy or the whip? And they can walk the pants off us no matter what they do. We're depending on them."

"I don't think we should sit around all day, that's all."

"Okay, Chris," Erich said, interjecting himself into what was narrowing into a sibling dispute. "*You* can guide us to Palanan."

Shaking his head in exasperation, Christopher ended the conversation by walking away. Bill wandered off. Erich shrugged and strode ahead to catch up with Paul, leaving Dario and me to bring up the rear again.

The brown cliffs to our left opened up to reveal a river valley shaped like an amphitheater, which allowed us a greater view of the interior of the Sierra than we had yet seen; there were no settlements here, no smoke, no sign of human habitation — only a lush jade forest rising steadily to a ridgeline perhaps two thousand feet high, where individual trees stood in contrast against the empty sky. High up in the mountains, a bare and open patch disclosed a path, perhaps of a recent landslide. A stream, greatly reduced by the encroaching dry season, flowed through this jungle; we leaped across it on glittering stones.

The illusion of coolness caused by the profuse greenery and space in that small valley evaporated once the mountain walls rose again. The sun was nearly overhead, baking the grapefruit-sized rocks we stumbled across, sending waves of heat up into tightening boots. The tide advanced and thundered against this mass of rocks, shifting and dislodging some of them so they realigned in the hissing foam and clattered like bones. I strode parallel to the breakers, my metal-tipped staff biting into gravel or sand or skittering loudly over stone, and my heavy boots knocked rocks loose at every step. In the heat, in my own silence, I fastened on these repetitious sounds — the cannonade of surf on a hard beach, the incessant rattle and stony clatter, out of the rocks a *clack, clack* that reminded me of the wooden beads' flogging the penitents' backs in Casiguran. As I grew more dazed and dehydrated, I lost touch with the beach and began to slow down. Even Dario passed me and disappeared ahead with the others, leaving me alone with my fatigue.

Struggling to the top of one large boulder, I saw that my friends were waiting for me at the foot of a lovely little waterfall, which fell fifty feet like a rainspout from the top of a crag. At its foot, a small basin spilled over and emptied among the rocks. My spirits soared! A cold dunking and an unrationed drink! When I got within fifty yards of this alluring scene, however, I was astounded to see my friends shouldering their packs and leaving; they had waited until I was in sight but, mean-spiritedly, not long enough for me to refresh myself as they had. What sort of fellowship was this? I stopped to fill my canteen and wet my head — the cliff was sweaty where water seeped from porous brown rock — but my enjoyment was tempered by bitterness, and when I hastened to catch up with them, my teeth ground in dull anger.

Forty minutes later, where strand poked into ocean in a distinctive spur and where eight elephantine boulders stood and absorbed crashing waves — every third surge sending up a plume of water and light — I found my friends eating a lunch of peanut butter and jelly on crackers. There was no waterfall, no fresh water, and no shade from that relentless sun. As I came up, my brother nodded and told me we had reached our place of rendezvous, pointing to a spot on his map. Bill handed me some crackers and a tube of jelly, which I took with a snarl. I walked five yards farther to sit apart.

To my amazement, sly Seanbuyan suddenly materialized before me — Seanbuyan, whom we had not seen since he waved good-bye from the deck of the *Marivie* below Dinapiqui. He had been moving south, following a deep notch among the boulders before emerging silently nearly at my feet. He had somehow passed us in the last few days. Carrying his bow and four arrows, he was shirtless and wore only his knife, loincloth, a necklace of red and white beads, and armbands that looked like pink garters. He nodded to me and looked curiously around — where were his companions? I pointed south and motioned to show that they were eating. He smiled and hurried off to find them, moving very quickly across the broken field, his bow and arrows held out for balance.

Sometime later the five Agtas appeared. They looked very displeased — including Seanbuyan, who had evidently been told of the bad manners of these white men. Bersosa brusquely signaled us to come on, let's get a move on, no time for lollygagging now. The boys sullenly did not meet our eyes — a bad sign.

I saw no profit in walking with my friends. So, fueled by residual anger, I struck out ahead and took pleasure at keeping up with the old man for more than an hour — across boulders, then a long, crescent-shaped beach of small pebbles, then up into more rocks. As my fellow Americans fell farther behind us, finally disappearing, I found myself musing on the cultural difficulties that were constantly emerging in our dealings with the Agtas, resulting in the erosion of simple trust and respect. Certainly this was nothing new in the history of the world, but nonetheless it was disturbing. Obviously stress was working on us all: the tropical heat, the harsh and unfamiliar terrain, the sudden exposure to a completely alien culture. The Agtas were at least as headstrong as my comrades. I hoped we could reach our destination before there was an explosion.

Large blocks of extrusive volcanic rock anchored the northern point of one concave stretch of beach. To cross them, I hauled myself up on sharp black rock as though I were climbing onto a stage apron from the orchestra pit. Several dozen yards along, I encountered a Tagalog man. In his fifties, he wore ragged shorts and his smile revealed many missing teeth.

"Hello," I said. "You surprised me."

"Where are you going, my friend?"

"To Palanan," I answered. "We took a boat from Baler to Dinalungan and walked most of the way from there to here."

"Oh, my friend, that is too long a distance," he said. "Are you with them?" — he gestured toward our guides, who had gone ahead — "those minorities?"

"Yes," I said, "and my five friends come behind me."

"Six Americans? Yes? I do not see any Americans here before." He shaded his eyes with one scarred hand and looked south for them, but they were yet too far away to be seen.

His name was Tomas: "You know — Doubting Tomas. That is me!" He offered me a hand-rolled cigarette, but I said I did not smoke. He told me he had moved his family to this deserted coastland seven or eight years earlier, and he had built a little nipa hut in a beachside grove. "The land is free," he said. "I raise everything I need right here. Nobody bothers me." He showed his picket fence teeth. "Nobody, that is, but the damn typhoons." Late summer storms often forced him to withdraw into the forest for safety. They had knocked down his house and crops one year out of every three. "But it's okay here," he said, showing me his hand and beginning to count off fingers. "No politicians! No guerrillas! No bandits! No priests! No loggers!" He ran out of fingers and laughed. "And . . . no Americans!"

On the far side of that tabled volcanic headland was Tomas's domain: a gracefully curving beach perhaps 2 miles long. It began as small pebbles but quickly became fine black sand. Molave trees, shrubs, and other littoral vegetation fringed a wide beach, and here the first bulwark of the Sierra Madre was a line of rounded hills only a few hundred feet above sea level. The Agtas had stopped to rest in a beachside grove of trees and looked pleased to see me.

"Your friends too slow," Bersosa informed me, which I suppose might have been a backhanded compliment at my managing to keep up with them until I met Tomas. I was fairly pleased myself, as a matter of fact. Sulimon and I had walked together for a time, he silently pointing at things that interested him — a crab in a tidal pool that might be good to eat, a shell that he indicated could be strung on a necklace, a splash and the shape of a leaping fish beyond the place where waves broke over coral reefs. Now, at this resting place, the old man sent Benchan and Udeng up a mountainside path to fetch drinking water, and they motioned for me to follow. After puffing over the top of one hill's flank, we passed through a grove and found a clear, delightful stream that burbled noisily down its rocky channel and cascaded off two miniature falls into a pool with a white sandy bottom. While the boys filled their jug, I flopped down on a flat rock and dunked my head underwater.

As we came back down onto the beach, the first of my friends was trudging up. Minutes later we were all together again and, my anger gone, I told them where to find water. When they had gone, Benchan and Udeng performed some little gymnastic tricks on the sand — turning cartwheels over each other, tumbling into a laughing heap. I sat down near Bersosa and Seanbuyan, who were relaxing as adults did with betel nuts. I reveled in this resurrecting afternoon, not knowing that a storm was brewing to the northeast — and also in our hearts.

Just north of us, the coast again was weighted under a sea of boulders — some of them as large as boxcars, but leaning this way and that as if they had been derailed. Something in the air changed, a drop in pressure, and eleven heads turned to see what was happening. Ten miles to the northeast, the familiar white curtain of a rainstorm closed rapidly across the sea in our direction.

The Agtas leaped to their feet, motioned for us to hurry, and began carrying their loads into the massed rocks. They failed to heed shouts to wait for us until we put on our shoes and socks. Once that was accomplished, we milled around — leadership forgotten, confusion reigning.

"I'm not moving in that rain across *rocks,*" Dario vowed. "It's too slippery. I'll break a leg, and then we'd really be in trouble."

"But if we move slowly . . ." said Paul.

"Nothing doing."

"I think we'd better follow the guides," said Erich, "or they'll leave us behind."

"Erich's right," I said. Large drops began falling.

"They won't go far," said Bill. "They'll crawl under a rock and wait."

"I don't know about that," said Paul. By then we had each thrown our dark blue ponchos over our heads. They whipped in the wind.

The storm struck. We gave up the discussion and any thought of progress and sat, looking like six nuns, on a fallen tree. Through the deluge we saw Sulimon crawling over a mammoth boulder to look for us. He shouted for us to come. But when we only motioned for him to come closer, he disappeared among the dark rocks. Half an hour later Udeng appeared in the rain and yelled at us, but he would not come closer either. I was sure they were all only a few dozen yards away, crouching under an overhang, waiting like us for the fierce rain to subside. I went over to sit against my pack at the base of a tree. Retracting my head from my hood, I drew my knees up to my chin in the dark, humid confines beneath my poncho and fell into a trance.

Sometime later — I don't know how long — the storm passed. In a diminishing drizzle, Erich and Paul entered the rocks to find our guides. When they returned they were worried. Their alarm flashed to us immediately.

"I got about a mile, guys," Erich told us, "and couldn't find them. But their footprints lead off down the beach, so I suggest we follow them immediately."

I flung a curse at the Agtas' backs — they carried our tents and food — and told Paul and Erich to come quickly with me; the rest were to follow at their own pace. The three of us took off across the tumbling beach, our backpacks bouncing and ponchos flapping furiously behind us like dark wraiths.

The cliff-walled coast undulated in a series of beaches shaped like fingernail parings, each separated from the next by a rising prominence of volcanic rock. We drew so far ahead of our friends that in the waning afternoon light we would stop and squint southward until we saw their antlike movement among the distant boulders, then we would continue. There was no sign of anyone ahead, though from time to time we saw our guides' footprints in the wet sand between the gray stone watermelons we fairly ran across. Paul got worried, finally, at the growing distance between us and our comrades, and he elected to wait for them to catch up. We left him behind.

As Erich and I hopped, we threw possibilities at each other. Might they climb the high cliffs so we would lose their trail? Perhaps they were angry enough to hide among the boulders and ambush us? Or maybe they would jettison our modern equipment along the way since they could hardly sell it for fear of alerting the authorities.

We came to a wide river that descended through a notch in the mountains on its way to the sea. Its surface was broken by strewn boulders too far apart from one another to form a bridge, so we waded through the water barefoot. By now the sun had rolled beyond the Sierra and total darkness was not far off. Still, there was no sight of our guides. Soon, I looked north and saw a mile ahead to where the high tide was lapping at the talus from a colossal landslide, making safe passage to the far side of the rockpile impossible. Clearly it was time to make camp.

As the others trailed in, we divided naturally into teams to get ready for the night, which was soon upon us. We did our tasks more smoothly than we had since arriving on the coast; at last we were working in concert under stress! In the hope that the guides had not intentionally abandoned us, we piled up wood for a bonfire that sent a pillar of flames some ten or twelve feet up into the night.

We crouched around the fire and drew reassurance from its light. My brother was the first to speak.

"I think there's a *forty percent chance* that they'll wait for us," said Christopher.

Everyone nodded at this authority, staring into the flames. Then I realized the craziness of this pronouncement, but before I could form a retort, something flickered in the corner of my vision. I jumped up, ran down to the water's edge, and strained to spot the faraway torch I thought I had just seen a mile or two to the north. When Erich and Paul heard what I had seen, they immediately set off with flashlights to investigate, saying they planned to cross the ocean-lapped talus slope in the dark. I was able to stop them only by warning that if I had seen anything, it might not be our guides.

Back around the campfire, Erich suggested that if they were gone for good, we should strike out over the mountains toward the Cagayan Valley — an insane idea that he quickly withdrew.

If we were only temporarily separated from them, we would find them in the morning by striking camp before daybreak. If the guides had left us, our best chance seemed to lie in pressing ahead. Even with our maps it was hard to say where we were, but Christopher thought we might be halfway to Palanan, which would mean about three days' walk. So long as we did not lack water and avoided the midday heat, we stood a good chance of making it. We had already taken inventory of our food: ten pounds of rice but no cooking pot; a quart of powdered milk; six little packets of nuts and fruit.

"We can cook the rice in our drinking cups," said Bill. "It'll take a long time, but it'll work out okay."

"If we struck a settlement we could buy a pot," offered Paul. But everyone knew the chances of finding even a tribal encampment were slim.

"And don't forget the IVs," said Dario.

We looked at him blankly.

"The IVs — in my medical kit," he said. "*Intra-venous.* That's food, too. If it comes right down to it, we can rig up the fluid pouches and stick a needle in and get by with that."

I shuddered at the idea of being reduced to that kind of desperation — still, I was glad Dario had elected to pack that extra weight of fluid pouches in case one of us was seriously hurt. When we finally turned in to sleep among the rocks — as we had the night before — I dreamed of stark white operating rooms, each decorated with dozens of potted palms.

10

CASIGURAN AND THE CONTRACOSTA, 1901

All of the inhabitants of Casiguran turned out to bid farewell to Funston's counterfeit patriots when, at six o'clock on the morning of March 17, 1901, the soldiers drew into formation in the town square under a gloomy and rainy sky. The five American captives were brought downstairs from their confinement in the mayor's house. Out in the fresh air for the first time in days, they took their place in the center of the column. Lazaro Segovia waited at the front, along with the twelve men from Casiguran who would come along. Each villager bore a small bale of supplies. Because of the fearful nature of the trail these men were very lightly laden; the bulk of the meat was packed in the Macabebes' gear. The column was to be guided the entire distance by an Ilongote tribesman.

"The *vice-presidente* and a number of the principal men of the town accompanied us for a couple of miles," Funston would write, "finally saying *adios* and *buen viaje* to all, including the 'prisoners.' I wonder what this simple and really good-hearted fellow thought when he found how he had been tricked. Of the numerous ones that we made fools of, he was the only one that I ever had the slightest qualms about. I hope he is gifted with a sense of humor."

The soldiers passed through muddy rice fields until they reached an immense, ancient forest, and from this point on they were forced into single file by the narrowness of the path. They walked in a generally northeasterly direction, pausing at the bed of one small creek to answer the queries of several curious Negrito hunters out with their dogs. For four and a half hours they tramped under a dark canopy of hardwood trees that towered some two hundred feet over their heads, their trail a furrow through a tangle of climbing rattan and bamboo, palms, and giant ferns, until finally they left the dimness for the salty, drizzly air of the Pacific beach.

Apparently the Ilongote guide wearied of his job at this point, for he slipped off into the forest and was seen no more. One of the Casiguran men said that he felt he could show them the way to Palanan.

Since the bearers were commingling with the other marchers, Funston noted, great care had to be exercised. "The presence of these men made it necessary for us to keep up the deception on the march and in camp," he wrote, "as the slightest word might send one of them scurrying ahead to Palanan." The Macabebes were forced to speak, of course, solely in the Tagalog dialect instead of their own.

Two miles farther up the coast, the column halted at a creek emptying into the sea. Segovia noticed soon after the cooking fires were lit that the Macabebes were broiling large pieces of meat; they showed no regard for the long journey that lay ahead and the serious need to use the scarce supplies with economy. He reproached them severely, warning that "should they eat it all in a day or two, we would die of hunger on the road, or turn cannibals." Only some of the scouts heeded his words.

After the meal, they set off on their afternoon march. This took them for some distance up a sandy beach that allowed them a lively gait. Then it became necessary to detour through a grove of trees to circle a rough-looking rocky area blocking their path. Regaining the beach sometime thereafter, they continued for the rest of the afternoon without incident.

It was during the evening meal that Lazaro Segovia began to see how serious their food problem would be. While some scouts had gone out with bolos to cut poles and brushes to shelter the men from the rain that was by then falling continuously, others had prepared cooking fires for dinner, and they jostled each other for large portions when it was ready. As before, most of the soldiers ate without regard for the morrow. Before he shut his eyes for the night, the Spaniard ordered all the provisions piled around him to safeguard against theft. Upon arising at six in the morning, he made an inventory of what was left. He discovered to his disgust that the Macabebes had already squandered more than half the entire meat supply. In addition, three of the chickens had mysteriously disappeared during the night. Of the two carabao yearlings they had bought in Casiguran, not more than seven pounds of salted meat remained. A third of their store of rice was also gone. All of this in one day.

"If this keeps on," Segovia exclaimed angrily, "the third day will find us without beef and rice."

The Spaniard made sure none of the Casiguran guides were near. He sidled over to Frederick Funston — reduced to passivity by his prisoner's guise, squatting on the beach with his fellow captives — and told him of their troubles. The dismayed general told Segovia to redistribute all the food among their village guides with strict orders to allow no one anything but what the Spaniard would issue himself. "I was greatly troubled in mind," Segovia confessed later. He followed Funston's whispered orders to the letter, making a great show of taking the food away from his scouts. But the damage had been done.

The men formed into their usual ranks and started the morning's march without breaking their fast. The day was relatively clear and very hot. They marched through burning, ankle-deep sand, which made walking agony for the scouts; their unshod feet throbbed and soon blistered.

All during the morning Segovia pondered what he could do to keep the men from dying of hunger during the march. Their path was taking them through a veritable desert and there were no further settlements on which to rely. The mountain range towered over their heads, its forested flanks appearing to shelter no game. So far as the vast ocean was concerned, he would learn that they could not hope to rely on it either.

"There was only one remedy," Segovia decided, "to reduce everybody's ration to one-fourth of the ordinary ration." Thus, at each of their two daily meals, four soldiers would share a portion barely satisfactory under normal occasions for one man. By increasing their pace and taking advantage of the light in the late afternoon and early evening, he hoped to reduce the overall suffering by cutting time off the march. But he worried about the stamina of his fellow soldiers: their path was difficult, and they would steadily weaken from lack of nourishment. "I was also afraid that sickness might break out among us," he noted, "and ruin completely our plans." Under the circumstances, it seemed only a matter of time before that happened.

"Still," Segovia recalled, "I trusted in the iron will of our soldiers, who like true Orientals would resign themselves to their kismet, and undergo unflinchingly hunger and sufferings." Segovia hoped that poor fat Hilario Talplacido would undergo the trial as well — although, the Spaniard observed, he normally required a carabao daily. As for the Americans, their will would have to see them through. Frederick Funston appeared to Segovia to have a delicate constitution, though not so weak as that of Burton Mitchell, who was so far able to eat only the small portions of chicken that fell to his share. The two Kansans would survive only through will power, the Spaniard decided. Looking at Newton and the Hazzard brothers, he could see that they were used to prolonged hardship, though "even they were pale and emaciated owing to the short rations, entirely inadequate to the craving of healthy stomachs and good appetites."

The column paused at midday, and Segovia addressed the assembled marchers, telling them the bad news that henceforth they would be issued quarter rations. There was no grumbling; by this time everyone had seen the nature of the countryside and they seemed to believe the Spaniard: to have patience for five days until their hardship would end in Palanan, where food was abundant.

Their noon meal on that bare beach consisted of rice, the last four chickens, and a broth made of beef extract. After the men had eaten, Segovia noticed that one of their bearers had deserted. "He had undoubtedly taken to the woods and went homeward, preferring the flesh pots of Casiguran to the hunger and hardships of our expedition," the Spaniard observed. "As the rations just issued had been his load, we were not very sorry to miss him, as it was one mouth less to feed."

The sandy beach ended soon after they resumed hiking. They came up against a sheer mountain face that squarely blocked their path where it advanced into the ocean. They began climbing; as Funston noted, "The footpath was fearfully steep, in some places more than forty-five degrees. In such places we were compelled to use not only feet, but hands also. But for the roots and branches of trees, which gave us something to hold to, I do not see how we could have surmounted some of the difficulties." Climbing nearby, Harry Newton would recall that "nothing but mountain goats or Filipinos could follow . . . the slightest misstep would result in instant death." It was necessary to maintain a quick pace, even with the trial of a difficult ascent, so they could sleep on the far side of the mountain and take advantage of the low tide. Otherwise they would be forced to wait out the high tide until noon.

As they reached the peak and began an equally perilous descent, the sky was lowering. Large drops of rain began falling with increasing frequency. Before they reached sea level again they forded a stream of fast, waist-deep water. Once on the beach, the Macabebes and guides erected the crude huts that had sheltered them the previous night.

The scouts spread out and attempted to catch small fish with their hands. A few succeeded while others scraped limpets from rocks or gathered snails. One Macabebe returned to the communal stewpot with a small devilfish; despite its forbidding appearance, it was added to the meal by the ravenous soldiers. "I cannot recommend devilfish to the fastidious," Funston said later, but on the beach he made no objections.

Rain poured on and through their palm leaf roofs throughout the night, and the men got an early start the next morning. Their path for that entire day, their third since leaving Casiguran, lay through virgin forests, as the seacoast had risen to unclimbable cliffs. For nearly five miles they walked along the bank of a stream, and here Hilario Talplacido grew so weak he could no longer walk. Since his presence was crucial upon their arrival in Palanan, he was afforded special treatment: he was hoisted and carried by a constant relay of two men. "It was hard and disagreeable marching," Segovia would write, "over the sharp pebbles strewn along our course." It was especially so for the Spaniard, for the walking had already destroyed one pair of canvas shoes, and the knife-edged stones forced him to throw away a ruined second pair in disgust. Now he was walking barefoot — so he could pay his respects to Don Emilio while being properly outfitted with his third and last pair. Such dignity would certainly be required for such a historic moment — though Segovia would regret not having brought sturdier footgear.

The midday camp came and went while they were still in the depths of the forest. The quarter rations were swallowed and immediately forgotten in the overweening gnawing of their empty stomachs. When they returned to plodding down the trail they were light-headed, dull in mind as well as shaky in constitution, and discipline and individual will crumbled. Two hours into the afternoon's march, the men in the rear of the column fell so far behind that they shouted pitifully to those ahead to wait. Funston, at the head of the line, glumly sat with the others for an hour until the last stragglers stumbled up.

During this time, Oliver Hazzard lay down on the ground near a thick bush and absent-mindedly tugged at a branch. Suddenly, out swarmed an angry horde of bees. "A general stampede took place," Segovia remembered. "We all ran into the woods, the Macabebes fired their guns, pandemonium reigned supreme for a few seconds [and] the bees were the victors." Once the air had cleared of gunsmoke and furious insects and the men had regrouped, one of the carriers from Casiguran suggested a splendid means of revenge: where there were bees there must certainly be honey, he said, so let us smoke them out. The Macabebes instantly set about this operation, and soon the smoke curling up to envelope the bush drove away the bees. But when the hungry adventurers crowded forward to collect their reward, they found no honey, only wax. Nonetheless, they ate it all.

The soldiers walked all afternoon through the forest, not reaching the beach until six in the evening. A short time later the advance men came upon fresh water and Segovia called a halt for the night. Many of the scouts were too fatigued to eat, though they had consumed next to nothing in two days.

After everyone was asleep, Segovia conferred with Funston and his staff. He was worried about the declining strength of his men. The general assured him that he was right to enforce a quick pace. Slow starvation was the inevitable outcome of any other plan. They also talked of Hilario Talplacido, enfeebled so that he was unable to walk, and they speculated whether he would survive the two or more days remaining of their journey. Success at the close of their trek might depend on the presence of that prone and groaning bulk of a man.

As the sun was low over the Pacific on the following day, March 20, 1901, the expedition was already under way on its fourth day's march. The guides predicted that the path would become increasingly difficult and that this would be the worst day. The men could only shrug listlessly.

For two hours they plodded across the soft sand, then ascended a small mountain that reared out of the beach. As they came down the far side, the men could readily see what they were facing. The coastline below stretched northward, and as far as they could see it was heavily littered by a sea of boulders that, noted Funston, "varied in size from that of a watermelon to a freight car. This was the hardest marching of all."

Forced to clamber over and around the fields of geological debris, Segovia would observe that "this would have been a beautiful and picturesque journey for a party of pleasure-seekers . . . but for us, tramping barefoot and starved, it was certainly not a pleasure trip." Indeed it was not. Great care was necessary with every step to avoid twisting an ankle or breaking a neck "in that chaos" — the Spaniard's words — "resembling more than anything else an ocean of rocks."

The column came upon a small rivulet that wound down along a declivity between two bare, brushless hills until it emptied into the sea. They paused to cook their first meal of the day — sweet potatoes and cracked corn mixed with a little rice. Because of the inordinate amount of rain, it had become, to General Funston's disgust, "a soggy and fermenting mess." During the meal, Segovia could be seen massaging his foot. It had begun to pain him during the morning, but since their path was hard and rocky, the Spaniard thought a night's rest might improve what he assumed was a simple case of sore feet.

A brief but furious tropical shower fell on the marchers in midafternoon, and as it struck while they were scattered about the rock field with no shelter available, they finished the day's slow progress completely soaked across slippery rocks. At five o'clock the men built two bonfires beside a creek. At least firewood was plentiful; many logs had been washed down from the heights and left strewn along the banks when the rainy season had ended and the water receded.

The meal that night was again "a revolting mess," recalled the general, consisting of the moldy rice and another stew of snails, limpets, and tiny fish. Poor Burton Mitchell, with his delicate stomach and aversion to any food save meat and potatoes, was suffering badly, but, as Funston noted, that night he was as ravenously hungry as always. He "drew a fish about three inches long," recalled the general, "and had downed it before he realized it had not been dressed. Then and there his gorge rose and he became violently 'sea-sick.' "

The night did not pass easily, for the march had been hard and everyone was in pain. "I was tortured day and night with muscular rheumatism," complained Funston, for though he had lived a strenuous life his age was catching up with him, especially with such rigorous exercise in the damp. Meanwhile, to Segovia's horror, he saw that his foot was swelling — developing an abscess, which was a serious matter in the tropics, where infections run their course with deadly speed.

The entire next day they struggled across the enormous rocky field. Segovia, though limping badly, was among the first men to reach the end of the desert, at five o'clock. He breathed an earnest prayer of thanks. It was another hour before the rest of the marchers reached him. The men were now declining rapidly. Many scouts again refused food and collapsed on the ground without bothering to dry their clothing. Talplacido had been borne to their camping place by two men, and he thereupon swore he would rather die than go ahead. The Americans were looking no better. Once Funston stopped walking, he felt nearly paralyzed by rheumatic pains. The Hazzard brothers and Newton were steadily losing weight, but clearly Mitchell was in bad trouble. He looked more like a victim of the Spanish Crown's *reconcentrado* camps than an American soldier raised on Texas beef and Kansas corn. He was weak, emaciated; his sunken eyes stared listlessly out from their sockets, and his clothes hung pitiably from his shoulders.

While the bearers and a few stronger scouts prepared their camp for the night, one of the men from Casiguran came in trailing two

Negrito hunters whom he had encountered while cutting down poles for shelter. Lazaro Segovia asked if they possessed any venison. They told him all they had was a small amount of wild boar, then disappeared for a short while, returning from their own camp bringing bones to which clung bits of malodorous, badly cured boar meat. A payment of one peso was offered, but the Negritos had no use for money and were satisfied with a few ounces of rice. They crouched down to eat their reward beside the soldiers, who devoured the boar meat and with it their tiny rations of rice and corn. To this meager allotment, Burton Mitchell recalled, was added the paltry yield from the sea: "The natives caught a few fresh fish along the beach, and one lad caught an octopus. We roasted the fish over some coals and ate them without salt, scales and all, and also got a little of the octopus soup."

Such fare hardly made a difference. With this meal finished, they had only one more remaining.

As if their impending starvation was not enough, the adventurers had begun to fret about the runners they had dispatched from Casiguran some five days previously. Funston and Segovia had faith that their forgeries were good enough to deceive Urbano Lacuna himself as well as Don Emilio, but why had they not encountered the Casiguran messengers? By then they should have been returning from Palanan with some sort of acknowledgment. Had someone sold them out?

Funston came up with a solution for not only this but the food problem; it might even prevent their being ambushed. He surreptitiously conferred with Segovia. Their carriers and Cecilio Segismundo had made it known that their next day's march lay along the beach and that they might reach a rebel outpost only eight miles from Aguinaldo's headquarters by the evening. After he and Funston had talked, the Spaniard immediately went over to crouch near Talplacido. Together they concocted another letter to Emilio Aguinaldo:

After five days of a distressing march we reached this place called Laguyo. The condition which our troops are in is deplorable; we are without food and our soldiers can not continue marching, exhausted as they are by hunger and fatigue. Taking advantage of the Negritos which we have met on the road, the bearers of this letter, we pray of Your Honor to be pleased and send us without loss of time, rice and food. If this is not done many of our soldiers will fall on the road before we can reach our destination.

The hunters agreed to take the message to Palanan. They soon disappeared northward up the beach.

Several soldiers were lying dully on the ground and told the Spaniard they could not go on. Before the men went to sleep, Segovia tried to rally their fortitude, if not their enthusiasm, by promising the Macabebes that only one more day's forced march lay before them; by the end of the morrow they would reach an outpost where food would await them — thanks to the Negrito hunters bearing their plea for aid.

At four o'clock the next morning, while it was still pitch dark, they began marching. Some of the scouts were burning up with fever while many others were so weak they reeled as they walked. It was necessary for several to clutch their companions' shoulders to keep vertical and moving. By now, the tormented Segovia could hardly bear to put his weight on the injured foot, though he somehow maintained his place at the head of the column. "The plucky Spaniard never faltered," marveled Funston. As Segovia limped and looked back at the Americans, he saw them walking silently, stoically, and he wondered, perhaps, if their Yankee assurance would ever light their eyes or quicken their pace again.

All that day they anxiously peered up at the cliffs that rose over the narrow beach; they were looking for rifle muzzles protruding from behind rocks or trees, and their necks crawled with the anticipation of a volley of insurgents' bullets that might rain down on them or a hail of spears from invisible tribesmen. The presence of Emilio Aguinaldo grew in their minds as the sun moved implacably toward its zenith.

Four hours after beginning their march, they halted to rest. Talplacido limply tumbled to the sand, moaning that he was dying. Segovia could get him up at the close of their break only with great persuasion. It was now necessary to carry the corpulent officer with the combined powers of four men because he had become more of a deadweight as the soldiers grew weaker.

They had hardly gone one mile farther when someone noticed an object up ahead on the beach. As they neared, Segovia saw that it was a staff thrust into the sand. Still closer, he saw the stick was cleft, inside which someone had put a piece of paper.

To their unutterable chagrin, they discovered their own note pleading for help from the insurgent chief, sent the previous day as their only chance of survival. Slowly the knowledge filtered into their consciousness that the Negrito hunters had apparently lost interest in the soldiers' mission — and their welfare — and had returned what was entrusted to them in this fashion.

In other words, they could expect no food by nightfall.

Funston, this is a desperate undertaking. I fear I shall never see you again.

How MacArthur's words must have echoed through the Kansan's feverish mind!

Brigadier General Frederick Funston, war hero and relentless adventurer, despaired. "It was plain that the end was at hand," he would recall. "It seemed impossible that the madcap enterprise could succeed, and I began to have regrets that I had led all these men to such a finish."

11

ON THE COAST TO DIGUYO, 1982

I

Abandoned by our guides after an absurd misunderstanding, shelterless and without provisions through lack of foresight, weak from having had no substantial meal for two days, close to panic — we were a wretched group of adventurers.

But up and moving north along our rocky coast before the ruddy tropical dawn, we were infused with an angry and fearful will to catch up with the vanished Agtas whether they wanted us to or not, though we staggered over tumbling rocks and panted in fatigue and growing dehydration. Erich, however, was the one exception to our shaky lot. He was in superb condition and leaped ahead like a jackrabbit across the boulders. Soon he had disappeared around an outstretched headland. Then we had only his cairns of stones and footprints in the sand to follow.

Hours and miles later I halted. The others were far behind me. I was where the boulders gave out at the bank of a fairly wide river, which drained a sloping, forested valley. I was too numb to feel relief or surprise to see Erich, and with him Bersosa, Benchan, and Udeng, all squinting at me without expression from the opposite bank. They sat in a circle as if for tea. There was no sign of Seanbuyan or Sulimon.

I took my time crossing the river (it was only thigh deep), filling my canteen, and then bending low to soak my head in the rushing water. Erich gave me a thumbs-up signal as I came ashore and I wordlessly turned to wave my walking staff at our friends, who now had become visible among the rocks.

"The two others are *not good!*" Bersosa told me in his reedy voice, shading his eyes with a hand as he looked up at me. "They see deer trail, they go up to hunt. But *we* stay to wait for you."

"You are good Agtas," Erich said. He explained to me that from their camp our guides had seen our signal fire the night before and had raised a torch in reply. Bersosa claimed they had not meant to leave us stranded. If this was true, then they had certainly walked a good distance since breaking camp, requiring a good chase on our part. Perhaps mischevious Seanbuyan was at the bottom of it all, sowing whispered words of dissent. Erich told me he had promised Bersosa we would hereafter respect their eating schedule and try to keep up with them. This made sense. They were leading us; we should consent to be led. I expected a scene when our comrades walked up, but they, like I, were too tired and demoralized to make an issue out of the debacle. It seemed (almost too easily, I thought) that reason would prevail from then on. We got some nuts and dried fruit that had begun to ferment out of Benchan's gear. He had found an empty plastic cooking oil jug that had been tossed ashore by the tides, and with his knife he had turned it into a yellow hat, which he wore.

We elected to press on a little farther before cooking a meal. The boulders gave way to beaches paved with gray pebbles, and after crunching across these we progressed to vast stretches of hot, dark sand. We came to a place where an abrupt escarpment of volcanic rock some forty feet tall stood perpendicularly across our path like a large black ship thrown up onto land. Waves smashed against the cliff, dousing us with spray. A few dry, yellowed vines dangled down from the top. Without hesitation, Bersosa shinnied up one like a buccaneer and disappeared over the top. Benchan and Udeng, looking not nearly as confident, gingerly took hold of the vines. But when one broke in Udeng's hands they both backed away, shaking their heads. The old man reappeared above and yelled down at them. The boys shook their heads again.

"Don't want to climb, eh?" said Bill. "Just hold on a second." He and Erich crouched in the sand and extracted nylon ropes and steel crampons from their packs while looking critically at the cliff. They had climbed together all through the Rockies in the States. Finally Bill muttered, "Here goes" and swarmed up one of the vines. He tied a rope around a boulder, anchored himself, and dropped the line down to Erich, who joined him above. Together they hauled up all our equipment; when it came our turn to climb, they kept a safety rope taut while we each pulled ourselves up and aboard the black deck of that rocky ship. Getting down to the beach on the far side was an exercise in caution — going over sharpened boulders, a thousand cutting edges slick with seaspray.

We might have regained a sense of teamwork and fellowship after being reunited with our guides and helping each other over the escarpment, but we lost most of it not very long after when we stopped to cook breakfast in a feathery patch of shade under a couple of stunted pandanus pines. When Christopher retrieved our cooking pot from Udeng's backpack, he found old grains of rice sticking to the interior, a generous meal for the squadron of bugs crawling around inside. He lost his temper and declared that since the guides could not clean up after themselves, they should be denied use of the pot. I said this seemed rather severe, since it was the only pot for all of us and the Agta could hardly be expected to take that lying down, as it were. But the notion of punishment struck responsive chords among the others. We were all soon squabbling again over the familiar issues of diplomacy versus authority. Finally it ended with Christopher washing out the pot with sand from a streambed while Erich lectured our guides on elementary hygiene. But even after we had filled ourselves with stew, the bitter exchange echoed in the air around us, and it was not until some hours later, after we stopped to rest, that we were able to meet each other's gaze.

On a stretch littered with an enormous amount of driftwood bleached white and resembling nothing less than bones, it seemed as though we had walked onto an old battlefield or the scene of some revolting massacre. When we trudged past real bones a few minutes later — a femur, scattered ribs, a jawbone, and grinning teeth — I thought for a frightful moment that they were a child's. Then it dawned on me that they were only those of a monkey shot or trapped by hunters, dismembered, picked clean, and left to whiten in the sun.

Our littoral highway continued to unwind in a series of shallow coves, the blue surf pounding monotonously on our right, and on the left, an unbroken palisade supporting scant vegetation. Every two miles or so the ridge would curve out, only to retreat from the waves and make room for another beach. Edging around these cliffy promontories usually called for boulder hopping and often a cautious scramble over sharp rocks. Coming around one point and discovering a soft and flat stretch ahead, I saw two things: the guides had stopped where the toboggan track of a nesting female sea turtle extended from the surf to dry land, and two tiny figures were making their way down the beach in our direction. It was the errant Seanbuyan and Sulimon. Bersosa and the young men were scrabbling where the mother turtle had buried her eggs; they sent up a plume of sand behind them. The old man grinned in anticipation — a fearsome sight!

I kept going. On the far side of a threading creek our two mighty hunters awaited me with nothing to show for their expedition. There seemed to be so little game on this bare coast.

Once we had all collected, no one objected when Seanbuyan demanded time to eat. After the anxiety of the day before, all were content to take a rest. And what more assurance did we need that luck had returned to us: Erich and I followed the creek with our eyes and beheld a waterfall plummeting forty feet down the cliff into an enchanting little rocky grotto and pool sheltered by a grove of trees. It was a paradisiacal place for a rest, a swim, a much-needed bath. I lost no time in pulling out my soap and immersing myself in the pool with a splash, upsetting a number of crayfish that scuttled to safety beneath a rocky overhang. My friends joined me, looking as ridiculous naked as I: skinnier than when we had started, sunburned raw in odd places. After a delightful bath, we washed our clothes in the creek and hung them on a fallen tree to dry. I watched an inch-long black wasp digging industriously in the sand, vanishing inside her hole for a while, backing out then with a small amount of sand she would leave in a pile outside.

After watching a number of repetitions of this, I got up and found a shady place beneath a tree to take up my dog-eared copy of Rizal's *Noli Me Tangere.* His witty anticlerical novel of the Philippines in the last years of the Spanish Empire was, I found, a nice contrast to the scene before me. Paul was washing out his socks in the stream. Dario was sitting on a rock and examining his feet for signs of wear and tear. Bill was napping among herbaceous creepers. Erich was doggedly but unsuccessfully trying to surprise a crayfish with a sharpened stick. Christopher was snapping photographs of the ocean and of Benchan and Udeng, who were tossing his Frisbee with growing authority. The older guides were boiling rice and turtle eggs, scarcely able to contain their enthusiasm at discovering such a bounty, talking excitedly and rubbing their stomachs. Later they offered Erich some of the golf ball–sized eggs, which he scrambled and passed around. They tasted like scrambled eggs seasoned with the vile kind of Thai fish sauce I brought home and used only once during an infatuation with my wok.

When none of us could think of a reason to sit around any longer, we rose and set off up the coast, which continued in short, regular curves like little bites along the edge of a slice of bread. All eleven of us marched together at a comfortable pace. The coastal moun-

tains appeared to be declining steadily to a place several miles ahead
where two large, mound-shaped promontories edged into the sea. I
was getting better at reading the topography and predicted they would
flank a wide river; when we arrived at the base of the first I was proven
right: it was the largest we had encountered yet — a wide, deep river
with a rocky bed flowing swiftly between the hills and spilling mightily into the surf.

Hill fell into cliff, cliff fell into river, and there seemed to be no
way to cross the torrent without a boat or raft. I was curious to see
what Bersosa would suggest — knowing by then his dislike for swimming. Addressing the brown cliff, he raised an arm and took hold
of a protruding rock, found an invisible toehold, found another and
another, and began edging along the wall without any visible support. The cookie tin dangling on his back caught the sun's reflection
in the river, which boiled a few inches beneath his bare soles. Sulimon gamely followed; the others raised their eyebrows in doubt but
joined them. Finally we were all strung out on the cliff face shouting
at each other — things like "What do I do now?" — words that were,
nonetheless, drowned out by the river's roar. At the end, we each
took an alarming backward and downward step into the eddies.
Finding firm ground, we splashed onto a brush-strewn riverbank. It
was three-thirty in the afternoon.

Bersosa announced that this place would be our campground for
the night. The seasoned campers among us — Erich, Bill, and Christopher — grumbled that we had another two hours of daylight in
which to hike, but after the old man told them that another couple
of hours' walk would put us on a mountainside with no water, they
were silent. Then they began to appreciate this riverside site.

In a rocky, level valley covered by an irregular forest of hagachac
lauans and, below these medium-high hardwoods, a jumble of screw
pines, nipa palms, creepers, and brush, the river flowed down to an
extensive sandbank, through which it moved in a serpentine curve
before passing in a final surge between the last hills and to do battle
with the waves. A dry, sandy streambed intersected the river where
we dropped our gear. On the opposite bank sat six abandoned and
decaying Agta huts. If they had been inhabited, Bersosa would have
exercised mightily to get us across somehow to their stewpots and
gossip.

When the sun fell behind the Sierra it created a palette of blue
and gray across the sky. Firewood, though hard to burn, was plentiful, and we built two huge fires, cooking our dehydrated beef stew
for all. A swarm of insane flying beetles descended upon us as we
finished. We wearied of flailing away and spitting them out when they

crawled inside our mouths and finally took refuge in the tents. The lulling, peaceful sound of the river flowing only yards away quickly put us to sleep.

II

We awoke at sunrise. I felt stronger and more relaxed than I had in days, and after a breakfast of granola and reconstituted milk I was ready to tackle almost anything. We walked a hundred yards upstream from our campsite to where the watercourse broke into six rivulets that rushed through a group of rocky islands. We crossed there, straight-arming our packs high in the air in waist-deep water, then balancing on logs and islets, then wading through more water, trying at once to move across and upstream to keep from being swept off our feet in the very fast-moving channels. Paul lost his footing a few yards from the riverbank and the weight of his pack threw him forward. He fell onto all fours, but he balanced himself there and kept his backpack high and dry, looking like a turtle on stilts, until someone went and collected him.

The forest grew down almost to the riverbank. Seanbuyan took the younger guides up a muddy embankment, and they padded off into the shadows with nary a backward glance to where we sat or hopped around on one foot and laced up our boots. Bersosa told me they were going ahead to hunt.

Once we entered the jungle — here a double canopy, with lauans stretching sixty or seventy feet above us — we followed a faint and winding trail, climbing over or crawling beneath the rotten tree trunks that blocked our path, dodging spiny palms and vines studded with thorns, repeatedly wedging backpacks between saplings and requiring a shove to get free. As Paul crawled beneath one tree, he saw a tubular movement inches away and froze. But it was not a snake, only a marching column of ants following a tree root into the undergrowth. For the first time in many days I heard a chorus of birds. Their cheery and effortless "burgee-burgee" and "ber-whippy" did not abate once as we crashed through the undergrowth beneath them. The trail wandered, became soggy, and meandered into a desultory brook, and we followed it until we came to a boggy opening in the trees, large enough for seven to stand together.

"Here we wait," said Bersosa. He crouched and brought out his little container of betel nut and paid us no more mind for two hours. We swatted mosquitoes and tried to get comfortable. Someone pulled out a slingshot, and we got some slight amusement taking turns defoliating a palm with pebbles. When we tired of this there was nothing to do.

Splashing announced the arrival of Benchan. He appeared around the bend in the creek and asked in sign language to borrow a cigarette lighter. He thanked us with an apologetic grin that plainly meant "We won't be much longer," then ran away again. I could not imagine what they could be hunting (Bersosa would reply only with his enigmatic yes when I questioned him). I got my answer about forty-five minutes later, when they all came wading down the creek with hands full of dripping honeycombs, triumphant at last — at least in smoking bees out of their hive. Seanbuyan carried a glass bottle filled to the top with honey. The boys cut off chunks of the sticky combs and passed them around. Seanbuyan handed me the bottle with a wide smile and I drank it like water; it was the sweetest, most liquid honey I have ever had. I took care to spit out the larvae. The Agtas laughed at such delicacy and crunched theirs like raisins.

When we set out again the ground began to rise, and we zigzagged up the side of a mountain, actually a series of four steep hills, each one separated at the shoulder by a trickle of a brook and each covered by a molave forest; the gnarled splay-topped trees grew at a distance from one another, with the forest floor a carpet of decaying leaves and wide-leafed creepers. Dark brown, almost black coral limestone was exposed wherever I looked. It discouraged all but the smallest growth on the hilltops. Ground water quickly drains away from the scant peaty soil into the honeycombed limestone structure of this type of hill, giving the vegetation a sparse, plucked look. Cicadas buzzed loudly. Bright shafts of sunlight caught us unawares as we climbed, making us blink and sneeze. Between the third and fourth hills a brook had worn its way into a seven-foot-deep fissure that was traversed by a felled sapling. The Agtas ran nimbly over it, but when it came time for Paul to cross, he stepped on it with a nervous heaviness. The sapling snapped beneath his foot and tumbled into the little gorge. He flailed forward, seeming to defy gravity, and someone yanked him over. Erich unsheathed his bolo knife and hacked down another bridge for the rest of us. "Finally I get to use this thing," he said happily.

I pulled myself up the last hillside using tree roots and leaning heavily on my walking staff, panting and cursing my stamina, which so often deserts me on inclines. Coming onto the summit, I looked down to where our guides were carefully descending an extremely steep slope toward the beach, some three hundred feet below. We followed. The ground was soft, moist, slippery, perilous; vines caught at our feet. Saplings, clinging dispiritedly to the shallow, rocky soil, were of no help when lost footing threatened to send us flying toward the sharp coral rocks. Christopher slipped off the path, and as he began tumbling he grabbed a sapling to stop himself, but with no root structure it came out in his hand. So did the next three — until he planted his feet and stopped. When we finally reached the beach, we had left behind a huge swath of broken trees and disturbed ground to mark our path. Of course, the surefooted Agtas, preceding us, had moved down the slope without a trace.

We sat on some logs in the shade to repair our bruised and blistered feet. The tide was receding; I hoped the afternoon walk would be easier because of it. Christopher produced cheese and crackers. I motioned for the Agtas to join us, but they were uninterested in a snack and sat glaring a few yards away. They looked increasingly impatient — with us, our rest breaks, and our tender feet. Abruptly Bersosa stood and strapped on his cracker tin. He picked up his weapons.

"*Must go!*" he shouted.

"Wait a minute," protested Erich. "We waited for you in the swamp, you wait for us!"

"No, must go!" By now the other Agtas had picked themselves up. Shaking their heads at our slowness, our guides stalked away, leaving us caught with our shoes off, as it were.

"Wait!" Erich's boots were on. He grabbed his pack, planted his bush hat, and began following them. He yelled over his shoulder to us: "*Keep me in sight!*"

His tall figure was our beacon for several miles as we alternately raged and worried at this new abandonment. We plodded across soft beach sand until we arrived one by one at another vast and stony field, very distinctive in that the smooth fist-sized stones were a spray of pinks and grays, but they were also treacherous — not well seated, prone to shifting away under our boots, and slippery. Black cuboid rocks began appearing ahead. They grew larger as we approached, finally dwarfing us as we skirted between some, climbed over others, and slipped on all. Seaspray and some sort of green algae had coated them like oil.

The beach widened as it curved out to a headland that was thickly overgrown down to the sand. We had finally closed the distance between us and Erich. He shouted back that our guides were not far ahead; in fact, their dark backs could now be seen as they hopped over rocks near the end of the little point.

In the jungle to my left I saw a hut. Two brown-skinned men stood in front, looking at this chase scene being played out on their beach. They wore loincloths; their straight hair was long, shoulder length,

and cut straight just above the eyebrows — Ilongotes, mountain people. In the few seconds that I took my attention away from the ground
I slipped, falling forward over my staff and against a boulder. I struck
my head and saw stars and cut both my hands.

Immediately Paul and Chris were at my side. They got me back
on my feet and I shook my head, trying to clear it. Paul told me that
when he saw me fall he thought I had surely crushed my head in —
"That stick of yours broke your fall." I had a goose egg on the side
of my head and my hands and wrists dripped blood, but when I saw
that Erich had stopped to see if I was all right, I shouted to him to
keep going. The guides had been too far away to see the accident,
and by now they were out of sight beyond the point. Erich followed
them.

It did not seem as though much time had elapsed by the time we
walked around the little peninsula. Perhaps it took me longer to clear
my head than I thought. We found the next beach empty for nearly
a mile — no Erich, no Agtas, just rocks. We took advantage then of
the low tide and walked out onto tidal flats — a rocky lunar surface
of coral slippery with brown algae. Each shallow depression was filled
with water and brimming with life — crayfish, pink crabs, newts. I
was weary and still stunned by the accident, and I blundered continuously into clear tidal pools — seeing only the sandy bottom, thinking they were dry.

A depressing drizzle began to fall. Dario and Bill took shelter under a slanting boulder and refused to come out. We left them, continuing to jump from rock to rock, heedless of the growing danger
of a bad fall and unmindful that for us, accidents had begun to occur in bunches as we grew more tired and careless.

Then it was Christopher's turn: he struggled over two rocks the
size of automobiles and on the far side slipped and abruptly disappeared from view — his legs flew up over his head and there was a
tremendous noise. I let out a cry, and in a trice my backpack was off
and I was vaulting over the rock. I found him lying on his back, the
wind knocked out of him, but he had landed on his pack, and luckily
he had somehow missed striking his head against a sharp rock only
inches away. Paul and I picked him up; we waited until he could walk
and then Chris and I continued. Paul fell behind to encourage our
lagging friends. The sun emerged from behind clouds.

We came to another cove of pastel-hued rocks. The drizzle had
made them glossy, and they began to put off steam in the brightening sun. We reached another promontory — this a black perpendicular wall some sixty feet high and running straight out into the sea.
Erich's rock cairn and an arrow scored in the sand told us to skirt

the base of the massif, which we did, edging out over booming waves on ledges, wedging hands and toes into cracks. We passed a deep, water-filled cavern through which we could see daylight from the other side.

Relief awaited us on the next beach. There were no rocks, which was a blessing since our feet had taken just about as much punishment as they could stand. Then we saw two Agtas waving to us from afar. When we drew nearer, we saw it was Sulimon and Benchan. They told us in sign language that we had only two more coves to cross before we got to our camp. So — characteristically for this emotional roller-coaster ride of an expedition — our fearful anger dissolved.

At the place where a small river (later I learned it was called the Dilaguas) left a forest and joined the ocean, we found a temporary settlement of rattan pickers — half a dozen lean-tos and a tent made from a yellow tarpaulin, with large bundles of peeled green rattan stacked nearby. We splashed across the river and saw Erich sitting on a raised bamboo platform shaded by a lean-to. He had removed his hat and shoes and was eating lychee nuts from a can with his hunting knife. Then I recognized his host, who was the boss of this small outfit: Danny Mangalapus, the skipper of the M.S. *Marivie*, which I now saw anchored in the lee of a barrel-shaped islet a few hundred yards offshore. He asked me whether I was enjoying our hike. I told him it had had its ups and its downs.

We set up camp under the scrutiny of the rattan pickers and Danny. Our bright nylon tents provoked much curiosity, especially in that magical moment when Christopher, who enjoyed the drama, fitted the last truss into place and snapped his wrists, producing an instant dome. Again I was reminded of how much our caravan was like a traveling carnival — our tents, our flashlights and camping gear, our powdered food, and especially our antics. Even then, as a handful of men and boys watched Bill put together his folding saw and begin cutting down a tree, I saw Bersosa relaxing near a cooking fire and slapping an Agta woman's knee and pointing to where Udeng and Benchan performed Frisbee tricks on a pebbly beach with Paul and my brother. Meanwhile, Bill had left some new friends to finish chopping up his tree; then he juggled tennis balls and sticks of firewood to the squealing delight of little naked children while a spotted puppy ran around their feet and yipped excitedly.

Our fire now blazing, we cooked dehydrated food, which interested our hosts less than fresh crayfish that two men had caught for them while wading in the river. They had battery packs strapped onto their backs and stunned crayfish by the score, sweeping them up in nets until boys had to rush out into the river to help them carry the catch ashore.

After dinner, Danny came over into our firelight. He brought over a fourteen-year-old boy who had wrapped a towel around his waist like a skirt.

"Do you like my boy?" Danny asked us. "He is a pretty boy, isn't he?" The boy giggled, rolled his eyes, and stuck out his tongue. He sashayed in a circle around the skipper. "I think he is the prettiest boy on the whole coast, maybe even prettier than those in Manila." He ruffled the boy's hair. "Do you like him?" We were polite but did not indicate any interest. They went away after a while. Throughout the evening, as we walked through the little encampment to talk with people, the boy glided nearby, making suggestive gestures and being studiously ignored.

A woman asked Dario to look at her husband. The man was weak and feverish, too sick to get up from his pallet. He had been unable to work for days and his wife said she was frightened he would die. Most of the people stood around the lean-to while Dario questioned the man through Danny, who acted as interpreter. Our doctor said it sounded like a bad flu. He gave him a shot for his discomfort and a supply of antibiotic pills to fight the infection, and he sat with him until he slept. Dario reassured the man's wife that everything would be all right soon. When he headed back to our tents, the people parted for him like the Red Sea, and even the boy who wore a towel as a skirt forgot to make a face.

III

The next morning, as we were stuffing our gear into the backpacks, Danny Mangalapus came over and made a terse offer. "Three days on the beach," he said, "or three hours by boat."

But we had walked too far to accept a ride now. For each of us, Palanan — that obscure village — was becoming more tangible with every passing day, and though we found our strength and certainly our alertness rapidly melting away as we lost weight, our resolve had become unshakable. We thanked Danny for his offer but refused it. He shook his head in wonder at our folly, but insisted on presenting us with ten kilos of rice for the last leg.

We had not walked far when we found ourselves on the bank of a deep and very wide river. Rain began to fall, and it was unusually chilly for the tropics. Bersosa said that a ferryman lived on the other side of the river and sent the three young men off to find a way across.

They disappeared into the woods that lined the riverbank and found an ancient *banca*, which they paddled across vigorously, bailing frantically with their hands since the boat was taking on an enormous amount of water. This reminded me of something Jurien de la Gravière had written in a nineteenth-century book, *Voyage en Chine*, about Philippine *bancas*. He compared them to cigar boxes, "in which the traveler is so tightly packed that he would have little chance of saving his life if it happened to upset."

Our young guides presently returned in a slightly more seaworthy craft — a dugout *banca* piloted by an ancient man in a big coolie hat who had draped large palm leaves over his shoulders to protect him from the rain. He took us across in three shifts, loading his fragile-looking boat until only its gunwales were visible above the water. When he finished he would take no money. Instead, he mimed taking a pill and smacked his lips. Apparently Bersosa had promised that our doctor would treat the old ferryman in exchange for our passage. Dario questioned him carefully to find out what was wrong, but the ferryman could not come up with anything other than a desire for attention, since doctors were never seen in those parts, so Dario gave him aspirin. The ferryman tipped his big hat, and his lined old face cracked open with pleasure when he clutched the plastic vial of pills. He was still in his boat looking at them as we climbed over some rocks and followed Bersosa into the woods.

Later, when I tried to reconstruct that day, my notes were indecipherable, nothing more than exhausted hieroglyphics smeared by seaspray and raindrops. Polling the rest of our crew turned up little intelligence: the day had begun at the Dilaguas River and ended in despair at the banks of another, yet the great bulk of our time was lost to us, with only the vaguest recollection remaining. Half-blinded by sweat and stuporous from accumulated fatigue and hunger, we marched through an awful heat goaded by the exhortations of our elderly guide — and we liked him less with every step we took.

Green tunnels through dank and tangled jungles took us across a procession of hills. We left the bursting silence of the forests for the roar of the sea when we finally rejoined the coast. It undulated drearily despite a growing drama of contrasts: sandy coves were paved with small stones, each beach distinctive — a dichromatic mottle of russet and tan or olive and ultramarine or umber and slate — each cove joined to the next by an extruding cliff or a tumble of boulders. The sea, under a hot, clear sky, was a brilliant aquamarine broken and churned by lines of dull coral. A growing number of bushy islets poked out of the sea like doorknobs. Rounding each point, we were slammed against the rocks by ferocious waves. Gusts of wind rolled over us from the north and made each step a struggle. We walked north in a heavy dream.

Somewhere on that strand we encountered an Agta woman of startling beauty. She had clear eyes and a full figure and wore only a skirt of some purplish cloth. She looked all the more exotic because she had painted her lips scarlet. The woman stared at each of us boldly as we passed her in a field of boulders. Soon, on a sandy beach, we came upon her settlement — six huts nestled among the trees above the high-water mark. We were too tired to cook food or even to eat. Dario curled up under a lean-to and went to sleep. The Agta boys with us coaxed others from the settlement into a comical game of Frisbee while a white-haired and toothless old crone watched and laughed, hugging her bare chest in mirth. Sly Seanbuyan found a tamed monkey and played with it in the cool shade of a hut. When it came time for us to resume the march he stayed put, smiling in his devilish way and promising to catch up to us later. I wonder whether it was because of the siren with the scarlet lips. We never saw him again.

In the late afternoon we came around a promontory to see a long, cursive beach ahead, which stretched beneath the cliffs to a large waterfall, finally ending where the mountains marched into the sea. A tree that once must have towered over all live things in spectacular solitude now lay uprooted and defeated on the ground, its branches rilling the water of a small creek.

Dario seemed to be close to the point of giving up. He walked erratically in desperate, truncated steps and occasionally gasped to himself. I had seen his feet during a rest stop: his ankles had swollen badly and his feet looked as if they were a dead man's. Exhausted myself, I waited for him at the creek. He sat heavily for a few minutes on a tree branch and stared mutely at the beach ahead. I could get him going only by telling him what Erich had told me — that Bersosa planned for us to sleep not far from the lovely waterfall, which dropped into a series of clear pools. "Another mile to go, Dario," I said, "and we stop for the night. You can make it!" My words sounded hollow because I was doing only slightly better — and we both knew it.

We trudged across soft, ankle-deep sand and stumbled down a collapsing bank into another creek; climbing only three feet onto the other sandbank seemed an incredible task. When we finally reached the base of the waterfall, we let our packs slide to the ground and filled our emptied canteens, then lay across the rocks and held our

Along the Pasig River, Manila

Manila street scene along the Plaza de Cervantes, where army supply wagons vied with horse-drawn trolleys and caromatas *(Library of Congress)*

One of the entrances to the Walled City (Intramuros) *(National Archives)*

"Filipino women are very beautiful" was a saying with as much currency at the turn of the century as today. These maidens are scowling, however—whether because of the harsh midday sun or the impertinence of the American photographer is impossible to say. *(Library of Congress)*

Members of the aboriginal tribe—called variously Negritos, Balugas, Aetas, or, as they prefer, Agtas—taken around the turn of the century *(National Archives)*

OFFICERS COMPRISING
THE EXPEDITION THAT
CAPTURED AGUINALDO.

The counterfeit prisoners of war: Burton Mitchell, Russell Hazzard, Harry Newton, and Oliver Hazzard stand behind Frederick Funston, 1901. *(Courtesy of Dorothy Hazzard Ignatieff)*

Russell and Oliver Hazzard, holding the flag captured from Emilio Aguinaldo, pose with their Macabebe scout company, 1901. *(Kansas State Historical Society)*

The U.S.S. *Vicksburg* at anchor in Manila Harbor *(National Archives)*

The Macabebe company aboard the U.S.S. *Vicksburg*. Talplacido, in front, is in white; Segismundo, the ill-starred courier, is at his right. *(National Archives)*

Aboard the *Vicksburg*: the Macabebe sergeant Pedro Bustos, the problematic Colonel Hilario Talplacido, and the Spanish mercenary Lazaro Segovia, all of whom played important roles in the capture of Aguinaldo *(National Archives)*

Palanan, March 23, 1901: Aguinaldo's headquarters, a former schoolhouse, is in the background. Sergeant Dionisio Bâto strides toward the photographer, Lieutenant Burton Mitchell. *(National Archives)*

The "prisoners of war": (from left) Harry Newton, Burton J. Mitchell, Oliver Hazzard, Frederick Funston, and Russell Hazzard after their trek. Palanan, March 24, 1901 *(National Archives)*

Colonel Simeon Villa, winged by Segovia's bullet, sits aboard the *Vicksburg* in Manila Bay as word of his chief's capture begins flashing across the world.
(National Archives)

Dr. Santiago Barcelona, on board the *Vicksburg (National Archives)*

Palanan, Isabela province, March 24, 1901: Colonel Simeon Villa, Emilio Aguinaldo, Frederick Funston, Dr. Santiago Barcelona *(National Archives)*

The counterfeit insurgents: (from left) Cecilio Segismundo, Gregorio Cadhit, Hilario Talplacido, Dionisio Bâto, and Lazaro Segovia, in Palanan, March 24, 1901 *(National Archives)*

Above: Aguinaldo salutes his American captors as he is taken aboard the *Vicksburg,* March 25, 1901. Burton Mitchell stands behind him on the gangplank as Villa and Barcelona are helped from the launch. *(National Archives)*

Right: General Funston aboard the *Vicksburg* after the capture of Aguinaldo *(National Archives)*

Opposite: The *Vicksburg* as it would have appeared from the landing boat carrying Aguinaldo to imprisonment, Palanan Bay, 1901. *(National Archives)*

Frederick Funston in San Antonio shortly
before he died *(National Archives)*

Below: Emilio Aguinaldo relaxes in his
Kawit home with his children in November 1929, under the benign gaze of
former president Calvin Coolidge.
(National Archives)

The famous corncob pipe–clenching profile: Douglas MacArthur, "for Filipinos the one true American hero" *(National Archives)*

Below: The Bataan Death March of 1942 followed the surrender of General Edward P. King on April 9. Out of 78,000 troops, some 6,000 died during the forced march. *(National Archives)*

Top: Part of the opening American salvo against Japanese holders of Manila, 1944. To the left of this 2,000-pound bomb, the Pasig River divides old Manila and the Paco district from Quiapo. The Ila de la Convalencia, a hospital island, lies just north of the Ayala Bridge. *(National Archives)*

Bottom: American tanks patrolling the Plaza de Espana within the Walled City during the two-month battle to flush out the last Japanese holdouts. *(National Archives)*

Right: An American tank enters a hole in the Fort Santiago gate, 1945. This wrecked bastion, the headquarters of Spanish military might during the colonial period and the place where Americans were held prisoner during the Japanese occupation, is now a peaceful open-air theater and park. *(National Archives)*

Below: The elegant old Manila Hotel, built in the heyday of American colonization around 1912, became Douglas MacArthur's home in the thirties; he personally directed its recapture in 1945. It was later rebuilt. *(National Archives)*

Manila after the 1945 liberation, showing the wrecked districts of Malate and Ermita. Eisenhower called the city the most devastated of all the world's capitals, surpassed only by Warsaw. *(National Archives)*

One hundred thousand Filipino civilians were killed by the Japanese in the months before the liberation. Those who survived contended with a Manila that was more than 80 percent destroyed and a complete breakdown of society. *(National Archives)*

heads under the cool water until we gasped. The guides and our friends were resting in some shade about fifty yards ahead. We finally collapsed, panting, on the ground next to them. I thought thankfully of a bath in the waterfall and a long night of rest. Just then Bersosa stood.

"*Must go!*"

"What?" I cried. "Forget it! This is fine right here. In another hour it will be dark." My friends loudly echoed me.

"No," he said to all our clamor, "*must go!* Next day tide catch us on other side of mountain! Will lose half day!" He turned and walked through some bushes to the base of a very steep — nearly perpendicular — hillside. "Must go *now!*"

"*Wait!*"

He ignored us. The young guides looked as if they wanted to remain neutral, but Sulimon and Udeng hurriedly grabbed their packs and scampered through the underbrush in Bersosa's furious wake.

"*Wait!*"

The old man began to climb. Paul stood and pointed a threatening finger at Benchan, our youngest guide, took a few steps toward him, and thundered at him to stop. The boy shifted his weight as if considering bolting, glanced nervously at his vanishing companions, and finally looked resigned. He waited until we struggled into our shoes and hoisted our gear. We began to climb after Bersosa, who by that time had disappeared into the gloom far above our heads.

Rage propelled me up that horrible, horrible climb, a pure white rage borne out of sudden, limitless fear and a profound sense of being betrayed once too often, patience evaporating for good as if in a furious burst of steam. Hand over hand, clutching at vines and roots, my backpack a deadweight pulling me off balance, I slipped in the soft dirt. I fell backward against a tree and wrenched my back. Snarling, I jammed my staff into the ground to push away and upward. Young Benchan looked down at me in dismay; wrath was pouring off me like sweat while my comrades below gnashed their teeth and struggled upward like a maddened posse, hands turning raw from rocks and stained green from grabbing at vines. Six hundred feet, seven hundred, eight hundred, nine hundred feet and more.

The mountainside began to level off, and we climbed tree roots as if mounting a steep and slippery staircase, the foliage nearly impenetrable, a mist forest of giant ferns and aerial roots, of dripping leaves, saturated ground, rotting logs, a dank mulch of decaying vegetation, with soft moss and liverworts carpeting the ground and clinging like tumors to dwarfed oaks, iguems, balakbaks. Wispy clouds drifted down from above, obscuring the path in the already dim jungle light. Saw-toothed plants slashed out and cut my face and bloodied my arms, and I used my staff to hack, slash, slam them back with a homicidal fury — fantasizing they were the gray pate of our devilish guide. Rage lost me my balance; I slipped off the trail a dozen times, and each time I caught myself with the staff only an inch short of beginning an unstoppable roll down the steep hillside toward a cliff and the roaring, invisible sea far below.

We toiled through the woods, thoroughly soaked in a stew of sweat, dirt, and drops from leaves. Finally we began meandering downward. Every time Benchan drifted more than five yards ahead of me I called him back, but he kept straining away from me and my flailing stick. The ground became firm and the path straight, and momentum carried us down at a trot until we burst through the last wall of palms to the edge of the sea.

A rocky beach. Empty. There was no sign of the old man, but there was no reason to doubt that we could catch up to him before darkness. Wide coral flats stretched away toward the breaking waves. Offshore knobs marched beside the coast. The failing afternoon light was blue-gray, like veins in the great piles of marble we trudged past. I slipped on scummy rock and splashed through craters filled with seawater.

The coast fell away at the mouth of a dark and very swift river. Over the noise I thought I heard someone screaming. I strained to see into the shadows of the opposite bank — an ominous tangle of mangroves and heavy brush — but I could make out no one, and I heard nothing more. Following the riverbank and peering across the surface of the river for signs of a fording place, we were dwarfed by cliffs rising high above us. We passed a heap of charred wood and several decaying lean-tos — an abandoned hunters' campground. A muddy path took us into thick brush between the cliffs and the river. Large trees had been flung across the path. The river narrowed to about thirty yards, and Benchan pointed without conviction — he knew as little as we about the terrain — at an outcropping of volcanic rock in the torrent. For want of an alternative, we entered the river and struggled across to the islet over black, razor-sharp boulders. The river bottom was treacherous: irregular, a floor of jagged and pitted lava. Dario slipped backward off a rock into the water, soaking his dry boots but keeping his pack from immersion.

We stood clustered and awkward on a sharp and very rough little perch not even halfway across the river. Benchan was at a loss. He looked out over an impossible distance to the opposite riverbank — dark, dank, overgrown. He threw up his hands.

"*Well, go in!*" I was shouting to be heard over the river's roar. I pointed to the black water. Benchan looked scared and shook his head. I took off my pack with an exasperated oath and climbed down into neck-deep water.

"Be careful!" My brother had helped me down with a hand and now crouched over the rocky edge. He was only a silhouette in the waning light. I could not see the bottom, could only feel the way with my feet. I began to move in cold rushing water and — it was horrifying! — went in over my eyes, my foot nearly wedged tight in a jagged hole. I had fulfilled another nightmare.

I climbed back up and vowed loudly not to go back in again.

"Well, let's not just stand here," shouted Erich. "Let's swim across."

"Nothing doing," I retorted.

"We can't just stay here all night!"

"You want to cross that tonight?" shouted Chris.

"Hell, yes! Can't be much forest before we hit the beach again. The old man's *got* to be down there."

"You want to go through that jungle in the dark? You're *crazy!*"

Seven travelers stood shoulder to shoulder in dark midstream, damnable panic raging through us like electricity through a circuit. We could hardly see each other now, and Benchan looked at us in fright as Christopher, gesturing furiously, screamed to be heard over the roar, his voice flung out at us and the encroaching darkness:

"Decide!"

12

ON THE WAY TO PALANAN, 1901

I

For General Funston, the morning of March 22, 1901, had begun as a dream and ended in despair as he discovered their last hope — a written plea for food — thoughtlessly discarded upon the beach. As he began to regret leading his men so far only to see them wither away from hunger and fatigue, Funston recalled the rumor they had heard in Casiguran, that Aguinaldo's encampment might now be fortified by General Tinio and his four hundred Ilocano soldiers. Watching the Macabebe scouts stumbling across the rocks and dragging deep furrows in the sand, he wondered whether "there was any fight left in this outfit."

At noon the men paused to rest. Lazaro Segovia cut their last meal into halves "so that we might have something, even if only a morsel, to eat at night." Two hours after they resumed the march, a bearer pointed ahead to the distant outpost that marked their day's goal. It was five miles up the coast. Then several Negritos came into view. Upon sighting nearly a hundred men bearing rifles, the tribesmen naturally ran away as fast as they could. Segovia called for his soldiers to stop. He sent two bearers ahead to induce one of the frightened hunters to approach them. They succeeded; and when Segovia asked the hunter to run ahead to the outpost to announce them, he complied. They resumed the trek.

In the late afternoon, Funston saw two men approaching from the north. When they drew near they began talking with Talplacido and

Segovia, and the Spaniard gestured for the group to halt. The soldiers weakly attempted to close ranks while the conversation up front continued. Funston could not tell what was going on, being in the center of the column and out of earshot. He watched as the Spaniard finished talking, fell out of line, and limped back toward the rear. He appeared to be seeing to his men. As Segovia passed the captives he hissed out to Funston in Spanish.

"It's all right," he said. *"We have them!"*

Their ruse had been believed. The two men were from Palanan, and they had been sent to escort General Lacuna's reinforcements to *Presidente* Aguinaldo. "What a load was lifted from our minds!" Funston exulted. "We were now ten miles from our quarry."

Dusk was falling when the soldiers reached the outpost. Called Dinundungan, it consisted of only a few small shelters for sentries; in addition, a work team of six Negritos under the quarrelsome supervision of an elderly man from Palanan was finishing the roofs of two sheds. The five American prisoners were taken to these shelters, their Macabebe guards making much of their posture as captors by scolding their charges harshly. Segovia distributed the remaining rations, but eating these small morsels of food only made them more ravenous. Separated from Segovia and learning nothing from their Macabebe guards, the Americans bided their time throughout the evening, as hungry for information as they were for sustenance.

Only after everyone at the outpost was soundly asleep did the Spaniard feel it was safe to approach them. Once at Funston's side, Segovia showed him a letter handed to him by the elderly Tagalog foreman. It had been sent from Palanan by Aguinaldo's chief of staff, Colonel Simeon Villa; it was addressed to Lieutenant Colonel Hilario Talplacido:

> In accordance with the instructions of our Honorable President, at receiving these presents, you will leave the prisoners under a guard at Dinundungan and you will set out immediately for here, but without the prisoners, as it would be a serious matter should they see this village.

While Funston pondered the implications of the letter, the Spaniard went on to tell him that he hoped to have solved their severe food problem. Obviously the soldiers could not perform their coup on the morrow while they were still starved and devastated from the effects of their forced march. Segovia had already dispatched a reply to Villa, which he had had signed by poor Hilario Talplacido:

> In this moment I am in receipt of your communication in reference to the prisoners, but I beg to state that it is impossible for me to continue the march, as our soldiers are in a very bad condition. Therefore I pray of you to send sufficient rice for one day, and also sufficient provisions for the guard which is to remain here, as we are entirely out of food. If this is done, we can continue our march tomorrow.

With luck a Negrito would deliver the message to Palanan that night and food would be supplied from Don Emilio's storehouse in the morning. "We entertained our empty stomachs with the hope of a square breakfast," Segovia recounted.

Upon learning all this information, Funston's satisfaction was mingled with uneasiness. It was good that Aguinaldo had received the packet of letters the conspirators had sent from Casiguran seven days earlier. It would have been the first news *el presidente* would have received that Cecilio Segismundo's quest for insurgent reinforcements — which had begun when Aguinaldo entrusted him with the mission (and his fateful courier pouch) more than two months before — had been successful. The letters they had written over General Urbano Lacuna's forged signatures to heighten the deception had clearly hoodwinked the rebels in Palanan. Aguinaldo had even elevated the corpulent Talplacido's rank — as the counterfeit letter from Lacuna had recommended.

With all this good news, Funston realized, there was one problem, and "it brought us nearer to disaster than any other thing connected with the expedition." Aguinaldo had ordered the prisoners to remain under guard at Dinundungan, a few miles from where the final act would be played in a drama in which Funston and his companions desperately wanted parts. Segovia told the general he was afraid to go off without the moral support of the American officers. The Macabebes had lost their courage along the route, he said, and "if left to themselves, they will open fire at the sight of the first enemy, and try to take Palanan by assault." This would obviously spoil all their well-laid plans.

But what could they do about Aguinaldo's orders?

They could not expect the elderly Tagalog from Palanan, nor the soldiers with him, to allow Aguinaldo's orders to be disobeyed so flagrantly. And if there was a struggle, with shots fired, anyone within earshot would run to alert the village and Don Emilio would slip away.

While the Hazzards, Newton, and Mitchell listened, none of them clear-headed enough to offer any suggestions, Funston and Segovia talked into the night.

II

They were all awake at about five o'clock on the morning of March 23, 1901, intoxicated by the mixture of dread and excitement that had colored their dreams — and that had not been dissipated upon awakening.

The Macabebes' spirits had improved a little overnight. Before they went to sleep they had pestered Segovia with their worries, for the scouts had questioned the insurgent sentries guarding the Dinundungan outpost. These men told them that Aguinaldo was being protected by a force of between seventy and a hundred men. Some badly scared scouts had urged that they be permitted to rush the village and open fire at once. It had taken all Segovia's powers of eloquence to convince them that by strictly obeying his orders they would incur no danger — and Emilio Aguinaldo would, the following day, be in their hands. Then Segovia had set them to cleaning their rifles to keep their doubts at a minimum.

Now, on the morning that would witness either their success or utter failure — possibly their death — the Spaniard drilled them again and again on the importance of discipline on this crucial day.

The rice they had requested from Palanan did not arrive by eight. Rather than incur any further delay, Segovia ordered his men into formation for their final march. Funston, Mitchell, Newton, and the Hazzards stood nearby. They were told they would remain at Dinundungan under the guard of eleven soldiers of the reinforcement column until further notice. After roll call, four men hoisted up the invalid Talplacido. Segovia took his place at the front. His infected foot had continued to swell, and he could hardly bear to stand on it.

The seventy-two soldiers left the nipa huts, the beach, and the five Americans; they struck inland along a narrow, muddy path through a dense forest. Half an hour along, the starving adventurers met two men carrying some food from Aguinaldo. The villagers assured Segovia that provisions were abundant in Palanan. On the previous day they had produced an elaborate fiesta for *el presidente*'s birthday. Today, said the villagers, the esteemed and welcome relief troops would be received in Palanan with music.

"Aguinaldo will have to pay the fiddler," Lazaro Segovia said to himself.

He took enough rice for his men, sending the carriers to Dinundungan with the rest to give to the men who had remained behind. The adventurers broke their long and excruciating fast with cheerful abandon.

A quarter-hour after they resumed walking, Segovia put up his hand for the single-file column to halt. He extracted from his pocket an envelope of his own manufacture, which he handed to one of his soldiers with instructions to return to the outpost. He was to give the letter to his Macabebe comrade in charge of the American captives and to explain to any questioners that a runner had come from Palanan with the orders he now bore: *the prisoners were to come to the village after all.* This scout turned back while the main column once again began slowly moving through the dark and humid jungle. By noon they had crossed several rivulets and finally came to a creek where it was necessary to splash along its length for part of an hour.

Segovia and his men were still in the streambed when they encountered the soldiers.

There were a dozen of them, each clothed in a clean new uniform of the insurgency. At the very sight of these men the Macabebes were transfixed. *Aguinaldo's own soldiers on Aguinaldo's undisputed territory!* Segovia's quickly raised hand for his men to halt was a wasted gesture — the scouts had turned into statues.

"This was for me the most critical moment of the whole expedition," recalled Segovia. He wondered whether his men would hold their peace; their rifles had been loaded since leaving the outpost. For a fleeting moment his impulse was to unleash them on these rebel soldiers, but he did not give in to it. Any shots might be overheard, and the Casiguran bearers would escape and give alarm.

The enemy sergeant advanced and saluted the Spaniard. He produced a letter from his commanding officer in Palanan, Colonel Simeon Villa:

> At receipt of this you will give the necessary orders that the prisoners in Dinundungan be delivered to Sergeant Andres, commanding the guard which will escort said prisoners. You will also order the guard of your column to march for this place.

Gripping the letter as if it were his life preserver and with nothing in his mind but alarm, Segovia began to speak.

"Very well, boys," he said to the soldiers, "how are things up there? Is everything all right in the village — is there sufficient food, plenty of troops?"

"Yes sir," Sergeant Andres replied. "We were expecting you yesterday in the village. There are not many soldiers, because this morning the outposts left, but yesterday we had more than a hundred."

Segovia asked him his commanding officer's name.

"I belong to Major Alhambra's troops," answered the sergeant.

"Well," said Segovia, anxious to stall for time by keeping the conversation going in this polite fashion, "what are your instructions?"

"You are to turn over the prisoners left behind in Dinundungan," said Andres, "and I am to take them into a part of the woods from which they cannot escape."

The soldier had regrettably returned them to the issue at hand.

By this time Funston and the others were marching in their rear to join them. What could Segovia do to get free of this tangle?

"Come on," the Spaniard proposed. "Let us get out of the creek and sit down. In the meantime I shall write the order which you must take to my corporal, for without an order from his superior officer, he will refuse to hand the prisoners over to you."

"Very well, sir," conceded Andres.

Hilario Talplacido was summoned. Segovia told him he would have to sign a letter addressed to their corporal in charge of the captives. Talplacido, in turn, told Gregorio Cadhit to make out the order. Under his breath, Segovia muttered to Cadhit to spend as much time as possible with it. While Talplacido and Cadhit were occupied, the Spaniard stepped aside and went to the rear. He approached one of his sergeants.

"Go as fast as your legs will carry you," he whispered, "until you meet the prisoners, and warn them to hide until this detachment has passed them."

The man slipped off into the trees.

Frederick Funston and his fifteen companions were traveling at a slow pace along the muddy path that ran up to the northwest from the beach. Though they had eaten all of the emergency rations sent by Aguinaldo to Dinundungan, they were still drastically weak. Every few hundred yards the general would have to lie down flat on the ground to rest for a moment or two. His companions were in similar shape.

They had waited at the outpost as agreed until the Macabebe scout returned from the main column, summoning the Americans to Palanan. Though he examined the letter suspiciously, the elderly Tagalog was finally content. He grumbled that he did not see why they had put him to so much trouble if they did not intend to use the shelters he had so hastily constructed, and he watched sourly as the soldiers herded their charges into the woods and out of sight. Hidden inside the Americans' bedrolls were five loaded Krag-Jorgenson rifles.

"We were now in a perilous position," recounted Harry Newton, "and the slightest miscalculation might mean annihilation."

"We were very weak," recalled Funston, but at least they had only their own people with them "and were relieved from the trying necessity of watching every action for fear it would arouse suspicion."

About two hours after they had left the beach, they heard a furious thumping of feet ahead. Suddenly, a Macabebe sergeant came rushing down the path, nearly colliding with them in his haste. He was so out of breath, he could only gesture frantically for them to get off the trail and conceal themselves in the undergrowth. As they pressed themselves against the moist earth, the scout explained what had transpired ahead. In a few moments, the party of insurgents passed within thirty feet of them. They watched through a tangle of brush as the group splashed along a creek, laughing and talking, unaware of the men lying rigidly so close by, almost fearing to breathe. After the contingent had passed and could no longer be heard, Funston and his group emerged from the bushes. They brushed themselves free of dirt and leaves and breathed a fervent sigh of relief at their narrow escape. "We resumed our march," recounted Funston, "having had a fine scare." Almost tiptoeing through the dense and gloomy woods, they kept well back from the main column.

The trees began to thin out around Lazaro Segovia's men at about two in the afternoon, giving way here and there to muddy rice patches and a few inhabited thatch huts. Two farmers looked curiously at the soldiers from their field as the column came near, and they told Segovia that Palanan was a short distance away, less than two miles. Not long after, they came within sight of their long-awaited goal.

The village, on the opposite bank of the swiftly moving Palanan River, was surrounded by a thick wall of jungle that carpeted the lowland plain and grew over the face of the cordillera. Many people were grouped in the town square in front of the village's largest structure — a one-story building perched, as was the custom, on stilts near the river's edge. A blue, red, and white Filipino nationalist flag snapped on a high pole attached to the building's peaked, palm-leaf roof. Perhaps eighty thatched houses stood behind the town square in neat rows. Segovia's column of soldiers neared the fording place, where three boats were tied. The metallic clang of a gong floated over the water from the village. As Segovia took in the awe-inspiring sight of Emilio Aguinaldo's final stronghold, he caught the glint of field glasses from a window of the main building.

13

ON THE WAY TO PALANAN, 1982

Pursuing the pursuers, and separated now by only one day's march and eighty-one years, I awoke before the others. I was rickety from sleeping on rocks and tottered in the predawn quiet to wash in a bamboo sluice near the abandoned and decrepit lean-tos we had appropriated to get out of the night's showers.

I had been overwhelmed by rage at our willful old guide's latest abandonment, and while I slept, residues glowed within me like embers, tingeing my dreams with violent images. Even as rocks clattering away from my feet woke my companions, I found one part of my mind automatically plotting various kinds of revenge I knew would never take place. Apparently a similar process was going on in my friends' minds, for a few minutes after they were fully awake we heard hunters' cries floating across the river from the jungle beyond, and as they echoed off the overhanging cliffs we exchanged narrow glances. It would be Udeng and Sulimon, out searching for their young friend whom we had taken hostage. I muttered to no one in particular that I hoped their worry about him had equaled our consternation — that they might have lost sleep thinking that we had vented our anger against old Bersosa on the hapless person of Benchan. We had, as a matter of fact, done no such thing — since a modicum of forethought and a great deal of chance had put packets of freeze-dried dinner in Bill's backpack and the expedition's only cooking pot in Benchan's. After all seven ate, we regained enough generosity of spirit to contribute an Ensolite pad and sleeping bag for our hostage's comfort against the dank night. His friends would be waiting for us in the morning; we had a living and breathing guarantee.

As far as the earlier party was concerned — Funston attenuated and creaky with rheumatism, Segovia gimpy, the others mere wraiths — it felt as though we were narrowing the gap. What was more, if Christopher's map reading was correct, the bay we had skirted the previous day was Dikadioan Bay, and the prominent tree-capped offshore island that stood at its head, just north of where we had camped, was Digoyo Island. This meant that we had a good chance of reaching Palanan by the next sundown.

Our gear stowed away and packs shouldered, we retraced our footsteps to where the river tumbled around its sharp outcropping of rock at midstream — the rock upon which we had entered chaos the night before. On the opposite bank in the shadows, Sulimon and Udeng waited. They emerged into the light at our appearance, looking relieved to see Benchan intact.

They pointed out a fording route we never would have found ourselves that crisscrossed from the islet into the swiftest part of the river. Caution was plainly called for. We used two-man teams to hold the packs aloft, and, after struggling against the current and stumbling into hidden pits and tripping over rocks, we reached the far side and a stinking muddy bank overhung with mangroves. A large white bird, a Great Egret whose greenish head announced that for him it was breeding season, launched himself from the nearest tree and flapped off over our heads before losing himself among the treetops.

None of us had much forgiveness for the two young guides. They waited awkwardly for us, and under our glares they meekly led the way along a muddy trail that cut through the woods and over a rise to the beach. A hundred yards up the strand was a temporary-looking cluster of lean-tos, which sheltered several Agta families and their curmudgeonly guest, Bersosa. Obviously it was the lure of these people and their stew pots that had propelled our chief guide and diplomat over yesterday's mountain.

As we approached, he began muttering to a middle-aged man sitting next to him on the sand. The others looked at us with curiosity. The sight of his six American charges dropping their packs against the trees and beginning to empty their hiking boots of river water unfolded him from the ground.

"*Must go!*" he shouted.

Six angry, husky-voiced American adventurers yelled at him to sit down and wait. He shrugged, sat down, and waited.

It took only a few minutes to prepare for the hike. As we clomped across the ten yards of sand separating us from Bersosa, there was no room but for mutual glares.

"You are too slow," Bersosa said to us, nudging his friend to pay close attention to us in all of our hulking gear and appalling inexperience. "Too slow," he repeated. "We will have to sleep on beach tonight."

"*No,*" said Erich in his most determined voice. "We will reach Palanan *tonight!*"

"You will eat our dust," I added.

Bersosa did not seem impressed at our resoluteness, but he had no idea how Palanan had begun to pull us forward as we drew within its range, nor did he estimate the amount of reserve strength available in us all when the finish was close at hand. Before we pushed off from the group of Agta huts the loads were adjusted; the guides' packs had grown disproportionately light in the previous two days and we could think of no reason why they should remain so. Dario, like the good doctor he was, refused to part with any of his medical supplies, claiming he could handle the load that had nearly beaten him flat the day before. Now I saw that he had, in the night, crossed some sort of barrier. He had lost twenty-five or thirty pounds in a little more than a week and suffered for it, but whereas he had looked haggard a day earlier, today he looked fit and ready. The same could be said for my other friends — and we had only the proximity of our goal to thank for it.

The terrain was cooperative at first. We crossed a beach under a hot and bright sky. The guides marched in front without outdistancing us — perhaps their adjusted loads kept them close, perhaps it was because we kept poor Benchan within grabbing distance. We presently left the coast to cross a succession of rises, having entered a territory called the Kanaipang Hills. Mariners' charts indicate this land area as "The Knobs," for apparently from the ocean one sees prominent land forms standing from eight hundred to a thousand feet high silhouetted against the rising Sierra. Of course, any geological significance was lost on us at ground level, though the hilly terrain did yield some flora new to us on this trip. We ascended and descended through masses of elephant ears, pitcher plants, and African violets, which surprised us nicely. When we had eventually worked our way back to the seashore, we crossed long expanses of sandy beaches strewn with pink rocks, each beach anchored to the coastline by the protruding headlands of bruising, tumbled-down rocks that we edged through with no little care.

The beach began to narrow as it was squeezed between the ocean and abrupt cliffs, which rose a hundred feet like fortress walls now overgrown with vines and scraggly bushes. The appearance of a noisy little brook gave us the opportunity to rest while canteens were refilled. While we were thus occupied I admired the walls overhead. Bersosa, looking at me and then the cliffs, nodded. Presently I saw why, for when we had walked a little farther he stopped, appraised the rocks and the encroaching sea, and began to climb straight up toward the top. My Ifugao staff was quite a hindrance in this climb, the most vertical in days, but it had saved my head from being cracked more than once and had supported me in my hours of weakness, and I would not jettison it now.

Finally we puffed over the crest seventy or eighty feet above the beach to find ourselves in a lush jungle. A path snaked off through the underbrush, and we followed it, finding the usual fallen trees requiring an occasional crawl beneath them. Birds and other wildlife being absent, the only sound was that of our thrashing and, somewhere, the muted roar of the sea. We began to descend a steep path, clinging to trees and bushes for fear of misstepping and tumbling over the edge. Then, after entering a fissure in the rock and climbing down exposed tree roots as cautiously as one would, I imagine, lower oneself in an empty elevator shaft, we stepped out onto a small table of beach sand and coral that revealed itself plainly as a cul-de-sac surrounded by cliffs and surf. Standing crowded together, we split the air with Agta and American curses before throwing our hands up in exasperation and, choosing another fissure, ascending once again toward the jungle above.

Sometime later Bersosa found the correct route to an unrestricted coastline and soon we saw a farmer, the first nontribal man we had seen since Danny Mangalapus and his rattan pickers. He was hoeing a vegetable plot next to a shack, and he paused to look at us with mingled surprise and distrust as we appeared, all ten of us, out of a grove of trees. We skirted his tilled ground. The momentum of our eleven days on the Contracosta was urging me forward, and I could spare him only a neighborly wave (returned halfheartedly) as I passed him. The explanation for our presence on this coast — offered so readily before — seemed now to be redundant. We were *there*, nearly as incongruous as those exhausted officers of the Western states had been, and my business lay not with this astonished farmer but somewhere ahead, where the past and present would intersect.

There was an embankment and a bluff overlooking the sea and the next beach as well as a long, steep, muddy slope down which we traveled on the seats of our pants, our backpacks thrown across our knees. Another beach, crescent-shaped and bisected by two tiny creeks, poured out of ferny overgrowth. There were some shacks and dogs and chickens somewhere, and pigs rooting beneath the shacks, and a few people who exclaimed when they saw old Bersosa leading his parade of fools up the sand to the settlement.

Paul approached a Tagalog man who seemed to be in charge, which he was, for this was another place for gathering and bundling rattan, and the dozen or so tribal people were his workers. Paul asked the man whether he spoke English.

"Of course," said the man. "Where are you going?"

"Palanan."

"Oh, Palanan is not far," said the foreman. "You can follow the road."

"The *road*?" We must have looked a sight — unkempt and dirty and dehydrated and obviously not believing our ears, for we gathered around him, our mouths agape, and repeated the word as if it were new to our ears. "The *road*?"

"Yes," he answered, "the logging road. It runs from here to Palanan, maybe fourteen kilometers."

I saw I was standing near the edge of a dirt road, which extended from where we stood through the trees until it curved out of sight. I felt like Dorothy in *The Wizard of Oz* when she has just been shown the beginning of the Yellow Brick Road — yet I was near the end, and the prospect of a road without boulders or cliffs nearly made me weep with relief.

"What is the name of this place?" I asked.

"Dinundungan," the foreman said.

Not far down the road from where bundles of rattan were drying in the sun, a stream tumbled down a hill to form a pool shaded by feathery saplings and bushes. Here, while we ate and rested and bathed in the cool water, I tried to convey my enthusiasm at having gained the first verifiable geographic place name mentioned by our predecessors since we had left Casiguran. (Later I realized that our last riverside camp, opposite Digoyo Island, had been cited by Segovia as "Laguyo," the place where they had traded with the Agta hunters for bad-smelling boar bones and sent the undependable Negritos forward as messengers.) Learning that this rattan-gathering station at Dinundungan had once been the revolutionary outpost where Funston was nearly undone, however, interested my friends less than peanut butter and crackers and the question of whether our socks would be dry enough for the afternoon's hike.

Bersosa and his young companions seemed in no mood to hurry off, we discovered, when we quit that enchanting glade for the dust of the road. Bersosa introduced me to a number of people standing in front of a neatly maintained board house. "They are my cousins," he croaked, looking pleased that his appearance had prompted the dusting off of a jug of locally produced *bino*. I saw no evidence of blindness or infirmity about, so I accepted a swig from the jug with a grin. All of our enmity had finally evaporated. The old man indicated that he was content to stay and relax for a while and would meet us in the central barangay later. The boys wanted to stay also. Apparently Benchan and Udeng could see why their more worldly friend Sulimon had earlier changed from his mission pants to a bright, patterned loincloth and beaded armbands. He stood out in the crowd of Agtas (who were attired less traditionally), a young and handsome hunter. He had already attracted the attention of several young women (at whose half-draped figures we tried not to stare). I wondered if Sulimon, who was reputed to be looking for a wife, would follow us to the end or remain in these parts.

Alone again but with lighter hearts, we six followed the rutted and neglected track. It ran parallel to the coast through tall palms and undergrowth for perhaps a mile before depositing us in the most surprising place, a sandy hollow in which had been left a rusty fleet of heavy earth-moving machinery, flatbed trucks, and other industrial vehicles, even several large scows that had been beached above the high-water mark. Flaked and peeling fuel storage tanks and decaying buildings completed the picture of desolation. It all seemed as though the inhabitants had been spirited away years before. Later I learned that the ghost town was part of a logging enterprise that had run into trouble. Its owner had attempted to bribe the mayor of Palanan. From what my informant told me, this was a standard business practice for the logger, who because of his wealth and connections in Manila thought he was as above the law as most of his fellow magnates were. He had not reckoned on the mayor's unflagging honesty. Though I never learned what happened to the logging baron, his whole business in Palanan had been turned over to the townspeople by a magistrate. Unfortunately, they were not equipped to manage the operation or able to arrange for the profitable disposal of the machinery for use elsewhere. It was thus abandoned, and now millions of dollars of equipment was rusting away for want of care. While that may or may not have been fitting, the whole place was not only a shock to eyes grown unaccustomed to modern technology but also extremely creepy. We hurried through that huge industrial graveyard as fast as we could.

The road crept up the steep side of a hill that afforded us a parting view of the sea. We followed it as it curved west through rolling

unpopulated jungle — the hilly terrain that would unfold in the Palanan River floodplain. When the incline became difficult and I lagged
behind the others, noting ruefully that Dario was out in front, I realized that my stamina was all but gone. Among the trees the humid-
ity afforded little breathable air, and my heart raced alarmingly. I
called Erich back to my side and insisted he begin telling me stories
to keep me going, which he did with much patience and humor.

A heavy rain fell, turning the road into ankle-deep mud. It was
pointless to bother with ponchos; we were already soaked in sweat.
An undependable old log bridge took us across a deep ravine. We
passed several tilled fields, dogs barking and children calling to us
from the windows of nipa farmhouses. But they received no answers, for we were all gasping with the effort now. From time to time
we walked through swarms of yellow butterflies. We splashed across
a creek and later waded through a knee-deep river without bothering to change shoes. The water filled our boots, making it feel as if
we were moving in fishbowls; we sloshed as we walked, and I could
feel my feet softening and the skin finally breaking down, but I did
not call a halt to empty my boots and neither did my friends. We
were hiking now as if hypnotized, and, whereas in the past we had
sung when talking seemed too much of an effort, now even singing
would have taken too much energy, so we were silent.

The land became level and we passed more farms. The rain had
stopped. We encountered a shy young couple walking hand in hand
with their pants legs rolled up; they knew so little English that we
hardly paused, but thirty yards later we found ourselves at the bank
of another river and realized that we needed them to tell us how to
cross — it was a hundred yards wide and looked very deep. Christopher and Erich ran back to find them, but they had disappeared.
When they approached a farmer way out in his field with a carabao
hitched to a plow, he only understood what they wanted when they
shouted, *"Palanan? Palanan?"*

By the time they returned, Paul had in his fearless way found the
ford himself by advancing out into the brown current and feeling his
way with his toes, an extremely difficult task since he was up to his
neck the entire way. We ferried our gear across in three-man teams,
again straight-arming the backpacks and trying not to slip on the rocks.

Several miles down the road we found another farmer. *"Palanan?
Palanan?"* I shouted, and he shrugged and pointed up a branching
lane. This turned out to be wrong, for presently I came to a house
(by then I was far ahead of the others) and was told that the central
barangay was not on this lane but rather at the end of the larger road
we had been directed to leave. "Everything is in the central barrio,"

said a man who later was introduced to me as the vice mayor, "the church, the school, everything." I simply nodded, furious at the mile-long walk for nothing, and headed off my friends as they attempted to cross a deep mud puddle on a shaky log.

Now my feet were in very bad shape; sharp pains flashed every time I took a step, and I leaned on my staff like a cripple. I saw my glazed eyes mirrored in my brother's pallid stare. Two women, two boys, and a donkey fell into step ahead of me. The women said they were going to the central barangay and we should follow. They kept looking back at us: me with my cap pulled over my eyes in the after-noon glare, stumbling along the road twenty or thirty yards ahead of the others, who walked in a clump and kept their eyes on their feet. I paid no one alive any attention. Sweat was in my eyes; I kept blinking through it to see the mountains and the fields and began to hallucinate, the ground shimmering below my feet and my perspec-tive shifting. I felt unstuck in time, closer to the pursuers and the pursued of eighty-one years before than to the men who had helped me retrace their footsteps. I felt as though I were a hundred years old. I *was* a hundred years old.

We came to another bend of the Palanan River — just silently say-ing that name filled me with an excitement I had never felt before. The river was thigh-deep here and flowed swiftly over a pebbly bot-tom, and I splashed across without looking back. A muddy road, some soggy cornfields, windbreaks, more cornfields — all while I kept thinking "the village is just up ahead," but there were only wind-breaks and more cornfields.

Finally the path rose slightly and cut through some high foliage; I walked through it as if it was a gate and found myself once again on a bank of the river, a high place that put me almost on the same level as the one opposite. Above a sandy beach and an overgrown bluff was a wall of coconut palms, and visible through the swaying fronds were the red roofs of the *convento* and church buildings of Palanan.

PART THREE

THE VILLAGE

14

PALANAN, 1901

I

Emilio Aguinaldo y Famy awaited his reinforcements from General Lacuna. A message from their colonel, Talplacido, indicated they had less than a hundred men. It was, however, a beginning. More troops would make the trek, and inaccessible as this coastal village was, it would serve as a place from which to attack the foreign invaders in the Cagayan Valley, and from there the rest of Luzon and beyond.

Two weeks before, *el presidente* had received a letter from Apolinario Mabini, his adviser, that had taken about three months to reach him. Mabini had told him that General MacArthur wanted Don Emilio to know that independence was a dream he would never see become reality; the American commander had had the temerity to invite him to return to Manila and take up residence with him in Malacañang Palace. The two of them together! Aguinaldo had no reason to think that he would be given anything to live in but a plain wooden box — nailed shut and buried deep. Mabini had closed his letter begging for instructions: now that President McKinley had defeated William Jennings Bryan in the presidential election — thus, Mabini thought, ending any hope that a change in administration might alter the invaders' course — what did *el presidente* want to do, plead for independence or autonomy?

Aguinaldo replied that the Filipinos in arms had no other desire except Philippine independence. He had no idea that by then Mabini had been packed off to Guam with others of Aguinaldo's subordinates.

In the weeks before his birthday, Aguinaldo occupied himself as he had for months, in supervising various petty details regarding the running of the town (he was, after all, a former mayor) and making sure the defenses around Palanan were adequate. He heard a rumor that an American ship might try to approach them, so he left town briefly to reconnoiter a mountaintop that commanded a full view of the sea.

On March 22, some hundred visitors arrived for his birthday fiesta — soldiers from his outposts in the mountains, farmers from the barrios beyond the village outskirts, even a delegation of people from Casiguran. Invitations to some of his senior officers in other provinces had been dispatched awhile before — many with the little Ilocano courier who had left Palanan in January — but none of them, including General Tinio, had been able to attend. "We celebrated the day with horse races, dancing, serenades, and amateur theatricals," Aguinaldo recalled with pleasure. "The near approach of our reinforcements furnished an added incentive to the festivity of the day."

The next morning, while his subordinates saw to dispatching food to Talplacido's column, Aguinaldo closeted himself with his physician and adviser, Dr. Santiago Barcelona, who had served him so faithfully during their arduous flight through the two mountain ranges to Palanan. They worked on preparations "for the formation of a Red Cross league among the ladies who had come up from Casiguran for my birthday." The women had been given a three o'clock appointment to see *el presidente*.

Around two o'clock in the afternoon, the expected column of reinforcements came out of the trees to stand on the opposite bank of the Palanan River. Aguinaldo, standing at the window of his headquarters, examined the officers with his field glasses.

Below him, pacing outside the building, Major Nazario Alhambra kept voicing his doubts about the soldiers — who by then had begun to cross the river in relays. Alhambra asked *el presidente* for permission to order the honor guard to fire a volley over the strangers' heads — to find out whether they were enemies or friends.

El presidente became angry. How could Alhambra doubt these men, their "brothers and allies"? Why should they be welcomed in such a way after their toilsome journey? Aguinaldo flatly refused to give them such a distrustful reception.

II

The process of transferring the men across the river in three boats took fifteen minutes. Segovia went over in the first vessel with four scouts, and upon stepping ashore he was embraced by a captain from Aguinaldo's staff, who welcomed them in the name of *el presidente*. It was regrettable, he told the Spaniard, that the reinforcements had not arrived earlier; they had been expected for two days, and the marchers would have been rewarded with the splendid birthday fiesta they had held only the previous day. Segovia explained that their long ordeal up the northeastern coast had made it impossible to reach Palanan sooner, but he asked the aide-de-camp whether he had enjoyed himself at the party.

"Yes, as far as I am concerned, very much so," replied the captain. "We had music, balls, theaters with local artists and different other pastimes. Furthermore, all of us officers made speeches in praise of our president, congratulating him." The officer fumbled inside a pocket, producing a scrap of paper. "Here, see, this is my speech. If you had been there, you also would have partaken of everything."

Segovia agreed that it was a shame.

"Well," the captain said, brightening, "we still have music, and I believe you can still have some fun."

By this point, all of the scouts had ferried across the water, and Bâto and Cadhit organized them into formation. Talplacido stood next to the Spaniard, for once unaided. Segovia turned to address his soldiers.

"Boys, when we are now in the presence of our President," Segovia said loudly, "I want you to go through a drill — and when I say 'Present Arms' you must do it well so it may not be said you are deficient in the soldier's art. Have you heard me?"

"Yes sir," the Macabebes answered.

They proceeded up the riverbank and into the village, where they were joined by Major Alhambra, the chief of Aguinaldo's troops. He also embraced the Spaniard and the procession continued.

The houses were resplendent with garlands and wreaths of flowers and bamboo ornaments from the celebration. A decorative wooden triumphal arch had been raised in the town square along with two gazebo-like bandstands attended by rows of benches. There was a summer pavilion as well as the village church.

Sixty soldiers wearing blue uniforms and white hats were lined up in the square. Each held a Mauser rifle. Segovia prayed that his men would not panic. They marched into the town square and halted not ten yards from the honor guard. Told to present arms, the scouts performed nervously — but in correct military fashion.

Leaving Cadhit and Bâto to attend to the Macabebes, Segovia approached Aguinaldo's house with Talplacido. Several men looked down on the pair from a window. They mounted the steps and were greeted with wide smiles by Santiago Barcelona; in addition to his other duties, the slight, wispy-bearded doctor was the treasurer of the Filipino republic.

With a sweeping gesture Barcelona conducted them inside the building, through a short hall, and into a sitting room containing only a table and a few benches. They were introduced to the men standing by the table: Colonel Simeon Villa and several other officers. Major Alhambra had meanwhile appeared. Barcelona begged them to be seated, explaining that *el presidente* was in his room dressing and would shortly join them. Segovia and Talplacido accepted cigarettes and glasses of sugared water from an officer, and while they waited, Villa sympathetically questioned the Spaniard about their arduous expedition.

Presently a door off the entry hall opened. A small man dressed in a starched khaki uniform appeared and entered the sitting room. As soon as they saw him, Talplacido and Segovia leaped to their feet and gave him a crisp military salute. It was Emilio Aguinaldo.

He had an air of command about him, though he was not physically impressive. Dressed in a plain khaki uniform and fancy Spanish riding boots, he was of average Filipino height and slight of build. He wore his dark hair in a pompadour over a wide, high brow that spoke of intelligence. His eyes were friendly, clear, and serene. He walked straight up to Segovia and Talplacido, welcomed them with a firm handshake, and asked them to stand at ease. He politely began to question Segovia in Castilian. Apparently Aguinaldo did not recall meeting Segovia before — which he had, briefly, eighteen months earlier, when the Spaniard had been a genuine revolutionary under General Manuel Llanera.

"How many days have you marched?" Aguinaldo asked.

"Twenty-six," answered Segovia. He saw there were, besides Aguinaldo and Barcelona, six officers in the room.

"How are the provinces in Central Luzon?"

"Very well, my President," replied Segovia. "We are under fire there every day. Many convoys and provisions have been captured from the Americans. The generals operating in those provinces have taken a large number of prisoners."

All of the officers in the room were wearing revolvers.

"The people of the villages willingly render all kinds of assistance to their brothers who are in arms and carry on the war in the mountains and woods," said Segovia. "The general state of affairs in the provinces is very favorable for us."

Two windows and one door afforded the only egress from the room.

"Very well, very well," Aguinaldo was saying. "I am glad to hear such news. How about ammunition? Did you bring much?"

"Yes sir," said Segovia. "The soldier who has the least carries a hundred cartridges."

One of the officers excused himself and left the room.

"Oh, well, very well. Here we are short of ammunition. My men have only twenty-five rounds, but now we can rest tranquilly with the company you gentlemen bring."

Aguinaldo noticed that the Spaniard's foot was hurt.

"What is the trouble with your foot?" He motioned for Segovia to be seated.

"I do not know," he replied. "About four days ago it began to become inflamed and now causes me great trouble."

"Do not be scared," Aguinaldo assured him. "Dr. Barcelona will soon cure you. He has medicine here and in three or four days you will be well."

He turned to question the fatigued and dazed Hilario Talplacido in Tagalog, asking him the same questions put to his companion. Funston had told the officer to speak as little as possible, so Talplacido kept his answers brief.

While they conversed, Aguinaldo's officers continued to excuse themselves, one by one, and leave the house. Finally only Alhambra, Villa, and Barcelona remained in *el presidente*'s company. Half an hour had passed since Segovia's men arrived in the town square; the Macabebe company awaited them outside, still at attention and still only ten yards from their hereditary enemies. The time had come.

"Lieutenant Colonel," said Segovia to his corpulent companion, "the soldiers require rest."

"Very well," said Talplacido, "ask for permission."

Aguinaldo, who was telling Villa to have food prepared for the newcomers, turned to them.

"Gentlemen, you will dine today with us."

"Sir," Segovia said, "the soldiers must have something to eat as well as rest. They have been very short of both for nearly a month."

"Good. Quarters are ready for them to rest," said Aguinaldo, pointing out the window to a house across the square. "As soon as the rations are cooked they will be notified and can then eat."

The Spaniard saluted Aguinaldo in anticipation of taking his leave.

"Before you go," *el presidente* said, "I congratulate you for your gallantry to have brought me five prisoners." He planned to have the Americans taken to Ilagan, in the Cagayan Valley, and set free.

"Many thanks, my President," Segovia answered. "You know that we are ready for everything necessary against the Americans."

"Thanks," said Aguinaldo. "The country will reward your services."

Segovia limped outside and paused at the top of the steps. The scouts stood rigidly at attention below; their bearers from Casiguran were nearby. Members of the Palanan bamboo orchestra had taken their places close to Aguinaldo's honor guard and were adjusting their instruments. There was going to be a salute.

Segovia carefully made his way down the stairs. A boy approached him and asked which of his soldiers knew how to blow a bugle. The Spaniard ignored the boy.

Gregorio Cadhit looked over at him. Segovia nodded slightly, removing his hat from his head, and raised it in signal.

"Now is the time, Macabebes!" Cadhit bellowed from the bottom of his lungs, *"Give it to them!"*

The column fired a ragged volley into the midst of the troops opposite, completely surprising them.

Segovia whirled, pistol drawn, and staggered back inside. Another, more disciplined volley rang out as the Macabebes overcame their fright and began to take aim.

Aguinaldo, thinking his troops were firing a welcoming salute, rushed to the window.

"Stop that foolishness," he cried. *"Don't waste ammunition!"* He saw his troops taking flight, their cartridges not in their rifles but on their belts. Some paused behind cover and frantically tried to load their guns. There was a lot of shouting. Someone lay on the ground, dead. Perplexed, Aguinaldo quickly turned from the scene.

Talplacido snapped out of his torpor and lunged toward Aguinaldo, forgetting to draw his pistol, and was brought up short by Barcelona, Villa, and Alhambra, who had drawn their guns and leaped to *el presidente*'s side. At that moment Segovia rushed in, waving his gun.

The scene was frozen in an eternity of seconds: Aguinaldo, shielded by his three officers; Talplacido, standing helpless and dazed; and Segovia, who finally found words.

"You are our prisoners," he cried. "We are not insurgents, we are Americans! Surrender or be killed!"

Barcelona, struggling with Aguinaldo as he attempted to pull his pistol out of its holster, warned Segovia not to shoot. But the Spaniard saw an abrupt movement and opened fire. Alhambra reeled, shot in the face, and managed to vault through a window into the river below, where he was swept away. Villa sank to the floor momentarily, shot in the wrist and back, but sprang up and through the same window. Barcelona had succeeded in stilling his leader's hand, and as the smoke cleared, the doctor pulled a white handkerchief from his breast pocket.

"We surrender," said Barcelona. "This is the flag of peace."

General Funston's small group had just reached the Palanan riverbank when the Macabebes' volley rang out. Shouting and firing their guns into the air to simulate an attacking force, they clambered into a boat tied up onshore and frantically paddled across the river.

Segovia went outside to stop the Macabebes. Aguinaldo's soldiers had fled into the jungle. Emboldened by their easy victory, the scouts were running through Palanan, shooting at the fleeing villagers and laughing wildly. The terrified Casiguran bearers had disappeared into the forest. One of the honor guard lay dead in the square, about ten yards from the village musician, who had been walking between the two groups when the first volley erupted. The bodies looked like piles of white rags in the grass.

Segovia left Bâto and Cadhit to discipline the Macabebes when he spied Funston's familiar form at the prow of the *banca*. Forgetting his injured foot in the excitement, the Spaniard ran down to the water to meet the Americans. He was splattered with the blood of Villa and Alhambra, and when Funston saw the gore his face went wild — *what had happened, was Aguinaldo dead?*

"It is all right," Segovia shouted in Spanish. "We have him!" Together they sprinted up to the headquarters. Nearby, several Macabebes were dragging Colonel Villa out of the river, his wounds still bleeding heavily.

The five Americans stomped into the room with Segovia at their side. Talplacido had flung himself to the floor when the shooting started, but when it was safe he recovered his wits enough to grasp Aguinaldo — as if he had captured him alone — when the general entered.

"You are a prisoner of war of the Army of the United States of America," the Kansan said. "I am General Funston, commander of the expedition." Aguinaldo was pale; there were tears in his eyes. "You will be treated with due consideration," Funston was saying, "and sent to Manila at the first opportunity in a steamer, which is coming to take us on board in the bay of this village."

The enormity of what was happening had not fully sunk in. Aguinaldo was still in a daze.

"Is this not some joke?" he asked.

III

The afternoon sun began to set to the mournful sound of spades hastily breaking the hard Palanan soil as the Macabebes dug graves for the dead and shallow trenches for themselves.

"It was all over," said Funston, "and after two years of war the elusive Filipino chieftain was at last a prisoner." For Segovia, now relegated to sixth in command, after the American officers, he could relish that "we were absolute masters of the situation."

Earlier, the scouts had been delirious with joy at their success. All five Americans had been smothered in one hysterical Macabebe embrace after another, "whether we willed or not," recalled the general. The famished scouts had foraged through the deserted village, gathering what food they could find. The adventurers' stomachs were soon filled for the first time in a week. Then the Macabebes had again looted the houses, this time selecting new clothing to replace their soiled rags. During one of the searches they discovered two terrified civilians hiding in their houses: the village mayor and a small boy. While the scouts helped themselves to the civilians' stores, Funston had ordered the contents of the headquarters inventoried and confiscated. They found fourteen hundred pesos and an enormous number of official documents. While men collected the abandoned rifles scattered around the grassy square, Burton Mitchell produced a small pocket camera he had hidden at the expedition's start and began snapping pictures of the village for posterity.

As night fell, the dead men were put into the ground. "It was regrettable that . . . these men had been killed, but there was no help in it," Funston rationalized.

> If we had sent our cards to them, told them who we were, and invited them to retire, as some lady-like persons in the United States afterward insisted that we should have done, it would merely have exposed our own men to a volley from them, and it scarcely could have been less fatal than the one that they received from us. The lives of these two men were of small moment counted against those that would have been lost had the insurrection continued. Few men have died to better purpose.

At the general's order, Gregorio Cadhit produced a signal-flare pistol he had carried up the coast. He fired a rocket into the air for the benefit of those on the steamship, but no one but themselves saw the fireworks — unless one counted whoever was lurking out in the jungle, watching them.

Aguinaldo was confined to a room that he shared with Barcelona and Villa, who by that time had been bandaged by the doctor and had his arm in a sling. Sentries stood outside the door and beneath each window of their cell. Fearing treachery, *el presidente* begged Funston not to leave them alone with the Macabebes; he felt a tribe that was responsible for dreaming up the water cure torture could not be trusted to adhere to any articles of war. Funston saw some merit in Aguinaldo's worries and made sure that one of the five Americans was within calling distance of the prisoners at all times. In addition, they all billeted themselves, along with Segovia, in an adjoining room in the house. The rest of the scouts clambered into their trenches for fear they would be attacked that night by Aguinaldo's honor guard — should they regroup — or by any of the guerrilla bands that might hear of the coup and attempt to free the prisoners.

That night, according to Simeon Villa's recollection, he, Aguinaldo, and Barcelona were confined to their room and left alone except for the occasional presence of a Macabebe, who had been assigned as their orderly. While the scout was serving food, Aguinaldo began talking very softly to him, "persuading him and his companions to change their minds and think of the future of their country." If the Macabebes wished, "the five Americans need not be killed but merely captured and imprisoned."

Incredibly, the Macabebe's heart was touched. He replied that he was willing to carry out *el presidente*'s plan, but he had to convince the other scouts first.

The next day the Macabebe whispered to Aguinaldo that he had convinced "half" of his fellows, but he wanted to be sure he had a majority on his side before taking any action.

After the tantalizing hope of a countercoup had been raised, Villa noted, before they left Palanan "the plot failed — because the Macabebes were not united, and in the face of a feared disaster, those who had earlier consented, also withdrew."

Frederick Funston's agreement with the navy was for Commander Barry to bring the *Vicksburg* to just outside Palanan Bay on March 25. There he would await their signal.

The victorious conspirators were able to spend the next day, the twenty-fourth, relaxing around the town. "We had no further suffering from lack of food, as we found cracked corn, rice, sweet-potatoes, and chickens . . . so we merely helped ourselves," Funston recalled. "There was no destruction of property," he asserted, though the scouts had done their looting earlier, "and we left the town in as good shape as we found it."

Funston spent some of the time with his illustrious prisoner, answering his many questions about the way he had been tricked. "Is there no limit to what you Americans can do!" *el presidente* exclaimed at one point, throwing his hands up in a manner that the normally quiet and withdrawn Aguinaldo was not often seen to do during his life. Later, the Kansan left to begin reading the captured dispatches and records. Lazaro Segovia visited Aguinaldo several times during the course of the day. He found him to be a polite but reserved conversationalist, as did Funston, who would iater call him "always courteous and self-possessed." Nonetheless, he was intensely curious about how the elaborate ruse had come about and insisted on knowing every last detail.

"I should never have believed it that I could be deceived in this manner," he told Segovia. "I would not have dared to do such a thing." He would tell Funston later that the deception had been sealed by the conspirators' use of Lacuna's forged hand on his own official stationery.

Aguinaldo asked the Spanish captain whether he would be executed. Segovia tried to convince him that "the Americans shoot nobody unless he is a criminal." *El presidente* mentioned the possibility of his exile to Guam. To this the Spaniard could not provide an answer, but nonetheless he assured Aguinaldo that his life would improve once he publicly accepted American sovereignty over the islands.

"The whole thing seems yet to be a nightmare," Aguinaldo said. "I can hardly believe myself to be a prisoner." He confided later that he was "deeply angered, then distressed, then almost completely numbed" by the treachery and betrayal that had led to his capture, and he was overwhelmed by a "feeling of disgust and despair for I had failed my people and my motherland."

Lieutenant Mitchell was busy with his camera all the day of the twenty-fourth. He snapped a group portrait of the Macabebe company, then one of the Filipino officers and Segovia, and then had one taken of himself with the other Americans. He arranged for a photograph of their prisoners, who stood in the sunlit square with uncomfortable expressions. The captured *presidente* insisted that one be taken with Funston standing next to him, and this was done.

Continuing what was under the circumstances a remarkable courtesy, Aguinaldo wrote a short note of congratulations that he signed and handed to the general. "His gameness and general bearing won our hearts," wrote Funston later.

Refreshed by their rest and newfound fellowship, the men in Palanan arose early on the morning of March 25, 1901. At six, all was in readiness. The prisoners appeared with their belongings; Aguinaldo was dressed in his khakis and his black riding boots and he wore a white pith helmet. His clothes and papers, and those of Villa and Barcelona, were stowed in a canoe along with the grievously wounded musician, who needed hospitalization. The *banca* was to be piloted down the Palanan River to the ocean by two men from Casiguran, who had cautiously rejoined them after the shooting was over. Aguinaldo wrote a letter of transit to safeguard them from anyone hiding in the woods and desiring revenge:

> I beg of you not to ill-treat or trouble the bearers, who take my baggage down to the bay, where I shall embark upon an American steamer which will carry me to Manila.
>
> The Prisoner, E. Aguinaldo

The party walked through a maze of fields outside Palanan and put the last houses behind them when they entered the woods. Each of the three captives was closely guarded by an American officer. The soldiers puzzled through a multiplicity of trails; having no guide, they lost their way repeatedly. They finally settled on sticking to a generally northeasterly direction.

When Major Nazario Alhambra had leaped out of Aguinaldo's window into the river and disappeared around a bend, he was not drowned or eaten by crocodiles, and he did not perish from the head wound inflicted by Segovia's revolver. He allowed himself to drift with the current for a while before crawling up onto dry land. In the woods he encountered a demoralized encampment of Palanan townsfolk and the remainder of his soldiers.

Alhambra feared that *Presidente* Aguinaldo might be executed. His bloody presence roused the gathering, and when he asked if they would follow him in an attack upon the town, saying, "Are you ready to die, to fight until the last moment?" the crowd roared its assent.

"Immediately they set out for town," wrote a contemporary who later interviewed Alhambra, "passing through cogon and talahib like mountain people running after wild beasts. Heading them was Alhambra, who seemed to possess an amulet and did not care for the shadow of death; his pants were rolled up to the knees and his feet were covered with mud."

Nearing the town, the crowd divided into sections and poured out into the municipal square, rushing into the convent, the rectory, the school building where their *presidente* had been confined. The town was deserted.

They ran across the Palanan fields and through the jungle, tracing their enemies' footsteps.

But their pursuit was too late.

Some miles out to sea, Major William Carey Brown sat in the captain's cabin aboard the U.S.S. *Vicksburg*. An inspector general under Funston's command back in the Fourth Luzon District, Brown had been one of the few people in the islands to know about the grand scheme from start to finish.

He had implored General Funston to be allowed to go along on the trek, but because he had been weakened by a severe attack of influenza, and because the general felt that the staff he had selected would be sufficient, Brown was left out — to his everlasting disappointment.

His life had been such that his being part of the expedition would have been appropriate. Born in 1854 and graduated from West Point in 1877, Brown had seen much action as a cavalry lieutenant during the Indian Wars, fighting against the Bannock tribes in Oregon and the Sheepeater Indians in Idaho. This, he always said, was poetic justice, for when he was eight, his family had been fugitives during the Sioux uprising. During the Spanish-American War, Brown was the captain of one of the troop contingents that charged at San Juan Hill, and it was there that he became a lifelong friend of Theodore Roosevelt.

Not being able to play the part of prisoner of war during Funston's expedition, Brown was gratified when the general secured permission for him at least to accompany them on the sea voyage. After the conspirators had disappeared into the rainy and foggy night of March 14, the *Vicksburg* had steamed south to anchor in Baler Bay.

"During my stay here," Brown wrote, "to prevent any possibility of the real mission of the *Vicksburg* being known, no communication between ship and shore was permitted except by officers." He, however, was allowed ashore with another officer, in order to deliver a ninety-nine-year sentence to a Filipino insurgent lieutenant who had been convicted of burying alive a wounded American prisoner. "To deceive the natives further the *Vicksburg* proceeded to Casiguran Bay on March 18," recounted Brown, "where it remained for six days while landing parties made inquiries concerning the five American prisoners who were being carried off to the north by insurgents." According to the major, the villagers lied cleverly and gave no reply or hint that the expedition had been their guests for two days.

Before leaving Casiguran Bay, Captain Barry had ordered a landing party to examine the beach where they had dropped off Funston. The men reported finding only the conspirators' footprints leading off in the direction of the head of the bay.

The gunboat sailed north toward Palanan, coming to anchor on March 25. "About one o'clock on that day Captain Barry came to his cabin," wrote Brown, "and remarked hurriedly to me that a column of smoke, evidently a signal, could be seen on the beach."

They all hastened to the bridge. Brown had his field glasses, and a naval lieutenant standing nearby had the ship's telescope — but they could see nothing. "The situation for a few moments was extremely tense," Brown said, "and we were about to conclude that we were going in to the shore too soon and would 'flush the game.' "

As they continued to peer through their glasses, Brown recalled with relish, "I detected a small white patch on the beach and a moment later noticed that it moved."

He called out that he could see some sort of signal, and all the men on the deck strained to make out something in the area toward which Brown was excitedly pointing.

A strong wind sprang up almost immediately after the signal fire was lit, and the column of smoke was spread low and dispersed along the beach. Someone produced a bedsheet he had stolen from the village, and they hurriedly rigged it to a pole and began violently waving it back and forth. Slowly the distant ship came about and began moving in toward shore. When it was closer, Harry Newton used the sheet to wigwag a message: WE HAVE HIM. SEND BOATS FOR ALL. Just as soon came back the reply: BULLY. A tiny cheer could be heard across the water from the ship's deck, which they could now see was aswarm with sailors and marines.

The gunboat came to anchor about two miles out from land. The longboats were lowered as well as the little steam launch that had been used so effectively to dislodge the *Vicksburg* when it went aground in Atimonan Harbor exactly two (eternally long) weeks before.

Waiting for the boats to reach land through a heavy surf, conspirators and captives alike sat on the sand. Several gathered under a tree by the edge of a stream that emptied into the sea. Now that the ruse was completely finished, and with it the excitement, Segovia and the former rebels who had played the part of officers now felt that "they appeared to have been merely invited to join the trip" instead of the ones who had ensured its success.

To pass the time, Gregorio Cadhit began to tell a story to entertain the men sitting with him under the tree. "Despite the beautiful conduct of Jesus towards his twelve Apostles," he said in a joking tone, "one turned out to be a traitor — Judas, who plotted against and sold his Master."

"What?" Cecilio Segismundo interrupted. "What is the point of your story?"

"Well," said Cadhit with a sly grin, "what I am relating has its parallel in the capture of the President of the Republic."

"What parallel?" Segismundo had been sitting on a big tree root, but now he stood up.

"Well," said Cadhit, enjoying his joke immensely, "the twelve Apostles of Jesus were like us. Aguinaldo is the Christ and you are Judas!"

Enraged, Segismundo pulled out his revolver. Cadhit also drew his gun. As they faced each other, ready to shoot it out, Frederick Funston intervened. There was no bloodshed.

As the first landing boat crashed through the last breakers to grind onto the beach, the tension evaporated. Captain Barry, "his face radiant with smiles," leaped into the froth to congratulate Funston as the other Americans and Macabebes sent up a yell of greeting. "There was no attempt by anybody to conceal his feelings," recalled Funston.

Emilio Aguinaldo was taken on the first launch to the *Vicksburg*. Mitchell came along as escort and helped him up the gangplank as the crew drowned out the sound of the sea with their cheers. Don Emilio's clothes hung sodden from the heavy surf, and he looked, frightened, at the swarm of shouting sailors and the American officers who waited nearby to receive their distinguished prisoner. He summoned up a nervous smile.

He saluted.

15

PALANAN, THE END OF THE TRAIL

I

Standing in a haze of exhaustion on the bank of the Palanan River, I heard the sound of a crowd cheering. It was not my imagination — at first I thought it was — but came from a group of people just beyond our sight near the Palanan church. Were we being congratulated upon successfully completing our journey? Another cheer floated across the river, and I realized we were hearing a group of teenagers playing basketball on the court adjoining the rectory. I could see one of the hoops. A few boys paused in their game, one holding the ball, to stand on the little bluff over the river and look at us. They soon returned to their sport.

Our ferryboat appeared: a very shaky canoe piloted by a boy who had not yet mastered it. Christopher and I went over in the first load with the two women and a youngster who had walked with us the last two miles. Though the ride was not long, the women kept shifting their positions, making the boat rock dangerously. I finally barked at them to be still. After our long hike I had no desire to be dumped — backpacks, notebooks, tape recorder, cameras, and all — ignominiously into the drink in sight of the whole town.

On the opposite bank we found a path that mounted the rise through dense bushes; had it been there when Funston and his crew ran up into the town? Leaving our backpacks in front of the rectory, a plain one-story concrete building with a shady verandah, we went looking for someone to give us permission to sleep there. The regular pastor, I had been told in Manila, had forsaken the priesthood to be married, leaving the churchgoers in the town without a spiritual leader and the rectory without someone looking after it.

The basketball game was breaking up by then; a few boys said, "Good afternoon, sir," as I passed by them. I spied a man who looked at us curiously from beyond a low, stone, churchyard wall.

"Good afternoon," said the man, who was gray and very thin and in his sixties. "Where have you come from?"

"Baler, Dinalungan, Casiguran, Dinapiqui," I said, relishing the sounds of the names as well as the accomplishment.

"You came by boat?"

"No, by foot."

Of course, he was astounded at such an expense of energy. After learning that we were not anthropologists, linguists, or missionaries but six historically minded people chasing a pair of generals who had met in Palanan eighty-one years earlier, the man introduced himself. He was Crispulo Villena, the telegraph operator for Palanan. "Unfortunately," he added, "the telegraph is out of order." From his tone I deduced this was an occurrence to which he had become accustomed.

Villena offered to escort us to see the municipal police chief — the only town official around since the mayor had gone beyond the mountains to Ilagan, in the Cagayan Valley, on business.

Already I had not walked so far without my backpack in a week, and though I relished feeling so light on my feet, I could have stretched out in the dust and gone to sleep. Despite my fatigue, I took note of this central barangay of Palanan, and it was not simply my relief at having arrived that made the town look so attractive. In all of my wanderings across Luzon I had not seen a prettier town. The streets were dry and clean, with no drainage ditches evident, and they were shaded by palm trees; laid out in a rectangular fashion, they even bore hand-painted signs on intersections denoting, for instance, Gen. Aguinaldo Street, Gen. Antonio Luna Street, and Andres Bonifacio Street. The houses they bordered were well built and maintained — mostly of gray weathered pine with red tin roofs and jalousie windows, standing on stilts and enclosed by fences and rows of flowers or clipped hedges. Roosters crowed and chickens clucked from beneath the houses, and I heard the occasional grunt of a pig. Every other house seemed to have a tiny store counter set up at street level, each staffed by children.

"Good afternoon, sir." We passed a friendly boy who was leading a bullock and cart. "Good afternoon, sir." A woman leaned out of her window to greet us. "Hello, sir." An elderly woman clutching the shoulder of a shy girl for support. "Good afternoon, sir." One of the basketball players. Only one other town — Sagada in the Central Cordillera, a place visited by Emilio Aguinaldo in 1899 and by myself a few weeks before — equaled Palanan for friendliness.

Villena could find us no officials to whom we could present ourselves. We turned back toward the church side of town, beginning to pass many men who turned off the street to enter a low building. A few carried roosters under their arms. "It is time for the cockfights," our guide told us. "We have very few diversions here."

When Christopher and I had said good-bye to the telegraph operator and returned to the rectory, we took along a case of cold San Miguel beer for our friends, having nicely surprised the owner of a tiny store with our order. After everyone had claimed a bottle we sat in the common room, shoeless, splay-legged, sunburned, and haggard, and I met Berto, the lay priest who had moved to take his predecessor's place. "I can perform mass," he said, "but the villagers have to wait for confession until the Order flies in a priest, every couple of months." Berto was fortyish and extremely thin. Smoking an endless chain of cigarettes, he answered our questions softly, pausing often to cough, his eyes glowing over prominent cheekbones. He agreed to lodge us for a few days if we didn't mind the floor. ("At least it's flat," Paul quipped.) When we had cooked up a dinner of freeze-dried beef Stroganoff Berto only picked at his food, seeming to prefer to draw his sustenance from his Marlboros. "I don't eat very much," he apologized.

At exactly 8:00 P.M. we heard talking out beyond the perimeter of the churchyard, and who should appear but Bersosa, Sulimon, Udeng, and Benchan with the rest of our equipment.

"What took you so long?" I inquired of Bersosa.

After the Agtas had been given dinner and were bedded down for the night in a little guest house across the yard, another visitor arrived. It was the police chief, Marciano Q. Salazar, who had been attending the cockfights when we could not find him. Over a beer we talked about Palanan's historical significance.

"My grandmother was a young girl when Aguinaldo was here," Salazar told us. "In fact, she was courted by several of the president's soldiers. There were many parties held during that time, and she said the soldiers were dashing and glamorous to her. But they left when the Americans came in, so she married my grandfather.

"Aguinaldo's soldiers were good to our people," he continued. "They shared their food, and when they went out fishing in Palanan Bay

they returned with so many, their *bancas* were heavy in the water" —
he indicated a catch up to the gunwales. *"Everyone* would eat well that
night."

I asked him to place his town within a modern perspective.

"Sometimes we feel as if we are not a part of Isabela province, or
of the Philippines," he said. "We have only two ways out of Palanan:
by boat to Baler, which takes eighteen hours, or by private plane to
Cagayan, which is very expensive. Otherwise you must walk for one
week over very rough paths through the mountains." He shook his
head. "The Philippine government acknowledges our part in history, but not to the extent of providing roads, or doctors, or dentists,
or enough social programs, or any of those tangible things that might
connect us to the rest of the country."

Berto customarily fired up a gasoline generator on Saturday nights
to build up a charge in the bank of truck batteries he used for power
during the week. Thus, of every building in that darkened town, the
rectory was ablaze with lights just as long as the generator was on.
While we talked with Captain Salazar we would hear the sound of a
little motor, like a model plane's, and then a large palmetto bug would
zoom in from the dark palm trees lining the riverbank into our light,
sailing around the room and dashing itself against the walls in a mad
ecstasy before banging itself senseless and dropping to the floor. A
few minutes later we would hear the little motor rev up again as the
palmetto bug returned to consciousness and its frenetic pattern.

After the generator was turned off, the lights extinguished, and
we turned in for the night, four or five of the little motors could be
heard still careening from wall to wall — *eeeeeer-bam! eeeeeeer-bam!* We
dispatched them with our shoes, but sleep was still not to be had, for
squadrons of large Philippine roaches emerged to crawl across our
faces as we tried to get comfortable. This soon got to be pretty un-
nerving, and one would think that as tired as we were, we might have
lost our sense of humor. But as one after another we cursed and
grabbed a flashlight to look for the vermin in vain, a voice spoke out
of the darkness.

"There's one thing I can't figure out," said Erich.

"What?" we all asked.

"Which way are these roaches crawling — clockwise or counter-
clockwise?"

In the sixteenth century, Franciscan Fathers had worked their way
from the mouth of the Cagayan River and the tip of Cape Engano

south along the beach of the Contracosta until they discovered the level Palanan River floodplain and founded a mission dedicated to Santa Maria Magdalena. The friars began to convert the occupants of the area, but the remoteness of the mission and the many epidemics to which the clerics were prone made the place as undesirable to the priests as the missions in Casiguran and Baler had seemed to their brethren. The Augustinians took over the administration of the missions in the seventeenth century. One of their chroniclers, while admitting that the task was hard, still allowed himself a little boasting: "From the admission of that territory by our province to the year 1704, the multitude of infidels who were turned by the preaching of our brothers from the unhappy liberty of paganism to the mild yoke of the Catholic faith, was vast." Nonetheless, in 1704, like a hot potato, Palanan was tossed back into the Franciscans' laps.

As Captain Salazar had said, the remoteness of Palanan had not abated much through the centuries despite the invention of the telegraph, the short-wave radio, and the diesel engine. The telegraph was constantly out of order, and we learned on our second day in Palanan that the police radio was only a little more dependable. Wanting to let the outside world know that we had survived the hike, we prevailed upon the police chief to send a message to our friends in Manila. But the radio link was broken — somewhere between his colleagues on the cordillera's western slope and the central command in Manila — so we had to be content with Salazar's promise to try to get word to the capital by other channels. Whatever these were, none would succeed.

It was market day, and the ferryman was kept busy bringing people across the river to town. In droves they strolled through the streets, some men carrying roosters and others leading small Philippine ponies. A marketplace was set up in the center of town, but there was not an extensive selection of goods. Palanan is, even today, trying to recover from the effects of four typhoons that struck in 1980 and destroyed two separate plantings of crops. The people who live in town, or in the scattered settlements that dot the floodplain and follow the river into the hills, are still very poor. The goods they buy and sell are meager and cost little — there are no handicrafts of any sort — and the goods spread out on cloths in the street are identical to those at the little shops — one-pound packets of corn meal and rice, little cakes, cigarettes. I bought a piece of sugared bread and a bowl of cold noodles in chicken broth from a woman who crouched on the street. She implored me to buy everything else she had — "You are a big strong man, you need to eat *more*," she said. I declined, though I later sent my friends over with a recommendation for her cuisine.

While I had been at the police station waiting for the chief to raise an answer on his old short-wave, he had asked me about Dario. "I cannot believe that he is not Filipino," Salazar exclaimed. "Dario Gonzalez is a Filipino name, and there are many people named Gonzalez in this town. And another thing I cannot understand. Is Dario a Negro? No? But he has curly hair, like a Negro."

"There are many people in America who have curly hair but are not Negro," I replied. "European Jews, Italian Catholics, and Hispanic Americans, for instance. In fact, it's very popular to have one's hair curled artificially."

A patrolman had been standing in the doorway listening to this colloquy, but he abruptly disappeared, returning five minutes later with an Agta man he found somewhere. "You see," said the patrolman, affectionately grabbing a fistful of the Agta's locks, "just like Dario Gonzalez."

Eventually I strolled back to the rectory to see what Dario was up to. In the early morning he had decided that because the expedition part of his trip was over, there was little danger of our requiring any of the services he had been prepared to perform. From his backpack he could have set and splinted broken limbs, pulled or repaired smashed teeth, sewn up gashes, treated burns, replaced lost fluids, fought off diseases with antibiotics, lessened discomfort from injuries with sedatives, hypnotics, barbiturates, or opiates, and, he had assured me, any number of other mishaps he declined to name. There was no point in his carrying it back home again, so he had Berto, Villena, and the nearby shopkeepers announce to everyone they knew that the doctor would be available for consultation all of market day.

When I returned the clinic was bustling, with a line stretching out of the rectory to the street. No one I asked could remember the last time a doctor had been here. The town had relied on paramedic nurses, who sometimes were forced to treat problems beyond their knowledge.

As I arrived, Dario had just returned with the paramedics from visiting a patient in the church guest house. A man had been stabbed during a dispute several days before. "They sew over knife wounds here," said Dario in amazement, "which is the worst thing you can do — you form a pocket of infection that way." At the Bronx hospital where Dario works, he sees a depressing number of stab wounds. "I just opened the sutures, cleaned it out, put a drain in and a gauze bandage," he said. "Mostly what I've seen today are things that would be no big deal at home, but here — isolated, in the tropics — could cause problems, like infections, bad cuts, or abscesses. A lot of tooth problems. Usually what they do here is yank a tooth if it starts hurting. I must have had a dozen people come in today and ask me to pull teeth. But I couldn't bring myself to do it for cavities or little infections." He showed me an ugly pair of dental pliers. "Instead of this, I used some temporary filling material — it might last a couple of months if they're lucky — and I told them to try to see a dentist." He looked out the window at the mountains and snorted. "Fat chance. These people should have a full-time doctor, they *deserve* a full-time doctor."

After seeing what seemed to be most of the town, Dario pulled aside the paramedics and Berto. "You might as well keep this stuff," he said, handing over his tools. He divided the medicine and supplies into three piles: a handful of vials he later destroyed; a collection of bottles of medicine with which the nurses were familiar and that would be useful in their work; and some relatively sophisticated tools, which he instructed them to put away in a drawer. "If a doctor comes to town," he said, "let him know you have this stuff. Maybe he can find a use for it here."

Dario looked over at Berto — frail, coughing, staring dreamily as was his habit with a wistful smile — lighting another cigarette.

"Don't you know those are bad for you?" Dario demanded.

"I heard something about that somewhere."

"How old are you?"

"Forty-one."

"You might make forty-two."

I had asked Villena to help me by scouting up some of the old folks of Palanan. Late in the afternoon he introduced me to Anastacia M. Palogan, who by his own account was the oldest person in Palanan with his wits still about him. He was a thin reed of a man with a firm handshake, who looked at me with a direct gaze from very pale eyes.

Palogan was born on January 7, 1901. "My parents were in the mountains overlooking Palanan when I was born," he told me. "Some American soldiers had been seen coming toward the town, so General Aguinaldo ordered all the people to flee to the mountains with everything they owned. They had stayed up there for a long time before my mother gave birth." Dr. Santiago Barcelona had been a close friend of Palogan's father, he said, and treated the family when they were ill. Later, after the war was over, Barcelona had kept in touch with the Palogan family until he died. By then Palogan had become a schoolteacher; appointed by the Americans to the Palanan post in 1917, he later opened the first local school for Agta children, in the 1930s.

"Did anyone ever tell you stories about when the Americans came and captured Aguinaldo?" I asked.

"Oh yes," he said, "my parents were there," and taking me by the hand, Palogan led me out onto the grassy lawn between the rectory and the guest house, to that coconut palm–fringed bluff overlooking the Palanan River. Beyond was the dim cordillera.

As he told me the story, he gestured about the churchyard — and the concrete walls of the nearby buildings seemed to melt away, and with them the neat board houses, and it seemed as if I could see the grassy municipal square, and the houses bedecked for a birthday celebration, and the soldiers lined up in their blue uniforms and white hats where a basketball court would be built, and the Macabebes standing perpendicularly and ready for their treachery, and a large schoolhouse (topped with a flag) built on land that has since eroded into the river.

And when the Spaniard had raised his hat in signal and the Tagalog officer had screamed out his command and the scouts had fired their first volley, a seventeen-year-old cornet player named Benjamin Ligardo had begun running toward the schoolhouse, whether in panic or patriotism no one knew, and the Tagalog officer had ordered the Macabebes to shoot him, and he was wounded in the wrist, arm, leg, and then the other leg, and still he stumbled and reeled toward the schoolhouse until the officer stepped forward and fired his pistol point blank into the boy's face, shooting away his nose, but luckily the bullet had deflected along his cheekbone and thus did not kill him, and he finally sank to the ground. And then someone waved a white flag from the window and later they took away the president and his aides and the wounded boy, and nothing more was heard from Benjamin Ligardo until he returned to Palanan, a grown man, and lived to be very old before he died.

II

At six o'clock on the morning of March 28, 1901, Frederick Funston left the *Vicksburg* at its mooring in Manila Bay, taking the ship's steam launch for himself and his three prisoners. "We steamed into the mouth of the Pasig River and up through the city to the Malacañang Palace, the home of the division commander, where we went ashore," recalled Funston.

General MacArthur was just rising, and came out in a wrapper to meet me. He shook hands, looked at me in a quizzical way, but did not ask a question. I said, "Well, I have brought you Don Emilio." The general could scarcely believe it, and asked, "Where is he?" I replied, "Right in this house." As soon as he could dress the general came out and greeted cordially all of the three. We all sat down to breakfast, but Aguinaldo was not very talkative, being apparently somewhat overcome. But the general put him at his ease finally, and told him he would immediately send for his family, whom he had not seen for a long time. The general got off his official despatch, and then the news was made public. To say that the city was wild with excitement mildly expresses the condition.

The headlines burst upon the United States with the force of an artillery shell. By the spring of 1901, the American people had grown weary of that war with its murky beginning and no promise of an ending, and they instantly took the diminutive adventurer from Kansas to their hearts for granting them even a moment's respite.

AGUINALDO IS SURPRISED IN HIS MOUNTAIN
RETREAT AND TAKEN AFTER A LIVELY FIGHT
The Thrilling Story of
Funston's Daring Exploit
Ninety-mile March Through Rugged Moun-
tains — Little Party on the Verge of
Starvation When They Reached Insurgent
Camp
BLOW TO REBEL CAUSE
Insurgents Disheartened by Aguinaldo's
Capture — May End War in Philippines

The excited readers of the *San Francisco Chronicle*, having hurriedly digested these banner headlines that took fully half of the front page, read on to discover that "the Captor of Aguinaldo Has Been the Hero of Scores of Thrilling Incidents." On the other side of the continent, the editors of the *Baltimore Sun* were similarly enthusiastic and printed a long biography of "Funston, The Captor: A Life Full of Adventure Crowned At Last By Notable Feat." Meanwhile, in New York, the *Times* reported: KANSAS WILD WITH JOY. Business in the sleepy prairie town of Iola was suspended, according to the newspaper's informant, and he rode out to the proud parents' farm to tell them the news; Funston's father paused in his field to wipe the sweat from his brow before replying, "That is certainly gratifying." The hero's mother stood in her Kansas kitchen, her eyes growing dim, telling the reporter that "I never lost faith in Fred's lucky star." And across the state, proud jayhawkers took up the call "Funston for governor," a fitting reward for the farmboy turned war hero. The Kansas State Legislature issued a congratulatory proclamation. It was only the first of many similar government bodies to do so. Though no statement came out of the White House, the *Washington Evening Star* disclosed: PRESIDENT PLEASED AT THE CAPTURE OF AGUINALDO. On street corners and in taverns, in the corridors of power and the halls of state, debates ensued on what could be an adequate reward for such a heroic feat.

While most of the reactions to the expedition were positive, still, as with everything else Funston did, protests — even outraged objections — surfaced amid the tumult of praise.

"As a lover of liberty I deplore the capture of Aguinaldo," said the elderly abolitionist William Lloyd Garrison to the *Boston Herald*. "A brave patriot and lover of liberty hunted down by troops of a powerful nation, a professed champion of self-government, is a sad sight for the opening of the 20th Century." The deposed Populist senator Richard F. Pettigrew, on vacation in New York from his South Dakota home, buttonholed a *Times* reporter in the lobby of the Fifth Avenue Hotel and issued his statement: "The capture of George Washington would not have ended the American Revolution. Others would have been found to take his place . . . I consider our treatment of the Filipinos constitutes one of the blackest pages in American history. Aguinaldo was one of our allies and his people should have been given their independence when the Americans took possession of the islands."

From Hartford, Mark Twain would eventually dictate a sarcastic diatribe, "In Defense of General Funston," in which he took up the issue of Funston's begging for food and then capturing his benefactor. "It would be [clearly unfair] to blame him because his conscience leaked out through one of his pores when he was little," Twain said. Elsewhere, though William Jennings Bryan believed Funston's deed "may end the war for the present," he could derive no satisfaction. "We cannot administer an empire in the Orient and maintain a republic in America," he intoned. Meanwhile, in London, the *Saturday Review* proclaimed Funston guilty of a "gross act of treachery."

But America paid little heed. Garrison was probably senile, Pettigrew a crank, Twain good only so long as he kept to humor, Bryan a case of sour grapes, the Brits with their own dirty Boer laundry in South Africa. America needed a hero, and "Fightin' Fred Funston of Kansas" was the likeliest candidate — at least for the moment.

In Manila, Emilio Aguinaldo was kept in seclusion under heavy guard with only his family and Filipino Americanistas allowed to see him. Meanwhile, the question of his future had to be settled. Admiral Dewey suggested that he be shot — and some American journals echoed him. "It is impossible to forget even now that he directed the burning of Manila and the assassination of all Americans, without distinction of sex," argued the *Philadelphia Press.* "Any power but England and the United States would execute him in a few hours." The *New York Tribune* agreed, calling Aguinaldo "vain, deceitful, cruel, tyrannical." Less bloodthirsty observers such as the American-owned *Manila Times* put forward the idea of making him "become a passenger for Guam" unless he could be persuaded to "throw his influence in favor of American arms."

As it turned out, this is exactly what the vanquished and demoralized leader would do after the administration decided it could not shoot or deport him for fear of having a martyr on their hands. Twenty-three days after he was ushered into Malacañang Palace, after vigorous lobbying from his wife, his mother, his sisters, and a number of prominent *illustrados,* Emilio Aguinaldo issued his last wartime proclamation, on April 19, 1901. "The country has declared unmistakably in favor of peace; so be it," he wrote, though his gauging of Filipino sentiments had undeniably been limited by his confinement. "Enough of blood; enough of tears and desolation . . . by acknowledging and accepting the sovereignty of the United States throughout the entire Archipelago, as I do now, without any reservation whatsoever, I believe that I am serving thee, my beloved country. May happiness be thine!" He was released from house arrest, finally, on July 4, 1902.

For a while it seemed as if the bottom had dropped out of the Filipino camp. Within a few months Generals Tinio, Alejandrino, Sandico, Mascardo, and Baldomero Aguinaldo, among others, had turned over their commands to the Americans and sworn the required oath. But the swift ending was only an illusion, for resistance continued — with renewed savagery on both sides — in Batangas province on Luzon, on the island of Samar, and increasingly in the southernmost Islamic islands of Mindanao, Jolo, and Bohol. Theodore Roosevelt succeeded McKinley as president after his assassination in September 1901; he presided over the continuation of the war. An old cavalryman and Indian fighter named General Adna Chaffee had stepped into the shoes of Arthur MacArthur the previous July. Judge William Howard Taft took over the management of the archipelago as the first of seven civilian colonial governors. Roosevelt had prescribed "stern measures" in putting down the "Injuns" and "bandits" of the Philippines, an order he did not rescind after July 4, 1902, when he proclaimed the war officially "ended." Henceforth all revolutionists in the north and central islands were to be treated as common criminals; the "Moro problem" would continue to bedevil the American military for most of the century's first decade.

The events of March 1901 left their mark on many, not the least on those who were directly involved — all of whom lived out the rest of their lives in the shadow or the spotlight of Funston's capture of Aguinaldo. It is safe to say that none rose so high or sank so low as they had during that one month, the most important of all their lives.

The doctors Barcelona and Villa eventually returned to the practice of medicine after swearing the American loyalty oath. Barcelona died at the age of seventy-four, in 1937, after a quiet life. Not so Villa, who fled to Japan soon after his capture with an old war atrocity charge hanging over his head. A general amnesty in 1902 allowed him to return. He attempted to enter politics in Manila, but election irregularities and a tarnished reputation kept him from assuming municipal office. Villa was killed during the 1945 liberation of Manila while trying to save the life of a daughter.

Funston's counterfeit patriots — the Macabebe scouts, the Tagalog officers, and the Spaniard Lazaro Segovia — were all offered posts, if they wanted them, in the Philippine Constabulary or the Native Scouts regiment. Each was rewarded with cash — ranging from the $25 to $50 given to the Macabebes to $500 in gold granted the Spaniard. Cecilio Segismundo, whose cooperation as Aguinaldo's courier was so important, later tearfully complained to Burton Mitchell that he had been cheated out of his reward by his expedition companions, who then teased him by calling him Judas. The ends of these men are shrouded in obscurity except for that of Segovia, who died a violent but mysterious death at the age of thirty-two. According to William Carey Brown, onetime inspector of Funston's command, "Segovia's loyalty to the United States proved eventually to be his undoing. He was assassinated about 1910 by some of his old enemies." Brown provided no further details, even among his private papers and diaries, and though I searched for information in the National Archives and in Manila, it seems as if the exact circumstances shall remain an enigma. This is especially true since he apparently had so many "old enemies," having fought under three flags in as few years. I asked Teodoro Agoncillo about this "assassination" in 1910. It was news to him; the historian replied, "I knew nothing about the death of Segovia. If he had enemies, I am sure they came from the Filipino camp. A double-dyed man like him deserved his

fate. Rather unkind, but men of his cast usually end up dying ignominiously."

Of all the other warriors, only one more would die violently. Russell Hazzard was rewarded for his part in the capture, like the other
American volunteers, with a Silver Star and an appointment in the
regular army in addition to other military and state legislature awards.
As a first lieutenant of the First Cavalry, he imitated Funston's ruse
in August 1901, on the island of Mindoro, by capturing an American deserter, Arthur Howard, who had commanded a Filipino detachment. Disguised as a revolutionary soldier and with eight Macabebe scouts, Hazzard penetrated the enemy lines, located the deserter,
and spirited him away to American military justice. Though his supervisors recommended him for a Medal of Honor, he modestly (ill-
advisedly, some said) declined to let the application go through, saying that "a soldier should perform all duty asked of him without special recognition."

At the height of his military career, Russell Hazzard began to have
problems; they came to a head in 1908. While stationed with the
Seventh Infantry at Fort Wayne, Michigan, Hazzard was arrested after
forging a superior officer's check to pay for wedding expenses. The
scandal intensified when it was learned that he already had a wife
and two daughters in Oakland, California, which he had concealed
from his new wife. Hazzard's court-martial was halted by a telegram
from the War Department; the secretary had received information
that the defendant was mentally incompetent, a result of an illness
contracted in the Philippines (as it was later declared). Apparently
his problems had surfaced within a few years of the expedition but
had been kept under wraps until he could control his behavior no
longer. He was treated at the Presidio military hospital and retired
by an army hearing board.

Divorced from his first wife, Russell Hazzard moved to Boise with
his second, and for a number of years he worked as an engineer for
the state highway department. But his mental deterioration continued. In August 1921, when he was fifty-five, Hazzard disappeared
from his home in Twin Falls. He surfaced in Seattle and registered
at a hotel under an assumed name. Old friends who dined with him
there saw that he was acting irrationally and notified his wife. Her
reply wire warned that he was demented and that none of his checks
should be honored, but it was too late. Already Hazzard had cashed
checks in the amount of $124. These were returned from the bank,
and with police reports from Portland against him for other bad
checks, private detectives went to his room and extracted a promise
that he would make good on his debts in a few days, on September

3. On that date a detective found him in his room, a pistol clutched in his hand, a suicide. His body was shipped back to Twin Falls for burial.

As tragic as Russell Hazzard's life became, his younger brother had a military career and a life built on one success after another. After the capture, he was commissioned a second lieutenant in the regular army but soon thereafter was promoted one notch to equal his brother's rank. He came away from six years' duty in the Philippines with many awards, including three Silver Stars; he was on staff duty in San Francisco during and after the earthquake and fire; and he was a member of Pershing's Punitive Expedition into Mexico. During the First World War, Oliver served as a colonel with the Horse Cavalry in France and Germany — including the battles of St.-Mihiel and Meuse-Argonne — and emerged with citations and another Silver Star. He retired in 1931 after serving at diplomatic missions in Japan and China, and except for recommission during the Second World War in Washington, D.C., he lived the rest of his life in California. He died in 1960, at the age of eighty-three, and was buried in San Francisco after a military funeral at the Presidio. While his daughter and niece were closing up his apartment, they found among his mementos the Philippine nationalist flag that had flown over Aguinaldo's headquarters in Palanan. They arranged for the flag to be returned to its rightful place, and it is now on exhibit at the University of the Philippines, Quezon City.

In the years immediately after the capture, Harry Newton enjoyed great celebrity in his home state of Wisconsin, adding a ceremonial sword (from his home town of Superior) and a gold medal of honor (from the legislature) to his collection of awards, citations, and, of course, his commission in the regular army as a first lieutenant. "The capture of Aguinaldo dealt the rebellion a crushing blow," he told the *Superior Telegram* when given a hero's welcome in August 1901. "The grief of Aguinaldo who saw everything fading from him in a moment . . . was indeed touching. His tears were not the tears of a coward; but those of a man without hope." However, Newton told the reporter that he doubted Aguinaldo would keep his oath of loyalty. "The Malay does not consider an oath as sacred," he said. "He has broken faith before with others and may do it again with us."

After service in the Coast Artillery Corps at various domestic posts, including the span of the First World War, Newton retired with the rank of lieutenant colonel in 1920. He lived in Coronado, California, near San Diego, until his death in 1946, at the age of seventy-nine.

Burton Mitchell, a first cousin and aide-de-camp to Frederick Funston, was rewarded with a Silver Star and commissioned as first lieutenant in the aftermath of the capture. He remained on Funston's staff and in his shadow for the rest of his military career with the exception of a year at Fort Niagara, New York, during which time he married into a prominent old Niagara Falls family. Thereafter he spent an additional year as Funston's aide at Fort Leavenworth, Kansas, but resigned his commission in 1910 to purchase a building supply company in Niagara Falls. During the First World War, Mitchell was recommissioned for domestic duty, but with that one exception he devoted the remainder of his life to his business, becoming a pillar of that western New York community. He died in 1941, at the age of sixty-nine, only a few months, it was noted, after receiving several hundred dollars in government travel expenses he incurred during the Philippine-American War.

The names of the two chief actors of the drama — the captive and the captor — are linked for all time, and their lives have come to stand for the respective aspirations of their people at the century's turn: an embryo republic yearning at once for self-definition and approval from those it emulated, a difficult task; and a nation, opportunistic and perpetually adolescent, compensating for its self-perceived lack of stature.

Emilio Aguinaldo returned to Kawit, where he lived for the rest of his life, managing the family plantations and other holdings and growing relatively well off by prewar Philippine standards. Aguinaldo was active in efforts to set up rural development banks to offset the devastation of the war; also, he became a prominent spokesman for veterans' interests, being elected head of the Asociacion de los Veteranos de la Revolucion in 1915. The Philippine legislature awarded him a lifetime pension in 1920. For nearly fifty years Aguinaldo wore a black bow tie of mourning for the republic that was never recognized, and for most of that time he stayed out of politics, living as a revered revolutionary hero. But when the 1930s arrived, bringing the Philippines commonwealth status and new expectations for independence, he attempted to stage a political comeback in a presidential race against the charismatic mestizo Manuel Quezon, whom he thought to stand for a government "not of law but of men." His platform called for a shortening of the transition period Quezon had accepted. Aguinaldo suffered a decisive defeat, dissolved his party, and retired, though he still retained his old revolutionary eminence.

This was nearly destroyed during the Second World War. The aging soldier (in his seventies by then) fell prey to Japanese Pan-Asia propaganda along with a host of eminent Filipinos during the Japanese invasion and occupation. Though he later claimed he had been "helplessly misused" (which today sounds self-serving), Aguinaldo broadcast pleas for Douglas MacArthur to stop his resistance. MacArthur was withdrawn from Corregidor in favor of Australia within a month anyway, but Aguinaldo's statements that the Filipinos desired only peace and independence and that Japan had promised them this aroused enmity in Washington. The War Department promptly branded him a "sort of Filipino Quisling." But after the war, when the other collaborators had been pardoned and had entered the republic's government, the old man from Kawit was not prosecuted.

During the Independence Day parade of July 4, 1946, Aguinaldo carried the 1898 revolutionary flag that he had raised against the Spanish in Kawit. On that day he ceremoniously removed his black bow tie. As the years went on, he continued to preserve his military dignity with a starched white uniform and a high choker collar, his stiff demeanor enforced by his shock of white hair that stood up straight in the pompadour he had made famous in 1898.

Emilio Aguinaldo always attributed his longevity to a lack of vices — he did not drink, smoke, or gamble — and to exercise. At least into his early seventies he used a chest expander and swam in a small pool excavated beneath his house. When this became too much, he insisted on climbing the three flights of stairs to the tower of his house several times a day.

Apparently his regimen worked well for him. Aguinaldo outlived all the men — Roosevelt, Lodge, McKinley, Dewey, Otis, MacArthur — who had precipitated the war against the Philippines in 1899 and, perhaps more poignantly, all the men connected to his capture in 1901. After an attack of coronary thrombosis, he died on February 6, 1964, just short of his ninety-fifth birthday. He was interred at the rear of his home in Kawit in a white marble tomb, which is shaded by tamarind trees and overlooks the Marulas River and the olive salt beds beyond.

Five and a half months after Frederick Funston received his appointment as brigadier general of the regular army, he was stricken with chronic ulcerative appendicitis and removed from his post at San Isidro, Nueva Ecija, to the military hospital in Manila. He failed to improve after the operation. Surgeons petitioned for his transfer back to the States, warning that he was "suffering from a general debility following an operation for an appendicitis. General Funston's vitality has been decidedly depressed by long residence in a tropical climate with a resultant lack of recuperative power . . . a change of climate is necessary for the restoration of his health."

Funston arrived in San Francisco early in January 1902 and

underwent another abdominal operation. His recuperation was slow — during the next six months he would have a malarial remission and undergo a third operation to clean out a sinus in his appendectomy wound — but his peppery temperament was unaffected. Sick leave granted Funston many opportunities to bask in the limelight and speak his mind about the war situation, and as usual he spoke before he thought; his celebrity as Aguinaldo's captor was still with him, enhanced by his serialized magazine account of the capture that had appeared early the previous fall. Invitations for lectures and dinner speeches poured in, and he cheerfully granted interviews to all comers. "The Filipino doesn't love us a bit," he said in San Francisco. "He doesn't know what gratitude is. He has no sense of appreciation, and I believe he'd like us better if we dealt more severely with him." Heading east, he stopped to receive his home town's adulation before moving on to address dinner audiences in Chicago and in New York at the Lotos Club. In his latter speech he blamed his fellow citizens for dragging on the war through their lack of fortitude.

> All of those men who have fallen since December 1900 have been victims of a lot of misinformed and misguided people here in the United States. It is perfectly proper for us to have all sorts of opinions as to what we should do with the Philippines, but for heaven's sake let us keep them to ourselves until every square inch of that territory recognizes the sovereignty of the United States.

It had grown simple to talk so in the Philippines, but at home it had become a different matter; Funston might have been a moving target, but he was at least closer and prone to overreacting to criticism. Anti-imperialist newspaper editorials blasted him and he replied with characteristic overkill. To make things worse, at the same time a senatorial committee chaired by Henry Cabot Lodge began to hear testimony from a former captain of the Twentieth Kansas. It was not the sort of information Lodge — or Funston — wanted to hear: the captain charged his former commander with administering the water cure and ordering his men "to take no prisoners." Lodge hustled the witness away as soon as he could manage.

The criticism of the bantam general mounted. Newspaper editors called for Funston's court-martial, and he replied by suggesting they should be strung up to the nearest lamppost. Senators Carmack and, more infuriating to the general, George F. Hoar rose to scold him for his words and deeds. Funston's retorts culminated in a speech before the Colorado Society of Sons of the Revolution in Denver. "I have only sympathy for the senior Senator from Massachusetts, who is suffering from an overheated conscience," Funston said. He also expressed contempt for men who at the beginning of the war would have had the United States take everything from Spain but who were now "playing at peanut politics and gambling in the blood of their countrymen."

His malarial fever had returned two days earlier; friends wondered if he was delirious. Hardly — but what was his ideological twin in the White House thinking at that point? By any stretch of the imagination, could Funston be referring to Roosevelt as "playing at peanut politics and gambling in the blood" of his countrymen?

Directly after the news of Aguinaldo's capture had flashed across the continent, Roosevelt had written to the hero from his summer house at Oyster Bay: "This is no perfunctory or formal letter of congratulation. I take pride in this crowning exploit of a career filled with feats of cool courage, iron endurance and gallant daring, because you have added your name to the honor roll of American worthies." Roosevelt had drifted from his praise to speculate at length on whether the United States would soon have to pit itself against a major world power now that the Philippine war seemed to have reached its climax; there would be a need to develop "fighting material." "I am one of many millions who would look with confidence to what you would do," he wrote. "Incidentally, if that day is not too far distant I shall hope to be serving under or along side of you. I think I could raise at once a brigade of three or four such regiments as that I commanded before Santiago."

Many things had changed since that letter of gushing hero worship. Roosevelt's peroration had earlier been as colorful as Funston's, but the mantle of the presidency was now upon him. His administration's Philippine policy had come under increasing fire long before Funston returned home. Perhaps he also saw in Funston's barnstorming a reflection of his own intemperate self-promotion before he gained national office. There had been talk of a Roosevelt-Funston ticket in 1904 (prompting the anti-administration *Springfield Daily Republican* to worry about that "militaristic nightmare"). No, Funston had to be silenced; so Roosevelt ended their years of rhapsodic mutual admiration. He sent a letter to the secretary of war:

> The reference to the senior senator from Massachusetts is entirely improper in a general of the army. I think that General Funston will have to be requested not to make any more public speeches. I appreciate to the full his great services and I am in cordial sympathy with his general view on the Philippines, but he expresses himself at times in a way that is very unfortunate.

William Allen White hurried at the president's behest to caution his old chum, coming away from the meeting worrying about Funston's drinking habits. But even White's intercession was not enough, for Roosevelt had decided that only a public rebuke would take the heat off his policies and silence the general. Funston was ordered to grant no further interviews or accept any more banquet invitations. A letter of censure was inserted into his military record.

Funston returned to put his energy into his army duties and the controversy receded. He and Eda had by then begun a family — apparently Arthur MacArthur Funston was conceived upon his father's return from Palanan; the boy died before he was ten. The Funstons raised another son and two daughters, who grew up on a series of army posts. Funston gained back his hero's luster on April 16, 1906, while serving as head of the military department of California under Major General A. W. Greely, his divisional commander. The San Francisco earthquake reduced much of the city to rubble, setting numerous fires. General Greely happened to be away at the time, so Funston took command — using army troops to prevent looting, blasting buildings as firebreaks, organizing emergency stations for the wounded and shelter for the homeless, and setting food price ceilings to prevent profiteering. Eda Funston made herself useful by directing a nurses' corps. Greely hurried back to San Francisco, his mild protest at Funston's assumption of power lost in the general acclaim.

Postings followed in Cuba, the Philippines, Hawaii, and at the service school at Fort Leavenworth, Kansas. But promotion eluded him; he was repeatedly passed over in favor of less deserving officers. Funston had contended with the animosity of his fellow officers since he had become, at thirty-four, the youngest general in the army. Those desk commanders with experience in the Indian Wars or an education at West Point resisted the frequent calls for Funston's elevation with great bitterness. Also, Funston had never disguised his contempt for William Howard Taft, which effectively scotched his chances so long as the former circuit judge and Philippine governor was vice president or president, as he was until 1913. Moreover, there had been rumors throughout the army and the War Department regarding Funston's heavy drinking habits. Though he seemed to have become "practically a teetotaler" by 1912, as his commander wrote to the War Department, still, the reputation died hard.

With the 1914 American intervention in Mexico, Funston commanded the troops sent to occupy Vera Cruz. As military governor of that city, he surprised many by his diplomacy under adverse conditions. Finally, at the age of forty-nine, Funston was promoted to major general. He was put in command of the army's Southern Department in 1915, and a year later, when Pancho Villa's guerrillas attacked the town of Columbia, New Mexico, killing many Americans, Funston recommended that a force under Brigadier General John ("Black Jack") Pershing be sent into Mexico to apprehend Villa.

A new era was beginning. While the United States and Mexico seemed on the brink of war, marines were being landed in Santo Domingo, beginning a continuous eight-year occupation; the Great War had already been raging for eighteen months in Europe, and the furor over the sinking of the *Lusitania* was making the "peace candidacy" of the presidential incumbent, Woodrow Wilson, a contradiction in terms. It seemed as if Frederick Funston would be named commander of a European Expeditionary Force.

On February 19, 1917, Funston attended dinner with friends at a San Antonio hotel. The hotel orchestra began playing "The Blue Danube" as the party finished eating, and Funston, who had bent down to play with a friend's child, said of the waltz, "How beautiful it is." Immediately he collapsed — and died of heart failure within minutes.

Frederick Funston, who was fifty-one, left his wife, Eda, and three children. Services at the Presidio in his adopted city of San Francisco were marred by a driving rain, but, as observers noted, "the sun flashed out for a moment from a rift in the clouds as the great Presidio guns boomed out thirteen times, a last salute," and for two minutes after that signal, all activity in the city ceased.

III

Bersosa and the younger guides seemed eager to begin their return trip, so I walked over to Palanan's little branch outlet of the National Grain Authority to buy bulk rice for them. Paul came along for company.

The building stood in the center of town near the marketplace. People strolling by greeted us with friendly nods or the "Good morning, sir" that we had already become used to hearing. Some stared curiously at my T-shirt, which I had just finished washing and pounding on the rocks of the Palanan riverbank. It was the shirt in which I had begun the expedition, sailed across a moonlit Baler Bay, and camped for the first time on the Contracosta; the shirt upon which Frederick Funston's stern image was printed and which was now torn in places by jungle thorns and stained ineradicably with the red Philippine mud.

Paul and I went up to a counter set in a window of the small rice storehouse. Two or three men inside, lounging over the counter, heard my request for bags of rice. They instructed us to go around the building and enter from the other side.

"I'd like to buy some rice in bulk," I repeated once we had entered the room, which held a table, some chairs, and a few shelves.

"That's what we are here for," a young man said as one of his friends scurried into the room with extra chairs. "Sit down," he said. We sat down and I saw that courtesies were in order. Would we like a beer? The first dispatched a small boy for some bottles and packets of crackers while the second and third maneuvered a heavy lauan table into the center of the room and moved us and our chairs over. The beer arrived. Would we like some food? No? Well, did we mind if they ate? Plates of steaming rice appeared from somewhere.

"We need some privacy," said one. "We can't talk with all these people walking by," pointing to the counter window, and they jumped up to lower the shutter and close the outside door. "So we won't be interrupted," they explained. In the dimness Paul and I looked quizzically at each other, and I saw he was judging whether he would have to karate his way out of the house.

The first young man, Eddie, had once gone away to college. He told me he had heard why we were visiting their town. "You know," he said, "we don't much respect Aguinaldo in Palanan."

"Do you mean everyone or just the younger people who have been away to college?"

"Right. The younger people."

I asked him why.

"He betrayed the poor in the revolution against the Spanish," Eddie promptly replied.

"I see you have read some Constantino," I said.

"A little," he admitted.

Renato Constantino is a popular political scientist whose writings have reflected his worthwhile attempts at "intellectual decolonization," presenting what he calls "a fuller, more balanced picture of reality." In his quest to find "a usable past," which is the redefining and retelling of Philippine history to present a political view stressing the class struggle, Constantino produced, in 1975, *The Philippines: A Past Revisited*. The ideas in the book may be said to have influenced a good portion of the country's younger generation.

His writings present Andres Bonifacio, the founder of the Katipunan, as a symbol of the Philippine working class and Aguinaldo as a tool of the *illustrado* elite — and thus a betrayer of the non-Hispanicized, non-Westernized Filipino masses. There are elements of truth to absolutely any position regarding history, but in Constantino's eagerness to stretch his ideological model to fit the facts, he has left out parts of the story, emphasized others, and glossed over still others, which make his telling asymmetrical.

In one typical instance, Constantino briefly retells the story of Aguinaldo's odyssey through the northern Luzon mountains to Palanan, relying, as all historians have, upon the diaries of Villa and Barcelona. He chooses to present the journey as one of abject retreat, and of all the occurrences during those ten months, he cites only the four instances when the guerrillas were resting or relieving their fatigue and tension by imagining, as most soldiers do, how they would live after the war was over. Thus the odyssey is presented as a span of time in which the retreating general holds horse races, fantasizes about trips abroad and retirement *haciendas,* and gives fiestas. Not only is the maintenance of troop morale on four occasions used to paint the mountain wanderings as a lark and a betrayal of the peasant class, but Constantino ignores the dangers to which the men were exposed and the many expressions and demonstrations of revolutionary fervor — the raids and ambushes, the moves at linking with other guerrilla units, the attempts to give central command to a widely scattered army. Constantino may make good points for debate among those who have studied history with care, but he leaves himself open to the criticism: In the end, are history and truth served?

Constantino thinks so. When we talked in Manila, I told him that his name was on the lips of nearly every young person whom I had met and told of my project. Unfortunately, few had actually read his books, and most were under the impression that what he was presenting was a "new nationalist history" as opposed to a political scientist's tool for nationalists to *look* at history.

"Yes, there is a difference," he said, "and it's unfortunate that people get these wrong ideas, that they don't take the time to actually study either the historical record or what my theories are about it. In time, perhaps, a Philippine-oriented educational system will make such intellectual tools available to all."

I was aware of — and sympathetic to — Constantino's views on education; he writes elsewhere of "Filipinos who do not have a mastery of English because it is foreign, and who do not have a mastery of their native tongue because of the deliberate neglect of those responsible for the education of the citizens of the nation." The problem is intensified by the same regionalism, the same scores of regional dialects that are learned from the cradle, that bedeviled efforts to establish an independent republic at the turn of the century. With the partial illusions of modernity and cosmopolitanism, of universal literacy and scholastic attainment, Constantino's "educated nationalism" will reach Filipinos — like Eddie in the National Grain Authority office in Palanan — giving them a distorted picture of their nation's historical legacy.

"I see you have read some Constantino," I had said to Eddie in Palanan.

"A little."

"Tell me what you learned."

"Aguinaldo sold out to the Americans for twenty million dollars," he said.

"Wrong. You're confusing two things. In the pact of Biaknabato, the Spanish governor promised to pay eight hundred thousand pesos to the revolutionaries if they would stop. Aguinaldo got one third, spending part of it on weapons and losing the rest to a crooked American diplomat. Another third was stolen by some of the so-called revolutionaries who stayed in the Philippines. The rest was pocketed by the Spaniards. After the Spaniards surrendered Manila to the Americans, they eventually agreed to quit their claim on the islands for twenty million dollars. That was the Treaty of Paris."

"That is very interesting," said Eddie, but the answer was more complicated than his mistaken belief, to which he would continue to cling. He pointed to my shirt. "What do you think of Funston?"

"He was a cad," I said, "and he was a hero. Like all of us, he was a product of his times."

"I heard that Funston did not ever come to Palanan," said Eddie. "He stayed in Casiguran until the shooting was over — and then appeared to get all the credit."

"Also not true," I answered. "He was crossing the river just as the shooting broke out." I gestured in the direction of the river fording. But I was growing weary of discussing his historical fantasies in that darkened room. I pushed my chair back from the table abruptly enough to signal that it was time to transact business about some rice. A few minutes later Paul and I were outside in the light and air with the guides' food.

The shutter on the counter window banged open as we came around the building. "Come back anytime," called Eddie. "We enjoy intellectual discussions very much."

Bersosa and the other guides were waiting when we returned to the rectory. I handed the bags of rice to the old man, who placed them inside his battered cracker tin and closed the lid with a little tap. On this last day of our knowing him, he seemed to have forgotten all of his English words but one, and so replied with his all-purpose "yes" when I counted out his pay, his boat fare, added a bonus, and clapped him on the back in thanks.

We had no Agta words with which to thank Sulimon and Udeng and Benchan; they had been faithful to the old coot when he left us in his dust, but it was clear that the trek had been a great adventure for them, too. After I paid the three, my friends presented them with a few gifts: a Frisbee, a small penknife, some flashlights and batteries, all of which they kept, and the two torn and zipperless backpacks Sulimon and Udeng had used, which they later sold for ten pesos to a villager.

Waving, they padded down to the riverbank.

Later I went over to examine the historical marker that stands just outside the churchyard overlooking the Palanan River and the mountains beyond. The marker had been defiled. It stood beneath a flagless flagpole surrounded by a small, well-tended flower garden, a concrete block perhaps three feet high and two wide. A bronze tablet read:

Marker commemorating
THE LAST STAND
of the
FIRST PHILIPPINE REPUBLIC
under General Emilio Aguinaldo
and his subsequent capture in Palanan
by American General Frederick Funston
on March 23, 1901.
Erected on Independence Day
June 12, 1962
Palanan, Isabela

Below this plaque were the scars of bolts yanked out of the stone. The tablet that had been placed there was gone, and in its place someone had defaced the stone with an indecipherable scrawl of pink spray paint. Fifteen feet away was the edge of the bluff, and the people of Palanan say it is steadily falling into the river as the riverbed shifts. In a few more years the marker will fall also, for the villagers do not have the money or technology to save it. Maintenance of the marker has been assigned to an official in the provincial capital on the far side of the cordillera. It is general knowledge in the town that he pockets the yearly allotment and does nothing.

I had heard in Manila that the government was considering erecting a statue of Aguinaldo in Palanan. When I mentioned this to the lay priest, Berto, he could only shake his head in his wistful way and say, "Let them send medicine instead." Who could argue with him?

Standing in front of that stone marker, I thought about my other "interesting intellectual discussions" with people like Eddie, who are so eager to be different, to be as "radical" as they deem safe — which is to blame the United States for every one of their problems and concoct half-truths about their national beginnings while studiously avoiding any utterances against their own government. And I mused about how the possibly valuable "tools" handed down to them by intellectuals were like giving computers to perfectly competent adults — but without the instruction books that would make them usable. And I thought about something Constantino had once said: "Philippine history must be rewritten from the point of view of the Filipino." Unfortunately, I reflected, the scramble to elevate some in their pantheon of heroes and to minimize or discredit others comes precisely in an age when the Philippines, as do we all, needs as many heroes as it can get.

There is no historical marker to commemorate the other occurrence for which the town of Palanan is famous, for the Philippine government is not in the habit of placing them for such things.

Nearly four months before President Marcos imposed martial law on the Philippines, members of the communist New People's Army guided a ship under North Korean registry to anchorage off the northeastern Luzon coast — below Palanan and near the Diguyo River (where, ten years later, my companions and I would take one of our Agta guides as "hostage" for our last night on the beach). During the process of unloading the ship's cargo of automatic rifles, antitank guns, and other sophisticated weapons of Chinese manufacture, the ship, the M.S. *Karagakatan,* ran aground as the tides shifted. The rebels unloaded as much more of the cargo as they could before dawn, finally abandoning the ship and attempting to move the weapons to a cave in the mountainous interior before they might be discovered.

The ship was spotted. On July 9, 1972, Marcos ordered a full-scale military assault on the area. The infantry, backed by armed helicopters, fighter planes, and reconnaissance aircraft, attacked suspected NPA positions. In the ensuing battles, the rebels finally withdrew — but not before taking more than half of the hidden armament with them.

It is generally thought in the Philippines that this first major clash with the reestablished Maoist New People's Army was one of the last straws that precipitated the imposition of martial law in September 1972. Paradoxically, there are still many who suspect that the battle was a sham, that the guerrillas were not there at the time, and that "the boat was Imelda's," a Marcos manufacture to justify his taking full control of a country he would lose under the Constitution with the expiration of his current term.

One night in Manila I was driven around for several hours until I was thoroughly lost, then taken to a nondescript bar somewhere in the city. A folk singer was announcing a break as I took a seat with four men — one of whom had been among the crew of the *Karagakatan*, two who had helped unload the ship, and one who had known of the plans though he had not gone north. All four had served from three to five years in prison — they showed me the scars on their arms and calves from that time — but for offenses such as picketing, distributing leaflets, or organizing unions, like most of those arrested. None had been prosecuted for his part in the *Karagakatan* unloading or the battle that followed because no one in the government suspected their complicity.

They were talking with me solely to correct, they said, the historical record: the boat was emphatically *not* "Imelda's"; in fact, it had been purchased with funds donated personally by one of the Chinese Gang of Four, and its cargo was put aboard in a Chinese port. Though the Marcos government had claimed that it had recovered "most" of the weapons, the former crew member said this was nonsense, that they had abandoned half on the ship and rescued half of the remainder from the cave before the soldiers pushed them back. That was all, they said. The record should be corrected.

The folk singer returned to his chair and began to sing. In English, he performed "Blowing in the Wind" followed by "The Times They Are A-Changin'" and "Masters of War." Everyone in the bar knew the words; some mouthed them as he sang. The songs were as well done as I had heard them in coffee houses in Cambridge and Greenwich Village and Georgetown fourteen years before. I had been in college then, like the men I had just talked with, and though our experiences had taken us in vastly different directions since, we were bonded for a moment by the music. When the singer stopped playing, though, the gulf between us reappeared. The musician spoke into the microphone, asking, "Are we all friends here?" and twenty heads rose to look around the room to see who was present.

"We're all friends," called the man who had driven me to the bar. The singer launched into a Tagalog song of protest that has been banned. It likens the soul to a bird that someday will rise, free. The people joined in.

The men at the table grew maudlin and I saw they were drinking to become senseless. By the end of the song, one was crying softly while he fingered a small plastic figurine that commemorates prisoners of conscience. Another had passed out, his head down on his folded arms. A third ordered another round for us all.

I declined, saying I had to get up early the next day. The man who had driven me appeared and escorted me outside.

"Can you catch a jeepney back to your hotel?" he asked. "I look after them when they get like this."

Despite the reputation of northern Luzon as a hotbed, there is not much reason for insurrection among the citizens of Palanan. They are isolated but they partly cherish this, for their isolation keeps the problems of modern civilization out, and they admit there is a tradeoff: disenfranchisement for tranquillity and the survival of traditions. The tactic of the New People's Army, which operates in the mountains above Palanan, is simply to establish good will in the town. There is some recruitment among the populace but their main goal is educational.

In 1978 or 1979, this delicate balance was disturbed when the government placed a unit of the Philippine Constabulary, fresh from combat in Mindanao, in Palanan. Though they were what one might call "hard-ass," one soldier in particular was a troublemaker — lewd, obstreperous, drunk, and trigger-happy. Even his comrades were uncomfortable around him. They asked that he be transferred, a request that was ignored. So the soldiers took him out into the woods and shot him. Later they coerced the villagers to sign statements that the trooper had been killed by guerrillas. The NPA prided itself on its reputation in the district, and several rebels went to Palanan to let the civilians know that they wanted to pick no quarrels in the town. But two local policemen, I was told, decided to be "heroes" and tried to shoot it out with the guerrillas, Wild West style. The policemen were killed. There have been no further incidents, and the soldiers were withdrawn.

We had marched up that coast with no concrete thought about how we would leave Palanan, planning to improvise once we arrived. Now we looked at our options, not surprised to see how few there were.

We found the telegraph broken and the radio link interrupted. Someone told us that a pilot in the Cagayan Valley owned a four-seater prop plane of relatively antique vintage that he used to fly through the mountains to the coast, but he was said to be as unreliable as the weather. If we wanted to hire him, we were told, we must sit out in the shed on the town's grassy airstrip and hope the pilot's whim took him in our direction. We set up two-man shifts and waited around for most of one day, but before noon, clouds sailed down along the cordillera like a curtain and effectively closed us off.

I happened to be talking with Berto at the rectory when a gap opened in the clouds and the pilot sailed through. Paul came back to tell me that things looked bad for this option. The pilot was a swaggering, bellicose air pirate. He would have to make two or possibly four trips and wanted all of his exorbitant fee ahead of time — and he would not say when he would return. "When I feel like it — what's it to you?" he had apparently said and then flew away.

Not only his price but his terms were out of the question. I began to think drearily about the *banca* we were told would leave in a few days on the eighteen-hour trip on miserable seas for Baler — beyond which would be a ten-hour bus ride to Manila.

Just then my friends returned to the rectory, and we dejectedly ate plates of beans and rice.

Then came the sound of an engine.

Berto cocked his ears. "That sounds like an air force ten-seater," he said, prompting us to look at him with great surprise. "You'd better get down to the airstrip."

All six of us hobbled through the town as fast as we could, outstripped by excited children and teenagers. The entire central barangay turned out whenever a strange aircraft landed.

The plane passed over the town and continued north, but then it lazily turned around, having apparently determined that the airstrip was secure since it had drawn no fire.

After the silver prop plane landed the crowd pressed forward to greet its sole passenger — their mayor, who because he was bringing in medical supplies had convinced the air force to send him across the mountains in a plane. I had an instant rapport with Mayor Bernardo, and I am sorry we were not able to talk longer than the time it took for the pilot, an air force major, to finish his flight log and get out to stretch his legs. I went over and told him we were historians on an expedition — blah, blah, blah — and asked if we could hitch a ride with him. He thought that would be all right.

"Where are you going?" I asked.

"Cavite," he said.

It was a fitting end in many ways: leaving the town of Aguinaldo's last stand, to be dropped off just south of Manila in his home province, only miles from where he is buried.

We packed hastily — tearing clothing off a clothesline and stuffing it into our backpacks, which now looked more like old lumpy pillows than efficient trailblazers' aids. Berto said good-bye, as did Villena and a few neighbors we had gotten to know, and we six adventurers hobbled under our equipment for the last time on that coast. All of the townspeople waved and shouted as we disappeared inside the aircraft.

The pilot readied the aircraft to taxi down the grassy runway for takeoff. We sat weary and a little unbelieving that our good fortune was extracting us from the coast precisely when we were ready to go, with all bones — and our friendship — intact. Arthur Miller once said that "fear, like love, is difficult to explain after it has subsided, probably because it draws away the veils of illusion as it disappears." In time, therefore, it was likely that we would not be able to account for all our deeds or decisions. We had been confronted by both an alien culture and inhospitable terrain and had shared moments of strength and weakness. The two of us who were brothers — coming of age as we had in two different eras, the sixties with its mandate for social change and the seventies with its penchant for turning inward — had responded to our fears in ways akin to our time, and since our fears were even then beginning to subside, we could begin to relax with one another; fellowship was affirmed.

Outside the plane, the people stopped waving and simply stared at us — we were leaving, after all, and they were being left behind. We were squeezed shoulder to shoulder in that small plane with nothing to do with our hands and nothing to say to each other: Christopher, the photographer; Erich, the carpenter; Dario, the doctor; Paul, the engineer; Bill, the cabinetmaker; and me, the chronicler. The aircraft began to bump down the strip.

Aloft, we circled over Palanan Bay, where the *Vicksburg* had awaited Funston's party, where Aguinaldo had first raised his hand in salute to the Stars and Stripes. Banking over the ocean, the pilot took us down along that beach of toil, the old Contracosta, across great tumbled masses of boulders, and rivers and streams, and intervening cliffs, and large stretches of jungle, and occasional hunters' huts above the high-water mark. The waves broke far below on the coral reefs marching in tandem with the strand. At last the major put his plane on automatic pilot and picked up a comic book. The clouds closed in below us and the coast disappeared.

EPILOGUE

Three days after I bundled up a clean typescript of this book and sent it off to my editor in Boston, my wife and I drove up to Middlebury, in the Green Mountains of Vermont, to attend the fifty-eighth annual Bread Loaf Writers' Conference. For us the summer had been blurred by my labors to finish the book before going on vacation. We looked forward to allowing the subject that had dominated our lives for four years to slide off center stage for at least a fortnight while we enjoyed the conviviality of old and new friends and the relentless, exhausting pace of daily lectures, readings, classroom discussions, and nightly bacchanals.

Only a week later, the insularity of the conference — where television and radio are banned and newspapers lie unread — was shattered. I finished a student's manuscript conference and headed over to the faculty lounge cottage with not much on my mind but admiration of the mountains that overlook the sprawling Victorian settlement that is Bread Loaf. I heard a car door slam and turned to see a friend hurrying toward me.

"Did you hear?" he blurted. "They killed Benigno Aquino in Manila yesterday."

There was little I could say when colleagues asked me, "What does it all mean?" Even in the months following the assassination it was difficult to pinpoint what "it all" would mean to the Marcos dictatorship, to the Philippine people, and to relations between our two nations, for there were just too many variables.

"You can't talk to a single Filipino, except one connected with Marcos, who will tell you the country is in good shape," said Benigno Aquino, the former senator from Tarlac province, to a Washington journalist shortly before leaving his self-imposed exile in the United States to return to the Philippines. It seemed an understatement. The budgets of all government departments had been slashed by 18 percent in January 1983 in response to pressure from international lenders to reduce deficits if more loans were to be forthcoming. Like a terminally ill patient, wasting away and beyond human intervention, the deficits continued to mount: President Marcos had overspent by $1.14 billion in 1982, but controls failed to make a difference, for a total of some $1.3 billion more than the treasury held would dissipate by the end of the third quarter of 1983. Two separate devaluations of the peso — 7 percent in June, 21 percent in October — did little to lighten economists' gloom; one predicted that the inflation rate might rise from the 1983 level of 14 percent to "the mid-twenties" in 1984. A bad drought in the summer of 1983, coupled with a vicious cycle of late summer typhoons, destroyed nearly half of the nation's sugar crop and devastated already low food supplies. As hunger spread, thousands flocked from the rural areas into the teeming shantytowns blighting the major cities. A growing number of strikes showed that those Filipinos with jobs were also hurting. They could not have avoided hearing that unemployment forecasts for 1984 threatened a catastrophe.

Even starving people can yearn for liberty — and the events preceding Aquino's decision to return home signaled that matters had changed little after the announced cessation of martial law in 1981. A thousand secret marshals assigned to ride jeepneys throughout Manila in the fall of 1982 were equipped with machine pistols and instructed to "fight street crime," which they proceeded to do like vigilantes. In their first week they captured only six for trial but killed forty-one before their guilt or innocence could be determined by the courts. The government closed the newspaper We Forum that December and arrested its publisher and a number of its writers and columnists on charges of subversion and conspiracy to overthrow the government. In May 1983, the Associated Press reported the existence of a secret decree, in force since the "end" of martial law, that provided the death penalty for anyone publishing articles criticizing the government. The president admitted the law was in place; three months later it was withdrawn. There was no substantive comment to the opposition's charge that Marcos had issued a thousand secret decrees in the past decade and that any number of others yet undiscovered might duplicate the draconian penalties of the one re-

moved. At about the same time — August 1983 — the president re-
scinded the dreaded Presidential Commitment Orders (which put
unrestrained police powers in Marcos's hands), but instituted something called Preventive Detention Actions in their place. These dif-
fered little from the earlier laws, since they in effect authorized in-
definite imprisonment for all acts and the advocacy of "insurrection,
subversion, rebellion, conspiracy."

Internal strife in areas outside the capital continued. The Muslim
separatist movement in the southern islands picked up renewed energy, and the army and paramilitary groups responded to ambushes
and other small-scale military actions by pressing the populace; strategic hamleting, the widespread displacement of peasants that had
been official policy for years, grew. In the far north, in Kalinga-Apayo
province, the long-term project to construct a series of dams threatened to displace more than a hundred thousand farmers from ancestral rice terraces and burial grounds. These peasants, growing more
desperate as the dreaded date approached, defected to the ranks of
NPA guerrillas in large numbers.

Though Aquino knew the moderate opposition needed a figure of
his stature to rally around (they had told him so by sending a delegation in the spring to request his return), he decided to face an uncertain future in the Philippines with relatively benign goals. "The
tragedy of tragedies," he said, "is that only Marcos can bring us back
to democracy." He believed that Marcos alone could decree an honest election, and with two scheduled, for 1984 and 1987, he thought
to form a partnership to encourage a relaxation of the president's
iron rule so that the opposition parties would have a fair chance.
"Imagine," Aquino said, "Mr. Marcos could be the only leader to take
his people's liberties and give them back. If he does that, posterity
may even forgive some of his mistakes." Aquino had known Marcos
for a long time, and his friendship with the First Lady had probably
saved his life in the past. But even Aquino's closest friends worried
that perhaps he was too optimistic about his bitterest rival. Marcos
had, after all, eliminated Aquino as a potential presidential candidate in 1972 by accusing him of murder, subversion, and illegal possession of firearms; Marcos had condemned him to Fort Bonifacio
under a death sentence.

Aquino's imprisonment had lasted eight years before his deterio-
rating health allowed him a reprieve for a triple-bypass heart operation in the United States. Ironically, though it was the question of
his own illness that gave Aquino three years of freedom, it was a worry
about the health of his tormentor that provided Aquino with the final impetus for his return. Marcos was reputed to be seriously ill.

Under the pretext of withdrawing from the public eye for three weeks "to write two books," the president was scheduled for critical surgery in August 1983, according to Aquino's private sources within Malacañang Palace. (This was never verified by government spokesmen, who consistently maintained that Marcos was in robust health despite his obvious growing appearance of frailty.)

Aquino planned his return like the skillful politician he was, arranging to fly into Manila with false papers on a Sunday to ensure that thousands could witness his return. If he had lived to deliver his speech under the hot sun at the airport, he would have told the twenty thousand supporters waiting for him that "I have returned of my free will to join the ranks of those struggling to restore our rights and freedoms through nonviolence. I seek no confrontation. . . . I feel it is my duty, as it is the duty of every Filipino, to suffer with his people especially in time of crisis." But Aquino would not be given the few minutes it would have taken to deliver the speech. Like thousands of his fellow citizens, none of them with his social standing or wealth, he was silenced. It is very likely that a part of Benigno Aquino knew he was going to his death and accepted it, knowing that perhaps only a martyr could make a difference.

A few days after the murder, government-controlled television stations began the saturation broadcasting of a bizarre "documentary" around the Philippines, purporting to reenact Aquino's death. For verisimilitude, the filmmakers spliced in footage taken by news photographers inside the China Airlines jet, showing Aquino as he smilingly threaded his way through friends and reporters in the aisle and left the plane accompanied by security guards. From this point the film turned into a clumsy propaganda vehicle, with suspenseful music added to the soundtrack. An actor dressed in white clothes resembling Aquino's descended onto the runway to be welcomed by more security guards. Suddenly, a lone figure darted from under the plane's fuselage and shot the Aquino character with an automatic, and was just as quickly mowed down by shocked guards. The music swelled to a finish.

Such a bald attempt to imprint an image of the government's version of events upon the public may have been the most sinister perversion of television news we have yet witnessed. But it converted very few from the common belief that the alleged assassin, a petty thug by the name of Rolando Galman, had been set up to shift the blame away from the government. Among other early objections, Galman was shorter than the victim — and an autopsy showed the bullet path in Aquino's skull to be downward, as if fired from above; also, a Japanese journalist claimed to have viewed the assassination from a porthole of the China Airlines jet, and he went into hiding soon after stating that Aquino had been murdered by one of the guards who escorted him off the plane. Early in 1984, a book by two California writers, *The Aquino Assassination,* thoroughly examined still and motion pictures, witnesses' testimony, and audiotape recordings of the seconds preceding the murder; it argues convincingly that the senator *was* killed by the military escort.

Whether the orders came directly from the president or from an associate mattered little to the hundreds of thousands of Filipinos who took to the streets in the widest protests in the country's history. After a commission of inquiry made up of Marcos stalwarts was replaced by a body only slightly more independent, civilian witnesses risked the focused ire of the military and surfaced to dispute the government's claim of innocence. It seemed, after the New Year, that sooner or later other scapegoats would materialize to interrupt the line stretching from the bloodstained tarmac at Manila International Airport to the chamber of power at Malacañang — if not low-level soldiers, then perhaps an expendable officer or cabinet minister. Marcos had hardly waited for the dead man to be identified before branding him a communist hit man, though few were persuaded since the communists, even in their disagreement with many of Aquino's positions, viewed him as a tactical ally. It seemed likely that this original motive for removing the moderate opposition's strongest alternative to the president would be replaced by a new one: the purifying right-wing fanaticism of the new scapegoats.

"Marcos will negotiate," Aquino once told an interviewer, "only out of fear." It was the unlikely sight of the financial district of Makati — the Wall Street of the Philippines — awash with suit-and-tie protesters that drove Marcos to allow a trickle-down of concessions, especially after President Reagan canceled a state visit set for November 1983. He authorized a 19 percent wage increase, bringing the minimum daily pay to $2.88, and he released thirty-seven of some eight or nine hundred political prisoners. But he refused to go much farther. "I warn the opposition," he said; "do not force my hand. Do not compel me to move into the extreme measures that you know of. If necessary, I will do so." The editors and publisher of the *Philippine Times* discovered this was no bluff when they were arrested for suggesting that the military was involved in the Aquino killing. Comfortable and well-to-do citizens aroused from years of fear or simple complacency by the death of Aquino got used to the novelty of public protest rather quickly and were not discernibly cowed by Marcos's promise to "hunt them down" for their daily demonstrations. (How-

ever, there still remained "the inner circle" of wealthy families rallying around the First Couple.) Marcos told television viewers that
the police had taken photographs and videotapes of businessmen "in
coats and ties" participating in street demonstrations. He promised
to deal with them "even if it takes one year." He answered the petitions and press conferences of prominent businessmen calling for some
rather basic guarantees of freedom and a token loosening of his grip
by warning that he possessed dossiers on those involved in white-col-
lar crimes like tax evasion and currency smuggling. Thirty-three ex-
ecutives were taken into custody in November, with more arrests
promised for later.

If not everyone agreed with Benigno Aquino's intuition that only
Marcos could save the country, at least most fretted about the question of succession. Indeed, the steadfast struggle to get the president
to indicate that the country might have a future after his death or
incapacity took on an enlarged significance.

The office of vice president and the line of succession were abol-
ished when Marcos declared martial law in 1972. It was not for another decade that anything else was heard of this matter, though the
president and the First Lady periodically denied that Madame Marcos was being groomed for the job. Creating a ten-member Executive Committee in 1982 to take over if he died or was disabled fueled
these rumors because Imelda Marcos was its preeminent member; it
seemed plausible that compliant committee members would make way
for a second Marcos on the throne, though the president began hint-
ing that Prime Minister Cesar Virata would be his most likely successor. This possibility pleased international bankers, since Virata, also
the nation's finance minister, was well respected among the various
noteholders.

The Aquino murder made the succession issue more urgent. Opposition members of the Marcos-dominated National Assembly called
for a revival of the vice presidency. "We are too deeply concerned
with too many problems," the president replied, "to be changing the
concept of government right now." But within a month, after announcing that the revival of the succession issue was "part of a conspiracy," he allowed the leaders of his New Society party to vote to
restore the office in time for the next national election, in 1987, the
fifteenth anniversary of martial law. In the interim, their plan called
for Speaker of the Assembly Querube Makalintal, a former chief justice and a Marcos loyalist, to be named as acting chief executive if
Marcos died, pending a new election within two months. Almost at
the same time Madame Marcos announced that she intended to step
down from a number of elected and appointed positions, including

her assembly seat and her posts as mayor of Metropolitan Manila and minister of human settlements. Furthermore, she resigned from the Executive Committee, claiming to have no plans to seek the presidency. After but one month's retirement, however, she was flying to China on an official diplomatic mission and being mentioned as a possible successor to Foreign Minister Carlos Romulo, who had resigned pleading ill health. Imelda Marcos had threatened to return to private life many times in the past; observers saw no reason to doubt that her ambitions were unabated.

What is often missed in the United States is the First Lady's role within the national power structure. During the time I spent in Manila, in 1982, the common view held that behind the government's seamless façade lay several struggling factions. One, the president's, was built upon his loyal and pervasive Ilocano roots and the New Society party structure he had created. Another, the First Lady's, represented the industrial and agricultural barons without whose finances the Marcos star would have dimmed long ago. A third was controlled by the Harvard-educated defense minister, Juan Ponce Enrile, whose ambition and control of the military had put him into a balance of power with the First Couple. But Enrile, once a threat, became one no longer after Madame Marcos forged a coalition with the army chief of staff, General Fabian Ver, who was viewed by the time of Aquino's assassination as a man with powerful ambitions himself. Their new rival seemed to be the hard-liner General Fidel Ramos. A scenario for the future — one with which Aquino was familiar — predicts that if the president should die or be disabled, Imelda Marcos would provide a rallying point that would prevent various factions from dividing and falling. But ultimately, and especially if the Filipino people continued to be "difficult," she might be used by the generals as a scapegoat for all of the ills besetting Philippine society. She would be ousted and the military would then take over — a situation not unlike that in Argentina after Perón.

Throughout his three-year exile, Benigno Aquino worked to influence American policy toward the Philippines, feeling that the moderate opposition's only chance would be if the United States "adopted" them. There had been positive indications of this trend during the Carter administration, with its erratically applied doctrine of human rights; indeed, Aquino often said that he owed his life and the circumstances of his reprieve to pressure applied by the U.S. State Department on his behalf. But after 1981 and the ascendance of the Reagan doctrine, the opposition began to lose hope. However, there is some evidence that career State Department experts, along with senior intelligence analysts, will continue to press for recognition of those oppositionists who, like Aquino, remain friendly to American interests and the multinationals even in the face of Washington's support of Marcos. (It has been suggested that Aquino was killed precisely because he looked so attractive to the State Department and CIA.) In the end, exiles such as Heherson Alvarez and Raul Manglapus might be viewed by these experts as people to back should the Philippine situation change. In Manila, the three major moderate oppositionists, all former senators, present not insurmountable problems. Lorenzo Tanada, while seen as too old, carries weight with other moderates. José Diokno is greatly respected (especially among the students and labor unions) for his courage and honesty, but he has a relatively weak power base and his quite vocal opposition to American bases in the Philippines might lose the support of not only Washington but of business interests in Manila and elsewhere; Diokno, though, is at heart as much a realist as he is an idealist. Salvador Laurel recently awoke from a prolonged benign period to resign angrily from the Marcos-dominated National Assembly, and perhaps, as a born-again oppositionist, he is intent on capturing the banner of the major moderate rival now that Aquino is gone. Laurel, who was arrested briefly in February as he was leaving on an American speaking tour, has yet to prove his mettle. The murder brought together disparate moderate groups that unfortunately have had a tendency toward splintering; it remains to be seen whether the unification will hold.

I hope someone emerges soon. The country seems poised on the brink of chaos. Within a month of Aquino's assassination, foreign human rights groups again visited the Philippines. The Lawyers Committee for International Human Rights in New York reported that their delegation heard testimony of a pattern of beatings, torture, and routine harassment of civilians and anyone working with slumdwellers or rural peasants. These findings were seconded by a joint survey team representing three American medical associations. "There has been a continuing pattern," they reported after interviewing in rural and urban areas and in military detention camps all over the country, "of gross violations of really very basic human rights, much of it induced by agents of the state." Along with Amnesty International, groups such as Americas Watch, Helsinki Watch, the International Red Cross, and the International Commission of Jurists have continued to deplore the government's crimes against its own people. If the political situation deteriorates further, the suffering is bound to increase.

Jaime Cardinal Sin, the archbishop of Manila, has called for a return to the original Constitution of 1935 and open, free elections. It is a transformation that the slain senator from Tarlac had hoped his presence in the Philippines would begin. Though there have been a few anti-American demonstrations outside the embassy in Manila, and though some anti-Marcos groups there and in the United States have called for the complete and utter withdrawal of American dollars and influence, it seems evident that a majority of Filipinos would welcome assistance — *positive* assistance — from the United States. Ours has been a constant and ubiquitous presence in that nation for more than eighty years: ours, rightly or wrongly, was their first common language, and it was an American-inspired curriculum, however ill suited to the Filipinos, that educated generations of Philippine students. Our cultural and spiritual ties are deep, as they always are with former colonies; and there is the matter of the eighty-six-year-old blood compact that has grown out of shared conflicts: a revolution against Spain, a colonial war, a mutual struggle against the invaders from across the Pacific.

Benigno Aquino offered a prescription in the months before he was murdered that, though not original, deserves to be repeated often and in a context encompassing not only the Philippines but the whole world. "It is my contention that where Americans have no leverage, it is foolish to intervene," he said, and he gave as an example the situation with the Russian invasion of Afghanistan in 1980. "But," Aquino continued, "when America *has* leverage and does not use it to further democracy, then I say America is as guilty as the dictator."

Aquino struggled, as he viewed the countries' mutual involvement, with the thorny issue of American bases in the Philippines. While still in prison in 1978, he told one reporter that the United States should be allowed to retain their use if they compensated the Philippines reasonably. By 1983, with a new multimillion-dollar treaty all but completed, he seemed to have changed his mind, saying that sooner or later, America would have to go.

The naval station at Subig Bay, which shelters the ships of the Seventh Fleet when they are not patrolling the Pacific all the way to the Persian Gulf, is the largest American naval base outside the United States. (It also seems to be the main storage facility for nuclear weapons in Asia, which makes many Filipinos nervous that they would be a target in event of a war between the superpowers.) Clark Field, the home of the Thirteenth Tactical Wing, is the largest U.S. Air Force installation in Asia. In the middle of 1983 a $900 million pact was concluded, renewing what is called the American lease on the bases. Though the nation needs money, the agreement is a disservice to the Filipino people. American forces would be guaranteed, in effect, to support the Marcos government against insurrection. It allows short-

and medium-range nuclear missiles in the country, increasing the likelihood of peril to the Filipinos if America went to war. It provides for the Philippines to be drawn into military operations involving the interests of SEATO nations like Australia, New Zealand, Great Britain, France, Pakistan, Northern Ireland, Thailand, and the United States. (Some critics, though, might welcome the departure of Marcos's overlarge national force from villages and hamlets to elsewhere.) The payment for the lease, which is contingent upon congressional appropriations, calls for some $300 million in foreign military sales credits (in effect, loans repayable within thirty years); $125 million would take the form of outright military assistance and $475 million would be used for economic and social aid — which critics such as José Diokno say will be used principally in the areas around the bases, including the rest and recreation cities of Angeles and Olongapo, and not for roads, schools, or power but to improve the camp towns and their hotels and nightclubs. When some American congressmen protested the terms of the agreement and the reaffirmation of Washington's support of Marcos's policies, the president had a swift retort. "If you feel that [the burden of commitment] is too heavy for you, just let us know," Marcos said. "Pull out and we will know how to take care of ourselves. We would have to enter some kind of modus vivendi with the Soviet power, which would mean that all of Southeast Asia, perhaps all of Asia, would be under the control of the Soviet Union." No one took his threat seriously, though Washington is not unmindful that, as in 1898, several countries have their eyes on the strategic placement of the Philippines.

Some analysts claim the bases could never be moved without sacrificing "vital American interests"; others admit that stations in Australia, Singapore, Guam, Tinian Island in the Marianas, Thailand, and Diego Garcia could be strengthened to offset the loss. But is this advisable in view of the long Philippine-American connection? So many years of support for the Marcos government have diminished the luster of "the great North American nation" (in poor Aguinaldo's words, back before our true mission was revealed). Perhaps, however, the light has not gone out completely and there is still a possibility for the kind of equitable partnership (with rulers like Marcos gone) that now exists only in dreams.

Two quotations spring to mind, and coming as they do from opposite ends of the Philippine-American involvement, they seem particularly appropriate.

The first comes from the old abolitionist and anti-imperialist United States senator from Massachusetts, George F. Hoar. The words were spoken heatedly, in the disappointment of defeat, for the senator saw tragedy brewing even in 1903, when the archipelago was firmly within the American sphere, and he lambasted the victorious expansionists.

> You chose war instead of peace. You chose force instead of concilia-tion . . . talked of the wealth of the Philippine Islands and about the advantage to our trade . . . declared in the Senate Chamber and on the hustings that the flag should never be hauled down. . . .
>
> You, my imperialistic friends, have had your ideals and sentimen-talities. One is that the flag shall never be hauled down where it has once floated. Another is that you will not talk or reason with a people with arms in their hand. Another is that sovereignty over an unwilling people may be bought with gold. And another is that sovereignty may be got by force of arms. . . .
>
> What has been the practical statesmanship which comes from your ideals and sentimentalities? You have wasted six hundred millions of treasure. You have sacrificed nearly ten thousand American lives, the flower of our youth. You have devastated provinces. You have slain uncounted thousands of the people you desire to benefit. You have established reconcentration camps. Your generals are coming home from their harvest, bringing their sheaves with them, in the shape of other thousands of sick and wounded and insane. . . .
>
> Your practical statesmanship has succeeded in converting a [grate-ful] people . . . into sullen and irreconcilable enemies, possessed of a hatred which centuries cannot eradicate. . . .

And then there are the words of Benigno Aquino, whose grand-father fought in the Revolution and against "the great North Amer-ican nation," whose father fought the Japanese in the Second World War, and whose words shall end this:

"All I'm asking from you is, if you must interfere, interfere for good, not evil. Help us bring back freedom of the press. Help us bring back free elections. That is *your* ethos. That is *your* tradition. That is *your* belief. Now what's so hard about that?"

Indeed.

New York
April 1984

ACKNOWLEDGMENTS

First of all, I should like to thank Mary Smyth Duffy, my wife, for her patience and good editorial advice, her forbearance during the six difficult weeks I was in the Philippines, and her acceptance of the financial stringencies during this four-year project. Without her strength and humor this book would not have come about. Special thanks are also due to our respective parents, David Bain (1915–1984) and Rosemary Bain and Jack and Kaye Duffy, for their encouragement, and likewise to Terry and Lisa Bain and Sarah and John Duffy.

Christopher Bain, my brother and colleague, showed great enthusiasm when I first broached the idea of a joint expedition to the Philippines' northeastern coast. His resourcefulness in seeing to the many details of our advance preparations and his steadiness once we arrived in the country ensured our success. My debt to him is enormous. Thanks also to Dario Gonzalez, Erich Vogt, William Allen, and Paul Kirtland, for their strength and courage during our coastal adventures, and to I. Herbert Gordon, for his counsel.

Ron Powers, Tim O'Brien, Michael Arlen, Mally Cox-Chapman, Steven Bauer, and Bob Reiss read the manuscript at various stages and offered valuable criticism; whatever defects remaining are my sole responsibility. I am grateful to Paul Mariani and Robert Pack for their enthusiasm, likewise to Stanley Bates, Carol Knauss, the late John Gardner, and to friends and colleagues at four sessions of the Bread Loaf Writers' Conference of Middlebury College. My resourceful agent and friend, Ellen Levine, will always have my thanks, as will my splendid editor, Gerard Van der Leun, my copy editor,

Luise M. Erdmann, and publishers, Nan A. Talese and Austin Olney. Special acknowledgments are due to the following friends for moral support and advice: Randall Warner, John Russell, Anita McClellan, Wyndham Anderson, Dr. Norman Moyes, Robert Houston, Penny Allen, Shere Hite, Robert Watts, Melissa White, Robert Brodsky, Antoinette Treadway, Donald Moser, Bernardo Lopez, Mark Ingebretsen, Wendy Lowe, Dr. James Cox-Chapman, John Silva, Joseph Esposito, John Grafton, Howard and Diana Kohn, Richard Fernandez, Eric Levin, Heherson Alvarez and Cecile Guidote-Alvarez, Bev Chapman, and Michael Schneider.

Thanks to the Lebensburger Foundation and the New York State Council on the Arts/PEN-NY Center, for material support.

I am grateful to the staffs of the following institutions: the Old Army and Navy Branch, National Archives and Records Service; the Library of Congress; the research libraries of the New York Public Library, the Boston Public Library, and the Brooklyn Public Library; the Kansas State Historical Society and its Frederick Funston Collection; the Western Historical Collections of the University of Colorado, Boulder; the U.S. Army Military History Research Collection at Carlisle Barracks, Carlisle, Pa.; and to the university libraries at Columbia, Harvard, Princeton, and Boston. Thanks in particular to Walter Hazzard Twiss and Dorothy Hazzard Ignatieff for information on the Hazzard brothers; to Paul H. Gaboriault, director of the Superior (Wis.) Public Library, for tracking down information on Harry Newton; to Virginia M. Howard, Youngstown, New York, and Donald E. Loker of the Earl W. Brydges Public Library, Niagara Falls, New York, for shedding light on Burton Mitchell. Thanks also to Grove Koger, Boise Public Library; Janet Bonneville-McGhee, Tacoma Public Library; Frank L. Green, Washington State Historical Society; Margaret L. Shields, Lewis County (Wash.) Historical Society; Jean Treloggen Peterson, Department of Human Development and Family Ecology, University of Illinois at Urbana-Champaign; Dr. J. E. Spencer, Department of Geography, UCLA; Dr. Frederick Wernstedt, Department of Geography, The Pennsylvania State University; Thomas C. Headland, Summer Institute of Linguistics, Bagabag, Philippines; Dr. Daniel Boone Schirmer, Cambridge, Mass.; and Mary Riggs Dawson.

In the Philippines, I should like to express my gratitude to the following: Carlos P. Romulo, Dr. Teodoro A. Agoncillo, Dr. Renato Constantino, Dr. Serafin Quiason and his staff at the National Historical Institute and National Library, and Dr. Carlos Quirino (some may disagree with my views or interpretation of facts); also, to a large group of friends whose identification here would cause problems ranging from embarrassment to imprisonment or death.

My research trip and expedition in the Philippines were made smoother by the cooperation and courtesies of others ahead of time in the United States and during the trip. Thanks to William Danner, Danner Shoe Manufacturing Company; Peter Landry, Diamond Brand Canvas Products Company; Skip Yowell, Jansport, Inc.; Claudia Krage, Nike, Inc.; Woods Bag & Canvas Company; Sylvia Gordon, Nikon, Inc.; and Robert Weinreb, Tenba, Inc. I should also like to extend my thanks for courtesies shown by José D. Aspiras, Romulo De Los Reyes, and Godfrey Lumauig of the Philippines Tourism Ministry; Roman Cruz, Philippine Airlines; Frans Schutzman and Margie David, Manila Hotel; Richard Chapman, Manila Hilton International. Each of the above provided discounts on their services, which made an underfunded expedition easier to make.

Finally, my abiding gratitude for the work performed by Amnesty International and Amnesty International USA (304 West Fifty-eighth Street, New York, N.Y. 10019) and by the Friends of the Filipino People (P.O. Box 2125, Durham, N.C. 27702). Readers are encouraged to contact them for further information on the Philippines and for suggestions as to how to become involved. *Philippine News*, a weekly newspaper (148 South Spruce Avenue, South San Francisco, Calif. 94080), is a good source of news on Philippine and Philippine-American affairs, as is the fortnightly publication *Ibon* (P.O. Box SM-447, Santa Mesa, Manila), which provides voluminous data on Philippine issues. Yearly bound volumes are available beginning with 1978 — an inexpensive but valuable source of information.

NOTES

(FFP *refers to the Frederick Funston Papers in the Kansas State Historical Society;* NARS, *to the National Archives and Records Service in Washington, D.C.*)

Prologue

2   "The Battle Hymn": Twain, *A Pen Warmed-Up in Hell*, 4. "The War Prayer": Twain, *The War Prayer* (New York: Harper Colophon, 1970).

3, 4   "To the Person": Twain, *A Pen Warmed-Up in Hell*, 64–65, 72.

Chapter 1: An American and His Country

10–11   "We had almost": Funston, *Memories*, 385–86.

13   Raccoon hunt: Scott, 817–18; E. F. Eckdall, 20–21.

14–15   Funston early childhood: E. F. Eckdall, 2–9, 25–29; Gleed, 322–24; notes on Funston family in E. H. Funston papers.

15–16   Funston family and Indians: E. F. Eckdall, 14–16.

17   "the tremendous desire": White, *Autobiography*, 141.
White and Kellogg backgrounds: Ibid.; Hinshaw.

18–20   College years: White, *Autobiography*, 142–43, 169; Riggs, 44–45; Canfield, 578–80; Hinshaw, 35; Funston, "Reminiscences"; *Boston Herald*, February 20, 1917; Crouch, "Funston: Formative Years," 189ff.; Young and Northrup, 342; E. F. Eckdall to Eda Funston, October 25, 1925, FFP; *New York Times*, April 30, 1899.

20   "We roamed the city": White, *Autobiography*, 210–11.

20–21   Fort Smith escapade: Scott, 818; *New York Times*, April 30, 1899; *Boston Herald*, February 20, 1917.

21   Rowdy cowboys: *Boston Herald*, February 20, 1917; Hinshaw, 37–38; *Kansas City Star*, February 21, 1917.

22   Camping trip: White, *Autobiography*, 173–74; Riggs, 44–47; Hinshaw, 35.

23   Funston's climb: Funston, "Storm Bound."

24　　Agricultural expeditions: Scott, 819; *New York Times*, February 25, 1917; Funston to E. C. Franklin, March 8, 1891, Funston to Ann M. Funston, May 3, 1891, FFP; F. V. Coville, "Sketch of the Flora of Death Valley," *Science* (December 16, 1892): 342; Eda B. Funston, "Notes on Frederick Funston," Funston Family Papers; Funston to C. F. Scott in *Iola Daily Register*, July 17, 1891, FFP.

26　　"fever brought on": *New York Times*, February 25, 1917.
　　　"were permanently disabled": Scott, 819.
　　　Yakutat Bay: Funston, "Field Report," in F. V. Coville, "Botany of Yakutat Bay, Alaska," *Contributions from the U.S. National Herbarium* 3, no. 6, 325–55; "Introductory Note," Ibid., 334; Funston and Jocelyn, 711–13; Funston to Ann Funston, August 19, 1890, FFP; Funston to E. C. Franklin, August 20, 1892, FFP.

27　　"There are a great many": Scott, 819.
　　　"I do not need": Ibid.
　　　Second Alaskan trip: Funston, "Over the Chilkoot Pass," 572; Funston's serialized letters to the *Iola Daily Register*, 1893 and 1894, FFP; *Report of the Expedition . . . Through Alaska and the British Northwest Territory . . .* , submitted to Dr. F. V. Coville, May 20, 1895, FFP, roll 3.
　　　"The Indians carried": *New York Times*, February 25, 1917.
　　　"My temper had been": Young and Northrup, 344.

28　　"with the speed of": Funston, "Chilkoot."
　　　"It was the very": Ibid.
　　　River descriptions: Ibid.

29　　Miles Canyon: Ibid.

30　　Forty Mile Creek: Ibid.
　　　Trek to Rampart House: White, "Frederick Funston's Alaskan Trip"; Funston to Ann Funston, May 8, 1894, FFP.

31　　"They are well-disposed": Funston, "Across the Great Divide," 1236.
　　　"well-disposed": Funston to Scott, *Iola Daily Register*, July 17 and September 11, 1891, FFP.
　　　Mirages: Funston to A. M. Funston, May 3, 1891, FFP.
　　　"nomads, constantly": Funston, "Across the Great Divide," 1236.

32　　Mania for fighting: Ibid.
　　　"stung like the cut": Ibid.

33　　"When they saw": Ibid., 1237.
　　　"The view was superb": Ibid.
　　　"I had a pretty serious row": Funston to E. H. Funston, May 30, 1894, FFP.

34　　Kipling: "Annual Meeting," *Kansas Historical Quarterly* 12 (1943): 97; "Persons in the Foreground," *Current Opinion* (June 1914): 428.
　　　Whaling fleet: White, "Alaskan Trip," 492; Gleed, 326; Funston, "Along Alaska's Eastern Boundary," 103.

35   Yukon voyage: White, "Alaskan Trip," 492, "Gen. Frederick
       Funston," 496; Young and Northrup, 345; Funston, "Along
       Alaska's Eastern Boundary," 103.

36   "I am going to resign": Funston to E. H. Funston, May 30, 1894,
       FFP.
       Drifts to New York: Scott, 819; Gleed, 326.

36–37 "Nothing was said": White, "Alaskan Trip," 492.
       Bond department: Gleed, 327.

37   Madison Square Garden: Funston, *Memories*, 3; Nathan Silver,
       Lost New York (New York: Schocken, 1971), 50–51; *New York Times*,
       April 3, 19, 29, May 14–17, 24, 1896.

38ff. Politics and panic: Williams, 27–57; Dulles, 21–39; Hofstadter,
       "Cuba, the Philippines, and Manifest Destiny," *Paranoid Style*, 145–
       87; Zinn, 290–313; Silk and Catton, 3–15; Karp, 3–96.
       "Uncertainty and fear": *Washington Post*, in H. Wayne Morgan,
       From Hayes to McKinley: National Party Politics, 1872–1896 (Syra-
       cuse: Syracuse University Press, 1969), 448–49.

39   "If this keeps on": "Correspondence of the Secretary of State,
       1894," NARS; also in Karp, 26.

40   "The frontier had dissolved": Millis, 5.

40–41 Pattern of interventions: see Dean Rusk's 1962 memo to Senate
       Foreign Relations Committee, "Instances of the Use of U.S.
       Armed Forces Abroad, 1798–1945," and Zinn, 290–91, for ex-
       planation.

42   "It is time": Millis, 29.

43   "From the Rio Grande": Lodge, "Our Blundering Foreign Pol-
       icy," *Forum* (March 1895): 8–17.
       Cuban nationalism: Williams, 39–48; Alger; Hofstadter, *Para-
       noid Style*, 145–87; Dulles, 21–39; Millis, 10–72; Karp, 49–68;
       Philip Foner, *The Spanish-Cuban-American War* (New York:
       Monthly Review, 1972).

44   "What is the occasion": *Journal of Commerce and Commercial Bul-
       letin* (January 12, 1898).
       "by any means necessary": *Cong. Rec.*, 54th Cong., 1st sess., 2249.
       "Spain is the most wicked": Ibid.

45   "I have sometimes": in Millis, 48.
       "Cross of Gold": for text, see Hofstadter, *Great Issues*, 166–73,
       or W. J. Bryan, *The First Battle* (Chicago, 1896).
       "We want no wars": *Cong. Rec.*, 55th Cong., 1st sess., 2–5.
       "having seen a salute": Funston, *Memories*, 6.

46ff. Funston in Cuba: Funston, *Memories*, 1–61, "To Cuba as a Fili-
       buster," 305–18, "Cascorra," 385–401; *New York Tribune*, May 26,
       1896, 8; Arthur Royal Joyce, "Scripps-McRae Dispatches," FFP,
       folder C-5; Prats-Lerma, "La Actuacion del Teniente Coronel
       Frederick Funston (Norteamericano) en la Guerra de Indepen-
       dencia de Cuba de 1895–1898," FFP, roll 3.
       "We lay about": Ibid., 16.

"swift and inevitable": Ibid.

47   "Well, you cannot know": Ibid., 30.
      "It was plain": Ibid., 40.

48   "The air was suddenly": Ibid., 44.
      "I did not exactly like": Ibid., 57.

49   Cavalry charge: Funston, "Desmayo," 225–26.

50   Cuban charge: Ibid.
      Light Brigade: Phillip Knightly, *The First Casualty* (New York: Harcourt Brace Jovanovich, 1975), 11.

51   Guáimaro: Funston, *Memories*, 62–97, "The Fall of Guáimaro," 579–95.
      "I slunk": Funston, *Memories*, 95.
      Weyler: Millis, 59–61, 74–76.

52   Jiguaní: Funston, *Memories*, 98–116, "A Defeat and a Victory," 735–55; Scott, 820; White, "Frederick Funston," *Harper's Weekly* (March 5, 1898): 226; Funston to E. H. Funston, March 5, 1897, FFP, Box 75; Funston to Ella Funston, May 10, 1897, ibid.; Funston to C. F. Scott, August 31, 1897, ibid.

53   "kicking up the dust": Funston to C. F. Scott, November 9, 1896, ibid.
      "a pretty big fool": Funston to Ella Funston, May 10, 1897, ibid.
      "I have gone past": Funston to C. F. Scott, May 10, 1897, ibid.
      "from the full vigor": Ibid.
      Lung wound: Gleed, 327; Scott, 820; *New York Tribune*, January 11, 1898, 4; Funston to C. F. Scott, August 31, 1897, FFP, Box 75.

54   Tunas: Funston, *Memories*, 116–46, "A Defeat and a Victory," 742–44, 750–51; E. W. Fenn, "Ten Months with the Cuban Insurgents," *Century* (June 1898).
      "I fairly shook": Funston, *Memories*, 131.
      "I saw the general": Ibid., 125–26.

55   "It was a shocking spectacle": Ibid., 138.
      Thigh wound: Gleed, 327; Scott, 820; White, *Autobiography*, 306.
      Escape from Cuba: *Topeka Daily Capital*, January 12, 1898; *New York Sun*, April 29, 1899; *New York Times*, February 25, 1917; White, "Frederick Funston," 226; Funston to C. F. Scott, May 10, 1897, FFP, Box 75.

56   "playing a damnable": Ibid.
      Cuban situation: for a fuller discussion, see Hofstadter, *Paranoid Style*, 152–87; Williams, 40–45; Zinn, 290–305; Millis, 73–150; Foner; Alger.
      McKinley's character: I am indebted to Walter Karp, who showed me the light. See Karp, 69–95; Williams, 40–45; Paolo Coletta, ed., *Threshold to American Internationalism: Essays on the Foreign Policy of William McKinley* (New York: Exposition Press, 1970). For a more conventional view, see the analyses of McKinley in Leech, Morgan, Olcott, and Morris.

"first Genius": Henry Adams, *Letters* (Boston: Houghton Mifflin, 1930–38), 2:191.

57 "No triumph of peace": Roosevelt to Goodrich, June 18, 1897, Roosevelt, *Letters*, vol. 1; Morris, 569–75; Millis, 81; Pringle, *Theodore Roosevelt*, 408–9.

Metropolitan Club: Morris, 568; Hofstadter, *Paranoid Style*, 163–64.

58 "a large number": *Cong. Rec.*, 55th Cong., 1st sess., 1081.

"in the name of," "a reasonable time": U.S. Dept. of State, 560–84.

59 "it will be a duty": Ibid.

Lee's dispatches: Millis, 92–96.

"After warning": Karp, 87.

Maine in Havana: Charles D. Sigsbee, *The Maine* (New York: Century, 1899); Millis, 96; Morris, 593–99.

60 "no more backbone": Millis, 114; Morris, 610; J. F. Rhodes, *The McKinley and Roosevelt Administrations* (New York: Macmillan, 1923).

"There may be an explosion": Lodge to Henry White, January 31, 1898, Pringle, *Theodore Roosevelt*, 203; Julius Pratt, *The Expansionists of 1898* (Baltimore: Johns Hopkins, 1936), 226.

"was an act of": Roosevelt to B. J. Diblee, *Letters*, 775.

Improvement of economy: Williams, 44–45.

61 "I cannot assume": U.S. Dept. of State, 711–13.

62 War message: Ibid., 750–60.

63 Handbill: Collection of Kansas State Historical Society.

Funston in Topeka: *Emporia* (Kans.) *Gazette*, n.d., *Topeka Daily Capital*, n.d., FFP, Box 75.

Arrival in New York: *New York Tribune*, January 11, 1898; *New York Sun*, April 29, 1899; White, "Frederick Funston," 226; Scott, 820; Ella Eckdall, 28; *Topeka Daily Capital*, January 12, 1898.

64 Governor's appointment: Funston, *Memories*, 150–51.

65 "I was staying": Ibid., 155.

In Tampa: Ibid., 156–58; White, "Gen. Frederick Funston," 496.

66 "The most ultimately righteous": Roosevelt, *Winning of the West*, 57–58.

66–67 Roosevelt and Mahan: Peter Karstein, "The Nature of 'Influence': Roosevelt, Mahan, and the Concept of Sea Power," *American Quarterly* 23, no. 4 (1971), for which I am indebted to Edmund Morris. See also Morris, 424–25, 572–75.

67 "Peace is a goddess": Pringle, *Theodore Roosevelt*, 172.

Kimball war plan: Grenville, 43.

Roosevelt-McKinley carriage ride: Millis, 81; Morris, 585–86.

"blockade, and if possible": Roosevelt, *Letters*, 685, 717.

68 "American factories": Claude Bowers, *Beveridge and the Progressive Era* (Boston: Houghton Mifflin, 1932), 169.

Manila the key: Williams, 43–44.

Roosevelt and Dewey: Dewey, *Autobiography;* Morris, 586–88; Philip Nicholson, "George Dewey and the Expansionists of 1898," *Vermont History* 42, no. 3 (1974); Millis, 85–87.

69   "all the charts": Millis, 86.

The acting secretary: Morris, 601–3.

70   "DEWEY": Roosevelt, *Letters,* 784.

"during my short absence": John D. Long, *Journal,* Massachusetts Historical Society, cited in Morris.

"DEWEY": Dewey, 178–79.

Battle of Manila Bay: Ibid.; Millis, 173–95; Wilcox, 29–40.

71   Alger's recollection: Alger, 326.

72   "constant work and anxiety," "Give my best love": Millis, 224.

"the truth is": Olcott, 2:110–11; Leech, 327–41.

"While we are conducting": Olcott, 2:165.

73   Complaint against Kansans: Wesley Merritt to the sec. of war, "Corres. Adj. Gen. Off.," NARS.

"That horse quivered": Funston, *Memories,* 163–64.

"One big ruffian": Ibid., 164–65.

74   "the great day": Roosevelt to Hagedorn, August 14, 1917, in Theodore Roosevelt Collection, Harvard.

McKinley cables Dewey: *Cong. Rec.,* 56th Cong., 1st sess., 33, 1:895.

"investigate and report": Sec. of state to Edward Hardin, August 2, 1898, U.S. Dept. of State.

75   "I hear talk": Lodge to Roosevelt, in Millis, 320.

"TWENTIETH KANSAS": Alger; Wolff, 90–91.

76   "desperately in love": White, *Autobiography,* 142–43.

"as a musician": Gleed, 329.

"by all odds": Funston, *Memories,* 171–72.

"Nobody supposed": Ibid., 172.

"it seems more than probable": Wolff, 83.

Manila tensions: J. F. Bass dispatch, *Harper's Weekly* (January 27, 1899); A. G. Robinson, 56–62; Wolff, 202–5; Miller, 58–59.

"Almost without exception": 57th Cong., 1st sess., S. Doc. 331, 884.

77   "We have to kill": W. Christner, January 17, 1899, U.S. Army Military History Research Collection, Carlisle Barracks, Carlisle, Pa.; Miller, 58.

"if a bullet": Funston, *Memories,* 176.

Benevolent Assimilation: 57th Cong., 1st sess., S. Doc. 331, 776–78, 764–68.

"Come out here, Colonel": Funston, *Memories,* 177–78.

78   "They have commenced": "Mrs. Funston in Filipino Costume," *Harper's Bazar* (January 13, 1900): 38; see also "Soldier's Wife in the Philippines," *Cosmopolitan* (May 1900): 65–72.

"The first blow": McKinley, *Speeches and Addresses, 1897–1900*

(New York: Doubleday & McClure, 1900), 211–17.

79 "mediocre poetry": Roosevelt to Lodge, January 12, 1899, in Roosevelt, *Selections from the Correspondence*, 1:384.

"Take up the": *McClure's Magazine* (February 1899): 291.

Philippine-American hostilities: For a fuller discussion, see Miller; Agoncillo, *Malolos;* Mahajani; Wolff; Sexton; Gates.

3,000 killed: Wolff, 227.

"There goes Kansas," "CALOOCAN TAKEN": Sexton, 95–96; Faust; Steele.

80 "Until I am mustered out!": *Boston Herald*, February 10, 1917.

repeatedly kicking them: Funston, *Memories*, 191–92.

"When I tell them": Gleed, 322.

MacArthur background: Manchester; Petillo, 1–54.

"Sometimes one had to decide": Manchester, 16.

81 "If anyone can do it": *Baltimore Sun*, March 29, 1901.

"goldfish": Wolff, 105.

82 Otis background: Wolff, 140–41; Miller, 46–47.

"pincushion of an old woman": Fuchs and Antler, 216.

83 Journalists' protest: Robinson, 82–84.

"We make everyone": *San Francisco Call*, April 15, 1899.

84 "With an enemy like this," "Our fighting blood": *Soldiers' Letters*, 3, 13.

Wheaton reprisal: Sexton, 95–98.

"last night": *Literary Digest* 18 (1899): 601.

Red Cross official: *San Francisco Call*, March 31, 1899.

85 "How the order started": 57th Cong., 1st sess. (1902), S. Doc. 331, 2550–51.

"Western States": White, "Gen. Frederick Funston," 496.

"With my own hands," "natives fell dead": *Soldiers' Letters*, 19, 5.

85–86 "The stories of brutalities": G. H. Fitch, "General Funston on Philippine Problems," *Harper's Weekly* (November 11, 1899).

86 "maintained and supported": 57th Cong., 1st sess. (1902), S. Doc. 331, 1443–45.

Secret orders: *Mass Meetings of Protest*, New England Anti-Imperialist League (Boston, 1903).

Brenner's charges: Storey and Codman, 12–15.

"attempted to escape": *Albany Press-Knickerbocker* story reprinted in *Public Opinion* 28 (1900): 485.

"The natives": Fitch, 1143.

87 "I am afraid that": *New York Times*, April 24, 1899.

"Not only is Funston": Gleed, 329.

"he is not a notoriety": Scott, 820.

"leads to his sentiments": E. S. Martin, "This Busy World," *Harper's Weekly* (July 15, 1899).

88 "He has to talk": Morris, 524.

Roosevelt's views: H. K. Beale, *Theodore Roosevelt and America's Rise to World Power* (Baltimore: Johns Hopkins, 1956), 34; Speech of Sen. Edward Carmack, 57th Cong., 1st Sess., S. Doc. 35, 5:4673; Edward Wagenknecht, *The Seven Worlds of Theodore Roosevelt* (New York: Longmans, 1958), 98, 118.

"and rawhide": Funston, in Martin.

88–89 "A Filipino is": *San Francisco Call*, October 12, 1899.

89 "A cold-blooded murderer": Funston, Lotos Club speech, in Wolff, 360–61.

"though not a bitter one": *Springfield Daily Republican*, July 3, 1899.

"I am a Protestant": Fitch, 1143.

"the real test": Funston, *Memories*, 233.

90 "Funston, who was rising": White, *Autobiography*, 501.

"well-known correspondent": Funston, *Memories*, 233.

"a dashing and aggressive soldier": Ibid., 223, 266.

91 "Brave! Brave!": Wolff, 236.

"He seemed to enjoy": Funston, *Memories*, 266.

"Although I had got into": Ibid., 274.

92 "I realized perfectly well": Ibid., 282.

"It's the Maxim": Ibid., 285–86.

"There were some vigorous": Ibid., 287.

93 "I felt a most terrific": Ibid., 292–93.

"I was highly gratified": Ibid., 295–96.

Twentieth Kansas record: Ibid., 311.

94ff. Aguinaldo capture plot. General references used: Funston, *Memories*, 384–426; Funston, "Official Report," Corres. Adj. Gen. Off., NARS; Funston, "How Aguinaldo Was Captured," "The Capture of Emilio Aguinaldo" (hereinafter cited as "Capture"); Segovia; Brown, "The Capture of Aguinaldo," document sent to Roosevelt (hereinafter cited as TR Letter); Brown, "Incidents in Aguinaldo's Capture" (hereinafter cited as "Incidents"), personal diary, Western Historical Collections; Abad; Aguinaldo, "The Story of My Capture" (hereinafter cited as "Story"); Aguinaldo and Pacis; Talplacido; and various official documents, letters, and periodical accounts.

94 "with all possible speed": Funston, *Memories*, 386.

95 "I am glad to": "How Lieut. Taylor Located Aguinaldo."

peaceful and agreeable: Segovia, 13–22.

96 Water cure: Aguinaldo and Pacis, 126–27.

Segismundo background: Funston, *Memories;* Abad.

97 Segovia background: Segovia, 1–3. His maternal name can be found on his Philippine National Army commission of December 21, 1898, FFP.

Filipino wife: Funston, "Capture," 263. Funston, true to his racial beliefs, wrote, in part: "He had the questionable taste to marry a native woman."

98 Cipher: Segovia, 25–31.

98–99 "After many and risky": Segovia, 32. There exist almost as many versions of the letters used in the plot as there are versions of what happened. Teodoro Agoncillo asserts that he has at least some of the letters in his possession (cf. *Malolos*) — but there are several authentic-looking ones in FFP, in a folder labeled "Cuban and Philippine Documents." Inasmuch as all communicate the basic information in varying styles, I have chosen the ones that most ring true, with the admission that there is no way to determine the greatest authenticity.

99   "we were": Funston, *Memories*, 390.

100   "to get him": Ibid., 393.

Chapter 2: Manila, 1982

103   "to see its poverty": Naipaul, *An Area of Darkness* (New York: Vintage, 1981), 47.

105   Pedestrian deaths: *Bulletin Today* (Manila), March 21, 1982.

107ff.   Spanish colonization: See John D. Phelan, *Hispanization of the Philippines* (Madison: University of Wisconsin Press, 1959); Eufronio Alip, *Political and Cultural History of the Philippines* (Manila: Alip & Brion, 1945); Zafra, 27–39; Agoncillo and Guerrero, 22–70; Craig; Blair and Robertson, vols. 7, 16, 40; Wernstedt and Spencer, 115–20.

109–10   "The pearls and": Bernad, 18.

110   Anson's voyage: Walter.

          Walled City taxes: Zafra, 58.

114–16   World War II: See Manchester; Petillo; Samuel Eliot Morison, *The Rising Sun in the Pacific* (Boston: Little, Brown, 1960); Louis Morton, *The Fall of the Philippines* (Washington, D.C.: U.S. Army Office of Military History, 1953); Agoncillo, *Fateful Years*.

115   "I am prepared": Petillo, 169.

116   "Japanese troops": Agoncillo, *Fateful Years*, 863.

117   "The American troops": Ibid.

          Postwar rebuilding: National Historical Commission, *Manila Since Independence*, 29–31, 85, 97, 102–3.

118   "The United States": Agoncillo and Guerrero, 496; also Constantino and Constantino, 198–203.

          "swung from periods": Shaplen, *Time Out of Hand*, 230.

119   Marcos background: Spence.

          Murder case: See Spence's bathetic account, ibid., 45–120.

120   Medals: See *Washington Post* article, reprinted in *Newsday*, February 3, 1984.

122   Huks: Saulo, *Communism;* Constantino and Constantino, 189–225; Agoncillo and Guerrero, 517–39.

124   President and deity: *New York Times*, November 29, December 3, 1972.

126   Weddings: *Time*, June 20, 1982; *San Francisco Chronicle*, June 11, 1982.

Manotoc: *New York Times*, January 2, 6, 1982, February 9, 1982.

129   Foreign workers: *New York Times*, January 31, 1982.

134   Systematically disregarded: *Amnesty International 1981 Report*, 9.
Human rights abuses: Ibid., 95–97, 99–101, 105.

136   Housing situation: *New York Times*, June 30, 1982; *Manila Daily Express*, February 15, 1981; *Ibon* 3 (1980), no. 52.

137–38   BBC documentary: "To Sing Our Own Song," narrated by José Diokno, 1982.

138   National debt: Benigno Aquino, *The MacNeil-Lehrer Report*, September 16, 1982; *Ibon* 4 (1981), no. 64, 4; *New York Times*, June 23, 1983.

140   Opera company, "frivolity and wealth": *New York Times*, February 7, 1982, September 16, 1982, January 6, 1983, October 30, 1983; Kamm.

142   Prostitution: *Ibon* 4 (1981), no. 68, 7; *Ibon* 3 (1980), no. 49, 1–10.

147   Mail-order brides: *New York Times*, March 13, 1982.

148   Colonial education: See Constantino, *Miseducation; Ibon* 4 (1981), no. 66.

150   "They are carrying": *Bulletin Today* (Manila), April 5, 1982.
Submarine and contraband: Ibid., April 4, 6, 1982.

Chapter 3: A Filipino and His Country

154   "They were just ready": Aguinaldo, *Memoirs*, 1; Alip, 5.
"This probably explains": Aguinaldo, *Memoirs*, 2.

154–55   "Among my brothers": Ibid.

155ff.   Filipino revolution: For a fuller discussion, see Agoncillo, *Short History* and *Revolt of the Masses;* Agoncillo and Guerrero; Constantino, *The Philippines;* De Los Santos; Mahajani.

155   "of Protestant ideas": Alzona, 50.

156   "unable to steer": Agoncillo, *Revolt,* 17.

157   Father's funeral: Aguinaldo, *Memoirs,* 4.
"Instead of attending to": Ibid., 7–8.
"although I was not": Ibid., 8.

158   "Alvarez found no difficulty": Ibid., 24.

159   "That was the beginning": Ibid.
Bonifacio background: De Los Santos; Agoncillo, *Revolt;* Constantino, *The Philippines.*
"the streets were as crooked": Agoncillo, *Revolt,* 64.

160   "displaying their beautiful legs": Aguinaldo, *Memoirs,* 13–15.

161   "In Vigan": Foreman, 522–23.

162   "Our hearts beat fast": Aguinaldo, *Memoirs,* 47.

163   "When I arranged them": Ibid., 71.
"I shouted": Ibid., 71–72.

164   Aguirre's sword: Ibid., 78.

165   "acted as if": Agoncillo, *Revolt,* 203–5.

166ff. Tejeros convention: Ibid., 209–14.
167 "It is clear": Ibid., 221.
  "I was amazed": Aguinaldo, *Memoirs,* 137.
  "I patiently accepted": Ibid.
168 Black spots: Ibid., 138.
  "Had the enemy": Ibid., 143.
168ff. Aguinaldo and Bonifacio: Ibid., 155–56, 161–63; Aguinaldo and Pacis, 26–27; Agoncillo, *Revolt* and *Writings and Trial of Bonifacio.*
171 Biaknabato manifestoes: Taylor, 1:33; Agoncillo, *Malolos,* 13–17.
172 Pedro Paterno: Ibid., 50–52; Foreman, 557–59.
174 Agoncillo's proposal: Le Roy, 1:147–48; 55th Cong., 3d sess. (1899), S. Doc. 62, pt. I, 333–34.
  "The United States": Aguinaldo and Pacis, 30–31.
175 Artacho's suit: Aguinaldo and Pacis, 31; 56th Cong., 1st sess., vol. 2, S. Doc. 208, 2–10.
  Pratt: Aguinaldo and Pacis, 32–34; *Singapore Free Press,* May 4, 1898, in 55th Cong., 3d sess. (1899), S. Doc. 95, "Articles Relating to Islands, February 1, 1899"; Welsh, 235–41.
176 Return to Hong Kong: Aguinaldo and Pacis, 36.
176–77 Dewey and Aguinaldo: Ibid., 37–39. See the illuminating transcript of Dewey's appearance at a Senate hearing on the origins of the war: S. Doc. 331, 2934–47, 2955, 2958–59.
178 Junta proclamation: Robinson, 44–45.
  "The great North American nation": 55th Cong., 3d sess. (1899), S. Doc. 62, vol. 1, 88–89.
  Declaration of Independence: See text in Zaide, *Philippine Revolution,* 195–99, 206–7.
179 "entire sympathy": Kalaw, *Philippine Politics,* 108–9.
  "the good will": Aguinaldo and Pacis, 74.
  "You are being tragic": Ibid., 75.
  Mabini background: Agoncillo, *Malolos;* Kalaw, *Philippine Politics;* Cesar Majul, *Mabini and the Philippine Revolution* (Quezon City, 1960).
180 "the first duty": Aguinaldo and Pacis, 70.
181 "The Republic we established": Ibid., 71.
  Dewey and ships: Kalaw, *The Case for the Filipinos,* 68–69; Le Roy, 1:214; *Diary of Lt. Frederick Sladen,* October 30, 1898, U.S. Army Military History Research Collection, Carlisle Barracks, Carlisle, Pa.
182 "like a combination": Miller, 113. For a fuller discussion of the anti-imperialist movement, see Schirmer, *Republic or Empire;* Pettigrew; Storey and Lichauco; and Miller, 104–28.
182–83 "Whatever may be thought": *Boston Times-Herald,* in *Literary Digest* 18 (1899): 541–42.
183 "What would have happened": *Philadelphia Press,* in *Literary Digest* 19 (1899): 336–37.

"True oppressors": S. Doc. 208, 1:101–3.

184   Otis's maneuvers: S. Doc. 331, 789–92; E. S. Otis, "Official Report" (1899), 88–93, Adj. Gen. Off., NARS.
185   Outbreak of war: Sexton, 91.
       "Armageddon": Aguinaldo and Pacis, 94.
       Armistice rebuffed: S. Doc. 331, 789–92; Aguinaldo and Pacis, 94.
       "We had no honorable": Ibid., 98.
       "an army of Tagalogs": Philippine Information Society, "Outbreak of Hostilities," no. 6, 20.
186   "the original beachhead": Aguinaldo and Pacis, 100.
       Luna background: Agoncillo, *Malolos*, 499–503, 515–18.
187   "a fiery and fanatical": Aguinaldo and Pacis, 100.
       "a despot": Mabini, *Letters*, 135.
       "the humane, pacific": Agoncillo, *Malolos*.
188   Malolos Congress: see Aguinaldo and Pacis, 102; Agoncillo, *Malolos*, 396.
       "since war is": Kalaw, *Philippine Politics*, 186–87.
189–90 Luna assassination: Ibid., 526–28; Aguinaldo and Pacis, 105. See also Agoncillo's "Aguinaldo: A Profile in Humility," *Archipelago Magazine* (August 1975).
190   "The loss of Luna": Aguinaldo and Pacis, 105. Note that an embittered Mabini accused Aguinaldo, without proof, of ordering Luna's death. Constantino, in *The Philippines*, admits there is no solid evidence but seems to be arguing that rumors about a coup may have led Aguinaldo to order, or condone, the murder.
191   Del Pilar: Kalaw, *Acceptable Holocaust*.
       "Read these booklets": Ibid., 7.
192   "His traveling bags": Ibid., 28.
193   "It rained continuously": Villa diary, November 15, 1899, in Villa and Barcelona.
194   "The Americans could never": Kalaw, *Acceptable Holocaust*, 47.
       "We arrived in Angake": Ibid., 49.
195ff. Tirad Pass battle: John T. McCutcheon, "Aguinaldo's Rear Guard," in Wilcox, 317–20.
       "heroically and successfully": Kalaw, *Acceptable Holocaust*, 50.
196ff. Del Pilar death: McCutcheon, 317–20; Richard Henry Little, *Chicago Tribune*, in Wolff, 286–88.
197   "We placed him": Kalaw, *Acceptable Holocaust*, 55.

Chapter 4: *Manila, 1901*

199   "mud and filth": Hamm, 27.
201   Binondo description: Browne, 106–7; Lala, 120–22; Hamm, 55–64.
       Hotel de Oriente: Hamm, 36–37.

204   Aguinaldo rumors quashed: *Army and Navy Journal* (April 6, 1901): 773.

Malacañang description: Lala, 130.

204–5   Mitchell background: *Niagara Falls Gazette*, June 16, 1941; *New York Times*, June 17, 1941.

205   Newton background: Funston, *Memories*, 395; *Commemorative Biographical Record of the Upper Lake Region* (1905), 395–96; E. Rossiter, "Right Forward, Fours Right, March!" (1900), Superior Public Library; *Superior* (Wis.) *Evening Telegram*, April 25, 1901, May 24, 1901; *Superior Leader*, April 23, 1897.

"A great scheme": Ibid.

206   "The selection": Funston, *Memories*, 395.

Talplacido background: Ibid., 396; Abad, 210–11; Talplacido.

Bâto and Cadhit background: Funston, *Memories*, 396; Abad, 214.

207   Crisanto de la Fuente: Abad, 211–12.

Segovia at hotel: Segovia, 50–51, 88; Abad, 213.

208   Hazzards' background: *Chehalis* (Wash.) *Bee-Nugget*, April 5, 1901, June 23, 1899, July 3, 1900; *Tacoma Daily News*, March 29, 1901.

209   Only five Americans: Funston, *Memories*, 397.

"All Manila": Segovia, 53.

210   "the poor woman": Funston, *Memories*, 398.

"Funston, this is": Ibid., 398.

Arrival at wharf: Segovia, 53–54.

Vicksburg: All weather and ocean conditions taken from U.S. Naval Records Collection, *Deck Log*, U.S.S. *Vicksburg* (March–April 1901 bound volume). It also contains a complete handwritten roster of Macabebe scouts seemingly unavailable elsewhere. W. C. Brown's diary (at both the Carlisle Barracks and the University of Colorado) lists the naval officers on duty aboard the *Vicksburg* and other interesting details.

Funston's earlier visit: *Deck Log*, March 6, 1901.

211   "I can't do it": Segovia, 59.

211–12   Dispensed punishment: *Deck Log*, March 7, 1901.

212   "Don't worry": Segovia, 61.

213   "My general": Funston, *Memories*, 399; Abad, 217.

Summary execution: Funston, *Memories*, 399: "If they were faithful they would be well-rewarded, if not there would be but one penalty and that would be inflicted, if it was the last thing done." Also, Funston, *Official Report*, 7: "They were warned that any treachery or disobedience of orders would be punished by the summary execution of the offenders." Note that in later accounts, the Filipinos' fears were minimized.

213–14   Lacuna incident: Funston, *Memories*, 378–79.

Lacuna letters: Texts appear in Funston, "Capture," 267–68. Also, compare Segovia, 78–81; Funston, *Memories*, 402–3; Funston, *Official Report*, 7–8. Note that Abad discloses the translator-forger's name, Roman Rocque, a former revolutionary officer.

214   "some mere rubbish": Funston, *Memories*, 403.

215   "They are terrors": Miller, 183.
       "Treat all men": Segovia, 66.

216   *Vicksburg* aground: The only admission of this incident was by
       Captain Barry and in a terse diary entry of Brown. See *Report* of
       Captain E. B. Barry, U.S.S. *Vicksburg*, March 1901, in *Area File
       of the Naval Records Collection, 1901*, Roll 387, NARS; and Barry
       to commander in chief, U.S. Naval Force on Asiatic Station, March
       28, 1901 (grounding incident report), in *Area File.* For compar-
       ison, see Funston's various accounts; Brown's diary, letter to
       Roosevelt, and "Incidents"; and Segovia.

217   Funston's mustering out: Funston, *Memories*, 398–99, 312.
       make a fortune: Eda Funston to Elizabeth Cullen, Manila, De-
       cember 17, 1898, FFP.

218   Polillo Island: Brown, diary, letter to Roosevelt, and "Incidents";
       Barry, *Report;* Funston, *Memories*, 401; Segovia, 73–75.

218–19 *Bancas* lost: Brown diary; Funston, "Capture," 266–67, *Memo-
       ries*, 402; Segovia, 82.

219–20 Landing: Funston, *Memories*, 404, "Capture," 268; Segovia, 82–
       87; U.S. Naval Records, *Area File; Deck Log.*

Chapter 5: Dinalungan, Aurora Province, 1982

234   Geological data: Wernstedt and Spencer, 423–24, 19.

237   Timber and erosion: Ibid., 78, 618–19; *Ibon* 3 (1980), no. 53.

239–40 Salcedo: William Henry Scott, 9–10.

Chapter 6: Casiguran Sound, 1901

244   "Now we were": Segovia, 87.
       "I was so scared": Ibid., 88.

295   "Everything was": Funston, *Memories*, 405.
       "savage Balugas": Funston, "Capture," 270.

246   "They thought their last days": "Lieut. Newton Among Sav-
       ages," *Superior Evening Telegram*, July 23, 1900; see also Funston,
       Memories, 320–23.
       Newton rescues friar: "Newton Lay on a Rock 3 days," *Superior
       Evening Telegram*, April 7, 1901.

247   Letter to Casiguran: Segovia, 92.

247–48 Conversation: Ibid., 93–94.

248   "like a bale": Ibid., 95.
       "We entered the town": Funston, *Memories*, 407.
       Segismundo sweetheart: Segovia, 95.

249   "They crowded around us": Funston, *Memories*, 408.
       "We had now stepped": Segovia, 99.
       Conversation: Segovia, 100–102.

250   Rice lost: Brown, "Incidents," 629.

"Do not worry": Segovia, 103–4; Funston, *Memories*, 409.
250–51 "I know the Philippine": Segovia, 105.
251–52 Conversations: Ibid., 107–9.
252–53 Forged letters: Ibid., 112–13; compare with Funston, "Capture," 271.
253–54 "I have no intention": Segovia, 116.
254 "Captain, take the gun": Ibid., 118–19.
"This yarn caused us": Funston, *Memories*, 410.
255 "All right": Segovia, 120.
"Though I must confess": Funston, "Capture," 272.

Chapter 7: From Casiguran to Casapsapan Bay, 1982

258 Agtas: See Noval-Morales and Monan.
Chain gangs: Wilfrid Turnbull, "Bringing a Wild Tribe Under Government Control," part 2, *Philippine Magazine* 27, no. 1, 40.
Reservation closed: *Annual Report of the Governor-General 1924* (Washington, D.C., 1926), 63.
259 Hunting decline: Headland, 10.
Headland quotes: letter to author, May 31, 1983.
263 Rexford: *Philippine Panorama*, April 4, 1982, 16–18.
264ff. church-state relations: See Yu and Bolasco; Agoncillo and Guerrero; Carlos Abesamis, *Salvation: Historical and Total* (Quezon City: JMC Press, 1978); "Servant of Humanity: Church Social Action in the Philippines, 1966–1980" (Manila: NASSA, 1981); *Ibon* 4 (1981), no. 61; Amnesty International, "Arrest, Detention, and Political Killing."
265 bishops' letter: Yu and Bolasco, 74–75.
"the defense of the poor": Ibid., 79–80.
267 "admonished us": *New York Times*, October 17, 1982.
272 "The crucial point": Joaquin, 123–24.

Chapter 8: The Odyssey to Palanan, 1899–1901

Inasmuch as Aguinaldo did not refer to his journey to Palanan in his writings, all historians have necessarily relied on the diaries of Colonel Simeon Villa and Dr. Santiago Barcelona, found in Taylor, *The Philippine Insurrection Against the United States*, and in a more satisfactory translation in Villa and Barcelona, *Aguinaldo's Odyssey*, 1963. Citations given below indicate the source (i.e., Barcelona or Villa), the date, and the page in the 1963 edition.

275 "I'm getting more nervous": Barcelona, May 20, 1900, 118–19.
278 "Those in Banaue": Villa, December 16, 1899, 11.
279 "We did not mind": Villa, January 7, 1900, 22.
281 "infamous, cowardly": Villa, February 5, 1900, 27.
283 "a supernatural man": Villa, March 5, 1900, 45.

284   "invincible liberator": Villa, March 22, 1900, 52.
          "The greetings were": Ibid.
286   "Every wail of the wind": Villa, May 16, 1900, 63.
287   "seeming to wait": Villa, May 17, 1900, 64.
289   Butterfly incident: Barcelona, May 20, 1900, 118–19.
290   "Americans behind": Barcelona, May 20, 1900, 119.
291   "They are Americans": Barcelona, May 20, 1900, 121.
          "Everybody looked like corpses": Ibid.
292   "Determination": Barcelona, May 20, 1900, 122.
          "they had him": Villa, May 29, 1900, 74.
293   "usurping the power": Villa, May 29, 1900, 79.
          "We slept with nothing": Villa, August 29, 1900, 84.
          "Everybody": Villa, September 6, 1900, 87.
294   Swim in ocean: Villa, September 19, 1900, 88.

Chapter 9: From Dinapiqui to North of Dinatadmo Point, 1982

306   "This would have been": Segovia, 137.

Chapter 10: Casiguran and the Contracosta, 1901

318   "The *vice-presidente*": Funston, *Memories*, 412.
319   "The presence of these men": Ibid.
          "should they eat it": Segovia, 124.
320   "I was greatly troubled": Ibid., 126–27.
321   "even they were pale": Ibid., 124–28.
          "He had undoubtedly": Ibid., 129.
          "The footpath was fearfully steep": Funston, "Capture," 472.
          "nothing but mountain goats": "Capt. Newton Tells of Aguinaldo's Capture," *Superior Evening Telegram*, May 23, 1901.
322   "I cannot recommend": Funston, "Capture," 472.
          "It was hard": Segovia, 131.
          "A general stampede": Ibid., 132.
323   "varied in size": Funston, *Memories*, 412, "Capture," 472; Segovia, 135.
          "this would have been": Segovia, 137.
          "a soggy and fermenting": Funston, *Memories*, 413.
324   "drew a fish": Ibid., 413–14.
325   Octopus: Mitchell, 508.
          Letter to Aguinaldo: Segovia, 139–40; compare with Funston, "Capture," 472.
326   "The plucky Spaniard": Funston, *Memories*, 414.
          Note left: Segovia, 141–42; Abad, 222.
          Funston, this: Funston, *Memories*, 398.
327   "It was plain": Ibid., 414.

Chapter 11: On the Coast to Diguyo, 1982

339   "in which the traveler": De la Gravière, 345.

Chapter 12: On the Way to Palanan, 1901

344   "there was any fight": Funston, *Memories*, 414.
      "so that we might have": Segovia, 143.
345   *"It's all right":* Funston, *Memories*, 414.
      "What a load": Ibid.
      Villa's letter: Segovia, 143–44.
346   Segovia's reply: Ibid., 144.
      "We entertained": Ibid., 145.
      "it brought us": Funston, *Memories*, 415.
      "if left to themselves": Segovia, 147.
347   "Aguinaldo will have to": Ibid., 152.
348   Segovia meets soldiers: Ibid., 153–55; Abad, 224–25.
349   Every few hundred yards: Funston, *Memories*, 417.
      "We were now": "Capt. Newton Tells of Aguinaldo's Capture," *Superior Evening Telegram*, May 23, 1901.
      "We were very weak": Funston, *Memories*, 419.
350   Segovia sights Palanan: Segovia, 156–57.

Chapter 14: Palanan, 1901

361   Regrouping plans: Villa (in Villa and Barcelona), 81, 88–90, 95–98; Aguinaldo, "The Story of My Capture" (hereinafter cited as Aguinaldo, "Story"), 134; Aguinaldo and Pacis, 115–16.
      Mabini letters: Villa, March 7 and 8, 1901, 101–2.
362   Reconnoiter mountaintop: Villa, March 16, 1901, 102.
      "We celebrated": Aguinaldo, "Story," 137.
      "for the formation of": Ibid.
      Aguinaldo and Alhambra: Abad, 226 (based on his interview with Alhambra around 1919).
363   Segovia's conversation: Segovia, 160–61.
      Description of Palanan: Funston, "How Aguinaldo Was Captured"; diagram in Funston, "Capture."
364   Segovia and Aguinaldo: Segovia, 163–66; Aguinaldo, "Story," 138–39; Aguinaldo and Pacis, 128–29.
366   A boy approached: Abad, 227.
      "Now is the time": Funston, "Capture," 474, *Memories*, 420.
      "Stop that foolishness": Ibid.
      Talplacido lunges; helpless: Aguinaldo and Pacis, 127–28.
      "You are our prisoners": Segovia, 168.
366–67   Shooting: Funston, *Memories*, 420–21.
367   "We surrender": Segovia, 168.
      Macabebes shooting: Ibid.

368

369

370

371

372

373

374

The bodies: Signal Corps photo, NARS.

"It is all right": Funston, *Memories*, 421.

Villa dragged: Funston, "Capture," 475.

Talplacido on floor: Abad, 229; Aguinaldo, "Story," 139.

"You are a prisoner": Segovia, 169.

"Is this not some joke": Funston, *Memories*, 421, "Capture," 474.

"It was all over": Funston, "Capture," 474.

"we were absolute masters": Segovia, 170.

"whether we willed": Funston, "Capture," 475.

Macabebes looting: Segovia, 170, 174; Funston, "Capture," 476.

Civilians found: Segovia, 170.

"It was regrettable": Funston, *Memories*, 422.

Signal-flare pistol: Abad, 231.

Aguinaldo's worries: Funston, "Capture," 475, *Memories*, 424; Mitchell, 510.

Countercoup attempt: Abad, 231–32.

"We had no further suffering": Funston, *Memories*, 423.

"Is there no limit": Brown to Roosevelt, Camp Wallace, Manila, April 27, 1901, in Theodore Roosevelt Papers, Ser. 1, Reel 13.

"always courteous," "The whole thing": Segovia, 173.

"I should never have believed": Segovia, 173.

"deeply angered": Aguinaldo and Pacis, 128–29.

"His gameness": Funston, *Memories*, 423.

Musician: *Deck Log* identifies him as Benjamin Ligardo.

"I beg of you": Segovia, 174.

Alhambra's rescue attempt: Abad, 234–35.

Brown's influenza: Brown, diary, February 12, 1901.

Brown background: Brimlow; Mitterling.

"During my stay": Brown, "Incidents," 629, diary; Brown to Roosevelt, Camp Wallace, Manila, April 27, 1901, in Theodore Roosevelt Papers, Ser. 1, Reel 13. *Note:* Brown's diary entry for March 25 contains Aguinaldo's and Barcelona's autographs. Villa, being winged and disgruntled, did not sign.

Footprints on beach: *Deck Log.*

Brown sees signal: Brown, "Incidents," 630–31.

Bedsheet: Funston, "Capture," 477.

"they appeared to have been": Abad, 232.

Cadhit's joke: Ibid., 233–34.

"his face radiant": Funston, "Capture," 477.

"There was no attempt": Ibid.

Aguinaldo boards ship: Described from photographs in possession of Signal Corps, NARS (111-SC-85795); and in W. C. Brown papers, University of Colorado; also, Brown, "Incidents."

Chapter 15: Palanan, The End of the Trail

382　　"We steamed": Funston, "Capture," 478; also *Manila Times*, March

29, 1901 (morning and afternoon editions).

383   AGUINALDO IS SURPRISED: *San Francisco Chronicle,* March 29, 1901. Also March 28, 30, and 31. Note that news of the expedition was leaked to the U.S. press as early as March 23, 1901: see *New York Daily Tribune* and *San Francisco Call,* March 24, 1901, and *Boston Herald,* March 25, 1901.

"Funston, The Captor": *Baltimore Sun,* March 28, 1901.

KANSAS WILD WITH JOY: *New York Times,* March 29, 1901.

384   PRESIDENT PLEASED: *Washington Evening Star,* March 29, 1901.

"As a lover of liberty": *Boston Herald,* March 29, 1901.

"The capture of George Washington": *New York Times,* March 29, 1901.

"It would be": Twain, "In Defense of General Funston," *North American Review* (May 1902): 613–24.

"gross act": In *New York Times,* March 30, 1901.

385   Dewey's suggestion: *Literary Digest* 22 (1901): 402–3; also *New York Times,* March 29, 1901.

"It is impossible": *Literary Digest* 22 (1901): 402–3.

"vain, deceitful": Ibid.

"become a passenger": *Manila Times,* March 29, 1901.

"Enough of blood": *Annual Report,* War Department, 1901, 1:100–101.

386   Barcelona and Villa: Quirino, introduction to Villa and Barcelona, x–xii.

Cash rewards: Corres. Adj. Gen. Off., Doc. 469262 (A, B, C, D) and 1058335, NARS.

Judas: Abad, 238.

Segovia's fate: Brown, "Incidents," 628.

"I knew nothing": letter to author, December 7, 1981.

387   "a soldier should": *Chehalis* (Wash.) *Bee-Nugget,* August 30, 1901.

387–88   Russell Hazzard's fate: Ibid., January 10, 24, 31, 1908, August 7, 1908, September 4, 1908, September 9, 1921; *Seattle Times,* September 4, 6, 1921; *Idaho Daily Statesman,* September 5, 1921; undated clipping (c. 1908) from the *Milwaukee Daily Free Press,* "Hazzard Sent to Hospital"; private correspondence with Dorothy Hazzard Ignatieff (his daughter) and Walter Hazzard Twiss (his nephew), 1983.

388   Oliver Hazzard: *Chehalis* (Wash.) *Bee-Nugget,* January 24, 1960; "Hazzard," 319–20; correspondence with Ignatieff and Twiss (see above note).

"The capture of Aguinaldo": *Superior Evening Telegram,* August 31, 1901.

"The grief of Aguinaldo": Ibid., August 30, 1901.

Harry Newton: Ibid., November 26, 1920, August 8, 1946; *Commemorative Biographical Record* (1905), 396.

388–89   Burton Mitchell: *Niagara Falls Gazette,* May 7, June 16, 1941; *New York Times,* June 17, 1941.

389ff.   Emilio Aguinaldo: Aguinaldo and Pacis, 176–79, 182–87, 277; Carmen Aguinaldo Melencio, "My Father," in Garcia, *Aguinaldo in Retrospect*, 11–17; Saulo, *Emilio Aguinaldo;* National Historical Institute, *Aguinaldo Shrine*, 5–6, 30–37; Associated Press Biographical Service, Sketch 3591 (1950); *New York Times*, February 6, 7, 1964.

390   "suffering from a": "Surgeon's Report, First Reserve Hospital, November 29, 1901," in *Funston — Medical Record*, Corres. Adj. Gen. Off., NARS.

391   "The Filipino doesn't love us": *San Francisco Call*, January 10, 26, 1902.
"All of those men": *New York Tribune*, March 9, 12, 1902; *San Francisco Call*, March 9, 1902.
"to take no prisoners": *New York Times*, April 10, 1902.
"I have only sympathy": Unattributed Denver news article (April 20, 1902) appended to Roosevelt letter to secretary of war, April 21, 1902, in Roosevelt presidential correspondence.

392   "This is no perfunctory": Roosevelt to Funston, March 30, 1901, Theodore Roosevelt Papers, Ser. 2, vol. 28, reel 325.
"militaristic nightmare": *Springfield* (Mass.) *Daily Republican*, March 20, 1902.
"The reference to": Roosevelt to secretary of war, April 21, 1902, in Roosevelt presidential correspondence.
White's intercession: White, *Autobiography*, 501.

393   San Francisco earthquake: *Annual Report*, War Department, 1906, 3:165; Funston, *Official Report*, San Francisco, May 17, 1906, in Corres. Adj. Gen. Off., NARS; Funston, "How the Army Worked to Save San Francisco," *Cosmopolitan* 41 (July 1906).
"practically a teetotaler": Coded War Department telegram, Bell to Wood, April 16, 1912, Corres. Adj. Gen. Off., Doc. 1901789, NARS.

394   "How beautiful it is": *Boston Herald*, February 20, 1917; Roy Miller to Captain David Potter, Houston, Texas, January 29, 1932, FFP.
"the sun flashed out": *Boston Herald*, February 20, 1917; *New York Times*, February 24 and 25, 1917. *Note:* Eda Blankart Funston died in June 1932. In her later years she was known for her devotion to charitable causes. In the 1920s she began collecting material for a boy's book on her husband's life, and shortly before her death she began a collaborative biography, with Captain David Potter of the Naval Supply Corps, which seems to have been abandoned at her death. Mrs. Funston had attempted to interest various figures in Hollywood, including Douglas Fairbanks, in a Funston film, but this also failed. Correspondence in FFP.

395ff.   Revisionist views on Aguinaldo: Constantino, *The Philippines*, 8, 231–36.

396   "Filipinos who do not have": Constantino, *Miseducation*, 16–17.

399   "Philippine history must be rewritten": Constantino, *The Philippines*, 4–5.
        M.S. *Karagakatan*: *New York Times*, July 10, 11–12, 1972.

Epilogue

406   "You can't talk": Interview with Spencer Sherman, *Mother Jones* (January 1984): 17.
        Economics: *New York Times*, January 23, October 6, 11, 1983.
        Secret marshals: *New York Times*, August 9, 1982; *Time*, September 20, 1982.
        We Forum: *New York Times*, December 8, 10, 1982.
        Secret decrees: *All Things Considered*, National Public Radio broadcast, May 16, 1983; *New York Times*, May 17, August 7, 1983.

407   "The tragedy": *Mother Jones* (January 1984): 22.
        "Imagine": *PAG–ASA Newsletter* 2, no. 4 (August 1983).

408   "I have returned": *New York Times*, August 22, 1983.
        "documentary": Given limited showing on various U.S. news shows, including ABC's *Nightline*.

408–9   Japanese witness: *New York Times*, August 23, 1983; *Philippine News*, August 31, 1983.

409   "Marcos will negotiate": *Mother Jones* (January 1984): 19.
        Wages: *New York Times*, November 8, 1983.
        "I warn the opposition": *New York Times*, September 23, 1983.
        Newsmen arrested: *New York Times*, September 29, 1983.
        "hunt them down": *New York Times*, September 26, October 15, 1983.

410   Virata named: *New York Times*, February 22, 1983.
        "We are too deeply": *New York Times*, October 25, 1983.
        "part of a conspiracy": *New York Times*, December 4, 1983.
        acting chief executive: *New York Times*, November 21, December 4, 6, 1983.
        Madame Marcos: *New York Times*, November 21, 1983, January 9, 1984.

411   Human rights: "The Philippines: A Country in Crisis," Lawyers Committee for International Human Rights, New York, October 1983; *New York Times*, December 18, 1983.

413   American leverage: *Mother Jones* (January 1984): 20.
        Aquino on bases: *New York Times*, March 13, 1978; *Mother Jones* (January 1984): 22.

414   Diokno: recorded during his June 1983 U.S. tour.
        Soviets and bases: *New York Times*, July 9, 1983.

414–15 Senator Hoar: Wolff, 361–62.

415   "All I'm asking": *Mother Jones* (January 1984): 18.

BIBLIOGRAPHY

Manuscripts

Austin, Eduardo Diaz. "A Study of the Rise and Fall of the First Democratic Republic in the Far East: The Philippines, 1898–99." Ph.D. diss., Georgetown University, 1957.

Brown, William Carey. "The Capture of Aguinaldo." Report dispatched to Vice President Theodore Roosevelt from Manila, April 1901. Brown Papers, Western Historical Collections, University of Colorado, Boulder, Colo.

———. Papers. U.S. Army Military History Research Collection, Carlisle Barracks, Carlisle, Pa.

———. Papers. Western Historical Collections, University of Colorado, Boulder, Colo.

Dewey, George. Papers. Library of Congress, Washington, D.C.

Fernandez, Leandro. "The Philippine Republic." Ph.D. diss., Columbia University, 1926.

Funston, E. H. Papers. Kansas State Historical Society, Topeka, Kans.

Funston, Frederick. Papers. Kansas State Historical Society, Topeka, Kans.

Funston family. Papers. Kansas State Historical Society, Topeka, Kans.

Hazzard, O. P. M. "The Capture of Emilio Aguinaldo." Fort Bragg, N.C. Supplied by Dorothy Hazzard Ignatieff.

Headland, Thomas C. "Imposed Values and Aid Rejection Among Philippine Negritos." Paper delivered before the Second International Philippine Studies Conference, Honolulu, June 1981.

McKinley, William. Papers. Library of Congress, Washington, D.C.

Philippines in the Third World. Papers. Third World Studies Center, University of the Philippines, Quezon City.

Roosevelt, Theodore. Papers. Library of Congress, Washington, D.C.

Root, Elihu. Papers. Library of Congress, Washington, D.C.

Public Documents

U.S. Adjutant General's Office. *Correspondence Relating to the War with Spain* [and the] *Insurrection in the Philippine Islands . . . April 15, 1898, to July 30, 1902.* Washington, D.C., 1902.
————, Department of the Army, National Archives and Records Service. Philippine Insurrection Service Records, Pension Indices, General Correspondence, Officers' Records.
U.S. Congress. 55th Cong. S. Doc. 29, 55, 62, 82, 148, 161, 208, 214. H. Doc. 2.
————. 56th Cong. S. Doc. 66, 134, 138, 148, 167, 179, 196, 208, 218, 221, 387, 426, 432, 435. H. Doc. 1, 2.
————. 57th Cong. S. Doc. 166, 205, 213, 259, 273, 286, 331, 347, 390, 422. H. Doc. 2, 596.
U.S. Department of State. *Papers Relating to the Foreign Relations of the United States, 1898–1903.* Washington, D.C., 1899–1904.
U.S. Library of Congress, Bibliography Division. *List of Works Relating to American Occupation of the Philippines, 1898–1903 (with some additions to 1905).* Washington, D.C., 1905.
U.S. Naval Records Collection, National Archives and Records Service. *Area File of the Naval Records Collection,* "Official Report of Capt. Edward B. Barry, March, 1901."
————. *Deck Log of the U.S.S. Vicksburg, 1901.*
————. Muster and pay rolls of the U.S.S. *Vicksburg,* 1901.
U.S. Navy Department Library. *U.S. Naval History: A Bibliography.* 5th ed. Washington, D.C., 1969.
U.S. Quartermaster General's Office, National Archives and Records Service. General correspondence; records and rolls of the Native Scouts, Macabebes.
The United States and the Philippine Islands, 1900–1904. Washington, D.C., 1905.
U.S. War Department. *Reports of the Secretary of War, 1899–1903.* Washington, D.C., 1900–1904.

Newspapers

Baltimore American	*Manila Times*
Baltimore Sun	*Milwaukee Free Press*
Boston Evening Transcript	*New York Evening Post*
Boston Globe	*New York Herald*
Boston Herald	*New York Journal*
Brooklyn Eagle	*New York Sun*
Chehalis (Wash.) *Bee-Nugget*	*New York Times*
Chicago Tribune	*New York Tribune*
Idaho Daily Statesman	*New York World*
Louisville Courier-Journal	*Niagara Falls Gazette*
Manila American	*San Francisco Call*
Manila Freedom	*San Francisco Chronicle*

Seattle Post-Intelligencer
Seattle Times
Springfield (Mass.) Daily Republican
Superior (Wis.) Leader

Superior Telegram
Tacoma Daily News
Washington Evening Star
Washington Post

Periodicals

The American Monthly Review of
  Reviews
Army and Navy Journal
The Atlantic Monthly
Collier's Weekly
Cosmopolitan
Everybody's Magazine
Frank Leslie's Weekly

Harper's Weekly
The Independent
Infantry Journal
Journal of the West
Kansas Historical Quarterly
Literary Digest
The Nation
Scribner's Magazine

Books, Articles, and Pamphlets

Abad, Antonio K. *Ang Pagkanulo Kay Heneral Emilio Aguinaldo.* Munoz, Nueva Ecija: The Student Press, 1919.

Achutegui, Pedro de, and Miguel Bernad. *Aguinaldo and the Revolution of 1896.* Quezon City: Ateneo de Manila University Press, 1972.

"Adventurous Career of Frederick Funston." *Current Opinion* 56, no. 6 (June 1914).

Agoncillo, Teodoro A. *The Fateful Years: Japan's Adventure in the Philippines, 1941–45.* Quezon City: Garcia, 1965.

———. *Filipino Nationalism, 1872–1970.* Quezon City: Garcia, 1974.

———. *Malolos: The Crisis of the Republic.* Quezon City: University of the Philippines Press, 1960.

———. *The Revolt of the Masses: The Story of Bonifacio and the Katipunan.* Quezon City: University of the Philippines Press, 1956.

———. *A Short History of the Philippines.* New York: New American Library, 1975.

———, ed. *The Writings and Trial of Andres Bonifacio.* Manila: Bonifacio Centennial Commission, 1963.

———, and Milagros Guerrero. *History of the Filipino People.* 5th ed. Quezon City: Garcia, 1977.

Aguinaldo, Emilio. *Memoirs of the Revolution.* Translated by Luz Colendrino-Bucu. Manila, 1967.

———. "The Story of My Capture." *Everybody's Magazine* 5, no. 24 (August 1901).

———. *True Version of the Philippine Revolution.* Malolos, 1899.

———, and Vicente Albano Pacis. *A Second Look at America.* New York: Robert Speller, 1957.

"Aguinaldo A Prisoner." *Army and Navy Journal* 38, no. 31 (March 30, 1901).

444 BIBLIOGRAPHY

Alfonso, Oscar M. *Theodore Roosevelt and the Philippines, 1877–1909*. Quezon City: University of the Philippines Press, 1970.

Alger, R. A. *The Spanish-American War*. New York: Harper's, 1901.

Alip, Eufronio Melo. *In the Days of General Emilio Aguinaldo*. Manila: Alip & Sons, 1969.

———. *Philippine Presidents: From Aguinaldo to Marcos*. Manila: Alip & Sons, 1968.

Alzona, Encarnacion. *A History of Education in the Philippines*. Manila: University of the Philippines Press, 1932.

American League of Philadelphia. "The Self-Governing Filipino. An Open Letter to Bishop Potter of New York." Philadelphia, 1900. In New York Public Library.

Ames, Charles Gordon. "Let There Be Light!" Address of Mass Meeting of Protest Against the Suppression of the Truth About the Philippines. Faneuil Hall, Boston, March 10, 1903. In Widener Library, Harvard University, Cambridge, Mass.

Amnesty International. *Annual Reports*. 1978–83.

———. *Arrest, Detention, and Political Killing of Priests and Church Workers in the Philippines*. New York: AIUSA Publications, 1982.

———. *Arrests and "Disappearances" of Urban and Rural Workers in the Philippines*. New York: AIUSA Publications, 1982.

———. *Human Rights Violations in the Philippines*. New York: AIUSA Publications, 1982.

———. *Report of an Amnesty International Mission to the Republic of the Philippines, 22 November–5 December 1975*. 2d ed. London: AI Publications, 1976.

———. *Report of an Amnesty International Mission to the Republic of the Philippines, 11–28 November 1981*. London: AI Publications, 1982.

Atkinson, Edward. "Criminal Aggression: By Whom Committed" and "The Cost of a National Crime." Brookline, Mass., 1899. In New York Public Library.

Baker, Charles F. *History of 30th Infantry, U.S. Volunteers, 1899–1901*. Clarkston, Wash., 1934.

Bello, Waldon, and Elaine Elinson. *Elite Democracy or Authoritarian Rule?* Manila: Nationalist Resource Center, 1981.

Bemis, Samuel Flagg. *A Diplomatic History of the United States*. New York: Holt, 1942.

Bernad, Miguel A. *The Western Community of Manila: A Profile*. Manila: National Historical Commission, 1974.

Blair, Emily H., and James A. Robinson. *The Philippine Islands, 1493–1898: Explorations by Early Navigators*. 55 vols. Cleveland: Arthur H. Clark, 1909.

Blount, James Henderson. *The American Occupation of the Philippines, 1898–1912*. New York: Putnam's, 1912.

Bonsal, Stephen, ed. *The Golden Horseshoe: Extracts From the Letters of Capt. H. L. Herndon, 21st U.S. Infantry, Philippines*. New York: Macmillan, 1900.

Bowring, Sir John. *A Visit to the Philippine Islands*. London: Smith, Elder, 1859.

Bradley, Claudia, ed. *List of Logbooks of U.S. Navy Ships Deposited in the U.S. National Archives and Records Service, 1801–1947*. Washington, D.C., 1978.

Bradley, Harold W. "Observations Upon American Policy in the Philippines." *Pacific Historical Review* 11 (1942).

Bridgeman, Raymond Landon. *Loyal Traitors: A Story of Friendship for the Filipinos.* Boston: J. H. West, 1903.

Brimlow, G. F. *Cavalryman Out of the West: The Life of General William Carey Brown.* Caldwell, Idaho: Caxton, 1944.

Brooks, F. A. "An Arraignment of President McKinley's Policy of Extending by Force the Sovereignty of the U.S. over the Philippine Islands." Boston: A. Mudge, 1899. In New York Public Library.

Brooks, Francis Augustus. "Objections to the President's Proposed Subjugation of the Filipinos Under License from Spain." Boston: A. Mudge, 1899. In New York Public Library.

Brown, William Carey. "Incidents in Aguinaldo's Capture." *Infantry Journal* 26, no. 6 (June 1925).

Browne, George Waldo. *Pearl of the Orient.* Boston: Estes, 1900.

Bruce, T., ed. *Views of the American Press on the Philippines.* New York: Este & Este, 1899.

Bryan, William Jennings. *Republic or Empire: The Philippine Question.* Chicago: Conkey, 1900.

Buencamino, Felipe. "Memorial to the U.S. Congress Relating to Conditions in the Philippines." (Also known as U.S. Congress, 56th Cong., 1st sess., S. Doc. 66.) Washington, D.C., 1900.

Canfield, James H. "Funston A Kansas Product." *Monthly Review of Reviews* 23, no. 6 (June 1901).

"Capt. Henry W. Newton." In *Commemorative Biographical Record of the Upper Lake Region.* Chicago: Beers, 1905.

Carmack, Edward Ward. "Conditions in the Philippines." Appendix to speech of Carmack in U.S. Senate, December 16, 1904.

———. "Courts Martial in the Philippines." Speech, U.S. Senate, February 9, 1903.

Cerezo, Saturnino. *Under the Red and Gold: The Siege of Baler.* Translated by F. L. Dodds. Kansas City: Hudson, 1909.

Chamberlain, L. T. "The Colonial Policy of the United States." Remarks before the Quill Club, New York, March 21, 1899. In New York Public Library.

Chamberlin, Frederick Carleton. *The Blow from Behind.* Boston: Lee & Shepard, 1901.

———. *The Philippine Problem, 1898–1913.* Boston: Little, Brown, 1913.

"Confidential State Papers of General Emilio Aguinaldo." Manila: Asociacion de los Veteranos de la Revolucion, 1942–44. In National Historical Library, Manila.

Constantino, Renato. *Dissent and Counter-Consciousness.* Quezon City: Foundation for National Studies, 1980.

———. *A History of the Philippines from the Spanish Colonization to World War Two.* New York: Monthly Review Press, 1975.

———. *Neocolonial Identity and Counter-Consciousness.* London: Merlin Press, 1978.

——. *The Miseducation of the Filipino*. Quezon City: Foundation for Nationalist Studies, 1982.

——. *The Philippines: A Past Revisited*. Quezon City: Foundation for Nationalist Studies, 1975.

——, and Letizia Constantino. *The Philippines: The Continuing Past*. Quezon City: Foundation for Nationalist Studies, 1978.

Craig, Austin. *The Former Philippines Through Foreign Eyes*. New York, 1917.

Crouch, Thomas W. "Frederick Funston in Alaska, 1892–1894." *Journal of the West* 10, no. 2 (April 1971).

——. "Frederick Funston of Kansas: His Formative Years, 1865–1891." *Kansas Historical Quarterly* 40, no. 2 (Summer 1974).

——. *A Yankee Guerrillero: Frederick Funston and the Cuban Insurrection, 1896–1897*. Memphis: Memphis State University Press, 1975.

"Daring Little Colonel Funston." *New York Sun*, April 29, 1899. Reprinted in the *New York Times*, April 30, 1899.

Davis, Oscar King. "Beginning of the End." *Harper's Weekly* 45 (March 7, 1901).

——. *Our Conquests in the Pacific*. New York: Stokes, 1899.

——. "The Real Aguinaldo." *Everybody's Magazine* 5, no. 24 (August 1901).

Day, Beth. *The Philippines: Shattered Showcase of Democracy*. New York: M. Evans, 1974.

De Los Santos, Epifanio. *Marcelo H. del Pilar, Andres Bonifacio, Emilio Jacinto*. Manila, 1955.

De Veyra, Jaime. "La Tragedia de Palanan: 23 Marzo 1901." *El Ideal*, March 23, 1912.

Dewey, George. *Autobiography of George Dewey, Admiral of the Navy*. New York: Scribner's, 1913.

Diokno, José W. *Justice Under Siege: Five Talks*. Manila: Nationalist Resource Center, 1981.

Dulles, Foster Rhea. *America's Rise to World Power, 1898–1954*. New York: Harper Torchbooks, 1963.

Dumia, Mariano A. *The Ifugao World*. Quezon City: New Day, 1979.

Eckdall, Ella Funston. *The Funston Homestead*. Emporia, Kans., 1949.

Eckdall, Frank F. "Fighting Fred Funston of Kansas." *Kansas Historical Quarterly*, Spring 1956.

Elliott, Charles B. *The Philippines to the End of the Commission Government: A Study in Tropical Democracy*. Indianapolis: Bobbs-Merrill, 1917.

——. *The Philippines to the End of the Military Regime*. Indianapolis: Bobbs-Merrill, 1917.

Ellis, Edward S. *The Life Story of Admiral Dewey . . . Together with a Complete History of the Philippines and Our War with Aguinaldo*. Philadelphia, 1899.

Faust, Karl Irving. *Campaigning in the Philippines*. San Francisco: Hicks-Judd, 1899.

"Fighting Fred Funston," *Literary Digest* 48 (May 23, 1914).

"Fightin' Fred Funston," *Kansas City Times*, January 14, 1936, p. D-16.

Fighting in the Philippines: Authentic Original Photographs. London: Neely, 1899.

Fitch, G. H. "General Funston on Philippine Problems." *Harper's Weekly* 43 (November 11, 1899).

Foreman, John. *The Philippine Islands*. New York: Scribner's, 1899.

Forbes, William Cameron. *The Philippine Islands*. Boston: Houghton Mifflin, 1928.

Freeman, James H. *True Story of the Capture of Emilio Aguinaldo*. Knoxville: Trent, 1927.

Freeman, Needom N. *A Soldier in the Philippines*. London: Neely, 1901.

Fuchs, Elinor, and Joyce Antler. *Year One of the Empire*. Boston: Houghton Mifflin, 1973.

Funston, Frederick. "Across the Great Divide in Midwinter." *Harper's Weekly* (December 22, 1900).

――――. "Along Alaska's Eastern Boundary." *Harper's Weekly* (February 1, 1896).

――――. "The Capture of Emilio Aguinaldo." *Everybody's Magazine* 5, no. 25, 26 (September and October 1901).

――――. "Cascorra, The First Cuban Siege." *Scribner's Magazine* (October 1910).

――――. "A Defeat and a Victory." *Scribner's Magazine* (December 1910).

――――. "Desmayo, The Cuban Balaklava." *Harper's Weekly* (March 5, 1898).

――――. "The Fall of Guáimaro." *Scribner's Magazine* (November 1910).

――――. "Field Report." In "Botany of Yakutat Bay, Alaska." In *Contributions from the U.S. National Herbarium* 3, no. 6 (January 15, 1896).

――――. "How Aguinaldo Was Captured: Report of Brig. Gen. Frederick Funston." *Army and Navy Journal* 38, no. 47 (July 20, 1901).

――――. *Memories of Two Wars*. New York: Scribner's, 1911.

――――. "Over the Chilkoot Pass to the Yukon." *Scribner's Magazine* (November 1896).

――――. "Reminiscences of Kansas University." *Kansas Magazine*. Wichita, 1909.

――――. "Storm Bound Above the Clouds." *St. Nicholas Magazine* (July 1891).

――――. "To Cuba as a Filibuster." *Scribner's Magazine* (September 1910).

――――, and S. P. Jocelyn. "Alaska — The Land and the Climate — Excerpts." *The Review of Reviews* (June 1896).

Ganzorn, John W. *I've Killed Men*. London: Robert Hale, 1940.

Garcia, Mauro, ed. *Aguinaldo in Retrospect*. Manila: Philippine Historical Commission, 1969.

Gates, John Morgan. *Schoolbooks and Krags: The U.S. Army in the Philippines*. Westport, Conn.: Greenwood Press, 1973.

Gatewood, W. B. *Black Americans and the White Man's Burden, 1898–1903*. Urbana: University of Illinois Press, 1975.

"General Funston's Report." *Army and Navy Journal* 38, no. 47 (July 20, 1901).

Gleed, Charles S. "Romance and Reality in a Single Life: General Frederick Funston." *Cosmopolitan* (July 1899).

Graff, Henry F. *American Imperialism and the Philippine Insurrection*. Boston: Little, Brown, 1969.

Grenville, J., and G. Young. *Politics, Strategy, and American Diplomacy*. New York, 1966.

"Guerrilla War in the Philippines." *Collier's* 28, no. 25 (March 27, 1902).

Guerrero, Amado. *Philippine Society and Revolution*. Manila, 1971.

Hagedorn, Hermann. *Leonard Wood, A Biography*. New York: Harper's, 1931.

Hahn, Emily. *The Islands*. New York: Coward, McCann, 1981.

Halstead, Murat. *Aguinaldo and his Captor.* Cincinnati: Halstead, 1901.

———. "The Politics of the Philippines: Aguinaldo a Traitor to the Filipinos and a Conspirator against the U.S. The record of a transformation from a beggar to a tyrant." Akron, Ohio: Allied Printing Trades Council, 1899.

Hamm, M. A. *Manila and the Philippines.* New York: Neely, 1898.

Hannaford, Ebeneezer. *Our New Wonderland.* Springfield, Ohio: Crowell & Kirkpatrick, 1899.

Hayden, Joseph Ralston. *The Philippine Policy of the U.S.* New York: Institute of Pacific Relations, 1939.

———. *The Philippines, A Study in National Development.* New York: Macmillan, 1942.

"Hazzard, Oliver P. M." In *Indiana Book of Merit.* Courtesy of Dorothy Hazzard Ignatieff.

"Health and Poverty, A Collection of Selected In-Depth Articles on the Health Conditions of the Filipino People." Manila: Inter-Agency Committee for Primary Health Care, 1981.

Higham, Robin, ed. *A Guide to the Sources of U.S. Military History.* Hamden, Conn.: Archan, 1975.

Hinshaw, David. *A Man from Kansas: The Story of William Allen White.* New York: Putnam's, 1945.

Hoar, George F. "The Attempt to Subjugate a People Striving for Freedom." Speech in the U.S. Senate, May 22, 1902. Washington, D.C., 1902.

———. *An Autobiography of Seventy Years.* New York: Scribner's, 1911.

———. "The Conquest of the Philippines." Extracts from speech in the U.S. Senate, April 12, 1900. In New York Public Library.

———. "The Lust of Empire." Speech in the U.S. Senate, April 17, 1900. New York: Tucker, 1900.

Hofstadter, Richard, ed. *Great Issues in American History: From Reconstruction to the Present Day, 1864–1969.* New York: Vintage, 1969.

———. *The Paranoid Style in American Politics and Other Essays.* New York: Vintage, 1965.

———, and Michael Wallace. *American Violence: A Documentary History.* New York: Vintage, 1971.

"How Lieut. Taylor Located Aguinaldo." *Army and Navy Journal* 38, no. 45 (July 6, 1901).

Ibon Facts and Figures. Vols. 1–5 (1978–82). Manila: Ibon Databank, P.O. SM-447, Manila.

Joaquin, Nick. *A Question of Heroes.* Manila: National Book Store, 1981.

Kalaw, Maximo M. *The Case for the Filipinos.* New York: Century, 1916.

———. *Development of Philippine Politics.* Manila: Oriental Commercial Company, 1926.

———. "The Filipinos' Side." *The Nation* 117.

Kalaw, Teodoro M. *An Acceptable Holocaust: Life and Death of a Boy-General.* Manila: National Historical Commission, 1974.

———. *Aide-de-Camp to Freedom.* Manila: Kalaw Society, 1965.

———. *The Philippine Revolution.* Manila: Manila Book Company, 1925.

Kamm, Henry. "Creating a Dynasty in the Philippines." *New York Times Magazine*, May 24, 1981.

Karp, Walter. *The Politics of War*. New York: Harper & Row, 1979.

Karsten, Peter. "The Nature of 'Influence': Roosevelt, Mahan, and the Concept of Sea Power." *American Quarterly* 23, no. 4 (1971).

Keesing, Felix M. *The Ethnohistory of Northern Luzon*. Stanford: Stanford University Press, 1962.

Kennedy, Crammond. "The Capture of Aguinaldo: A Review of the Facts and the Law, with Some Observations on the Question Whether Aguinaldo Owed Allegiance to the U.S. Before He Took the Oath." Washington, D.C.: McGill & Wallace, 1902. In New York Public Library.

Kimball, John C. *Uncensored Manila News*. Cambridge: Cooperative Press, 1900.

La Feber, Walter. *The New Empire: An Interpretation of American Expansion, 1860–1898*. Ithaca: Cornell University Press, 1963.

Lala, Ramon R. *The Philippine Islands*. New York: Continental, 1898.

Le Roy, James A. *The Americans in the Philippines*. Boston: Houghton Mifflin, 1914.

Leech, Margaret. *In the Days of McKinley*. New York: Harper's, 1959.

Lichauco, Alejandro. *The Lichauco Paper: Imperialism in the Philippines*. New York: Monthly Review Press, 1973.

"Lieut. Taylor and Aguinaldo's Capture." *Army and Navy Journal* 38, no. 38 (May 18, 1901).

"Lieutenant Taylor's Service." *Army and Navy Journal* 38, no. 45 (July 6, 1901).

Link, Arthur S., and William B. Catton. *American Epoch: A History of the United States Since the 1890's*. Vol. 1, 1897–1920. 3d ed. New York: Knopf, 1967.

Mabini, Apolinario. *The Letters of Apolinario Mabini*. Manila: National Heroes Commission, 1965.

———. *The Philippine Revolution*. Manila, 1903.

Mahajani, Usha. *Philippine Nationalism: External Challenge and Filipino Response, 1565–1946*. St. Lucia: University of Queensland Press, 1971.

Majul, Cesar Adib. *Apolinario Mabini: Revolutionary*. Manila: National Heroes Commission, 1964.

———. *The Political and Constitutional Ideas of the Philippine Revolution of 1896*. New York: Oriole Editions, 1967.

"The Man Who Always Made Good." *The Independent*, March 5, 1917.

Manchester, William. *American Caesar: Douglas MacArthur, 1880–1964*. Boston: Little, Brown, 1978.

"Manifesto by Aguinaldo." *Army and Navy Journal* 38, no. 35 (April 27, 1901).

March, Alden. *The History and Conquest of the Philippines and Our Other Island Possessions*. Philadelphia: World Bible House, 1899.

Marcos, Ferdinand. *The Democratic Revolution in the Philippines*. Englewood Cliffs, N.J.: Prentice-Hall, 1974.

———. *Progress and Martial Law*. Manila: Republic of the Philippines, 1981.

Mass Meetings of Protest. New England Anti-Imperialist League, Boston, 1903.

Merk, Frederick. *Manifest Destiny and Mission in American History: A New Interpretation*. New York: Knopf, 1963.

Miller, Stuart Creighton. *Benevolent Assimilation: The American Conquest of the*

Philippines, 1899–1903. New Haven: Yale University Press, 1982.

Millet, Frank D. *The Expedition to the Philippines.* New York: Harper, 1899.

Millis, Walter. *The Martial Spirit.* New York: Literary Guild of America, 1931.

"Minister's Meeting of Protest Against the Atrocities in the Philippines." Boston, 1902. In New York Public Library.

Mitchell, Burton J. "Aguinaldo's Capture." *Frank Leslie's Popular Monthly* (September 1901).

Mitterling, Doris. *Guide to the William Carey Brown Papers, 1854–1939.* Boulder: Western Historical Collections, University of Colorado Libraries, 1978.

Morgan, H. Wayne. *William McKinley and His America.* Syracuse: Syracuse University Press, 1963.

Morris, Edmund. *The Rise of Theodore Roosevelt.* New York: Coward, McCann, 1979.

"Mrs. Funston in Filipino Costume." *Harper's Bazar* (January 13, 1900).

"Muzzled Voices, Struggling Spirits." Manila: First National Conference on Human Rights, February 17–18, 1982.

National Historical Commission. *Manila Since Independence.* Manila: National Historical Commission, 1974.

———. *Preliminary Bibliography on Emilio Aguinaldo.* Manila: National Historical Commission, 1969.

National Historical Institute. *Aguinaldo Shrine.* Manila: National Historical Institute, 1978.

Nevins, Allen. *Henry White.* New York: Harper's, 1930.

Noble, Lela Garner. "The Moro National Liberation Front in the Philippines." *Pacific Affairs,* Fall 1976.

"Notes from the Capital — General Funston." *The Nation* (March 1, 1917).

Noval-Morales, Daisy, and James Monan. *A Primer on the Negritos of the Philippines.* Manila: Philippines Business for Social Progress, 1979.

Noyes, Theodore W. *Conditions in the Philippines: Editorial Correspondence of the Evening Star.* Washington, D.C., 1900.

Olcott, Charles S. *Life of William McKinley.* Boston: Houghton Mifflin, 1916.

"Peace Factors in the Philippines." *Army and Navy Journal* 38, no. 32 (April 6, 1901).

Peralta, Jesus T., and Lucila A. Salazar. *Pre-Spanish Manila: A Reconstruction of the Pre-History of Manila.* Manila: National Historical Commission, 1974.

"Persons in the Foreground: The Adventurous Career of Frederick Funston." *Current Opinion* (June 1914).

Peterson, Jean Treloggen. *The Ecology of Social Boundaries: Agta Foragers of the Philippines.* Urbana: University of Illinois Press, 1978.

Petillo, Carol Morris. *Douglas MacArthur: The Philippine Years.* Bloomington: Indiana University Press, 1981.

Pettigrew, Richard Franklin. *The Course of Empire.* New York: Boni and Liveright, 1920.

Philippine Information Society. "Aguinaldo and the American Generals." Boston, 1901. In New York Public Library.

———. "Iloilo — An Episode of January 1899." Boston, 1901. In New York Public Library.

————. "Luzon Campaign, From February to December, 1899." Boston, 1901. In New York Public Library.

————. "Outbreak of Hostilities, February 4, 1899." Boston, 1901. In New York Public Library.

Pier, Arthur S. *American Apostles to the Philippines.* Boston: Beacon Press, 1950.

Pringle, Henry F. *The Life and Times of William Howard Taft.* New York: Farrar and Rinehart, 1939.

————. *Theodore Roosevelt.* New York: Harcourt, Brace, 1931.

Pringle, Robert. *Indonesia and the Philippines.* New York: Columbia University Press, 1980.

Psinakis, Steve. *Two Terrorists Meet.* San Francisco: Alchemy Books, 1981.

Quirino, Carlos. *The Young Aguinaldo from Kawit to Biaknabato.* Manila: Bookmark, 1960.

Riggs, Henry Earle. *Our Life Was Loved While the Old Order Changed: A Story for Our Children.* Privately published, 1948.

Rizal, José. *El Filibusterismo.* Translated by Leon Ma. Guerrero. London: Longmans, 1980.

————. *Noli me Tangere.* Translated by Leon Ma. Guerrero. London: Longmans, 1980.

Robinson, A. G. *The Philippines, the War, and the People.* New York, 1901.

Romulo, Carlos P. *Identity and Change: Towards a National Definition.* Manila: Solidaridad, 1965.

————. *I Saw the Fall of the Philippines.* New York: Doubleday, Doran, 1942.

————. *I Walked with Heroes.* New York: Holt, Rinehart, 1961.

Roosevelt, Theodore. *Letters of Theodore Roosevelt.* Edited by E. E. Morison. Cambridge: Harvard University Press, 1951–54.

————. *Selections from the Correspondence of Theodore Roosevelt and Henry Cabot Lodge, 1884–1918.* New York: Scribner's, 1925.

————. *The Winning of the West.* Vol. 7 of *The Works of Theodore Roosevelt.* Edited by Hermann Hagedorn. National edition. 20 vols. New York: Scribner's, 1926.

Root, Elihu. *Elihu Root Collection of U.S. Documents Relating to the Philippine Islands.* 178 vols. Washington, D.C., 1898–1906.

Russell, Henry Benjamin. *The Story of Two Wars.* Hartford: Hartford Publishing Company, 1899.

Samson, Laura Lorenzo. *Images of America: Mystification and De-Mystification in Philippine Popular Literature.* Quezon City: University of the Philippines, Third World Studies Center, no. 2, July 1976.

Santos Cristobal, Epifanio. *The Revolutionists.* Manila, 1928.

Saulo, Alfredo B. *Communism in the Philippines: An Introduction.* Manila: Ateneo de Manila University Press, 1969.

————. *Emilio Aguinaldo.* Quezon City: Phoenix Press, 1983.

Schirmer, Daniel Boone. *The Reagan Administration and the New Threat of U.S. Military Intervention.* Quezon City: University of the Philippines, Third World Studies Center, no. 23, June 1981.

————. *Republic or Empire: American Resistance to the Philippine War.* Cambridge: Schenkmann, 1972.

Scott, Charles F. "Frederick Funston." *The Independent* (April 11, 1901).

Scott, William Henry. *The Discovery of the Igorots.* Quezon City: New Day, 1977.

————. *On the Cordillera.* Manila: MCS Enterprises, 1969.

Segovia, Lazaro. *The Full Story of Aguinaldo's Capture.* Translated by Frank de Thoma. Manila: Amigos del Pais, 1902.

Sexton, William Thaddeus. *Soldiers in the Sun: An Adventure in Imperialism.* Harrisburg, Pa.: Military Service Publishing Company, 1939.

Shaplen, Robert. *Time Out of Hand: Revolution and Reaction in Southeast Asia.* New York: Harper & Row, 1969.

————. *A Turning Wheel.* New York: Random House, 1979.

Sheridan, Richard Brinsley. *The Filipino Martyrs: A Story of the Crime of February 4, 1899, by an Eyewitness.* London: John Lane, 1900.

Simbulan, Roland G. *U.S. Foreign and Military Policy in Asia: A Third World Perspective.* Quezon City: University of the Philippines, Third World Studies Center, no. 26, May 1981.

Smith, Edward Burritt. "Republic or Empire." Chicago, 1900. In New York Public Library.

"Soldiers' Letters." Boston: Anti-Imperialist League, 1899. In Boston Public Library.

"Soldier's Wife in the Philippines." *Cosmopolitan* (May 1900).

Sommers, Richard J. *Manuscript Holdings of the Military History Research Collection.* Carlisle Barracks, Pa.: U.S. Army Military History Research Collection, 1972–75.

Sonnichsen, A. *Ten Months A Captive Among Filipinos.* New York: Scribner's, 1901.

Spence, Hartzell. *Marcos of the Philippines.* Manila: Republic of the Philippines, 1982.

Stanley, Peter W. *A Nation in the Making: The Philippines and the United States, 1899–1921.* Cambridge: Harvard University Press, 1974.

Steele, J. M. "Official History of the Operations of the Twentieth Kansas Infantry, U.S.V., in the Campaign in the Philippine Islands." San Francisco, 1899. In Kansas State Historical Society, Topeka, Kans.

Stickney, Joseph L. *Admiral Dewey at Manila.* Philadelphia: Moore, 1899.

Storey, Moorfield, and Julian Codman. "Secretary Root's Record: 'Marked Severities' in Philippine Warfare." Boston: Ellis, 1902. In New York Public Library.

Storey, Moorfield, and M. P. Lichauco. *The Conquest of the Philippines by the U.S., 1898–1925.* New York: Putnam's, 1926.

"Stories About Funston." *Kansas City Star,* June 6, 1949.

"Stories About Funston." *Topeka Daily Capital,* February 20, 1917.

"The Strategic Hamlets of Mindanao." Manila: Mindanao Documentation Committee for Refugees, 1982.

Tadem, Eduardo C. *Mindanao Report: A Preliminary Study of the Economic Origins of Social Unrest.* Davao City: AFRIM Resource Center, 1980.

Talplacido, Hilario. "Account of the Capture of Aguinaldo at Palanan, March 23, 1901." Cabanatuan, 1918. In National Library, Manila.

Taylor, John R. M., ed. *The Philippine Insurrection Against the United States.* 5 vols. Pasay City: Lopez Foundation, 1971.

"Three Men and Three Destinies." *Overland Monthly,* San Francisco (May 1908).

Turnbull, Wilfred. "Bringing a Wild Tribe Under Government Control." *Philippine Magazine* 27, no. 1 (1930).

Turot, Henri. *Emilio Aguinaldo: First Filipino President, 1898–1901* [Paris, 1901]. Translated by Pacifico A. Castro. Manila: Foreign Service Institute, 1981.

Twain, Mark. *The Autobiography of Mark Twain.* Edited by A. B. Paine. New York: Harper's, 1949.

―――. *Europe and Elsewhere.* New York: Harper's, 1923.

―――. "In Defense of General Funston." *North American Review* (May 1902).

―――. *Letters From the Earth.* Edited by Bernard De Voto. New York: Fawcett, 1963.

―――. *A Pen Warmed-Up in Hell: Mark Twain in Protest.* Edited by Frederick Anderson. New York: Harper & Row, 1972.

University of the Philippines. *Union List of Philippine Materials of Sixty-four Government Agency Libraries of the Philippines.* Manila, 1973.

Villa, Simeon, and Santiago Barcelona. *Aguinaldo's Odyssey.* Manila: Philippine Bureau of Public Libraries, 1963.

Villarroel, Fidel. *Apolinario Mabini: His Birth Date and Student Years.* Manila: National Historical Institute, 1979.

Walter, Richard. *Anson's Voyage Round the World in the Years 1740–44.* New York: Dover, 1974.

Welch, Herbert. *The Other Man's Country: An Appeal to Conscience.* Philadelphia: Lippincott, 1900.

Welch, Richard E. *Response to Imperialism.* Chapel Hill: University of North Carolina Press, 1979.

Wernstedt, Frederick L., and Joseph E. Spencer. *The Philippine Island World: A Physical, Cultural, and Regional Geography.* Berkeley: University of California Press, 1967.

White, William Allen. *The Autobiography of William Allen White.* New York: Macmillan, 1946.

―――. *Forty Years on Main Street.* New York: Farrar & Rinehart, 1937.

―――. "Frederick Funston's Alaskan Trip." *Harper's Weekly* (May 25, 1895).

―――. "General Frederick Funston." *Harper's Weekly* (May 20, 1899).

Wilcox, Marrion. *Harper's History of the War in the Philippines.* New York: Harper's, 1900.

Wildman, Edwin. *Aguinaldo: A Narrative of Filipino Ambitions.* Boston: Lothrop, 1901.

Williams, Daniel R. *The Odyssey of the Philippine Commission.* Chicago: McClure, 1913.

―――. *The United States and the Philippines.* New York: Doubleday and Page, 1924.

Williams, H. L. *Taking Manila, or, In the Philippines with Dewey.* New York: Hurst, 1899.

Williams, William Appleman. *The Tragedy of American Diplomacy.* New York: Delta, 1972.

Willis, Henry Parker. *Our Philippine Problem: A Study of American Colonial Policy.* New York, 1905.

"Within the President's Prerogative." *New York Morning Journal* item in *Army and Navy Journal* 38, no. 33 (April 13, 1901).

Wolff, Leon. *Little Brown Brother: America's Forgotten Bid for Empire Which Cost 250,000 Lives.* London: Longmans, 1961.

Worcester, Dean Conant. *The Philippines Past and Present.* New York: Macmillan, 1914.

Yap-Diangco, Robert. *The Filipino Guerrilla Tradition.* Manila, 1971.

Yu, Rolando, and Mario Bolasco. *Church-State Relations.* Manila: St. Scholastica's College, 1981.

Young, Louis S., and Henry D. Northrup. *Life and Heroic Deeds of Admiral Dewey, Including Battles in the Philippines.* Philadelphia, 1899.

Younghusband, G. J. *The Philippines and Round About.* New York: Macmillan, 1899.

Zafra, Nicolas. *The Colonization of the Philippines and the Beginnings of the Spanish City of Manila.* Manila: National Historical Commission, 1974.

Zaide, Gregorio F. *Manila During the Revolutionary Period.* Manila: National Historical Commission, 1973.

———. *The Philippine Revolution.* Manila: Modern Book, 1954.

Zinn, Howard. *A People's History of the United States.* New York: Harper Colophon, 1980.

Zornow, William Frank. "Funston Captures Aguinaldo." *American Heritage* 5, no. 2 (February 1958).

———. *Kansas: A History of the Jayhawk State.* Norman: University of Oklahoma Press, 1957.

INDEX